Lecture Notes in Computer Scien

Commenced Publication in 1973
Founding and Former Series Editors:
Gerhard Goos, Juris Hartmanis, and Jan van Leeuwen

Kenji Suzuki   Teruo Higashino
Keiichi Yasumoto   Khaled El-Fakih (Eds.)

Formal Techniques for Networked and Distributed Systems – FORTE 2008

28th IFIP WG 6.1 International Conference
Tokyo, Japan, June 10-13, 2008
Proceedings

 Springer

Volume Editors

Kenji Suzuki
The University of Electro-Communications
Department of Computer Science
1-5-1 Chofugaoka, Chofu-shi, Tokyo 182-8585, Japan
E-mail: suzuki@cs.uec.ac.jp

Teruo Higashino
Osaka University
Graduate School of Information Science and Technology
Department of Information Networking
Suita, Osaka 565-0871, Japan
E-mail: higashino@ist.osaka-u.ac.jp

Keiichi Yasumoto
Nara Institute of Science and Technology
Graduate School of Information Science
Ikoma, Nara 630-0192, Japan
E-mail: yasumoto@is.naist.jp

Khaled El-Fakih
Verimag – Université Joseph Fourier
Centre Equation, 2 rue de Vignate, 38610 Gières, France
E-mail: Khaled.Elfakih@imag.fr

Library of Congress Control Number: 2008927452

CR Subject Classification (1998): C.2.4, D.2.2, C.2, D.2.4-5, D.2, F.3, D.4

LNCS Sublibrary: SL 2 – Programming and Software Engineering

ISSN   0302-9743
ISBN-10   3-540-68854-4 Springer Berlin Heidelberg New York
ISBN-13   978-3-540-68854-9 Springer Berlin Heidelberg New York

Springer is a part of Springer Science+Business Media

springer.com

© IFIP International Federation for Information Processing 2008

Typesetting: Camera-ready by author, data conversion by Scientific Publishing Services, Chennai, India
Printed on acid-free paper   SPIN: 12278343   06/3180   5 4 3 2 1 0

Preface

This volume contains the proceedings of FORTE 2008, 28th IFIP WG6.1 International Conference on Formal Techniques for Networked and Distributed Systems. FORTE 2008 was held at the Campus Innovation Center in Tokyo, Japan during June 10–13, 2008. FORTE denotes a series of international working conferences on formal description techniques applied to computer networks and distributed systems. The conference series started in 1981 under the name PSTV. In 1988 a second series under the name FORTE was set up. Both series were united to FORTE/PSTV in 1996. In 2001 the conference changed the name to its current form. Recent conferences of this long series were held in Berlin (2003), Madrid(2004), Taipei(2005), Paris(2006), and Tallinn(2007).

As in the previous year, FORTE 2008 was collocated with TESTCOM/ FATES 2008: the 20th IFIP International Conference on Testing of Communicating Systems (TESTCOM) and the 8th International Workshop on Formal Approaches to Testing of Software (FATES). The co-location of FORTE and TESTCOM/FATES fostered the collaboration between their communities. The common spirit of both conferences was underpinned by joint opening and closing sessions, invited talks, as well as joint social events.

This year we received 44 submissions. The Program Committee finally selected 19 full papers and 1 short paper for presentation at the conference. The special focus of FORTE 2008 was on formal approaches to new areas of networked and distributed systems such as ubiquitous, grid, and mobile computing systems, and also on the application of formal techniques to service-oriented architectures as well as security issues in networked systems. Together with the invited presentation by Wolfram Schulte from Microsoft Research, USA, the 20 accepted papers formed the very strong and high-quality program of FORTE 2008. In addition, the conference included two more invited presentations on behalf of TESTCOM/FATES by Yutaka Yasuda from KDDI Corporation, Japan and Paul Baker from Motorola, UK. A tutorial day preceded the conference.

It took tremendous efforts to organize this event. We would like to thank all the contributors for the success of FORTE 2008. In particular we are grateful to the Local Organization Chair, Tomohiko Ogishi from KDDI R&D Laboratories, who handled issues related to the conference venue, social events, and registration, and Takaaki Umedu from Osaka University, who managed the conference website and paper submission system. We also owe special thanks to all members of the FORTE 2008 Steering Committee, Program Committee, and co-reviewers for their support in selecting high-quality papers. Without these contributions, these proceedings would not exist. We thank the International Communications Foundation, Support Center for Advanced Telecommunications Technology Research, Foundation, Microsoft Research, and KDDI Corporation for their financial support, and Springer for publishing the proceedings.

Last but not least, we would also like to express our sincere appreciation to The University of Electro-Communications, Osaka University, Nara Institute of Science and Technology, Verimag, Université Joseph Fourier, and to all members of the Local Organization team for their continuous support of this conference.

March 2008

Kenji Suzuki
Teruo Higashino
Keiichi Yasumoto
Khaled El-Fakih

Conference Organization

General Chairs

Kenji Suzuki (The University of Electro-Communications, Japan)
Teruo Higashino (Osaka University, Japan)

Program Chairs

Keiichi Yasumoto (Nara Institute of Science and Technology,
    Japan)
Khaled El-Fakih (Verimag, Université Joseph Fourier, France, and
    American University of Sharjah, UAE)

FORTE Steering Committee

Gregor v. Bochmann (University of Ottawa, Canada)
John Derrick (University of Sheffield, UK)
Ken Turner (University of Stirling, UK)

Program Committee

Jiri Adamek (Charles University in Prague, Czech Republic)
Jonathan Billington (University of South Australia, Australia)
Gregor v. Bochmann (University of Ottawa, Canada)
Kirill Bogdanov (University of Sheffield, UK)
Mario Bravetti (University of Bologna, Italy)
Ana Cavalli (INT Evry, France)
Jose M. Colom (University of Zaragoza, Spain)
John Derrick (University of Sheffield, UK)
David de Frutos-Escrig (Complutense University of Madrid, Spain)
Reinhard Gotzhein (University of Kaiserslautern, Germany)
Susanne Graf (Verimag, France)
Serge Haddad (Lamsade-Paris Dauphine, France)
Teruo Higashino (Osaka University, Japan)
Dieter Hogrefe (University of Gottingen, Germany)
Gerard J. Holzmann (NASA/JPL, USA)
Claude Jard (ENS Cachan - Bretagne, France)
Ferhat Khendek (Concordia University, Canada)
Myungchul Kim (ICU, South Korea)
Hartmut Koenig (Brandenburg University of Technology, Germany)

David Lee (Ohio State University, USA)
Luigi Logrippo (University of Quebec - Outaouais, Canada)
Jose C. Maldonado (University of San Carlos, Brazil)
Elie Najm (ENST, France)
Masakatsu Nishigaki (Shizuoka University, Japan)
Manuel Nunez (Complutense University of Madrid, Spain)
Kazuhito Ohmaki (AIST, Japan)
Olaf Owe (University of Oslo, Norway)
Doron A. Peled (University of Warwick, UK)
Alexandre Petrenko (CRIM Montreal, Canada)
Jean-Francois Pradat-Peyre (Cedric-Cnam, France)
Wolfgang Reisig (Humboldt University, Germany)
Ichiro Satoh (NII, Japan)
Hiroyuki Seki (NAIST, Japan)
Jean-Bernard Stefani (Inria, France)
Kenji Suzuki (The University of Electro-Communications, Japan)
Stavros Tripakis (Cadence, USA)
Ken Turner (University of Stirling, UK)
Hasan Ural (University of Ottawa, Canada)
Juri Vain (Tallinn University of Technology, Estonia)
Farn Wang (National Taiwan University, Taiwan)
Jianping Wu (Tsinghua University, China)
Nina Yevtushenko (Tomsk State University, Russia)
Xia Yin (Tsinghua University, China)

Local Organization

Tomohiko Ogishi (KDDI R&D Laboratories Inc.) (Chair)
Takaaki Umedu (Osaka University)

Additional Reviewers

Saleh Al-Shadly	Irfan Hamid	Shin Nakajima
Cesar Andres	Chuanming Jing	Fernando Rosa-Velardo
Beatrice Berard	Einar B. Johnsen	Alper Sen
Faycal Bessayah	Guy-Vincent Jourdan	Soonuk Seol
Sergiy Boroday	Sungwon Kang	Andrey Shabaldin
Patricia Bouyer	Rajesh Karunamurthy	Natalia Shabaldina
Marius Bozga	Felix Klaedtke	Carron Shankland
David Cairns	Nimrod Lilith	Xingang Shi
Robert G. Clark	Lin Liu	Sebastian Schmerl
Arnaud Dury	Luis Llana	Martin Steffen
Lars-Ake Fredlund	Amel Mammar	Koichi Takahashi
Guy Gallasch	Mercedes G. Merayo	Min Tang

Erik Tschinkel   Zhiliang Wang   Denis Wolf
Michael Vogel   Bachar Wehbi   Hirozumi Yamaguchi
Sebastian Vogel

Sponsoring Institutions

International Communications Foundation, Tokyo, Japan
Support Center for Advanced Telecommunications Technology Research,
    Foundation, Tokyo, Japan
Microsoft Research, Redmond, USA
KDDI Corporation, Tokyo, Japan

Table of Contents

Application

Specification Framework II

Theory

Reliability of Networked Systems

Model Generation for Horn Logic with Stratified Negation

Ethan K. Jackson and Wolfram Schulte

Microsoft Research,
One Microsoft Way, Redmond, WA
{ejackson,schulte}@microsoft.com

Abstract. Model generation is an important formal technique for finding interesting instances of computationally hard problems. In this paper we study model generation over Horn logic under the closed world assumption extended with stratified negation. We provide a novel three-stage algorithm that solves this problem: First, we reduce the relevant Horn clauses to a set of non-monotonic predicates. Second, we apply a fixed-point procedure to these predicates that reveals candidate solutions to the model generation problem. Third, we encode these candidates into a satisfiability problem that is evaluated with a state-of-the-art SMT solver. Our algorithm is implemented, and has been successfully applied to key problems arising in model-based design.

1 Introduction

Informally, *model generation* is a procedure that takes as input some mathematical statement ψ, and produces as output some data M (a model) that, when substituted back into ψ, makes the statement true. For example, if ψ is a boolean satisfiability problem, then M is an assignment of boolean variables to truth values. Similarly, if ψ is a set of linear inequalities, then M is an assignment of variables to the real numbers. Note that model generation can be used to check satisfiability, but not all techniques for checking satisfiability are able to generate models. In this paper we study model generation for an important type of non-classical logic called *Horn logic with stratified negation*.

Horn logic has important applications in computer science and new applications continue to arise. Recently, Horn logic extended with *negation as failure* was used to formalize the non-context-free languages arising in modern software engineering methodologies[1] such as *Model Driven Architecture*[2][3] (MDA), *Model Integrated Computing*[4] (MIC), and *Platform-based Design*[5][6] (PBD). This particular application adds a new and interesting twist: An effective means of model generation is essential if the Horn paradigm is to be truly useful.

In this paper we present a novel approach to model generation for *non-recursive Horn logic* extended with *stratified negation*. Our approach employs a three stage process:

1. We simplify the problem by reducing the relevant Horn clauses to a set of non-monotonic predicates that we call *non-monotonic acceptors*.

K. Suzuki et al. (Eds.): FORTE 2008, LNCS 5048, pp. 1–20, 2008.
© IFIP International Federation for Information Processing 2008

2. We apply a fixed-point procedure to the non-monotonic acceptors that reveals the candidate solutions to the model generation problem.
3. We encode these candidates into a satisfiability problem that is evaluated with the state-of-the-art SMT solver Z3.

We show that this procedure is sound, but incomplete.

This paper is organized into six sections. Section 2 informally describes the class of Horn logic targeted for model generation. Section 3 provides the key formal definitions. The first stage of the algorithm is explained in Section 4 as a modified form of backwards chaining. Section 5 describes the elimination of quantification over closed-worlds and the reduction to a boolean satisfiability problem. We conclude in Section 6.

2   Background and Running Example

Model-based approaches to software engineering rely on high-levels of abstraction to simplify the design process. The left-hand side of Figure 1 shows a *metamodel* describing a simple abstraction layer. This diagram defines an abstract language for scheduling problems without regard to the particular details of the tasks being scheduled. This language contains objects of type `Task` and `Processor`. Tasks can be assigned to processors by directed edges of type `TaskMap`. Resource constraints between tasks prevent two tasks from being scheduled on the same processor. Resource constraints are modeled as undirected edges of type `Constraint` connecting tasks. The right-hand side of Figure 1 shows a member of this language. There are three tasks T_1, T_2, T_3 and two processors P_1, P_2. Tasks T_1 and T_2 have a resource constraint, as do tasks T_2 and T_3. Tasks T_1, T_3 are scheduled on processor P_1 while T_2 is scheduled on P_2.

Metamodels (and other artifacts) can expressed a set of axioms using *Horn logic with stratified negation* [7]. Consequently, model generation on this logic is a key tool for reasoning about abstraction layers. For example, we might demand a model generator to *"Construct a model that contains three tasks and two processors"*. The procedure must find a model satisfying the rules of the abstraction that also meets this goal. Model generation is a difficult problem, as this example illustrates. A correct mapping from tasks to processors is precisely a graph coloring problem[8] where the processors are the colors. This illustrates

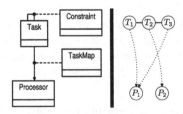

Fig. 1. (Left) Scheduling abstraction (Right) Example scheduling instance

that any procedure capable of constructing non-trivial instances must solve difficult subproblems.

The task scheduling language is defined with the following set of non-recursive and stratified Horn clauses:

$$task(x) \leftarrow taskmap(x, y) \tag{1}$$
$$processor(y) \leftarrow taskmap(x, y) \tag{2}$$
$$task(x) \leftarrow constraint(x, y) \tag{3}$$
$$task(y) \leftarrow constraint(x, y) \tag{4}$$
$$no\_map(task(x)) \leftarrow task(x), \neg taskmap(x, y) \tag{5}$$
$$bad\_map(task(x), task(y)) \leftarrow taskmap(x, z), taskmap(y, z), constraint(x, y) \tag{6}$$

The first four clauses declare that the end-points of task mappings and resource constraints always exist. Clause 5 deduces a term $no\_map(task(x))$ for any task x that is not mapped to a processor. Clause 6 deduces $bad\_map(task(x), task(y))$ anytime two tasks x, y are improperly scheduled. We now examine the semantics of this logic in detail.

2.1   Classical Horn Logic

Classical Horn logic restricts first-order logic by requiring each conjunct of a DNF (disjunctive normal form) formula ψ to have at most one non-negated literal. A collection of Horn formulas has a more natural representation in *implicative normal form*, as shown below:

$$\forall x, y, z \; taskmap(x, z), taskmap(y, z), constraint(x, y) \Rightarrow bad\_sched(x, y) \tag{7}$$

This classical clause looks similar to Clause 6, however its meaning is quite different. For the sake of discussion, assume that $taskmap(\cdot, \cdot)$, $constraint(\cdot, \cdot)$, $bad\_sched(\cdot, \cdot)$ are predicates. From this clause we know that $bad\_sched(x, y)$ must be true for tasks x and y that have resource constraint between them and are scheduled onto the same processor. Given two particular tasks t_1, t_2 without a resource constraint between them, what can we conclude about $bad\_sched(t_1, t_2)$? Rewriting Equation 7 yields:

$$\forall z, \; \neg taskmap(t_1, z) \vee \neg taskmap(t_2, z) \vee \neg constraint(t_1, t_2) \vee bad\_sched(t_1, t_2) \tag{8}$$

Since $\neg constraint(t_1, t_2)$ is true, Equation 8 is satisfied without forcing a particular truth value to $bad\_sched(t_1, t_2)$. In other words, there exists a model satisfying Equation 7 for which tasks 1 and 2 are badly scheduled, but there also exists a model where they are not badly scheduled. Both of these possibilities exist because we have used classical implication. However, there exists a commonly employed extension to Horn logic that closes this loop-hole.

2.2   Closed World Assumption

The *Closed World Assumption* (CWA) is applied whenever a set of Horn clauses is intended to capture *all* the necessary information for a domain[9]. In order for CWA to work properly there must exist some information known to be true from the outset. These pieces of information are called *facts*, which are of the form $true \Rightarrow h$ where h is a non-negated literal. For example:

$$true \Rightarrow taskmap(\mathbf{t}_1, \mathbf{p}_1) \tag{9}$$

Intuitively, a predicate $f(x, y, z)$ is true for some x, y, z if $f(x, y, z)$ is a fact or if there is a sequence of derivations starting at facts that force $f(x, y, z)$ to be true. If there is no such derivation, then $f(x, y, z)$ is false. This rule eliminates the case where tasks $\mathbf{t}_1$ and $\mathbf{t}_2$ are badly scheduled.

This slight adjustment to classical implication profoundly effects the underlying formal machinery by introducing a fixed-point operator $\widehat{\Gamma}$. This operator, called the *immediate consequence operator*, deduces new facts from existing facts using the clauses. All facts not deduced by $\widehat{\Gamma}$ are false, so any model generation procedure must reason over this operator. If M is an initial set of facts and Λ is a set of non-fact Horn clauses, then the set of facts deducible by Λ is the least set X such that $M \subseteq X$ and $X = \widehat{\Gamma}(X)$. CWA can also be understood from a different angle under the name *existential fixed-point logic* [10].

The Closed World Assumption is used in most applications of Horn logic, so it must be taken into account by any model generation procedure. However, CWA forces a rephrasing of the model generation problem: Let Λ be a set of non-fact Horn clauses and a *goal* $G = \{l_1, l_2, \ldots, l_n\}$ be a set of non-negated literals. Loosely speaking, the *finite* model generation problem is to find a finite set of facts M so that (1) $M \subseteq X$, (2) X is a least fixed-point of $\widehat{\Gamma}$, and (3) X contains the goal literals (with respect to some substitution.) Thus, any model generation procedure must reason carefully about the fixed-points of $\widehat{\Gamma}$.

2.3 Negation-as-Failure

Classical Horn logic (without CWA) restricts the use of negation, which restricts the expressiveness of the fragment. *Negation-as-failure* (NAF) attempts to reintroduce a form of negation that is compatible with CWA and does not recreate full first-order logic. However, this new form of negation is very different from its classical counterpart. Intuitively, a negated literal $\neg l$ is true if l *cannot* be proved true under Horn logic with CWA. Thus, negation is defined in terms of a proof procedure.

In order to distinguish our Horn clauses from the classical fragment we write a clause this way:

$$h \leftarrow s_1, s_2, \ldots, s_m, \quad \neg t_1, \neg t_2, \ldots, \neg t_k \tag{10}$$

The literal h is called the *head* of the clause and $\{s_1, \ldots, s_m, t_1, \ldots, t_k\}$ is the *tail* of the clause. Each $\neg t_i$ is a *negated* literal where negation refers to non-classical NAF. Consider Clause 5 containing the negated term $\neg taskmap(x, y)$. This negation does not directly ask if $taskmap(x, y)$ is false for some x, y. Instead, it asks if $taskmap(x, y) \notin \widehat{\Gamma}(M)$ for some x, y. Unlike classical negation, NAF must be used carefully otherwise logical inconsistencies can arise. For example, under NAF we might simultaneously conclude $f \in \widehat{\Gamma}(M) \wedge f \notin \widehat{\Gamma}(M)$ for some fact f. This is a more dangerous inconsistency than $b \wedge \neg b$ for some boolean variable b, which has a well-defined meaning. Much work has been done on generalized forms of NAF that do not suffer from inconsistencies [11][7][12]. We avoid these problems by using only a restricted form of NAF called *stratified negation*. Our approach to handling NAF is similar to the *non-monotonic rules* described in [13].

3 Definitions

We now formally describe the style of Horn logic for which we generate models; this logic incorporates both CWA and NAF. Note that our definitions are biased to make the presentation of model generation simpler.

3.1 Basic Concepts

Let Υ denote a finite signature, Σ an infinite alphabet of constants, and $\mathcal{V}$ a infinite alphabet of variable names. We use the letters f, g, h for variables ranging over function symbols of some signature Υ. We use `typewriter` script to denote constants from Σ. Finally, we use x, y, z for variables ranging over *terms*. Let $arity(f)$ denote the arity of some function symbol f. A *term* is a combination of function symbols, constants, and variables:

Definition 1. *Given Υ, Σ, and $\mathcal{V}$, the set of all finite terms $\mathcal{T}$ is defined inductively*

1. *Each $c \in \Sigma$ is a term*
2. *Each $x \in \mathcal{V}$ is a term*
3. *If $f \in \Upsilon$ and $t_1, t_2, \ldots, t_{arity(f)} \in \mathcal{T}$ then $f(t_1, t_2, \ldots, t_{arity(f)})$ is a term.*

If it is unclear from context, we write $\mathcal{T}(\Upsilon)$ to denote the finite terms constructed from function symbols of signature Υ. A *ground term* is a term without variables; we use $\mathcal{T}_G$ to denote the set of all ground terms. If t is a term, then s is a *subterm* of t (written $s \sqsubseteq t$) if $s = t$ or s is a subterm of one of the arguments of t. If t is a term, then $vars(t)$ is the set of subterms that are also variable names. Similarly, $consts(t)$ is the set of subterms that are also constants. These functions are extended to sets of terms $S \subseteq \mathcal{T}$ in the natural way: $vars(S)$ (or $consts(S)$) are the variables (or constants) appearing in a set of terms.

3.2 Substitutions and Unifiers

Terms are related to one another through special homomorphisms called *substitutions*.

Definition 2. *A substitution $\varphi : \mathcal{T} \to \mathcal{T}$ is a mapping from terms to terms such that:*

1. *φ fixes constants, i.e. $\forall c \in \Sigma$, $\varphi(c) = c$.*
2. *φ is a term homomorphism, i.e. $\varphi(f(t_1, t_2, \ldots, t_n)) = f(\varphi(t_1), \varphi(t_2), \ldots, \varphi(t_n))$.*

Let Φ be the set of all substitutions for some T. Two terms s, t are said to *unify* if there exists a substitution φ that makes them the same: $\varphi(s) = \varphi(t)$. Essentially, a substitution makes two terms the same by replacing variables in the terms with new subterms. The essence of this replacement is easily characterized in terms of the *kernel* of φ.

Definition 3. *The kernel of a homomorphism φ (e.g. a substitution) is:*

$$\mathbf{ker}\ \varphi = \{(s, t) \in T^2 \mid \varphi(s) = \varphi(t)\} \tag{11}$$

The kernel characterizes which subterms are equated by a substitution without regard to the particular values assigned to variables. Some important properties of kernels are: (1) Every kernel is an equivalence relation. (2) The intersection of two equivalence relations is also an equivalence relation. (3) The least equivalence relation Θ containing two equivalence relations Θ_1, Θ_2 is the transitive closure of $(\Theta_1 \cup \Theta_2)$. This shall be written $\Theta = \Theta_1 \oplus \Theta_2$.

The *most general unifiers* (mgu) of two terms s, t is an equivalence relation between the variables of s and t that must hold for any substitution unifying s and t. This equivalence relation represents the weakest set of constraints over the variables of s and t that ensures unification. The most general unifiers have the following properties:

Lemma 1. *Given two terms s, t that unify, let $mgu(s, t)$ denote the most general unifiers.*

1. *The $mgu(s, t)$ is unique.*
2. $mgu(s, t) = \bigcap_{\varphi} \{\mathbf{ker}\ \varphi \mid \varphi(s) = \varphi(t)\}$

If terms s and t do not unify, then we write $mgu(s, t) = \emptyset$.

3.3 Horn Logic with CWA and NAF

Given $\Upsilon, \Sigma, \mathcal{V}$ a Horn clause λ is a triple $\lambda = (h, P, N)$ where h is a term and P, N are sets of terms. $P = \{s_1, \ldots, s_m\}$ is the set of non-negated tail terms and $N = \{t_1, \ldots, t_k\}$ is the set of negated tail terms. A Horn clause is written:

$$h \leftarrow s_1, s_2, \ldots, s_m, \quad \neg t_1, \neg t_2, \ldots, \neg t_k \tag{12}$$

Furthermore, P must be non-empty and $vars(h) \subseteq vars(P)$. (We shall explain these restrictions shortly.) Let Λ be a finite set of Horn clauses, then there exists a binary relation $\prec$ over clauses, where $(h', P', N') \prec (h, P, N)$ if there exists some $s_i \in P$ or $t_j \in N$ that unifies with h'.

Definition 4. *Let Λ be a finite set of clauses, then Λ is non-recursive and stratified if $\prec$ is a strict partial order.*

Restricting $\prec$ to a strict partial order yields a simple semantics for evaluating the set of facts derivable by Λ. Order the clauses $\lambda_1, \lambda_2, \ldots, \lambda_k$ so that $\lambda_i \prec \lambda_j$ implies $i < j$, then for each clause define an immediate consequence operator:

$$\widehat{\Gamma_i}(X) = \bigcup_\varphi \{\varphi(h_i) \mid \alpha(P_i, N_i, \varphi, X)\} \cup X \tag{13}$$

This equation states that the facts deducible by a single clause λ_i are calculated by finding all the substitutions that satisfy a special predicate $\alpha_i(P_i, N_i, \varphi, X)$; each substitution is applied to the head h_i to derive a new fact. Earlier we restricted the variables of h_i to be a subset of the variables of P_i, so each substitution maps h_i to a well-defined ground term.

The predicate $\alpha(P_i, N_i, \varphi, X)$ captures the CWA and NAF semantics.

Definition 5. $\alpha : \mathcal{P}(\mathcal{T})^2 \times \Phi \times \mathcal{P}(\mathcal{T}) \rightarrow \mathbb{B}$ *is called a non-monotonic acceptor:*

$$\alpha(P, N, \varphi, X) \overset{def}{=} (\varphi(P) \subseteq X) \wedge \forall \varphi' \left[(\varphi(P) = \varphi'(P)) \Rightarrow (\varphi'(N) \cap X = \emptyset) \right] \tag{14}$$

The acceptor $\alpha(P, N, \varphi, X)$ is true for some substitution φ and some set of terms (e.g. facts) X if the positive terms P can be found in the set of facts through the substitution φ. The negative terms N must not be found in the facts X for any extension of φ to φ' that agrees on P.

Lemma 2. *Let Λ be a finite set of non-recursive and stratified Horn clauses, and M a finite set of ground terms. Let the clauses of Λ be ordered $\lambda_1, \lambda_2, \ldots, \lambda_k$ to respect $\prec$ then:*

1. *The set of all facts deducible from M by Λ is $\Gamma(M)$ where:*

$$\Gamma(M) = \widehat{\Gamma_k}(\ldots \widehat{\Gamma_2}(\widehat{\Gamma_1}(M)) \ldots) \tag{15}$$

2. *It can be decided in finite time if any ground term $t_g \in \Gamma(M)$, i.e. the logic is decidable.*

3.4   The Model Generation Problem

Solving the model generation problem requires the construction of a set of facts M that satisfies a *goal*. A goal $G = (P_G, N_G)$ is comprised of two sets of terms: the positive terms P_G, and the negative terms N_G. A goal is satisfied if there exists some M such that all the facts deduced from M (i.e., $\Gamma(M)$) include P_G and do not include N_G. More precisely, M satisfies the goal if $\exists \varphi, \; \alpha(P_G, N_G, \varphi, \Gamma(M))$ holds.

In order to construct meaningful solutions, the model generation procedure must know which terms are allowed to appear as facts. Consider the problem of creating a badly scheduled set of tasks for the scheduling abstraction:

$$G = (\{bad\_map(x, y)\}, \emptyset)$$

then we expect the model generation procedure return a solution similar to this one:

$$M = \left\{ \begin{array}{c} task(\mathbf{t}_1), task(\mathbf{t}_2), processor(\mathbf{p}_1), \\ taskmap(\mathbf{t}_1, \mathbf{p}_1), taskmap(\mathbf{t}_2, \mathbf{p}_1), constraint(\mathbf{t}_1, \mathbf{t}_2) \end{array} \right\}.$$

Without additional information, the solution $M = \{bad\_map(\mathbf{c}, \mathbf{c})\}$ is also trivially valid. This extra information is expressed by partitioning the signature Υ into two parts: the *fact signature* Υ_F and the *derived signature* Υ_D. We call a term $t \in \mathcal{T}(\Upsilon_F)$ a *fact term* and call all other terms *derived terms*. The model generation procedure only considers solutions that are sets of fact terms. For example, the partitioning:

$$\Upsilon_F = \{task(\cdot), processor(\cdot), taskmap(\cdot, \cdot), constraint(\cdot, \cdot)\},$$
$$\Upsilon_D = \{no\_map(\cdot), bad\_map(\cdot, \cdot)\}$$

forces all solutions to be built from tasks and processors. The goal G contains a derived term $bad\_map(x, y)$, but the solution M will never contain this term directly. We now define the finite model generation problem.

Definition 6. *The finite model generation problem - Given:*

1. *A finite signature Υ partitioned into $\Upsilon_F \neq \emptyset$ and Υ_D,*
2. *A finite set of clauses Λ that are non-recursive and stratified,*
3. *A goal $G = (P_G, N_G)$ where P_G, N_G are finite subsets of terms.*

Construct a finite set of ground terms $M \subset \mathcal{T}_G(\Upsilon_F)$ so that

$$\exists \varphi \; \alpha(P_G, N_G, \varphi, \Gamma(M)) \tag{16}$$

4   Utilizing Backwards Chaining

The semantics of non-recursive and stratified Horn logic has a succinct characterization in terms of Γ. However, it is difficult to construct a set of constraints from Γ that guide model generation. Fortunately, there is a well-known technique for computing the truth values of goals, called *backwards chaining*, which addresses this problem. Imagine that a set of facts M is already known, and the only task is to check if a goal G is satisfied by these facts. Backwards chaining works backwards from the goal, through the clauses, to the facts M to check satisfiability. If the goal is satisfied, then the procedure yields a proof tree showing exactly how the facts derive the goal. Formally, this process is called *SLD resolution* [14] for Horn logic and *SLDNF resolution* [15] for Horn logic with NAF. These resolution procedures are sound and complete for non-recursive and stratified Horn logic. We modify SLDNF resolution to return "possible" proof trees, and then search for models that satisfy these proof trees. We utilize soundness/completeness results [16] to argue soundness for model generation.

The key modification to SLDNF is a new termination condition that does not rely on M. Typical backwards chaining terminates when it encounters a fact, i.e. a clause of the form $f \leftarrow true$. This termination condition must be modified for model generation because initially no facts are known. We modify backwards chaining so that it terminates when a fact term is encountered, even though this fact term may not exist in the solution M. Let a clause $\lambda \in \Lambda$ be partitioned as follows:

$$h \leftarrow p_1, \ldots, p_m, \ u_1, \ldots, u_{m'}, \ \neg n_1, \ldots, \neg n_k, \ \neg w_1, \ldots, \neg w_{k'} \qquad (17)$$

where (1) each p_i is a positive fact term, (2) each u_i is a positive derived term, (3) each n_i is a negative fact term, and (4) each w_i is a negative derived term.

Associated with each clause λ is a backwards chaining predicate $\beta_\lambda(\varphi, M, \Theta)$ where M is a set of terms, φ is a substitution, and Θ is an equivalence relation.

Definition 7. *Let λ be a clause, then associate with λ a backwards chaining predicate[1] $\beta_\lambda(\varphi, M, \Theta)$:*

$$\beta_\lambda(\varphi, M, \Theta) \overset{def}{=}$$

1. $\left(\Theta \subseteq \ker \varphi \right) \wedge$

2. $\alpha \left(\{p_1, p_2, \ldots, p_k\}, \{n_1, n_2, \ldots, n_m\}, \varphi, M \right) \wedge$

3. $\displaystyle\bigwedge_{1 \le i \le m'} \left(\bigvee_{mgu(u_i, h_{\lambda'}) \ne \emptyset} \beta_{\lambda'} \left(\varphi, M, \Theta \oplus mgu(u_i, h_{\lambda'}) \right) \right) \wedge$

4. $\displaystyle\forall \varphi' \left[\left(\forall v \in vars(P_\lambda) \ \varphi'(v) = \varphi(v) \right) \Rightarrow \left(\bigwedge_{1 \le j \le k'} \bigwedge_{mgu(w_j, h_{\lambda''}) \ne \emptyset} \neg \beta_{\lambda''} \left(\varphi', M, \Theta \oplus mgu(w_j, h_{\lambda''}) \right) \right) \right]$

The backwards chaining predicate is defined recursively and terminates on fact terms; these parts of the tail simplify to non-monotonic acceptors (Def. 7.2). On the other hand, derived terms must be understood through additional clauses. The backwards chaining process recurses into derived terms by locating clauses that unify with these terms. The equivalence relation Θ is used to collect unification constraints during this process. For every positive derived u_i there must exist some unifying clause λ' so that $\beta_{\lambda'}$ is satisfied (Def. 7.3). Contrarily, every negative derived term w_j must have no clause λ'' that derives w_j for any extension of φ to φ' agreeing on positive variables (Def. 7.4). It is possible that some unification constraints cannot be satisfied by any substitution φ. If this occurs then Def. 7.1 fails to hold. We assume that each time a clause λ' (or λ'') is examined for unification its variables are renamed to new variables that have not appeared before. This is called *standardizing apart*, and it prevents clauses from improperly interacting through variable names.

Backwards chaining is used to reduce any goal into a set of non-monotonic acceptors. However, there is one problem with the simple definition presented here:

---

[1] We follow the convention that the OR of the empty set is false and the AND of the empty set is true.

It does not recurse through clauses with heads that are fact terms. (Consider clause 1 from the previous example.) This definition assumes that fact terms do not appear as heads. Fortunately, we can always rewrite the clauses of Λ to enforce this rule; this is discussed later. For the moment, assume that facts do not appear as heads then the following important theorem holds:

Theorem 1. *Given $\Upsilon_F, \Upsilon_R, \Lambda$ such that fact terms do not appear as heads, and a goal G, then*

$$\forall M \subset \mathcal{T}(\Upsilon_F), \ \forall \varphi \quad \alpha(P_G, N_G, \varphi, \Gamma(M)) \Leftrightarrow \beta_G(\varphi, M, \mathcal{ID}_T) \qquad (18)$$

for M finite and Λ non-recursive and stratified.

This theorem shows that evaluating the non-monotonic acceptor over all the facts deducible from Γ gives the same result as working backwards from the goal G through the backwards chaining predicates. We use this result to eliminate the fixed-point operator Γ from the model generation problem. Note that the backwards chaining process is initiated without any constraints on the variables as described by the identity relation $\mathcal{ID}_T = \{(t, t) | t \in \mathcal{T}\}$.

4.1   Simplification of Backwards Chaining

The backwards chaining formulation eliminates Γ, but generates many constraints across many recursions. In this section we show how to aggregate these constraints into convenient pieces. To facilitate this discussion we give names to particular parts of the backwards chaining predicate:

$$\omega(\varphi, \varphi', P) \overset{def}{=} \left(\forall v \in vars(P) \ \varphi'(v) = \varphi(v) \right) \qquad (19)$$

$$\psi_\lambda^-(\varphi', M, \Theta) \overset{def}{=} \bigwedge_{1 \le j \le k'} \bigwedge_{mgu(w_j, h_{\lambda''}) \ne \emptyset} \neg \beta_{\lambda''} \left(\varphi', M, \Theta \oplus mgu(w_j, h_{\lambda''}) \right) \qquad (20)$$

Definition 7.4 becomes $\forall \varphi' \ \omega(\varphi, \varphi', P_\lambda) \Rightarrow \psi_\lambda^-(\varphi', M, \Theta)$.

Consider the action of the goal backwards chaining predicate $\beta_G(\varphi, M, \Theta)$, as shown in Figure 2. The predicate β_G introduces a non-monotonic acceptor α_1 and some constraints on the kernel of φ via Θ_1. (Note that we index the constraints $1, 2, \ldots$ as the recursion proceeds.) Similarly, a subformula containing ψ_1^- is introduced due to negative derived terms. The positive derived terms

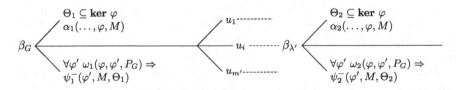

Fig. 2. A single expansion of the backwards chaining predicate for some unification choices of positive derived terms

$u_1, u_2, \ldots, u_{m'}$ act as choice-points, because there may exist many clauses that unify with each u_i. Consider some choice of unifications for each u_i, then the recursion introduces more kernel constraints, non-monotonic acceptors, and negative subformulas. Let $\widehat{\beta}$ be an expansion of some β for particular unification choices of the positive derived terms appearing through the recursion. Then this expansion has the following form:

$$\widehat{\beta}(\varphi, M, \Theta) =$$
$$\left(\bigwedge_i (\Theta_i \subseteq \mathbf{ker}\ \varphi) \right) \wedge \left(\bigwedge_i \alpha(P_i, N_i, \varphi, M) \right) \wedge \left(\bigwedge_i \begin{array}{c} \forall \varphi'\ \omega(\varphi, \varphi', V_i^+) \Rightarrow \\ \psi_i^-(\varphi', M, \Theta_i) \end{array} \right)$$
$$(21)$$

The following lemmas help to simplify the expansion.

Lemma 3. *Non-monotonic acceptors compose over conjunction for fixed φ and X.*

$$\alpha(P_a, N_a, \varphi, X) \wedge \alpha(P_b, N_b, \varphi, X) = \alpha(P_a \cup P_b, N_a \cup N_b, \varphi, X) \qquad (22)$$

Lemma 4. *Constraints on the kernel of φ compose over conjunction.*

$$(\Theta_a \subseteq \mathbf{ker}\ \varphi) \wedge (\Theta_b \subseteq \mathbf{ker}\ \varphi) = (\Theta_a \oplus \Theta_b) \subseteq \mathbf{ker}\ \varphi \qquad (23)$$

Applying the lemmas simplifies Equation 21 to:

$$\widehat{\beta}(\varphi, M, \Theta) = (\Theta' \subseteq \mathbf{ker}\ \varphi) \wedge \alpha(P', N', \varphi, M) \wedge \left(\bigwedge_i \begin{array}{c} \forall \varphi'\ \omega(\varphi, \varphi', V_i^+) \Rightarrow \\ \psi_i^-(\varphi', M, \Theta_i) \end{array} \right) \quad (24)$$

where

$$\Theta' = \Theta \oplus \left(\bigoplus_i \Theta_i \right) \qquad (25)$$

$$P' = \bigcup_i P_i, \quad N' = \bigcup_i N_i \qquad (26)$$

In summary, for a particular set of unification choices the backwards chaining reduces to:

1. Constraints on the kernel of φ, which equate variables,
2. A single non-monotonic acceptor containing only fact terms,
3. A number of backwards chaining predicates for negative derived terms.

A clause λ may have an exponential number of expansions $\widehat{\beta}$. Label these expansions $\widehat{\beta}_1, \ldots, \widehat{\beta}_{c_\lambda}$, then they relate to the original predicate through disjunction:

$$\beta_\lambda(\varphi, M, \Theta) = \bigvee_{1 \leq i \leq c_\lambda} \widehat{\beta}_i(\varphi, M, \Theta) \qquad (27)$$

This decomposition also allows the ψ^- terms to be rewritten in terms of the expansion:

$$\psi^-(\varphi, M, \Theta) = \bigwedge_{mgu(w_i, h_{\lambda'}) \neq \emptyset} \bigwedge_{1 \leq j \leq c_{\lambda'}} \forall \varphi' \begin{bmatrix} \omega(\varphi, \varphi', V^+) \Rightarrow \\ \neg \widehat{\beta}_j(\varphi', M, \Theta \oplus mgu(w_i, h_{\lambda'})) \end{bmatrix} \quad (28)$$

The decomposition of β_λ shows that each ψ^- term will expand into some number of non-monotonic acceptors depending on the depth of the negation, which is certainly finite. Unlike the positive derived terms, each ψ^- must examine all the relevant $\widehat{\beta}$ predicates to ensure that the negated derived term is not satisfied. Furthermore, the simplification lemmas cannot be directly applied to expansions of ψ^- because the non-monotonic acceptors appear in negated form. In the following sections we use these expansions to generate models from the backwards chaining proof trees.

4.2   Restratification

The previous analysis assumed that backwards chaining terminates at fact terms. This assumption can be violated if Λ contains clauses with fact terms as heads. The clause $task(x) \leftarrow taskmap(x, y)$ is an example. Fortunately, there is a simple syntactic operation that soundly manipulates Λ so that no fact terms appear as heads. We call this process *restratification*, because it changes the ordering $\prec$.

Definition 8. *Given Υ_F, Υ_D, Λ, and a goal G, then the* restratified *system is Υ_F, Υ_D^*, Λ^*, G^* where:*

1. *Introduce a new unary derived function symbol $restrat(\cdot)$ to Υ_R.*

$$\Upsilon_D^* = \Upsilon_D \cup \{restrat(\cdot)\} \quad (29)$$

2. *For each clause $\lambda \in \Lambda$ where the head h is a fact term, add the modified clause λ^* to Λ^*:*

$$restrat(h) \leftarrow \neg h, \quad s_1, s_2, \ldots, s_n, \quad \neg t_1, \neg t_2, \ldots, \neg t_m \quad (30)$$

3. *For each clause $\lambda \in \Lambda$ where the head h is derived term, add λ to Λ^**
4. *Modify the goal $G = (P_G, N_G)$ to include the negative derived term $\neg restrat(x)$ where x is a variable that does not appear in G.*

$$G^* = \left(P_G, N_G \cup \{restrat(x)\} \right) \quad (31)$$

Lemma 5. *If Λ is a set of non-recursive and stratified Horn clauses, then the restratified clauses Λ^* are also non-recursive and stratified where no clause has a fact term as head.*

Theorem 2. *The models that satisfy G are related to the models that satisfy G^* according to:*

$$\forall M \subset \mathcal{T}_G(\Upsilon_F), \left(\Gamma_\Lambda(M) \cap \mathcal{T}_G(\Upsilon_F) = M \right) \Rightarrow$$
$$\left(\exists \varphi \ \alpha(P_G, N_G, \varphi, \Gamma_\Lambda(M)) \Leftrightarrow \exists \varphi' \ \alpha(P_G^*, N_G^*, \varphi', \Gamma_{\Lambda^*}(M)) \right) \quad (32)$$

If M is a set of ground fact terms such that $\Gamma_A(M)$ does not grow the number of fact terms, then the restratified system will be in agreement with G. Conversely, when models are found that satisfy the restratified system, then these models do not grow fact terms under the original system. Of course, ground derived terms can still grow under either system. This is not a limitation, because solutions to G that are not solutions to G^* will accumulate fact terms under Γ_A until the set of ground fact terms is exactly a solution to G^*.

4.3   Generating Schedules: Part 1

We now apply these techniques to the running example of a scheduling abstraction. Our goal is to find a model that contains three tasks T_1, T_2, T_3 and two processors P_1, P_2 so that the tasks are scheduled onto the processors. Furthermore tasks T_1 and T_2 cannot be on the same processor; the same constraint holds for task T_2 and T_3. In order to make the example more interesting the tasks are not introduced in the goal:

$$P_G = \{\, processor(p_1), processor(p_2), constraint(t_1, t_2), constraint(t_2, t_3)\,\} \tag{33}$$
$$P_N = \{no\_map(x), bad\_map(y, z)\}$$

for $\Upsilon_R = \{no\_map(\cdot), bad\_map(\cdot, \cdot)\}$ and all other function symbols in Υ_F.

Applying restratification to the original clauses yields:

$$restrat(task(x)) \leftarrow taskmap(x, y), \neg task(x) \tag{34}$$
$$restrat(processor(y)) \leftarrow taskmap(x, y), \neg processor(y) \tag{35}$$
$$restrat(task(x)) \leftarrow constraint(x, y), \neg task(x) \tag{36}$$
$$restrat(task(y)) \leftarrow constraint(x, y), \neg task(y) \tag{37}$$
$$no\_map(task(x)) \leftarrow task(x), \neg taskmap(x, y) \tag{38}$$
$$bad\_map(task(x), task(y)) \leftarrow taskmap(x, z), taskmap(y, z), constraint(x, y) \tag{39}$$

and the restratified goal is $G^* = (P_G, N_G \cup \{restrat(w)\})$.

Next, the backwards chaining predicates are expanded until the goal is expressed by a system of non-monotonic acceptors defined with only fact terms. In this example the ω terms are trivial and have been removed.

$$\exists M,\ \exists \varphi\ \beta_{G^*}(\varphi, M, \mathcal{ID}_T) =$$
$$\exists M,\ \exists \varphi,\ \forall \varphi'\ \alpha(P_G, \emptyset, \varphi, M)\ \wedge$$
$$\neg\alpha\bigg(\{task(x_1)\}, \{taskmap(x_1, y_1)\}, \varphi', M\bigg)\ \wedge$$
$$\neg\alpha\bigg(\{taskmap(x_2, y_2)\}, \{task(x_2)\}, \varphi', M\bigg)\ \wedge$$
$$\neg\alpha\bigg(\{taskmap(x_3, y_3)\}, \{processor(y_3)\}, \varphi', M\bigg)\ \wedge \tag{40}$$
$$\neg\alpha\bigg(\{constraint(x_4, y_4)\}, \{task(x_4)\}, \varphi', M\bigg)\ \wedge$$
$$\neg\alpha\bigg(\{constraint(x_5, y_5)\}, \{task(y_5)\}, \varphi', M\bigg)\ \wedge$$
$$\neg\alpha\bigg(\{taskmap(x_2, z_2), taskmap(y_2, z_2), constraint(x_2, y_2)\}, \emptyset, \varphi', M\bigg)$$

After the goal has been reduced, the quantifiers must be eliminated from the formula. This elimination procedure is described in the next section.

5   Eliminating the Closed World

The formula $\exists M$, $\exists \varphi\, \beta_G(\varphi, M, \mathcal{ID}_T)$ contains a second-order variable M ranging over all the closed worlds, of which there are an infinite number. The next step in model generation is the elimination of the variable M. The *elimination* of M means that we construct a new formula $\exists \varphi\, \beta'_G(\varphi)$ that does not contain M, but the solutions to this formula can be used to construct a finite set of facts M satisfying the original formula.

Elimination is accomplished by constructing a finite candidate set M_C of non-ground terms with the property that there exists a satisfying M if and only if there exists a subset $M'_C \subseteq M_C$ where $\exists \varphi\, \beta_G(\varphi, \varphi(M'_C), \mathcal{ID}_T)$. Once M'_C is discovered, all that remains is to arbitrarily choose an assignment of variables to constants to get a concrete M.

In the interest of space, we describe the solution when all backwards chaining paths pass through at most one negated derived term. The results here are easily generalized to arbitrary depth of negation. (The previous example fits into this restricted case.) Consider any expansion $\widehat{\beta}_G$ of the goal predicate. The results from the previous section guarantee that it has the following simplified form:

$$\exists M,\ \exists \varphi\ (\Theta' \subseteq \ker \varphi)\ \wedge\ \alpha(P', N', \varphi, M)\ \wedge \forall \varphi'$$
$$\left[\neg\omega_1(\varphi, \varphi', V_1^+)\ \vee\ (\Theta_1' \not\subseteq \ker \varphi')\ \vee \neg\alpha(P_1', N_1', \varphi', M)\right]\ \wedge$$
$$\left[\neg\omega_2(\varphi, \varphi', V_2^+)\ \vee\ (\Theta_2' \not\subseteq \ker \varphi')\ \vee \neg\alpha(P_2', N_2', \varphi', M)\right]\ \wedge \qquad (41)$$
$$\vdots$$
$$\left[\neg\omega_k(\varphi, \varphi', V_k^{\,|})\ \vee\ (\Theta_k' \not\subseteq \ker \varphi')\ \vee \neg\alpha(P_k', N_k', \varphi', M)\right]$$

The simplification results in exactly one non-negated acceptor $\alpha(P', N', \varphi, M)$, where P' and N' are the composition of many non-monotonic acceptors according to Lemma 3. Each negated derived term also creates a backwards chaining tree according to Equation 28 and these trees can be simplified in the same way. After simplification, the negative derived terms yield disjunctions of negated ω formulas, kernel constraints, and non-monotonic acceptors. These negated sub-formulas are arbitrarily numbered $1, \ldots, k$ and primed to remind the reader that they result from simplification.

Recall that every clause has a least one positive term in the tail, so every P_i' must be non-empty. However, the goal G might not have positive terms, in which case $P' = \emptyset$. If this holds, let $M = \emptyset$, then M trivially satisfies $\alpha(\emptyset, N', \varphi, \emptyset)$ and trivial satisfies $\forall \varphi'$, $\neg\alpha(P_i', N_i', \varphi', \emptyset)$. Thus, we focus on the interesting case where the goal G contains some positive terms, i.e. $P' \neq \emptyset$.

Assume $P' \neq \emptyset$, then by definition of α it must be that $\varphi(P') \subseteq M$. The set P' must have a homomorphic image in any solution M. Therefore, let the candidate solution $M_C = P'$. It may be that the negative part N' disallows some of these terms, but this can be discovered later. Next, consider the negated acceptors. It could be that some acceptor $\alpha(P'_i, N'_i, \varphi', M)$ is satisfied by the candidate model M_C. A necessary condition for this to occur is:

$$\exists \varphi' \; \omega_i(\varphi, \varphi', V_i^+) \wedge (\Theta'_i \subseteq \ker \varphi') \wedge (\varphi'(P'_i) \subseteq M_C) \tag{42}$$

This situation is only problematic if no term from N'_i has a homomorphic image in M_C. These problematic situations are mitigated by expanding M_C with the maximum number of negative terms: $M_C^{new} = M_C^{old} \cup \varphi'(N'_i)$. This expansion is performed for every possible φ', of which there are a finite number (if M_C is already finite). If N'_i contains variables not found in P'_i, then these variables are given new names.

Expanding M_C may provide new opportunities for negated acceptors to fail (i.e. the acceptor evaluates to *true*, so its negation is *false*). These new opportunities must be identified and may require further expansion of M_C. The strategy is to add the maximum number of terms to M_C that allow all the negated acceptors to succeed. For each negated acceptor assign an operator C_i^-:

$$C_i^-(\varphi, X) = \bigcup_{\varphi'} \left\{ \varphi'(N'_i) \; \middle| \; \omega_i(\varphi, \varphi', V_i^+) \wedge (\Theta'_i \subseteq \ker \varphi') \wedge (\varphi'(P'_i) \subseteq X) \right\} \cup X \tag{43}$$

For the single non-negated acceptor $\alpha(P', N', \varphi, M)$ assign the operator C^+:

$$C^+(\varphi, X) = X \cup \varphi(P') \tag{44}$$

The problem of finding the maximum M_C can now be stated in terms of a least fixed-point equation:

$$M_C = C^+(\varphi, M_C) = C_1^-(\varphi, M_C) = C_2^-(\varphi, M_C) = \ldots = C_k^-(\varphi, M_C) \tag{45}$$

These operators have two important properties: (1) *monotonic*: $X \subseteq C^{+/-}(X)$ (2) *extensive*: $X \subseteq Y \Rightarrow C^{+/-}(X) \subseteq C^{+/-}(Y)$. These properties lead to the important lemma:

Lemma 6. *If the least fixed-point M_C exists, then it is unique for a given φ.*

In fact, φ serves as a book-keeping mechanism to remember constraints over variables, and it can be constructed while solving the fixed-point equation. However, in the interest of space we omit the algorithm that constructs the fixed-point M_C.

Theorem 3. *For some expansion $\widehat{\beta}_G$, if the fixed-point M_C exists, then*

$$\forall M, \; \forall \varphi \;\; \widehat{\beta}_G(\varphi, M, \mathcal{ID}) \Rightarrow \left(\exists M'_C \subseteq M_C, \; \exists \varphi' \;\; \varphi'(M'_C) = M \right) \tag{46}$$

where φ' assigns variables to constants, and M is a minimal solution.

```
┌─────────────────────────────────────────────────────────────────────┐
│  Model Generation Algorithm                                           │
├─────────────────────────────────────────────────────────────────────┤
│ 1:  enumeration Results = { satisfiable, unsatisfiable, unknown };    │
│ 2:  let result := unsatisfiable;                                      │
│                                                                       │
│ 4:  Restratify(ϒ_F, ϒ_D, Λ, G);                                       │
│ 5:  let goal_expansions := {β̂_1, β̂_2, ..., β̂_k};                     │
│ 6:  for each β̂_i ∈ goal_expansions {                                  │
│ 7:      if (fixed_point_exists(β̂_i) ) {                               │
│ 8:          let M_C = fixed_point(β̂_i);                               │
│ 9:          for each M'_C ⊆ M_C and each interesting φ' {             │
│ 10:             if ( ∃φ β̂_i(φ, φ'(M'_C), ID)) {                       │
│ 11:                 result := satisfiable;                            │
│ 12:                 return φ'(M'_C);                                   │
│ 13:             }                                                     │
│ 14:         }                                                         │
│ 15:     else result := unknown;                                       │
│ 16: }                                                                 │
└─────────────────────────────────────────────────────────────────────┘
```

Fig. 3. Eliminating the closed world using fixed-points of goal expansions $\widehat{\beta}_i$

This key theorem explains that if a least fixed-point M_C exists for some expansion of the goal $\widehat{\beta}_G$, then a definite conclusion can be drawn about the satisfiability of this expansion: If there is a finite model that satisfies the subgoal, then there is some minimal model M that satisfies the subgoal. The minimal model M is exactly some subset $M'_C \subseteq M_C$ where the variables of M'_C have been assigned to constants. The least fixed-point M_C is finite, so there are a finite number of subsets M'_C. Furthermore, there are only a finite number of *interesting* ways that variables can be assigned constants. This result leads to an algorithm for model generation:

5.1   Generating Schedules: Part 2

We apply these results to generate non-trivial models for the scheduling language. Recall that Equation 40 is the simplification of the goal predicate β_G and this predicate has only one expansion to $\widehat{\beta}$. The task is the calculation of the fixed-point M_C from $\widehat{\beta}$. Initially M_C contains only the positive part of the goal:

$$M_C^0 = \{processor(p_1), processor(p_2), constraint(t_1, t_2), constraint(t_2, t_3)\} \qquad (47)$$

This candidate model may violate the negated acceptors:

$$\forall \varphi' \ \neg \alpha(\{constraint(x_4, y_4)\}, \{task(x_4)\}, \varphi', M) \ \wedge$$
$$\forall \varphi' \ \neg \alpha(\{constraint(x_5, y_5)\}, \{task(y_5)\}, \varphi', M)$$

The substitution $\varphi'(x_4) = \varphi'(x_5) \mapsto t_1$, $\varphi'(y_4) = \varphi'(y_5) \mapsto t_2$ is a witness to this possibility. (There exists a similar substitution for t_2, t_3.) These substitutions expand the candidate set to include the three tasks:

$$M_C^1 = M_C^0 \cup \{task(t_1), task(t_2), task(t_3)\} \tag{48}$$

This candidate set does not contain *taskmap* terms from tasks to processors, violating the subformula:

$$\forall \varphi' \ \neg \alpha(\{task(x_1)\}, \{taskmap(x_1, y_1)\}, \varphi', M)$$

The expansion of M_C introduces the *taskmap* terms and also new variables:

$$M_C^2 = M_C^1 \cup \{taskmap(t_1, x), taskmap(t_2, y), taskmap(t_3, z)\} \tag{49}$$

Finally, new processor terms are introduced for the end-points of the *taskmap* terms:

$$M_C^3 = M_C^2 \cup \{processor(x), processor(y), processor(z)\} \tag{50}$$

This set is the fixed-point, i.e. $M_C = M_C^3$.

The model generation problem can be solved by examining subsets of the fixed-point M_C. Some subsets will not produce satisfying models:

$$M_{fail} = \left\{ \begin{array}{c} task(t_1), task(t_2), task(t_3), \\ taskmap(t_1, x), taskmap(t_2, y), taskmap(t_3, z) \\ constraint(t_1, t_2), constraint(t_2, t_3), processor(p_1), \end{array} \right\} \tag{51}$$

where $x = y = z = p_1$. This subset will fail for any assignment of variables to constants because there are not enough distinct processors. On the other hand, the set

$$M_{success} = M_{fail} \cup \left\{ processor(p_2) \right\} \tag{52}$$

where $x = z = p_1$ and $y = p_2$ and $x \neq y$ satisfies the goal. In fact, any choice of constants that respects the equalities/disequalities satisfies the goal. In the next section we show how these subsets can be calculated using boolean satisfiability.

5.2 A Better Algorithm Using SMT

The simple algorithm in Figure 3 is a brute force approach for finding a model that satisfies the goal. It tries every subset of M_C and every interesting assignment φ' of variables to constants. In general, there are an exponential number of (M_C', φ') pairs to test. This exponential blow-up cannot be eliminated entirely, but it can be mitigated by translating the problem into a SAT problem. Mature SAT algorithms can be used to suppress the exponential blow-up. The encoding described here assumes a modern solver capable of reasoning about equalities among a set of non-boolean variables. We use an SMT solver (*Satisfiability Modulo Theories*) called *Z3* [17] to accomplish this task. Z3 utilizes efficient SAT algorithms to solve problems that are not purely boolean; e.g. problems with equalities over non-boolean variables.

The first step of the encoding is the translation of complex terms to boolean variables. At this stage all the terms that need to be considered already exist in M_C, so the encoding is simple. Assign a boolean variable τ_i to each term t_i in the candidate set M_C. If τ_i is true then the corresponding term t_i is in the solution, otherwise t_i is not in the solution. Furthermore, introduce a set of non-boolean variables X, which are the variables occurring as subterms in M_C: $X = vars(M_C)$. We provide these non-boolean variables so the SAT solver can decide if some variables x_i, x_j in M_C should take the the same values ($x_i = x_j$), or different values ($x_i \neq x_j$), or a fixed value ($x_i = c$).

The non-negated acceptor $\alpha(P', N', \varphi, M)$ defines terms P' that must be in any solution. Let $t_1^+, t_2^+, \ldots, t_k^+$ be the terms in M_C that were added according to P', then the following boolean formula must be true:

$$\bigwedge_{1 \leq j \leq k} \tau_j^+ \tag{53}$$

Next, consider any negated acceptor $\neg\alpha(P_i', N_i', \varphi', M)$. Let φ' be such that $\omega_i(\varphi, \varphi', V_i^+)$ holds, $\Theta_i' \subseteq \ker \varphi'$, and $\varphi'(P_i') \subseteq M_C$. Let $\varphi'(P_i') = \{t_1^-, t_2^-, \ldots, t_k^-\}$. (Note φ' may not exist.) The negated acceptor is satisfied if one of the following holds:

1. One of the t_j^- terms is not in the solution.
2. There exists a pair of variables $(x, y) \in vars(\varphi'(P_i'))$ that is also in the kernel of φ', but $x \neq y$.
3. There exists a variable $x \in vars(\varphi'(P_i'))$ and a constant c where $(x, c) \in \ker \varphi'$, but $x \neq c$.
4. There exists an extension of φ' to φ'' and some $t^+ \in M_C$ so that $t^+ \in \varphi''(N_i')$.

Conditions (1)-(3) yield the following encoding:

$$\left(\bigvee_{1 \leq j \leq k} \neg\tau_j^- \right) \vee \left(\bigvee_{\substack{x,y \in vars(\varphi'(P_i')), \\ (x,y) \in \ker \varphi'}} x \neq y \right) \vee \left(\bigvee_{\substack{x \in vars(\varphi'(P_i')), c \in \Sigma, \\ (x,c) \in \ker \varphi'}} x \neq c \right) \tag{54}$$

Condition (4) has a more complicated encoding:

$$\bigvee_{t^+} \left[\tau^+ \wedge \left(\bigwedge_{\substack{x,y \in vars(\varphi''(P_i') \cup t^+)), \\ (x,y) \in \ker \varphi''}} x = y \right) \wedge \left(\bigwedge_{\substack{x \in vars(\varphi''(P_i') \cup t^+)), \\ c \in \Sigma, (x,c) \in \ker \varphi''}} x = c \right) \right] \tag{55}$$

Such an encoding must be generated for all relevant φ' and φ''. A similar translation encodes the negative part N' of the non-negated acceptor α'. We omit it this in the interest of space.

In this discussion we have ignored the relationship between variables and terms. For example, two terms $f(x)$, $f(y)$ are affected by equating (or disequating) the variables: If $x = y$ ($x \neq y$) then $f(x) = f(y)$ ($f(x) \neq f(y)$).

In this case the relationship can be easily encoded because all the variables in M_C will only take constant values. Let t_i, t_j be two terms that unify by equating variables to other variables or constants. Then the following must hold:

$$(\tau_i \Leftrightarrow \tau_j) \vee \left(\bigvee_{(x,y) \in mgu(t_i, t_j)} x \neq y \right) \vee \left(\bigvee_{(x,c) \in mgu(t_i, t_j)} x \neq \mathsf{c} \right) \quad (56)$$

Terms that unify by assigning some variables to complex terms are ignored.

6   Conclusion and Future Work

Model generation is an important tool for the model-based design of software systems. It can be used to generate non-trivial solution instances from domain-specific abstractions, perform design-space exploration, and reason about model-transformations. We have given a sound algorithm that generates models from non-recursive and stratified Horn logic. These algorithms have been implemented in a tool called *FORMULA* (FORmal Modeling Using Logic Analysis). The SMT (SAT Modulo Theories) solver Z3 is used to solve the SAT encodings output by FORMULA.

Future work includes extending model generation to encompass *constraint logic programming* (CLP) frameworks. CLP combines Horn logic with constraints, as in the following clause:

$$bad\_sched(critial\_task(x)) \leftarrow critical\_task(x), task(y), priority(x) < priority(y)$$

Assume there is a new type of task called a *critical_task*. This clause states that a bad schedule assigns a high priority to a non-critical task. Priorities are expressed by the ordering $<$ over integers, resulting in a combination of Horn logic with the theory of integers. We will utilize additional theories available at the SMT level to generate models for CLP extensions.

Acknowledgments

We would like to thank Nikolaj Bjørner for his invaluable feedback and his insight into Z3.

References

1. Jackson, E.K., Sztipanovits, J.: Towards a formal foundation for domain specific modeling languages. In: Proceedings of the Sixth ACM International Conference on Embedded Software (EMSOFT 2006), pp. 53–62 (2006)
2. Object Management Group: Mda guide version 1.0.1. Technical report (2003)
3. Bezivin, J., Gerbé, O.: Towards a precise definition of the omg/mda framework. In: Proceedings of the 16th Conference on Automated Software Engineering, pp. 273–280 (2001)

4. Karsai, G., Sztipanovits, J., Ledeczi, A., Bapty, T.: Model-integrated development of embedded software. Proceedings of the IEEE 91(1), 145–164 (2003)
5. Burch, J., Passerone, R., Sangiovanni-Vincentelli, A.: Modeling techniques in design-by-refinement methodologies. Integrated Design and Process Technology (June 2002)
6. Lee, E.A., Neuendorffer, S.: Actor-oriented models for codesign: Balancing re-use and performance. In: Formal Methods and Models for Systems. Kluwer, Dordrecht (2004)
7. Przymusinski, T.C.: Every logic program has a natural stratification and an iterated least fixed point model. In: PODS 1989: Proceedings of the eighth ACM SIGACT-SIGMOD-SIGART symposium on Principles of database systems, pp. 11–21. ACM, New York (1989)
8. Jensen, T.R., Toft, B.: Graph Coloring Problems. Wiley-Interscience, New York, ISBN 0-471-02865-7
9. Reiter, R.: On closed world data bases, pp. 300–310 (1987)
10. Blass, A., Gurevich, Y.: Existential fixed-point logic. In: Börger, E. (ed.) Computation Theory and Logic. LNCS, vol. 270, pp. 20–36. Springer, Heidelberg (1987)
11. van Gelder, A., Ross, K., Schlipf, J.S.: The well-founded semantics for general logic programs. Journal of the ACM 38, 620–650 (1991)
12. Gelfond, M., Lifschitz, V.: The stable model semantics for logic programming. In: Kowalski, R.A., Bowen, K. (eds.) Proceedings of the Fifth International Conference on Logic Programming, pp. 1070–1080. The MIT Press, Cambridge (1988)
13. Marek, V.W., Nerode, A., Remmel, J.B.: A context for belief revision: Forward chaining - normal nonmonotonic rule systems. Ann. Pure Appl. Logic 67(1-3), 269–323 (1994)
14. Emden, M.H.V., Kowalski, R.A.: The semantics of predicate logic as a programming language. J. ACM 23, 733–742 (1976)
15. Apt, K.R., Doets, K.: A new definition of SLDNF-resolution. The Journal of Logic Programming 18, 177–190 (1994)
16. Dantsin, E., Eiter, T., Gottlob, G., Voronkov, A.: Complexity and expressive power of logic programming. ACM Comput. Surv. 33(3), 374–425 (2001)
17. de Moura, L., Bjørner, N.: Z3: An Efficient SMT Solver. In: Proceedings of Fourteenth International Conference on Tools and Algorithms for the Construction and Analysis of Systems (TACAS 2008). LNCS, vol. 4963, pp. 337–340. Springer, Heidelberg (2008)

Counterexample Guided
Spotlight Abstraction Refinement*

Tobe Toben

Carl von Ossietzky Universität Oldenburg, Germany
toben@informatik.uni-oldenburg.de

Abstract. This paper addresses the formal verification of distributed systems comprising a dynamically changing and potentially unbounded number of processes. We employ the spotlight principle to obtain a concise finitary abstraction of the system and devise an abstraction refinement strategy guided by the analysis of abstract counterexamples.

It turns out that the key problem for spotlight refinement is the identification of spurious counterexamples. We observe that the problem is in general undecidable, and provide a sound but incomplete method that is able to solve the problem for many practically relevant systems. Our method is driven by a *three-valued* satisfaction relation for temporal specifications that accounts for the fact that concrete counterexamples can be identified in the abstracted system if they occur within the spotlight.

1 Introduction

Distributed systems comprising a dynamically changing and potentially unbounded number of processes naturally occur in various areas of ubiquitous computing, ad-hoc networking and traffic management systems. For example, processes may represent mobile devices entering a wireless network, or trains approaching a railway controller that is responsible for granting movement authorisations (as proposed e.g. in the ETCS Level 3 standard [1]). The correct treatment of at run-time appearing and disappearing processes adds a new level of complexity when designing safety-critical distributed systems.

The use of formal methods can help to avoid errors early in the system development phase. Formal verification of *dynamic* behaviour however imposes two challenges. Firstly, it requires an appropriate formal description of the system behaviour. This formalism has to go beyond standard notations for reactive systems like Kripke structures [2,3], because the local states of arbitrary many alive processes have to be representable. Secondly, automatic verification techniques like model-checking [3] are a priori only applicable to (small) finite-state systems. One approach to deal with this problem is to use finitary abstraction [4], that is, to devise a finite abstraction of the system and to show that the analysis of the abstract system is sufficient to ensure the correctness of the original system.

---

* This work was partly supported by the German Research Council (DFG) as part of the Transregional Collaborative Research Centre "Automatic Verification and Analysis of Complex Systems" (SFB/TR 14 AVACS).

K. Suzuki et al. (Eds.): FORTE 2008, LNCS 5048, pp. 21–36, 2008.

This paper proposes a solution for both of these problems. Inspired by early work in the area of first-order modal logic [5], we use *first-order logical structures* as a formal representation of a global system state. These structures comprise a set of process identities and an interpretation of predicates for these process identities. With this, the behaviour of a dynamic system can be represented as an infinite-state transition system over logical structures. Consequently, we use a *first-order* variant of linear temporal logic for the formal requirement specification, that is, we allow to quantify over variables denoting process identities.

By a finitary abstraction of the considered systems, we are able to use any of the highly optimised verification engines (like VIS [6] or SPIN [7]) that are available for finite-state systems. The employed abstraction follows the spotlight principle [8] by representing only a finite number of processes exact and collapsing the rest into one dedicated *summary process*. The number of concrete processes can easily be determined by the number of variables in the requirement specification. Formally, the abstraction yields *three-valued* logical structures, because the predicate interpretation for the summary process may neither become *true* nor *false* but "*maybe*" in order to remain sound. The abstract system yields a sound but incomplete overapproximation of the original system, i.e. the satisfaction of properties transfers from the abstract to the original system, but in general not vice versa: Not every property that is valid for the original system can be proven in the abstraction. This entails the existence of *spurious counterexamples* which demonstrate the violation of a property in the abstraction, although the property actually holds for the original system. Thus, an abstract counterexample can not be "trusted" unless it has been validated. However, due to the heterogeneous nature of the underlying abstraction, we are also able to obtain *concrete* counterexamples directly in the abstracted system, namely if they occur within the spotlight part of the abstraction. We will formalise this intuition in the course of this paper, again by the usage of three-valued logic.

Running Example. We use the car platooning scenario to illustrate our approach. In this case study, cars driving on a highway are supposed to autonomously form car platoons, i.e. series of interlinked cars driving with only little distance. To do so, a car can *merge* with a car driving in front (cf. Fig. 1), and a car being the head of a platoon can *split* from its followers. As cars can freely enter and leave a highway, no finite upper bound on the number of cars can be made.

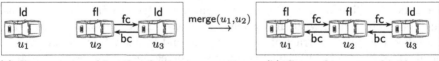

(a) Car u_1 approaching the platoon.   (b) Car u_1 has merged with u_2.

Fig. 1. Car platooning. A car at the head of a platoon is called a leader (ld), where a single car is represented as a platoon of size one. A car driving within a platoon is called a follower (fl). The platoon itself is organised as a doubly-linked list, where each car has a (communication) link to its front car (fc) and a link to its back car (bc).

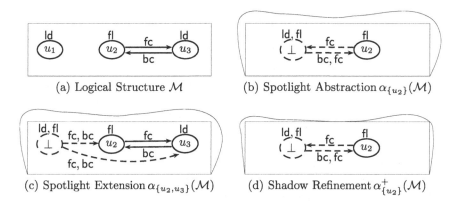

(a) Logical Structure $\mathcal{M}$

(b) Spotlight Abstraction $\alpha_{\{u_2\}}(\mathcal{M})$

(c) Spotlight Extension $\alpha_{\{u_2,u_3\}}(\mathcal{M})$

(d) Shadow Refinement $\alpha^+_{\{u_2\}}(\mathcal{M})$

Fig. 2. Spotlight abstraction (cf. Def. 2) and possible refinements

Spotlight Abstraction and Refinement. Figure 2(a) graphically represents the logical structure according to the global state of the car platooning system in Fig. 1(a). It comprises three process identities, u_1, u_2 and u_3, and provides the predicate interpretation by labelling the nodes and arcs by those predicates that are true for these nodes. For example, the unary predicate ld is true for u_1 and u_3 and false for u_2, and the binary predicate fc is true only for (u_2, u_3).

Figure 2(b) shows the abstraction of this structure with only u_2 in the spotlight. The truth values of the predicates are kept only among the processes in the spotlight, i.e. the abstraction preserves that there exists a *follower* car with a fc link to (at least) one abstract car. Any information about the processes in the shadows however is neglected, i.e. any predicate yields *maybe* for the summary process $\bot$, as indicated by dashed lines. Hence the summary process in general considerably *overapproximates* the original structure, as indicated by the gray area exceeding the box. This coarse representation is special to spotlight abstraction and is the key for easily obtaining the abstract transition system. It provides a sound abstraction, thus every temporal specification that holds for the spotlight abstracted transition system also holds for the original transition system. Besides overapproximating the shadows, the spotlight abstraction also maintains an *underapproximation* of the original system regarding the finite set of spotlight processes. Thus, a natural refinement of the abstraction consists of enlarging the spotlight. In Fig. 2(c), the spotlight comprises u_2 and u_3, and the abstraction now preserves the existence of a valid platoon of size two. But note that we can only ensure the validity of this spotlight configuration if the system run leading to Fig. 2(c) is not illegally influenced by the summary process.

In general, the overapproximative behaviour of $\bot$ may result in spotlight configurations that are not reachable in the original system. Another important refinement is thus to eliminate spurious behaviour of the summary process, as graphically indicated by a reduced gray area in Fig. 2(d). We will use temporal assumptions for refining the behaviour of $\bot$, stating that certain interactions of $\bot$ are not possible in certain spotlight configurations. These assumptions will be derived from the validation of abstract counterexamples that have been obtained for the verification of a given requirement specification. Following the discussion above, we propose to regard the satisfaction of a temporal specification in a three-valued fashion, namely as *true* if it is satisfied in all system runs, *false* if it is violated in some run independent of ⊥, and *unknown* else. In the latter case, we aim at concretising the abstract counterexample via spotlight extension, that is, we try to reproduce the behaviour of ⊥ by concrete processes. For this, we add additional spotlight processes. If the behaviour is not possible with concrete processes, an assumption for shadow refinement has been obtained and a new verification task is started under the refined abstraction. If the behaviour can be validated with concrete processes, we may obtain a concrete counterexample and are done. But it is also possible that the behaviour of the new spotlight processes is again influenced by the abstract process, hence we may obtain another abstract counterexample that itself has to be validated. Therefore, we *successively* add concrete processes until a definite answer has been obtained.

The major contribution of this paper is an instantiation of the framework of counterexample guided abstraction refinement [9] for spotlight abstraction, that is, we automate the refinement of spotlight abstraction. We observe that, due to the coarse abstraction, the validation of abstract counterexamples becomes difficult (and undecidable in general) while the shadow refinement can be shown to be very effective. We devise a translation from counterexamples to temporal specifications that on the one hand allows us to validate the counterexample, and on the other hand is a source for a refinement assumption. The translation and refinement loop has been evaluated on the basis of a verification toolset [10] for dynamic systems, and first experimental results are given in Sect. 5.

Related Work. In [11], spotlight abstraction is applied for the verification of UML models, and the abstraction is manually refined by separately established assumptions. Our approach allows us to compute such kind of assumptions automatically. [12] uses a variant of spotlight abstraction for the verification of parameterised communication models, but they leave out abstraction refinement as future work. [13] proposes a general strategy for spotlight abstraction refinement by inferring and integrating so-called non-interference lemmata. This idea is realised in [14] resp. [15], where two particular kinds of invariants, namely non-interference properties resp. topology invariants, are automatically computed and integrated into a refinement procedure. These approaches however have no immediate potential for iteration, i.e. if the refinement by the inferred invariants is not accurate enough to prove the specification, one remains inconclusive.

Other approaches for analysis of dynamic systems work on graph transformation systems and define tailored abstraction techniques like Partner Abstraction [16] or approximation in terms of Petri nets [17]. The latter approach also applies a CEGAR loop to reduce spurious behaviour stemming from the merge of graph nodes during the abstraction. However, the unique nature of the spotlight abstraction principle requires new validation and refinement strategies.

Abstracting a set of concrete nodes to summary nodes is also the underlying principle of parametric shape analysis [18]. Their abstraction mechanism is more precise (and therefore more expensive) by creating *multiple* summary nodes for different equivalence classes of concrete nodes. However, concrete nodes may migrate from one summary process to another, thereby losing their identity (cf. [8]). In contrast, spotlight abstraction allows us to trace process identities over the time, which enables the analysis of full temporal properties. On the other hand, our logic is not expressive enough to reason about the shape of the *overall* heap structure, because the transitive closure operator does not fit well with spotlight abstraction.

2   Preliminaries

In general, abstraction comes hand in hand with a loss of information. To formally characterise partial impreciseness, we use the framework of three-valued logic according to Kleene [19]. Here, the boolean domain comprises three values, namely $\mathbb{B}_3 := \{0, 1/2, 1\}$. Besides the *value order* $\leq$ on $\mathbb{B}_3 \times \mathbb{B}_3$, we consider the *information order* $\sqsubseteq$ on $\mathbb{B}_3 \times \mathbb{B}_3$ defined as $b_1 \sqsubseteq b_2$ iff $b_1 = 1/2$ or $b_1 = b_2$.

As we do not impose an upper bound on the number of currently alive processes, we assume an infinite set $Id = \{u_1, u_2, \ldots\}$ of *process identities*. By $\bot \notin Id$ we denote the *summary process*, and we set $I^\bot := I \dot\cup \{\bot\}$ for any $I \subseteq Id$. The actual configuration and evolution of the system will be characterised by a number of predicates, i.e. we define a *signature* $\mathcal{S} = (\mathcal{X}, \mathcal{P}_S, \mathcal{P}_L, \mathcal{P}_E)$ as a collection of a finite set of logical variables $\mathcal{X}$, a finite set of unary state predicates $\mathcal{P}_S$, a finite set of binary link predicates $\mathcal{P}_L$, and a finite set of evolution predicates $\mathcal{P}_E$. For convenience, we set $\mathcal{P}_{SL} := \mathcal{P}_S \cup \mathcal{P}_L$, and $\mathcal{P} := \mathcal{P}_S \cup \mathcal{P}_L \cup \mathcal{P}_E$, and denote the arity of a predicate $p \in \mathcal{P}$ by k_p. With this, a configuration of the system can be faithfully represented as a first-order logical structure, i.e. a tuple $(\mathcal{U}, \iota)$ comprising a set of currently alive processes $\mathcal{U} \subseteq Id^\bot$ and an interpretation of the state and link predicates, i.e. ι yields for each $p \in \mathcal{P}_{SL}$ a function $\iota(p) : \mathcal{U}^{k_p} \to \mathbb{B}_3$. For a subset of identities $I \subseteq Id^\bot$, we use $\mathbf{M}_\mathcal{S}(I) := \{(\mathcal{U}, \iota) \mid \mathcal{U} \subseteq I\}$ to denote the set of logical structures where at most the identities from I are present. In the following, we will represent an interpretation ι by the tuple $(\iota_1, \iota_{1/2})$ with

$$\iota_1 := \{p(u_1, \ldots, u_{k_p}) \mid \iota(p)(u_1, \ldots, u_{k_p}) = 1\}$$
$$\iota_{1/2} := \{p(u_1, \ldots, u_{k_p}) \mid \iota(p)(u_1, \ldots, u_{k_p}) = 1/2\}.$$

3   Dynamic Systems

The behaviour of a dynamic system can be formally characterised by a (infinitely large) labelled transition system where the states are logical structures and the transitions are labelled by evolution predicates. To actually model such systems, we introduce a symbolic description of a dynamic system as a set of evolution rules D, each of them comprising a *label*, a *guard* and a sequence of *actions*. The label is a *term* over evolution predicates $\mathcal{P}_E$, i.e. it is of the form $p(x_1, \ldots, x_{k_p})$ with $x_i \in \mathcal{X}$. The guard is a *formula* over state and link predicates, generated by the grammar $\psi ::= t \mid x_1 = x_2 \mid \neg\psi \mid \psi_1 \wedge \psi_2$ where t is a term over $\mathcal{P}_{SL}$. Finally, an action sequence is generated by the grammar $a ::= a_1; a_2 \mid t \mid \neg t \mid \circledast x \mid \ominus x$. Here, a positive term t over $\mathcal{P}_{SL}$ turns the corresponding predicate to true, and a negative term $\neg t$ sets it to false. The action $\circledast x$ will create a new process denoted by $x \in \mathcal{X}$, and $\ominus x$ will kill the corresponding process. We require that each label comprises exactly those variables that are used in its guard and in its actions.

Before defining the formal semantics, let us formalise the car platooning example as a dynamic system Car over signature $(\mathcal{X}, \mathcal{P}_S, \mathcal{P}_L, \mathcal{P}_E)$ with $\mathcal{P}_S = \{\mathsf{ld}, \mathsf{fl}\}$, $\mathcal{P}_L = \{\mathsf{bc}, \mathsf{fc}\}$ and $\mathcal{P}_E = \{\mathsf{new}/1, \mathsf{merge}/2, \mathsf{split}/2\}$. The evolution rules are

$$\mathsf{new}(x) \bullet \neg \mathsf{alive}(x) \blacktriangleright \circledast x; \mathsf{ld}(x)$$
$$\mathsf{merge}(x_1, x_2) \bullet \mathsf{ld}(x_1) \wedge \mathsf{alive}(x_2) \wedge x_1 \neq x_2 \blacktriangleright \neg \mathsf{ld}(x_1); \mathsf{fl}(x_1); \mathsf{fc}(x_1, x_2); \mathsf{bc}(x_2, x_1)$$
$$\mathsf{split}(x_1, x_2) \bullet \mathsf{ld}(x_1) \wedge \mathsf{bc}(x_1, x_2) \blacktriangleright \mathsf{ld}(x_2); \neg \mathsf{fl}(x_2); \neg \mathsf{fc}(x_2, x_1); \neg \mathsf{bc}(x_1, x_2)$$

written in the form $label \bullet guard \blacktriangleright actions$. The first rule allows to freely create cars as leaders, that is, any structure where some process identity u is currently not alive (see below for the definition of alive) may evolve into a structure where u exists and $\mathsf{ld}(u)$ holds. The second rule allows to merge a leader car with some other alive car, that is, the leader becomes a follower and communication links are established. The third rule allows a leader car to split from its back car.

Now to formally characterise when two logical structures are in transition relation according to a dynamic system, we need to define the satisfaction of a guard and the effect of applying actions to a logical structure. Let $\mathcal{M} = (\mathcal{U}, \iota) \in \mathbf{M}_S(I)$ be a logical structure and $\mathcal{V} \in Vals_I(X)$ a valuation, i.e. a function $X \to I$ of variables $X \subseteq \mathcal{X}$ to identities $I \subseteq Id^\perp$. Then

$$\mathcal{M}[\![p(x_1, \ldots, x_{k_p})]\!](\mathcal{V}) := \mathcal{V}(x_1), \ldots, \mathcal{V}(x_{k_p}) \in \mathcal{U} \wedge \iota(p)(\mathcal{V}(x_1), \ldots, \mathcal{V}(x_{k_p}))$$
$$\mathcal{M}[\![x_1 = x_2]\!](\mathcal{V}) := \mathcal{V}(x_1), \mathcal{V}(x_2) \in \mathcal{U} \wedge \mathcal{V}(x_1) = \mathcal{V}(x_2)$$
$$\mathcal{M}[\![\neg \psi]\!](\mathcal{V}) := \neg \mathcal{M}[\![\psi]\!](\mathcal{V})$$
$$\mathcal{M}[\![\psi_1 \wedge \psi_2]\!](\mathcal{V}) := \mathcal{M}[\![\psi_1]\!](\mathcal{V}) \wedge \mathcal{M}[\![\psi_2]\!](\mathcal{V})$$

inductively defines the (possibly three-valued) *satisfaction* of a guard. We decided that a term can only be satisfied if all its arguments are currently alive, that is, in $\mathcal{U}$. In particular, this allows for the abbreviation $\mathsf{alive}(x) := x = x$. The action *update* of $\mathcal{M} = (\mathcal{U}, \iota)$ under valuation $\mathcal{V}$ is inductively defined as

$$\mathcal{M}\langle a_1; a_2; \ldots; a_n \rangle(\mathcal{V}) := \mathcal{M}\langle a_1 \rangle(\mathcal{V})\langle a_2; \ldots; a_n \rangle(\mathcal{V})$$
$$\mathcal{M}\langle p(x_1, \ldots, x_{k_p}) \rangle(\mathcal{V}) := (\mathcal{U}, \iota[p \mapsto \iota(p)[(\mathcal{V}(x_1), \ldots, \mathcal{V}(x_{k_p})) \mapsto 1]])$$
$$\mathcal{M}\langle \neg p(x_1, \ldots, x_{k_p}) \rangle(\mathcal{V}) := (\mathcal{U}, \iota[p \mapsto \iota(p)[(\mathcal{V}(x_1), \ldots, \mathcal{V}(x_{k_p})) \mapsto 0]])$$
$$\mathcal{M}\langle \circledast x \rangle(\mathcal{V}) := (\mathcal{U} \cup \{\mathcal{V}(x)\}, \iota)$$
$$\mathcal{M}\langle \ominus x \rangle(\mathcal{V}) := (\mathcal{U} \setminus \{\mathcal{V}(x)\}, \iota)$$

where $f[x \mapsto y]$ denotes substitution for some function $f : X \to Y$, i.e. it alters the function f to yield $y \in Y$ for argument $x \in X$, and $f(x')$ for all $x' \in X \setminus \{x\}$.

Starting at the empty structure $(\emptyset, (\emptyset, \emptyset))$, the semantics of a dynamic system is computed by iteratively applying evolution rules that are *enabled*, i.e. there is a valuation $\mathcal{V}$ into the infinite domain of identities Id s.t. the guard is satisfied. Note that the evolution steps are labelled by the applied rule and the subset of involved identities. This information will be exploited later when evaluating temporal specifications and for performing spotlight extension as refinement.

Definition 1 (Concrete Semantics). *The concrete semantics of a dynamic system* D *over* $\mathcal{S}$, *denoted* $[D]$, *is the labelled transition system* $(\mathbf{S}, \mathbf{S}_0, \mathbf{L}, \mathbf{R})$ *with*

- *states* $\mathbf{S} := \mathbf{M}_\mathcal{S}(Id)$ *with initial state* $\mathbf{S}_0 := (\emptyset, (\emptyset, \emptyset))$,
- *labels* $\mathbf{L}$ *and transitions* $\mathbf{R} := \{(\mathcal{M}, label[V], \mathcal{M}\langle actions\rangle(\mathcal{V})) \in \mathbf{S} \times \mathbf{L} \times \mathbf{S} \mid$
$$\exists (label \bullet guard \blacktriangleright actions) \in D, \mathcal{V} \in Vals_{Id}(\mathcal{X}) : \mathcal{M}[\![guard]\!](\mathcal{V})\}.$$

where $p(x_1, \ldots, x_{k_p})[\mathcal{V}] := p(\mathcal{V}(x_1), \ldots, \mathcal{V}(x_{k_p}))$ *for* $p \in \mathcal{P}_E$.   ◇

The concrete semantics induces a set of runs of a dynamic system D as follows. A run of $\mathsf{T} = (\mathbf{S}, \mathbf{S}_0, \mathbf{L}, \mathbf{R})$ is an infinite sequence $((L_i, S_i))_{i \in \mathbb{N}_0}$ of labels $L_i \in \mathbf{L}$ and states $S_i = (\mathcal{U}_i, \iota_i) \in \mathbf{S}$ such that $S_0 = \mathbf{S}_0$ and $(S_i, L_{i+1}, S_{i+1}) \in \mathbf{R}$ for all $i \geq 0$. The runs of T are denoted by $Runs(\mathsf{T})$. An example run of $[\mathsf{Car}]$ is

$$((\emptyset, (\emptyset, \emptyset))),$$
$$(\mathsf{new}(u_1), (\{u_1\}, (\{\mathsf{Id}(u_1)\}, \emptyset))),$$
$$(\mathsf{new}(u_2), (\{u_1, u_2\}, (\{\mathsf{Id}(u_1), \mathsf{Id}(u_2)\}, \emptyset))),$$
$$(\mathsf{merge}(u_1, u_2), (\{u_1, u_2\}, (\{\mathsf{fl}(u_1), \mathsf{Id}(u_2), \mathsf{fc}(u_1, u_2), \mathsf{bc}(u_2, u_1)\}, \emptyset))),$$
$$(\mathsf{split}(u_2, u_1), (\{u_1, u_2\}, (\{\mathsf{Id}(u_1), \mathsf{Id}(u_2)\}, \emptyset))), \ldots$$

where two cars u_1, u_2 appear, merge to a platoon of size two and split again.

Note that the unbounded number of processes in a dynamic system renders the verification problem undecidable. In [20] we show how to encode the transitions of a two-counter-machine by a set of evolution rules as introduced above. The basic idea is to simulate an unbounded counter as a linked list of processes.

3.1 Spotlight Abstraction of Dynamic Systems

To obtain a finite representation of the infinite-state transition system, we apply spotlight abstraction [8]. It takes a finite set of "spotlight identities" $I \subseteq Id$ and collapses all identities from $Id \setminus I$ into the abstract identity $\perp$, for which all predicates then evaluate to $1/2$ in order to obtain a sound abstraction.

Definition 2 (Spotlight Abstraction). *The spotlight abstraction of a logical structure is the function* $\alpha.(\cdot) : 2^{Id} \times \mathbf{M}_\mathcal{S}(Id^\perp) \rightarrow \mathbf{M}_\mathcal{S}(Id^\perp)$ *with* $\alpha_I((\mathcal{U}, \iota)) := (\alpha_I(\mathcal{U}), \alpha_I(\iota))$ *where* $\alpha_I(\mathcal{U}) := (\mathcal{U} \cap I) \cup \{\perp\}$ *and*

$$\alpha_I(\iota)(p_l)(\perp, u_1) := 1/2 \qquad\qquad \alpha_I(\iota)(p_s)(u_1) := \iota(p_s)(u_1)$$
$$\alpha_I(\iota)(p_l)(u_1, u_2) := \iota(p_l)(u_1, u_2) \qquad\qquad \alpha_I(\iota)(p_s)(\perp) := 1/2$$
$$\alpha_I(\iota)(p_l)(u_1, \perp) := 1/2 \text{ if } \exists u' \in \mathcal{U} \setminus I : \iota(p_l)(u_1, u'), \text{ and } 0 \text{ else}$$

for $p_s \in \mathcal{P}_S$, $p_l \in \mathcal{P}_L$, *and* $u_1, u_2 \in \mathcal{U} \cap I$.   ◇

Note that a binary predicate p_l for some concrete process u_1 and the summary process $\perp$ becomes $1/2$ if there was at least one collapsed process u' where the predicate was true. By this we actually lose the *number* of links to abstracted processes (cf. Fig. 2(b)). The fact that the abstraction neglects all information about the processes outside of the spotlight allows the abstract transition relation to be easily computed. We simply restrict the set of states to finite three-valued structures $\mathbf{M}_S(I^\perp)$, apply the action update as in the concrete semantics, and then blur the resulting structure via the abstraction function α_I from Def. 2.

Definition 3 (Abstract Semantics). *The abstract semantics of a dynamic system* $D \in \mathcal{D}_S$ *and a set of identities* $I \subseteq Id$, *denoted* $[D]_I^\sharp$, *is the labelled transition system* $(\mathbf{S}, \mathbf{S}_0, \mathbf{L}, \mathbf{R})$ *with*

- *states* $\mathbf{S} := \mathbf{M}_S(I^\perp)$ *with initial state* $\mathbf{S}_0 := \alpha_I((\emptyset, (\emptyset, \emptyset)))$,
- *and transitions* $\mathbf{R} := \{(\mathcal{M}, label[V], \alpha_I(\mathcal{M}\langle actions\rangle(\mathcal{V}))) \in \mathbf{S} \times \mathbf{L} \times \mathbf{S} \mid$
  $\exists\,(label \bullet guard \blacktriangleright actions) \in D, \mathcal{V} \in Vals_{I\perp}(\mathcal{X}) : \mathcal{M}[\![guard]\!](\mathcal{V}) \geq 1/2\}.$ ◇

Remark 1. Let D be a dynamic system and $I \subset Id$ a finite set of identities, i.e. a finite spotlight. Then $[D]_I^\sharp$ is finite, i.e. it comprises only finitely many states. ◇

We proceed by introducing the syntax and semantics of a specification logic for dynamic systems, and provide a generalised soundness theorem for spotlight abstraction in terms of the information order of three-valued logic.

3.2   Specification Logic for Dynamic Systems

Temporal logic [21] has become a standard formalism to reason about system behaviour. In this paper, we use a variant of first-order linear time logic with implicit universal quantification. The specification language over signature $\mathcal{S} = (\mathcal{X}, \mathcal{P}_S, \mathcal{P}_L, \mathcal{P}_E)$, denoted $Specs_{\mathcal{S}}$, is defined by the grammar

$$\phi ::= \mathbf{tt} \mid t \mid \neg\phi \mid \phi_1 \wedge \phi_2 \mid \phi \geq 1/2 \mid \mathsf{G}\,\phi \mid \mathsf{F}\,\phi$$

where t is a term over $\mathcal{P}$. For example, the following specification for the Car system states that for all cars x_1, whenever x_1 is in its ld ("leader") state it has no fc ("front car") connection to any car x_2:

$$\phi_{\mathsf{ld}} := \mathsf{G}\,(\mathsf{ld}(x_1) \rightarrow \neg \mathsf{fc}(x_1, x_2))$$

In the case of overapproximative abstraction, the satisfaction of a temporal specification transfers from the abstract to the concrete system, i.e. $D^\sharp \models \phi \rightarrow D \models \phi$. In the case of spotlight abstraction, we observe special cases where also the converse holds, i.e. where $D^\sharp \not\models \phi \rightarrow D \not\models \phi$. We can easily identify these cases by exploiting the fact that the transitions are annotated by the set of involved identities: Any violation where $\perp$ is not involved is by construction a concrete violation in the original system. This finding leads to a new three-valued definition of a run satisfying a temporal specification as follows, and is the basis for identifying non-spurious abstract counterexamples.

Definition 4 (Satisfaction Relation). *Let* T *be a labelled transition system over signature* $\mathcal{S}$. *The satisfaction of* $\phi \in Specs_{\mathcal{S}}$ *in a run* $\pi = ((L_i, S_i))_{i \in \mathbb{N}_0} \in Runs(\mathsf{T})$ *under valuation* $\mathcal{V} \in Vals_{Id^\perp}(vars(\phi))$ *is defined inductively as follows, where* $p_s \in \mathcal{P}_S$, $p_l \in \mathcal{P}_L$ *and* $p_e \in \mathcal{P}_E$.

$$\pi[\![p_s(x)]\!]^i(\mathcal{V}) := S_i[\![p_s(x)]\!](\mathcal{V}) \qquad \pi[\![\phi \geq {}^1\!/{}_2]\!]^i(\mathcal{V}) := \pi[\![\phi]\!]^i(\mathcal{V}) \geq {}^1\!/{}_2$$

$$\pi[\![p_l(x_1, x_2)]\!]^i(\mathcal{V}) := S_i[\![p_l(x_1, x_2)]\!](\mathcal{V}) \qquad \pi[\![\neg\phi]\!]^i(\mathcal{V}) := \neg\,\pi[\![\phi]\!]^i(\mathcal{V})$$

$$\pi[\![p_e(x_1, \ldots, x_{k_{p_e}})]\!]^i(\mathcal{V}) := L_i = p_e(\mathcal{V}(x_1), \ldots, \mathcal{V}(u_{k_{p_e}})) \qquad \pi[\![\mathbf{tt}]\!]^i(\mathcal{V}) := 1$$

$$\pi[\![\phi_1 \wedge \phi_2]\!]^i(\mathcal{V}) := \pi[\![\phi_1]\!]^i(\mathcal{V}) \wedge \pi[\![\phi_2]\!]^i(\mathcal{V})$$

$$\pi[\![\mathsf{G}\,\phi]\!]^i(\mathcal{V}) := \begin{cases} 1 & if\ \forall\, k \geq i : \big(\pi[\![\phi]\!]^k(\mathcal{V}) = 1\big) \\ 0 & if\ \exists\, k \geq i : \big(\pi[\![\phi]\!]^k(\mathcal{V}) = 0 \wedge \\ & \qquad \forall\, j \in \{i \ldots k\} : \perp \notin L_j\big) \\ {}^1\!/{}_2 & else \end{cases}$$

$$\pi[\![\mathsf{F}\,\phi]\!]^i(\mathcal{V}) := \neg\,\pi[\![\mathsf{G}\,\neg\phi]\!]^i(\mathcal{V})$$

The satisfaction of ϕ *in* T *under* $\mathcal{V}$ *is defined as the minimum over all runs:*

$$\mathsf{T}[\![\phi]\!](\mathcal{V}) := \min\{\pi[\![\phi]\!]^0(\mathcal{V}) \in \mathbb{B}_3 \mid \pi \in Runs(\mathsf{T})\}. \qquad \diamond$$

By this, we obtain an *embedding* (with respect to the information order) of the three-valued satisfaction for the abstracted semantics into the satisfaction for the concrete semantics. That is, whenever $[\mathsf{D}]_I^\sharp[\![\phi]\!](\mathcal{V})$ evaluates to a definite value, then $[\mathsf{D}][\![\phi]\!](\mathcal{V})$ evaluates to the same value. If $[\mathsf{D}]_I^\sharp[\![\phi]\!](\mathcal{V}) = {}^1\!/{}_2$, we remain inconclusive. The following theorem formally states this property.

Theorem 1 (Embedding). *Let* D *be a dynamic system over* $\mathcal{S}$ *and* $\phi \in Specs_{\mathcal{S}}$. *Then*

$$[\mathsf{D}]_I^\sharp[\![\phi]\!](\mathcal{V}) \sqsubseteq [\mathsf{D}][\![\phi]\!](\mathcal{V})$$

for any spotlight $I \subseteq Id$ *and valuation* $\mathcal{V} \in Vals_I(vars(\phi))$. $\qquad \diamond$

Based on the satisfaction relation from Def. 4, we define the satisfaction of the quantified specification for a dynamic system in two variants, namely for the concrete and the abstract semantics of a dynamic system. For the latter, we allow to fix a subset of the variables that will bind to the $\perp$ identity, and we set the range of the actual valuation function as the content of the spotlight.

Definition 5 (Quantified Satisfaction). *For a dynamic system* D *over signature* $\mathcal{S}$, *a specification* $\phi \in Specs_{\mathcal{S}}$ *and variables* $X \subseteq vars(\phi)$ *we define*

$$\mathsf{D}[\![\phi]\!] := \min\{\,[\mathsf{D}][\![\phi]\!](\mathcal{V}) \in \mathbb{B}_3 \mid \mathcal{V} \in Vals_{Id}(vars(\phi))\}$$

$$\mathsf{D}_X^\sharp[\![\phi]\!] := \min\{\,[\mathsf{D}]_{ran(\mathcal{V})\backslash\{\perp\}}^\sharp[\![\phi]\!](\mathcal{V}) \in \mathbb{B}_3 \mid \mathcal{V} \in Vals_{Id^\perp}(vars(\phi))\ with$$
$$\mathcal{V}(x) = \perp \iff x \in X\}. \qquad \diamond$$

Note that $D[\![\phi]\!] \in \{0,1\}$. For the abstract semantics, we compute the minimal value according to $\leq$, i.e. if there is an abstract run and a valuation that yields a definite violation, we obtain a definite violation of the quantified specification, and if all runs under all valuations yield a definite satisfaction, we obtain a definite satisfaction. In all other cases, we obtain the indefinite value $1/2$.

The above definition requires to analyse the system under *infinitely many* valuation functions. However, we observe that dynamic systems induce transition systems that are symmetric in identities [22], i.e. whenever a set of processes I satisfies (violates) a specification, then any permutation on process identities $\sigma(I)$ satisfies (violates) the specification. This is because the behaviour of a process does not depend on its actual identity. Given a specification comprising N variables, we may reduce the number of valuations to a finite number N' of representative cases, where N' lies in $O(N!)$ [22]. These cases now only distinguish between the pairwise (in-)equality of process identities. For example, for the verification of ϕ_{ld} it is sufficient to consider two valuations, e.g. $[x_1 \mapsto u_1, x_2 \mapsto u_1]$ and $[x_1 \mapsto u_1, x_2 \mapsto u_2]$, because all other cases are symmetric. Note that in [23] the term Query Reduction was coined for such kind of exact reductions.

Theorem 1 directly transfers to the quantified case when no variable in $vars(\phi)$ evaluates to the $\perp$ identity, that is, $D_\emptyset^\sharp[\![\phi]\!] \sqsubseteq D[\![\phi]\!]$. In practice, this relation is only of interest when obtaining a definite value for the abstract system. However, the coarse representation of the spotlight environment allows for many (spurious) interferences with the spotlight (see an example below), hence we expect to often obtain the inconclusive result $1/2$. In the next section, we devise an iterative algorithm to suppress these interferences.

4   Spotlight Abstraction Refinement

In the following, let D be a dynamic system over signature $\mathcal{S}$ and $\phi \in Specs_\mathcal{S}$. Whenever $D_X^\sharp[\![\phi]\!] \leq 1/2$, we can present a counterexample δ to demonstrate the (abstract) violation. By remark 1 such a counterexample can be finitely represented by a finite prefix of a run (possibly with a looping part as suffix, i.e. lasso-shaped [24]). We define the set of counterexamples

$$\delta = \langle \bar{\pi}, \mathcal{V} \rangle \in Cex(D_X^\sharp[\![\phi]\!])$$

where $\bar{\pi} = ((L_i, S_i))_{0 \leq i \leq n}$ is a finite prefix of a run $\pi \in Runs([D]_I^\sharp)$ and $\mathcal{V} \in Vals_{I\perp}(vars(\phi))$ is a valuation such that $\pi[\![\phi]\!]^0(\mathcal{V}) \leq 1/2$.

A counterexample in $Cex(\mathsf{Car}_\emptyset^\sharp[\![G(\mathsf{ld}(x_1) \to \neg\mathsf{fc}(x_1, x_2))]\!])$ is $\delta_{\mathsf{ld}} =$

$$\langle\ \alpha_{\{u_1,u_2\}}(\{\perp\}, (\emptyset, \emptyset)),$$
$$(\mathsf{new}(u_1),\ \alpha_{\{u_1,u_2\}}(\{u_1, \perp\}, (\{\mathsf{ld}(u_1)\}, \emptyset))),$$
$$(\mathsf{new}(u_2),\ \alpha_{\{u_1,u_2\}}(\{u_1, u_2, \perp\}, (\{\mathsf{ld}(u_1), \mathsf{ld}(u_2)\}, \emptyset))),$$
$$(\mathsf{merge}(u_1, u_2),\ \alpha_{\{u_1,u_2\}}(\{u_1, u_2, \perp\}, \{\mathsf{fl}(u_1), \mathsf{ld}(u_2), \mathsf{fc}(u_1, u_2), \mathsf{bc}(u_2, u_1)\}, \emptyset)),$$
$$(\mathsf{split}(\perp, u_1),\ \alpha_{\{u_1,u_2\}}(\{u_1, u_2, \perp\}, \{\mathsf{ld}(u_1), \mathsf{ld}(u_2), \mathsf{fc}(u_1, u_2), \mathsf{bc}(u_2, u_1)\}, \emptyset)),$$
$$[x_1 \mapsto u_1, x_2 \mapsto u_2]\ \rangle$$

This run yields a possible violation of the specification because the last evolution $\mathsf{split}(\bot, u_1)$ yields a structure where $\mathsf{ld}(u_1) \wedge \mathsf{fc}(u_1, u_2)$, i.e. there is a leader car with a link to a front car. The question is whether those evolution transitions that affect the $\bot$ identity correspond to real behaviour of an (abstracted) process in the spotlight environment, or whether it is spurious behaviour stemming from the abstraction. In this example, we can manually argue that the $\mathsf{split}(\bot, u_1)$ is spurious because the prefix up to this transition indicates that no car in the spotlight environment is in a platoon with car u_1. In general, we consider a counterexample spurious if it has no concretisation, where a concretisation is possible if we can reproduce the behaviour of $\bot$ by concrete processes as follows.

Definition 6 (Concretisation). *Let* D *be a dynamic system over signature* $\mathcal{S}$. *A run* $\pi = ((L_i', S_i'))_{i \in \mathbb{N}_0} \in Runs([\mathsf{D}])$ *is a concretisation of a counterexample*

$$\delta = \langle ((L_i, S_i))_{0 \leq i \leq n}, \mathcal{V} \rangle \in Cex(\mathsf{D}_X^\sharp \llbracket \phi \rrbracket),$$

written $\pi \succ \delta$, *if* $\pi \llbracket \phi \rrbracket^0 (\mathcal{V}) = 0$ *and a monotone function* $f : \bot(\delta) \to \mathbb{N}$ *exists s.t.*

$$\forall i \in \mathsf{dom}(f) : L_i = L_{f(i)}'[Id \setminus \mathsf{ran}(\mathcal{V}) \mapsto \bot] \wedge S_i = \alpha_{\mathsf{ran}(\mathcal{V})}(S_{f(i)}')$$

where $\bot(\delta)$ *denotes the interferences of the abstract process in* δ, *i.e.* $\bot(\delta) := \{i \in \{1, \dots, n\} \mid \bot \in L_i\}$. *The set of concretisations of* δ *is defined as* $\gamma(\delta) := \{\pi \in Runs([\mathsf{D}]) \mid \pi \succ \delta\}$, *and* δ *is called spurious, written* $F(\delta)$, *if* $\gamma(\delta) = \emptyset$.   ◇

The function f in Def. 6 ensures that each interference of the $\bot$ process is reproduced in the concretisation run in the same order. For example, Fig. 3 shows an abstract counterexample δ_{fl} for the specification $\phi_{\mathsf{fl}} := \mathsf{G} \neg \mathsf{fl}(x)$ where the only spotlight process u merges with the abstract process $\bot$. This counterexample is concretised by the run π_{fl} where the interference with the abstract process is replaced by interaction with a concrete process u'.

The identification of counterexample as being spurious requires to show that no concretisation exists, which reduces to an (in general undecidable) verification problem of the original system (see Lemma 1 below). However, the information contained in the counterexample allow a more specific verification task to be constructed where all evolution steps of the abstract process are now required to be performed by concrete processes. This provides a natural source for *spotlight extension* by introducing new variables in the specification as follows.

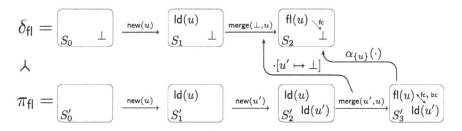

Fig. 3. Concretisation of an abstract counterexample for ϕ_{fl} with $f(2) = 3$

Definition 7 (Counterexample Formula). *Let* D *be a dynamic system over* S *and* $\delta = \langle((L_i, S_i))_{0 \leq i \leq n}, \mathcal{V}\rangle \in Cex(D_X^\sharp[\![\phi]\!])$ *a counterexample. We define the counterexample formula of* δ *recursively as* $\varphi(\delta) := \varphi(\delta)^1$ *where*

$$\varphi(\delta)^i := \begin{cases} \mathsf{F}\left(label(L_i, \mathcal{V}, i) \wedge state(S_i, \mathcal{V}) \wedge (\varphi(\delta)^{i+1})\right) & \textit{if } i \in \bot(\delta) \\ \varphi(\delta)^{i+1} & \textit{if } i \notin \bot(\delta) \wedge i \leq n \\ \mathsf{tt} & \textit{else} \end{cases}$$

where

$$label(p_e(u_1, \ldots, u_{k_p}), \mathcal{V}, i) := p(\mathcal{V}_+^{-1}(u_1, i, 1), \ldots, \mathcal{V}_+^{-1}(u_{k_p}, i, k_p)), \textit{ with}$$

$$\mathcal{V}_+^{-1}(u, i, j) := \begin{cases} \mathcal{V}^{-1}(u) & \textit{if } u \neq \bot \\ x_{i,j} \in \mathcal{X} \setminus \mathsf{dom}(\mathcal{V}) & \textit{else} \end{cases}$$

and

$$state(S, \mathcal{V}) := \bigwedge_{x_1 \in \mathsf{dom}(\mathcal{V}), p_s \in \mathcal{P}_S} \left(val(p_s(x_1), S, \mathcal{V}) \wedge \bigwedge_{x_2 \in \mathsf{dom}(\mathcal{V}), p_l \in \mathcal{P}_L} val(p_l(x_1, x_2), S, \mathcal{V})\right)$$

with $val(t, S, \mathcal{V}) = t$ *if* $S[\![t]\!](\mathcal{V}) = 1$ *and* $val(t, S, \mathcal{V}) = \neg t$ *else for any term* t. *By* $fresh(\varphi(\delta)) := vars(\varphi(\delta)) \setminus \mathsf{dom}(\mathcal{V})$ *we denote the new variables in* $\varphi(\delta)$. ◇

As an example, the counterexample δ_{ld} translates to $\varphi(\delta_{\mathsf{ld}}) =$

$$\mathsf{F}\left(\mathsf{split}(x_{4,1}, x_1) \wedge \mathsf{ld}(x_1) \wedge \neg\mathsf{fl}(x_1) \wedge \mathsf{fc}(x_1, x_2)\right) \wedge \neg\mathsf{bc}(x_1, x_2)) \wedge$$
$$\mathsf{ld}(x_2) \wedge \neg\mathsf{fl}(x_2) \wedge \neg\mathsf{fc}(x_2, x_1)) \wedge \mathsf{bc}(x_2, x_1) \wedge (\mathsf{tt}))$$

with $fresh(\varphi(\delta_{\mathsf{ld}})) = \{x_{4,1}\}$. The translation introduces nested F ("finally") expressions for each interference of the abstract $\bot$ process. In the *label* translation phase, each occurrence of $\bot$ in a transition label is substituted by a fresh process variable. The translation of the *state* part ensures that the configuration of the spotlight processes is preserved in the concretisation run. We have the following correspondence between the translation from Def. 7 and the definition of counterexample concretisation according to Def. 6.

Lemma 1 (Counterexample Validation). *Let* D *be a dynamic system over signature* S, $\phi \in Specs_S$ *and* $\delta \in Cex(D_X^\sharp[\![\phi]\!])$ *a counterexample. Then*

$$F(\delta) \iff D[\![\neg\varphi(\delta) \vee \phi]\!]. \qquad ◇$$

In other words, if and only if no concrete run exists that both satisfies the counterexample formula and violates the specification, then the counterexample is spurious. For the car platooning case study, we can verify (cf. Sect. 5) that

$$Car_\emptyset^\sharp[\![\neg\varphi(\delta_{\mathsf{ld}}) \vee \phi_{\mathsf{ld}}]\!] = 1$$

because the counterexample formula $\varphi(\delta_{\mathsf{ld}})$ is unsatisfiable under abstraction with three concrete processes in the spotlight. This entails $Car[\![\neg\varphi(\delta_{\mathsf{ld}}) \vee \phi_{\mathsf{ld}}]\!] = 1$ by the embedding theorem 1 and thus $F(\delta_{\mathsf{ld}})$ by Lemma 1, i.e. δ_{ld} is spurious.

We can not yet conclude that $\mathsf{Car}[\![\phi_{\mathsf{ld}}]\!]$ holds, obviously because there may be other counterexamples besides δ_{ld}. However, the fact that a counterexample is spurious allows us to reduce the satisfaction analysis to those runs where the counterexample formula is definitely violated. Thus by Lemma 1, we can use the counterexample formula as a source for shadow refinement simply by binding the fresh variables of the counterexample formula to $\bot$. By this, we eliminate behaviour of $\bot$ that was shown to be not possible with any concrete processes.

Lemma 2 (Shadow Refinement). *Let* D *be a dynamic system over signature* $\mathcal{S}$, $\phi \in \mathit{Specs}_{\mathcal{S}}$ *and* $\delta \in \mathit{Cex}(\mathsf{D}_X^{\sharp}[\![\phi]\!])$ *a counterexample with* $F(\delta)$. *Then*

$$\mathsf{D}_F^{\sharp}[\![\varphi(\delta) \geq {}^{1}\!/{}_{2} \vee \phi]\!] \sqsubseteq \mathsf{D}[\![\phi]\!]$$

for $F := \mathit{fresh}(\varphi(\delta))$. $\diamond$

Applied to the case study, we check

$$\mathsf{Car}_{\{x_4,1\}}^{\sharp}[\![\varphi(\delta_{\mathsf{ld}}) \geq {}^{1}\!/{}_{2} \vee \phi_{\mathsf{ld}}]\!]$$

for which we obtain the result 1, intuitively because ϕ_{ld} holds on all runs where $\varphi(\delta_{\mathsf{ld}})$ is definitely violated. From Lemma 2, we conclude that $\mathsf{Car}[\![\phi_{\mathsf{ld}}]\!] = 1$.

This procedure of validation and refinement can be iterated in a standard refinement loop, where the iteration runs as long as we obtain an indefinite result. We must however be prepared that a counterexample may not be (in-)validated via a single verification run, because checking the counterexample formula according to Lemma 1 *under spotlight abstraction* may not yield a definite answer. In this case we can use the same validation and refinement procedure for the counterexample of the counterexample formula. Algorithm 1 called $\mathsf{check}(\mathsf{D}, \phi)$ implements our idea of counterexample guided spotlight abstraction refinement by recursively calling itself for iterative counterexample validation. By the above lemmata 1 and 2, we have that $\mathsf{D}[\![\phi]\!] \iff \mathsf{check}(\mathsf{D}, \phi)$.

Algorithm 1. $\mathsf{check}(\mathsf{D}, \phi)$ returns $\mathbb{B}$

1: let $F := \emptyset$
2: let $b := \mathsf{D}_F^{\sharp}[\![\phi]\!]$
3: **while** $b = {}^{1}\!/{}_{2}$ **do**
4:     let $\delta \in \mathit{Cex}(\mathsf{D}_F^{\sharp}[\![\phi]\!])$
5:     **if** $\mathsf{check}(\mathsf{D}, \neg\varphi(\delta) \vee \phi)$ **then**
6:         let $F := F \cup \mathit{fresh}(\varphi(\delta))$
7:         let $\phi := \varphi(\delta) \geq {}^{1}\!/{}_{2} \vee \phi$
8:         let $b := \mathsf{D}_F^{\sharp}[\![\phi]\!]$
9:     **else**
10:         $b := 0$
11:     **end if**
12: **end while**
13: **return** b

As a consequence of the undecidability of the verification problem, algorithm 1 does not terminate in general. However, in each recursion depth the spotlight is enlarged and each iteration eliminates a new source for spurious interference. In fact it can be shown [20] that the only source for divergence of the algorithm is the recursive counterexample validation, whereas the iterative refinement is guaranteed to finally terminate. We thus anticipate that the overall algorithm terminates for a relevant class of dynamic systems, namely for those where counterexamples can be (in-)validated via a finite number of concrete processes. First promising experiments are given in the next Section.

5   Evaluation

We use an existing verification environment for dynamic systems, which has been developed in the course of [10], for a first experimental evaluation of our approach. The toolset comprises a compiler from XML descriptions of dynamic systems to input languages of finite-state model-checkers, and integrates the spotlight abstraction implementation of [25]. The experiments were performed by the VIS 2.1 model-checker [6] on a Linux host with 3 GHz and 2 GB of RAM. In Table 1 below, 'rec' denotes the actual recursion depth of algorithm 1, 'iter' the iteration counter in this depth, and 'spot' the maximal size of the spotlight, that is, the number of concrete processes.

The upper part of Table 1 shows the verification tasks that are necessary to verify the running example property ϕ_{ld} for the car platooning system. As a second experiment, we demonstrate that we are able to obtain *concrete* counterexamples under spotlight abstraction. This is of special importance as a typical debugging application of model-checking is to check whether a certain *desired* configuration is reachable. Therefore, one claims that the negation of the configuration is globally true and expects a counterexample. The lower part of Table 1 shows the verification tasks necessary to disprove the property $\phi_{\text{fl}} := G \neg fl(x)$, that is, to find a concrete witness for a car becoming a follower car (cf. Fig. 3).

We furthermore evaluated our approach on a case study concerning a scatternet formation [26] roughly following the bluetooth connection scenario. In this protocol, mobile devices are grouped into piconets comprising one master device and a finite set of slave devices connected in a star topology. Piconets may then merge into scatternets where one slave device serves as a bridge, that is, it is

Table 1. Task flow of check(Car, ϕ_{ld}) and check(Car, ϕ_{fl})

rec	iter	task	spot	result	time	memory
0	0	$\text{Car}_{\emptyset}^{\#}[\![\phi_{\text{ld}}]\!]$	2	$^{1}/_{2}$ (δ_{ld})	6 s	2 MB
1	0	$\text{Car}_{\emptyset}^{\#}[\![\neg\varphi(\delta_{\text{ld}}) \vee \phi_{\text{ld}}]\!]$	3	1	42 s	3 MB
1	0	return 1				
0	1	$\text{Car}_{\{x_{4,1}\}}^{\#}[\![\varphi(\delta_{\text{ld}}) \geq {}^{1}/_{2} \vee \phi_{\text{ld}}]\!]$	2	1	8 s	2 MB
0	1	return 1				
0	0	$\text{Car}_{\emptyset}^{\#}[\![\phi_{\text{fl}}]\!]$	1	$^{1}/_{2}$ (δ_{fl})	3 s	2 MB
1	0	$\text{Car}_{\emptyset}^{\#}[\![\neg\varphi(\delta) \vee \phi_{\text{fl}}]\!]$	2	0 (π_{fl})	7 s	2 MB
1	0	return 0				
0	0	return 0				

a slave in two different piconets at the same time and is routing information from one piconet to the other. The case study consists of seven evolution rules, and the running times of the verification tasks are below two minutes each. We needed a recursion depth of two with a maximal spotlight size of three to prove that a device is able become a bridge device. Two iterations and a recursion depth of one allows us to verify the safety property that a pure slave device has a connection to exactly one master device.

6   Conclusion

We have presented an iterative refinement scheme for spotlight abstractions that allows us to formally verify dynamic systems against first-order temporal specifications. To the best of our knowledge, this is the first iterative refinement approach in this research direction. Although spotlight abstraction can be formulated [8] as an instance of the canonical abstraction framework [18], our results reveal a quite different nature for refinement: While predicate abstraction allows us to identify spurious counterexamples by simulation but may diverge during the refinement steps, spotlight abstraction shifts the problem into the validation of counterexamples while the refinement itself can be done very effectively.

A strong point of our approach is that we may start with a minimal number of concrete processes, and enlarge the spotlight only *gradually* driven by abstract counterexamples. In doing so we keep the number of concurrent processes as small as possible in order to avoid combinatorial explosion of the model-checking tasks. The running times of the experiments confirm the importance of this issue.

For future work, we aim at a more in-depth investigation of termination properties of our algorithm. It will be worthwhile to integrate existing techniques for shadow refinement [14,15] in order to reduce the number of iterations. Also, the application of spotlight abstraction refinement in the area of heap manipulating programs [18] is of interest (see the discussion on related work on page 24).

References

1. UNISIG: Subset 026-ch. 3; vers. 2.2.2 (srs) (March 2002), http://www.aeif.org/ccm/default.asp
2. Kripke, S.: Semantical Considerations on Modal Logic. Acta Phil. Fennica 16, 83–94 (1963)
3. Clarke, E.M., Grumberg, O., Peled, D.A.: Model Checking. The MIT Press, Cambridge (1999)
4. Kesten, Y., Pnueli, A.: Control and Data Abstraction: The Cornerstones of Practical Formal Verification. International Journal on Software Tools for Technology Transfer 2(4), 328–342 (2000)
5. Fitting, M., Mendelsohn, R.L.: First Order Modal Logic. Kluwer, Dordrecht (1998)
6. Brayton, R.K., Hachtel, G.D., Sangiovanni - Vincentelli, A.L., Somenzi, F., Aziz, A., Cheng, S.T., Edwards, S.A., Khatri, S.P., Kukimoto, Y., Pardo, A., Qadeer, S., Ranjan, R.K., Sarwary, S., Shiple, T.R., Swamy, G., Villa, T.: VIS: a System for Verification and Synthesis. In: Alur, R., Henzinger, T.A. (eds.) CAV 1996. LNCS, vol. 1102, pp. 428–432. Springer, Heidelberg (1996)

7. Holzmann, G.J.: The SPIN model checker: Primer and reference manual. Addison-Wesley, Reading (2004)
8. Wachter, B., Westphal, B.: The Spotlight Principle. On Combining Process-Summarising State Abstractions. In: Cook, B., Podelski, A. (eds.) VMCAI 2007. LNCS, vol. 4349, pp. 182–198. Springer, Heidelberg (2007)
9. Clarke, E.M., Grumberg, O., Jha, S., Lu, Y., Veith, H.: Counterexample-Guided Abstraction Refinement. In: Emerson, E.A., Sistla, A.P. (eds.) CAV 2000. LNCS, vol. 1855, pp. 154–169. Springer, Heidelberg (2000)
10. Rakow, J.: Verification of Dynamic Communication Systems. Master's thesis, Carl von Ossietzky Universität Oldenburg (April 2006)
11. Westphal, B.: LSC Verification for UML Models with Unbounded Creation and Destruction. Electr. Notes Theor. Comput. Sci. 144(3), 133–145 (2006)
12. Miller, A., Calder, M.: An automatic abstraction technique for verifying featured, parameterised systems. Theor. Comput. Sci. (to appear, 2007)
13. Damm, W., Westphal, B.: Live and let die: LSC-based verification of UML-models. Science of Computer Programming 55(1–3), 117–159 (2005)
14. Toben, T.: Non-Interference Properties for Data-Type Reduction of Communicating Systems. In: Davies, J., Gibbons, J. (eds.) IFM 2007. LNCS, vol. 4591, pp. 619–638. Springer, Heidelberg (2007)
15. Bauer, J., Toben, T., Westphal, B.: Mind the Shapes: Abstraction Refinement via Topology Invariants. In: Namjoshi, K.S., Yoneda, T., Higashino, T., Okamura, Y. (eds.) ATVA 2007. LNCS, vol. 4762, pp. 35–50. Springer, Heidelberg (2007)
16. Bauer, J., Wilhelm, R.: Static Analysis of Dynamic Communication Systems by Partner Abstraction. In: Riis Nielson, H., Filé, G. (eds.) SAS 2007. LNCS, vol. 4634, pp. 249–264. Springer, Heidelberg (2007)
17. König, B., Kozioura, V.: Counterexample-Guided Abstraction Refinement for the Analysis of Graph Transformation Systems. In: Hermanns, H., Palsberg, J. (eds.) TACAS 2006 and ETAPS 2006. LNCS, vol. 3920, pp. 197–211. Springer, Heidelberg (2006)
18. Sagiv, S., Reps, T.W., Wilhelm, R.: Parametric shape analysis via 3-valued logic. ACM Trans. Program. Lang. Syst. 24(3), 217–298 (2002)
19. Kleene, S.C.: Introduction to metamathematics. Bibl. Matematica. North-Holland, Amsterdam (1952)
20. Toben, T.: Spotlight Abstraction Refinement by Evolution Constraints. PhD thesis, Carl von Ossietzky Universität Oldenburg (to appear, 2008)
21. Pnueli, A.: The temporal logic of programs. In: Proc. FOCS, pp. 46–57. IEEE, Los Alamitos (1977)
22. Westphal, B.: Specification and Verification of Dynamic Topology Systems. PhD thesis, Carl von Ossietzky Universität Oldenburg (2008)
23. Xie, F., Browne, J.C.: Integrated State Space Reduction for Model Checking Executable Object-oriented Software System Designs. In: Kutsche, R.-D., Weber, H. (eds.) ETAPS 2002 and FASE 2002. LNCS, vol. 2306, pp. 64–79. Springer, Heidelberg (2002)
24. Vardi, M.Y., Wolper, P.: An Automata-Theoretic Approach to Automatic Program Verification. In: Proc. LICS 1986, pp. 332–344. IEEE Computer Society, Los Alamitos (1986)
25. Westphal, B., Cook, B.S.: LSC Verification for UML Models with Unbounded Creation and Destruction. In: B. Cook, S., Stoller, W.V. (eds.) Proc. SoftMC 2005. ENTCS, vol. 144(3), pp. 133–145. Elsevier B.V, Amsterdam (2005)
26. Haartsen, J.: Bluetooth – the universal radio interface for adhoc, wireless connectivity. Ericsson Review 3 (1998)

An Experimental Evaluation of Probabilistic Simulation*

Jonathan Bogdoll, Holger Hermanns, and Lijun Zhang

Department of Computer Science, Saarland University, Saarbrücken, Germany
{bogdoll,hermanns,zhang}@cs.uni-sb.de

Abstract. *Probabilistic* model checking has emerged as a versatile system verification approach, but is frequently facing state-space explosion problems. One promising attack to this is to construct an abstract model which *simulates* the original model, and to perform model checking on that abstract model. Recently, efficient algorithms for deciding simulation of probabilistic models have been proposed. They reduce the theoretical complexity bounds drastically by exploiting parametric maximum flow algorithms. In this paper, we report on experimental comparisons of these algorithms, together with various interesting optimizations. The evaluation is carried out on both standard PRISM example cases as well as randomly generated models. The results show interesting time-space tradeoffs, with the parametric maximum flow algorithms being superior for large, dense models.

1 Introduction

System performance and dependability becomes more and more important with the ubiquity of computing systems. Discrete-time and continuous-time Markov chains (DTMCs and CTMCs) [18] are widely used to model and analyze performance and dependability of such systems. A related model, which in addition supports nondeterminism, is the model of probabilistic automata (PAs) [17]. For all these three models, tool support is available, in the form of probabilistic model checkers such as PRISM [12] or MRMC [15]. They enable the automatic verification of performance and dependability models for specifications expressed by PCTL [11,6] or CSL [1,3] formulas. PCTL is a discrete probabilistic variant of the temporal logic CTL interpreted over DTMCs and PAs, and CSL is its continuous stochastic extension, tailored to CTMCs.

Despite the remarkable versatility of this approach, its power is limited by the infamous state space explosion problem. Several approaches are being pursued to alleviate that problem. Notably, minimizing the system to the bisimulation quotient is a favorable approach [14]. As a more aggressive attack to the problem, simulation relations [13,4,5] have been proposed for these models, which, in correspondence to the non-probabilistic setting, preserve relevant fragments

---

* This work is supported by the NWO-DFG bilateral project VOSS and by the DFG as part of the Transregional Collaborative Research Center SFB/TR 14 AVACS.

K. Suzuki et al. (Eds.): FORTE 2008, LNCS 5048, pp. 37–52, 2008.

of the logics PCTL and CSL, respectively. In particular, they provide the principal ingredients to perform abstractions of the models, while preserving *safe* fragments of the respective logics [5,17].

The kernel of simulation, simulation equivalence, preserves both safe and live fragments of PCTL. Since simulation equivalence is coarser than bisimulation, the induced quotient is thus smaller. This means that as long as one is interested in safety or liveness properties, it is favorable to perform model checking on the simulation equivalence quotient. To strive for the quotient, an algorithm for deciding simulation preorder is needed. Since the bisimulation algorithm is generally faster than the simulation algorithm, one can combine them by constructing the simulation quotient based on the bisimulation quotient.

In many applications the specification can not be easily expressed by the logic PCTL or CSL: it is rather a probabilistic model itself. Examples of this kind include various recent wireless network protocols, such as ZigBee [10], Firewire Zeroconf [7], or the novel IEEE 802.11e, where the central mechanism is selecting among different-sided dies, readily expressible as a probabilistic automaton [16]. For such cases, a decision algorithm for simulation preorder can be applied as a specification checker: The model satisfies the specification if the automaton for the specification *simulates* the automaton for the model. We believe that such specification checking is the only formal validation technique that is in reach for verifying implementations of the above protocols. Given the emergence of ever more wireless standards of that sort, there is an obvious motivation to study the principal technological basis: the decision algorithm for probabilistic simulation. This paper attacks the very problem of efficient decision algorithms for probabilistic simulation.

Let n denote the number of states, and m denote the number of transitions. Baier *et al.* [2] introduced a polynomial decision algorithm for simulation with time complexity $\mathcal{O}(n^7/\log n)$ and space complexity $\mathcal{O}(n^2)$, by tailoring a network flow algorithm to the problem, embedded into an iterative refinement loop. This complexity can be improved to time complexity $\mathcal{O}(m^2n)$ by exploiting the parametric maximum flow algorithm [8] to solve the maximum flows for the arising sequences of similar networks [21]. This improvement however comes with a penalty in space complexity $\mathcal{O}(m^2)$, since one has to store networks across iterations. Lately, the algorithm developed in [21] has been extended to handle probabilistic automata and their continuous-time extension [20].

The purpose of this paper is to complement the theoretical complexity results with practical evidence concerning which algorithmic approach has the most potential in practical applications. We provide, for the first time, systematic experimental results of the space and time requirements of the available algorithms, also comparing several optimizations and heuristics to accelerate the algorithm. As a base algorithm we use an implementation of decision algorithm [2] without any optimizations. The parametric maximum flow variation is treated as one particular optimization. We also consider the effect of the following optimizations which can be applied selectively:

- Partitioning: By grouping states with identical probabilistic structure into equivalence classes, computations can be performed on representative elements for each class.
- Invariant checking: Some pairs can be removed from the simulation by asserting an invariant on the arc capacities in the corresponding maximum flow network, which is computationally less complex than the maximum flow algorithm. This invariant is referred to as the P-Invariant in the remainder of this paper.
- Significant arcs: As the algorithm progresses, arcs will be deleted from maximum flow networks as a result of pairs being removed from the simulation relation. If deleting such an arc will cause the network's flow to be less than 1, it is called significant. By deciding which arcs are significant in advance, some networks will be discarded as part of the update process and do not have to be considered in the following iteration.

We apply our approach to a variety of case studies taken from the PRISM webpage http://www.prismmodelchecker.org. In order to avoid a bias in the selection of models, we also evaluate the algorithms on randomly generated Markov models. This is inspired by [19] where the authors experimentally evaluated algorithms for classical automata constructions on random generated automata. Our experimental approach follows the same strategy. On randomly generated Markov chains, we have two interesting parameters to adjust in our studies: the density of transitions and the density of labels. We study the performance curve for various density combinations.

In a nutshell, we observe that state partitioning performs best on models with low to medium transition densities while P-Invariant checking, significant arc detection and parametric maximum flow perform better on models with medium to high transition densities. We also observe that significant arc detection and parametric maximum flow is not commendable in cases where memory usage is a concern.

Organization of the paper. Section 2 recalls the decision algorithm. We discuss various optimization strategies in Section 3. In Section 4 different combinations of the optimizations are compared on regular models, uniform random models and non-uniform random models. Section 5 concludes the paper.

2   Preliminaries

Let AP be a fixed, finite set of atomic propositions. For a finite set S, a distribution μ on S is a function $\mu : S \to [0,1]$ satisfying the condition $\mu(S) \leq 1$. We let $Dist(S)$ denote the set of distributions over the set S. The support of μ is defined by $Supp(\mu) = \{s \mid \mu(s) > 0\}$, and the size of μ is defined by $|\mu| = |Supp(\mu)|$. The distribution μ is called stochastic if $\mu(S) := \sum_{s \in S} \mu(s) = 1$, absorbing if $\mu(S) = 0$, and sub-stochastic otherwise. We use an auxiliary state (not a *real* state) $\bot \notin S$ and set $\mu(\bot) = 1 - \mu(S)$. Further, let $S_\bot$ denote the set $S \cup \{\bot\}$, and let $Supp_\bot(\mu) = Supp(\mu) \cup \{\bot\}$ if $\mu(\bot) > 0$.

Probabilistic Automata [17]. A probabilistic automaton (PA) is a tuple $\mathcal{M} = (S, Act, \mathbf{P}, L)$ where S is a finite set of states, Act is a finite set of actions, $\mathbf{P} \subseteq S \times Act \times Dist(S)$ is a finite set, called the probabilistic transition matrix, and $L : S \to 2^{AP}$ is a labeling function.

For $(s, \alpha, \mu) \in \mathbf{P}$, we use $s \xrightarrow{\alpha} \mu$ as a shorthand notation, and call μ an α-successor distribution of s. The PA $\mathcal{M}$ is a *fully probabilistic system* (FPS) if $Act = \{\alpha\}$ is a singleton and for $s \in S$, there is at most one transition $s \xrightarrow{\alpha} \mu$. A discrete-time Markov chain (DTMC) is an FPS where all distributions are either stochastic or absorbing. For ease of notation, we give a simpler definition for FPSs by dropping the single action: An FPS is a tuple $\mathcal{M} = (S, \mathbf{P}, L)$ where S, L as defined for PAs, and $\mathbf{P} : S \times S \to [0, 1]$ is the probabilistic transition matrix such that $\mathbf{P}(s, \cdot) \in Dist(S)$ for all $s \in S$. The *fanout* of the FPS $\mathcal{M}$ is defined by $\max_{s \in S} |\mathbf{P}(s, \cdot)|$.

Simulation requires that every α-successor distribution of one state have a corresponding α-successor distribution of the other state. The correspondence of distributions is naturally defined with the concept of *weight functions* [13]. For $\mu, \mu' \in Dist(S)$ and $R \subseteq S \times S$, a weight function for (μ, μ') with respect to R, denoted by $\mu \sqsubseteq_R \mu'$, is a function $\Delta : S_\perp \times S_\perp \to [0, 1]$ such that

1. $\Delta(s, s') > 0$ implies $(s, s') \in R$ or $s = \perp$,
2. $\mu(s) = \Delta(s, S_\perp)$ for $s \in S_\perp$,
3. $\mu'(s') = \Delta(S_\perp, s')$ for $s' \in S_\perp$.

The relation $R \subseteq S \times S$ is a *simulation* [17] on $\mathcal{M}$ iff for all s_1, s_2 with $(s_1, s_2) \in R$: $L(s_1) = L(s_2)$ and if $s_1 \xrightarrow{\alpha} \mu_1$ then there exists a transition $s_2 \xrightarrow{\alpha} \mu_2$ with $\mu_1 \sqsubseteq_R \mu_2$. We say that s_2 simulates s_1, denoted by $s_1 \precsim_\mathcal{M} s_2$, iff there exists a simulation R on $\mathcal{M}$ such that $(s_1, s_2) \in R$. Obviously $\precsim_\mathcal{M}$ is the coarsest simulation relation for $\mathcal{M}$.

For $(s_1, s_2) \in R$, we say that s_2 simulates s_1 up to R, denoted $s_1 \precsim_R s_2$, if $L(s_1) = L(s_2)$ and if $s_1 \xrightarrow{\alpha} \mu_1$ then there exists a transition $s_2 \xrightarrow{\alpha} \mu_2$ with $\mu_1 \sqsubseteq_R \mu_2$. Otherwise we write $s_1 \not\precsim_R s_2$. Note that $s_1 \precsim_R s_2$ does not imply $s_1 \precsim_\mathcal{M} s_2$ unless R is a simulation, since only the first step is considered for $\precsim_R$.

Algorithm for deciding simulation. The algorithm [2] takes as a parameter a model, which, for now, is an FPS $\mathcal{M}$. To calculate the simulation relation for $\mathcal{M}$, the algorithm starts with the trivial relation $R_{init} = \{(s_1, s_2) \in S \times S \mid L(s_1) = L(s_2)\}$ and removes each pair (s_1, s_2) if s_2 cannot simulate s_1 up to the current relation R, i.e., $s_1 \not\precsim_R s_2$. This proceeds until there is no such pair left, i.e., $R_{new} = R$. Invariantly throughout the loop it holds that R is at least as coarse as $\precsim_\mathcal{M}$. Hence, we obtain the simulation preorder $\precsim_\mathcal{M} = R$, once the algorithm terminates.

The decisive part of the algorithm is the check whether $s_1 \precsim_R s_2$. As the condition $L(s_1) = L(s_2)$ is easy to check, it remains to check whether $\mathbf{P}(s_1, \cdot) \sqsubseteq_R \mathbf{P}(s_2, \cdot)$ holds. This is reduced to a maximum flow computation on the network $\mathcal{N}(s_1, s_2, R)$ constructed out of $\mathbf{P}(s_1, \cdot)$, $\mathbf{P}(s_2, \cdot)$ and R. This network is constructed via a graph containing a copy $\bar{t} \in \overline{S_\perp}$ of each state $t \in S_\perp$ where $\overline{S_\perp} = \{\bar{t} \mid t \in S_\perp\}$ defined as follows: Let $\nearrow$ (the source) and $\searrow$ (the sink) be two additional vertices not contained in $S_\perp \cup \overline{S_\perp}$. For $\mu, \mu' \in Dist(S)$ and a relation $R \subseteq S \times S$ we define the network $\mathcal{N}(\mu, \mu', R) = (V, E, u)$ with the set of vertices

$$V = \{\nearrow, \searrow\} \cup Supp_\perp(\mu) \cup \overline{Supp_\perp(\mu')}$$

and the set of edges (or arcs) E defined by

$$E = \{(s, \overline{t}) \mid (s, t) \in R \vee s = \perp\} \cup \{(\nearrow, s), (\overline{t}, \searrow)\}$$

where $s \in Supp_\perp(\mu)$ and $t \in Supp_\perp(\mu')$. The capacity function u is defined as follows: $u(\nearrow, s) = \mu(s)$ for all $s \in S_\perp$, $u(\overline{t}, \searrow) = \mu'(t)$ for all $t \in S_\perp$, $u(s, \overline{t}) = \infty$ for all $(s, t) \in E$ and $u(v, w) = 0$ otherwise. Obviously, $\mathcal{N}(s_1, s_2, R)$ is a bipartite network. For two states s_1, s_2, we let $\mathcal{N}(s_1, s_2, R)$ denote the network $\mathcal{N}(\mathbf{P}(s_1, \cdot), \mathbf{P}(s_2, \cdot), R)$.

The crucial relationship exploited in [2] is that $\mathbf{P}(s_1, \cdot) \sqsubseteq_R \mathbf{P}(s_2, \cdot)$ iff the maximum flow in $\mathcal{N}(s_1, s_2, R)$ is 1. Thus we can decide $s_1 \precsim_R s_2$ by computing the maximum flow in $\mathcal{N}(s_1, s_2, R)$. A key observation we made in [21] is that the networks $\mathcal{N}(s_1, s_2, \cdot)$ constructed later in successive iterations are very similar: They differ from iteration to iteration only by deletion of some edges induced by the successive clean up of R. The algorithm, hence, exploits this fact by leveraging maximum flow already computed in the last iteration rather than re-starting maximum flow computation from scratch each time. In more detail, we consider the initial network $\mathcal{N}(s_1, s_2, R_{init})$ for an arbitrary pair $s_1, s_2 \in S$. Recall R_{init} denotes the initial relation $\{(s_1, s_2) \in S \times S \mid L(s_1) = L(s_2)\}$. Let $D_1, \ldots, D_k$ be pairwise disjoint subsets of R_{init}, which correspond to the pairs deleted from R_{init} in iteration i. Let $\mathcal{N}(s_1, s_2, R_i)$ denote $\mathcal{N}(s_1, s_2, R_{init})$ if $i = 1$, and $\mathcal{N}(s_1, s_2, R_{i-1} \setminus D_{i-1})$ if $1 < i \leq k+1$. Let f_i denote the maximum flow of the network $\mathcal{N}(s_1, s_2, R_i)$ for $i = 1, \ldots, k+1$. The problem of checking $|f_i| = 1$ for all $i = 1, \ldots, k+1$ can be checked efficiently by exploiting a variation of the parametric maximum flow algorithm [8] (called algorithm for a sequence of maximum flows in [21]). Based on this, an algorithm with time complexity $\mathcal{O}(m^2 n)$ is introduced for FPSs, CTMCs in [21], and for PAs in [20]. This improvement however comes with a penalty in space complexity: it is increased from $\mathcal{O}(n^2)$ to $\mathcal{O}(m^2)$, due to the need to store of the maximum flow values of the corresponding networks across iterations.

3 Optimization Options

Our implementation of the principal algorithm uses the following optimizations and heuristics to eliminate redundant or trivial computations. All of the optimizations and heuristics presented apply to DTMCs, CTMCs and PAs directly. Throughout this section, we fix an FPS $\mathcal{M}$ and a pair of states s_1, s_2. The same considerations can also be directly applied to CTMCs and PAs. Let n denote the number of states and m denote the number of transitions of $\mathcal{M}$. Let $\mathcal{N}(s_1, s_2, R)$ denote the network as defined earlier. Furthermore, let V denote the set of the vertices, and E denote the set of the edges of $\mathcal{N}(s_1, s_2, R)$.

Compact Maximum Flow. The algorithm used to compute the maximum flow is based on the existing push-relabel based preflow algorithm [9] and tailored specially to the needs of the decision algorithm in order to save memory and to omit computations for cases that never arise in the scenario considered. In a complete maximum flow implementation, the value of the flow is computed. However, for the purpose at hand, it is sufficient to determine whether or not the flow equals 1. To decide the simulation preorder, we consider bipartite networks in which source and sink and all arcs connected with them are not relevant to the computation and can be omitted. Furthermore, the fact that all remaining (not connected to source or sink) arcs have infinite capacity allows us to ignore the concept of arc capacity altogether.

The use of this tailored algorithm greatly reduces the memory usage (by a factor of approximately 4 to 6) in comparison to a more generic implementation while its runtime stays almost unchanged in most cases. It should be noted that this implementation does not use certain known optimizations for the push-relabel based method and is inferior in speed to implementations which use these optimizations.

Parametric Maximum Flow. Premise: By saving the result of previous maximum flow computations and keeping the network consistent with the constraints of a valid flow when deleting arcs as described in [8], the time required to recompute the maximum flow repeatedly on the same network can be reduced.

This adds a $\mathcal{O}(|E|)$ time overhead for updating each network. Additional space in the order of $\mathcal{O}(m^2)$ is needed to store all the networks ($\mathcal{O}(|E|)$ per network) such that they can be passed to the next iteration. Depending on the structure of a maximum flow network, the time needed to compute the flow varies greatly.

State Partitioning. Premise: In large models, many states will be structurally identical. This can be exploited by grouping states with identical probabilistic structure together into an equivalence class. This forms a partition of the state space. The equivalence classes are also referred to as blocks. Given two blocks B_1 and B_2 of the partition, simulation algorithm will yield the same result for any pair (s_1, s_2) with $s_1 \in B_1$ and $s_2 \in B_2$. Thus, it suffices to decide simulation once for an arbitrary pair of states picked from B_1 and B_2.

Two states s_1 and s_2 have an identical probabilistic structure if their successors have pairwise the same labels and the same respective transition probabilities. It is important to note that state partitioning is only correct in the first iteration of the simulation algorithm when the initial relation is defined solely on the basis the labels, thus is an equivalence relation. As soon as the relation is not an equivalence relation any more, state partitioning can no longer be applied.

State partitioning adds an overhead of $\mathcal{O}(n \log n)$ for sorting states and successor sets. This is necessary for being able to compute the partition and to be able to test whether two states should belong to the same block in linear time with respect to the number of transitions in the model. State partitioning uses an extra $\mathcal{O}(n + h^2)$ space, where h is the number of blocks in the partition. In order to store which block a state belongs to we need $\mathcal{O}(n)$, and in order to store the result of whether one block simulates another block we need $\mathcal{O}(h^2)$.

P-Invariant Checking. Premise: For a relation $R \subseteq S \times S$, we define $R(s) := \{s' \in S \mid (s, s') \in R\}$ and $R^{-1}(s) := \{s' \in S \mid (s', s) \in S\}$. The maximum flow of a network can only be 1 if the following two constraints are met:

1. $\mu(s) \leq \mu'(R(s))$ for all $s \in S$,
2. $\mu'(s') \leq \mu(R^{-1}(s'))$ for all $s' \in S$.

The complexity of verifying these constraints is in the order of $\mathcal{O}(|E|)$ per network and $\mathcal{O}(m^2)$ overall. This operation needs an additional $\mathcal{O}(|V|)$ space while performing the checks. Additionally, if the condition $\mathbf{P}(s_1, S) > \mathbf{P}(s_2, S)$ holds, $(s_1, s_2) \notin R$ is implied. The test of this constraint can be performed in $\mathcal{O}(n)$ time once before the simulation algorithm and it requires $\mathcal{O}(n)$ space during the operation.

Significant Arc Detection. Premise: The P-Invariant constraints are only checked when a network is created. However, it would be desirable to check whether or not the constraints are still fulfilled after a certain arc has been deleted as a result of its corresponding pair having been removed from the relation. This can be done as follows: For a network which satisfies the P-Invariant constraints, an arc is called *significant* iff its removal would cause the network to violate the constraints. The detection of these arcs takes $\mathcal{O}(|V|^2)$ time in addition to that of P-Invariant checking and $\mathcal{O}(|E|)$ space per network for storing the flag for every arc. Removing an arc takes constant time if the arc is significant, otherwise $\mathcal{O}(|E|)$ time to recompute the significance of the remaining arcs.

Significant arc detection is an extension of parametric maximum flow. It requires that networks be stored rather than recomputed from scratch, otherwise it is equivalent to P-Invariant checking.

4   Case Studies

The following section examines the performance of the algorithm with the various optimizations turned on and off in respect to different models.

In the case studies, we refer to the different configurations of optimizations considered in this paper by binary numbers constituting combinations of the following strategies: State Partitioning (0001), P-Invariant Checking (0010), Significant Arcs (0100), Parametric Maximum Flow (1000). Reported run-times measure the amount of CPU time (user mode only) spent computing the simulation. Time used on parsing the model prior to simulation and cleaning up memory after simulation is not accounted for. By omitting time spent in system mode, the result is not affected by virtual memory operations. The code was compiled with compiler optimizations turned off to demonstrate the advantage achieved by the heuristics alone. With compiler optimizations turned on, an additional speed-up of up to three times is achieved in some cases. The lowest amount of time/memory is marked in bold print in the tables.

Table 1. Time and memory used for Leader Election models under various optimizations. Memory statistics represent peak values throughout the process of deciding simulation preorder, excluding memory used by the relation map which is present in all configurations (Map size).

States	439	1031	2007	3463	439	1031	2007	3463
Trans.	654	1542	3006	5190	654	1542	3006	5190
Unit	Time (sec)		Time (min)		Space (kB)			
Map size					47.158	259.763	983.900	2928.669
0000	6.62001	196.25106	47.409	421.233	*754.500*	*4156.195*	*15742.382*	*46858.687*
0001	0.22081	2.07773	0.234	1.181	754.515	4156.210	15742.398	46858.703
0010	0.14801	0.69684	0.049	0.209	754.500	4156.195	15742.382	46858.687
0011	0.09101	0.39202	0.026	0.113	754.516	4156.211	15742.398	46858.703
1000	6.59761	196.70669	47.632	422.430	3910.007	20711.601	81310.734	266355.210
1001	0.19201	2.04513	0.235	1.180	2589.883	13113.180	53140.984	182841.039
1110	0.10681	0.59084	0.043	0.170	4015.472	21263.984	83497.390	273674.011
1111	*0.06600*	*0.32102*	*0.022*	*0.084*	2651.290	13412.281	54388.648	187375.586

4.1 Regular Case Studies

Leader Election Models. The leader election family of models have a very simple structure, namely that of one state in each model with a large number, denoted by k, of successors while the remaining states have only one successor. As such, these models are a prime example for a successful application of partitioning. Due to the structural similarity of the models, the number of blocks of the state partition is 4 for all leader election models and the number of times that the maximum flow algorithm is actually invoked is drastically decreased. For the simulation of three leaders and $k = 8$ (1031 states, 1542 transitions) with uniform distribution of three different labels, the maximum flow algorithm is invoked 369859 times without any optimization, and 228109 times with state partitioning.

The time advantage achieved by this becomes apparent in Table 1 (0000 vs. 0001). Due to the simplistic structure of the models, parametric maximum flow yields only a small advantage on the leader election models as recomputing from scratch is not very complex. In general, using the parametric maximum flow algorithm by itself is not desirable for sparse models because the advantage is negligible in comparison to the time and memory overhead. Table 1 illustrates the additional amount of time and memory required for parametric maximum flow (1000) versus the approach without any optimizations (0000).

Additionally, maximum flow usage statistic shows that the maximum flow algorithm is invoked more often (although by a relatively small margin) with parametric maximum flow enabled than not. This is due to the fact that certain trivial networks are discarded during construction without ever computing their maximum flow. However if a network was not initially trivial but becomes trivial after an arc is deleted, this is only detected upon reconstruction of the same network, but not upon updating and recomputing the network if it was saved. Significant arc detection works against this by effectively performing P-Invariant checking every time an arc is removed from a network.

P-Invariant checking and significant arc detection have little effect in reducing the number of times that the maximum flow algorithm is used on models similar to leader election when used alone. This is due to the fact that almost all states (all except for the first) have exactly one successor and consequently almost all networks have either one arc or none at all. Those with no edges at all are filtered out in advance and those with one edge have $\sum_{s' \in S} P(s, s') = 1$ for both s_1 and s_2 so that P-Invariant checking cannot achieve any additional filtering. The small reduction in maximum flow usage is due to the first state which has more than one successor but is unfortunately negligible.

We also note that the time advantage achieved by P-Invariant checking and significant arc detection is exceptionally large compared to the reduction in maximum flow usage. This is because a small number of networks which appear in the leader election models and are filtered out by these optimizations, are inefficient to compute under the maximum flow implementation used in this study. Therefore, the time spent computing maximum flow decreases significantly even though the algorithm is still used almost as much.

Overall, it is notable that the minimum time for simulating leader election is consistently achieved by the configuration 1111. It can be said that in general, the combination of all presented optimizations is beneficial for extremely sparse models such as leader election. If memory usage is a concern, 0011 should be preferred over 1111 as it works without ever storing more than one maximum flow problem in memory at a time (cf. Table 1) while only slightly inferior to 1111 in speed.

Molecular Reactions. For CTMCs we consider the Molecular Reactions as a case study. In particular, we focus on the reaction $Mg + 2Cl \longleftrightarrow Mg^{+2} + 2Cl^-$. Models for other reactions found on the PRISM web-site are very similar in structure and do not offer any additional insight.

While the structure of this family of models is relatively simple, few optimizations show any notable effect. All states have between 1 and 4 successors with the average being around 3.8 for all models, but the transition rates are different between almost all states. As a consequence, state partitioning fails entirely. With a few minor exceptions, all blocks of the partition contain exactly one state, which means that no speed-up can be achieved at all. In particular, the reduction in maximum flow usage is always below 1%.

Although the optimizations are not very effective, you will note that in comparison to the leader election models, the algorithm terminates very quickly on this family of models (See also Table 1 and Table 2): 7 hours for Leader Election with 3463 States and 5190 Transitions (cf. 0000), 9 seconds for Molecular Reaction with 4032 States and 15750 Transitions (cf. 0000). This is because the simulation relation is empty except for the identity relation for all these models which is known after just two iterations of the algorithm. The leader election family on the other hand needs four iterations and does not have a trivial simulation relation, which makes the process of deciding simulation preorder more complex. (Additionally, the leader election family also has some networks for which the maximum flow is hard to compute.) This is also why the memory

Table 2. Time and memory used for Molecular Reaction models under various optimizations. Memory statistics represent peak values throughout the process of deciding simulation preorder, excluding memory used by the relation map which is present in all configurations (Map size).

States	676	1482	2601	4032	5776	676	1482	2601	4032	5776
Trans.	2550	5700	10100	15750	22650	2550	5700	10100	15750	22650
Unit	Time (ms)		Time (sec)			Memory (MB)				
Map size						0.11	0.52	1.61	3.88	7.95
0000	226.0	1158.9	3.622	9.261	19.840	*0.88*	*4.28*	*13.19*	*31.72*	*65.12*
0001	234.8	1169.3	3.751	9.487	20.650	1.33	6.42	19.79	47.60	97.70
0010	204.0	976.1	3.059	*7.660*	16.960	0.88	4.28	13.19	31.72	65.12
0011	212.0	1039.3	3.375	8.321	18.552	1.33	6.42	19.79	47.60	97.70
1000	227.2	1139.3	3.610	9.039	19.458	1.09	5.50	17.16	40.99	85.49
1001	232.8	1181.7	3.788	9.571	20.386	1.52	7.44	23.08	55.73	114.53
1110	*194.8*	*954.1*	*3.027*	7.761	*16.754*	0.90	4.37	13.53	32.54	66.88
1111	215.2	1077.7	3.349	8.744	19.107	1.46	7.21	22.29	53.92	110.80

values are all relatively close to each other (see Table 2), specifically the configurations which use parametric maximum flow (1***). Intuitively this is true because almost every pair is immediately discarded and does not have to be saved for later iterations. This implies that parametric maximum flow does not hold any benefit for this type of model.

The only optimization which shows some promise for this type of model is P-Invariant checking (0010). Only surpassed by configuration 1110 in a few cases, it has the greatest performance boost of all, although it is relatively small when compared to the approach without any optimizations (0000). While P-Invariant checking consistently reduces maximum flow computation by about 99.2%, the largest part of the run-time is taken up by the remaining set of pairs which are not discarded until the second iteration. Significant arc detection, which builds upon P-Invariant checking and parametric maximum flow computation, does not hold any benefit for this model due to the failure of parametric maximum flow. While faster than pure P-Invariant checking in some cases as a result of the left-over pairs not discarded in the first iteration, the speed-up is not consistent and only in the range of about 1.5% to 5.25%.

Dining Cryptographers. We use the Dining Cryptographers model from the PRISM web-site to study the performance of our algorithm on PAs. In this study, we reduce the set of configurations to 0000, 0001, 0010 and 0011, excluding significant arcs and parametric maximum flow which have not yet been implemented.

Table 3 shows that state partitioning (0001) is clearly the best choice for this model. While the average size of the partition is relatively small, a speedup of about 50% is achieved on average.

It is notable that P-Invariant checking is actually slower on this model than approach 0000. This is because of the structure of the models. Since every action

Table 3. Time and memory used on Dining Cryptographers models

Cryptographers	3	4	5	3	4	5
States	381	2166	11851	381	2166	11851
Trans.	780	5725	38778	780	5725	38778
Actions	624	4545	30708	624	4545	30708
	Time			Space (MB)		
Map size				0.03488	1.11959	33.49911
0000	71.00 ms	2.037 s	86.788 s	*0.36649*	*11.91495*	*357.08298*
0001	*40.00 ms*	*0.977 s*	*39.839 s*	0.36916	11.95903	357.72893
0010	79.01 ms	2.248 s	89.793 s	0.36649	11.91495	357.08298
0011	42.00 ms	1.068 s	42.056 s	0.36916	11.95903	357.72893

has either one or two equally likely successors, a pair will almost never be discarded due to violating the P-Invariant constraint which can be seen as follows. All networks have at most two vertices on the left and two on the right. Consider a network and assume first that there is at least a vertex which has no arcs connected to it. In this case the network is discarded as trivial since the maximum flow must be below 1. Now assume that each vertex in the network has at least an arc connected to it. In this case it is easy to see that the maximum flow of the network is 1. Consequentially, the benefit of P-Invariant checking is very low in the first iteration, which accounts for the bulk of the total runtime and the computational overhead prevails.

For the same reason as described above, the combination of state partitioning and P-Invariant checking does not outperform state partitioning on its own.

4.2   Randomly Generated Models

Uniform models. In addition to regular case studies, we consider randomly generated DTMCs with uniform distributions, that is, all transitions from a state s have equal probabilities. If not stated explicitly, we also use three different labels which are uniform distributed. Furthermore, these random models can be described by three parameters n, a and b such that $|S| = n$ and $a \leq |post(s)| \leq b \; \forall s \in S$. We will reference random uniform model by the parameters n, a, b. Table 4 illustrates required time, memory and number of invocations of the maximum flow algorithm with respect to different model sizes for random uniform models.

This study is particularly remarkable because it demonstrates the strength of parametric maximum flow. In comparison to other cases studied above, leading configurations in the study at hand use parametric maximum flow. This is due to the density of the model, i.e. the larger number of successors per state in comparison to the other case studies in this paper. It is also remarkable that, in contrast to other case studies above, all optimizations hold some (even though limited) benefit.

State partitioning performs well on the lower end of the range, yielding a speed-up of about 80% at best and about 20% at worst. While a larger speed-up

Table 4. Comparison of all optimizations on uniform random models $400, 1, B$ with varying numbers of B. Values are in milliseconds

B	10	20	30	40	50	60	70	80
0000	7.93	36.60	83.81	140.34	224.68	372.66	650.67	718.48
0001	3.13	28.04	66.64	117.97	185.61	303.72	521.30	573.94
0010	6.90	34.37	81.47	151.68	229.28	395.62	649.67	671.28
0011	*2.77*	*26.43*	*60.64*	97.14	196.08	276.15	473.63	520.97
1000	8.00	34.80	78.97	126.47	195.01	319.29	543.03	612.57
1001	3.17	27.37	64.54	109.37	166.64	272.08	*449.16*	510.20
1010	7.10	34.54	80.57	138.21	211.98	349.39	573.07	637.74
1011	2.77	26.50	61.24	*96.44*	183.28	*268.75*	455.56	*493.56*
1100	9.47	40.30	89.01	137.24	214.05	356.22	601.07	685.98
1101	3.90	31.04	72.24	117.64	181.38	296.05	490.80	555.77
1110	7.37	36.87	84.64	132.37	207.65	344.99	583.04	660.61
1111	2.90	27.47	63.24	99.57	*174.71*	278.78	469.56	509.00

may be desirable, this is a very good result since it means that state partitioning will never slow down the process on this kind of model.

P-Invariant checking is beneficial in most cases, particularly towards the upper end of the range, but in a few cases ($40 \leq B \leq 65$) it is actually slower than approach 0000 and it is also slower than state partitioning in general. Consequentially, P-Invariant checking should not be applied on its own. Coupled with state partitioning however (see configuration 0011), P-Invariant checking performs better and is in fact one of the best configurations in the study at hand.

While faster in a few cases, significant arc detection does not yield a consistent performance boost in any configuration. Significant arc detection is most powerful in gradual simulation decision processes where few arcs are deleted in one iteration. The simulation relations in this study however are decided in only three to four iterations, indicating that most pairs of states are deleted from the relation in the first iteration already, but significant arc detection can only speed up the decision on pairs which are not deleted immediately. It stands to reason that significant arc detection would perform better in models with a larger minimum number of successors per state.

Parametric maximum flow shows good results in this study. Clocking in at speeds faster than P-Invariant checking in many cases, this is the kind of model for which parametric maximum flow is beneficial. At its worst, parametric maximum flow is about 4% slower than approach 0000. At its best, it is faster by 18%.

The best configuration for this model is a tie between 1001 and 1011. While 1111 sometimes achieves times better than 1001 or 1011, it also requires more memory and has about the same average performance as either 1001 or 1011.

Consider also Figure 1 which compares the performances of all configurations[1] on uniform random models with different numbers of labels. All optimizations except state partitioning (0001) and configurations making use of it have monotone

---

[1] To get a readable picture, we plot only the representative configurations, i.e., configurations showing extreme performances. This holds also for Figure 2.

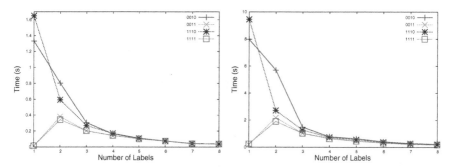

Fig. 1. Comparison of configurations on random uniform models $200, 1, 25$ (left)and $200, 1, 50$ (right) with respect to varying numbers of labels. Values are averaged over 4 independently generated models of the same class.

falling curves because more labels means that the initial relation will be smaller. Configurations using state partitioning however are affected in a different manner, displaying a very low value at one label, a maximum at two labels and a monotone curve after that. The reason for this behavior is that having only one label works in favor of the partitioning algorithm, enabling it to partition the state space into fewer blocks.

Non-uniform models. In addition to random uniform models, we also briefly consider randomly generated DTMCs with varying degrees of structure. For this purpose, we define several structural features called biases which loosely represent the probability that a certain feature is present or not. We define the following biases:

- Probability Bias, $pb \in [0; 1]$, defines whether or not the transition probabilities are distributed uniformly ($pb = 0$) or randomly ($pb = 1$)
- Fanout Bias, $fb \in [-1; 1]$, defines if a state is more likely to have the minimum ($fb < 0$) or maximum ($fb > 0$) number of successors

It must be noted that, in case of $pb > 0$, the generated probabilities are not random values. Rather, the partition of the successor set into subsets of successors, each of which have different transition probabilities, is random. This means that the distribution for state s is equal to the distribution for state s' w.r.t. transition probabilities iff $|post(s)| = |post(s')|$ and the successor sets are partitioned into subsets of equal sizes. As a consequence, the state partitioning optimization is still likely to find useful partitions, even though the same optimization would be useless for models with truly randomized transition probabilities.

Consider Figure 2 (first row) which plots the time needed for simulation for $200, 10, 20$ models with different values of probability bias. On the left, we have all configurations which use state partitioning (***1). On the right, we have all remaining configurations. We observe that state partitioning (left) performs best with uniform distributions and gets progressively slower for higher values of the bias. Intuitively this is because the partitioning algorithm is able to create fewer blocks when more distributions are uniform. All other configurations are only

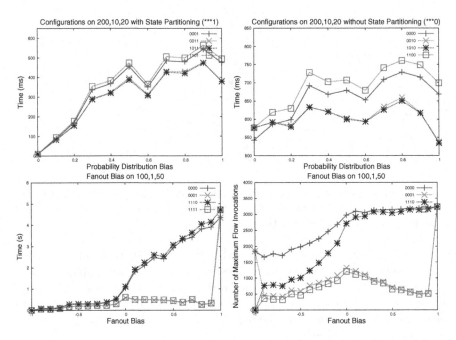

Fig. 2. Comparison on random nonuniform models with probability bias and fanout bias

insignificantly affected by the bias (right). In these cases, only the complexity of computing the maximum flow depends on the distributions, which accounts for a comparatively small portion of the run-time in models with a low number of successors per state. In both subsets, the configurations using P-Invariant checking (**1*) perform better compared to the remaining configurations for higher values of the bias, because nonuniform distributions are more likely to violate the P-Invariant constraints.

In Figure 2 we also compare the impact of different fanout biases on the set of representative configurations. We observe, as one might expect, that a higher fanout bias increases the run-time of the algorithm. An exception to this are configurations which use state partitioning (***1), which are only insignificantly affected by the bias, except for the special case of $fb = 1$. For this value, all states are in the same block and thus state partitioning cannot improve the run-time. The right plot shows that the increase in run-time is not directly linked to the number of times the maximum flow algorithm is invoked. In particular, the maximum (disregarding corners) for configurations which use state partitioning (***1) is at $fb = 0$, the value which represents the highest entropy and the highest number of blocks. For other configurations (***0), the maximum is reached by $fb > 0$, in which case only a statistically insignificant number of maximum flow computations is trivial. However, the run-time of the algorithm still rises because the complexity of the individual maximum flow computations increases. We conclude that this result depends to a high degree on the complexity of maximum flow computation more than the number of such computations, which means that it will vary greatly for different ranges of numbers of successors.

5   Conclusions

This paper has investigated an experimental approach to algorithm design, especially for Markov models. Starting off with a published simulation algorithm, we experimented with different models to determine ways of further improving upon this algorithm. At the end of this empirical process we have several promising concepts, implemented as optimizations to the fundamental algorithm. Using a collection of well-chosen case studies as well as randomly generated models we studied the practical performance of the concepts.

One of the most interesting observations of our experimental studies is the not uncommon imbalance between theoretical complexity and runtime in practice. While the parametric maximum flow based method [21,20] offered a tremendous drop in theoretical complexity, its practical implementation comes with an overhead that makes it considerably weaker in many practical applications than more straightforward approaches. Its strength are large, dense models which require several iterations to terminate. These cases seem seldom in models commonly used for case studies. The gap between theoretical and practical efficiency is not caused by "the constant factors" but by the fact that the corner cases that blow up the worst case complexity are rare in practice.

We were surprised to find that simpler and more intuitive approaches like state partitioning and P-Invariant checking actually produced promising results in general in our practical studies, in comparison to our theoretically proven algorithm. In particular, state partitioning works very well on models with low to medium transition densities and near-uniform or uniform probability distributions. On the other hand, P-Invariant checking performs very well on models with non-uniform probability distributions.

As future work we plan to make the tool available such that the optimizations and achievements are at hand for deciding simulation preorders for Markov chains and probabilistic automata. We also plan to extend the implementation to compute weak simulation for Markov chains. Additionally, we plan to develop heuristics to determine internally where to selectively apply optimizations to achieve an even better performance. Another direction is to compute the preorders symbolically, i. e., using MTBDDs (multi-terminal BDDs) to fight state space explosion problems.

References

1. Aziz, A., Sanwal, K., Singhal, V., Brayton, R.K.: Verifying continuous time Markov chains. In: Alur, R., Henzinger, T.A. (eds.) CAV 1996. LNCS, vol. 1102, pp. 269–276. Springer, Heidelberg (1996)
2. Baier, C., Engelen, B., Majster-Cederbaum, M.E.: Deciding bisimilarity and similarity for probabilistic processes. J. Comput. Syst. Sci. 60(1), 187–231 (2000)

3. Baier, C., Haverkort, B.R., Hermanns, H., Katoen, J.-P.: Model-checking algorithms for continuous-time Markov chains. IEEE Trans. Software Eng. 29(6), 524–541 (2003)
4. Baier, C., Katoen, J.-P., Hermanns, H., Haverkort, B.: Simulation for continuous-time Markov chains. In: Brim, L., Jančar, P., Křetínský, M., Kucera, A. (eds.) CONCUR 2002. LNCS, vol. 2421, pp. 338–354. Springer, Heidelberg (2002)
5. Baier, C., Katoen, J.-P., Hermanns, H., Wolf, V.: Comparative branching-time semantics for Markov chains. Inf. Comput. 200(2), 149–214 (2005)
6. Bianco, A., de Alfaro, L.: Model Checking of Probabilistic and Nondeterministic Systems. In: Thiagarajan, P.S. (ed.) FSTTCS 1995. LNCS, vol. 1026, Springer, Heidelberg (1995)
7. Bohnenkamp, H.C., van der Stok, P., Hermanns, H., Vaandrager, F.W.: Cost-optimization of the ipv4 zeroconf protocol. In: DSN, pp. 531–540 (2003)
8. Gallo, G., Grigoriadis, M.D., Tarjan, R.E.: A fast parametric maximum flow algorithm and applications. SIAM J. Comput. 18(1), 30–55 (1989)
9. Goldberg, A.V., Tarjan, R.E.: A new approach to the maximum-flow problem. J. ACM 35(4), 921–940 (1988)
10. Groß, C., Hermanns, H., Pulungan, R.: Does clock precision influence ZigBee's energy consumptions? In: Tovar, E., Tsigas, P., Fouchal, H. (eds.) OPODIS 2007. LNCS, vol. 4878, pp. 174–188. Springer, Heidelberg (2007)
11. Hansson, H., Jonsson, B.: A logic for reasoning about time and reliability. Formal Asp. Comput. 6(5), 512–535 (1994)
12. Hinton, A., Kwiatkowska, M.Z., Norman, G., Parker, D.: PRISM: A Tool for Automatic Verification of Probabilistic Systems. In: Hermanns, H., Palsberg, J. (eds.) TACAS 2006. LNCS, vol. 3920, pp. 441–444. Springer, Heidelberg (2006)
13. Jonsson, B., Larsen, K.G.: Specification and refinement of probabilistic processes. In: LICS, pp. 266–277 (1991)
14. Katoen, J.-P., Kemna, T., Zapreev, I., Jansen, D.N.: Bisimulation minimisation mostly speeds up probabilistic model checking. In: Grumberg, O., Huth, M. (eds.) TACAS 2007. LNCS, vol. 4424, pp. 87–101. Springer, Heidelberg (2007)
15. Katoen, J.-P., Khattri, M., Zapreev, I.S.: A Markov reward model checker. In: QEST, pp. 243–244 (2005)
16. Mangold, S., Zhong, Z., Hiertz, G.R., Walke, B.: Ieee 802.11e/802.11k wireless lan: spectrum awareness for distributed resource sharing. Wireless Communications and Mobile Computing 4(8), 881–902 (2004)
17. Segala, R., Lynch, N.A.: Probabilistic simulations for probabilistic processes. Nord. J. Comput. 2(2), 250–273 (1995)
18. Stewart, W.J.: Introduction to the Numerical Solution of Markov Chains. Princeton University Press, Princeton (1994)
19. Tabakov, D., Vardi, M.Y.: Experimental evaluation of classical automata constructions. In: Sutcliffe, G., Voronkov, A. (eds.) LPAR 2005. LNCS (LNAI), vol. 3835, pp. 396–411. Springer, Heidelberg (2005)
20. Zhang, L., Hermanns, H.: Deciding simulations on probabilistic automata. In: Namjoshi, K.S., Yoneda, T., Higashino, T., Okamura, Y. (eds.) ATVA 2007. LNCS, vol. 4762, pp. 207–222. Springer, Heidelberg (2007)
21. Zhang, L., Hermanns, H., Eisenbrand, F., Jansen, D.N.: Flow faster: Efficient decision algorithms for probabilistic simulations. In: Grumberg, O., Huth, M. (eds.) TACAS 2007. LNCS, vol. 4424, pp. 155–169. Springer, Heidelberg (2007)

An SMT Approach to Bounded Reachability Analysis of Model Programs

Margus Veanes[1], Nikolaj Bjørner[1], and Alexander Raschke[2],[*]

[1] Microsoft Research, Redmond, WA, USA
{margus,nbjorner}@microsoft.com
[2] University of Ulm, Ulm, Germany
alexander.raschke@uni-ulm.de

Abstract. Model programs represent transition systems that are used to specify expected behavior of systems at a high level of abstraction. The main application area is application-level network protocols or protocol-like aspects of software systems. Model programs typically use abstract data types such as sets and maps, and comprehensions to express complex state updates. Such models are mainly used in model-based testing as inputs for test case generation and as oracles during conformance testing. Correctness assumptions about the model itself are usually expressed through state invariants. An important problem is to validate the model prior to its use in the above-mentioned contexts. We introduce a technique of using Satisfiability Modulo Theories or SMT to perform bounded reachability analysis of a fragment of model programs. We use the Z3 solver for our implementation and benchmarks, and we use AsmL as the modeling language. The translation from a model program into a verification condition of Z3 is incremental and involves selective quantifier instantiation of quantifiers that result from the comprehension expressions.

1 Introduction

Model programs [20] are used to describe protocol-like behavior of systems at a high level of abstraction, the main application area being application-level network protocols. Model programs typically use abstract data types such as sets and maps, and comprehensions to express complex state updates. Protocols are abundant; we rely on the reliable sending and receiving of email, multimedia, and business data. But protocols, such as the Windows network file protocol SMB (Server Message Block), can be very complex and hard to get right. They require careful design to guarantee reliability and failure resilience; they require careful and efficient implementations; and they require careful documentation and interoperability testing, so that different vendors understand the same protocol. The use of model programs to model such complex protocols is an emerging practice in the software industry [14].

---

[*] Part of this work was done during the authors visit at Microsoft Research.

K. Suzuki et al. (Eds.): FORTE 2008, LNCS 5048, pp. 53–68, 2008.

Correctness assumptions about the model itself are usually expressed through state invariants. An important problem is to validate the model prior to its use in the above-mentioned contexts. We introduce a technique of using incremental SMT solving to perform bounded reachability analysis of a fragment of model programs. We define the formal framework and describe the implementation to Z3 [28,11]. The translation from a model program into a verification condition of Z3 is and involves lazy elimination of quantifiers that result from the comprehension expressions.

The use of SMT solvers for automatic software analysis has recently been introduced [2] as an extension of SAT-based bounded model checking [5]. The SMT based approach makes it possible to deal with more complex background theories. Instead of encoding the verification task of a sequential program as a propositional formula the task is encoded as a quantifier free formula. The decision procedure for checking the satisfiability of the formula may use combinations of background theories [22]. The formula is generated after preprocessing of the program. The preprocessing yields a normalized program where all loops have been eliminated by unwinding the loops up to a fixed bound.

Unlike traditional sequential programs, model programs typically operate on a more abstract level and in particular make use of (set and bag) comprehensions as expressions that are computed in a single step, rather than computed, one element at a time, in a loop. In this paper we consider an extension of the SMT approach to reachability analysis of model programs where set comprehensions are supported at the given level of abstraction and not unwound as loops. Allowing arbitrary comprehensions quickly leads to undecidability. We identify a fragment of model programs using the array property fragment [7] that remains decidable for bounded reachability analysis.

The construction of the formula for bounded reachability of sequential programs is based on the semantics of the behavior of the program as a transition system. The resulting formula encodes reachability of some condition within a given bound in that transition system. If the formula is satisfiable, a model of the formula typically is a witness of some bad behavior. The semantics of a model program on the other hand, is given by a *labeled* transition system, where the labels record the actions that caused the transitions. Using the action label is conceptually important for separating the (external) trace semantics of the model program from its (internal) state variables. The trace semantics of model programs is used for example for conformance testing. When composing model programs, shared actions are used to synchronize steps. We illustrate how composition of model programs [26] can be used for scenario oriented or user directed analysis.

2   Model Programs

The semantics of model programs in their full generality builds on the abstract state machine (ASM) theory [15]. Model programs are primarily used in model-based testing tools like Spec Explorer [1,25] where one of the supported input languages is the abstract state machine language AsmL [4,16]. The NModel tool [23,20] and Spec Explorer 2007 [14] use plain C# for describing model programs. Spec Explorer 2007 uses, in addition, a coordination language Cord for scenario control [13] and model composition. Typically, a model program makes use of a rich background theory [6] $\mathcal{T}$, that contains integer arithmetic, finite collections (sets, maps, sequences, bags), and tuples, as well as user defined data types.

2.1   Background Theory

Let the signature of $\mathcal{T}$ be Σ. For each *sort* S (representing a type) the theory for S and its signature are denoted by $\mathcal{T}_S$ and Σ_S, respectively. All function symbols and constants in Σ, and all variables are typed, and when referring to terms over Σ we assume that the terms are well-typed. For a term t, the set of symbols that occur in it is called the *signature of t* and is denoted by $\Sigma(t)$. Boolean sort $\mathbb{B}$ is explicit, and formulas are represented by Boolean terms. We use the notation $t[x]$ to indicate that the free logical variable x may occur in t. Given term s we also use the notation $t[s]$ to indicate the substitution of s for x in t. The integer sort is $\mathbb{Z}$. Given sorts D and R, $\{D \mapsto R\}$ is the *map sort* with *domain sort D* and *range sort R*. The map sort $\{D \mapsto \mathbb{B}\}$ is also denoted by $\{D\}$ and called a *set sort* with domain sort D. For each sort S there is a designated constant $default_S$ denoting a special value in (the type represented by) S. For Booleans, that value is *false*. The use of $default_S$ is to represent partial maps, with range sort S, as total maps that map all but finitely many elements to $default_S$. In particular, sets are represented by their characteristic functions as maps.

Maps. For each map sort $S = \{D \mapsto R\}$, the signature Σ_S contains the binary function symbol $read_S$, the ternary function symbol $write_S$ and the constant $empty_S$. The function $read_S : S \times D \longrightarrow R$ retrieves the element for the given key of the map. The function $write_S : S \times D \times R \longrightarrow S$ creates a new map where the key has been updated to the new value. The constant $empty_S$ denotes the empty map. The theory $\mathcal{T}_S$ contains the classical map axioms (see e.g. [7]), which we repeat here for clarity and to introduce some notation:

$$\forall m \, x \, v \, y(read(write(m,x,v),y) = Ite(x = y, v, read(m,y))), \qquad (1)$$
$$\forall m_1 \, m_2(\forall x(read(m_1,x) = read(m_2,x)) \rightarrow m_1 = m_2). \qquad (2)$$

All symbols are typed, i.e. have the expected sort, but we often omit the sort annotations as they are clear from the context. The value of an if-then-else term $Ite(\varphi, t_1, t_2)$ (in a given structure) is: the value of t_1, if φ holds; the value of t_2, otherwise. The second axiom above is extensionality. $\mathcal{T}_S$ also contains the axiom for the empty map:

$$\forall x(read(empty, x) = default_R). \qquad (3)$$

Sets. For each set sort $S = \{D\}$, the signature Σ_S contains additionally the binary set operations for union $\cup_S$, intersection $\cap_S$, set difference $\setminus_S$, and subset $\subseteq_S$. The theory $\mathcal{T}_S$ contains the appropriate axiomatization for the set operations. We write $x \in s$ and $x \notin s$ as abbreviations for $read(s, x)$ and $\neg read(s, x)$, respectively. A *set comprehension term* s of sort S has the form $Compr(t[x], x, r, \varphi[x])$ or

$$\{t[x] : x \in r, \varphi[x]\}, \tag{4}$$

where $t[x]$ is a term of sort D called the *element term of* s, x is a logical variable of some sort E called the *variable of* s, r is a term of sort $\{E\}$ called the *range of* x, and $\varphi[x]$ is a formula called the *restriction condition of* s. When the restriction condition is *true*, we write the set comprehension as $\{t[x] : x \in r\}$. Given a closed set comprehension term s as (4), the constant $\bar{s}$ *defines* s by (5).

$$\forall y(y \in \bar{s} \leftrightarrow \exists x(y = t[x] \land x \in r \land \varphi[x])). \tag{5}$$

The element term $t[x]$ of s is *invertible for* x, if 1) the function $\mathbf{f} = \lambda x.t[x]$ is injective, 2) there exists a formula $\psi_t[y]$ that is true iff y is in the range of $\mathbf{f}$, and 3) there exists a term $t^{-1}[y]$ such that $t^{-1}[y] = \mathbf{f}^{-1}(y)$ for all y such that $\psi_t[y]$ holds. If $t[x]$ is invertible, then the existential quantifier in (5) can be eliminated and (5) can be simplified to (6). (Just extend the body of the existential formula with the conjunct $t^{-1}[y] = x \land \psi_t[y]$ and substitute $t^{-1}[y]$ for x.)

$$\forall y(y \in \bar{s} \leftrightarrow t^{-1}[y] \in r \land \varphi[t^{-1}[y]] \land \psi_t[y]) \tag{6}$$

We say that a set comprehension term s is *normalizable* if the element term of s is invertible for the variable of s. The form (6) is called the *normal form definition for* s.

Range expressions. For the sort $S = \{\mathbb{Z}\}$ of integer sets, Σ_S contains the binary function symbol $Range : \mathbb{Z} \times \mathbb{Z} \longrightarrow S$. A term $Range(l, u)$ is called a *range expression* with l as its *lower bound* and u as its *upper bound*. We also use the notation $\{l..u\}$ for $Range(l, u)$. The interpretation of a range expression is the set of integers from its lower bound to its upper bound. $\mathcal{T}_S$ contains the axiom (7) for range expressions, where it is assumed that $\mathcal{T}_\mathbb{Z}$ includes Pressburger arithmetic.

$$\forall x\, l\, u(x \in \{l..u\} \leftrightarrow l \leq x \land x \leq u) \tag{7}$$

Note that a formula $t \in \{l..u\}$ simplifies to $l \leq t \land t \leq u$, and a formula $t \notin \{l..u\}$ simplifies to $l > t \lor t > u$. More generally, any formula that is a Boolean combination of range expressions and set operations can be simplified to linear equations. Similarly, range expressions that are used as sets and that do not depend on bound variables (inside nested comprehesion terms) can also be eliminated by introducing fresh constants and adding constraints corresponding to (7).

The theories for sets are assumed to contain definitions for all closed set comprehension terms. When considering particular model programs below, the signature Σ is expanded with new application specific constants. However, for technical reasons it is convenient to assume that all those constants are available in Σ a priori, so that the extension with set comprehension definitions is already built into the theories.

Example 1. Let s be $\{m + x : x \in \{1..c\}\}$ where m and c are application specific integer constants. The term $m + x$ is invertible for x; let ψ_{m+x} be *true* and let $(m + x)^{-1}$ be $y - m$. The normal form definition for s is $\forall y(y \in \bar{s} \leftrightarrow y - m \in \{1..c\})$, which reduces to $\forall y(y \in \bar{s} \leftrightarrow 1 \leq y - m \land y - m \leq c)$.

Example 2. Let s be $\{x + x : x \in \{1..c\}\}$ where c is an application specific constant. The term $x + x$ is invertible provided that $\mathcal{T}_{\mathbb{Z}}$ supports divisibility by a constant; let $(x + x)^{-1}$ be $y/2$ and let ψ_{x+x} be $Divisible(y, 2)$. The normal form definition for s is $\forall y(y \in \bar{s} \leftrightarrow y/2 \in \{1..c\} \land Divisible(y, 2))$, or equivalently $\forall y(y \in \bar{s} \leftrightarrow 2 \leq y \land y \leq 2 \cdot c \land Divisible(y, 2))$.

Arrays. A class of model programs, e.g. those used typically in protocol specifications, do not depend on the full background theory but only on a fragment of it. The particular fragment of interest is when all map sorts have domain sort $\mathbb{Z}$ and $\mathcal{T}_{\mathbb{Z}}$ is Pressburger arithmetic, with $\Sigma_{\mathbb{Z}}$ including $\{+, -, <, =\}$ and integer numerals. In particular, multiplication is omitted. Multiplication by a numeral is used as a convenient shorthand for repeated addition. In this case, the set comprehension term in Example 1 is normalizable. This fragment is called *array theory* [7] and has useful properties that are exploited below.

Note that it *is* possible to express divisibility constraints by for example introducing auxiliary variables and eliminating positive occurrences of $Divisible(t, k)$ by $k \cdot z = t$, and negative occurrences by $k \cdot z + u = t \land 1 \leq u < k$ for fresh z and u. One can even consider extending the array fragment to Büchi arithmetic [18].

2.2 Variables and Values

We refer to the part of the global signature Σ that only includes symbols whose interpretation is fixed by the background theory $\mathcal{T}$ as Σ^{static}; including for example arithmetic operations and numerals and set operations. We let $\Sigma^{\text{var}} = \Sigma \setminus \Sigma^{\text{static}}$ denote the uninterpreted symbols. We let Σ_S^{var} and Σ_S^{static} indicate the corresponding signatures restricted to the sort S. Note that Σ^{var} includes an unlimited supply of variables for all sorts, treated as uninterpreted constants.

A ground term over Σ^{static} is called a *value term*. The interpretation of a value term t is uniform in all models of $\mathcal{T}$ and is denoted by $[\![t]\!]$, i.e., $[\![t]\!] = \{s : s =_{\mathcal{T}} t\}$. As the *universe of values* we consider the set of all $[\![t]\!]$ for value terms t.

2.3 Actions

There is an *action sort* $\mathbb{A}$. The theory $\mathcal{T}_{\mathbb{A}}$ axiomatizes a collection $\Sigma_{\mathbb{A}}$ of *action symbols* as free constructors. For each action symbol f of arity n, the sort of f is $\mathbb{A}$ if $n = 0$ and the sort of f is $S_1 \times \cdots \times S_n \longrightarrow \mathbb{A}$ otherwise, where each S_i is a sort distinct from $\mathbb{A}$. In other words, actions cannot take actions as parameters. A term $t = f(x_1, \ldots, x_n)$ where $x_i \in \Sigma_{S_i}^{\text{var}}$, for $1 \leq i \leq n$, is called a *signature term for f*.

An *action* is value term $f(t_1, \ldots, t_n)$ where f is an action symbol. We also say *action* for $[\![f(t_1, \ldots, t_n)]\!] = f([\![t_1]\!], \ldots, [\![t_n]\!])$

2.4   Update Rules

As update rules we consider basic ASMs [15] enriched with $\mathcal{T}$. Thus, update rules are built using: the empty update rule or skip; simple assignment of a term to a state variable; conditional update rule; parallel update rule; update rule with a local let-binding. As the concrete language in this paper we use the corresponding fragment of AsmL [16].

2.5   Model Program Definition

Intuitively, a model program describes a transition system with a set of states and transitions labeled by actions where the transition relation is induced by the action rules of the model program.

Definition 1. A *model program* P is a tuple (V_P, A_P, I_P, R_P), where

- V_P is a finite subset of Σ^{var}, called the *state variables of P*;
- A_P is a finite subset of $\Sigma_{\mathbb{A}}$, called the *action symbols of P*;
- I_P is a formula over $\Sigma^{\mathrm{static}} \cup V_P$, called the *initial state condition of P*;
- R_P is a family $\{R_P^f\}_{f \in A_P}$ of *action rules* $R_P^f = (F_P^f, G_P^f, U_P^f)$, where
    - F_P^f is a signature term for f called the *action signature term of R_P^f*.
    - G_P^f is a formula called the *guard* or *enabling condition of R_P^f*;
    - U_P^f is an update rule called the *update rule of R_P^f*.

It is required that all symbols that occur in R_P^f are in $\Sigma^{\mathrm{static}} \cup V_P \cup \Sigma(F_P^f)$.

Let P be a fixed model program. Let $\Sigma(P)$ stand for $\Sigma^{\mathrm{static}} \cup V_P$. A *P-state* is a first-order $\Sigma(P)$-structure that models $\mathcal{T}$. Given a P-state S, an extension of S with parameters $\{x_i \mapsto v_i\}_{1 \leq i \leq n}$ is denoted by $(S; \{x_i \mapsto v_i\}_{1 \leq i \leq n})$. Given a first-order structure S, the *reduction* of S to a sub-signature X is denoted by $S \upharpoonright X$.

Definition 2. Let $f \in A_P$, let S be a P-state and let $f(x_1, \ldots, x_n) = F_P^f$. An action $f(t_1, \ldots, t_n)$ is *enabled* in S if $(S; \{x_i \mapsto [\![t_i]\!]\}_{1 \leq i \leq n}) \models G_P^f$.

We use the notion of *firing* of an update rule U in a state S [15], denoted here by $Fire(S, U)$, that yields the updated state.

Definition 3. Let S_1 be a P-state and let $a = f(t_1, \ldots, t_n)$ be an action that is enabled in S_1. Let $f(x_1, \ldots, x_n) = F_P^f$ and let

$$S_2 = Fire((S; \{x_i \mapsto [\![t_i]\!]\}_{1 \leq i \leq n}), U_P^f) \upharpoonright \Sigma(P).$$

Then a *causes a transition from S_1 to S_2*, or S_2 is the result of *executing a* from state S_1.

A *labeled transition system* or *LTS* is a tuple $(\mathcal{S}, \mathcal{S}_0, L, T)$, where $\mathcal{S}$ is a set of states, $\mathcal{S}_0 \subseteq \mathcal{S}$ is a set of *initial states*, L is a set of labels and $T \subseteq \mathcal{S} \times L \times \mathcal{S}$ is a *transition relation*.

Definition 4. Let P be a model program. The *LTS of P*, denoted by $[\![P]\!]$ is the LTS $(\mathcal{S}, \mathcal{S}_0, L, T)$, where $\mathcal{S}_0$ is the set of all P-states s such that $s \models I_P$; L is the set of all actions over A_P; T and $\mathcal{S}$ are the least sets such that: $\mathcal{S}_0 \subseteq \mathcal{S}$, and if $s \in \mathcal{S}$ and $a \in L$ causes a transition from s to s' then $s' \in \mathcal{S}$ and $(s, a, s') \in T$.

A *run* of P is a sequence of transitions $(s_i, a_i, s_{i+1})_{i<k}$ in $[\![P]\!]$ where s_0 is an initial state of $[\![P]\!]$. A run may be empty.

2.6   Composition of Model Programs

Under composition, model programs synchronize their steps for the same action symbols. The guards of the actions in the composition are the conjunctions of the guards of the component model programs. The update rules are the parallel compositions [15], denoted by '$\|$', of the update rules of the component model programs. The formal definition is a simplification of the parallel composition of model programs from [26].

In order to avoid parameter renaming, it is convenient to assume that action rules that are composed, use fixed formal parameter names, i.e. the signature term for each action symbol is fixed and can be omitted from the definition of an action rule.

Definition 5. Let P and Q be model programs such that $A = A_P = A_Q$. The *composition* $P \oplus Q$ is $(V_P \cup V_Q, A, I_P \wedge I_Q, (G_P^f \wedge G_Q^f, U_P^f \parallel U_Q^f)_{f \in A})$.

Composition can be used to do scenario oriented modeling [26]. In Section 5 we illustrate how composition can also be used to do scenario oriented analysis, or assist the theorem prover with lemmas.

3   Bounded Reachability of Model Programs

Let P be a model program and let φ be a $\Sigma(P)$-formula. The main problem we are addressing is whether φ is reachable in P within a given bound.

Definition 6. Given φ and $k \geq 0$, φ *is reachable in P within k steps*, if there exists an initial state s_0 and a (possibly empty) run $(s_i, a_i, s_{i+1})_{i<l}$ in P, for some $l \leq k$, such that $s_l \models \varphi$. If so, the action sequence $\alpha = (a_i)_{i<l}$ is called a *reachability trace for φ* and s_0 is called an *initial state for α*.

Note that, given a trace α and an initial state s_0 for it, the state where the condition is reached is reproducible by simply executing α starting from s_0. This provides a cheap mechanism to check if a trace produced by a solver is indeed a witness. In a typical model program, the initial state is uniquely determined by an initial assignment to state variables, so the initial state witness is not relevant.

Note also that an important use of action parameters is to make all non-determinism explicit, by providing a parameter and making a choice based on that parameter using a conditional update rule. Therefore update rules considered here do not have the nondeterministic *choose* construct of nondeterministic ASMs [15].

3.1   Step Formula Creation

The basic idea of generating a reachability formula for bounded model checking and to use SAT to check this formula was introduced in [5]. Here we use a similar translation scheme and apply it to model programs. Given a state variable or action parameter x we use $x[i]$ to denote a new variable or parameter for step number i. For step 0, we assume that $x[0]$ is x, i.e. the original variable is used.

For a term t, $t[i]$ produces a term by induction over the structure of terms where all state variables and action parameters are given step number i. During the translation all set comprehension terms are replaced by constants that define them as described above. If a comprehension term is normalizable, the generated definition has the form as shown in (6).

A translation from an update rule U to a step formula for step nr i, denoted by $U[i]$, is defined by induction over the structure of update rules. For an assignment update rule '$x := t$', $(x := t)[i]$ is the equality $x[i+1] = t[i]$. If U is a conditional update rule '$if\ \varphi\ then\ U_1\ else\ U_2$' let $X_j \subseteq V_P$ be the state variables assigned in U_k but not in U_j, for $\{j,k\} = \{1,2\}$. The translation of $U[i]$ is

$$(\varphi[i] \wedge U_1[i] \wedge_{x \in X_1} x[i+1] = x[i]) \vee (\neg\varphi[i] \wedge U_2[i] \wedge_{x \in X_2} x[i+1] = x[i])$$

For a parallel update rule, $(U_1 \parallel U_2)[i]$ is $U_1[i] \wedge U_2[i]$.

Consider an action symbol $f \in A_P$. Let $X \subseteq V_P$ be the state variables not assigned in f. The step formula for step i generated for the action rule R_P^f is:

$$R_P^f[i] \quad \stackrel{\text{def}}{=} \quad G_P^f[i] \wedge U_P^f[i] \wedge \bigwedge_{x \in X} x[i+1] = x[i]$$

Intuitively this means that the updates can take place provided that the action is enabled and all state variables not assigned by the action rule preserve their old values.

There is a variable $action[i]$ of sort $\mathbb{A}$ for each step nr i. Let $skip = default_{\mathbb{A}}$ be the action that "skips" a step. Let $Skip[i]$ be the formula:

$$Skip[i] \quad \stackrel{\text{def}}{=} \quad \bigwedge_{x \in V_P} x[i+1] = x[i]$$

Finally, the step formula $P[i]$ for P is:

$$P[i] \quad \stackrel{\text{def}}{=} \quad (action[i] = skip \wedge Skip[i]) \vee \bigvee_{f \in A_P} (action[i] = F_P^f[i] \wedge R_P^f[i])$$

The translation assumes that the signatures of all signature terms of all actions are pairwise disjoint. In other words, each action uses unique parameter names for its parameters.

3.2   Reachability

The *bounded reachability formula* for a given model program P, step bound k and reachability condition φ is:

$$Reach(P, \varphi, k) \quad \stackrel{\text{def}}{=} \quad I_P \wedge (\bigwedge_{0 \leq i < k} P[i]) \wedge (\bigvee_{0 \leq i \leq k} \varphi[i]) \tag{8}$$

Recall from above, that during the creation of $P[i]$ comprehension terms are given explicit definitions and replaced by corresponding Skolem constants in $P[i]$, thus the formula $P[i]$ is quantifier free (provided that quantifiers are not used in conditions of conditional update rules or in *if-then-else* terms). Recall also the assumption that these definitions are part of $\mathcal{T}_S$ for the corresponding set sort S. Introduce the function *RemoveSkips* which removes all the *Skip* actions from the trace. We can state the following theorem that follows from the construction of $P[i]$ and the definition of a model program.

Theorem 1. *Let P be a model program, $k \geq 0$ a step bound and φ a reachability condition. Then $Reach(P, \varphi, k)$ is satisfiable if and only if φ is reachable in P within k steps. Moreover, if M satisfies $Reach(P, \varphi, k)$, let $M_0 = M \restriction \Sigma(P)$, let $a_i = action[i]^M$ for $0 \leq i < k$, and let α be the sequence $RemoveSkips((a_i)_{i<k})$. Then α is a reachability trace for φ and M_0 is an initial state for α.*

3.3   Array Model Programs and Quantifier Elimination

We consider here the fragment of $\mathcal{T}$ when $\mathcal{T}_{\mathbb{Z}}$ is Pressburger arithmetic and all map sorts have domain sort $\mathbb{Z}$. We call model programs that only depend on this fragment of $\mathcal{T}$, *array model programs*. In the following lemma we refer to the *array property* fragment introduced in [7]. An example of a model program in this fragment is the Credits model program in Figure 1. The model program is explained in detail in [27].

```
var window as Set of Integer = {0}
var maxId as Integer = 0
var requests as Map of Integer to Integer = {->}

[Action]
Req(m as Integer, c as Integer)
   require m ∈ window and c > 0
   requests := requests.Add(m, c)
   window := window − {m}

[Action]
Res(m as Integer, c as Integer)
   require m ∈ requests and requests(m) ≥ c and c ≥ 0
   //require requests.Size > 1 or window <> {} or c > 0   <-- bug
   window := window + {maxId + i | i ∈ {1..c}}
   requests := requests.RemoveAt(m)
   maxId := maxId + c

[Invariant]
ClientHasEnoughCredits()
   require requests = {->} implies window <> {}
```

Fig. 1. *Credits* model program. Specifies how a client and a server need to use message ids, based on a sliding window protocol.

Lemma 1. *Let P be an array model program and assume that all set compre-hension definitions of P are normalizable and that P[i] is quantifier free. As-sume also that I_P and φ are in the array property fragment. Let $k \geq 0$. Then Reach(P, φ, k) is in the array property fragment.*

The following is a corollary of Lemma 1 and [7, Theorem 1], using the fact that the only range sort theory besides $\mathcal{T}_{\mathbb{Z}}$ is $\mathcal{T}_{\mathbb{B}}$ and thus this fragment of $\mathcal{T}$ is decidable. We also refer to SAT$_A$ in [7, Definition 9].

Corollary 1. *Let P and φ be as in Lemma 1. Then SAT$_A$ is a decision proce-dure for Reach(P, φ, k).*

The decision procedure SAT$_A$ eliminates universal quantifiers by restricting the universal quantification to a finite index set generated from the formula. In our case the formula under consideration is $\psi = Reach(P, \varphi, k)$. We assume here that the set (comprehension) definitions are conjuncts of the respective step formula.

Typically, a set comprehension uses a range expression, see e.g. the Credits example in Figure 1, and the index set for this formula yields at least four indices (the boundary cases for the range and its negation). The size of the index set grows at least proportionally to k, because each step formula introduces new indices, and thus the elimination process increases the size of the final quantifier free formula at least quadratically.

In our elimination scheme, the index set used to eliminate quantifiers of a given step formula, *only* originates from that step formula. For the set of model programs we have encountered so far, this restricted elimination preserves com-pleteness of SAT$_A$ for satisfiability of ψ. While we do not yet have identified a general class of model programs where this restriction remains complete, we can use Z3 to *lazily* augment the constraints we generate by model-checking the model returned by Z3. Section 4 explains the way we use Z3 lazily.

4   Implementation Using Z3

Z3 [11,28] is a state of the art SMT solver. SMT generalizes Boolean satisfi-ability (SAT) by adding equality reasoning, arithmetic, fixed-size bit-vectors, arrays, quantifiers, and other useful first-order theories. Of particular relevance to model-programs, Z3 exposes a theory of extensional arrays, which has a built-in decision procedure. Thus, terms built up using the array constructs *read* and *write* are automatically subjected to the axioms (1) and (2). Constant arrays are also supported natively, such that axiom (3) can be obtained as a side-effect of declaring a constant array *const(default)*. Enumerations are translated into integers, and for maps whose range consists of non-negative integers we assign *default* to a negative number.

Boolean algebras, also known as sets, are implemented natively in Z3 as a layer on top of the extensional array theory. Thus, adding and removing elements from a set is obtained by using *write*, set membership uses *read*, and the empty sets are the constant sets:

$$s' = s \cup \{x\} \leftrightarrow s' = write(s, x, true)$$
$$s' = s \setminus \{x\} \leftrightarrow s' = write(s, x, false)$$
$$x \in s \leftrightarrow read(s, x)$$
$$\emptyset \leftrightarrow const(false)$$

The set operations $\cup, \cap, \setminus$ are encoded using a generalized *write*, which we will call *write-set*. It has the semantics:

$$\forall m\, m'\, m''\, x \quad (read(write\text{-}set(m, m', m''), x) =$$
$$Ite(read(m, x) = read(m', x), read(m'', x), read(m', x)),$$

such that the set operations can be encoded using:

$$s \cup s' \leftrightarrow write\text{-}set(const(false), s, s')$$
$$s \cap s' \leftrightarrow write\text{-}set(const(true), s, s')$$
$$s \setminus s' \leftrightarrow write\text{-}set(s', const(false), s)$$

Z3 hides these encodings, such that expressions involving sets can be formulated directly using the usual set operations.

Map comprehensions, on the other hand, are not supported over Z3's API. As explained before, we are therefore using a reduction in the style of [7] in order to handle comprehensions. Our reduction, however, remains hybrid in two respects. First, our reduction does not require eliminating *write*, which would be necessary to follow the approach in [7] literally, instead we use the built-in support for extensional array constructs, together with *write-set*. Second, we are using the API of Z3 to supply an incremental decision procedure for comprehensions. We will explain how this is achieved in the following.

Z3's API exposes the method **AssertCnstr** - to assert a logical formula, and the method **CheckAndGetModel** - to check for satisfiability of the asserted constraints and return a model if the constraints are satisfiable, **Push**, **Pop** - to create logical contexts using a stack discipline. The life-time of an asserted formula follows the scoping indicated by **Push/Pop**. We use these facilities to implement theory specific extensions on top of Z3. Our implementation introduces axioms based on a potential partial index set explained in Section 3.3. These axioms are asserted to Z3 together with the input path constraint. Models returned by **CheckAndGetModel** are checked according to the semantics of the set comprehensions. If the current model can be extended to a model satisfying the comprehensions we are done, if not, additional assertions are added to the current scope, and the updated logical context is re-checked. The model-checking loop furthermore ensures that our reduction that retains *write* and *write-set* constructors in the input does not miss checking array indices that are introduced during Z3's search. For example, Z3 internally introduces Skolem constants for array disequalities. These constants should for completeness be counted into the index set in the SAT_A reduction, these indices are extracted lazily during model checking. Figure 2 illustrates a model refinement loop around

Z3 (using the .NET managed API calls with F#). The model refinement loop is iterated with additional assertions as long as Z3 returns a satisfying model which does not satisfy the model_check (not shown here) test on the set of extracted indices. The function model_check uses another API exposed by Z3 to evaluate terms in the context of a model $\mathcal{M}$. To describe the functionality of model_check by example, when encountering a subterm of the form $Range(l, u)$ of a formula φ, we call the evaluation function with the two formulas $i \in Range(l, u)$ and $l \leq i \wedge i \leq u$ for every i in the supplied index set. If their evaluations disagree on a given index i (one version evaluates to *true*, the other to *false*), we add the axiom $i \in Range(l, u) \leftrightarrow (l \leq i \wedge i \leq u)$. Note that Z3 supports quantifiers and therefore allows to add axioms such as $\forall i, l, u\{i \in Range(l, u)\}\ i \in Range(l, u) \leftrightarrow (l \leq i \wedge i \leq u)$, where $\{i \in Range(l, u)\}$ is a pattern. However, relying on such axioms is incomplete as they are only expanded if search explicitly builds a subterm that matches the pattern.

In the context of checking model-based programs we have an alternative way of checking and refining models produced by the SMT solver, Z3. We simply run the model program on the trace returned by the SMT solver. If the run deviates from the model by violating comprehensions on certain indices, we may augment the path constraint by the corresponding index constraints.

5   Experiments

As the concrete input language of model programs we use a subset of AsmL [4] that captures the fragment of ASMs described in Section 2. Model programs

```
let check formula =
    z3.Push();
    z3.AssertCnstr formula;
    let indices = get_indices formula in
    let m = ref (null : Model) in
    let rec refine_model() =
        if !m <> null then
            ((!m).Dispose(); m := null);
        if LBool.True = z3.CheckAndGetModel(m) then
            match model_check (!m) indices formula with
            | None -> ()
            | Some violated_comprehension ->
            z3.AssertCnstr violated_comprehension;
            refine_model()
    in
    refine_model();
    z3.Pop();
    if !m <> null then Some (!m) else None
```

Fig. 2. Model refinement loop with Z3

var *counter* **as** Map **of** Integer **to** Integer = {0->n, 1->n}
[Action]
Execute(*bar* **as** Integer)
  require *bar* $\in$ *counter*
  if *counter*(*bar*) = 1
    counter := *RemoveAt*(*counter*, *bar*)
  else
    counter(*bar*) := *counter*(*bar*) − 1

Fig. 3. *Count*(n) model program

have the same meaning as in the Spec Explorer tool [25] or in NModel [23]. The difference is that here the analysis is done symbolically using a theorem prover, rather than using explicit state exploration through execution. An action rule is given by a method definition annotated with the [Action] attribute, with the method name being the action symbol and the method signature providing the signature term for the action. The conjunction of all the require-statements defines the precondition. The main body of the method defines the update rule, where parallel update is the default in AsmL.

The *Credits* model program in Figure 1 illustrates a typical usage of model-programs as protocol-specifications. The actions use parameters, maps and sets are used as state variables and a comprehension expression is used to compute a set. Here the reachability condition is the negated invariant. One of the preconditions is missing (indicated by **bug**). There is a two-action trace leading to a state where the invariant is violated due to this. Asking Z3 with a bound of 2 or more steps (in an incremental mode) produces that trace **Req(0,1),Res(0,0)** in 21ms.

We are also investigating this analysis technique in the context of some embedded real time scheduling problems [19]. In some cases, in particular if the formula is not satisfiable, the solver may stall while trying to exhaust the search space. In this case it may be useful to apply composition to constrain the search space. This is reminiscent to adding user defined lemmas to the theorem prover. A typical example would be the use of a model program that fixes the order of some actions relative to some other actions, tantamount to user controlled partial order reduction. The *Count* example in Figure 3 is a distilled version of the counting aspect of the partiture model from [19]. There are a number of indexed counters that can be decremented. Each index corresponds to an atomic part of a schedule (called a *bar*) and the count for that bar specifies the total number of times that this bar can be executed. Suppose that there are two bars, 0 and 1, the initial count for both bars is some value n, and that we are interested in finding a sequence of actions that exhausts all the counters, i.e. the reachability condition φ is 'counter is the empty map'. If the step bound k is smaller than $2n$ then *Reach*(*Count*(n), φ, k) is clearly unsatisfiable. The size of the search space of the theorem prover grows exponentially in k in this case (see Table 1). In this simplified example we can use the knowledge that the order of decrementing the different counters is irrelevant and fix such an order using another model program *Order* shown in Figure 4.

var *current* **as** Integer
[Action]
Execute(*bar* **as** Integer)
    require *current* ≤ *bar*
    current := *bar*

Fig. 4. Model program *Order*. It imposes a linear order on the execution of bars where execution of bar i has to precede execution of bar j if $i < j$. For example, if the bars are a, b and c, where $a < b < c$, this model program essentially defines the regular expression Execute$(a)^*$Execute$(b)^*$Execute$(c)^*$.

Table 1. Running times of the bounded reachability checking of the *Count* example in Z3 for different values of the counting limit n and step bound k

Model program	Step bound	Verdict	Time (in seconds)
Count(5)	10	Sat	0.14
Count(5) ⊕ *Order*	10	Sat	0.14
Count(5)	9	Unsat	1.5
Count(5) ⊕ *Order*	9	Unsat	0.16
Count(8)	16	Sat	2.2
Count(8) ⊕ *Order*	16	Sat	1.4
Count(8)	15	Unsat	152
Count(8) ⊕ *Order*	15	Unsat	1

6   Related and Future Work

The unrolling of transition systems into SAT was introduced in [5] and the extension to SMT was introduced in [2] that also compares the SMT approach to other related program verification work. SMT solvers that support arrays are described in [3,24].

Our formula encoding into SMT [28,11,9,10] follows the same scheme but does not unwind comprehensions and makes the action label explicit. The explicit use of the action label is needed to compose model programs [26]. The composition by using actions and identifying an action signature is somewhat different from composition of modules through shared state variables as in SAL 2 [12], although it can be encoded by introducing a special shared action variable. However, in this case special projection functions need to be used in the semantics to eliminate the action, because in a labeled transition system the action label is not part of the state, i.e. the same target state can be reached through distinct actions. Compositional modeling and verification of physical layer protocols involving real time is done in [8] using SAL 2.

Our quantifier elimination scheme builds on [7], but refines it by using model-checking to implement an efficient incremental saturation procedure on top of the SMT solver of our choice. A recent application of the quantifier elimination scheme has been pursued by [21] in the context of railway control systems. Several areas have been left for future work. In particular model-programs use data structures that we are not yet handling with the SMT solver. For instance, a proper encoding of bags (multi-sets) has been left to future work. The class of array model programs is too restrictive for analysis of more general algorithms, see e.g. [17].

References

1. Spec Explorer, http://research.microsoft.com/specexplorer
2. Armando, A., Mantovani, J., Platania, L.: Bounded model checking of software using SMT solvers instead of SAT solvers. In: Valmari, A. (ed.) SPIN 2006. LNCS, vol. 3925, pp. 146–162. Springer, Heidelberg (2006)
3. Armando, A., Ranise, S., Rusinowitch, M.: A rewriting approach to satisfiability procedures. Inf. Comput. 183(2), 140–164 (2003)
4. AsmL, http://research.microsoft.com/fse/AsmL/
5. Biere, A., Cimatti, A., Clarke, E., Zhu, Y.: Symbolic model checking without BDDs. In: Cleaveland, W.R. (ed.) ETAPS 1999 and TACAS 1999. LNCS, vol. 1579, pp. 193–207. Springer, Heidelberg (1999)
6. Blass, A., Gurevich, Y.: Background, reserve, and Gandy machines. In: Clote, P.G., Schwichtenberg, H. (eds.) CSL 2000. LNCS, vol. 1862, pp. 1–17. Springer, Heidelberg (2000)
7. Bradley, A.R., Manna, Z., Sipma, H.B.: What's decidable about arrays? In: Emerson, E.A., Namjoshi, K.S. (eds.) VMCAI 2006. LNCS, vol. 3855, pp. 427–442. Springer, Heidelberg (2005)
8. Brown, G.M., Pike, L.: Easy parameterized verification of biphase mark and 8N1 protocols. In: Hermanns, H., Palsberg, J. (eds.) TACAS 2006 and ETAPS 2006. LNCS, vol. 3920, pp. 58–72. Springer, Heidelberg (2006)
9. de Moura, L., Bjørner, N.: Efficient E-matching for SMT solvers. In: Pfenning, F. (ed.) CADE 2007. LNCS (LNAI), vol. 4603, pp. 183–198. Springer, Heidelberg (2007)
10. de Moura, L., Bjørner, N.: Model-based theory combination. In: 5th International Workshop on Satisfiability Modulo Theories (SMT 2007), Berlin, Germany, July 2007, pp. 46–57 (2007)
11. de Moura, L., Bjørner, N.: Z3: An efficient SMT solver. In: Tools and Algorithms for the Construction and Analysis of Systems (TACAS 2008). LNCS, vol. 4963, Springer, Heidelberg (2008)
12. de Moura, L.M., Owre, S., Rueß, H., Rushby, J.M., Shankar, N., Sorea, M., Tiwari, A.: Sal 2. In: Alur, R., Peled, D.A. (eds.) CAV 2004. LNCS, vol. 3114, pp. 496–500. Springer, Heidelberg (2004)
13. Grieskamp, W., Kicillof, N.: A schema language for coordinating construction and composition of partial behavior descriptions. In: 5th International Workshop on Scenarios and State Machines: Models, Algorithms and Tools (SCESM) (2006)
14. Grieskamp, W., MacDonald, D., Kicillof, N., Nandan, A., Stobie, K., Wurden, F.: Model-based quality assurance of windows protocol documentation. In: First International Conference on Software Testing, Verification and Validation, ICST, Lillehammer, Norway (April 2008)
15. Gurevich, Y.: Specification and Validation Methods. In: Evolving Algebras 1993: Lipari Guide, pp. 9–36. Oxford University Press, Oxford (1995)

16. Gurevich, Y., Rossman, B., Schulte, W.: Semantic essence of AsmL. Theor. Comput. Sci. 343(3), 370–412 (2005)
17. Gurevich, Y., Veanes, M., Wallace, C.: Can abstract state machines be useful in language theory? Theor. Comput. Sci. 376(1), 17–29 (2007)
18. Habermehl, P., Iosif, R., Vojnar, T.: What Else Is Decidable about Integer Arrays? In: Amadio, R. (ed.) Proc. of the 11th Int. Conf. on Foundations of Software Science and Computation Structures (FoSSaCS 2008). LNCS, vol. 4962, Springer, Heidelberg (2008)
19. Helander, J., Serg, R., Veanes, M., Roy, P.: Adapting futures: Scalability for real-world computing. In: Proceedings Real-Time Systems Symposium (RTSS 2007), pp. 105–116. IEEE, Los Alamitos (2007)
20. Jacky, J., Veanes, M., Campbell, C., Schulte, W.: Model-based Software Testing and Analysis with C#. Cambridge University Press, Cambridge (2008)
21. Jacobs, S., Sofronie-Stokkermans, V.: Applications of hierarchical reasoning in the verification of complex systems. Electr. Notes Theor. Comput. Sci. 174(8), 39–54 (2007)
22. Nelson, G., Oppen, D.C.: Simplification by cooperating decision procedures. ACM Trans. Program. Lang. Syst. 1(2), 245–257 (1979)
23. NModel (released, May 2007), http://www.codeplex.com/NModel
24. Stump, A., Barrett, C.W., Dill, D.L., Levitt, J.R.: A decision procedure for an extensional theory of arrays. In: LICS 2001, pp. 29–37. IEEE, Los Alamitos (2001)
25. Veanes, M., Campbell, C., Grieskamp, W., Schulte, W., Tillmann, N., Nachmanson, L.: Model-Based Testing of Object-Oriented Reactive Systems with Spec Explorer. In: Hierons, R., Bowen, J., Harman, M. (eds.) Formal Methods and Testing. LNCS, vol. 4949, pp. 39–76. Springer, Heidelberg (2008)
26. Veanes, M., Campbell, C., Schulte, W.: Composition of model programs. In: Derrick, J., Vain, J. (eds.) FORTE 2007. LNCS, vol. 4574, pp. 128–142. Springer, Heidelberg (2007)
27. Veanes, M., Schulte, W.: Protocol modeling with model program composition. In: FORTE 2008. LNCS, Springer, Heidelberg (2008); In this volume
28. Z3 (released September 2007), http://research.microsoft.com/projects/z3

Parameterized Tree Systems

Parosh Aziz Abdulla[1], Noomene Ben Henda[1],
Giorgio Delzanno[2], Frédéric Haziza[1], and Ahmed Rezine[1]

[1] Uppsala University, Sweden
[2] Università di Genova, Italy
parosh@it.uu.se,
Noomene.BenHenda@it.uu.se,
giorgio@disi.unige.it,
Frederic.Haziza@it.uu.se,
Rezine.Ahmed@it.uu.se

Abstract. Several recent works have considered *parameterized verification*, i.e. automatic verification of systems consisting of an arbitrary number of finite-state processes organized in a *linear array*. The aim of this paper is to extend these works by giving a simple and efficient method to prove safety properties for systems with *tree-like* architectures. A process in the system is a finite-state automaton and a transition is performed jointly by a process and its parent and children processes. The method derives an over-approximation of the induced transition system, which allows the use of finite trees as symbolic representations of infinite sets of configurations. Compared to traditional methods for parameterized verification of systems with tree topologies, our method does not require the manipulation of tree transducers, hence its simplicity and efficiency. We have implemented a prototype which works well on several nontrivial tree-based protocols.

1 Introduction

In recent years, there has been an extensive amount of work on the verification of *parameterized systems*, e.g. [11, 18, 5, 9, 10]. Typically, a parameterized system consists of an arbitrary number of finite-state processes organized in a linear array. The task is to perform *parameterized verification*, i.e. to verify correctness of the system regardless of the number of processes inside the system. Examples of parameterized systems include mutual exclusion algorithms, bus protocols, telecommunication protocols, multi-threaded programs, and cache coherence protocols. This work aims at extending the paradigm of parameterized verification in order to verify systems which operate on tree-like architectures. More precisely, we consider analysis of safety properties for *parameterized tree systems*. Such a system consists of an arbitrary number of finite-state processes which operate on a tree-like architecture. Examples of parameterized tree systems include several interesting protocols such as the percolate protocol [18],the Tree-arbiter protocol [8], and the IEEE 1394 Tree identity protocol [17].

One of the most prominent techniques which have been used for verification of parameterized tree systems is that of *tree regular model checking* [14, 4, 18, 12, 7].

K. Suzuki et al. (Eds.): FORTE 2008, LNCS 5048, pp. 69–83, 2008.
© IFIP International Federation for Information Processing 2008

In tree regular model checking, configurations (states) of the system are represented by trees, sets of configurations by tree automata, and transitions by tree automata operating on pairs of trees, i.e. tree transducers. Safety properties can be checked through performing reachability analysis, which amounts to applying the tree transducer relation iteratively to the set of initial configurations. The main problem with transducer-based techniques, such as the ones mentioned above, is that they are very heavy and usually rely on several layers of computationally expensive automata-theoretic constructions; in many cases severely limiting their applicability.

In this paper, we propose a light-weight approach to parameterized tree verification which, in addition to its simplicity, also yields a much more efficient implementation than tree regular model checking. In our method, a configuration of the system is represented by a tree over a finite alphabet, where elements of the alphabet represent the local states of the individual processes. The behaviour of the system is induced by a set of rewriting rules which describe how the processes perform transitions. A transition performed by a process is conditioned by the current local state of the process and possibly the local states of neighboring processes, i.e. the parent and children processes. The transition may change the states of all involved processes. (see Figure 1).

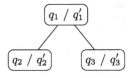

Fig. 1. A typical transition rule where a process and its two children change state from q_1, q_2, q_3 to q_1', q_2', q_3', respectively

Observe that the set of configurations is infinite since we are dealing with trees of an arbitrary size. In fact, parameterized verification amounts to analyzing an infinite family of systems; namely one for each size of the system and one for each tree of that particular size.

The main idea of our method is to consider a transition relation which is an over-approximation of the one induced by the tree parameterized system. To do so, we modify the semantics of the transition rules, such that a rule is applied to a node and two nodes in its left and right subtrees (rather than its left and right children). The approximate transition system obtained in this manner is *monotonic* with respect to the tree embedding relation on configurations (larger configurations are able to simulate smaller ones). Since the approximate transition relation is monotonic, it can be analyzed using symbolic backward reachability algorithm based on a generic method introduced in [2]. An attractive feature of this algorithm is that it operates on sets of configurations which are upward closed with respect to the tree embedding relation. This allows an efficient symbolic representation of upward sets of configurations, since such a set can be represented by (the finite set of) its minimal elements. Since the minimal elements are trees, reachability analysis can be performed by computing predecessors of trees, which is much simpler and more efficient than applying transducer relations on general tree regular languages. Also, as a side effect, the analysis of the approximate model is guaranteed to terminate. This follows from the fact that the embedding relation on configurations (trees) is a *well quasi-ordering* by Kruskal's theorem [19]. The whole verification process is fully automatic since both the approximation and the reachability analysis are carried out without user intervention. Observe that if the approximate transition system satisfies a safety property then we can safely conclude that the original system satisfies the property too.

Based on the method, we have implemented a prototype which works well on several tree-based protocols such as the percolate, leader election, Tree-arbiter, and the IEEE 1394 Tree identity protocols.

Outline. In the next section, we give some preliminaries on trees. In Section 3, we define the basic model of parameterized tree systems. In Section 4, we describe the induced transition system and in Section 5, we define the over-approximated transition system on which we run our algorithm. We present a generic scheme for deciding reachability of upward closed sets in Section 6, and we show how to instantiate it on our model in Section 7. In Section 9, we report our experimental results on several tree protocols. Section 10 concludes the paper and gives direction for future works. Some proofs as well as the details of the case studies can be found in [1].

2   Preliminaries

In this section, we give some basic definitions and notations needed in the rest of the paper. To simplify the presentation, we will only consider binary trees in this paper. However, all the concepts and algorithms can be extended in a straightforward manner in order to deal with trees of higher ranks.

For a set X, we use X^* to denote the set of words over X. We let ε denote the empty word and use $x \bullet x'$ to denote the concatenation of two words $x, x' \in X^*$. We extend the concatenation operation to sets of words $D \subseteq X^*$ by $x \bullet D :=\{x \bullet x' \mid x' \in D\}$. Given two words $x, x' \in X^*$, we use $x \leq x'$ to denote that x is a prefix of x'; and use $x < x'$ to denote that $x \leq x'$ and $x \neq x'$. In case $x \leq x'$, we use $x' - x$ to denote the word x'' where $x \bullet x'' = x'$.

Binary Trees. A *(binary) tree structure* N is a finite set of words over $\{0, 1\}$ which is closed under the prefix relation, i.e. $n \in N$ and $n' \leq n$ imply $n' \in N$. In the rest of the paper, we fix a finite set of symbols Σ and we use b as a variable ranging over $\{0, 1\}$.

A *binary tree* (*tree* for short) T over the alphabet Σ is a tuple (N, λ) where N is a tree structure and λ is a mapping from N to Σ. Each element of N is called *a node* of T. We say that a node n' is *the parent* of the node n iff $n' \bullet b = n$ for some b. In such a case, n is said to be *a child* of n'. A *leaf* in T is a node which does not have any children; and *the root* of T is the node ε. Given a node n, we define *the descendants of* n by $\text{Desc}(n) := \{n' \in N \mid n < n'\}$. We use $\text{Trees}(\Sigma)$ to denote the set of all trees over Σ.

Inclusions and Embeddings. Consider two trees $T = (N, \lambda)$ and $T' = (N', \lambda')$ in $\text{Trees}(\Sigma)$.

An *inclusion* of T in T' is an injection $f : N \to N'$ such that for any $n \in N$:

 − $n \bullet b \in N \implies f(n) \bullet b = f(n \bullet b)$, and
 − $\lambda(n) = \lambda'(f(n))$.

We write $T \subseteq_f T'$ to denote that f is an inclusion of T in T', and write $T \subseteq T'$ if $T \subseteq_f T'$ for some inclusion f. Informally, if $T \subseteq T'$ then T' contains a copy of T.

An *embedding* of T in T' is an injection $f : N \to N'$ such that for any $n \in N$:

 − $n \bullet b \in N \implies f(n) \bullet b \leq f(n \bullet b)$, and
 − $\lambda(n) = \lambda'(f(n))$.

We use $T \preceq_f T'$ to denote that f is an embedding of T in T', and write $T \preceq T'$ if $T \preceq_f T'$ for some embedding f. Observe that $\preceq$ is a weaker relation than $\subseteq$. The difference between the two relations is that an inclusion preserves the parent/child relation between nodes, while an embedding preserves a weaker relation, namely that of ascendant/descendant.

Operations on Trees. In this paragraph, we fix a tree $T = (N, \lambda) \in \text{Trees}(\Sigma)$.

For a node $n \in N$, we use $T(n)$ to denote the subtree of T rooted at n. Formally, we let $T(n) = (N', \lambda')$ where $N' := \{n'' - n \mid n'' \in N \wedge n \leq n''\}$; and for any $n' \in N'$, $\lambda'(n') := \lambda(n \bullet n')$.

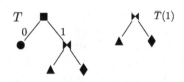

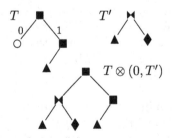

Now we fix a tree $T' = (N', \lambda') \in \text{Trees}(\Sigma)$ and define the the following operation: Given a node $n \in N$, we denote by $T \otimes (n, T')$ the tree $T'' = (N'', \lambda'')$ where $N'' := (N - \text{Desc}(n)) \bigcup (n \bullet N')$ and for any $n'' \in N''$, $\lambda''(n'') := \lambda(n'')$ if $n \not\leq n''$, and $\lambda''(n'') := \lambda'(n'' - n)$ otherwise. Intuitively, we obtain T'' by replacing in T the subtree rooted at n by T'.

Consider a (partial) function $f : N \rightharpoonup N'$. We define the *renaming of* T' *with respect to* f *and* T, denoted by $T' \odot_f T$, to be the tree $T'' = (N', \lambda'')$ where for any $n' \in N'$, $\lambda''(n') = \lambda'(n')$ if $n' \notin \text{Img}(f)$, and $\lambda''(n') = \lambda(f^{-1}(n'))$ otherwise.

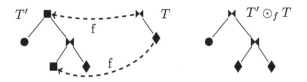

3   Parameterized Tree Systems

A parameterized tree system consists of an arbitrary (but finite) number of identical processes, arranged in a (binary) tree topology. Each process is a finite-state automaton. The transitions of the automaton are conditioned by the current local state and possibly the local states of other processes (parent, children, etc). A transition may change the states of all processes involved in the condition. A parameterized tree system induces an infinite family of finite-state systems, namely one for each size and each structure of the tree. The aim is to verify correctness of the systems for the whole family regardless of the number of processes in the system or the particular form of the tree.

Formally, a parameterized tree system $\mathcal{P}$ is a tuple (Q, R) where Q is a finite set of *local states*, and $R \subseteq \mathit{Trees}(Q \times Q)$ is a finite set of trees called *rewrite rules*. For each rule $r = (N, \lambda) \in R$, we associate two special trees in $\mathit{Trees}(Q)$ called *left* and *right* trees of r, and denoted respectively by $lhs(r)$ and $rhs(r)$. We define $lhs(r) := (N, lhs(\lambda))$ and $rhs(r) := (N, rhs(\lambda))$, where $lhs(\lambda)$ and $rhs(\lambda)$ are obtained from λ by projecting on the first and the second component of $Q \times Q$. More precisely, for any node $n \in N$, if $\lambda(n) = (q, q')$ then $lhs(\lambda)(n) := q$ and $rhs(\lambda)(n) := q'$.

Example 1. We consider the percolate protocol where the set of states Q is defined by $\{q_0, q_1, q_u\}$ and the transition rules $R = \{r_1, r_2, r_3, r_4\}$ are as depicted in Figure 2. The protocol evaluates the disjunction of the values in the leaves up to the root.

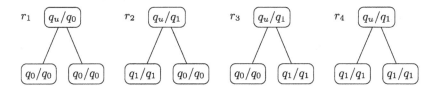

Fig. 2. The transition rules of the percolate protocol

4   Operational Semantics

The operational semantics of a parameterized tree system can be captured by a transition system. In this section, we first describe the induced transition system. Then we introduce the *coverability problem*.

Transition System. A *transition system* $\mathcal{T}$ is a pair $(C, \Longrightarrow)$, where C is an (infinite) set of *configurations* and $\Longrightarrow$ is a binary relation on C. We use $\overset{*}{\Longrightarrow}$ to denote the reflexive transitive closure of $\Longrightarrow$. Given an ordering $\trianglelefteq$ on C, we say that $\mathcal{T}$ is *monotonic with respect to* $\trianglelefteq$ if the following holds: For any configurations $c_1, c_2, c_3 \in C$ with $c_1 \Longrightarrow c_3$ and $c_1 \trianglelefteq c_2$, there is a configuration $c_4 \in C$ such that $c_2 \Longrightarrow c_4$ and $c_3 \trianglelefteq c_4$. We will consider several transition systems in this paper.

First, a parameterized system $\mathcal{P} = (Q, R)$ induces a transition system $\mathcal{T}(\mathcal{P}) = (C, \longrightarrow)$ where $C = \textit{Trees}(Q)$. Intuitively, a configuration $c = (N, \lambda) \in C$ represents an instance of the system with $|N|$ processes. These processes are arranged according to the tree structure N and their current local states are given by λ. More precisely, each node $n \in N$ represents a process in the state $\lambda(n)$.

Next, we define the transition relation $\longrightarrow$ on the set of configurations as follows. Let $r \in R$ be a rewrite rule. Consider two configurations c_1 and c_2. We write $c_1 \overset{r}{\longrightarrow} c_2$ to denote that there is an f such that the following conditions hold: (i) $lhs(r) \subseteq_f c_1$, and (ii) $c_2 = c_1 \odot_f rhs(r)$. Intuitively, c_2 can be derived from c_1 by changing the labels of all the nodes in $\textrm{Img}(f)$ according to the labeling function of $rhs(r)$. Below, we give informal explanations of the conditions. First, in condition (i), we identify the "active processes" (those which participate in the transition) by the inclusion f ($\textrm{Img}(f)$). Implicitly, we interpret $lhs(r)$ as a guard and therefore require, through condition (i), that the configuration c_1 contains a tree which is a copy of the left hand side of the rule. Then, in condition (ii), we interpret $rhs(r)$ as an operation and require that, in c_2, the processes in $\textrm{Img}(f)$ (the active ones) should all change state according to $rhs(r)$. Observe that the local states of the "passive processes", i.e. those not participating in the transition, should remain unchanged through the transition, and also that the transition does not change the structure of the tree [1] (see Figure 3).

We use $c \longrightarrow c'$ to denote that $c \overset{r}{\longrightarrow} c'$ for some rule $r \in R$.

Safety Properties. In order to analyze safety properties, we study the *coverability problem* defined below. For a parameterized tree system $\mathcal{P} = (Q, R)$, we assume that we are given a set of initial configurations *Init*, each of which characterizes a possible state of the system prior to starting the execution.

We recall the definition of the relation $\preceq$ defined in Section 2. A set of configurations $D \subseteq C$ is said to be *upward closed* (with respect to $\preceq$) if $c \in D$ and $c \preceq c'$ implies $c' \in D$. For sets of configurations $D, D' \subseteq C$ we use $D \longrightarrow D'$

---

[1] In fact, our method can also cope with non-structure preserving rules, such dynamic creation and deletion of processes. However, for simplicity of presentation, we choose not to do so.

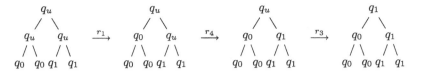

Fig. 3. A possible run of the percolate protocol. We highlight in white the zone where the rule applies (see Example 1).

to denote that there are $c \in D$ and $c' \in D'$ with $c \longrightarrow c'$. The *coverability problem* for parameterized tree systems is defined as follows:

PAR-TREE-COV

Instance

- A parameterized tree system $\mathcal{P} = (Q, R)$.
- An upward closed set F of configurations.

Question $Init \xrightarrow{*} F$?

It can be shown, using standard techniques (see [20, 15]), that checking safety properties (expressed as regular languages) can be translated into instances of the coverability problem. Therefore, checking safety properties amounts to solving PAR-TREE-COV (i.e. to the reachability of upward closed sets).

5   Approximation

In this section, we introduce an over-approximation of the transition relation of a parameterized tree system.

In Section 4, we mentioned that each parameterized tree system $\mathcal{P} = (Q, R)$ induces a transition system $\mathcal{T}(\mathcal{P}) = (C, \longrightarrow)$. A parameterized tree system $\mathcal{P}$ also induces an *approximate* transition system $\mathcal{A}(\mathcal{P}) = (C, \rightsquigarrow)$, where the set C of configurations is identical to the one in $\mathcal{T}(\mathcal{P})$ and the transition relation $\rightsquigarrow$ is defined below.

First, we define a special operation on trees needed in order to describe the semantics of $\rightsquigarrow$.

Tree Subtraction. In this paragraph, we fix two trees $T = (N, \lambda), T' = (N', \lambda') \in Trees(\Sigma)$ such that $T' \preceq_f T$ for some embedding f. We define $T \ominus_f T'$ to be the tree T'' obtained from T by performing a sequence of operations described below. First, we enumerate the nodes of T' in a bottom-up fashion. Formally, let $\{n_i\}_{1 \leq i \leq |N'|}$ be an enumeration of the set N' of nodes in T' such that for any $i, j : 1 \leq i \neq j \leq |N'|$, $n_i < n_j$ implies that $j < i$. In other words, if n_j is a descendant of n_i in T', then n_j occurs earlier than n_i in the enumeration. Based on the enumeration, we define a sequence of trees $\{T_i\}_{1 \leq i \leq |N'|-1}$ as follows. We let $T_1 := T$. For any $i : 1 \leq i \leq |N'| - 2$, we denote by n_i^p the parent of n_i, i.e. $n_i^p \bullet b = n_i$ for some b; and we define

$$T_{i+1} := T_i \otimes (f(n_i^p) \bullet b, T(f(n_i))).$$

Finally, we let $T'' := T_{|N'|-1}$. In other words, we go through the nodes of T' one by one in a bottom-up manner. For each node n_i and its parent n_i^p in T' (say $n_i^p \bullet b = n_i$ for some b), we consider their images $f(n_i^p)$ and $f(n_i)$ in T. We replace the subtree rooted in the child of the image $f(n_i^p) \bullet b$ by the one rooted in the image $f(n_i)$ (see Figure 4). Notice that the resulting tree T'' and the trees T', T are related by $T' \subseteq T'' \preceq T$. In the sequel, we denote by $\widehat{f}$ the inclusion of T' in T'' such that $\widehat{f}(\varepsilon) = f(\varepsilon)$ (such a function exists and is unique by the definition above).

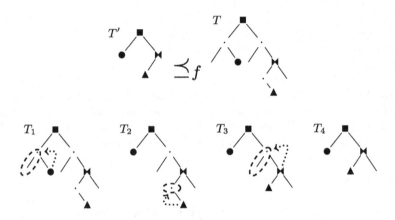

Fig. 4. In the first row, we give an example of two trees T, T' satisfying $T' \preceq_f T$ for some embedding f. In the second row, we give the sequence of trees used in the definition of $T \ominus_f T'$. In each of the trees, the arrow shows where subtrees are re-rooted, while the nodes surrounded by a dashed line are those which are removed.

The Approximate Transition Relation. Consider two configurations c_1, c_2 and a rule $r \in R$. We write $c_1 \overset{r}{\leadsto} c_2$ to denote that there is an f such that (i) $lhs(r) \preceq_f c_1$, and (ii) $c_2 = (c_1 \ominus_f lhs(r)) \odot_{\widehat{f}} rhs(r)$. Intuitively, starting from c_1 and an embedding f of $lhs(r)$ in c_1, we first remove all nodes in c_1 such that $lhs(r)$ is included in the resulting configuration. This is done by taking $lhs(r) \ominus_f c_1$ and the inclusion $\widehat{f}$. Then we apply the rule r and obtain c_2 from $lhs(r) \ominus_f c_1$ in a similar manner to how it is described in the previous section, i.e. by renaming the labels of the nodes in $\mathrm{Img}(\widehat{f})$ according to $rhs(r)$ (see Figure 5). We use $c_1 \leadsto_1 c_2$ if $c_1 \overset{r}{\leadsto} c_2$ for some $r \in R$.

Observe that the relation $\leadsto$ is an over-approximation of the transition relation defined in the previous section (i.e. $\leadsto \supseteq \longrightarrow$) by the following argument.

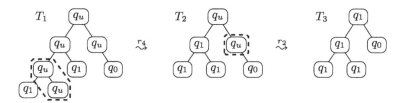

Fig. 5. A possible run of the approximate transition system induced by the percolate protocol (see Example 1). The nodes with a white background represent those where the rule will apply while the dashed lines surround the nodes which are removed.

Consider two configurations $c_1, c_2 \in C$ with $c_1 \longrightarrow c_2$. By definition, this implies the existence of a rule $r \in R$ and an inclusion f of $lhs(r)$ in c_1 such that $c_2 = c_1 \odot_f rhs(r)$. Observe that, by definition of the $\ominus$ operation, since f is an inclusion it follows that $c_1 \ominus_f lhs(r) = c_1$ and $\widehat{f} = f$. Therefore, we obtain $c_2 = c_1 \odot_f rhs(r) = (c_1 \ominus_f lhs(r)) \odot_{\widehat{f}} rhs(r)$, and as a consequence, $c_1 \overset{r}{\rightsquigarrow} c_2$.

We are now ready to state a key property of the approximated transition system.

Lemma 1. *The approximate transition system* $(C, \rightsquigarrow)$ *is monotonic with respect to* $\preceq$.

We define the coverability problem for the approximate system as follows.

APRX-PAR-TREE-COV

Instance

- A parameterized tree system $\mathcal{P} = (Q, R)$
- An upward closed set F of configurations.

Question $Init \overset{*}{\rightsquigarrow} F$?

Since $\longrightarrow \subseteq \rightsquigarrow$, a negative answer to APRX-PAR-TREE-COV implies a negative answer to PAR-TREE-COV.

6 Scheme

In this section, we recall a generic scheme from [2] for performing symbolic backward reachability analysis. The scheme in question is based on symbolic representations of infinite sets of configurations called *constraints*. Throughout this section, we fix a transition system $\mathcal{T} = (C, \Longrightarrow)$ and a set $Init \subseteq C$ of initial configurations.

Constraint Systems. A *constraint system* Ψ relative to the transition system $\mathcal{T}$ is a set whose elements are called constraints and can be finitely encoded, such that there is a function $\llbracket \cdot \rrbracket : \Psi \to 2^C$. For a finite set Φ of constraints, we let $\llbracket \Phi \rrbracket = \bigcup_{\phi \in \Phi} \llbracket \phi \rrbracket$. We say that a set $D \subseteq C$ is *computable* or *representable* (in the constraint system Ψ) if it is possible to compute a finite set of constraints $\Phi \subseteq \Psi$ such that $D = [\![\Phi]\!]$.

We define an *entailment relation* $\sqsubseteq$ on constraints, where $\phi_1 \sqsubseteq \phi_2$ iff $[\![\phi_2]\!] \subseteq [\![\phi_1]\!]$. For sets Φ_1, Φ_2 of constraints, abusing notation, we let $\Phi_1 \sqsubseteq \Phi_2$ denote that for each $\phi_2 \in \Phi_2$ there is a $\phi_1 \in \Phi_1$ with $\phi_1 \sqsubseteq \phi_2$. Notice that $\Phi_1 \sqsubseteq \Phi_2$ implies that $[\![\Phi_2]\!] \subseteq [\![\Phi_1]\!]$.

For a constraint ϕ, we let $\mathrm{Pre}(\phi)$ be the set of constraints, such that $[\![\mathrm{Pre}(\phi)]\!] = \{c | \exists c' \in [\![\phi]\!]. \ c \Longrightarrow c'\}$. In other words, $\mathrm{Pre}(\phi)$ characterizes the set of configurations from which we can reach a configuration in ϕ through the application of a single rewrite rule. Such a set does not necessarily exist, nevertheless, for our class of systems, we will show that such a set always exists and is in fact computable. For a set Φ of constraints, we let $\mathrm{Pre}(\Phi) = \bigcup_{\phi \in \Phi} \mathrm{Pre}(\phi)$.

Symbolic Backward Reachability. We present a scheme for a symbolic algorithm which, given a finite set Φ_F of constraints, checks whether $Init \stackrel{*}{\Longrightarrow} [\![\Phi_F]\!]$.

In the scheme, we perform a backward reachability analysis, generating a sequence $\{\Phi_i\}_{i \in \mathbb{N}} : \Phi_0 \sqsupseteq \Phi_1 \sqsupseteq \Phi_2 \sqsupseteq \cdots$ of finite sets of constraints such that $\Phi_0 = \Phi_F$, and $\Phi_{i+1} = \Phi_i \cup \mathrm{Pre}(\Phi_i)$. Since $[\![\Phi_0]\!] \subseteq [\![\Phi_1]\!] \subseteq [\![\Phi_2]\!] \subseteq \cdots$, the procedure terminates when we reach a point j where $\Phi_j \sqsubseteq \Phi_{j+1}$. Consequently, Φ_j characterizes the set of all predecessors of $[\![\Phi_F]\!]$. This means that $Init \stackrel{*}{\Longrightarrow} [\![\Phi_F]\!]$ iff $Init \cap [\![\Phi_j]\!] \neq \emptyset$.

Observe that, in order to implement the scheme (i.e. transform it into an algorithm), we need to be able to (i) compute Pre; (ii) check for entailment between constraints; and (iii) check for emptiness of $Init \cap [\![\phi]\!]$ for any constraint ϕ. A constraint system satisfying these three conditions is said to be *effective*. Moreover, in [2], it is shown that termination is guaranteed in case the constraint system is *well quasi-ordered (WQO)* with respect to $\sqsubseteq$, i.e. for each infinite sequence $\phi_0, \phi_1, \phi_2, \ldots$ of constraints, there are $i < j$ with $\phi_i \sqsubseteq \phi_j$.

7   Algorithm

In this section, we instantiate the scheme of Section 6 to derive an algorithm for solving APRX-PAR-TREE-COV. We do that by introducing an effective and well quasi-ordered constraint system.

Throughout this section, we assume a parameterized tree system $\mathcal{P} = (Q, R)$ and the induced approximate transition system $\mathcal{A}(\mathcal{P}) = (C, \leadsto)$. We define a constraint to be a tree in $Trees(Q)$. Although we use the same syntax as for configurations, constraints are interpreted differently. More precisely, given a constraint ϕ, we let $[\![\phi]\!] = \{c \in C | \phi \preceq c\}$.

An aspect of our constraint system is that each constraint characterizes a set of configurations which is upward closed with respect to $\preceq$. Conversely (by Higman's Lemma [16]), any upward closed set F of configurations can be characterized as $[\![\Phi_F]\!]$ where Φ_F is a finite set of constraints. In this manner, APRX-PAR-TREE-COV is reduced to checking the reachability of a finite set of constraints.

Below we show effectiveness and well quasi-ordering of our constraint system, meaning that we obtain an algorithm for solving APRX-PAR-TREE-COV. First, observe that the entailment relation can be computed in a straightforward manner since for any constraints ϕ, ϕ', we have $\phi \sqsubseteq \phi'$ iff $\phi \preceq \phi'$.

In order to check the initial condition, we rely on previous works on *regular tree languages* [13] and provide a sufficient condition on *Init* which guarantees effectiveness of *Init* $\cap \llbracket \phi \rrbracket = \emptyset$ for any constraint ϕ. More precisely, we require that the set *Init* can be characterized by a regular tree language.

For the computation of Pre we rely on the following result.

Lemma 2. *For any constraint ϕ, the set of constraints $Pre(\phi)$ is computable and finite.*

It was shown in [19] that the embedding relation on trees $\preceq$ is a well quasi-order (Kruskal's theorem). This combined with results in [2] guarantee termination of our scheme when instantiated on the constraints we have defined above.

8   Case Studies

In this section, we provide descriptions of two tree protocols we have analyzed using our method. For each protocol, we define the corresponding parameterized tree system model and we give the sets of unsafe (F) and initial (*Init*) configurations.

8.1   The Tree-Arbiter Protocol

The protocol supervises the access to a shared resource of a set of processes arranged in a tree topology. The processes competing for the resource reside in the leaves.

A process in the protocol can be in state *idle* (i), *requesting* (r), *token* (t) or *below* (b). All the processes are initially in state i. A node is in state b whenever it has a descendant in state t. When a leaf is in state r, the request is propagated upwards until it encounters a node which is aware of the presence of the token (i.e. a node in state t or b). A node that has the token (in state t) can choose to pass it upwards or pass it downwards to a requesting child (node in state r).

We model the tree-arbiter protocol with a parameterized tree system $\mathcal{P} = (Q, R)$ where $Q = \{q_s^n \mid s \in \{i, r, t, b\} \land n \in \{leaf, inner, root\}\}$ and R is as depicted in the figure below (figure 6). Observe that in the definition of Q, we use the scripts s and n to model respectively the state and the nature (leaf, inner or root) of the nodes. In the definition of the rules, we will drop the script(s) whenever we mean that it is arbitrary (it can take any value).

The rules to model this protocol are as follows: 2 rules to propagate the request upwards, 2 rules to propagate the token downwards, 2 rules to propagate the token upwards and one rule to initiate a request from a leaf.

The set of bad constraints F is represented by trees where at least two processes (i.e. two leaves) obtain the token (i.e. in state q_t^{leaf}).

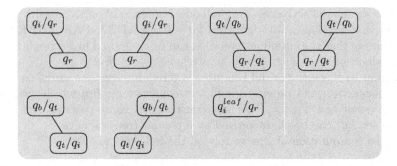

Fig. 6. The rewrite rules for the tree-arbiter protocol. We mention here that there are more rules in the model we have verified. For example, the rule in the top-left corner is represented in the concrete model by 2 rules, each of which corresponds to a particular combination of the natures of the parent and child nodes: For the parent there are 2 possibilities (q_i^{inner}/q_r^{inner} and q_i^{root}/q_r^{root}) while for the child, there are 2 (q_r^{inner} and q_r^{leaf}).

The set of initial configurations *Init* contains all trees where the leaf nodes are either idle or requesting, inner nodes are idle, and the root has the token.

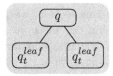

8.2 The IEEE 1394 Tree Identification Protocol

The 1394 High Performance serial bus [17] is used to transport digitized video and audio signals within a network of multimedia systems and devices.

The tree identification protocol is used in one of the phases implementing the IEEE 1394 protocol. More precisely, it is run after a bus reset in the network and leads to the election of a unique leader node.

In this section, we consider a version working on tree topologies. Furthermore, we assume that (i) each inner node is connected to 3 neighbors, (ii) the root is connected to 2 neighbors, and (ii) communication is atomic.

Initially, all nodes are in state *undefined* (u). We identify two steps in the protocol depending on the number n of neighbors which are still in state u. If $n > 1$, the node waits for ("be my parent") requests from its neighbors. If $n = 1$, the node sends a request to the remaining neighbor in state u. Observe that we implicitly assume that the leaf nodes are the first to communicate with their neighbors.

Formally, we derive a parameterized tree system model $\mathcal{P} = (Q, R)$ as follows. We define the set of states by $Q = \{q_s^n \mid s \in \{u, c, l\} \land n \in \{leaf, inner, root\}\}$ where the scripts s and n describe respectively the state and the nature of the node. In the definition of the state (s), the letters u, c and l stand respectively for *undefined*, *child* and *leader*. In a similar manner to the previous section, we

drop the script(s) whenever we mean that it can take any value (see caption of
Figure 6).

The rewrite rules R are described below.

− The leaves initiate the communications:

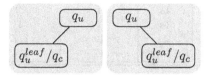

− The inner nodes become children or wait for requests:

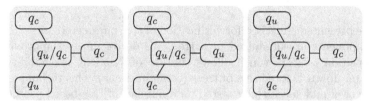

− The leader is chosen:

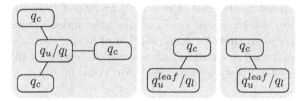

The set of initial configurations *Init* is represented by trees where all nodes
are in state undefined, and the set of bad constraints F is represented by trees
where at least 2 leaders are elected.

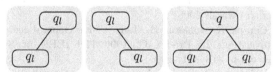

9   Experiments

We have implemented a prototype tool in C++ and run it on several models of
protocol with tree-like topologies. The experiments have been performed on a
dual Opteron 2.8 GHz, with 8 GB of RAM memory and the results are reported
in Table 1.

For each example, we give the number of iterations performed by the reachability algorithm, the largest number of constraints maintained at the end of the
execution, the time and total memory consumption. Full details of the examples
can be found in [1].

Table 1. Experimental Results

Protocol	Time	# iterations	# constraints	Memory
Token	1s	1	3	<1 MB
Two way token	1s	1	3	<1 MB
Percolate	1s	1	2	<1 MB
Leader	1s	4	41	63 MB
Tree Arbiter	37s	12	1173	70 MB
IEEE 1394	1h15m25s	17	4145	137 MB

10 Conclusions and Future Work

We have presented a method for verification of tree parameterized systems where the components are organized in a tree. We derive an over-approximation of the transition relation which allows the use of symbolic reachability analysis defined on upward closed sets of trees (configurations). This technique has been implemented and successfully tested on a number of tree-based protocols.

It would be interesting to see if one can extend our method to other classes of architectures such as unordered trees, DAGs, and more general classes of graphs. In a similar manner to the case of words [3] we intend to consider tree systems where the individual processes may contain unbounded variables. This would allow to analyze algorithms for manipulation of heaps, (balanced) binary trees, etc. Finally, we intend to extend our framework to check for liveness properties on tree-like architecture systems (as done for words in [6]).

References

1. Abdulla, P., Henda, N.B., Delzanno, G., Haziza, F., Rezine, A.: Parameterized tree systems. Technical Report 2008-010, Dept. of Information Technology, Uppsala University, Sweden (March 2008)
2. Abdulla, P.A., Čerāns, K., Jonsson, B., Tsay, Y.-K.: General decidability theorems for infinite-state systems. In: Proc. LICS 1996, 11th IEEE Int. Symp. on Logic in Computer Science, pp. 313–321 (1996)
3. Abdulla, P.A., Delzanno, G., Rezine, A.: Parameterized verification of infinite-state processes with global conditions. In: Damm, W., Hermanns, H. (eds.) CAV 2007. LNCS, vol. 4590, pp. 145–157. Springer, Heidelberg (2007)
4. Abdulla, P.A., Jonsson, B., Mahata, P., d'Orso, J.: Regular tree model checking. In: Brinksma, E., Larsen, K.G. (eds.) CAV 2002. LNCS, vol. 2404, Springer, Heidelberg (2002)
5. Abdulla, P.A., Jonsson, B., Nilsson, M., d'Orso, J.: Regular model checking made simple and efficient. In: Brim, L., Jančar, P., Křetínský, M., Kucera, A. (eds.) CONCUR 2002. LNCS, vol. 2421, pp. 116–130. Springer, Heidelberg (2002)
6. Abdulla, P.A., Jonsson, B., Nilsson, M., d'Orso, J., Saksena, M.: Regular model checking for s1s + ltl. In: Alur, R., Peled, D.A. (eds.) CAV 2004. LNCS, vol. 3114, pp. 348–360. Springer, Heidelberg (2004)

7. Abdulla, P.A., Legay, A., d'Orso, J., Rezine, A.: Tree regular model checking: A simulation-based approach. The Journal of Logic and Algebraic Programming 69(1-2), 93–121 (2006)
8. Alur, R., Brayton, R.K., Henzinger, T.A., Qadeer, S., Rajamani, S.K.: Partial-order reduction in symbolic state space exploration. In: Grumberg, O. (ed.) CAV 1997. LNCS, vol. 1254, pp. 340–351. Springer, Heidelberg (1997)
9. Boigelot, B., Legay, A., Wolper, P.: Iterating transducers in the large. In: Hunt Jr., W.A., Somenzi, F. (eds.) CAV 2003. LNCS, vol. 2725, pp. 223–235. Springer, Heidelberg (2003)
10. Bouajjani, A., Habermehl, P., Vojnar, T.: Abstract regular model checking. In: Alur, R., Peled, D.A. (eds.) CAV 2004. LNCS, vol. 3114, pp. 372–386. Springer, Heidelberg (2004)
11. Bouajjani, A., Jonsson, B., Nilsson, M., Touili, T.: Regular model checking. In: Emerson, E.A., Sistla, A.P. (eds.) CAV 2000. LNCS, vol. 1855, pp. 403–418. Springer, Heidelberg (2000)
12. Bouajjani, A., Touili, T.: Extrapolating Tree Transformations. In: Brinksma, E., Larsen, K.G. (eds.) CAV 2002. LNCS, vol. 2404, Springer, Heidelberg (2002)
13. Comon, H., Dauchet, M., Gilleron, R., Jacquemard, F., Lugiez, D., Tison, S., Tommasi, M.: Tree Automata Techniques and Applications (October 1999)
14. Dams, D., Lakhnech, Y., Steffen, M.: Iterating transducers. In: Berry, G., Comon, H., Finkel, A. (eds.) CAV 2001. LNCS, vol. 2102, Springer, Heidelberg (2001)
15. Godefroid, P., Wolper, P.: Using partial orders for the efficient verification of dead-lock freedom and safety properties. Formal Methods in System Design 2(2), 149–164 (1993)
16. Higman, G.: Ordering by divisibility in abstract algebras. Proc. London Math. Soc (3) 2(7), 326–336 (1952)
17. IEEE Computer Society. IEEE standard for a high performance serial bus. Std 1394-1995 (August 1996)
18. Kesten, Y., Maler, O., Marcus, M., Pnueli, A., Shahar, E.: Symbolic model checking with rich assertional languages. Theoretical Computer Science 256, 93–112 (2001)
19. Kruskal, J.: Well-quasi-ordering, the tree theorem, and Vazsonyi's conjecture. Transactions of the American Mathematical Society 95, 210–225 (1960)
20. Vardi, M.Y., Wolper, P.: An automata-theoretic approach to automatic program verification. In: Proc. LICS 1986, 1st IEEE Int. Symp. on Logic in Computer Science, June 1986, pp. 332–344 (1986)

Adapting Petri Nets Reductions to Promela Specifications

C. Pajault[1], J.-F. Pradat-Peyre[1], and P. Rousseau[2]

[1] LIP6, Université Pierre et Marie Curie, Paris,
{Christophe.Pajault,Jean-Francois.Pradat-Peyre}@lip6.fr
[2] Cedric-CNAM
rousseau@cnam.fr

Abstract. The interleaving of concurrent processes actions leads to the well-known combinatorial explosion problem. Petri nets theory provides some structural reductions to tackle this phenomenon by agglomerating sequences of transitions into a single atomic transition. These reductions are easily checkable and preserve deadlocks, Petri nets liveness and any LTL formula that does not observe the modified transitions. Furthermore, they can be combined with other kinds of reductions such as partial-order techniques to improve the efficiency of state space reduction. We present in this paper an adaptation of these reductions for Promela specifications and propose simple rules to automatically infer atomic steps in the Promela model while preserving the checked property. We demonstrate on typical examples the efficiency of this approach and propose some perspectives of this work in the scope of software model checking.

1   Introduction

The interleaving of concurrent processes actions leads to a combinatory explosion. In order to give a simple insight of this problem, let us consider a simple example: let $\{p_i\}_{i=1...n}$ be a set of stateless servers which infinitely execute a loop consisting in a sequence of two actions $accept_i$ and $execute_i$. The interleaving of these actions leads to a state space whose size is 2^n. Partial order methods (e.g. persistent sets [1], sleep sets [2], stubborn sets [3], ...), or symmetry based reductions [4,5] may reduce the size of the state space to a size of n. However, the simple fact of considering the sequence as atomic leads to a state space reduced to a singleton! Obviously, as for partial order techniques, such a reduction may be faulty since for instance, it could hide occurrence of deadlocks. The goal of a reduction theory is to (syntactically) characterize situations where a reduction is sound and how to perform it.

Based on this principle, we proposed in [6] some new Petri nets reductions that cover a large range of synchronization patterns. We extended these reductions to colored Petri nets (which are an abbreviation of Petri nets) in [7,8] and use them in the QUASAR [9] platform that performs verification of concurrent Ada programs by analyzing an intermediate colored Petri net generated from a given program.

These reductions yield very interesting results and we present in this paper how these reductions can be adapted to simplify program analysis without needing a translation step into a more formal model (such as Petri nets). We illustrate

K. Suzuki et al. (Eds.): FORTE 2008, LNCS 5048, pp. 84–98, 2008.

our approach with the Promela language since it's a simple and clear language associated to the very efficient model checker Spin [10].

More precisely, we define some syntactical rules based on Petri nets agglomerations which allow the automatic detection of sequences of statements that can be marked as "atomic" (using the **atomic** construction of Promela) while preserving analyzed properties. The interest of this transformation is to significantly reduce interleaving and thus the size of the state space.

2   Petri Nets Transitions Agglomerations

A Petri net reduction is characterized by some application conditions, a net transformation and a set of preserved properties (i.e. which properties are simultaneously true or false in the original net and in the reduced one). Before presenting the pre- and the post-agglomerations, we briefly recall some Petri nets definitions.

2.1   Brief Petri Nets Definitions and Notations

Definition 1 (Petri net model). *A marked net (N, m_0) is defined by a tuple (P, T, W^-, W^+, m_0) where: P is the finite set of places, T is the finite set of transitions disjoint from P, W^- (resp. W^+) an integer matrix indexed by $P \times T$ is the backward (resp. forward) incidence matrix, m_0 a integer vector indexed by P is the initial marking. The transitions linked to a place p are defined by $^\bullet p = \{t | W^+(p, t) > 0\}$ and $p^\bullet = \{t | W^-(p, t) > 0\}$.*

Definition 2 (Firing rule). *Let (N, m_0) be a marked net then a transition $t \in T$ is firable from a marking m (denoted by $m[t\rangle$) iff $\forall p \in P\ m(p) \geq W^-(p, t)$. The firing of $t \in T$ firable from m leads to the marking m' (denoted by $m[t\rangle m'$) defined by $\forall p \in P\ m'(p) = m(p) + W(p, t)$ where W the incidence matrix is defined by $W = W^+ - W^-$. A marking m such that $\forall t \in T$, $NOT(m[t\rangle)$ is called a **dead** marking.*

We use the following notations.

- T^* is the set of finite sequences of transitions and T^ω is the set of infinite sequences of transitions; λ defines the empty sequence of transitions;
- $\Pi_T(s)$ denotes the projection of the sequence s on a subset of transitions T' and is recursively defined by $\Pi_{T'}(\lambda) = \lambda$, $\forall t \in T'$, $\Pi_{T'}(s.t) = \Pi_{T'}(s).t$ and $\forall t \notin T'$, $\Pi_{T'}(s.t) = \Pi_{T'}(s)$;
- $|s|_{T'} = |\Pi_{T'}(s)|$ denotes the number of occurrences of transitions of T' in s;
- $Pref(s) = \{s' \mid \exists s'' \text{ s.t. } s = s'.s''\}$ denotes the set of prefixes of s.

Definition 3 (Firing rule extension). *Let (N, m_0) be a marked net. A finite sequence $s \in T^*$ is firable from m, a marking and leads to m' (also denoted by $m[s\rangle$ and $m[s\rangle m'$) iff either $s = \lambda$ and $m' = m$ or $s = s_1.t$ with $t \in T$ and $\exists m_1\ m[s_1\rangle m_1$ and $m_1[t\rangle m'$ We note $Reach(N, m_0) = \{m | \exists s \in T^*\ m_0[s\rangle m\}$ the set of reachable markings. An infinite sequence $s \in T^\omega$ is firable from m a marking (also denoted $m[s\rangle$) iff for every finite prefix s_1 of s, $m[s_1\rangle$.*

Definition 4 (Generated language). *Let (N, m_0) be a marked net then*

- $L(N, m_0) = \{s \in T^* | m_0[s\rangle\}$ *is the language of finite sequences,*
- $L^{Max}(N, m_0) = \{s \in T^* | \exists m\ dead\ marking\ m_0[s\rangle m\}$ *is the language of finite maximal sequences,*
- $L^{\omega}(N, m_0) = \{s \in T^{\omega} | m_0[s\rangle\}$ *is the language of infinite sequences.*

2.2   Petri Nets Agglomerations

We note (N, m_0) a Petri net and we suppose in the following definitions that the set of transitions of the net is partitioned as: $T = T_0 \uplus_{i \in I} H_i \uplus_{i \in I} F_i$ where I denotes a non empty set of indices. The underlying idea of this decomposition is that a couple (H_i, F_i) defines transitions sets that are causally dependent: an occurrence of $f \in F_i$ in a firing sequence may always be related to a previous occurrence of some $h \in H_i$ in this sequence. Starting from this property, we developed conditions on the behavior of the net which ensure that we can restrict the dynamics of the model to sequences where each occurrence $h \in H_i$ is immediately followed by an occurrence of some $f \in F_i$ without changing its behavior w.r.t. to a set of properties. This restricted behavior is the behavior of a reduced net, denoted (N_r, m_0), defined in Appendix.

From now, we note $H = \cup_{i \in I} H_i$ and $F = \cup_{i \in I} F_i$. The firing rule in the reduced net is noted $\rangle_r$ (i.e. $m[s\rangle_r m'$ denotes a firing sequence in the reduced net). We note also ϕ the homomorphism from the monoid T_r^* to the monoid T^* defined by: $\forall t \in T_0, \phi(t) = t$ and $\forall i \in I, \forall h \in H_i, \forall f \in F_i, \phi(hf) = h.f$ This homomorphism is extended to an homomorphism from $\mathcal{P}(T_r^*)$ to $\mathcal{P}(T^*)$ and from $\mathcal{P}(T_r^{\infty})$ to $\mathcal{P}(T^{\infty})$.

In order to obtain the preservation properties (such like deadlock occurrences) we have to introduce behavioral hypotheseses. The basic one, named *Potential agglomerability* ensures that an occurrence of a transition of F is always preceeded by an occurrence of a transition of H. For doing that we define a set of counting functions, denoted Γ_i, by $\forall s \in T^*, \Gamma_i(s) = |s|_{H_i} - |s|_{F_i}$.

Definition 5 (P-agglomerability). *A marked net (N, m_0) is potentially agglomerable (p-agglomerable for short) iff $\forall s \in L(N, m_0), \forall i \in I, \Gamma_i(s) \geq 0$.*

We define now the behavioral conditions that ensure that the agglomerations preserve properties of the net. Note that these behavioral conditions can be checked with efficient structural and algebraical sufficient conditions (not presented here) directly on the Petri net.

Pre-Agglomeration. The following definition states four conditions ensuring that delaying the firing of a transition $h \in H_i$ until some $f \in F_i$ fires does not modify the behavior of the net w.r.t. the set of properties we want to preserve.

Definition 6. *Let (N, m_0) be a p-agglomerable net. (N, m_0) is*

1. *H-independent iff $\forall i \in I, \forall h \in H_i, \forall m \in Reach(N, m_0), \forall s$ such that $\forall s' \in Pref(s), \Gamma_i(s') \geq 0, m[h.s\rangle \Longrightarrow m[s.h\rangle$*
2. *divergent-free iff $\forall s \in L^{\infty}(N, m_0), |s|_{T_0 \cup F} = \infty$*

3. **quasi-persistent** *iff* $\forall i \in I, \forall m \in Reach(N, m_0), \forall h \in H_i,$
   $\forall s \in (T_0 \cup F)^*,$ *such that* $m[h\rangle$ *and* $m[s\rangle$ $\exists s' \in (T_0 \cup F)^*$ *fulfilling:* $m[h.s'\rangle,$
   $\Pi_F(s') = \Pi_F(s)$ *and* $W(s') \geq W(s).$
   Furthermore, if $s \neq \lambda \Longrightarrow s' \neq \lambda$ *then the net is* **strongly** *quasi-persistent.*

4. **H-similar** *iff* $|I| = 1$ *or* $\forall i, j \in I, \forall m \in Reach(N, m_0), \forall s \in T_0^*,$
   $\forall h_i \in H_i, \forall h_j \in H_j, \forall f_j \in F_j$ $m[h_i\rangle$ *and* $m[s.h_j.f_j\rangle \Longrightarrow \exists s' \in (T_0)^*, \exists f_i \in F_i$
   such that $m[s'.h_i.f_i\rangle$ *and such that* $s = \lambda \Longrightarrow s' = \lambda.$

The H-independence roughly means that once a transition $h \in H_i$ is firable it can be delayed as long as one does not need its occurrence to fire a transition of F_i. When a net is divergent-free it does not generate infinite sequences with some suffix included in H. In the pre-agglomeration scheme, we transform original sequences by permutation and deletion of transitions to simulateable sequences. Such an infinite sequence cannot be transformed by this way into an infinite simulateable sequence. Therefore this condition is mandatory. The quasi-persistence ensures that in the original net a "quick" firing of a transition of H does not lead to some deadlock which could have been avoided by delaying this firing. At last, the H-similarity forbids situations where the firing of transitions of F is prevented due to a "bad" choice of a subset H_i.

Under previous conditions (or a subset of), fundamental properties of a net are preserved by the pre-agglomeration reduction. This result is stated in the following theorem whose demonstration is provided in [6].

Theorem 1. *If a p-agglomerable Petri net* (N, m_0) *is also*

1. *H-independent and divergent-free then*

$$\Pi_{T_0 \cup F}(L^{max}(N, m_0)) \supseteq \Pi_{T_0 \cup F}(\Phi(L^{max}(N_r, m_{0r})))$$

2. *H-independent, strongly quasi-persistent and H-similar then*

$$\Pi_{T_0 \cup F}(L^{max}(N, m_0)) \subseteq \Pi_{T_0 \cup F}(\Phi(L^{max}(N_r, m_{0r})))$$

3. *H-independent then*

$$\Pi_{T_0 \cup F}(\phi(L^{\infty}(N_r, m_0))) = \Pi_{T_0 \cup F}(L^{\infty}(N, m_0))$$

The first point defines which conditions ensure that the reduction does not introduce maximal blocking sequences (e.g. characterizing a deadlock) in the reduced net. The second one fixes when the reduction does not hide some maximal blocking sequences. At last, the third point focuses on the preservation of properties expressed with infinite sequences (e.g. fairness properties).

Post-Agglomeration. The main behavioral property that the conditions of the post-agglomeration implies is the following one: in every firing sequence with an occurrence of a transition h of H followed later by an occurrence of a transition f of F, one can immediately fire f after h. From a modeling point of view, the set F represents local actions while the set H corresponds to global actions possibly involving synchronization.

Definition 7. *Let (N, m_0) be a p-agglomerable marked net. (N, m_0) is*

1. **F-independent** *iff* $\forall i \in I, \forall h \in H_i, \forall f \in F_i, \forall s \in (T_0 \cup H)^*, \forall m \in$
   $Reach(N, m_0), m[h.s.f\rangle \implies m[h.s.f\rangle$
   (N, m_0) *is* **strongly F-independent** *iff* $\forall i \in I, \forall h \in H_i, \forall f \in F_i, \forall s \in T^*$
   s.t. $\forall s' \in Pref(s), \Gamma(s') \geq 0 \ \forall m \in Reach(N, m_0), m[h.s.f\rangle \implies m[h.f.s\rangle$

2. **F-continuable** *iff* $\forall i \in I, \forall h \in H_i, \forall s \in T^*$, *s.t.* $\forall s' \in Pref(s), \Gamma(s') \geq 0$
   $\forall m \in Reach(N, m_0) \ m[h.s\rangle \implies \exists f \in F_i$ *such that* $m[h.s.f\rangle$

We express the strong dependence of the set F on the set H with these two hypotheses. The F-independence means that any firing of $f \in F$ may be anticipated just after the occurrence of a transition $h \in H$ which "makes possible" this firing. The F-continuation means that an excess of occurrences of $h \in H$ can always be reduced by subsequent firings of transitions of F.

As for the pre-agglomeration, these conditions (or a subset of) ensure that fundamental properties of a net are preserved by the post-agglomeration reduction (the demonstration is provided in [6]).

Theorem 2. *If a p-agglomerable Petri net (N, m_0) is also*

1. *F-continuable and F-independent then*

$$\Pi_{T_0 \cup H}(L^{max}(N, m_0)) = \Pi_{T_0 \cup H}(\Phi(L^{max}(N_r, m_{0r})))$$

2. *F-continuable and strongly F-independent then*

$$\Pi_{T_0 \cup H}(\phi(L^\infty(N_r, m_0))) = \Pi_{T_0 \cup H}(L^\infty(N, m_0))$$

3   Simplifying Promela Model Analysis

3.1   The Promela Language

Promela is a verification modeling language associated with the Spin tool. Promela specifications consist of processes, message channels and variables. Processes are global objects. Message channels and variables can be declared either globally or locally within a process. Processes specify behavior while channels and global variables define the processes environment.

The execution of every statement is conditional on its executability. Statements are either executable or blocked. For instance, an assignment j=1 is always executable while a boolean condition j==1 is *executable* only when j is equal to 1.

An important feature of Promela is the ability given to processes to synchronize themselves through message channels which are used to model the transfer of data from one process to another. They are declared either locally or globally.

Figure 1 depicts an example of Promela specification. This simple producer/-consumer example spawns two processes: one of type **writer** and one of type **reader**. The writer sends N messages to the reader via a channel.

```
1  #define SIZE 255
2
3  int N = 100;
4  chan root = [SIZE] of {int};
5
6  proctype reader()
7  {
8      int i;
9      int j = 1;
10     do
11         :: ( j<= N ) -> root?i; j++
12         :: ( j > N ) -> break
13     od
14 }
15 proctype writer()
16 {
17     int j = 1;
18     do
19         :: ( j<= N ) -> root!j; j++
20         :: ( j > N ) -> break
21     od
22 }
23 init
24 {
25     atomic{
26         run writer();
27         run reader()
28     }
29 }
```

Fig. 1. A simple producer/consumer Promela model

On line 4, `chan root = [ SIZE ] of { int }`; declares a channel that can store up to `SIZE` messages of type `int`. The statement `root!j` (line 19) is a transmission of the value of `j` on the channel `root` (i.e. it appends the value to the tail of the channel). And `root?i` (line 11) models the reception on that channel (i.e. it retrieves it from the head of the channel, and stores it in the variable `i`). The send operation is executable only when the channel addressed is not full. The receive operation, similarly, is only executable when the channel is non empty. The channels pass messages in a first-in-first-out order.

The control flow in Promela can be defined with the selection, the repetition, and the unconditional jumps. For instance, The lines 18-21 in Figure 1 contains a repetition statement (`do ... od`). This repetition statement contains two sequences of statements, each preceded by a double colon. The first statements of these execution sequences are called *guards*. This repetition sequence will either execute the sequence starting with `:: ( j <= N )` or the sequence starting with `:: ( j > N )` regarding which guard is executable. If several guards are executables, one is randomly chosen. Once the sequence is executed, the repetition statement will be repeated. The normal way to terminate the repetition structure is the use of the **break** statement. The selection statement is similar to the repetition statement, but occurs only once.

3.2 Syntactical Promela Agglomerations

We define now some conditions under which it is possible to automatically infer agglomerations in a Promela specification. These agglomerations group sequential statements into an atomic block in order to reduce the combinatory. In other term we will fix simple conditions that allow us to transform a sequence [1]

---

[1] The case $k = 0$ is obvious and not studied.

$$i_0; \texttt{atomic} \ \{ \ i_1; \ i_2; \ \ldots; \ i_k \ \}$$

into the atomic sequence

$$\texttt{atomic} \ \{ \ i_0; \ i_1; \ i_2; \ \ldots; \ i_k \ \}$$

We study different cases for which this transformation preserves deadlock, non progress cycles or any LTL formula that does not observe the action i_0 (when we perform a pre-agglomeration) or any actions of i_j (when performing a post-agglomeration).

Methodology used The main principle is to explicitly use the behavioral conditions of Petri nets agglomerations for characterizing different cases in which the transformation is correct w.r.t. the analyzed property. Indeed, for any Promela specification, a corresponding Petri net with the same behavior can be generated (as in the QUASAR project for analyzing concurrent dynamic Ada programs) and adapted to Promela specification in [11]. Then, agglomeration conditions on Petri nets can be translated into syntactical and semantical conditions in the Promela program.

In order to interpret Petri net behavior into Promela behavior we classify Promela statements following three criteria (in the following examples we suppose that a statement i_0 is followed by a sequence of statement $s_f = \{i_1 \ldots; i_k\}$):

1. *is the statement blocking or not?* For instance, an assignment is a non blocking statement, because it is always executable while a boolean expression or a receive operation on a channel are blocking statements; this characteristic is related to the F-continuation hypothesis ;

   Indeed, if the statement i_0 is followed by a sequence of non blocking statements s_f, we know that the sequence will always be executed if i_0 is executed and so the F-continuation hypothesis is fulfilled (in the Petri net model, all the transitions modeling the sequence execution will be executable after firing i_0).

2. *does the statement refers local or global variables?* When the statement refers only local variables, the value for which the statement is executed by a process cannot change by the execution of other processes ; this characteristic is related to the H- and the F-independence ;

   For s_f referring only local variables or constants, the way the sequence s_f is executable cannot change after the execution of i_0. More precisely, suppose that i_2 refers a variable x and that s_f is executable after i_0 for a value x_0 of x ; as x is local, the value of x cannot change after i_0 is executed and before s_f execution, and then the way that s_f is executed does not change. So the F-Independence condition is fulfilled. As statements are executed by a process, i_0 cannot be re-executed before s_f has been executed. The strongly F-Independence condition is then also fulfilled (in the Petri net model, it would mean that the transitions of the sequence do not access places also accessed by a transition modeling another process execution).

   The same reasoning can be performed for i_0, but in this case would fulfill the H-independent and the strongly quasi-persistence conditions. As

i_0 accesses only variables that cannot change when the process is not active, the statement i_0 can be delayed and then the H-independent and the strongly quasi-persistence conditions are fulfilled.

3. *is the statement a guard (a first statement of a sequence in a branch of a selection)?* in that case, the statement is potentially in competition with other statements in other branches of the selection structure (the process may have a choice); this characteristic is related to the quasi-persistent and the H-similar hypothesizes.

   If there is no competition (the statement is not a guard) the H-similarity condition is fulfilled ($|I| = 1$). Others cases have to be discussed for each kind of statement.

The statement i_0 is followed by non blocking statements. The first case is when the sequence $s_f = \texttt{atomic\{ } i_1;\ldots; i_k\}$ is a non blocking sequence and $i_1; \ldots; i_k$ only refers local variables or constants (i.e. variables that are declared within the corresponding process or that are never assigned except at their declaration). In that case, a post-agglomeration of i_0 with the rest of the sequence can be performed. Indeed, as s_f is non blocking, it can be executed as soon as i_0 has been executed and then the F-continuation condition is fulfilled. Now, as $i_1 \ldots; i_k$ refers only local variables or constants the way the sequences s_f is executable cannot change after the execution of i_0. More precisely, suppose that i_2 refers a variable x and that s_f is executable after i_0 for a value x_0 of x; as x is local, the value of x cannot change before s_f is executed, and then the way that s_f is executed does not change when i_0 has been executed and s_f not. So the F-Independence condition is fulfilled. As statements are executed by a process, i_0 cannot be re-executed before s_f has been executed. The strongly F-Independence condition is then also fulfilled.

The statement i_0 is not a guard. We suppose here that i_0 is not a guard and we examine three kinds of statements for i_0: the blocking conditional statement $(\texttt{x == y})$ the assignment $(\texttt{x = y})$ and the receive operation on a channel $(\texttt{q?x})$

1. Suppose first that i_0 is an assignment that does not refer to global variables (except constants). As i_0 accesses only variables that cannot change when the process is not active, the statement i_0 can be delayed and then the H-independent and the strongly quasi-persistence conditions are fulfilled. As the statement i_0 is not a loop, the divergence freeness is ensured. Moreover, as we agglomerate a single statement (i_0) with a sequence (s_f), the H-similarity condition is fulfilled ($|I| = 1$). Now, if i_1 is a blocking statement and if i_1 does not use variables modified by i_0 and does not modify variables accessed by i_0, we can safely replace the statement $\texttt{atomic\{ } i_0; i_1; \ldots; i_k\}$ by the statement $\texttt{atomic\{ } i_1; i_0; \ldots; i_k\}$. By this way we put the "blocking" statement at the beginning of the sequence which disables a possible interruption in the atomic statement execution.

2. Now, suppose that i_0 is a boolean expression and suppose that this expression does not refer to global variables (except constants). Then using the same reasoning, a pre-agglomeration can be performed on i_0 and s_f.

3. When i_0 is a blocking reception on a channel we have to be careful. First, suppose that the channel is marked as "exclusive reader". This disables the possibility that a process takes a message that another process was waiting for (which will contradict the quasi-persistence condition). Then the H-independence condition implies that the reception of a message on the channel does not enable any action of an other process. In the general case this is not possible (a "reader" can unblock a "writer"). However, suppose that the user can mark a channel as "sufficient capacity" meaning that a writing statement on this channel will never be blocked; then, reading a message on such a channel cannot unblock a process waiting for writing. In such a case, a pre-agglomeration can be safely performed.

The statement i_0 is a guard. Now suppose that i_0 is the first statement of a selection structure (this applies also to a repetition statement)

if

    :: i_0; atomic{ i_1; ...; i_k}

    :: s_1

    :: ...

    :: s_n

    :: else s_e

fi

where s_1, ..., s_n and s_e are sequences of actions (atomic or not).

1. First, suppose that i_0 is an assignment or a boolean expression that uses only local variables or constants. Suppose also that atomic{ i_1; ...; i_k} is a non blocking sequence, that each statement s_j can be written $i_0^j.s_j'$ with s_j' a non blocking sequence and that i_0^j is an assignment or a boolean expression that uses only local variables or constants; then we can perform a pre-agglomeration of i_0 with the sequence atomic{ i_1; ...; i_k} simultaneously with a pre-agglomeration of each i_0^j with the first statement of s_j'. Indeed, the H-independence and the quasi-persistence are ensured due to the locality of variables used in statements. The H-similarity is obtained by the non blocking character of each sequence s_j' which ensures that if a given sequence s_j' is executable, then all other sequences $s_{j'}'$ are also executable.

2. Next, suppose that i_0 is a boolean expression using only local variables and constants. If all statements s_i also begin with a boolean expression using only local variables and constants and if at most one of this boolean expression is true at a time, then i_0 can be pre-agglomerated with atomic{ i_1; ...; i_k}. This is so because there is no really choice on the selection structure: at most one sequence is executable and the one which is executable does not change until it is executed.

3. The same reasoning can be applied when i_0 is a statement $q?v_0(x_0)$ such that q is a channel marked as an exclusive reader which does not block writers under the conditions that:

    (a) each s_i is also a statement $q?v_i(x_i)$, where $v_0 \ldots v_n$ denotes different constant values,

(b) $x_0, \ldots, x_i$ design local variables and

(c) there is no *else* part in the selection structure.

Indeed, in that case, there is no real choice (due to the different value of message type) and as there is no *else* part, the message reception can be delayed.

4. At last, suppose that all alternatives of a selection statement are atomic sequences; then, without modifying its behavior we can rewrite it into an atomic sequence that contains the selection statement as the unique statement.

The following algorithm (Algorithm 1) formalizes these Promela sources transformation rules.

4 Experimentations

We implemented these agglomerations in a tool (atomicSpin [12]). We applied our transformations on different models. Using the Spin tool (v. 4.3.0), we compute the total number of generated states when looking for all invalid end-states in the original and in the reduced model.

Consider the producer/consumer specification depicted on Figure 1. The resulting specification after agglomerations is depicted on Figure 2.

Consider process of type `Reader`: the sequence `root?i; j++` can be transformed into `atomic {root?i; j++}` using the first rule (3.1.2) which corresponds to a post-agglomeration. Indeed, `j++` is a non blocking statement using only local variable. Then, we can operate the transformation of the sequence `(j <= N); atomic {root?i; j++}` into the sequence `atomic{ (j <= N); root?i; j++}` using the second rules of subsection 3.1.4. Symmetric transformations can be applied in the code of the `Writer` process.

In the Table 1, we trace the number of reachable states for the original and the transformed model using the Spin partial order reduction in both cases (SPO

```
 1  #define SIZE 255
 2
 3  int N = 100;
 4  chan root = [SIZE] of {int};
 5
 6  proctype reader()
 7  {
 8      int i;
 9      int j = 1;
10      do
11          :: atomic { ( j<= N ) -> root?i; j++ }
12          :: atomic { ( j > N ) -> } break
13      od
14  }
15  proctype writer()
16  {
17      int j = 1;
18      do
19          :: atomic { ( j<= N ) -> root!j; j++ }
20          :: atomic { ( j > N ) -> } break
21      od
22  }
23  init
24  {
25      atomic{
26          run writer();
27          run reader()
28      }
29  }
```

Fig. 2. The simple producer/consumer with automatically inferred atomic blocks

---

Algorithm 1. Atomicspin algorithm

Require: i_0, i_1, s

  if atomic sequence s doesn't use global variables **then**

    if atomic sequence s doesn't contain any blocking statement **then**

      if i_0 is not a guard **then**

        add i_0 to the atomic sequence s

      else if i_0 is an assignment, printf, or general statement **then**

        add i_0 to the atomic sequence s

      else if i_0 is a boolean expression **and**

            all other choices are boolean expression **and**

            at most one choice is true at a time

      then

        add i_0 to the atomic sequence s

      else if i_0 is a channel reception **and**

            channel is exclusive reader **and**

            all choices are receptions on the same channel **and**

            there is no else part in the selection statement **and**

            there is only one reception computable at a time

      then

        add i_0 to the atomic sequence s

      else

        close the atomic sequence s

      end if

    else

      if i_0 is a guard **then**

        close the atomic sequence s

      else if i_0 is an assignment or a boolean expression **and**

            i_0 doesn't modify i_1 variables **and**

            i_0 access only local variables

      then

        add i_0 to the atomic sequence s

        swap i_0 and i_1

      else if i_0 is a reception on a channel **and**

            the channel is exclusive reader **and**

            the channel is sufficient capacity

      then

        add i_0 to the built atomic sequence

        swap i_0 and i_1

      else

        close the atomic sequence s

      end if

    end if

  else

    close the atomic sequence s

  end if

Table 1. Benchmarks

name	process	states		memory (Mo)	
		SPO	APO	SPO	APO
allocator	1	44	23	0	0
	2	1 818	646	0	0
	3	42 419	11 876	6	2
	4	637 398	160 242	107	26
	5	7.77e+06	1.89e+06	1 555	378
leader	20	367	267	0	0
	40	727	527	1	1
	60	1 087	787	2	2
	80	1 447	1 047	4	3
	100	1 807	1 307	7	5
leader2	2	84	60	0	0
	3	356	254	0	0
	4	2 074	1 482	0	0
	5	14 122	10 082	3	2
	6	106 514	75 986	29	21
petersonN	3	2 999	2 374	0	0
	4	533 083	383 478	21	21
	5	-	-	-	-
philo1	2	42	20	0	0
	4	1 525	236	0	0
	6	64 944	3 745	6	0
	8	2.91e+06	62 712	373	8
	10	-	1.02e+06	-	155
philo2	10	189 445	86 407	20	9
	11	706 565	292 125	84	35
	12	2.61e+06	955 822	334	122
	13	9.50e+06	3.14e+06	1 293	427
	14	-	1.02e+07	-	1 478
prod_cons	200	161 609	41 009	172	44
	400	558 529	214 789	596	229
	600	967 329	419 589	1 033	448
	800	1.37e+06	624 389	1 469	666
	1000	1.78e+06	829 189	1 906	885
sort	50	5 252	2 705	7	3
	100	20 502	10 404	51	26
	150	45 752	23 104	172	87
	200	81 002	40 804	406	204
	250	126 252	63 304	791	398

means Spin with partial order reductions, and APO means atomicSpin with the same partial order reductions). Agglomerations leads to a significant reduction of the state space size, with a quasi null cost in time (checking our conditions on Promela programs is a very simple task).

We also carried out experiments on classical examples of Promela models included in the standard distribution of Spin (the leader election, the distributed sort, the two versions of a cell-phone handoff strategy in a mobile network, the Peterson for N, the snooping cache) and some examples of our own (two version of the well known dining philosophers and a task allocator modeling a client-server application).

Agglomerations improve the state space reduction in all cases. Except for the leader election, the reduction factor is at least 2 even when partial-order reductions are enabled and agglomerations performed on the dining philosophers model achieved reductions of the state space by a factor 20.

5   Related Works on Syntactical Model Reductions

First works concerning reduction of sequences into atomic actions for simplification purpose was performed by Lipton in [13]. Lipton focused only on deadlock property preservation. Using parallel program notations of Dijkstra he defined "left" and "right" movers. Roughly speaking, a "left" (resp. "right") mover is a local process statement that can be moved forward (resp. delayed) w.r.t. statements of others processes without modifying the halting property. Lipton then demonstrated that, in principle, the statement P(S), where S is a semaphore, is a "left" mover and V(s) is a "right" mover. Then Lipton proved that some parallel program are deadlock free by moving P(S) and V(S) statements and by suppressing atomic statements that have no effect on variables. However, two difficulties arise: the reduction preserves only deadlocks and the application conditions are difficult to be checked.

Cohen and Lamport propose in [14] assumptions on TLA specifications under which they define a reduction theorem preserving liveness and safety properties. This work fixes the reduction theorem in a "high" level formalism which can be a clear advantage for defining specific utilization. However, it's also its main drawback since it is based on the hypothesis that some actions commute, but no effective way is proposed to check whether this assumption holds.

More recently, Cohen, Stoller, Qadeer, and Flanagan [15], [16], [17] leveraged Lipton's theory of reduction to detect transactions in multi-threaded programs (and consider these transactions as atomic actions in the model checking step). Stoller and Cohen propose in [15] a reduction theorem based on omega algebra that can be applied to models of concurrent systems using mutual exclusion for access to selected variables. However, they use a restricted notion of "left" mover and a better reduction ratio can be obtained by applying more accurate reductions (as demonstrated in [18]). Moreover, their reductions are justified by the correct use of "exclusive access predicates" and by the respect of a specific synchronization discipline. These predicates may be difficult to compute and no effective algorithm is given to test that the synchronization discipline is respected.

Flanagan and Qadeer noted in [17] that the previous authors use only the notion of "left" mover and proposed an algorithm that uses both "left" and "right" mover notions to infer transactions. However, this algorithm is based on access predicates that can be automatically inferred only for specific programs using lock-based synchronization. Moreover, as they use both "left" and "right" movers to obtain a better reduction ratio and as they do not fix sufficient restrictive application conditions, their reduction theorem do not preserve deadlock.

In Petri nets formalism, the first works concerning reductions have been performed by Berthelot [19]. The link between transition agglomerations (the most effective structural reductions proposed by Berthelot) and general properties, expressed in LTL formalism, is done in [20].

We proposed in [6] new Petri nets reductions that cover a large range of patterns by introducing algebraic conditions whereas the previously defined ones rely solely on structural conditions. We adapted them in [7] to colored Petri nets which are an abbreviation of Petri nets and define a concise formalism for the modeling of concurrent software. We showed here that these reductions can also be adapted to Promela specifications leading to simple syntactical rules which permit a significant reduction of the combinatory while preserving properties of the model.

6   Conclusion

We demonstrate in this paper that efficient Petri nets reductions can be used to significantly reduce the state space size of a Promela specification. We propose simple syntactical rules allowing the automatic building of atomic sequences. Our experiments highlight the efficiency of these approaches. A first implementation of these rules has already been developed [12]. Our experience with Petri nets allows us to expect even better reductions for more complex models. Based on these experimentations we plan to adapt these transformation rules to automatically infer transactions in concurrent software written in Ada or Java in the near future.

References

1. Wolper, P., Godefroid, P.: Partial-order methods for temporal verification. In: Best, E. (ed.) CONCUR 1993. LNCS, vol. 715, pp. 233–246. Springer, Heidelberg (1993)
2. Godefroid, P., Wolper, P.: Using partial orders for the efficient verification of deadlock freedom and safety properties. Form. Methods Syst. Des. 2(2), 149–164 (1993)
3. Valmari, A.: On-the-fly verification with stubborn sets. In: Courcoubetis, C. (ed.) CAV 1993. LNCS, vol. 697, pp. 397–408. Springer, Heidelberg (1993)
4. Emerson, A., Prasad Sistl, A.: Symmetry and model checking. In: Courcoubetis, C. (ed.) CAV 1993. LNCS, vol. 697, pp. 463–478. Springer, Heidelberg (1993)
5. Sistla, A.P.: Symmetry reductions in model-checking. In: Zuck, L.D., Attie, P.C., Cortesi, A., Mukhopadhyay, S. (eds.) VMCAI 2003. LNCS, vol. 2575. Springer, Heidelberg (2002)
6. Haddad, S., Pradat-Peyre, J.: Efficient reductions for LTL formulae verification. Technical report, CEDRIC, CNAM, Paris (2004)

7. Evangelista, S., Haddad, S., Pradat-Peyre, J.F.: New coloured reductions for software validation. In: Workshop on Discrete Event Systems (2004)
8. Haddad, S., Pradat-Peyre, J.-F.: New efficient petri nets reductions for parallel programs verification. Parallel Processing Letters 16(1), 101–116 (2006)
9. Evangelista, S., Kaiser, C., Pradat-Peyre, J.F., Rousseau, P.: Quasar: a new tool for analysing concurrent programs. In: Rosen, J.-P., Strohmeier, A. (eds.) Ada-Europe 2003. LNCS, vol. 2655. Springer, Heidelberg (2003)
10. Holzmann, G.J.: The model checker SPIN. Software Engineering 23(5), 279–295 (1997)
11. Pajault, C., Pradat-Peyre, J.: Static reductions for promela specifications. Technical Report 1005, Conservatoire National des Arts et Métiers, laboratoire Cedric, Paris, France (2006)
12. http://quasar.cnam.fr/atomicSpin/
13. Lipton, R.J.: Reduction: a method of proving properties of parallel programs. Commun. ACM 18(12), 717–721 (1975)
14. Cohen, E., Lamport, L.: Reduction in TLA. In: International Conference on Concurrency Theory, pp. 317–331 (1998)
15. Stoller, S.D., Cohen, E.: Optimistic synchronization-based state-space reduction. In: Garavel, H., Hatcliff, J. (eds.) ETAPS 2003 and TACAS 2003. LNCS, vol. 2619. Springer, Heidelberg (2003)
16. Flanagan, C., Qadeer, S.: A type and effect system for atomicity. In: Proceedings of the ACM SIGPLAN 2003 conference on Programming language design and implementation, pp. 338–349. ACM Press, New York (2003)
17. Flanagan, C., Qadeer, S.: Transactions for software model checking. In: Cook, B., Stoller, S., Visser, W. (eds.) Electronic Notes in Theoretical Computer Science, vol. 89. Elsevier, Amsterdam (2003)
18. Evangelista, S., Haddad, S., Pradat-Peyre, J.: Coloured Petri nets reductions for concurrent software validation. Technical report, CEDRIC, CNAM, Paris (2004)
19. Berthelot, G.: Checking properties of nets using transformations. In: Rozenberg, G. (ed.) Advances in Petri nets. LNCS, vol. 222. Springer, Heidelberg (1985)
20. Poitrenaud, D., Pradat-Peyre, J.: Pre and post-agglomerations for LTL model checking. In: Nielsen, M., Simpson, D. (eds.) ICATPN 2000. LNCS, vol. 1825. Springer, Heidelberg (2000)

A   Agglomerated Petri Net Definition

Proposition 1. *The incidence matrices W, W^- and W^+ can be extended to matrices indexed by $P \times T^*$ by the following recursive definition:*

- $W(p, \lambda) = W^-(p, \lambda) = W^+(p, \lambda) = 0$ *and* $W(p, s_1.t) = W(p, s_1) + W(p, t)$
- $W^-(p, s_1.t) = Max(W^-(p, s_1), W^-(p, t) - W(p, s_1))$
- $W^+(p, s_1.t) = W(p, s) + W^-(p, s)$

such that this extension is compatible with the firing rule, i.e.

$\forall s \in T^*,\ m[s\rangle m' \iff \forall p \in P,\ m(p) \geq W^-(p, s)$ *and* $m'(p) = m(p) + W(p, s)$

Definition 8 (Reduced net). *The reduced Petri net (N_r, m_0) is defined by:*

- $P_r = P$, $T_r = T_0 \cup_{i \in I} (H_i \times F_i)$ *(we note hf the transition (h, f) of $H_i \times F_i$);*
- $\forall t_r \in T_0, \forall p \in P_r,\ W_r^-(p, t) = W^-(p, t)$ *and* $W_r^+(p, t) = W^+(p, t)$
- $\forall i \in I, \forall hf \in H_i \times F_i, \forall p \in P_r\ W_r^-(p, hf) = W^-(p, h.f)$ *and* $W_r^+(p, hf) = W^+(p, h.f)$

Verification of a Hierarchical Generic Mutual Exclusion Algorithm

Souheib Baarir[1], Julien Sopena[2], and Fabrice Legond-Aubry[2]

[1] Univ. degli Studi del Piemonte Orientale. Department of Computer Science.
Via Bellini 25G, 15100 Alessandria, Italy
[2] LIP6 - Université de Paris 6
104, Avenue du President Kennedy, 75016 Paris, France
souheib.baarir@mfn.unipmn.it,
{julien.sopena,fabrice.legond-aubry}@lip6.fr

Abstract. In distributed environments, the shared resources access control by mutual exclusion paradigm is a recurrent key problem. To cope with the new constraints implied by recently developed large scale distributed systems like grids, mutual exclusion algorithms become more and more complex and thus much harder to prove and/or verify. In this article, we propose the formal modeling and the verification of a new generic hierarchical approach. This approach is based on the composition of classical already proof checked distributed algorithms. It overcomes some limitations of these classical algorithms by taking into account the network topology latencies and have a high scalability where centralized ones don't. We also have formalized the properties of the mutual exclusion paradigm in order to verify them against our solution. We prove that our compositional approach preserves theses properties under the assumption that all used plain algorithms assert them. This verification by formal method checkers was eased by the efficient use of already proved mutual exclusion algorithms and the reduction of state spaces by exploiting the symmetries.

Keywords: distributed algorithm, composition, mutual exclusion, grid computing, colored Petri nets, model checking.

1 Introduction

By gathering geographically distributed resources, a Grid offers a single large-scale environment suitable for the execution of computational intensive applications. A Grid usually comprises of a large number of nodes grouped into clusters. Nodes within a cluster are often linked by local networks (LAN) while clusters are linked by a wide area network (WAN). Therefore, Grids present a hierarchy of communication delays: the cost of sending a message between nodes of different clusters is much higher than that of sending the same message between nodes within the same cluster.

Distributed or parallel applications that run on top of a Grid usually require that their processes get exclusive access to some shared resources (critical section). Thus, the performance of mutual exclusion algorithms is critical to Grid

K. Suzuki et al. (Eds.): FORTE 2008, LNCS 5048, pp. 99–115, 2008.

applications and it is the focus of this paper. A mutual exclusion algorithm ensures that exactly one process can execute the critical section at any given time (*safety* property) and that all critical section (CS) requests will eventually be satisfied (*liveness* property). We choose not to discuss the necessity, advantages or drawbacks of distributed versions of such algorithms. Readers can learn more informations about them in [7].

The contribution of this paper is two fold : the design of a generic hierarchical mutual exclusion composition approach which easily allows the combination of different *inter-cluster* and *intra-cluster* algorithms on the contrary to the previous approach and the verification of its correctness.

The remainder of this paper is organized as follows. Section 3 presents our composition approach and shows its advantages comparatively to existing works. In section 4, we describe the Petri net (P.N.) modelization of our approach followed by the expression of the properties we verify in section 5. Afterward, we present results of these properties verification on our proposed approach in section 7. The last section concludes our work and proposes interesting perspectives of research.

2   Related Work

Several studies have proposed to adapt existing mutual exclusion algorithms to a hierarchical scheme. In Mueller [15], the author presents an extension to Naimi-Tréhel's algorithm, introducing the concept of priority. A token request is associated with a priority and the algorithm first satisfies the requests with higher priority. Bertier et al. [2] adopt a similar strategy based on the Naimi-Tréhel's algorithm which treats intra-cluster requests before inter-cluster ones.

Finally, several authors have proposed hierarchical approaches for combining different mutual exclusion algorithms. Housni et al. [8] and Chang et al. [3]'s mutual exclusion algorithms gather nodes into groups. Both articles basically consider hybrid approaches where the algorithm for intra-group requests is different from the inter-group one. In Housni et al. [8], sites with the same priority are gathered at the same group. Raymond's tree-based token algorithm [18] is used inside a group, while Ricart-Agrawala [19] diffusion-based algorithm is used between groups. Chang et al.'s [3] hybrid algorithm applies diffusion-based algorithms at both levels: Singhal's algorithm [20] locally, and Maekawa's algorithm [13] between groups. The former uses a dynamic information structure while the latter is based on a voting approach. Similarly, Omara et al. [17]'s solution is a hybrid of Maekawa's algorithm and Singhal's modified algorithm which provides fairness. In Madhuram et al. [12], the authors also present a two level algorithm where the centralized approach is used at lower level and Ricard-Agrawala at the higher level. Erciyes [6] proposes an approach close to ours based on a ring of clusters. Each node in the ring represents a cluster of nodes. The author then adapts Ricart-Agrawal to this architecture.

Our approach is close to these proposed solutions. However, we have found a more generic approach to achieve the scalability we need for large scale grid by finding a way to aggregate pre-existing algorithms and considering network latencies heterogeneity. It enables us to fit better the grid architecture and the application behavior. To do this, we have created glue code which coordinates two instance levels of plain mutual exclusion algorithms by just inserting well placed call traps in their inner code but without modifying their behavior. Practical results show significantly better performances [21] over classical distributed algorithms but no proof has been made to verify the correctness of the solution.

3   Our Composition Algorithm - An Informal Approach

Our approach consists in having a hierarchy of token-based mutual exclusion algorithms: a per cluster mutual exclusion algorithm that controls critical section requests from processes within the same cluster and a second algorithm that controls *inter-cluster* requests for the token. The former is called the *intra* algorithm while the latter is called the *inter* algorithm. An *intra* algorithm of a cluster runs independently from the other *intra* algorithms.

The application is composed of a set of processes which run on the nodes of the Grid. We consider one process per node and call it an *application* process. When an *application* process wants to access the shared resource, it calls the function *intra.CS_Request()*. It then executes its critical section. After executing it, the process calls the function *intra.CS_Release()* to release it. Both functions are provided by the *intra* token algorithm.

Within each cluster there is a special node, the *coordinator*. The *inter* algorithm runs on top of the *coordinators* allowing them to request the right of accessing the shared resource on behalf of *application* nodes of their respective cluster. *Coordinators* are in fact hybrid processes which participate in both the *inter* algorithm with the other *coordinators* and the *intra* algorithm with their cluster's *application* processes. However, even if the *intra* algorithm sees a *coordinator* as an *application* process, the *coordinator* does not take part in the application's execution *i.e.*, it never requests access to the CS for itself in the *intra* and *inter* layers but act as a **mandatory proxy for each layer**. As explained in the next sections, it forwards incoming *inter* requests and outgoing *intra* requests.

3.1   Coordinator Algorithm

The key feature of our approach is that the two hierarchical algorithms are clearly separated since an *application* process gets access to the shared resource just by executing the *intra* algorithm of its cluster. Another important advantage is that the behavior of the chosen algorithms of both layers do not need to be modified. Hence, it is very simple to have different compositions of algorithms.

An *intra* algorithm controls an *intra* token while the *inter* algorithm controls an *inter* token. Thus, there is one *intra* token per cluster but a single *inter* token of which only the *coordinators* are aware. **Holding the *intra* token must be sufficient and necessary for an *application* process to enter the CS** since the local *intra* algorithm ensures that no other local *application* node of the cluster has the *intra* token. **But, considering the hierarchical compo-sition of algorithms, our solution must then guarantee that no other** *application* **process of the other clusters is also in critical section when holding an** *intra* **token (per cluster** *safety* **property).** In other words, the *safety* property of the *inter* algorithm must ensure that at any time only one cluster has the right of allowing its *application* processes to execute the CS. This property can be asserted by the possession of the *inter* token by a *coordinator*.

Similarly to a classical mutual exclusion algorithm, the *coordinator* calls the *inter.CS_Request()* and the *inter.CS_Release()* functions for respectively asking or releasing the *inter* token. However, when a *coordinator* is in critical section, it means that *application* processes of its cluster have the right of accessing the resource. The *inter* token is held by the *coordinator* of this cluster which is then considered to be in critical section by the other *coordinators*.

```
1  Coordinator Algorithm ()
2  |   intra.CS_Request()                    19  CS_Request ()
3  |   /* Holds intra-token CS */            20  |   ...
4  |   while TRUE do                         21  |   mutexState ← REQ
5  |   |   if ¬ intra.PendingRequest() then  22  |   Wait for Token
6  |   |   |   state ← OUT                    23  |   mutexState ← CS
7  |   |   |   Wait for intra.PendingRequest()
8  |   |   state ← WAIT_FOR_IN               24  CS_Release ()
9  |   |   inter.CS_Request()                 25  |   ...
10 |   |   /* Holds inter-token. CS */        26  |   mutexState ← NO_REQ
11 |   |   intra.CS_Release()
12 |   |   if ¬ inter.PendingRequest() then
13 |   |   |   state ← IN
14 |   |   |   Wait for inter.PendingRequest()
15 |   |   state ← WAIT_FOR_OUT              27  pendingRequest ()
16 |   |   intra.CS_Request()                         ⎧ TRUE    if ∃ pending request
17 |   |   /* Holds intra-token CS */         28   return ⎨
18 |   |   inter.CS_Release()                         ⎩ FALSE   otherwise
```

Fig. 1. Coordinator Algorithm

Our composition solution does not require any change in the mutual exclusion algorithm. Providing such "plug in" feature is done by just inserting callbacks in the mutual exclusion implantation code. The algorithm themselves are not modified.

Only two trap callbacks are necessary: a *new request* trap and a *no more request* trap. The former, as its named suggest, must be invoked at each new token request processing while the latter must be invoked when there are no more pending request in the algorithm. These callbacks need no parameters and must be inserted in strategic code locations.

The guiding principle of our approach is described in the pseudo code of figure 1. Initially, every *coordinator* holds the *intra* token of its cluster and one cluster hold the *inter* token. When an *application* process wants to enter the critical section, it sends a request to its local *intra* algorithm by calling the *intra.CS_Request()* function. The *coordinator* of the cluster, which is the current holder of the *intra* token, will also receive such a request. However, before granting the *intra* token to the requesting *application* process, the *coordinator* must first acquire the *inter* token by calling the *inter.CS_Request()* function [line 9] of the *inter* algorithm. Therefore, upon receiving the *inter* token, the *coordinator* gives the *intra* token to the requesting *application* process by calling the *intraCS_Release()* function [line 11].

A *coordinator* which holds the *inter* token must also treat the *inter* token requests received from the *inter* algorithm. However, it can only grant the *inter* token to another *coordinator* if it holds its local *intra* token too. Having the latter ensures it that no *application* processes within its cluster is in the critical section. Thus, if the *coordinator* does not hold the *intra* token, it sends a request to its *intra* algorithm asking for it by calling the *intra.CS_Request()* function [line 16]. Upon obtaining the *intra* token, the *coordinator* can give the *inter* token to the requesting *coordinator* by calling the *inter.CS_Release()* function[line 18].

3.2   Coordinator Automaton

In a classical mutual exclusion algorithm, a process can be in one of the three following states : requesting the critical section (REQ), not requesting it (NO_REQ), or in the critical section(CS), as shown in figure 2(a).

The behavior of a *coordinator* process can be summarized by a state automaton. A *coordinator* process is in one of the above three states in regards to both layer algorithms. **Therefore, in the automaton of figure 2(b),** *Intra* **and** *Inter* **refer to the** *coordinator* **state related to the** *intra* **algorithm and** *inter* **algorithm instance respectively.** Thus, a *coordinator* has new states in respect with the global state of the composition, which can be one of the following: OUT, IN, $WAIT\_FOR\_OUT$, $WAIT\_FOR\_IN$. These new states are a tuple composed of the states of each layer state.

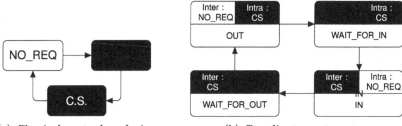

(a) Classical mutual exclusion   (b) Coordinator automaton
client automaton

Fig. 2. Coordinator and mutual exclusion client Automata

To ease the reader comprehension, we have had line references to the "**Co-ordinator algorithm**" pseudo-code in brackets and *inter* or *intra* layers state references of the automaton figure 2(b) in parenthesis. If the coordinator is in the state *OUT*, no local *application* processes of its cluster has requested the CS. Thus, it holds the *intra* token (*Intra* = *CS*)[line 2 or line 16] and does not hold the *inter* token (*Inter* = *NO_REQ*).

When the *coordinator* is in the state *WAIT_FOR_IN*, it means that there are one or more pending *intra* requests [line 1]. It still holds the local *intra* token (*Intra* = *CS*) but is waiting for the *inter* token (*Inter* = *REQ*)[line 9]

In the *IN* state, the coordinator holds the *inter* token (*Inter* = *CS*)[line 9]. but has granted the *intra* algorithm token (*Intra* = *NO_REQ*)[line 11] to one of its *application* processes.

Finally, when the coordinator is in the state *WAIT_FOR_OUT*, it still holds the *inter* token (*Inter*= *CS*)[line 9] but it is requesting the *intra* token to the *intra* algorithm (*Intra* = *REQ*)[line 16] in order to be able to satisfy an *inter* algorithm pending request [line 14].

It is worth remarking that only one coordinator can be either in *IN* or in *WAIT_FOR_OUT* state at any given time. All the other coordinators are either in state *OUT* or in state *WAIT_FOR_IN*.

4   Our Composition Algorithm - A Formal Model

High Level Petri Nets (*H.L.P.N.*) [9] formalism is an expressive model extending the representation of concurrency by Petri nets with a data management via the coloured domains and functions. It is well fitted for the representation of large distributed system like ours. Moreover, by use of Stochastic Well-Formed Petri nets (*S.W.N.*) [4], a particular category of H.L.P.N., we can check efficiently behavioral properties on the built representation. Thus, we have naturally choose this formalism over proof based methods.[1]

To obtain a good modelling, we have adopted an incremental and compositional methodology. We have isolated fundamental parts of our solution and defined Petri nets interfaces to bind them together. During the whole process, we have kept in mind the necessity to maintain the inherent symmetries of our approach. The preservation of behavioral symmetries is the key point to achieve our verification goals.

4.1   A Basic Mutual Exclusion Aware Application Modelization

Distributed applications which use mutual exclusion can be summarized by a potentially infinite ordered succession of three specific states like those exposed in the section 3.2 and on the automaton of figure 2(a): *NO_REQ*, *REQ* and

---

[1] It is worth noting that our models are described in the general framework of H.L.P.N., without taking into consideration the particular syntax of SWN. Actually, this simplifies considerably the modelling process without loss of generality.

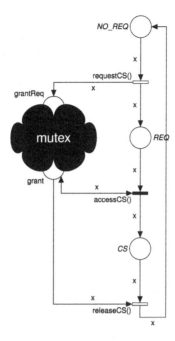

Fig. 3. Basic Mutual Exclusion modelling in *H.L.P.N.*

CS. These three states are represented by the three places at the right of the figure 3.

Initially, the place *NO_REQ* contains a colored token per application process. A process do some local work during an undefined time and does not require an access to the exclusive resources. The need for a process to get the exclusive access is expressed by the firing of transition *requestCS()*. The processes identified by the colored token must then wait for the critical section (CS) granting authorization by the mutual exclusion algorithm. Upon clearance, the process token is then able to fire the transition *AccessCS()* and will mark the place *CS*. The process can now execute its "critical section". As soon as it has finished (after an undefined time), it can get back to its local tasks by releasing the exclusive lock - *i.e.*, by firing the transition *releaseCS()*. Therefore the subnet composed of the places *NO_REQ*, *REQ*, *CS* and their adjacent transitions abstracts the behavior of our application processes.

The exclusive access to the place *CS* and the management of the request queue are ensured by a distributed mechanism: the mutual exclusion algorithm. This mechanism interacts with the application on every transitions. For now, we have no need to have a concret modelling of such an algorithm, hence we abstract it by the use a *clouded* Petri net named *"mutex"* (see figure 3). At the border-side of the cloud, two places can be seen. The place *grantRequest*, when marked by a token *x* asserts the fact that the request for CS has been sent by the process *x*. The second is the place *grant* which represents the mutual exclusion grant allowance for the process identified by the color of the token.

This model is in accordance with the classical A.P.I. of the mutual exclusion algorithms described in the pseudo-code of the figure 1: $CS\_Request()$ [line 19] and $CS\_Release()$ [line 24]. An application process use these two functions after a random elapsed time. This explains the temporisation of the corresponding transitions (white filled ⟹). On the contrary, the firing of the transition $AccessCS()$ depends on the return of the "*wait for token*" synchronized blocking instruction call of the figure 1 pseudo-code [line 22]. So, the sojourn time in the place REQ is, deterministically, dependent of the availability of the grant token. This explains the immediate character of transition $AccessCS()$ (black filled ▬). As soon as the authorization is granted (the place *grant* is marked by token x), the requesting process x enters the CS.

4.2   Our Composition Algorithm Petri Net

Using the previous section, the modelling of our composition algorithm is much more simple. It can be seen as a synchronized use of two distinct instances of a mutual exclusion service: one at the *inter* level and one at the *intra* level. The subnet of the figure 4 models our composition approach. Since section 3 postulates the use of the same *intra* algorithm for each cluster, we have chosen to fold all the *intra* algorithm instances (*i.e.*, of every cluster) in one unique clouded subnet named "*intra*" at the right of the figure 4. To do so, the color token $\langle i, c \rangle$ identifies the process i of the cluster c. Note that the process color $\langle 0, c \rangle$ identify the coordinator. The c color permits the isolation of each local instances.

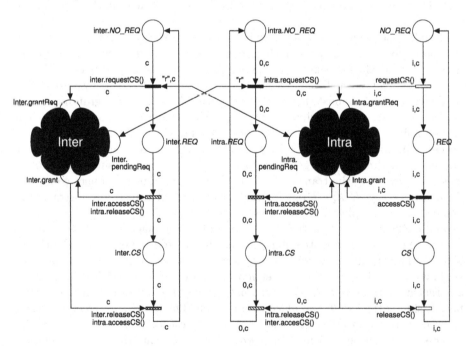

Fig. 4. *H.L.P.N.* of the composition algorithm

The subnet of the figure 4, composed of places NO_REQ, REQ and CS and its adjacent transitions abstracts the behavior of all the application processes inside each cluster. These are all the process $\langle i, c \rangle$ of each cluster c with $(i \neq 0)$ as explained later. From now on, we call it the "application subnet". Its places and transitions are not prefixed. Thus this subnet is nearly identical to the subnet of the figure 3 which illustrate the fact that the composition is nearly transparent from the application process point of view like described in the section 3.

However, inside each cluster, the coordinator processes which are identified by the color $\langle 0, c \rangle$ behave differently. In order to ease the interpretation of the global net, we unfold the application places of figure 3 for them. The places names will be prefixed by the "*intra*" mention. From now on, we call the subnet the "*intra* subnet". This subnet differs from figure 3 by its transitions. As explained in section 3, the coordinator does not act on its own initiative but just ensures the correctness of the solution (like uniqueness of the mutual exclusion grant token, ...). The three transitions between the three places "*intra.NO_REQ*", "*intra.REQ*" and "*intra.CS*" are not temporized and controlled by our composition mechanism. That is why we need them all immediate transitions.

Finally, we set the "*inter* subnet" as the net composed of the prefixed *inter* places and its adjacent transitions. It defines the coordinator behavior with respect to the *inter* algorithm. There are only one coordinator by cluster on the whole grid so they only are identified by the color c in the *inter* subnet. And like the *intra* subnet, and for same reasons the three transitions between the three places "*inter.NO_REQ*", "*inter.REQ*" and "*inter.CS*" are immediate transitions.

Each coordinator has an *intra* behavior, based on the marking sequences of token $\langle 0, c \rangle$ the *intra* subnet and an *inter* behavior, based the marking sequences of token $\langle c \rangle$ the *inter* subnet. This abstraction enlighten the main idea of our solution, exposed via the automaton of figure 2(b): each state of the coordinator is a combination of an *inter* and *intra* local states.

To synchronize this dual behavior, we first split the *inter* and *intra* subnets into two main parts. The first concerns the *inter.requestCS()* and *intra.requestCS()* immediate transitions which trigger the sending of a request in its counter-part level. The second concerns the two immediate transitions called *inter. releaseCS() / intra.accessCS()* and *intra.releaseCS() / inter.accessCS()* which enforce the coordinated release of the CS and the grant allowance of each level. **These two transitions have been split to ease the reading of the model but they are filled with the same patterns to clearly identify them.**

A coordinator request sending can be viewed as a *forward* from one level to the other. So the transition firing is enforced by the reception of an *inter* or *intra* request. We need to materialize this information inside the *inter* and *intra* algorithms for the coordinators to exploit them. Thus, in the figure 1 pseudo-code, we need to add a *pendingRequest()* function [line 27] to the standard A.P.I.. To ab- stract this reification we have added a new state called *pendingReq* at the *inter* and *intra* clouded P.N. border-side. The marking of the place *inter.pendingReq* (resp. *intra.pendingReq*) represents the registration of a request coming from the *inter* (resp. *intra*) layer.

The *inter* (resp. *intra*) critical section coordinated release is enforced by the real access (and thus the grant authorization) to the *intra* (resp. *inter*) section. Abstracting this behavior must be done by a cross-synchronization between the *accessCS()* action of one layer with the *releaseCS()* on the other - like on the figure 2(b). On figure 4, the *inter.accessCS()* / *intra.releaseCS()* [lines 9 and 11] and *intra.releaseCS()* / *inter.accessCS()* are the same immediate transition (▨▨▨▨) and represents this desired synchronization. So does the split transition *intra.accessCS()* / *inter.releaseCS()* (▨▨▨▨) [lines 16 and 18].

To finalize our model, we specify the initial global marking of the system. To achieve this, we define the following sets:

C : the finite set of all clusters

$C_{c'} = \{c \in C | c \neq c'\}$: the finite set of all clusters minus the cluster element c'.

A_c : the finite set of all processes of a single cluster c.

$A_c^* = \{i \in A_c | i \neq 0\}$: the finite set of all **application** processes of a single cluster c. The application processes are the set of all processes i of the cluster c minus the coordinator process (with index $i = 0$).

Under the hypothesis where $M(p)$ represents the marking of the place p, the initialisation is performed by the following markings:

- all the application nodes are not requesting the CS, thus are in the NO_REQ state.

$$M(NO\_REQ) = \sum_{c \in C} \sum_{i \in A_c^*} \langle i, c \rangle$$

- the coordinator c' is in the CS state) w.r.t. the *inter* algorithm but in the NO_REQ state w.r.t. the intra algorithm.

$$M(intra.NO\_REQ) = \langle 0, c' \rangle \quad \text{and} \quad M(inter.CS) = M(inter.grant) = \langle c' \rangle$$

- all other coordinators are in CS state w.r.t. the *intra* algorithm and are in the NO_REQ state w.r.t. the *inter* algorithm.

$$M(inter.NO\_REQ) = \sum_{c \in C_{c'}} \langle c \rangle \quad \text{and} \quad M(intra.CS) = M(intra.grant) = \sum_{c \in C_{c'}} \langle 0, c' \rangle$$

5   Fundamental Properties

The mutual exclusion paradigm was first introduced and informally defined by Dijkstra in 1965 [5]. This article has defined the bases of the mutual exclusion problem and was successively refined into more formal definitions [11]. Defining mutual exclusion is to define a set of properties that must be asserted by all algorithms of this paradigm. These properties are:

Well-formedness: all the processes must respect the classical automaton of mutual exclusion, as described in figure 2(a).

Mutual Exclusion: at any time, there is at most one process in the CS state (figure 2(a))

Progress: if there is at least one process in the REQ state and there is no process in the CS state, then eventually one process will enter in the REQ state.

Following the Lamport [10] taxonomy, the first two properties can be classified in the safety class properties. The last one can be put in the liveness class properties. However, the *Progress* liveness property does not guarantee for a process to access the CS. Rather, it is a global notion of liveness. So to avoid any starvation for a particular process, a mutual exclusion algorithm must verify a complementary property:

Weak fairness: if one process is in the REQ state and if the mutual exclusion section execution time is finite, then the process will eventually access to the CS state.

This weak fairness property implies the progress property because the individual liveness implies the system wide liveness. But as many applications can not afford to rely on the progress alone, many articles do not even consider progress and instead use the weak fairness property. In the remaining of this paper, we consider these two properties distinctively and we explicit which one is used.

5.1   Formal Expression of Properties

The aforementioned properties can all be expressed using the Linear Temporal Logic (LTL). We begin by defining some atomic propositions that will help us to translate mutual exclusion properties into LTL.

- P_1 : the process i of the cluster c does not require the CS nor is in CS $(M(NO\_REQ) \geqslant \langle i, c \rangle)$.
- P_2 : the process i of cluster c requests an access to the CS $(M(REQ) \geqslant \langle i, c \rangle)$.
- P_3 : the process i of the cluster c is in CS $(M(CS) \geqslant \langle i, c \rangle)$.
- P_4 : the process i of the cluster c is NOT in CS $(M(CS) < \langle i, c \rangle)$.
- P_5 : the number of application processes in CS is less or equal than 1 $(\#(CS) \leqslant 1)$.
- P_6 : there is no application process in CS (no one is in place CS). $(\#(CS) = 0)$.
- P_7 : there is a exactly one application process in CS $(\#(CS) = 1)$.
- P_8 : there is at least one application process which request an access to the CS $(\#(REQ) \geqslant 1)$.

Then the properties can be written down as follows:

Well-formedness: if a process marks the place NO_REQ (resp. REQ, CS), it will not be able to mark the place CS (resp. NO_REQ, REQ) without having previously marked the place REQ (resp. CS, NO_REQ).

$F_1 : G(P_1 \Rightarrow F(!P_3 \ U \ P_2)) \wedge G(P_2 \Rightarrow F(!P_1 \ U \ P_3)) \wedge G(P_3 \Rightarrow F(!P_2 \ U \ P_1))$

Mutual Exclusion: there is always at most one application process in the CS state.

$$F_2 : G(P_5)$$

Progression: always, if there is at least one application process requesting the CS (*i.e.*, a token $\langle i, c \rangle$ marks the place REQ) and if there is no process in CS, then an application process will be able to access the CS (*i.e.*, it will mark the place CS).

$$F_3 : G((P_8 \wedge P_6) \Rightarrow F(P_7))$$

Weak fairness: one application node will always be able to access the CS after having requesting it.

$$F_4 : G(P_2 \Rightarrow F(P_3))$$

6   Simplified Models for Mutual Exclusion Algorithms

To check the previously defined properties on our composed mutual exclusion algorithm we need to instantiate the *inter* and *intra* clouded nets. Two methods would have been possible. The first one consists in replacing each clouded net by a *H.L.P.N.* reflecting the exact behavior of some well known mutual exclusion algorithms like [22], [16] or [14]. However, this level of details is only useful for quantitative studies and to evaluate the effect of each algorithm on our composition for, for instance, the "mean delay transmission time" or "the mean number of exchanged requests", etc. The second method consists in simply modelling the properties they assert. The aim is then to check if our composition approach upholds the properties of the algorithms it uses.

In this paper, we have chosen the second approach which enables us a preliminary qualitative study of our solution. It is a necessary step prior any real quantitative study. Thus, we propose two H.L.P.N. models which verify the properties described in section 5. The figure 5(a) H.L.P.N. abstracts the *validity, mutual exclusion* and *progress* properties whereas figure 5(b) H.L.P.N. abstracts the *validity, mutual exclusion, progress* and *weak fairness*.

Consider figure 5(a), we observe the presence of the places *grantRequest, pendingReq* and *grant* at the border-side of figure 4. We also have a place *algo* which materializes the request treatment. The transition *latency* stands for the request reception event. Trivially, everyone can check we do not consider the request transmission method: it can be a simple message emission like in Suzuki-Kasami [22] or a sequence of them like in Martin algorithm [14]. As the network travelling time and the registering treatment time are undetermined, the transition is temporized (white filled ⊏⊐). The CS access is modeled by the *getGrant* transition. The exclusive access is ensured by the inhibitor arc on the place *grant*. The *progress* property on the registered requests (place *algo*) is provided by the immediate transition *getGrant* (black filled ▬).

To continue the description of the figure 5(a), lets notice that places *algo* and *pendingRequest* do not have the same color domains. This is due to the fact that our composition algorithm only need to know if there is any request that

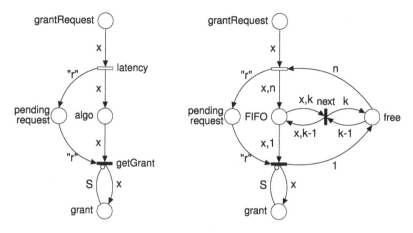

(a) Abstraction not asserting
Weak Fairness

(b) Abstraction asserting Weak Fairness

Fig. 5. Mutual Exclusion algorithm abstraction nets

must be treated but do not need to know which is the requesting process. So, when the transition *latency* is fired by a token $\langle x \rangle$, the *pendingReq* place is, at the same time, marked by a constant "r" (to notice the reception of the request by the algorithm). So, the requesting process identity remains unknown to the coordinator. To conclude, this H.L.P.N. does not guarantee *weak fairness*: some tokens in place *algo* can potentially never pass through the transition *getGrant*. They can be perpetually overtaken by new incoming requests.

Now, the figure 5(b) enhances the previous H.L.P.N. by substituting to the place *algo* a model of a fair request queue (in fact, it is a simple FIFO queue of size n). The queue is modelled by two places. The first one is the place $FIFO$ marked with colored token $\langle x, k \rangle$. When a request of process x, comes in, it is associated to a position k starting with the last position (index n). The second one is the place $free$ which is initially marked by all available positions - *i.e.*, all the k colors. When a request marks the place $FIFO$, its position will progress by firing the immediate transition *next*. But a request x with position k can only fire the transition $free$ if the $k - 1$ position is available (*i.e.*, only if its predecessor was able to progress). Thus all request are treated in their arrival order and the *weak fairness* property is asserted for all the registered requests - *i.e.*, all requests that have fired the transition *latency*. However, asserting this property for all sent requests (*i.e.*, for every token marking the *grantRequest*) is another problem. It requires the modelling of an additional hypothesis. Actually, all mutual exclusion algorithms make this following minimum hypothesis about their communication channels: we never lost the same message twice. So to say, a message sent an infinity number of times will be received an infinity number of times. This property is called the *"fair lossy channel"* property. The integration of this hypothesis can be done in two ways: the first one is to make the transition *latency* firing "fair". This materializes the fact that each request will be registered by the mutual exclusion algorithm. For each -infinite- execution of our model, if the transition *latency* is firable then it will eventually be fired. The second way is to take this constraint directly in the properties. We modify the properties in order to exclude all the scenarios where at least one specific x marking the place *grantRequest* do not fire the *latency* transition on the whole execution.

The second solution has been chosen because H.L.P.N in their classical definition do not enable us to set a transition as "fair'". Thus, we have rewritten the property F_4 and we use the following atomic propositions to do it:

- P_9 : an *intra* request of the process i' of the cluster c' has not been treated - *i.e.*, it was sent but not registered by the used mutual exclusion algorithm $(M(intra.grantRequest) \geqslant \langle i', c' \rangle)$.
- P_{10} : an *inter* request of the cluster c'' coordinator has not been treated - *i.e.*, it was sent but not registered by the used mutual exclusion algorithm $(M(inter.grantRequest) \geqslant \langle c'' \rangle)$.

Hence, the *weak fairness* property must be modified as follows:

weak fairness: always, if a process i of the cluster c request for the CS then, either in the future, it will have the CS, or at least one message for the process i' of the cluster c' will be treated, or at least one message of the coordinator of the cluster c'' will be treated.

$$F_4 = G(P_2 \Rightarrow (F(P_3) \vee FG(P_9) \vee FG(P_{10})))$$

7   Model Checking

The classical method to verify a model (*i.e.*, *model-checking* [23]) against LTL properties relies on automata theory. Within this approach, all possible executions of the studied application are produced and synchronized with the automaton representing the executions *invalidating* the desired property. If the resulting automaton is "not empty" then the property is not satisfied by the model. Here "not empty" means that the language recognized by the automaton is not reduced to the empty word.

The main problem of this approach is the excessive size of the generated automata. Actually, This size can be exponentially greater than the syntactic description of the model and the property (the well-known state space explosion problem). The explosion is essentially due to the concurrency of the system actions and thus the synchronisation of its elements. Many approaches were developed to overcome this problem. Their aims either are to drastically reduce the representation of the generated automata or to substitute context-equivalent smaller automata. One of these last such solutions is based on the observation that concurrent systems are composed of identical behaviors (up to a permutation). The factorisation of the representation of such similar behaviors leads to the construction of smaller automata which can be efficiently used for model checking [1].

Our composition approach is highly symmetric. In fact, we have identified and used symmetries at all levels: the application process of the same cluster behave the same and so do the coordinators process. Hence, we have kept and used them in all our modeling process. Moreover, by use of the rigorous syntax of SWN these symmetries are efficiently represented and exploited for an *automatic* construction of a reduced automaton representing the system executions [4,1]. These ends up by the verification of our properties.

The tool we used to generate the reduced automaton of our model is the well know and widely used GreatSPN[2]. It was connected to the Spot[3] model-checker tool. The verification is done in two steps. Firstly, we verified the mutual exclusion algorithm models (figure 5) by plugging them into the (abstract) model of the application process (figure 3). Secondly we have plugged the model of mutual exclusion algorithm (figure 5) in the abstract model of figure 4. Trivially, the first part was checked and the properties F_1 to F_3 were verified on the model of figure 5(a) and the properties F_1 to F_4 were verified on the model of figure 5(b).

For the second part, and the most important, the results show that all properties are preserved: when the used algorithm verify *validity, mutual exclusion* and *progress* for the *intra* and *inter* levels our solution validate the same properties. When the used *intra* and *inter* algorithms verify the *validity, mutual exclusion, progress* and *weak fairness* properties (F_1 to F_4) our algorithm does the same way whichever the topology we choose.

To give an idea on the complexity of the model-checking accordingly to a chosen deployment topology, we highlight in table 1 some of the obtained results. Here we represent the number of visited states for the verification of each of the described properties, when using the model of 5(b) to instantiate the composition approach model.

Table 1. Model-checking over different topologies

Topo. Propr.	6 process			8 process		
	6 a.	2 c. 3 a.	3 c. 2 a.	8 a.	2 c. 4 a.	4 c. 2 a.
F_1	1438	70823	145455	2888	619362	1793654
F_2	218	9988	20205	391	74817	212666
F_3	318	14548	30662	569	108295	320577
F_4	785	36844	76018	1716	345375	708019

Six topologies noted "$xc./ya.$" are reported into it. In our notation, x is the number of clusters (that is why it is postfixed by c) and y is the number of application processes by cluster (that is why it is postfixed by a). So, we have checked six topologies: three with 6 application processes gathered into 1, 2 and 3 clusters and three with 8 application processes gathered into 1, 2 and 4 clusters. The topology noted "$ya.$" is the plain algorithm used as complexity reference which

[2] http://www.di.unito.it/ greatspn/
[3] http://spot.lip6.fr/

is low comparing to our composition. Increasing the number of clusters generate more states because of the synchronizations implied by our composition.

8   Conclusion

This paper exposes a new algorithm to easily compose existing mutual exclusion algorithms in order to achieve better scalability on grids. This solution enable us to optimize the grant authorization time without a lost of the basic mutual exclusion properties. It is also totally transparent for applications.

To check the consistency of our solution, we have isolated mutual exclusion algorithm common A.P.I. We have modelled this generic A.P.I. into H.L.P.N. We take good advantages of this defined interface to compositionally put together our modelling. Based on these A.P.I., we were able to plug in mutual exclusion algorithm abstractions that assert the classical mutual exclusion paradigm properties. This simplification, sufficient for this first qualitative study, make possible to model-check our composition algorithm against the same properties. Concerning these properties, we have done their LTL conversion and integrated an underlying crucial hypothesis called *"fair lossy channel"* required by almost all mutual exclusion algorithms.

During the whole modelling process and verification, we always kept in mind the inner symmetries of our solution. After exhibiting them in our algorithm, we has exploited them to best model our solution and maximize the simplification the LTL properties. At last, the conservation of these symmetries was exploited in the model-checking by using specific algorithms.

This study has numerous research perspectives. The fine P.N. modelling of existing -classical- mutual exclusion algorithms like Suzuki and Kasami [22], Naimi-Tréhel [16] or Martin[14] could lead to numerical quantitative study of the influence of our solution with respect to the application processes. We will be able to calculate performance indices accordingly to the composed plain algorithms.

References

1. Baarir, S., Haddad, S., Ilié, J.-M.: Exploiting Partial Symmetries in Well-formed nets for the Reachability and the Linear Time Model Checking Problems. In: Proceeding of IFAC Workshop on Discrete Event Systems, part of 7th CAAP, Reims - France. Springer, Heidelberg (2004)
2. Bertier, M., Arantes, L., Sens, P.: Distributed mutual exclusion algorithms for grid applications: A hierarchical approach. Journal of Parallel and Distributed Computing 66, 128–144 (2006)
3. Chang, I., Singhal, M., Liu, M.: A hybrid approach to mutual exclusion for distributed system. In: IEEE International Computer Software and Applications Conference, pp. 289–294 (1990)
4. Chiola, G., Dutheillet, C., Franceschinis, G., Haddad, S.: Stochastic well-formed coloured nets for symmetric modelling applications. IEEE Transactions on Computers 42(11), 1343–1360 (1993)
5. Dijkstra, E.W.: Solution of a problem in concurrent programming control. Comm. ACM 8(9), 569 (1965)

6. Erciyes, K.: Distributed mutual exclusion algorithms on a ring of clusters. In: Laganá, A., Gavrilova, M.L., Kumar, V., Mun, Y., Tan, C.J.K., Gervasi, O. (eds.) ICCSA 2004. LNCS, vol. 3045, pp. 518–527. Springer, Heidelberg (2004)
7. Fu, S., Tzeng, N., Li, Z.: Empirical evaluation of distributed mutual exclusion algorithms. pp. 255–259
8. Housni, A., Trhel, M.: Distributed mutual exclusion by groups based on token and permission. In: International Conference on Computational Science and Its Applications, June 2001, pp. 26–29 (2001)
9. Jensen, K.: High-level petri nets. In: Pagnoni, A., Rozenberg, G. (eds.) Proceedings of the 3rd European Workshop on Application and Theory of Petri Nets, Varenna, Italy. Informatik - Fachberichte, vol. 66, pp. 166–180. Springer, Heidelberg (1983)
10. Lamport, L.: Proving the correctness of multiprocess programs. IEEE Trans. Software Eng. 3(2), 125–143 (1977)
11. Lynch, N.A.: Distributed Algorithms. Morgan Kaufmann, San Francisco (1996)
12. Madhuram, K.: A hybrid approach for mutual exclusion in distributed computing systems. In: IEEE Symposium on Parallel and Distributed Processing (1994)
13. Maekawa, M.: A $\sqrt{N}$ algorithm for mutual exclusion in decentralized systems. ACM-Transactions on Computer Systems 3(2), 145–159 (1985)
14. Martin, A.J.: Distributed mutual exclusion on a ring of processes. Sci. Comput. Program. 5(3), 265–276 (1985)
15. Mueller, F.: Prioritized token-based mutual exclusion for distributed systems. In: International Parallel Processing Symposium, March 1998, pp. 791–795 (1998)
16. Naimi, M., Trehel, M.: An improvement of the log(n) distributed algorithm for mutual exclusion. In: IEEE Intern. Conf. on Distributed Computing Systems, pp. 371–377 (1987)
17. Omara, F., Nabil, M.: A new hybrid algorithm for the mutual exclusion problem in the distributed systems. International Journal of Intelligent Computing and Information Sciences 2(2), 94–105 (2002)
18. Raymond, K.: A tree-based algorithm for distributed mutual exclusion. ACM Transactions on Computer Systems 7(1), 61–77 (1989)
19. Ricart, G., Agrawala, A.: An optimal algorithm for mutual exclusion in computer networks. Communications of the ACM 24 (1981)
20. Singhal, M.: A dynamic information structure for mutual exclusion algorithm for distributed systems. IEEE Trans. on Parallel and Distributed Systems 3(1), 121–125 (1992)
21. Sopena, J., Legond-Aubry, F., Arantes, L., Sens, P.: A composition approach to mutual exclusion algorithms for grid applications. In: Proc. of the International Conference on Parallel Processing, p. 65 (2007)
22. Suzuki, I., Kasami, T.: A distributed mutual exclusion algorithm. ACM Transactions on Computer Systems 3(4), 344–349 (1985)
23. Vardi, M.Y.: An automata-theoretic approach to linear temporal logic. In: Moller, F., Birtwistle, G. (eds.) Logics for Concurrency. LNCS, vol. 1043, pp. 238–266. Springer, Heidelberg (1996)

Distributed Semantics and Implementation for Systems with Interaction and Priority

Ananda Basu, Philippe Bidinger, Marius Bozga, and Joseph Sifakis

Université Grenoble 1 - CNRS - VERIMAG
Centre Équation, 2 av de Vignate, 38610 Gières, France

Abstract. The paper studies a distributed implementation method for the BIP (Behavior, Interaction, Priority) component framework for modeling heterogeneous systems.

BIP offers two powerful mechanisms for describing composition of components by combining interactions and priorities. A system model is layered. The lowest layer contains atomic components; the second layer, describes possible interactions between atomic components; the third layer includes priorities between the interactions. The current implementation of BIP is based on global state operational semantics. An Engine directly interprets the operational semantics rules and computes the possible interactions between atomic components from global states.

The implementation method is a translation from BIP models into distributed models involving two steps. The first translates BIP models into partial state models where are known only the states of the components which are ready to communicate. The second implements interactions in the partial state model by using message passing primitives.

The main results of the paper are conditions for which the three models are observationally equivalent. We show that in general, the translation from global state to partial state models does not preserve observational equivalence. Preservation can be achieved by strengthening the premises of the operational semantics rules by an oracle. This is a predicate depending on the priorities of the BIP model. We show that there are many possible choices for oracles. Maximal parallelism is achieved for dynamic oracles allowing interaction as soon as possible. Nonetheless, these oracles may entail considerable computational overhead. We study performance trade-offs for different types of oracles. Finally, we provide experimental results illustrating the application of the theory on a prototype implementation.

1 Introduction

A distributed system is a collection of loosely coupled independent components, communicating by explicit message passing. The components are intrinsically concurrent and their states may be known only through communication. We cannot determine the exact global state of a distributed system, we can only approximate it [4].

K. Suzuki et al. (Eds.): FORTE 2008, LNCS 5048, pp. 116–133, 2008.

The paper studies a distributed implementation method for the BIP (Behavior, Interaction, Priority) component framework for modeling heterogeneous systems [2]. The method consists of three steps:

• It starts from a *global state* model of the system to be implemented described in BIP. The model represents the system behavior as a transition system where transitions are atomic. The BIP execution platform uses an Engine which coordinates the execution of the components. Atomicity of transitions implies a strict alternation between the execution of components and the Engine: no interaction is possible when some component is performing a computation.

• From the global state model, a *partial state* model is derived where we distinguish between states from which components are *ready* for interaction and states where components are *busy* by executing some internal computation. For this model partial state knowledge may suffice for executing interactions. We study conditions for the partial state model to be equivalent to the global state model. The conditions are in the form of an *oracle* used by the BIP Engine to safely execute interactions in the presence of uncertainty about the global state.

• From the partial state model, a *distributed model* is obtained where atomic multiparty interactions of the partial state models are replaced by communication protocols. In this model, components exchange messages to communicate with the Engine represented by an additional component.

The main results of the paper are conditions for which the three models are observationally equivalent by considering as silent the actions corresponding to internal computations of the initial global state model. They are described in more details below.

BIP combines two powerful mechanisms for describing multiparty interactions between components: *interactions* and *priorities*. A system model is layered. The lowest layer contains atomic components whose behavior is described by state machines with data and functions described in C. As in process algebras, atomic components can communicate by using ports. The second layer contains interactions which are relations between communication ports of individual components. Priorities are used to express scheduling policies by selecting amongst the enabled interactions of the layer underneath.

The current implementation of BIP is based on global state semantics. From a BIP model, a compiler is used to generate C++ code for a dedicated platform. The platform uses an Engine that directly interprets the operational semantics rules. For a given global state, the Engine computes from the set of the communication ports offered by individual components and the set of interactions, the set of the enabled interactions. Amongst these, the Engine chooses a maximal one, according to the priorities of the third layer, and notifies the involved components which can continue their computation.

We define partial state semantics for BIP where the assumption of atomic execution of transitions does not hold. This is a straightforward generalization of global state semantics where interactions are separated from internal computation in the components. A component may be either in a busy state or in a ready state. A busy state corresponds to the execution of some internal computation. When the computation terminates, some ready state is reached. From this state the component can participate in interactions and move again to some busy state.

The implementation problem for a partial state model is to find an Engine that may execute interactions even for partially known states, while preserving (observational) equivalence with the corresponding global state model. The following example shows that in general, the two models are not equivalent.

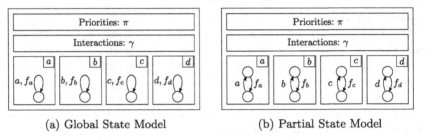

(a) Global State Model   (b) Partial State Model

Fig. 1. A System with Four Components

Example 1. Consider a BIP model consisting of four components A, B, C, D each one offering cyclically an interaction through ports a, b, c, d followed respectively by the execution of functions f_a, f_b, f_c, f_d (Figure 1(a)). We assume that A is a sender and B, C, D are receivers. A can broadcast a message through a and the set of the possible interactions is $\gamma = \{a, ab, ac, ad, abc, abd, acd, abcd\}$. Priority rules are used to ensure that amongst all the possible interactions from a state only a maximal one is possible. This is expressed by using a priority order on interactions π and rules of the form $x\pi xy$ where x and xy are interactions. These rules say that whenever both interactions x and xy are enabled, only interaction xy can be executed. That is, maximal progress is enforced. For this example, the only possible interaction is $abcd$ and thus the functions f_a, f_b, f_c, f_d are executed synchronously.

The partial state model for this system is shown in Figure 1(b). It is possible, due to the separation between interaction and internal computation, to reach a configuration where the receivers are in a busy state. In that case, only the ready components will be synchronized. Thus an arbitrary desynchronization of the receivers with respect to the sender is possible.

Example 2. Consider again the previous example where broadcast is replaced by three rendezvous: $\gamma = \{ab, bc, cd\}$ and π is such that $ab\pi bc$, $cd\pi bc$ in the global state system. This system executes forever the interaction bc. Consider the corresponding partial state system where interactions are separated from functions. For this system, it is possible to execute the sequence $ab.(f_a.cd.f_c.f_b.ab.f_d)^\omega$ which goes through states never enabling the interaction bc.

The above examples motivate the definition of partial state semantics where the premises of the operational semantics rules include an oracle, a predicate parameterized by a dependency relation between interactions. The dependency relation is an abstraction of the priorities of the initial BIP model. The oracle characterizes the partial states from which an interaction can be safely executed: if an interaction a_1 depends on an interaction a_2, then a_1 cannot be executed if the system has some internal evolution leading to a state enabling a_2. We show that there are many possible choices for oracles. If the time for computing them is negligible, best performance is achieved for oracles allowing interaction as soon as possible in order to reduce waiting times of ready components. The worst performing oracle is the one allowing interaction only when all the components are at ready states. For this oracle partial and global state semantics coincide.

We study a transformation from the partial state model to a distributed one. This consists in replacing atomic interactions by protocols using message passing. For distributed semantics, the Engine becomes an additional component. The results are applied to obtain a multi-threaded implementation for BIP. We analyze performance of this implementation for different types of oracles as well as with respect to the global state semantics model.

The presented method is not specific to BIP and can be applied for the implementation of systems in particular in two cases. First, for concurrent systems with fairness constraints which at implementation level, become scheduling policies expressed by dynamic priorities. Second, for systems involving communication by broadcast. This requires mechanisms for identifying the maximal set of interacting components that can be specified by using priorities. Consequently, the proposed method can be used for correct implementation.

The paper is organized as follows. In section 2, we present global state semantics and the associated partial state semantics for BIP. In section 3, we study oracles and their properties. We show correctness of partial state semantics enforced by an oracle with respect to global state semantics. In section 4, we study the transformation from partial state to distributed semantics. We also discuss experimental results for a multi-threaded implementation, in particular for different choices of oracles. The last section includes conclusions and description of future work. Proofs are omitted due to space limitation but appear in [1].

2   BIP – Basic Semantic Models

2.1   Global State Semantics

BIP is a component framework for constructing systems by superposing three layers of modeling: Behavior, Interaction, and Priority.

Atomic Components. We define *atomic components* as transition systems with a set of ports labeling individual transitions. These ports are used for communication between different components.

Definition 1 (Atomic Component). *An atomic component B is a labeled transition system represented by a triple $(Q, P, \rightarrow)$ where Q is a set of states, P is a set of communication ports, $\rightarrow \subseteq Q \times P \times Q$ is a set of possible transitions, each labeled by some port.*

For any pair of states $q, q' \in Q$ *and a port* $p \in P$, *we write* $q \xrightarrow{p} q'$, *iff* $(q, p, q') \in \rightarrow$. *When the communication port is irrelevant, we simply write* $q \rightarrow q'$. *Similarly,* $q \xrightarrow{p}$ *means that there exists* $q' \in Q$ *such that* $q \xrightarrow{p} q'$.

Interaction For a given system built from a set of n atomic components $\{B_i = (Q_i, P_i, \rightarrow_i)\}_{i=1}^n$, we assume that their respective sets of ports are pairwise disjoint, *i.e.* for any two $i \neq j$ from $\{1..n\}$ we have $P_i \cap P_j = \emptyset$. We can therefore define the set $P = \bigcup_{i=1}^n P_i$ of all ports in the system. An *interaction* is a set $a \subseteq P$ of ports. When we write $a = \{p_i\}_{i \in I}$, we suppose that for $i \in I$, $p_i \in P_i$.

Definition 2 (Composite Component). *A composite component (or simply component) is defined by a composition operator parameterized by a set of interactions* $\gamma \subseteq 2^P$. $B \stackrel{def}{=} \gamma(B_1, \ldots, B_n)$, *is a transition system* $(Q, \gamma, \rightarrow)$, *where* $Q = \bigotimes_{i=1}^n Q_i$ *and* $\rightarrow$ *is the least set of transitions satisfying the rule*

$$\frac{a = \{p_i\}_{i \in I} \in \gamma \quad \forall i \in I. \ q_i \xrightarrow{p_i}_i q'_i \quad \forall i \notin I. \ q_i = q'_i}{(q_1, \ldots, q_n) \xrightarrow{a} (q'_1, \ldots, q'_n)}$$

The inference rule says that a composite component $B = \gamma(B_1, \ldots, B_n)$ can execute an interaction $a \in \gamma$, iff for each port $p_i \in a$, the corresponding atomic component B_i can execute the transition labeled with p_i; the states of components that do not participate in the interaction stay unchanged.

Observe that, it is possible for a composite component to further communicate on the ports initially provided by its atomic components

Priorities In composite components, many interactions can be enabled at the same time, introducing a degree of non-determinism in the product behavior. Non-determinism can be restricted by means of priorities, specifying which of the interactions should be preferred among the enabled ones.

Definition 3 (Priority Model). *A priority on* $B = \gamma(B_1, \ldots, B_n)$ *is a relation* $\pi \subseteq \gamma \times Q \times \gamma$. *We write* $a_1 \pi_q a_2$ *for* $(a_1, q, a_2) \in \pi$. *Furthermore, we require that for all* $q \in Q$, π_q *is a strict partial order on* γ. $a_1 \pi_q a_2$ *means that interaction* a_1 *has less priority than* a_2 *at state* q.

Given a behavior $B = (Q, P, \rightarrow)$ defined as above, we construct a new behavior $\pi B = (Q, P, \rightarrow_\pi)$ as follows:

$$\frac{q \xrightarrow{a} q' \quad \forall a' \in \gamma. \ a\pi_q a' \implies q \not\xrightarrow{a'}}{q \xrightarrow{a}_\pi q'}$$

Example 3. The examples 1 and 2 are straightforward to define in BIP. The system Figure 1(a) is defined as $\pi\gamma(A, B, C, D)$ where A, B, C and D are atomic components with one state and one transition defined as $X = (\{q_X\}, \{x\}, (q_X, x, q_X))$ for $(X, x) \in \{(A, a), (B, b), (C, c), (D, d)\}$.

We have $\gamma = \{a, ab, ac, ad, abc, abd, abcd\}$. The system $\gamma(A, B, C, D)$ has only one state $q = (q_A, q_B, q_C, q_D)$ for which $\pi_q = \{(x, xy) \mid (x, xy) \in \gamma^2\}$. Example 2 is defined similarly for $\gamma = \{ab, bc, cd\}$ and $\pi_q = \{(ab, bc), (cd, bc)\}$.

Implementation The operational semantics rules are interpreted by the BIP *Engine*. At a given global state, each atomic component publishes the ports of the enabled transitions. From this information, the Engine computes the set of the possible interactions, that is the interactions of γ such that each one of their ports is published by some component. Amongst these interactions, the Engine chooses non-deterministically one that satisfies the priority rules π and notifies the involved components by communicating the corresponding port names.

2.2   Partial State Semantics

The model with global state semantics is based on the fact that transitions are atomic and a global state is always defined. To obtain the partial state model corresponding to a global state model, we 1) replace atomic components by their partial state models; 2) extend the operational semantics rules for interactions and priorities.

Atomic Components To model concurrent behavior, we associate with each atomic component, its corresponding *partial state model*. Atomic components with partial states behave as atomic components with the difference that each transition is decomposed into a sequence of two transitions: an interaction (visible transition) followed by an internal computation or *busy transition*. Between these two transitions, a new *busy* state is added. Busy states are transient states considered by the Engine as undefined states of the component.

Definition 4 (Atomic Component with Partial States). *Given an atomic component* $B = (Q, P, \rightarrow)$, *we define the associated partial state model as the transition system* $B^{\perp} = (Q \cup Q^{\perp}, P \cup \{\beta\}, \leadsto)$ *where*

- $Q^{\perp} = \{q_t \mid t \in \rightarrow\}$ *such that* $Q^{\perp} \cap Q = \emptyset$. $Q^{\perp}$ *is a set of busy states in bijection with the set of transitions* $\rightarrow$.
- β *is a port name not in* P
- $\leadsto \subseteq (Q \cup Q^{\perp}) \times P \cup \{\beta\} \times (Q \cup Q^{\perp})$ *where if* $t = (q_1, p, q_2) \in \rightarrow$, *then* $q_1 \overset{p}{\leadsto} q_t$ *and* $q_t \overset{\beta}{\leadsto} q_2$.

Interaction We define below interactions for partial state models.

Definition 5. *Given a BIP model built from a set of atomic components* $\{B_i = (Q_i, P_i, \rightarrow_i)\}_{i=1}^{n}$, *of the form* $\gamma(B_1, \ldots, B_n)$, *we define the corresponding partial state model* $\gamma^{\perp}(B_1^{\perp}, \ldots, B_n^{\perp})$ *such that*

- $B_i^{\perp}$ *is the partial state model* $B_i^{\perp} = (Q_i \cup Q_i^{\perp}, P_i \cup \{\beta_i\}, \leadsto_i)$
- $\gamma^{\perp} = \gamma \cup \{\beta_i\}_{i=1}^{n}$

Notice that $\gamma^{\perp}(B_1^{\perp}, \ldots, B_n^{\perp}) = (\bigotimes_{i=1}^{n}(Q_i \cup Q_i^{\perp}), \gamma^{\perp}, \leadsto)$. The transition relation $\leadsto$ can be equivalently defined by the rules:

$$\frac{a = \{p_i\}_{i \in I} \in \gamma \qquad \forall i \in I.\ q_i \overset{p_i}{\leadsto}_i q_i' \qquad \forall i \notin I.\ q_i = q_i'}{(q_1, \ldots, q_n) \overset{a}{\leadsto} (q_1', \ldots, q_n')}$$

$$\frac{q_i \overset{\beta_i}{\leadsto} q_i'}{(q_1, \ldots, q_i, \ldots, q_n) \overset{\beta_i}{\leadsto} (q_1, \ldots, q_i', \ldots, q_n)}$$

The first rule is the same as the composition rule for the global state semantics. The second rule defines the busy transitions of the composite system.

The state space can be split into two disjoint sets $\bigotimes_{i=1}^{n}(Q_i \cup Q_i^{\perp}) = Q^g \cup Q^p$. The set of *global states* $Q^g = \bigotimes_{i=1}^{n} Q_i$ which is the set of states of $\gamma(B_1, \dots, B_n)$. The set of *partial states* Q^p where at least one component is busy.

Definition 6. *For $q, q' \in Q^p \cup Q^g$, we write $q \overset{\beta}{\leadsto} q'$ if $q \overset{\beta_i}{\leadsto} q'$ for some i.*

Property 1. The relation $\overset{\beta}{\leadsto}$ is terminating and confluent. Thus, from any partial state, a unique global state is eventually reached by executing β-transitions.

Priority The above property is used to define priorities for partial state models. The priority relation at some partial state should agree with the priority relation at the global state reached by executing β-transitions.

Definition 7. *Given a BIP model $\pi\gamma(B_1, \dots, B_n)$, the corresponding partial state model is $\pi^{\perp}\gamma^{\perp}(B_1^{\perp}, \dots, B_n^{\perp})$ where $\pi^{\perp} \subseteq \gamma \times (Q^g \cup Q^p) \times \gamma$ such that $a_1 \pi_q^{\perp} a_2$ if $\exists q' \in Q^g$. $q \overset{\beta^*}{\leadsto} q' \wedge a_1 \pi_{q'} a_2$.*

Note that $\pi^{\perp}$ is a priority and it coincides with π on Q^g.

Example 4. The partial state model for Example 3 has the atomic components $A^{\perp}$, $B^{\perp}$, $C^{\perp}$ and $D^{\perp}$ with two states and two transitions defined by

$$X^{\perp} = (\{q_X, q_X^{\perp}\}, \{x, \beta_X\}, \{(q_X, x, q_X^{\perp}), (q_X^{\perp}, \beta_X, q_X)\})$$

where $(X, x) \in \{(A, a), (B, b), (C, c), (D, d)\}$. For the first system, $\gamma^{\perp} = \{a, ab, ac, ad, abc, abd, abcd\} \cup \{\beta_A, \beta_B, \beta_C, \beta_D\}$ and $\pi^{\perp}$ is such that for all states q in $\gamma^{\perp}(A^{\perp}, B^{\perp}, C^{\perp}, D^{\perp})$, we have $\pi_q^{\perp} = \{(x, xy) \mid (x, xy) \in \gamma^2\}$. For the second system, we have $\gamma^{\perp} = \{ab, bc, cd\} \cup \{\beta_A, \beta_B, \beta_C, \beta_D\}$ and $\pi^{\perp}$ is such that for all states q in $\gamma^{\perp}(A^{\perp}, B^{\perp}, C^{\perp}, D^{\perp})$, we have $\pi_q^{\perp} = \{(ab, bc), (cd, bc)\}$.

2.3   Comparing Global and Partial State Semantics

We study sufficient conditions for partial state models to be behaviorally equivalent to global state models. We use observational equivalence [8] for this comparison by considering that β-transitions are not observable. As noticed in the introduction (Example 1), observational equivalence is not preserved. The systems $\pi\gamma(A, B, C, D)$ and $\pi^{\perp}\gamma^{\perp}(A^{\perp}, B^{\perp}, C^{\perp}, D^{\perp})$ are not observationally equivalent. The global state model can perform only the maximal interaction $abcd$ while in the partial state model, non maximal synchronization is possible. For instance, we have the transitions:

$$(q_A, q_B, q_C, q_D) \overset{abcd}{\leadsto} (q_A^{\perp}, q_B^{\perp}, q_C^{\perp}, q_D^{\perp}) \overset{\beta}{\leadsto} (q_A, q_B^{\perp}, q_C^{\perp}, q_D^{\perp}) \overset{a}{\leadsto} (q_A^{\perp}, q_B^{\perp}, q_C^{\perp}, q_D^{\perp})$$

Thus, in general, a BIP model is not observationally equivalent to its partial state model. Nonetheless, the following theorem shows that if $\pi = \emptyset$, $\gamma(B_1, \dots, B_n)$ and $\gamma^{\perp}(B_1^{\perp}, \dots, B_n^{\perp})$ are observationally equivalent.

We define observational equivalence of two transition systems $A = (Q_A, L \cup \{\beta\}, \rightarrow_A)$ and $B = (Q_B, L \cup \{\beta\}, \rightarrow_B)$. It is based on the usual definition of weak bisimilarity where β-transitions are considered unobservable.

Definition 8 (Weak Simulation). *A weak simulation over A and B is a relation $R \subseteq Q_A \times Q_B$ such that we have $\forall (q, r) \in R,\ a \in L.\ q \xrightarrow{a}_A q' \implies \exists r'.\ (q', r') \in R \wedge r \xrightarrow{\beta^* a \beta^*}_B r'$ and $\forall (q, r) \in R.\ q \xrightarrow{\beta}_A q' \implies \exists r'.\ (q', r') \in R \wedge r \xrightarrow{\beta^*}_B r'*

A weak bisimulation over A and B is a relation R such that R and R^{-1} are simulations. We say that A and B are observationally equivalent and we write $A \sim B$ if for each state of A there is a weakly bisimilar state of B and conversely.

We use this definition to compare partial state and complete state semantics.

Theorem 1. $\gamma(B_1, \ldots, B_n) \sim \gamma^\perp(B_1^\perp, \ldots, B_n^\perp)$

3   Partial State Semantics with Oracles

Let $\gamma(B_1, \ldots, B_n)$ be a system obtained as the composition of atomic components $B_i = (Q_i, P_i, \rightarrow_i)$ by using a set of interactions $\gamma \subseteq 2^P$ where $P = \bigcup_{i=1}^n P_i$. The corresponding partial state system $\gamma^\perp(B_1^\perp, \ldots, B_n^\perp)$ consists of the components $B_i^\perp = (Q_i \cup Q_i^\perp, P_i \cup \{\beta_i\}, \rightsquigarrow_i)$ composed by using interactions in $\gamma^\perp$. As above, we take $\bigotimes_{i=1}^n (Q_i \cup Q_i^\perp) = Q^g \cup Q^p$. We also suppose that π is a priority for $\gamma(B_1, \ldots, B_n)$, and $\pi^\perp$ is its extension to partial states.

3.1   Basic Definitions and Properties

For a system $\gamma^\perp(B_1^\perp, \ldots, B_n^\perp)$, a state $q \in Q^g \cup Q^p$ and an interaction $a \in \gamma$, we say that a is *enabled* at state q and we write $\mathtt{enabled}(q, a)$, if the transition a is possible from state q. That is, $q \xrightarrow{a} q'$ for some state q'. We say that a is *disabled* at state q and we write $\mathtt{disabled}(q, a)$, if there is an atomic component in a *ready state* that prevents synchronization on a. That is, if $a = \{p_i\}_{i \in I}$ there is $i \in I, q_i \in Q_i$ such that $q_i \xrightarrow{p_i}$.

For global states, $\mathtt{disabled}(q, a)$ is equivalent to $q \xrightarrow{a}$ and in particular we always have either $\mathtt{disabled}(q, a)$ or $\mathtt{enabled}(q, a)$. However, for partial states the status (disabled or enabled) of an interaction a at a given state may be unknown if some components involved in a are in busy states.

To compare partialness of states, we define a partial order relation over the states of composite components.

Definition 9 (State Ordering). *For $q, r \in Q^g \cup Q^p$, $q \leq r \iff \forall i \in \{1..n\}.\ (r_i = q_i \vee q_i \in Q_i^\perp)$.*

For a given relation $\pi^\perp$, an oracle is a predicate $\mathcal{O}$ on $(Q^p \cup Q^g) \times \gamma$ used to strengthen the premises of the semantic rule for $\gamma^\perp(B_1^\perp, \ldots, B_n^\perp)$. Oracles are defined so that $\pi^\perp \gamma_{\mathcal{O}}^\perp(B_1^\perp, \ldots, B_n^\perp)$ is observationally equivalent to $\pi \gamma(B_1, \ldots, B_n)$

where $\gamma_{\mathcal{O}}^{\perp}(B_1^{\perp}, \ldots, B_n^{\perp})$ is the behavior restricted by the oracle. We introduce first a notion of composition with an oracle and in Subsection 3.2, we introduce oracles.

Definition 10 (Composite Components with Oracle). *Given an oracle $\mathcal{O}$ on $(Q^p \cup Q^g) \times \gamma$, we define $B \stackrel{def}{=} \gamma_{\mathcal{O}}^{\perp}(B_1^{\perp}, \ldots, B_n^{\perp})$ as the transition system $(Q^p \cup Q^g, \gamma^{\perp}, \rightsquigarrow)$ where $\rightsquigarrow$ is the least set of transitions satisfying the rules*

$$\frac{a = \{p_i\}_{i \in I} \in \gamma \qquad \forall i \in I.\ q_i \stackrel{p_i}{\rightsquigarrow}_i q_i' \qquad \forall i \notin I.\ q_i = q_i' \qquad \mathcal{O}(q_1, \ldots, q_n, a)}{(q_1, \ldots, q_n) \stackrel{a}{\rightsquigarrow} (q_1', \ldots, q_n')}$$

$$\frac{q_i \stackrel{\beta_i}{\rightsquigarrow}_i q_i'}{(q_1, \ldots, q_i, \ldots, q_n) \stackrel{\beta_i}{\rightsquigarrow} (q_1, \ldots, q_i', \ldots, q_n)}$$

The following proposition says that a system with an oracle $\mathcal{O}$ strongly simulates ([8]) a system with oracle $\mathcal{O}'$ such that $\mathcal{O} \implies \mathcal{O}'$.

Proposition 1. *Let $\mathcal{O}$ and $\mathcal{O}'$ be two oracles for the system $\gamma^{\perp}(B_1^{\perp}, \ldots, B_n^{\perp})$, such that $\mathcal{O} \implies \mathcal{O}'$. They define two systems $B = \gamma_{\mathcal{O}}^{\perp}(B_1^{\perp}, \ldots, B_n^{\perp}) = (Q^g \cup Q^p, \gamma^{\perp}, \rightarrow_{\mathcal{O}})$ and $B' = \gamma_{\mathcal{O}'}^{\perp}(B_1^{\perp}, \ldots, B_n^{\perp}) = (Q^g \cup Q^p, \gamma^{\perp}, \rightarrow_{\mathcal{O}'})$. Every state of B is strongly similar to some state of B'.*

3.2   Oracles

We defines oracles parameterized by a dependency relation $\sqsubseteq$ on interactions. This relation contains $\pi^{\perp}$ but it need not be an order as shown below.

Definition 11 (Oracle). *A $\sqsubseteq$-oracle for a system $\gamma^{\perp}(B_1^{\perp}, \ldots, B_n^{\perp})$ and a dependency relation $\sqsubseteq \subseteq \gamma \times (Q^g \cup Q^p) \times \gamma$, is a predicate $\mathcal{O}$ on $(Q^g \cup Q^p) \times \gamma$ such that:*
- *(Dependency Enforcement)*

$$\mathcal{O}(q, a) \implies (\forall a'.\ a \sqsubseteq_q a' \implies \mathtt{disabled}(q, a') \vee \mathtt{enabled}(q, a'))$$

- *(Soundness) $q \in Q^g \implies \forall a \in \gamma.\ \mathcal{O}(q, a)$*

The dependency enforcement condition means that the oracle allows execution of a from state q if the status (enabled or disabled) of the interactions a' that dominate a (*i.e.* $a \sqsubseteq_q a'$) is known.

Property 2. If $\sqsubseteq_1 \subseteq \sqsubseteq_2$ and if $\mathcal{O}$ is a $\sqsubseteq_2$-oracle, then it is a $\sqsubseteq_1$-oracle.

We will now define several $\pi^{\perp}$-oracles for the system $\gamma^{\perp}(B_1^{\perp}, \ldots, B_n^{\perp})$ providing various degrees of parallelism and cost of implementation. There is a compromise to make between the degree of parallelism allowed by an oracle, and the cost for its implementation.

Ideal Oracle. The best possible oracle is defined by

$$\mathcal{O}_{ideal}(q, a) \iff (\forall a'.\ a\pi_q^{\perp}a' \implies \mathtt{disabled}(q, a') \vee \mathtt{enabled}(q, a'))$$

However, such an oracle is difficult to implement. It requires that at a given partial state q, the Engine is able to compute the relation $\pi_q^\perp$ which according to the definition of $\pi^\perp$ (Definition 7) boils down to computing the global state q' reachable from q. For this, in the general case, the Engine has to know the transition relation of the global state system.

Dynamic Oracle. We use now a dynamic approximation $\sqsubseteq^{dyn}$ of $\pi^\perp$. The reachability condition $q \overset{\beta^*}{\rightsquigarrow} q'$ in the definition of $\pi^\perp$ is replaced by a comparison $q \leq q'$, i.e. $a \sqsubseteq_q^{dyn} a' \iff \exists q' \in Q^g . q \leq q' \wedge a\pi_{q'}a'$. The dynamic oracle is defined by:

$$\mathcal{O}_{dyn}(q, a) \iff (\forall a'. a \sqsubseteq_q^{dyn} a' \implies \texttt{enabled}(q, a') \vee \texttt{disabled}(q, a'))$$

For the dynamic oracle, the Engine does not need a complete knowledge of the state of the system in order to compute $\sqsubseteq_q^{dyn}$ for a given partial state q.

Static Oracle. The static oracle $\mathcal{O}_{static}$ is defined via a static approximation $\sqsubseteq^{st}$ of $\pi^\perp$: $a \sqsubseteq_q^{st} a' \iff \exists q' \in Q^g . a\pi_{q'}a'$. We write $\sqsubseteq^{st}$ instead of $\sqsubseteq_q^{st}$ as the relation does not depend on q. The static oracle is defined by:

$$\mathcal{O}_{static}(q, a) \iff (\forall a'. a \sqsubseteq^{st} a' \implies \texttt{enabled}(q, a') \vee \texttt{disabled}(q, a'))$$

Lazy Oracle. The lazy oracle forbids all interactions from partial states. It waits for all the atomic components to finish their computation in order to know all the possible interactions. It is defined by $\mathcal{O}_{lazy}(q, a) \iff q \in Q^g$.

Proposition 2. $\mathcal{O}_{ideal}, \mathcal{O}_{dyn}, \mathcal{O}_{static}$ and $\mathcal{O}_{lazy}$ are $\pi^\perp$-oracles and we have, $\mathcal{O}_{lazy} \implies \mathcal{O}_{static} \implies \mathcal{O}_{dyn} \implies \mathcal{O}_{ideal}$.

The above result with Proposition 1 shows that these oracles provide an increasing degree of parallelism.

3.3 Correctness with Respect to Global State Semantics

The systems $\pi\gamma(B_1, \ldots, B_n)$ and $\pi^\perp\gamma_{\mathcal{O}}^\perp(B_1^\perp, \ldots, B_n^\perp)$ are observationally equivalent when $\mathcal{O}$ is a $\pi^\perp$-oracle.

Theorem 2. *Let π be a priority relation for the system $\gamma(B_1, \ldots, B_n)$ and $\mathcal{O}$ a $\pi^\perp$-oracle for the system $\gamma^\perp(B_1^\perp, \ldots, B_n^\perp)$. The systems $\pi\gamma(B_1, \ldots, B_n)$ and $\pi^\perp\gamma_{\mathcal{O}}^\perp(B_1^\perp, \ldots, B_n^\perp)$ are observationally equivalent.*

4 Distributed Semantics

4.1 Implementation

The model of BIP components with partial states is a first step towards a distributed implementation of BIP by separating internal computations from interactions. However, this model uses strong synchronization and therefore is still not directly implementable on arbitrary platforms where rendezvous is usually not available as a communication primitive.

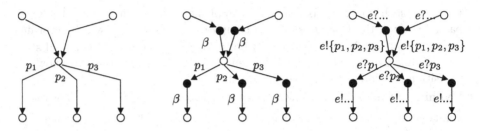

Fig. 2. Transformation from atomic BIP components (left) towards atomic components with partial states (middle) and io-machines (right)

We propose a second step towards a concrete distributed implementation of BIP components with partial states where multiparty interactions are replaced by asynchronous communication protocols (see Figure 2). The target model is *input-output systems* (io-systems) that are collections of parallel *input-output machines* (io-machines) communicating asynchronously by message passing through FIFO channels. This model is conceptually simple and directly encompasses primitives offered by languages used for modeling of distributed systems (such as SDL[7] or IO-automata[5]) or primitives usually available on distributed execution platforms (e.g. asynchronous execution of threads or processes, inter-process and inter-thread communication through FIFO queues, network protocols).

The principle of implementation is sketched in figure 3. Given $\pi^{\perp}\gamma^{\perp}(B_1^{\perp}, B_2^{\perp}, ..., B_n^{\perp})$ and a $\pi^{\perp}$-oracle $\mathcal{O}$, the implementation is an io-system consisting of io-machines B_i^{io} emulating the behavior of $B_i^{\perp}$ and an additional io-machine, the *Engine* $E(\gamma^{\perp}, \pi^{\perp}, \mathcal{O})$ realizing the coordination between them. Communication takes place only between the atomic components and the Engine, and never directly between different atomic components this leads to an io-system with a centralized architecture.

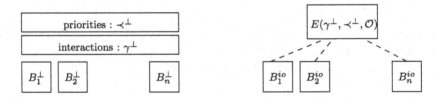

Fig. 3. Implementation: The Overall Structure

Formally, an io-system is a tuple $\mathcal{S} = (\mathcal{M}, Act, \{A_i = (Q_i, \hookrightarrow_i)\}_{i \in I})$ where

- $\mathcal{M}$ is a set of *messages*,
- Act is a set of actions α including *outputs* $j!m$ – output of the message $m \in \mathcal{M}$ to machine $j \in I$, *inputs* $j?m$ – input of message $m \in \mathcal{M}$ sent by machine $j \in I$ or *uninterpreted actions* a,

- $\{A_i = (Q_i, \hookrightarrow_i)\}_{i \in I}$ is a finite set of io-machines, where
  - Q_i is a finite set of states,
  - $\hookrightarrow_i \subseteq Q_i \times Act \times Q_i$ is a finite set of transitions labeled with actions.

States of io-systems are represented by configurations $\{(q_i, w_i)\}_{i \in I}$ where $q_i \in Q_i$ is a local state and $w_i \in (I \times \mathcal{M})^*$ is the FIFO-queue content of io-machine i. The semantics of io-systems is given as a labeled transition system on configurations. For each transition $q_i \xrightarrow{\alpha}_i q'_i$ of the io-machine i, we consider the following transitions on configurations corresponding respectively to input, output and uninterpreted actions:

- $\{..., (q_i, (j, m) \bullet w'_i), ...\} \xrightarrow{\tau} \{..., (q'_i, w'_i), ...\}$ when $\alpha = j?m$,
- $\{..., (q_i, w_i), (q_j, w_j), ...\} \xrightarrow{\tau} \{..., (q'_i, w_i), (q_j, w_j \bullet (i, m)), ...\}$ when $\alpha = j!m$
- $\{..., (q_i, w_i), ...\} \xrightarrow{a} \{..., (q'_i, w_i), ...\}$ when $\alpha = a$,

The implementations of atomic components are io-machines obtained as follows. Whenever a ready state is reached, they output a message to the Engine containing (1) the sets of ports on which they are willing to interact and (2) their local ready state. Then, they wait for a notification from the Engine indicating the port selected for interaction. Depending on this port, they continue their execution. Formally, given $B_i^\perp = (Q_i \cup Q_i^\perp, P_i \cup \{\beta_i\}, \leadsto_i)$, its corresponding io-machine $B_i^{io} = (Q_i \cup Q_i^\perp, \hookrightarrow_i)$ has the same set of states as $B_i^\perp$ and transitions defined by the following rules (see Figure 2):

- $q_i \xrightarrow{e!(X, q'_i)}_i q'_i$ *interaction request* whenever $q_i \xrightarrow{\beta_i}_i q'_i$ and $X = \{p \mid q'_i \xrightarrow{p}_i\}$
- $q_i \xrightarrow{e?p}_i q'_i$ *interaction notification* whenever $q_i \xrightarrow{p}_i q'_i$

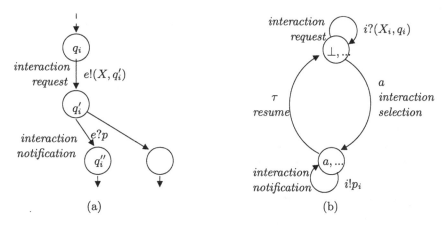

(a)   (b)

Fig. 4. Principle of Implementation: (a) io-machines for atomic components and (b) io-machine for the Engine

The Engine $E(\gamma^\perp, \pi^\perp, \mathcal{O})$ is an io-machine (see Figure 4) realizing the coordination between atomic io-machines for a given set of interactions $\gamma^\perp$, priorities $\pi^\perp$ and a $\pi^\perp$-oracle $\mathcal{O}$. Iteratively, the Engine receives and stores the sets of ports and the local states of components ready to interact. Depending on this information, it seeks a feasible interaction, which is maximal with respect to priorities and allowed by the oracle $\mathcal{O}$. If such an interaction exists, the Engine *executes* it by notifying sequentially, in some arbitrary order, all the involved components. Formally, given $\pi^\perp \gamma^\perp (B_1^\perp, B_2^\perp, ..., B_n^\perp)$ and an oracle $\mathcal{O}$, the Engine is the io-machine $(Q_e, \hookrightarrow_e)$ where

- $Q_e = (\gamma \cup \{\perp\}) \times \bigotimes_{i=1}^{n} 2^{P_i} \times \bigotimes_{i=1}^{n} (Q_i \cup \{\perp\})$ is the set of states of the form $(a^\perp, \mathbf{X}, \mathbf{q}^\perp)$ with $\mathbf{X} = (X_1, ..., X_n)$ and $\mathbf{q}^\perp = (q_1^\perp, ..., q_n^\perp)$ where

  - $a^\perp \in \gamma \cup \{\perp\}$ is the interaction being currently executed, $\perp$ if none;
  - $X_i \in 2^{P_i}$, is the set of ports on which component i is able to interact, empty if still busy;
  - $q_i^\perp \in Q_i \cup \{\perp\}$ is the state q_i if component i is ready to interact, $\perp$ if still busy.

- $\hookrightarrow_e$ contains the following transitions

  - $(\perp, \mathbf{X}, \mathbf{q}^\perp) \overset{i?X_i, q_i}{\hookrightarrow_e} (\perp, \mathbf{X}[X_i/i], \mathbf{q}^\perp[q_i/i])$ *interaction request*, stores information received from component i ready to interact.
  - $(\perp, \mathbf{X}, \mathbf{q}^\perp) \overset{a}{\hookrightarrow_e} (a, \mathbf{X}, \mathbf{q}^\perp)$ *interaction selection*, whenever an interaction a exists such that $a \subseteq \cup_{i=1}^{n} X_i$, a is maximal with respect to priorities $\pi^\perp$ and a is allowed by the oracle $\mathcal{O}$ at state $\mathbf{q}^\perp$. It consists in executing the interaction and moving to a state from which all the components involved will be notified.
  - $(a, \mathbf{X}, \mathbf{q}^\perp) \overset{i!p_i}{\hookrightarrow_e} (a, \mathbf{X}[\emptyset/i], \mathbf{q}^\perp[\perp/i])$ *interaction notification* and *cleanup* of the i component involved in the interaction a, that is when $a \cap X_i = \{p_i\} \neq \emptyset$,
  - $(a, \mathbf{X}, \mathbf{q}^\perp) \overset{\tau}{\hookrightarrow_e} (\perp, \mathbf{X}, \mathbf{q}^\perp)$ *resume*, when all atomic components have been notified, that is $a \cap \cup_{i=1}^{n} X_i = \emptyset$. It consists in moving back to a state where requests are handled.

The correctness of the implementation is formally established by the following theorem.

Theorem 3. *Composite components with partial states* $\pi^\perp \gamma_{\mathcal{O}}^\perp (B_1, B_2, ..., B_n)$ *are weakly bisimilar to* $(\mathcal{M}, Act, \{B_1^{io}, ..., B_n^{io}, E(\gamma^\perp, \pi^\perp, \mathcal{O})\})$, *i.e. their io-system implementation where* τ *is a silent action.*

4.2 Experimental Results

Distributed Execution Platform. We have implemented the distributed semantics of BIP programs and included it into the BIP toolset[2]. This toolset is a collection of tools dedicated to execution and analysis of BIP programs currently providing:

- *A compilation chain that transforms BIP programs into C/C++ code.* Compilation relies on model-based technologies available for Java under the Eclipse platform. Starting from BIP programs, the compiler generates BIP models conforming to a full-fledged BIP meta-model developed using EMF[1]. On the models, we can apply source-to-source transformations as well as static analysis techniques. Finally, models are used to generate C/C++ code to be executed on a dedicated platform, as follows.

- *A platform for execution and analysis of the generated C/C++ code.* The execution platform includes an Engine and the associated software infrastructure for multithreaded execution of the C/C++ code. Each atomic component is assigned to a thread, the Engine being a thread itself. The Engine implements the distributed semantics and is parameterized by a dynamic or lazy oracle. Iteratively, the Engine computes feasible interactions available on ready components. Then, if such interactions exist and the oracle allows them, the Engine selects one for execution and notifies the involved components.

Benchmarks. We present two examples illustrating the application of the results on a prototype implementation. We evaluate for two different types of oracles, the degree of parallelism over time, measured as the number of simultaneously executing atomic components. Before providing experimental results, we analyze the relationship between degree of parallelism and parameters of the system.

To simplify the analysis, consider a system consisting of n atomic components always able to interact through their ports. We distinguish the following cases, illustrated in Figure 5:

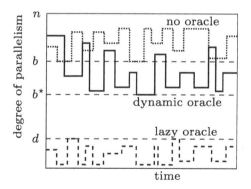

Fig. 5. Performance analysis

- For an implementation without oracle, the degree of parallelism is related to the minimal cardinality b of blocking subsets of atomic components. A subset of atomic components is *blocking* iff every interaction in the system requires at least one component of the subset to participate. Now, the degree of parallelism

---

[1] Eclipse Meta-modeling Framework.

l is such that $b \leq l \leq n$. In fact, whenever less than b components are running some interaction is possible and the Engine can eventually launch it;

• For an implementation with the lazy oracle, the maximal degree of parallelism is related to the maximal degree of interaction d, that is the maximal number d of components involved in a single interaction. In this case, the degree of parallelism l is such that $0 \leq l \leq d$. Interactions can be executed only from global states so there is no possibility of concurrency between interactions - the Engine is not able to keep running more than d atomic components at time;

• Finally, for dynamic oracles, the degree of parallelism is related again to the minimal cardinality $b^\star$ of some particular blocking sets of atomic components, the ones which block *all the maximal* interactions. We have $b^\star \leq b$ and the degree of parallelism l achieved in this case is such that $b^\star \leq l \leq n$. Using a similar reasoning as in the case without oracle, whenever less than $b^\star$ components are running, there should exist a maximal interaction ready and the Engine can eventually lauch it.

As a first benchmark, we consider a linear chain consisting of a set of identical components connected serially as shown in Figure 6. A component C_i has two ports, l_i and r_i. It has a single control state S_i, and two transitions labeled by l_i and r_i. The transition r_i is always enabled, its guard being *true*, whereas the transition l_i has a non-trivial guard g_i. We model broadcast from each component to its right neighbor by considering two types of interactions, 1) a set of singleton interactions consisting of the ports r_i; 2) a set of binary interactions $r_i l_{i+1}$ between the neighboring components, and 3) the priority $r_i \pi r_i l_{i+1}$ for the above interaction pair.

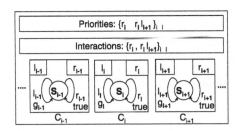

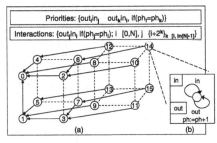

Fig. 6. The Linear Chain   Fig. 7. The Parallel Adder

Our experiment considers a system with 25 such components. Each component executes 100 steps (transitions), getting busy for 50-60 milliseconds on an l transition and 5-6 milliseconds on an r transition respectively. We performed the experiment on a single-processor PC running linux. The busy times of the atomic components were simulated by *sleep* system calls. We measured the degree of parallelism in the system with respect to the execution time. Figure 8 shows the results obtained for dynamic and lazy oracles.

Without oracle, the degree of parallelism is 25 continuously. In fact, whenever a component is ready, it can continue alone on the r interaction and the Engine notifies it immediately. For the lazy oracle, the maximal degree of parallelism equals the maximal degree of an interaction, which is 2. Whenever an interaction takes place, the two participating atomic components are active simultaneously for the first 5-6 ms, after which only the atomic component performing the l transition remains busy for 50-60 ms. Therefore, the degree of parallelism stays at an average close to 1. Finally, for dynamic oracle, the minimal blocking set has cardinality 12 (as for a linear chain with n atoms, the minimal cardinality is $n/2$, when every alternate atoms are busy blocking all the maximal interactions). Hence, we have at least 12 atomic components executing at any time. The measured degree of parallelism in this case, remains in average higher than 15.

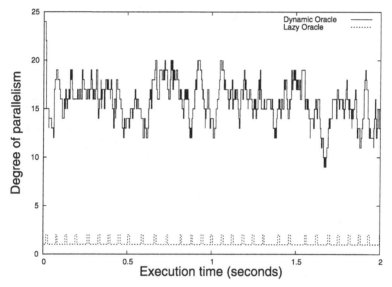

Fig. 8. Degree of Parallelism for Linear Chain

The second benchmark treats a parallel adder originally presented in [9], which adds 2^m values in a hypercube multi-processor machine. When the algorithm begins, the nodes hold the values to be added. On termination, the node labeled 0 contains their sum. Figure 7 presents the BIP model of a pipelined parallel-adder in a 4-dimensional hypercube with 2^4 nodes. Each node is modeled as a BIP component with ports *in* and *out*, labeling two transitions from a single control state, as shown in Figure 7(b). It also contains an array of values to be added (not shown on the figure) and the variable ph which records the index of current running addition on that node.

For each addition, every node receives partial addition results from its predecessors, adds them to its own value, sends the resulting sum to its unique successor and increments its ph variable. Communications between nodes are

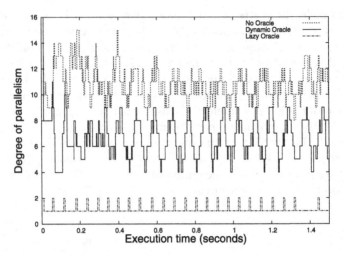

Fig. 9. Degree of Parallelism for Parallel Adder

modeled as interactions between the *out* port of a node and the *in* port of its successor, with a transfer of value from the node to the successor. Priorities are used to enforce correct order of the computation, *i.e.* a node cannot perform an *out* unless it has synchronized through its *in* port with all its predecessors. The final result of every addition is generated by the root node labeled 0.

The degrees of parallelism achieved, respectively without oracle and with lazy and dynamic oracles, are shown in Figure 9. Without oracle, the degree of parallelism is in average equal to 10. Let us notice that, without oracle, the functional behavior is completely wrong as priorities are used to enforce the right order of computation between nodes. With the lazy oracle, the maximal degree of parallelism equals the maximal degree of interaction which is 2. However, due to specific timing constraints on the execution of *in* and *out* transitions, the degree of parallelism stays in average close to 1. Finally, the dynamic oracle achieves a much better performance with an average degree of parallelism equal to 7.

5   Conclusion

We study a distributed implementation method for BIP, a framework for the description of component-based heterogeneous systems. BIP offers two powerful mechanisms for composing components by using interactions and priorities. The combination of interactions and priorities is expressive enough to express usual composition operators of other languages as shown in [3]. In particular to model broadcast, interactions do not suffice and other operators such as restrictions or priorities are needed. Furthermore, priorities are essential for describing scheduling policies, run-to-completion execution, urgency in real-time systems [6]. The proposed implementation method is quite general and can be easily adapted to other languages.

A key innovative idea is the translation of languages based on global state semantics to observationally equivalent distributed models from which implementation is straightforward. The decomposition of the translation in two steps allows separation of concerns in solving two main problems: the definition of partial state semantics and the expression of composition in terms of message passing primitives. Operational semantics provide an adequate framework for formalizing the translation. The models are obtained by successive refinements that preserve observational equivalence.

The main results show that whenever priorities are needed to express coordination between components, the operational semantics rules should be strengthened to take into account dependency between interactions. Oracles are very simple controllers enforcing preservation of semantics. Maximal parallelism is achieved for dynamic oracles allowing interaction as soon as possible. Nonetheless, these oracles may entail considerable computational overhead. As illustrated by experimental results the degree of parallelism depends on the type of the oracle and topology of the interactions.

There are many open problems to be investigated in the proposed framework for distributed implementation. These include the preservation of specific classes of properties, and less centralized implementations for the Engine.

References

1. Basu, A., Bidinger, P., Bozga, M., Sifakis, J.: Distributed semantics and implementation for systems with interaction and priority. Technical report, Verimag, Centre Équation, 38610 Gières (March 2008)
2. Basu, A., Bozga, M., Sifakis, J.: Modeling heterogeneous real-time components in BIP. In: SEFM, pp. 3–12 (2006)
3. Bliudze, S., Sifakis, J.: The algebra of connectors – structuring interaction in BIP. In: EmSoft, pp. 11–20 (2007)
4. Chandy, K.M., Lamport, L.: Distributed snapshots: Determining global states of distributed systems. ACM Trans. Comput. Syst. 3(1), 63–75 (1985)
5. Garland, S.J., Lynch, N.A.: The ioa language and toolset: Support for designing, analyzing, and building distributed systems. Technical Report MIT/LCS/TR-762, Laboratory for Computer Science, Massachusetts Institute of Technology, Cambridge, MA (August 1998)
6. Gößler, G., Sifakis, J.: Priority systems. In: de Boer, F.S., Bonsangue, M.M., Graf, S., de Roever, W.-P. (eds.) FMCO 2003. LNCS, vol. 3188, pp. 314–329. Springer, Heidelberg (2004)
7. ITU-T. Recommendation Z.100. Specification and Description Language (SDL). Technical Report Z-100, International Telecommunication Union – Standardization Sector, Genève (November 1999)
8. Milner, R.: Communication and concurrency. Prentice Hall International (UK) Ltd., Hertfordshire (1995)
9. Quinn, M.J.: Designing efficient algorithms for parallel computers. McGraw-Hill, Inc., New York (1986)

Checking Correctness of Transactional Behaviors[*]

Vincenzo Ciancia[1], Gian Luigi Ferrari[1], Roberto Guanciale[2],
and Daniele Strollo[1,2]

[1] Università degli Studi di Pisa, Dipartimento di Informatica
Largo B. Pontecorvo 3 I-56127, Pisa, Italy
{ciancia,giangi,strollo}@di.unipi.it
[2] Institute for Advanced Studies IMT Lucca
Piazza S. Ponziano 6, 55100, Lucca, Italy
{roberto.guanciale,daniele.strollo}@imtlucca.it

Abstract. The Signal Calculus is an asynchronous process calculus featuring multicast communication. It relies on explicit modeling of the communication structure of the network (communication flows), and on handling sessions, even *multi-party*. The calculus is strongly motivated by the practical needs of *Service-Oriented Computing*, and there exists a Java implementation, called JSCL, with a graphical modeling framework. To the aim of adding to SC (and JSCL) a verification environment, in this work we introduce the abstract semantics of SC, based on bisimulation. We show an example exploiting bisimilarity to prove the correctness of an SC model with respects to a transactional isolation requirement.

Keywords: Service Oriented Architectures, Event Notification, Coordination, Observational Equivalence.

1 Introduction

The Service Oriented Architecture (SOA) [1] main challenge consists in the definition of an architectural style where applications are built by composition of distributed functionalities, called services, that can be accessed in a uniform and platform independent manner, and communicate with each other by exchanging messages. The Web Service (WS) platform has become the universally accepted mechanism for implementing SOAs. The main contribution of this technology relies on the adoption of XML (eXtensible Markup Language) that has opened a new perspective for developers and service providers enabling language and platform independence (a.k.a. *interoperability*). The Web Service core specifications provide mechanisms for describing, publishing, retrieving and accessing services.

An open issue, in WS world, is the definition of a language for describing how these services interact and to check if the related implementations adhere to the

---

[*] Research supported by the EU FET-GC2 IST-2004-16004 Integrated Project SEN-SORIA and by the Italian FIRB Project TOCAI.IT.

K. Suzuki et al. (Eds.): FORTE 2008, LNCS 5048, pp. 134–148, 2008.

specifications. In our previous works, we provided and implemented a middleware, Java Signal Core Layer (JSCL), paired with a formal specification of the programming facilities that it offers. At the abstract level, the middleware takes the form of the *Signal Calculus* (SC) [10,12,8], an high level language inspired by the asynchronous π-calculus [15] enriched with the concepts of component locality and the needed primitives for dealing with Event Notification (EN) paradigm [18] (namely, multicast channels, that also give rise to multi-party sessions).

The adoption of EN yields to model services in terms of reactive entities that, autonomously, declare the set of events they are interested in and the behavior that they perform upon their occurrence. The main advantages of EN adoption rely on loosely coupling of services and on its flexibility. Specifically, EN features high level coordination mechanisms that allow programmers/designers to decouple components and rely entirely on event handling.

In this work we focus our attention on the verification of SC protocols. For this purpose, we introduce an abstract semantics of SC networks, based on the notion of *bisimulation*, which not only represents the behavior of sets of components interacting with each other, but also that of isolated subsystems. Behavioral semantics is important because it allows to distinguish isolated components that behave differently when "plugged" into a network. Our semantics is inspired by the π-calculus "direct HT bisimulation" [15]. Exploiting the notion of bisimulation, SC systems can be verified against abstracted versions of their design.

In this paper, we outline the main features of our approach by considering a simple, but illustrative case study, described in [24]. The case study is modeled by taking into account the transactional requirements given at specification level, proving that constraints on transactional isolation are maintained in the involved components. The verification of the scenario is done by checking that it is bisimilar to a "magic" property, i.e. an abstracted design that models properties of interest.

The paper is organized as follows. In Section 2 we review the main features and the operational semantics of the SC process calculus. Section 3 presents the abstract semantics of SCbased on a labeled transition system. Section 4 presents the case study, its abstract modeling and highlights how to exploit the bisimulation relation to prove transactional isolation of networks. Section 5 yields some concluding remarks.

2   Background: The Signal Calculus

In this section, we introduce the *signal calculus*. This is a process calculus suitable to describe service coordination, adopting the event notification paradigm. The communication mechanism is inspired by the asynchronous π-calculus. The calculus is centered around the notion of *component*, written as $a[B]_F^R$ and representing a service uniquely identified by a name a, the public address of the service, having internal behavior B, interfaces R, called *reactions*, and outgoing connections F, called *flows*.

We assume a countable set T of *topic* names (ranged over by τ), representing the available signal types, and a countable set of component names, ranged over by $a, b, c, ...$ The notation a indicates a set of component names.

Components exchange messages, called *signals*, in the form of pairs of topics $\tau\copyright\tau'$, where the first part is the signal type (which is, an unique name identifying an event kind), and the second one is a session identifier. Session identifiers and event kinds are freely interchangeable, and can be either freshly generated or received as input by reactions. When an event is raised by a component, it is notified to the components interested in handling it. Components are thus modeled in terms of reactive agents which declare, and can dynamically alter, the kind of events they are capable to handle.

Reactions describe available methods of a service in a given state. Their syntax is given by the following grammar:

$$R \quad ::= \quad 0 \quad | \quad \langle\alpha\rangle \to B \quad | \quad R|R$$

The *input prefix* $\langle\alpha\rangle$ is either $\tau\copyright\lambda\tau'$ or $\tau\copyright\tau'$, where τ' is bound in $\tau\copyright\lambda\tau'$. The *lambda reaction* $\tau\copyright\lambda\tau' \to B$ is triggered by signals having topic τ independently from their session, and binds τ' to the received session identifier. Conversely, the *check reaction* $\tau\copyright\tau' \to B$ reacts only to signals having topic τ issued for the specific session τ'. Once a signal reaction takes place, the behavior B will be executed in the component in parallel with the current internal behavior. *Reaction composition* $R|R$ allows a component to react to different kinds of signal in different ways. The *empty reaction* 0 cannot respond to any signal.

Each component has a *flow* describing the *choreography*, from the point of view of the component. Flows describe addressees of messages, for each topic τ. Flow syntax is defined as follows:

$$F \quad ::= \quad 0 \quad | \quad \tau \rightsquigarrow a \quad | \quad F|F$$

where the *empty flow* 0 does not deliver any kind of signal, the *single flow* $\tau \rightsquigarrow a$ delivers signals having topic τ to the components specified in the set a. Finally, new flows can be appended to component interfaces by using the parallel composition construct $F|F$.

Now, we introduce the syntax of *behaviors*, the basic programs that each service executes when a reaction is triggered by signals. Behaviors are described by the following grammar:

$$
\begin{array}{llll}
B & ::= & \mathbf{out}\langle\tau\copyright\tau'\rangle.B & \textit{(Signal emission)} \\
& | & (\nu\tau)B & \textit{(Topic restriction)} \\
& | & \mathbf{rupd}\,(R)\,.B & \textit{(Reaction update)} \\
& | & \mathbf{fupd}(F).B & \textit{(Flow update)} \\
& | & B \mid B' & \textit{(Parallel)} \\
& | & 0 & \textit{(Empty behavior)}
\end{array}
$$

The $\mathbf{out}\langle\tau\copyright\tau'\rangle.B$ primitive spawns a signal of topic τ having session τ', and then continues as B. A number of copies of the same message are created inside the network, one for each component listed in the flow of the component, for the topic τ. Topics can be freshly generated using *topic restriction*, a binder that declares local topics; namely, the occurrences of τ in $(\nu\tau)B$ are bound. The calculus provides two primitives to allow a component to dynamically change its interface: the *reaction update* **rupd** $(R).B'$ and the *flow update* **fupd**$(F).B'$. The former installs a new reaction R in the interface part of components and the latter appends F to its flows. The empty and parallel constructs have the obvious meaning.

Networks describe the component distribution and carry signals exchanged among components. Network syntax is defined as follows:

$$N ::= \quad \emptyset \quad | \quad a[B]_F^R \quad | \quad N \parallel N \quad | \quad \langle \tau © \tau' \rangle @a \quad | \quad (\nu\tau)N$$

A network can be empty $\emptyset$, a single component $a[B]_F^R$, the parallel composition of networks $N \parallel N'$, or the restriction of a topic in a (sub)network. Networks carry signals exchanged among components. The signal emission spawns into the network, for each target component, an "envelope" $\langle \tau © \tau' \rangle @a$ containing the signal and the target component name a. Finally, the last production allows to extend the scope of freshly generated topics over networks.

We assume that each service is identified by an unique name, and each name identifies at most one service, as it is usual in service-oriented computing.

We define a *network context* as a network having an "hole" where another network can be "plugged in". Formally, contexts are the terms generated by the grammar below, having only one occurrence of the symbol $-$:

$$C ::= \emptyset \quad | \quad a[B]_F^R \quad | \quad C \parallel C \quad | \quad \langle \tau © \tau' \rangle @a \quad | \quad (\nu\tau)C \quad | \quad -$$

The well formedness condition is also extended to contexts, so that a context is considered valid for a network when their component names are disjoint. This is formalized in the following definition.

Definition 1. *A network is* well formed *if the names of the components it contains are all different. We say that a context $C[-]$ is a* well formed context *of a network N if $C[N]$ is well formed.*

Free and bound names for networks, reactions, behaviors and flows are defined by structural induction in the usual way. We summarize the main rules in the following:

$$fn(\tau © \tau' \to B) = fn(B) \cup \{\tau, \tau'\} \qquad bn(\tau © \tau' \to B) = bn(B) \setminus \{\tau, \tau'\}$$
$$fn(\tau © \lambda \tau' \to B) = fn(B) \setminus \{\tau'\} \cup \{\tau'\} \qquad bn(\tau © \lambda \tau' \to B) = bn(B) \cup \{\tau'\} \setminus \{\tau'\}$$
$$fn((\nu\tau)B) = fn(B) \setminus \{\tau\} \qquad bn((\nu\tau)B) = bn(B) \cup \{\tau\}$$
$$fn((\nu\tau)N) = fn(B) \setminus \{\tau\} \qquad bn((\nu\tau)N) = bn(B) \cup \{\tau\}$$

We define structural congruence over the syntax of the calculus as the smallest congruence that satisfies the commutative monoidal laws for $(R, |, 0)$, $(F, |, 0)$, $(B, \mid, 0)$ and $(N, \parallel, \emptyset)$, α-conversion of bound names, and the rule s below. In particular, notice that τ is not in the scope of τ' in $\tau © \lambda \tau' \to B$.

$$\frac{N \to N'}{N \parallel M \to N' \parallel M} \; (npar)$$

$$\frac{a[B]_F^R \to a[B']_{F'}^{R'}}{a[B \mid B_1]_F^R \to a[B' \mid B_1]_{F'}^{R'}} \; (par) \qquad\qquad \frac{N \to N_1}{(\nu\tau)N \to (\nu\tau)N_1} \; (new)$$

$$a[\mathbf{rupd}\,(R')\,.B]_F^R \to a[B]_F^{R \mid R'} \quad (rupd) \qquad a[\mathbf{fupd}(F')\,.B]_F^R \to a[B]_{F \mid F'}^R \quad (fupd)$$

$$\frac{(F){\downarrow}_\tau = \{b_1, \ldots, b_n\}}{a[\mathbf{out}\langle \tau\copyright\tau'\rangle.B]_F^R \to a[B]_F^R \parallel \langle \tau\copyright\tau'\rangle@b_1 \parallel \ldots \parallel \langle \tau\copyright\tau'\rangle@b_n} \; (emit)$$

$$\langle \tau\copyright\tau'\rangle@a \parallel a[0]_F^{\tau\copyright\tau' \to B \mid R} \to a[B]_F^R \quad (check)$$

$$\langle \tau\copyright\tau'\rangle@a \parallel a[0]_F^{\tau\copyright\lambda\tau_1 \to B' \mid R} \to a[\{\tau'/\tau_1\}B]_F^{\tau\copyright\lambda\tau_1 \to B' \mid R} \quad (lam)$$

Fig. 1. Operational semantics

$$(\nu\tau)0 \equiv 0 \qquad\qquad ((\nu\tau)B) \mid B' \equiv (\nu\tau)(B \mid B'), \text{ if } \tau \notin fn(B')$$

$$(\nu\tau)(\nu\tau')B \equiv (\nu\tau')(\nu\tau)B \qquad\qquad (\nu\tau)(\nu\tau')N \equiv (\nu\tau')(\nu\tau)N$$

$$(\nu\tau)\emptyset \equiv a[0]_F^0 \equiv \emptyset \qquad\qquad ((\nu\tau)N) \parallel N' \equiv (\nu\tau)(N \parallel N'), \text{ if } \tau \notin fn(N')$$

$$\frac{F_1 \equiv F_2 \quad B_1 \equiv B_2 \quad R_1 \equiv R_2}{a[B_1]_{F_1}^{R_1} \equiv a[B_2]_{F_2}^{R_2}} \qquad\qquad \frac{\tau \notin fn(R) \cup fn(F) \cup \{a\}}{a[(\nu\tau)B]_F^R \equiv (\nu\tau)a[B]_F^R} \, .$$

2.1   Reaction Rules

We briefly recall the reduction semantics of SC [12]. This is defined using the previously introduced structural congruence and the *flow projection* function $((F){\downarrow}_\tau)$, defined as

$$(\tau \rightsquigarrow a){\downarrow}_\tau = a \qquad (\tau \rightsquigarrow a){\downarrow}_{\tau'} = (0){\downarrow}_{\tau'} = \emptyset \qquad (F_1 \mid F_2){\downarrow}_\tau = (F_1){\downarrow}_\tau \cup (F_2){\downarrow}_\tau$$

This function takes a flow and a topic and yields the set of target component names to which signals having topic τ have to be delivered.

The reduction semantics of SC explains how components, at each step, communicate and update their interface. The reduction relation $\to$ is depicted in Figure 1. We assume the set of rules to be augmented with structural congruence, i.e., the following additional rule is used:

$$\frac{N \equiv N' \quad N' \to M' \quad M' \equiv M}{N \to M} \; (struct)$$

Rules labeled *rupd* and *fupd* update, respectively, reactions and flows of a process. Rule *emit* introduces in the network a new envelope for the event kind τ targeted to each subscribed component $((F)\downarrow_\tau = \{b_1, \ldots, b_n\})$. Rules labeled *check* and *lam* model activation of *check* reactions, that exactly match the session identifier, and of *lambda* reactions, that receive a session identifier as argument. Rules *npar*, *struct* and *new* are usual in process calculi, while *par* allows behaviors to be added in parallel into a component, preserving reactions. This rule allows us to define the semantics only on components whose internal behavior has no parallel operation, avoiding the need for separate rules. This happens because synchronization of two internal behaviors of the same component is not possible in our framework.

3   LTS Semantics

Here we present the *behavioral* semantics of networks, in terms of a labeled transition system that represents not only the behavior of sets of components that interact with each other, but also of isolated subsystems. Having an LTS semantics is important because it allows to distinguish isolated components that behaves differently when inserted into a network (e.g. a component with an installed reaction, and the empty component).

The transition system is similar in spirit to work on the asynchronous π-calculus by Honda and Tokoro [15], and Amadio, Castellani and Sangiorgi [2]. The set of observable actions α is specified as follows:

$$\alpha ::= \emptyset \mid \langle \tau \copyright \tau' \rangle @a \mid \langle \tau \copyright (\tau') \rangle @a \mid \tau \copyright \tau' @a \mid \tau \copyright \tau' @(a)$$

In our syntax, $\emptyset$ models unobservable actions. $\langle \tau \copyright \tau' \rangle @a$ is *free* (asynchronous) output with event kind τ, session type τ' and addressee a. $\langle \tau \copyright (\tau') \rangle @a$ is *bound* output, and $\tau \copyright \tau' @a$ is free input. $\tau \copyright \tau' @(a)$ represents the action of receiving a message and storing it in parallel with the current process. This action is observable in any system, thus including the empty network. This behavior is the essence of asynchronous communication, and is similar to the transition rule named in_0 in [2], which is used to define the so-called "directed HT bisimulation", derived, on its turn, from the rules given in [15]. All names in the actions are free, with the exception of τ' in *bound* output action. Finally we use $n(\alpha)$ to denote the set of names occurred in the action α.

The labeled transition relation over networks is defined by the rules depicted in Figure 2. We briefly comment on the semantics. The *async* rule allows any system to perform an input, simply storing the received message for subsequent usage. The *out* rule makes observable the output capability of a system with pending messages. Rules *struct*, *par*, *rupd*, *fupd*, *new* and *npar* are very similar to their counterparts in the unlabeled semantics. Rules *check* and *lam* model the capability of a system to consume messages present on the network, the former strictly matching on the session identifier, and the latter receiving sessions as input. In a similar fashion to the π-calculus, *ext* and *bsync* model sending

$$\frac{N \equiv N' \quad N' \xrightarrow{\alpha} M' \quad M' \equiv M}{N \xrightarrow{\alpha} M} \ (struct)$$

$$\frac{}{a[\mathbf{rupd}\ (R')\ .B]_F^R \xrightarrow{\emptyset} a[B]_F^{R|R'}} \ (rupd) \qquad \frac{}{a[\mathbf{fupd}(F').B]_F^R \xrightarrow{\emptyset} a[B]_{F|F'}^R} \ (fupd)$$

$$\frac{(F)\!\downarrow_\tau = \{b_1, \ldots, b_n\}}{a[\mathbf{out}\langle\tau\textcircled{c}\tau'\rangle.B']_F^R \xrightarrow{\emptyset} a[B']_F^R \ \|\ \langle\tau\textcircled{c}\tau'\rangle@b_1 \ \|\ \ldots\ \|\ \langle\tau\textcircled{c}\tau'\rangle@b_n} \ (emit)$$

$$\frac{}{\langle\tau\textcircled{c}\tau'\rangle@a \xrightarrow{\langle\tau\textcircled{c}\tau'\rangle@a} \emptyset} \ (out) \qquad \frac{}{N \xrightarrow{\tau\textcircled{c}\tau'@(a)} N \ \|\ \langle\tau\textcircled{c}\tau'\rangle@a} \ (async)$$

$$\frac{R' = \tau\textcircled{c}\tau' \to B}{a[0]_F^{R|R'} \xrightarrow{\tau\textcircled{c}\tau'@a} a[B]_F^R} \ (check) \qquad \frac{R' = \tau\textcircled{c}\lambda\tau' \to B}{a[0]_F^{R|R'} \xrightarrow{\tau\textcircled{c}\tau''@a} a[\{\tau''/\tau'\}B]_F^{R|R'}} \ (lam)$$

$$\frac{N \xrightarrow{\alpha} N_1 \quad \tau \notin n(\alpha)}{(\nu\tau)N \xrightarrow{\alpha} (\nu\tau)N_1} \ (new) \qquad \frac{N \xrightarrow{\langle\tau\textcircled{c}\tau'\rangle@a} N' \quad \tau \neq \tau'}{(\nu\tau')N \xrightarrow{\langle\tau\textcircled{c}(\tau')\rangle@a} N'} \ (ext)$$

$$\frac{N \xrightarrow{\langle\tau\textcircled{c}(\tau')\rangle@a} N' \quad M \xrightarrow{\tau\textcircled{c}\tau'@a} M' \quad \tau' \notin fn(M)}{N \ \|\ M \xrightarrow{\emptyset} (\nu\tau')N' \ \|\ M'} \ (bsync)$$

$$\frac{N \xrightarrow{\langle\tau\textcircled{c}\tau'\rangle@a} N' \quad M \xrightarrow{\tau\textcircled{c}\tau'@a} M'}{N \ \|\ M \xrightarrow{\emptyset} N' \ \|\ M'} \ (sync)$$

$$\frac{a[B]_F^R \xrightarrow{\alpha} a[B']_{F'}^{R'}}{a[B \mid B_1]_F^R \xrightarrow{\alpha} a[B' \mid B_1]_{F'}^{R'}} \ (par) \qquad \frac{N \xrightarrow{\alpha} N' \quad bn(\alpha) \cap fn(M) = \emptyset}{N \ \|\ M \xrightarrow{\alpha} N' \ \|\ M} \ (npar)$$

Fig. 2. Behavioral semantics

a restricted name as an output message, and receiving it as a fresh name. Finally, rule *sync* allows communication by linking input reactions and output capabilities of pending messages.

Rule labeled with (*async*), first given by Amadio, Castellani and Sangiorgi in [2], is the essence of asynchronous communication. This rule allows any process (even those that do not perform input) to store a message without consuming it, so that one cannot directly observe *when* input actions actually happen. In the definition of bisimulation below, only asynchronous input transitions (that is, transitions obtained from the *async* rule) are kept in account, while "normal" input is not considered. This allows two processes that only differ in the way they interleave input with other actions to be considered bisimilar.

Even though they are similar, the semantics of the asynchronous π-calculus and that of SC differ in some key aspects. Namely, SC features dynamic multicast channels due to the dynamic nature of flows. Hence, the addressee of a message is not statically known. This is the reason why our calculus features the output primitive, that using rule (*out*) spawns a certain number of messages in parallel, while in the asynchronous π-calculus there is no such construct.

The notion of *weak* transition system is defined in the standard way:

$$N \stackrel{\emptyset}{\Longrightarrow} N' \quad \text{iff } N(\stackrel{\emptyset}{\rightarrow})^* N'$$
$$N \stackrel{\alpha}{\Longrightarrow} N' \quad \text{iff } N \stackrel{\emptyset}{\Longrightarrow} . \stackrel{\alpha}{\rightarrow} . \stackrel{\emptyset}{\Longrightarrow} N' \text{ for all } \alpha \neq \emptyset$$

The following theorem establishes a link between the reduction relation and the observational semantics.

Theorem 1. $N \rightarrow N'$ *if and only if* $N \stackrel{\emptyset}{\rightarrow} N'$.

Finally we provide the definition of SC-bisimulation ($\sim_{\text{SC}}$). This relation allows to distinguish isolated subsystems (e.g. a component, or a partition of a network) that behave differently when inserted into a network, even though, in isolation, they cannot react.

Definition 2. $\sim_{\text{SC}}$ *is the largest symmetric relation on* SC-*terms such that if* $N \sim_{\text{SC}} M$, $N \stackrel{\alpha}{\rightarrow} N'$, $\alpha \neq \tau \copyright \tau' @ a$, $bn(\alpha) \cap fn(M) = \emptyset$ *implies that* $M \stackrel{\alpha}{\rightarrow} M'$ *and* $N' \sim_{\text{SC}} M'$.

The notion of weak SC bisimulation ($\approx_{\text{SC}}$) is obtained substituting in the above definition the transition relation with the weak one.

Bisimulation allows one to check for properties that have to be satisfied by the implementation of a system against its design expressed in a high-level language. Sometimes the implementation is slightly modified in order to verify a subset of the system requirements, e.g. by inserting the implementation in a suitable *controlled* context or environment, where it can be formally shown that, by construction, only properties of interest can lead to violation of the design. We show an example of this technique in section 4, as an application of the behavioral modeling framework we are developing.

Theorem 2. *If* $N \sim_{\text{SC}} N'$ *then*

$$N \parallel \langle \tau_1 \copyright \tau_1' \rangle @ a_1 \ldots \parallel \langle \tau_k \copyright \tau_k' \rangle @ a_k \sim {}_{\text{SC}} N' \parallel \langle \tau_1 \copyright \tau_1' \rangle @ a_1 \ldots \parallel \langle \tau_k \copyright \tau_k' \rangle @ a_k$$

Proof. (outline) Since the rule *async* can be applied to any network and envelope, the network N can perform a transition step labeled $\alpha = \tau \copyright \tau' @ (a)$, going to $N \parallel \langle \tau \copyright \tau' \rangle @ a$. The same rule can be applied to the network N', that goes to $N' \parallel \langle \tau \copyright \tau' \rangle @ a$. Since N and N' are bisimilar, when they perform the same transition α, they must go in bisimilar state: $N \parallel \langle \tau \copyright \tau' \rangle @ a \sim_{\text{SC}} N' \parallel \langle \tau \copyright \tau' \rangle @ a$. This proves that two bisimilar network remain bisimilar if composed with the same envelope. This proof can be applied with any number of envelopes, proving the theorem. $\square$

Theorem 3. *For any context* C, *and any two networks* N *and* N', *such that* $N \sim_{\text{SC}} N'$, *with* C *a well formed context of both networks (see Definition 1), it holds that* $C(N) \sim_{\text{SC}} C(N')$.

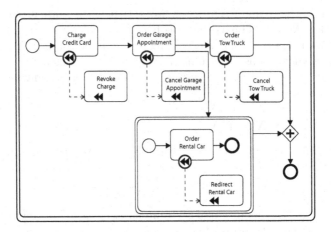

Fig. 3. Car repair scenario: the BPMN model

4   The Car Repair Scenario

In this section we adopt the SC calculus to model the service coordination issues of the SENSORIA car repair scenario [24], consisting of a car manufacturer service offering assistance support to their customers.

4.1   The Sensoria Scenario

A car manufacturer offers an assistance service to the customer once his/her car breaks down. Once contacted, such system attempts to locate a garage, a tow truck and a rental car service so that the car is towed to the garage and repaired meanwhile the customer may continue his travel. Several services are involved into the system and interact to reach a common goal. Their inter-dependencies are summarized as follows:

- before any service lookup is made, the credit card is charged with a security amount;
- before looking for a tow truck, a garage must be found as it poses additional constraints to the candidate tow trucks;
- if finding a tow truck fails, the garage appointment must be revoked;
- if renting a car succeeds and finding either a tow truck or a garage appointment fails, the car rental must be redirected to the broken down car's actual location;
- if the car rental fails, it should not affect the tow truck and garage appointment.

This scenario can be described through a business process language. We use the industry standard Business Process Modeling Language (BPMN [13]) to graphically describe the scenario and the inter-dependencies among services. The

BPMN model of this scenario is presented in Figure 3. Notice that the model exploits the transactional and compensation facilities of BPMN and that the car rental service is a sub-transaction, since it does not affect other activities. We briefly recall the graphical notation adopted in BPMN. A double-lined boundary indicates that the sub-process is a transaction. The single-lined boxes represent activities executed inside transactions and the activities linked through backward arrows represent the related compensation activities that must be executed when the process is rolling back. The blank circles represent the entry and exit points of a transaction. Finally, the diamond containing the plus symbol represents the joining of two activities. The full BMPN specification can be found in [13].

4.2   Modeling the Car Repair Scenario

Services involved into the Car Repair Scenario (CRS) scenario are described by SC components. To specify the interactions among participants, we introduce the following signal topics:

- τ_f is used to propagate *forward signals* to inform components about the completion of previous activities;
- τ_r is used to propagate *rollback signals* to components. Such signals are treated by executing the compensation activity and subsequently by propagating, backwards, the signal to the other participants;
- τ_n is used to implement the join mechanism among parallel activities executed inside the same workflow session.
- τ_{ok} is used internally by components to represent the successful termination of an activity.
- τ_{exc} is used internally by components to represent an internal failure, for example the throwing of an exception.

In SC, *transactional components* can be described as services reacting to both τ_f and τ_r notifications. At the reception of a τ_f signal, the component executes its main activity and installs the corresponding compensation reaction. At the reception of a τ_r signal, the previously installed compensation is executed. We suppose that each invocation of the transactional workflow has a unique session (in the following referred as τ). The consumer has to generate the session, that will be delivered with each signal to identify the workflow instance. Notice that, for a workflow session, the compensation activity must be executed only after the successful execution of the main activity. A transactional component having address a, a main activity A and a compensation C is translated to an SC model by the function TC. The connections to other components are described by the sets $next$ and $prev$ containing the target components to which, respectively, τ_f and τ_r signals must be forwarded. The TC function is defined as follows:

$$TC(a, A, C, prev, next) \triangleq (\nu \tau_{ok})(\nu \tau_{exc})a[0]_{F_{TC}(a,next,prev)}^{R_{TC}(A,C)}$$

where:

$$
\begin{aligned}
F_{TC}(a, next, prev) &\triangleq \tau_f \rightsquigarrow next | \tau_r \rightsquigarrow prev | \tau_{exc} \rightsquigarrow a | \tau_{ok} \rightsquigarrow a \\
R_{TC}(A, C) &\triangleq \tau_f \textcircled{C} \lambda\tau \rightarrow \mathbf{rupd}\,(R_{res}(C)) \mid A \\
R_{res}(C) &\triangleq \tau_{ok} \textcircled{C} \tau \rightarrow B_{ok}(C) | \tau_{exc} \textcircled{C} \tau \rightarrow B_{exc} \\
B_{ok}(C) &\triangleq \mathbf{rupd}\,(R_{rb1}(C))\,.\mathbf{out}\langle \tau_f \textcircled{C} \tau \rangle.0 \\
R_{rb1}(C) &\triangleq \tau_r \textcircled{C} \tau \rightarrow C \\
B_{exc} &\triangleq \begin{cases} \mathbf{rupd}\,(R_{rb2})\,.\mathbf{out}\langle \tau_f \textcircled{C} \tau \rangle.0 & \text{subtransaction} \\ \mathbf{out}\langle \tau_r \textcircled{C} \tau \rangle.0 & \text{otherwise} \end{cases} \\
R_{rb2} &\triangleq \tau_r \textcircled{C} \tau \rightarrow \mathbf{out}\langle \tau_r \textcircled{C} \tau \rangle.0
\end{aligned}
$$

Initially, the component has an installed reaction (R_{TC}) for handling the forward flow (τ_f notifications). Once the reaction is activated, it retrieves the signal session, that identifies the workflow instance, and executes the main activity A. The formalization of the activity A and of the compensation C are out of our scope; hereafter, we assume that:

1. if the main activity A successfully terminates, a signal τ_{ok} is internally raised, to inform the component that the flow can continue
2. if the main activity A fails, a signal τ_{exc} is internally raised, informing the component to start the backward flow
3. the last operation of the compensation C is the rising of a rollback signal ($\mathbf{out}\langle \tau_r \textcircled{C} \tau \rangle.0$).

Notice that the topics τ_{ok} and τ_{exc} are restricted to the local scope of component. Concurrently with the activity A, the component installs the reactions, defined by R_{res}, to check the termination state of A (τ_{ok} or τ_{exc}).

If the activity A successes, it internally delivers a τ_{ok} signal and the behavior B_{ok} is executed. It installs a check reaction (R_{rb1}), that is used to wait for a rollback notification from a successor component, and propagates the τ_f signal to the next components in the workflow (using $\mathbf{out}\langle \tau_f \textcircled{C} \tau \rangle.0$). If, later, a τ_r signal for the session τ is received, the compensation C is executed and the rollback signal is propagated to previous stages (since we suppose that the last operation of the compensation is $\mathbf{out}\langle \tau_r \textcircled{C} \tau \rangle.0$).

If the activity A fails, it internally delivers a τ_{exc} signal and the behavior B_{exc} is executed. Notice that two implementation of the behavior are provided: the first one is used if the component acts as an isolated sub-transaction (e.g. car rental service), while the second one is used if the components acts as a standard transactional activity. In the first case, the behavior propagates the τ_f signal, since an error of the sub-transaction should not affect the computation of the other components. Moreover the behavior installs a reaction for τ_r that just propagate the backward flow. In the second case, the behavior simply starts the backward flow, raising a rollback signal.

A sequential work-flow can simply be specified as a chain of transactional components by properly setting their *next* and *prev* sets. To model the parallel branch, we define the *collector* and *emitter* components as follows:

$Emitter(a, prev, next, collector) \triangleq$
$a[0]^{\tau_f \copyright \lambda \tau \rightarrow \mathbf{rupd}(\tau_r \copyright \tau \rightarrow \mathbf{rupd}(\tau_r \copyright \tau \rightarrow \mathbf{out}\langle \tau_r \copyright \tau \rangle.0).\mathbf{out}\langle \tau_n \copyright \tau \rangle.\mathbf{out}\langle \tau_f \copyright \tau \rangle.0)}_{\tau_f \rightsquigarrow next | \tau_r \rightsquigarrow prev | \tau_n \rightsquigarrow \{collector\}}$

$Collector(a, prev, next) \triangleq$
$a[0]^{\tau_n \copyright \lambda \tau \rightarrow \mathbf{rupd}(\tau_f \copyright \tau \rightarrow \mathbf{rupd}(\tau_f \copyright \tau \rightarrow \mathbf{rupd}(\tau_r \copyright \tau \rightarrow \mathbf{out}\langle \tau_r \copyright \tau \rangle.0.\mathbf{out}\langle \tau_f \copyright \tau \rangle.0)))}_{\tau_f \rightsquigarrow next | \tau_r \rightsquigarrow prev}$

The emitter represents the entry point of the parallel branch. Essentially it activates the forward flow of *next* components, representing the parallel activities, and synchronizes their backward flows. The synchronization mechanism is implemented by sequentially installing two reactions for the topic τ_r and the session τ (through $\mathbf{rupd}\,(\tau_r \copyright \tau \rightarrow \mathbf{rupd}\,(\tau_r \copyright \tau \rightarrow ...)))$. After that the synchronization mechanism has been installed, the emitter activates the forward flow ($\mathbf{out}\langle \tau_n \copyright \tau \rangle.\mathbf{out}\langle \tau_f \copyright \tau \rangle.0$). Notice that the component emits two signals: one having topic τ_f and the other one having topic τ_n. The first signal is delivered to the components representing the parallel activities. The other one is delivered to the collector, informing it of the received session that will be later used by it to implement its synchronization. When the synchronization of the backward flow takes place, the emitter forwards the rollback signal ($\mathbf{out}\langle \tau_r \copyright \tau \rangle.0$) to the *prev* components.

Similarly, the collector component is responsible to implement the synchronization mechanism for the forward flows and to activate the backward flows of the parallel components when a τ_r signal is received. Notice that the collector needs to be notified about the session τ via a τ_n signal. This is necessary since there is not mutual exclusion among executed behaviors.

The car repair scenario can be modeled by the following SC network:

$TC(card, ChargeCredit, RevokeCredit, \{\}, \{garage\}) \parallel$
$TC(garage, OrderGarage, CancelGarage, \{card\}, \{e\}) \parallel$
$Emitter(e, \{garage\}, \{truck, car\}, \{c\}) \parallel$
$TC(truck, OrderTowTruck, CancelTowTruck, \{e, car\}, \{c\}) \parallel$
$TC(car, OrderCar, RedirectCar, \{e\}, \{c\}) \parallel$
$Collector(c, \{truck, car\}, \{\})$

Notice that τ_r events raised by the *truck* component are notified to the *car* service, since an error occurred in the execution of a main activity must activate the compensations of all other concurrent components. Instead the τ_r events raised by the *car* component are notified only to the emitter, since car is a sub transaction.

4.3   Checking Sub-transaction Isolation

As discussed above, the rental car service is an isolated sub-transaction, namely, if the car rental fails, it should not affect the execution of the other components in the network. Regardless of the implementation details of the main activity and of the compensation, we model only the signal emissions that represent their termination. Hence, the car service that fails (Car_{exc}) and the other one that successes (Car_{ok}) are modeled as:

$$Car_{exc} \triangleq TC(car, \mathbf{out}\langle \tau_{exc} \mathbb{C} \tau_s \rangle.0, \mathbf{out}\langle \tau_r \mathbb{C} \tau_s \rangle.0, \{e\}, \{c\})$$
$$Car_{ok} \triangleq TC(car, \mathbf{out}\langle \tau_{ok} \mathbb{C} \tau_s \rangle.0, \mathbf{out}\langle \tau_r \mathbb{C} \tau_s \rangle.0, \{e\}, \{c\})$$

Now we prove the *transaction isolation property* of the car service by comparing its model with a *magic* car service. This is a transactional component that performs the ideal behavior: when it receives a τ_f signal, it propagates the signal to *next* components, while, when it receives a τ_r signal, it propagates the signal to *prev* components. Then, we check that, independently from the behavior executed internally by the car service, the whole transactional workflow performs the same action of the one containing the *magic* service. Formally the workflow containing the Car_{exc} (or Car_{ok}) must be bisimilar to the one containing the *magic* car service. This service can be model as:

$$Car_{magic} \triangleq car[0]_{\tau_f \rightsquigarrow next | \tau_r \rightsquigarrow prev}^{\tau_f \mathbb{C}\lambda\tau \rightarrow skip.(\,\dots\,).skip.\mathbf{out}\langle \tau_f \mathbb{C}\tau \rangle.\mathbf{rupd}(\tau_r \mathbb{C}\tau \rightarrow \mathbf{out}\langle \tau_r \mathbb{C}\tau \rangle.0)}$$
$$skip.B \triangleq \mathbf{fupd}(0)$$

In the above process, the *skip* action is used for internal computation steps. However, this is not a primitive of the calculus, but rather it is a derived operation, modeled by installation of an empty flow (hence, not altering the flow of the component).

The process describes a set of possible magic properties, parametrized by the number of *skip* actions. For the system to satisfy the required property, it is sufficient that there exists a number of *skip* actions that lets the bisimulation check succeed. We use the compositionality property of the bisimilarity (Theorem 3) as a "substitution principle": the statement $Car_{ok} \sim_{SC} Car_{magic}$ (and $Car_{exc} \sim_{SC} Car_{magic}$) ensures that the bisimulation result propagates to the whole workflows.

5   Future Work

We have presented an LTS semantics for the SC process calculus. The obtained abstract semantics, based on bisimulation, allows one to reason about behavioral properties of SC networks. The SC-JSCL framework has been designed to support the specification, the implementation and verification of coordination policies for services oriented applications. Our main goal is to provide general facilities to implement high-level languages for service oriented architectures (e.g. BPEL4WS [16], BPML [22], WS-CDL [23]). The strict interplay between SC and JSCL permits to drive and verify the implementation of such languages. A number of approaches have been introduced to provide the formal foundations of standards for service orchestrations and service choreographies. The SC-JSCL framework differs from these approaches (COWS [17], Global Calculus [5], λ_{req} [3] ORC [19], SCC [4], SOCK [14] to cite a few), since it focuses on a lower level of abstraction, merging the theoretical formalization with the implementation requirements. Indeed, the emphasis in SC-JSCL relies on the notion of event notification that strictly fits to the loosely coupling nature of services.

We foresee two development lines. In this work, bisimulation proofs have been done by hand, while one would expect automated checkers to be used. The fresh name generation construct of SC, even though giving it great expressive power (in particular, for the possibility to handle new sessions), makes it difficult to define and implement finite state algorithms for bisimulation checking and (in perspective) model checking. *History-Dependent* automata [20] are an operational model where garbage-collection of unused names can be exploited to obtain finite state models of systems featuring generation of fresh resources [7]. As a possible future development, thus, it would be interesting to express the semantics of SC using HD-automata, in order to be able to reuse work on minimization and bisimulation checking algorithms for nominal calculi [9].

In [12], we introduced an algebraic structure over topics. This allows us to implement more complex coordination logics directly encoded inside the signal type. The definition of bisimulation in this case should make use of the algebraic structure to obtain a suitable *quantitative* notion of bisimulation, allowing to express properties of a system with respects to e.g. a range of security policies. On the logical side, there is a close connection, which should be studied in detail, with the quantitative/spatial logic over c-semirings defined in [6].

The SC/JSCL framework is equipped with a programming environment, called *JSCL4Eclipse* [11], that allows one to graphically model JSCL networks and to automatically generate the stub implementation. As a long term research goal, we aim to integrate verification tools based on bisimulation and model checking techniques within our development framework.

References

1. Aiello, M., Aoyama, M., Curbera, F., Papazoglou, M.P. (eds.): Service-Oriented Computing - ICSOC 2004, Second International Conference, Proceedings, November 15-19, 2004. ACM, New York (2004)
2. Amadio, R.M., Castellani, I., Sangiorgi, D.: On bisimulations for the asynchronous pi-calculus. Theor. Comput. Sci. 195(2), 291–324 (1998)
3. Bartoletti, M., Degano, P., Ferrari, G., Zunino, R.: Secure service orchestration. In: Hertzberg, J., Beetz, M., Englert, R. (eds.) KI 2007. LNCS (LNAI), vol. 4667. Springer, Heidelberg (2007)
4. Boreale, M., Bruni, R., Caires, L., De Nicola, R., Lanese, I., Loreti, M., Martins, F., Montanari, U., Ravara, A., Sangiorgi, D., Vasconcelos, V.T., Zavattaro, G.: Scc: A service centered calculus. In: Bravetti, M., Núñez, M., Zavattaro, G. (eds.) WS-FM 2006. LNCS, vol. 4184, pp. 38–57. Springer, Heidelberg (2006)
5. Carbone, M., Honda, K., Yoshida, N.: Structured communication-centred programming for web services. In: De Nicola, R. (ed.) ESOP 2007. LNCS, vol. 4421, pp. 2–17. Springer, Heidelberg (2007)
6. Ciancia, V., Ferrari, G.L.: Co-Algebraic Models for Quantitative Spatial Logics. In: Quantitative Aspects of Programming Languages (QAPL 2007) (2007)

7. Ciancia, V., Montanari, U.: A name abstraction functor for named sets. Coalgebraic Methods in Computer Science (to appear, 2008)
8. Ferrari, G.L., Guanciale, R., Strollo, D.: Event based service coordination over dynamic and heterogeneous networks. In: Dan, A., Lamersdorf, W. (eds.) ICSOC 2006. LNCS, vol. 4294, pp. 453–458. Springer, Heidelberg (2006)
9. Ferrari, G.L., Montanari, U., Tuosto, E.: Coalgebraic minimization of hd-automata for the pi-calculus using polymorphic types. Theor. Comput. Sci. 331(2-3), 325–365 (2005)
10. Ferrari, G., Guanciale, R., Strollo, D.: Jscl: A middleware for service coordination. In: Najm, et al. [21], pp. 46–60.
11. Ferrari, G., Guanciale, R., Strollo, D.: An Eclipse plugin for designing and developing Web Service orchestrations in JSCL. Technical report (2007)
12. Ferrari, G., Guanciale, R., Strollo, D., Tuosto, E.: Coordination via types in an event-based framework. In: Derrick, J., Vain, J. (eds.) FORTE 2007. LNCS, vol. 4574, pp. 66–80. Springer, Heidelberg (2007)
13. Object Management Group. Business process modelling notation. Technical report, http://www.bpmn.org
14. Guidi, C., Lucchi, R., Gorrieri, R., Busi, N., Zavattaro, G.: A calculus for service oriented computing. In: Dan, A., Lamersdorf, W. (eds.) ICSOC 2006. LNCS, vol. 4294, pp. 327–338. Springer, Heidelberg (2006)
15. Honda, K., Tokoro, M.: An object calculus for asynchronous communication. In: America, P. (ed.) ECOOP 1991. LNCS, vol. 512, pp. 133–147. Springer, Heidelberg (1991)
16. IBM. Business Process Execution Language (BPEL). Technical report (2005)
17. Lapadula, A., Pugliese, R., Tiezzi, F.: A calculus for orchestration of web services. In: De Nicola, R. (ed.) ESOP 2007. LNCS, vol. 4421, pp. 33–47. Springer, Heidelberg (2007)
18. Liu, Y., Plale, B.: Survey of publish subscribe event systems. Technical Report 574, Department of Computer Science, Indiana University
19. Misra, J.: A programming model for the orchestration of web services. In: SEFM, pp. 2–11. IEEE Computer Society, Los Alamitos (2004)
20. Montanari, U., Pistore, M.: History Dependent Automata. Technical report, Dipartimento di Informatica, Università di Pisa, TR-11-98 (1998)
21. Najm, E., Pradat-Peyre, J.-F., Donzeau-Gouge, V.V. (eds.): FORTE 2006. LNCS, vol. 4229. Springer, Heidelberg (2006)
22. OMG. Business Process Modeling Language (2002), http://www.bpmi.org
23. W3C. Web Services Choreography Description Language (v.1.0). Technical report
24. Wirsing, M., Clark, A., Gilmore, S., Hölzl, M.M., Knapp, A., Koch, N., Schroeder, A.: Semantic-based development of service-oriented systems. In Najm, et al [21], pp. 24–45

Specifying and Verifying Web Transactions*

Jing Li, Huibiao Zhu, and Jifeng He

Shanghai Key Laboratory of Trustworthy Computing
East China Normal University
Shanghai, China, 200062
{jli, hbzhu, jifeng}@sei.ecnu.edu.cn

Abstract. New evolving internet technologies are extending the role of the World Wide Web from a platform of information exhibition to a new environment for service interactions. While new business opportunities are brought in under this new era of internet, novel challenges are coming out at the same time. Current technologies have been found lacking efficient support for web transactions. Because transactions in the context of web services have distinct features, such as autonomous and interactive, the traditional automatic mechanisms of resource locking and rollback are proved to be inappropriate. For this reason, we suggest that web transactions are constructed through a series of compensable transactions, using the concept of compensation to ensure a relatively relaxed atomicity. This paper formally expresses the composition structures and behavioral dependencies of compensable transactions. Based on the formal description for a transaction model, we are able to further verify its transactional behavior according to the specified requirement of relaxed atomicity and more precise behavioral properties with temporal constraints.

1 Introduction

Web Services are becoming the current most promising paradigm for enabling business interactions through the Internet. They have greatly influenced the way for application development. Web services can be regarded as computational entities, generally independent and autonomous. They are driven by XML related technologies which make services able to be described, discovered and invoked across the internet. Based on more and more accessible services over the Web, there is an opportunity to provide new value-added services to customers by combining individual services. Therefore, extensions of web service technologies have been considered. Several proposals for describing web service composition (XLANG, WSFL, BPEL and WSCDL) have been already put forward.

When a composite web service combines several existing services to complete a given task, a web transaction is required to orchestrate the loosely coupled services into a unit of work so as to guarantee a reliable execution. However, setting

---

* Supported by National Basic Research Program of China (No.2005CB321904), National High Technology Research and Development Program of China (No.2007AA 010302), National Natural Science Foundation of China (No.90718004).

K. Suzuki et al. (Eds.): FORTE 2008, LNCS 5048, pp. 149–168, 2008.

up an efficient web transaction is not a trivial task. First of all, web transactions usually require a long time to complete, due mainly to lengthy computation and pause for input from users, which may cause severe performance problems. Such long lived transactions greatly increase the contention for resources and finally lead to more deadlocks. Secondly, for a web transaction, its participating services may belong to different and even competing companies such that services are generally independent and autonomous. In such systems, there is no chance to intentionally block the resources residing in other services. Lastly, web transactions usually involve communications between companies and human beings, where the outcome of interactions cannot be physically undone. Thus, the pure rollback mechanism is not applicable at all. Therefore, the key features of traditional transactions become impracticable for web transactions. To solve this problem, the degree of atomicity needs to be relaxed. A weaker notion of atomicity based on compensation has been proposed to recover from failure.

The notion of compensation has its root to the seminal work of Sagas [8] which is one of the first proposals for extended transactional models. A saga is a long lived transaction which is partitioned into a set of sub-transactions. When a sub-transaction completes, it commits prior to the completion of the whole saga. This enables resources to be released earlier and thus reduces the possibilities of deadlock. However, partial effects have been exposed to the outside. In this case, each sub-transaction is associated with a compensation whose responsibility is to semantically undo the effect of its sub-transaction. Thus, whenever a sub-transaction aborts in the middle, the partial results made by the committed sub-transactions will be removed by executing their compensations.

This paper suggests to construct a web transaction in terms of compensable transactions. A compensable transaction is a new type of transaction whose effect can be semantically undone even after it has committed. Basically, a compensable transaction consists of two parts: forward flow and compensation flow. The forward flow describes the required normal logic according to system requirements, while the compensation flow is properly defined so as to undo the effect of its forward flow semantically. Unlike the traditional ACID transactions, a compensable transaction has distinct features. Its features allow web transactions to incorporate different transactional semantics as well as different behavioral dependency patterns. This provides a manner to enhance the flexibility and reliability of web transactions. In order to provide a precise description, we adopt the novel transactional language t-calculus [14] to model the composition structure of compensable transactions. Moreover, the behavioral semantics is precisely defined for different transactional constructs.

Compensation is a kind of backward recovery in the presence of failure. In order to promote the possibility of successful completion, our transaction model also supports forward recovery so as to survive the failure caused by a certain sub-transaction. In this case, there is no need to obey the strict requirement of all-or-compensated. The notion of *acceptable termination states* (ATS) is used to express the relaxed atomicity requirement. Given a web transaction, we are able to verify its behavior according to the specified ATS. Further, we can also

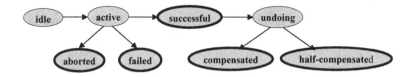

Fig. 1. The state transition diagram of compensable transactions

help to find inconsistencies if its behavior is proved to be invalid. In addition, depending on particular applications for which web transactions are designed, additional properties capable of expressing temporal constraints would be required. Here, we propose a specification language to specify this kind of transactional properties. The corresponding process for verifying whether these properties are satisfied is formally presented subsequently.

This paper is organized as follows. Section 2 gives a detailed description about compensable transactions whose execution structure is clearly depicted by a state transition diagram. The transactional model with the corresponding language is presented in Section 3, where related behavioral dependencies are formally specified. Section 4 presents strict solutions to the verification of web transactions according to the specified requirements. We discuss some related work in Section 5 and conclude this paper at last.

2   Compensable Transaction

Compensable transactions are the basic constituents for building web transactions in our approach. A compensable transaction aims to do a specific task as part of a business goal. Different from traditional transactions, a compensable transaction can withdraw its result after its commitment in case of error. On the transaction level, we do not model its internal operations but only deal with its external visible aspects. We adopt the *state transition diagram* to describe its behavior structure by providing a set of execution states and a set of transitions between these states. The Figure 1 shows the state transition diagram for an arbitrary compensable transaction.

A compensable transaction has eight states and five of them are terminal states shown by bold ellipses in Figure 1. Initially, its state is marked as *idle* and it becomes *active* when it is arranged for execution. Once it is active, it can be either *aborted* or *failed* due to the presence of failure, or it finally achieves its objective and leads to the *successful* state. Whenever some wrong has happened during its execution or within other concurrent transactions, it tries to erase its partial outcome as soon as possible. If all the partial effects have been erased, it becomes aborted as if nothing has ever been done. Otherwise, it turns into failed since some partial effect still exists. This case possibly results in data inconsistency. Especially, the effect after completion for compensable transactions does not remain for ever. When it has succeeded, its effect can be semantically undone by properly defined compensation. Once the system decides to undo a successful compensable transaction, this transaction enters into the *undoing* state. During this period, its associated compensation is executing. The final state is totally dependent on the execution result of its compensation. When the compensation fails in the middle, it is marked as *half-compensated*, otherwise as *compensated*.

Let $\mathcal{T}$ be a finite set of compensable transactions, and Σ be a finite set of transactional states. Here, Σ is defined as:

$$\Sigma = \{idl, act, suc, abt, fal, und, cmp, hap\}$$

where they stand for the fore-mentioned eight states (idle, active, successful, aborted, failed, undoing, compensated and half-compensated). Moreover, we let Δ be the set of terminal states, that is:

$$\Delta = \{suc, abt, fal, cmp, hap\}$$

An *action* a on $\mathcal{T}$ and Σ is a pair $(T, \sigma) \in \mathcal{T} \times \Sigma$, saying the transaction T enters into the state σ. Especially, a *terminal action* is a special kind of action, which is a pair satisfying $(T, \sigma) \in \mathcal{T} \times \Delta$. Actions may follow a specified order or conform to some other policies. Here, we propose five relations to enforce different constraints on the occurrence of actions:

1. $a < b$: only a can fire b.
2. $a \prec b$: b can be fired by a.
3. $a \ll b$: a is the precondition of b.
4. $a \leftrightarrow b$: a and b both occur or both not.
5. $a \not\leftrightarrow b$: the occurrence of one action inhibits the other.

The first three relations specify a kind of order, whereas the last two do not. $a < b$ indicates a must precede b when two actions both occur. In addition, the two actions must both appear or not, same as $a \leftrightarrow b$ in this sense. However, $a \leftrightarrow b$ does not enforce any temporal constraint on actions. $a \prec b$ tells that b can also be fired by other event except for a. In other words, b is able to occur without the previous occurrence of a. $a \ll b$ tells that a must occur earlier whenever b occurs. However, the occurrence of a does not guarantee a following occurrence of b. Finally, $a \not\leftrightarrow b$ denotes that the two actions must be mutually exclusive. These relations have some useful and interesting properties. $<$, $\prec$ and $\ll$ are anti-symmetric and transitive. $\leftrightarrow$ is reflexive, symmetric and transitive, while $\not\leftrightarrow$ is irreflexive, symmetric and intransitive. Besides, there are more useful properties when these relations are combined.

Law 1. If $a < b$ and $a \leftrightarrow c$ then $b \leftrightarrow c$

Law 2. If $a < b$ and $b \leftrightarrow c$ then $a \leftrightarrow c$

Law 3. If $a < b$ and $b \circ c$ ($\circ \in \{\prec, \ll\}$) then $a \circ c$

Law 4. If $a \circ b$ ($\circ \in \{\prec, \ll\}$) and $b < c$ then $a \circ c$

Law 5. If $a \circ b$ ($\circ \in \{<, \prec, \leftrightarrow\}$) and $b \not\leftrightarrow c$ then $a \not\leftrightarrow c$

Law 6. If $a \circ b$ ($\circ \in \{<, \ll, \leftrightarrow\}$) and $a \not\leftrightarrow c$ then $b \not\leftrightarrow c$

Table 1. Intra-constraints of a compensable transaction

$(T, idl) \ll (T, act)$	$(T, act) \ll (T, suc)$	$(T, act) \ll (T, abt)$	$(T, act) \ll (T, fal)$
$(T, suc) \leftrightarrow (T, abt)$	$(T, suc) \leftrightarrow (T, fal)$	$(T, abt) \leftrightarrow (T, fal)$	$(T, cmp) \leftrightarrow (T, hap)$
$(T, suc) \ll (T, und)$	$(T, und) \ll (T, cmp)$	$(T, und) \ll (T, hap)$	

As for an arbitrary compensable transaction T, all the actions occurring during its execution must satisfy some constraints which are clearly shown in Table 1. For instance, the compensation can only be activated when the transaction T has succeeded, expressed as $(T, suc) \ll (T, und)$. Besides, terminal states must be exclusive, e.g., $(T, suc) \leftrightarrow (T, abt)$, $(T, cmp) \leftrightarrow (T, hap)$.

3   The Transactional Model

Though the structure of a compensable transaction is relatively complex, its distinct properties provide the opportunity for engineers to resolve the performance problem caused by web transactions. In this section, we explain how to build reliable web transactions on the basis of compensable transactions. A novel transactional language t-calculus is adopted to describe the composition structure of compensable transactions. Its syntax is shown below:

$$S, T ::= BT \mid S; T \mid S \parallel T \mid S \sqcap T \mid S \otimes T \mid$$
$$S \rightsquigarrow T \mid S \trianglerighteq T \mid S \triangleright T \mid S * T$$
$$P ::= \{T\}$$

The basic transaction BT is the primary block to form a compensable transaction. Generally, BT is composed of two activities, one denotes the forward flow while the other one represents its compensation. More details of basic transactions can be found in [14] but not relevant in this paper. The key point is that compensable transactions support composition, that is, it can be constructed out of simpler ones and still preserves the features of compensable transactions. To deal with specific requirements of web transactions, we incorporate some distinct composition constructs in this transactional model. These new constructs help to build a web transaction with a higher quality which mainly comes from three directions:

– *Flexibility* is enforced by allowing users to provide functionally equivalent sub-transactions for a given objective. These equivalent transactions may have different or even priorities. Transactions with even priorities can be arranged to run in parallel, expressed as $S \otimes T$. Otherwise, the transaction with higher priority must be executed first, expressed as $S \rightsquigarrow T$. Note that if one of these transactions completes successfully, the objective is achieved.
– *Reliability* is enhanced by properly dealing with partial compensations. We have shown in Figure 1 that partial compensation will make a compensable transaction into the *half-compensated* state in which data consistency does not hold at all. In order to keep the whole system consistent, partial compensation needs further treatment which is referred as *exception handling*. $S \trianglerighteq T$ and $S \triangleright T$ are two kinds of proposed mechanisms for exception handling.

– *Specialization* is added by offering specialized compensations for specific applications. Basically, the compensation of a composite transaction is constructed by the accumulation of those of its sub-transactions. Concerning the requirement of a concrete application, it is more satisfactory for developers to directly define an appropriate compensation, expressed as $S * T$.

Finally, we use $\{T\}$ to stand for a complete web transaction. Once a web transaction completes, its effect holds for ever. An aborted web transaction looks like doing nothing from the view of an external observer. A failed web transaction causes some loss due to its inconsistent status. Our transactional model can not avoid inconsistency, but it helps to reduce the possibilities of such failure.

3.1 Behavioral Dependencies

In t-calculus, each composite construct stipulates distinct behavioral dependencies between compensable transactions. It specifies how simpler compensable transactions are coupled and how the behavior of a certain compensable transaction influences the behavior of the other. Further, it specifies how the behaviors of sub-transactions determine the behavior of their composite transaction. In the following, we formally describe the behavioral dependencies for all the transactional constructs.

Sequential composition: $S; T$ arranges the first transaction S to be executed first. Only when S finishes its task, the following transaction T will be activated to run. However, whenever T is aborted or compensated, the completed transaction S would be compensated so as to remove all the partial effects. The above description reflects the following behavioral dependencies:

$$(S, suc) < (T, act) \tag{; 1}$$
$$(T, abt) \prec (S, und) \tag{; 2}$$
$$(T, cmp) \prec (S, und) \tag{; 3}$$

Recall that any compensable transaction satisfies some internal constraints (Table 1), e.g., $(S, suc) \leftrightarrow (S, abt)$ and $(T, act) \ll (T, suc)$. By using (; 1) and Law 6, we have that $(T, act) \leftrightarrow (S, abt)$. Then using Law 6 and the symmetry property of $\leftrightarrow$, we get that $(S, abt) \leftrightarrow (T, suc)$ which says the abortion of S would never lead to the success of T. Similarly, we can deduce more dependencies as follows:

$$(S, suc) \ll (T, \alpha) \quad \alpha \in \Delta \tag{; 4}$$
$$(S, \alpha) \leftrightarrow (T, \beta) \quad \alpha \in \{abt, fal\}, \ \beta \neq idl \tag{; 5}$$
$$(S, \alpha) \leftrightarrow (T, \beta) \quad \alpha \in \{cmp, hap\}, \ \beta \in \{fal, hap\} \tag{; 6}$$

The last item (; 6) tells that if T is failed or half-compensated, the compensation of the former transaction S will never be enabled. Now we are going to investigate the relationship between the composite transaction and its sub-transactions. A composite transaction is also a compensable transaction and its terminal state is totally dependent on the terminal states of its sub-transactions. Here, we focus our attention on terminal actions which are associated with terminal states. The behavior of a composite transaction is recorded by sequences of terminal actions which are referred as *transactional traces*. For any composite transaction T, the symbol $[(T, \sigma)]$ denotes all these transactional traces which finally cause T to end in the terminal state σ ($\sigma \in \Delta$). Especially, if T is a basic transaction, then it just has one single transactional trace, that is:

$$[(T, \sigma)] = \{\langle (T, \sigma) \rangle\}$$

Next we define the behavior of T as the union of transactional traces for all terminal states, denoted as $[\![T]\!]$:

$$[\![T]\!] = \bigcup_{\sigma \in \Delta} [(T, \sigma)]$$

In the following, we will define the behavior of sequential composition in terms of transactional traces. We write st for the concatenation of two traces s and t. The successful completion of $S; T$ requires both S and T to succeed.

$$[(S; T, suc)] = \{st \mid s \in [(S, suc)] \wedge t \in [(T, suc)]\}$$

Abortion of $S; T$ is caused by either an abortion or a full compensation of S.

$$[(S; T, abt)] = [(S, abt)] \cup \{sts' \mid s \in [(S, suc)] \wedge t \in [(T, abt)] \wedge s' \in [(S, cmp)]\}$$

The failure of S or T directly leads to the failure of $S; T$. Besides, the half-compensation of S results in the same outcome too.

$$[(S; T, fal)] = [(S, fal)] \cup \{st \mid s \in [(S, suc)] \wedge t \in [(T, fal)]\} \cup \\ \{sts' \mid s \in [(S, suc)] \wedge t \in [(T, abt)] \wedge s' \in [(S, hap)]\}$$

A full compensation of $S; T$ means both sub-transactions have been compensated utterly. Note that sub-transactions are compensated in a reverse order to their original sequence.

$$[(S; T, cmp)] = \{ts \mid t \in [(T, cmp)] \wedge s \in [(S, cmp)]\}$$

A partial compensation of $S; T$ is rendered by a failed compensating execution of either sub-transaction.

$$[(S; T, hap)] = [(T, hap)] \cup \{ts \mid t \in [(T, cmp)] \wedge s \in [(S, hap)]\}$$

Note that the occurrences of $(S; T, cmp)$ and $(S; T, hap)$ require a precondition implicitly, that is, the whole transaction $S; T$ has already completed successfully.

Parallel composition: For $S \parallel T$, both branches S and T are executed in parallel. Likewise, their compensations are also activated concurrently when semantic rollback is needed. If one branch aborts or fails, the other branch is willing to disrupt its flow and yield to this failure. In other words, two branches must both succeed or both not. The related behavioral dependencies are formalized as follows:

$(S, act) \leftrightarrow (T, act)$ $(\parallel 1)$
$(S, und) \leftrightarrow (T, und)$ $(\parallel 2)$
$(S, suc) \leftrightarrow (T, suc)$ $(\parallel 3)$

More dependencies can be deduced:

$$(S, \alpha) \leftrightarrow (T, \beta) \ \alpha \in \{abt, fal\}, \beta \in \{suc, cmp, hap\} \tag{$\|$ 4}$$
$$(T, \alpha) \leftrightarrow (S, \beta) \ \alpha \in \{abt, fal\}, \beta \in \{suc, cmp, hap\} \tag{$\|$ 5}$$

The behavior of parallel composition needs to take interleaving into consideration. In the following, the symbol $s \, \| \, t$ denotes the set of transactional traces which are combinations of s and t.

The successful completion of $S \| T$ achieves only when both branches succeed.

$$[(S \| T, suc)] = \{r \mid r \in s \, \| \, t \wedge s \in [(S, suc)] \wedge t \in [(T, suc)]\}$$

The abortion of $S \| T$ is caused by the abortion of both branches.

$$[(S \| T, abt)] = \{r \mid r \in s \, \| \, t \wedge s \in [(S, abt)] \wedge t \in [(T, abt)]\}$$

The failure of either branch causes the failure of $S \| T$.

$$[(S \| T, fal)] = \{r \mid r \in s \, \| \, t \wedge s \in [(S, fal)] \wedge t \in [(T, abt)]\}$$
$$\cup \{r \mid r \in s \, \| \, t \wedge s \in [(S, abt)] \wedge t \in [(T, fal)]\}$$
$$\cup \{r \mid r \in s \, \| \, t \wedge s \in [(S, fal)] \wedge t \in [(T, fal)]\}$$

A full compensation of $S \| T$ means that both branches have been compensated successfully. Note that both branches are compensated in parallel too.

$$[(S \| T, cmp)] = \{r \mid r \in s \, \| \, t \ \wedge s \in [(S, cmp)] \wedge t \in [(T, cmp)]\}$$

A partial compensation of $S \| T$ arises from a failed compensation of either branch.

$$[(S \| T, hap)] = \{r \mid r \in s \, \| \, t \wedge s \in [(S, hap)] \wedge t \in [(T, cmp)]\}$$
$$\cup \{r \mid r \in s \, \| \, t \wedge s \in [(S, cmp)] \wedge t \in [(T, hap)]\}$$
$$\cup \{r \mid r \in s \, \| \, t \wedge s \in [(S, hap)] \wedge t \in [(T, hap)]\}$$

Internal choice: In some cases, only one branch is selected in accordance with internal decisions. In the construct of $S \sqcap T$, only S or T will be activated:

$$(S, act) \leftrightarrow (T, act) \tag{$\sqcap$ 1}$$

Further, we get that only one branch will terminate:

$$(S, \alpha) \leftrightarrow (T, \beta) \ \ \{\alpha, \beta\} \subseteq \Delta \tag{$\sqcap$ 2}$$

The behavior of $S \sqcap T$ is directly defined as follows:

$$[S \sqcap T] = [S] \cup [T]$$

Speculative choice: This construct provides a way for developers to design two or more threads to finish one task. If one thread is aborted, the other thread is still active trying to achieve the same target. In this construct of $S \otimes T$, S and T are two sub-transactions with equivalent functions. The two sub-transactions have even priorities and they are arranged to be executed concurrently. The choice is delayed when one sub-transaction has succeeded. That is, only one sub-transaction will be finally selected to achieve its business goal. When one sub-transaction terminates successfully, the other one cannot succeed but aborts either internally or forcibly. Especially, if one sub-transaction fails halfway, the other one should yield to this failure. The related behavioral dependencies are formalized below:

$$(S, act) \leftrightarrow (T, act) \qquad\qquad (\otimes\ 1)$$
$$(S, suc) \not\leftrightarrow (T, suc) \qquad\qquad (\otimes\ 2)$$
$$(S, suc) \not\leftrightarrow (T, fal) \qquad\qquad (\otimes\ 3)$$
$$(T, suc) \not\leftrightarrow (S, fal) \qquad\qquad (\otimes\ 4)$$

The above dependencies imply that only one sub-transaction can be compensated if compensation is needed.

$$(S, \alpha) \not\leftrightarrow (T, \beta) \quad \{\alpha, \beta\} \subseteq \{cmp, hap\} \qquad\qquad (\otimes\ 5)$$

Speculative choice is a construct which behaves partially like parallel composition by allowing concurrent executions and partially like internal choice by choosing one sub-transaction to fulfil the objective.

The successful completion of $S \otimes T$ realizes when one branch succeeds and another one aborts.

$$[(S \otimes T, suc)] = \{r \mid r \in s \;|||\; t \wedge s \in [(S, suc)] \wedge t \in [(T, abt)]\}$$
$$\cup \{r \mid r \in s \;|||\; t \wedge s \in [(S, abt)] \wedge t \in [(T, suc)]\}$$

The abortion of $S \otimes T$ is due to the abortion of both branches.

$$[(S \otimes T, abt)] = \{r \mid r \in s \;|||\; t \wedge s \in [(S, abt)] \wedge t \in [(T, abt)]\}$$

Likewise, the failure of either branch will finally lead to the failure of the whole composition $S \otimes T$.

$$[(S \otimes T, fal)] = \{r \mid r \in s \;|||\; t \wedge s \in [(S, fal)] \wedge t \in [(T, abt)]\}$$
$$\cup \{r \mid r \in s \;|||\; t \wedge s \in [(S, abt)] \wedge t \in [(T, fal)]\}$$
$$\cup \{r \mid r \in s \;|||\; t \wedge s \in [(S, fal)] \wedge t \in [(T, fal)]\}$$

Since only one branch can succeed, then just the successful one will be compensated. A full compensation or a partial compensation is determined by the successful branch.

$$[(S \otimes T, \alpha)] = \begin{cases} [(S, \alpha)] & \text{if } S \text{ has succeeded} \\ [(T, \alpha)] & \text{if } T \text{ has succeeded} \end{cases} \quad \alpha \in \{cmp, hap\}$$

Alternative forwarding: Similar to speculative choice, this construct also provides two functionally equivalent sub-transactions to achieve one business goal. The difference is that these two sub-transactions have distinct priorities. In addition, the one with the higher priority is executed first and the other is activated only when the first one has been aborted. In $S \rightsquigarrow T$, S is planed to run first and T is the backup of S. The related dependency is given below:

$$(S, abt) < (T, act) \qquad\qquad (\rightsquigarrow 1)$$

Then we get the following dependencies:

$$(S, abt) \ll (T, \alpha) \quad \alpha \in \Delta \qquad\qquad (\rightsquigarrow 2)$$
$$(S, \alpha) \leftrightarrow (T, \beta) \quad \alpha \in \Delta - \{abt\}, \beta \in \Delta \qquad (\rightsquigarrow 3)$$

The behavior of alternative forwarding corresponds to a sequential execution. Different from sequential composition, the right branch is enabled on abortion instead of on success of the left branch.

The successful completion of $S \rightsquigarrow T$ achieves when there is one branch which succeeds eventually.

$$[(S \rightsquigarrow T, suc)] = [(S, suc)] \cup \{st \mid s \in [(S, abt)] \wedge t \in [(T, suc)]\}$$

The abortion of $S \rightsquigarrow T$ is caused by the abortion of its alternative T.

$$[(S \rightsquigarrow T, abt)] = \{st \mid s \in [(S, abt)] \wedge t \in [(T, abt)]\}$$

The failure of $S \rightsquigarrow T$ is due to the failure of either branch.

$$[(S \rightsquigarrow T, fal)] = [(S, fal)] \cup \{st \mid s \in [(S, abt)] \wedge t \in [(T, fal)]\}$$

In this construct, only one branch can succeed in the end. Thus, the definitions of $[(S \rightsquigarrow T, cmp)]$ and $[(S \rightsquigarrow T, hap)]$ are as same as those for speculative choice.

Backward handling: Partial compensation leads to inconsistency which is unwelcome by the users. The failure of a composite transaction is ultimately caused by the half-compensated state of one of its sub-transactions provided that basic transactions cannot fail. Backward handling $S \triangleright T$ is such a construct that provides a backward handler T to remedy the failure thrown by S. This handler tries to undo all the remaining effects which are not covered by partial compensation. The handler T is triggered on the failure of S, that is:

$$(S, fal) < (T, act) \qquad\qquad (\triangleright 1)$$

Consequently, we get that:

$$(S, fal) \ll (T, \alpha) \quad \alpha \in \Delta \qquad\qquad (\triangleright 2)$$
$$(S, \alpha) \leftrightarrow (T, \beta) \quad \alpha \in \Delta - \{fal\}, \beta \in \Delta \qquad (\triangleright 3)$$

Note that this construct offers a kind of backward recovery mechanism, for the backward handler is devised to undo the remaining partial effects.

The successful completion of $S \triangleright T$ realizes when the left branch S succeeds.

$$[(S \triangleright T, suc)] = [(S, suc)]$$

The abortion of $S \triangleright T$ is caused by the abortion of the left branch S or the successful completion of the handler T.

$$[(S \triangleright T, abt)] = [(S, abt)] \cup \{st \mid s \in [(S, fal)] \wedge t \in [(T, suc)]\}$$

The failure of S fires the activation of T and the thrown failure can be thoroughly cleared only when the handler T succeeds. Hence, either failure or abortion of T will cause the final failure of the whole composition $S \unrhd T$.

$$[(S \unrhd T, fal)] = \{st \mid s \in [(S, fal)] \wedge t \in [(T, abt)] \cup [(T, fal)]\}$$

Since only the success of the left branch S leads to the successful composition of $S \unrhd T$, the compensation result is totally dependent on the compensation of S.

$$[(S \unrhd T, cmp)] = [(S, cmp)] \qquad [(S \unrhd T, hap)] = [(S, hap)]$$

Forward handling: This is another manner to deal with partial compensation apart from backward handling. In $S \rhd T$, T is the forward handler to fix the failure thrown by S. Different from backward handling, this construct adopts the forward recovery mechanism trying to fulfill the business goal in the presence of failure. In other words, if the forward handler completes, the whole composition is regarded as success though some error has occurred previously. Likewise, this handler T can only be activated by the failure of S:

$$(S, fal) < (T, act) \qquad\qquad\qquad (\rhd\ 1)$$

Consequently, we get that:

$$
\begin{aligned}
(S, fal) &\ll (T, \alpha) & \alpha \in \Delta & \qquad (\rhd\ 2)\\
(S, \alpha) &\leftrightarrow (T, \beta) & \alpha \in \Delta - \{fal\}, \beta \in \Delta & \qquad (\rhd\ 3)
\end{aligned}
$$

The successful completion of $S \rhd T$ realizes when either branch succeeds.

$$[(S \rhd T, suc)] = [(S, suc)] \cup \{st \mid s \in [(S, fal)] \wedge t \in [(T, suc)]\}$$

The abortion of $S \rhd T$ is caused by the abortion of S.

$$[(S \rhd T, abt)] = [(S, abt)]$$

The abortion of T means the handler does nothing essential and thus the previous failure has not been resolved at all. Then either failure or abortion of T will make the whole composition $S \rhd T$ into the failed state.

$$[(S \rhd T, fal)] = \{st \mid s \in [(S, fal)] \wedge t \in [(T, abt)] \cup [(T, fal)]\}$$

Since both branches can lead to the success of $S \rhd T$, we should first judge which branch has succeeded and then be sure whose compensation is activated while undoing. Hence, the definitions of $[(S \rhd T, cmp)]$ and $[(S \rhd T, hap)]$ are as same as those for speculative choice.

Programmable compensation: Primarily, the compensation is attached through the transactional pair which is a central construct to compose activities [14]. As for a composite transaction, the developers sometimes need to program a new compensation so as to satisfy a specific application requirement. Thus, the construct of $S \ast T$ is added to meet this demand. Formerly, the compensation of

S is constructed by the accumulation of those of its sub-transactions. Here, T is the newly programmed compensation for S, while the original accumulated one is simply discarded. When S has completed, its new compensation T is waiting to be enabled so that the effect of S can be semantically removed in case some error occurs later:

$$(S, suc) \ll (T, act) \qquad\qquad\qquad (* 1)$$

By using the transitive property of $\ll$ and dependencies listed in Table 1, we have that:

$$(S, suc) \ll (T, \alpha) \quad \alpha \in \Delta \qquad\qquad\qquad (* 2)$$

In our model, compensation is also a compensable transaction. Thus we allow this kind of composition, such as $S * (T_1 \rightsquigarrow T_2)$ in which S has two alternative compensations. Moreover, the actions (T, cmp) and (T, hap) have no chance to take place since compensation for compensation will never be used.

The behavior of $S*T$ is quite simple, S decides whether the whole composition is successful, aborted or failed. Whereas the new compensation T determines whether the whole composition is compensated completely or partially.

$$[(S * T, \alpha)] = [(S, \alpha)] \qquad \alpha \in \{suc, abt, fal\}$$
$$[(S * T, cmp)] = [(T, suc)]$$
$$[(S * T, hap)] = [(T, \alpha)] \qquad \alpha \in \{abt, fal\}$$

3.2   A Case Study

Now let us presents a real web transaction dedicated to the processing of customer orders. This description is carried out by compensable transactions illustrated in Figure 2. Firstly, an order request from a customer is accepted and this step is compensated by notifying the customer this request is canceled. Then money will be deducted from the credit card providing that the credit checking has passed. Afterwards, all the ordered items are packed for shipment and this step is compensated by unpacking. Simultaneously with packing items, the seller books shippers for delivery. In this example, we make an assumption that this seller has only two shippers (shipper A and shipper B) to contact with. Shipper A is cheaper but hard to book whereas shipper B is more expensive but always available. For the sake of saving money, shipper A is preferred and shipper B is booked only when shipper A is unavailable. At last, the selected shipper is responsible for delivering these items. Note that if the customer cancels the order during processing, the compensation for completed parts will be activated. When the compensation cannot properly undo the partial effects, the seller would ask for extra indemnities from the customer which is transacted by backward handling.

The transactional flow described above is not always satisfactory. Sometimes, the customer needs the goods urgently because of his timing requirement. However, the process of credit checking may cost so much time that transportation

$$OrderTrans = \{(ProcessRequest; OrderProcess) \trianglerighteq GetIndemnity\}$$
$$OrderProcess = PayByCard; (PrepareOrder \parallel ContactShipper); DeliverOrder$$
$$ProcessRequest = AcceptOrder * CancelOrder$$
$$PayByCard = (CheckCredit; DeductMoney) * RefundMoney$$
$$PrepareOrder = PackItems * UnpackItems$$
$$ContactShipper = BookShipperA \rightsquigarrow BookShipperB$$

Fig. 2. Transaction for order fulfillment

will be delayed. In this case, the seller would like to deal with payment in parallel with packing items. On the other hand, in order to be more reliable, sometimes transporting items by more than one shipper would be a better solution. Overall, the transactional flow designed in hand should satisfy specific application requirements. In the following section, we will introduce two kinds of representations to express application requirements. Further we will propose strict solutions to the verification of web transactions.

4 Verification

In this section, we mention two notions for specifying application requirements. One is referred as acceptable termination states (ATS) as a correctness criteria to specify relaxed atomicity requirements. Another one is a specification language used for expressing temporal constraints with regard to transactional properties.

4.1 Acceptable Termination States

Let $T.\sigma$ ($\sigma \in \Delta \cup \{idl\}$) represent the final state σ of the compensable transaction T. Especially, $T.idl$ denotes that T terminates without activation. As for a web transaction $\{T\}$, a termination state of $\{T\}$ is described by a set of final states of its sub-transactions $\{T_1.\sigma_1, T_2.\sigma_2, \ldots, T_n.\sigma_n\}$, where T_i is a sub-transaction of T. For example, given a transaction $T = \{(T_1 \trianglerighteq T_2); T_3\}$, one of its termination states is $\{T_1.fal, T_2.suc, T_3.idl\}$. It says that T terminates when T_1 fails and T_2 succeeds without activating T_3.

Let Ω be the set of transactions in which the designer is interested when investigating the termination states. Each transaction in Ω can be a composite transaction. Further, we require that for two arbitrary transactions $S, T \in \Omega$, T cannot be the sub-transaction of S and vice versa. An *acceptable termination state* of a web transaction $\{T\}$ is a termination state limited to Ω in which the designer expect to see $\{T\}$ ends without raising any inconsistency. In other words, an acceptable termination state is a termination state in which this transaction finally succeeds or aborts but not fails. The set of all acceptable termination states specified by the designer is denoted as ATS.

Let $\lfloor T.\sigma \rfloor$ be the set of termination states in which T ends in σ. A web transaction $\{T\}$ is invalid if there is a termination state belonging to ATS which cannot make $\{T\}$ successful or aborted.

Definition 4.1. *A web transaction* $\{T\}$ *is said to be valid according to its acceptable termination states* ATS *if and only if* $ATS \subseteq \lfloor T.suc \rfloor \cup \lfloor T.abt \rfloor$

It is worth noting that it is much better if there are more termination states in which $\{T\}$ cannot fail except for those in ATS. In order to verify a valid web transaction, we should know the values of $\lfloor T.suc \rfloor$ and $\lfloor T.abt \rfloor$. As mentioned before, the transactional behavior is recorded by transactional traces. Now we transform transactional traces to termination states such that $\lfloor T.\sigma \rfloor$ can be derived from $[(T, \sigma)]$. Five steps need to be done in sequence:

1. While computing transactional traces, every interested transaction does not expand. That is, $[(T, \sigma)](T \in \Omega)$ is defined as $\{\langle(T, \sigma)\rangle\}$ without considering its sub-transactions.
2. If there are two actions related to one transaction in a transactional trace, the first one is removed while the latter one is preserved.
3. For any transactional trace t, its element (S, σ) is removed if S is not in Ω. New element (S, idl) is inserted if S is in Ω but not mentioned in t.
4. Elements of a transactional trace are actions with the form of (T, σ), while elements of a terminate state are states with the form of $T.\sigma$. Thus the form of elements should be changed from (T, σ) into $T.\sigma$.
5. Elements in a transactional trace are ordered but elements in a termination state are not. Finally, we extract the order information from traces by turning sequences into sets.

When a transaction T is compensated, some transactional traces contain two actions about T. The first action is (T, suc) and the following action is either (T, cmp) or (T, hap). The second step above is intended to remove the first action which is actually an interim state.

So far, we are able to compute $\lfloor T.\sigma \rfloor$ $(\sigma \in \Delta)$ for any T. Further, we need one more definition to help compute $\lfloor T.idl \rfloor$:

$$\lfloor T.idl \rfloor = \{\{T.idl\}\} \qquad\qquad\qquad T \subset \Omega$$
$$\lfloor T.idl \rfloor = \{s \cup t \mid s \in \lfloor T_1.idl \rfloor \wedge t \in \lfloor T_2.idl \rfloor\} \qquad T \notin \Omega \wedge T = T_1 \odot T_2$$

The operator $\odot$ here and below denotes an arbitrary operator in t-calculus. Restricted by behavioral dependencies, not all pairs of final states can exist simultaneously. For instance, $T_1 \rightsquigarrow T_2$ does not have such a termination state $\{T_1.suc, T_2.abt\}$, since (T_1, suc) and (T_2, abt) are exclusive derived from ($\rightsquigarrow$ 3).

Definition 4.2. *Suppose* $T = T_1 \odot T_2$ *and* T_1, T_2 *are not expanded* [1], $T_1.\sigma_1$ *and* $T_2.\sigma_2$ *are said compatible with regard to* $\odot$ *if and only if* $\exists \sigma \bullet \{T_1.\sigma_1, T_2.\sigma_2\} \in \lfloor T.\sigma \rfloor$

When a web transaction is proved to be invalid, we further provide a solution to help designers to find the possible reason for this problem. Let $\mathcal{A}$ represent the set of termination states in ATS but not in $\lfloor T.suc \rfloor \cup \lfloor T.abt \rfloor$. Apparently, $\mathcal{A}$ is not empty when the web transaction $\{T\}$ is invalid. We try the two steps below to locate the error.

---

[1] While computing $\lfloor T.\sigma \rfloor$ for a composite transaction T with its sub-transactions T_1, T_2 not expanded, we temporarily set Ω to be $\{T_1, T_2\}$. Thus, $\lfloor T.\sigma \rfloor$ just includes the sets with two elements denoting the final states of T_1, T_2 respectively.

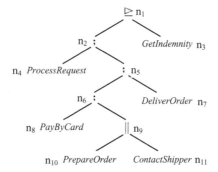

Fig. 3. The syntax tree of order transaction

1. Firstly, construct a syntax tree according to the structure of $\{T\}$. This is a binary tree and the contents of its nodes are either operators in t-calculus or transactions in Ω. All these transactions in Ω lie in the leaves of this tree.[2] Every node n relates to a compensable transaction denoted by $\mathbb{T}(n)$. For a leaf node n, $\mathbb{T}(n)$ is equal to its content. For a non-leaf node m with an operator $\odot$, $\mathbb{T}(m)$ is equal to $\mathbb{T}(m_1) \odot \mathbb{T}(m_2)$, in which m_1, m_2 are its children nodes.

2. Secondly, try to traverse this tree in post-order. Given a termination state θ, for any tree node n, its related transaction $\mathbb{T}(n)$ has a final state denoted by $\ell(n, \theta)$. While visiting a leaf node n, for each θ in $\mathcal{A}$, $\ell(n, \theta)$ is computed and it is equal to $\mathbb{T}(n).\sigma$ which is an element of θ. While visiting a non-leaf node m with an operator $\odot$ and two children nodes m_1, m_2, for each θ in $\mathcal{A}$, we need to check whether the two states $\ell(m_1, \theta)$ and $\ell(m_2, \theta)$ are compatible with regard to $\odot$. If something incompatible is found, it means this operator is wrongly written and the process of traverse is stopped. Otherwise, let $\ell(m, \theta)$ equal to $\mathbb{T}(m).\sigma$ where $\{\ell(m_1, \theta), \ell(m_2, \theta)\} \in \lfloor \mathbb{T}(m).\sigma \rfloor$ for each θ in $\mathcal{A}$. After that the next node in post-order is visited until there is a node associated with an improper operator.

Next, we take the example in Figure 2 to explain our method for locating the problem. Suppose the designer is interested in these sub-transactions below:

$$\Omega = \{ProcessRequest, PayByCard, PrepareOrder\}$$
$$\cup \{ContactShipper, DeliverOrder, GetIndemnity\}$$

The syntax tree for $OrderTrans$ is given in Figure 3. It has eleven nodes marked by $n_1, n_2, \ldots, n_{11}$. All the leaves denote the interested sub-transactions. While traversing the tree in post-order, the nodes are visited in the following order:

$$n_4, n_8, n_{10}, n_{11}, n_9, n_6, n_7, n_5, n_2, n_3, n_1$$

---

[2] If the transactions in Ω cannot cover all the leaves, the designer should provide more information by enlarging the elements of Ω until all the leaves can be covered.

For simplicity, we assume $\mathcal{A}$ just includes one termination state:

$$\theta = \{ProcessRequest.cmp, PayByCard.abt, PrepareOrder.abt\}$$
$$\cup \{ContactShipper.abt, DeliverOrder.idl, GetIndemnity.idl\}$$

When visiting the first four nodes in post-order, we get their related transactions and states as follow:

$$\mathbb{T}(n_4) = ProcessRequest \qquad \ell(n_4, \theta) = ProcessRequest.cmp$$
$$\mathbb{T}(n_8) = PayByCard \qquad \ell(n_8, \theta) = PayByCard.abt$$
$$\mathbb{T}(n_{10}) = PrepareOrder \qquad \ell(n_{10}, \theta) = PrepareOrder.abt$$
$$\mathbb{T}(n_{11}) = ContactShipper \qquad \ell(n_{11}, \theta) = ContactShipper.abt$$

Node n_9 is equipped with a parallel operator. The transaction related to n_9 is:

$$\mathbb{T}(n_9) = \mathbb{T}(n_{10}) \parallel \mathbb{T}(n_{11}) = PrepareOrder \parallel ContactShipper$$

It is not difficult to prove that $\ell(n_{10}, \theta)$ and $\ell(n_{11}, \theta)$ are compatible with regard to this parallel operator by figuring out $\lfloor \mathbb{T}(n_9).abt \rfloor$:

$$\lfloor \mathbb{T}(n_9).abt \rfloor = \{\{PrepareOrder.abt, ContactShipper.abt\}\}$$

Thus, we get that: $\ell(n_9, \theta) = \mathbb{T}(n_9).abt$. The next node n_6 is associated with a sequential operator and the transaction related to n_6 is: $\mathbb{T}(n_6) = \mathbb{T}(n_8); \mathbb{T}(n_9)$.

In the case, the states $\mathbb{T}(n_8).abt$ (i.e., $\ell(n_8, \theta)$) and $\mathbb{T}(n_9).abt$ (i.e., $\ell(n_9, \theta)$) are proved to be incompatible with regard to the sequential operator. It is easy to predict this result because in the sequential composition $S; T$, T does not have the chance to be activated without mentioning the possibility of abortion when S is aborted. Thus, we find that this sequential operator attached to n_6 is wrongly written. In fact, the designer here expects the credit check to be performed in parallel not in sequence with preparing order because such check normally succeeds. Moreover, the seller in this case has more time to process order so as not to delay the transportation unnecessarily.

4.2 Verifying Temporal Constraints

In order to express more specific transactional properties with temporal constraints, we devise a specification language whose syntax is given below:

$$\psi ::= \diamond a \mid a \prec b \mid a \ll b \mid a < b \mid a \leftrightarrow b \mid a \leftrightarrow b$$
$$\neg\psi \mid \psi \wedge \psi \mid \psi \vee \psi$$

where a, b are terminal actions. Except for these five relations $(<, \prec, \ll, \leftrightarrow, \leftrightarrow)$, one more unitary relation $\diamond$ is introduced. $\diamond a$ says that a will definitely occur in the future.

Let M be the set of all terminal actions, and M^* be the set of all finite sequences (including $\langle \rangle$) which are formed from elements of M. For a trace s, $s[i]$ denotes the ith element. From another view, a formula ψ can be regarded

$$
\begin{aligned}
(\!\lozenge\, a\!) \quad &= \{s : M^* \mid \exists i \bullet s[i] = a\} \\
(\!a \prec b\!) \quad &= \{s : M^* \mid \forall i \bullet (s[i] = a \Rightarrow \exists j \bullet (j > i \wedge s[j] = b))\} \\
(\!a \ll b\!) \quad &= \{s : M^* \mid \forall i \bullet (s[i] = b \Rightarrow \exists j \bullet (j < i \wedge s[j] = a))\} \\
(\!a < b\!) \quad &= \{s : M^* \mid \exists i, j \bullet (i < j \wedge s[i] = a \wedge s[j] = b) \vee \forall i \bullet (s[i] \ne a \wedge s[i] \ne b)\} \\
(\!a \leftrightarrow b\!) \quad &= \{s : M^* \mid \exists i, j \bullet (s[i] = a \wedge s[j] = b) \vee \forall i \bullet (s[i] \ne a \wedge s[i] \ne b)\} \\
(\!a \leftrightsquigarrow b\!) \quad &= \{s : M^* \mid \exists i \bullet s[i] = a \Rightarrow \forall j \bullet s[j] \ne b\} \\
(\!\neg \psi\!) \quad &= M^* - (\!\psi\!) \\
(\!\psi_1 \wedge \psi_2\!) &= (\!\psi_1\!) \cap (\!\psi_2\!) \\
(\!\psi_1 \vee \psi_2\!) &= (\!\psi_1\!) \cup (\!\psi_2\!)
\end{aligned}
$$

Fig. 4. Interpretations over traces for formulae

as a set of transactional traces defined by the function $(\!\cdot\!)$, whose definition is inductively given in Figure 4. Given a transaction T and a property ψ, the designer expects to verify whether ψ is satisfied by a specific behavior $[(T, \sigma)]$ for a concrete state σ ($\sigma \in \Delta$).

Definition 4.3. ψ *holds for* $[(T, \sigma)]$ *(written as* $[(T, \sigma)] \models \psi$*) if and only if* $[(T, \sigma)] \subseteq (\!\psi\!)$.

The problem is that the number of traces in $(\!\psi\!)$ is too large due to a large amount of elements in M. To improve this, we reset M for each formula ψ and make it be the set of actions only mentioned by ψ. In addition, we need to restrict the traces of $[(T, \sigma)]$ to the actions in M. For a trace s, we use the expression $s \restriction M$ to denote a new trace formed from s simply by omitting all actions outside M. Thus, the traces from $[(T, \sigma)]$ restricted to M is defined as follows:

$$[(T, \sigma)] \!\downarrow_M = \{t \mid \exists s \bullet (t = s \restriction M \wedge s \in [(T, \sigma)])\}$$

Then the verification process can be improved by getting rid of actions independent of properties.

Theorem 4.1. *Let M be the set of actions occurring in ψ. $[(T, \sigma)] \models \psi$ holds if and only if $[(T, \sigma)] \!\downarrow_M \subseteq (\!\psi\!)$.*

Example: Given a simple transaction $T = (T_1; T_2) \trianglerighteq T_3$ and a specified property $\psi = (T_1, hap) \prec (T_3, suc)$, we require to check whether $[(T, abt)] \models \psi$ holds.

First, we compute the behavior of T provided it is aborted.

$$
\begin{aligned}
[(T, abt)] = \; &\{\langle (T_1, abt) \rangle, \langle (T_1, suc), (T_2, abt), (T_1, cmp) \rangle\} \\
\cup \; &\{\langle (T_1, suc), (T_2, abt), (T_1, hap), (T_3, suc) \rangle\} \\
\cup \; &\{\langle (T_1, fal), (T_3, suc) \rangle, \langle (T_1, suc), (T_2, fal), (T_3, suc) \rangle\}
\end{aligned}
$$

This property only refers to two actions and we get that:

$$M = \{(T_1, hap), (T_3, suc)\}$$

Then we limit the traces of $[(T, abt)]$ to the set of M:

$$\langle (T_1, abt) \rangle \upharpoonright M \qquad\qquad\qquad\qquad = \langle \rangle$$
$$\langle (T_1, fal), (T_3, suc) \rangle \upharpoonright M \qquad\qquad = \langle (T_3, suc) \rangle$$
$$\langle (T_1, suc), (T_2, abt), (T_1, cmp) \rangle \upharpoonright M \qquad = \langle \rangle$$
$$\langle (T_1, suc), (T_2, fal), (T_3, suc) \rangle \upharpoonright M \qquad = \langle (T_3, suc) \rangle$$
$$\langle (T_1, suc), (T_2, abt), (T_1, hap), (T_3, suc) \rangle \upharpoonright M = \langle (T_1, hap), (T_3, suc) \rangle$$

Consequently, we have that

$$[(T, abt)] \downarrow_M = \{\langle \rangle, \langle (T_3, suc) \rangle, \langle (T_1, hap), (T_3, suc) \rangle\}$$

At last, we convert the property to a set of traces:

$$(\!|\psi|\!) = \{s : M^* \mid \forall i \bullet (s[i] = (T_1, hap) \Rightarrow \exists j \bullet (j > i \wedge s[j] = (T_3, suc)))\}$$
$$= \{\langle \rangle, \langle (T_3, suc) \rangle, \langle (T_1, hap), (T_3, suc) \rangle\}$$

Obviously, $[(T, abt)] \downarrow_M \subseteq (\!|\psi|\!)$ holds for this example.

A complex formula ψ possibly makes $(\!|\psi|\!)$ much bigger, which increases the difficulty of verification. A practical solution is that we change the formula into the *disjunctive normal form* as follows:

$$\psi = \psi_1 \vee \psi_2 \vee \cdots \vee \psi_n$$

Apparently, $(\!|\psi_i|\!)$ $(1 \leq i \leq n)$ is smaller than $(\!|\psi|\!)$. If we can verify that one sub-formula is satisfied, the whole formula holds obviously.

Theorem 4.2. *Suppose* $\psi = \psi_1 \vee \psi_2 \vee \cdots \vee \psi_n$. $[(T, \sigma)] \models \psi$ *if* $[(T, \sigma)] \models \psi_1 \vee [(T, \sigma)] \models \psi_2 \vee \cdots \vee [(T, \sigma)] \models \psi_n$.

5   Related Work

Due to limitations of classical transactions, some models have adopted the concept of compensation to satisfy the autonomy requirement in distributed environment. Elmagarmid et al. [5] supported mixed transactions allowing compensable and noncompensable sub-transactions to coexist. Levy et al. [11] proposed a formal model to unify the two dual methods of compensation and retry. In their work, a whole transaction was modeled as a static partial order of steps. A new approach called XIP [17] was proposed to present an optimistic commit protocol to enable the Internet transaction semantics. In contrast with these works, we develop a formal language to explicitly model the logical precedence, causality and synchronization constraints among compensable transactions.

In recent literatures, process calculus is adopted extensively to formalize long-lived transactions. Several proposals [1,10,15] took the well-known π-calculus as a starting point and extended it with some transactional features. Another language cCSP [3] as an extension of CSP supports automatic compensation on transactional failure. It is equipped with a simple operational semantics [4] and this semantics is made executable by encoding the rules in Prolog. Bruni et al. [2]

have developed a sagas calculus with similar operators to cCSP. The difference is mainly that while considering parallel execution, cCSP encourages synchronized compensation whereas sagas calculus supports distributed compensation. None of these transactional languages treats compensations as compensable transactions like t-calculus [14] we proposed earlier does. The operational and algebraic semantics of t-calculus was studied and a kind of linking theory has been established [13,12]. Unlike our previous works, this paper specifies web transactions by investigating compensable transactions in a higher level of granularity. In addition, the semantics of each transactional construct is explored in a different way by formally describing its behavioral dependencies. Moreover, this work proposes strict solutions to verify transactional behavior.

With regard to verification, there are already a series of work focusing on analyzing and verifying web service properties. Foster et al. [6] discussed a model-based approach to verify web service compositions, in which implementations were mechanically translated to FSP to perform an equivalence trace verification process. Temporal logics for compositional reasoning about web service interfaces have been proposed in [18]. Nakajima used model checking to analyze web service flow by translating BPEL descriptions into Promela [16]. The interactions of composite web services were analyzed by modeling them as conversations [7]. Service processes were first translated into guarded automata and then verified using SPIN. Pu et al. [9] adopted a similar approach to use the model checker UPPAAL to verify BPEL programs including timed properties. However, we find no relevant work on verifying web transactions with the feature of compensation. This paper is the first attempt in this area to the best of our knowledge.

6 Conclusion

Web transactions in this paper are built upon a set of compensable transactions which help to ensure a relatively relaxed atomicity. Compensable transactions support composition in different manners, aiming to enhance the reliability and flexibility of web transactions. Distinct transactional constructs correspond to different behavioral dependencies which have been explored from two aspects. On the one hand, the dependency between two sub-transactions on the same syntactic level is described by a series of relations between actions. On the other hand, the dependency among a composite transaction and its sub-transactions is defined in terms of transactional traces. Transactional traces are more precise than relations of actions, since they can assist designers to track the behavior of a whole web transaction.

The formal description of web transactions helps to clarify ambiguous concepts and it provides the basis for the following process of verification. At first, this paper has provided a method to verify web transactions according to the relaxed atomicity requirement. Besides, the problem can be located if inconsistency exists. Afterwards, a specification language has been proposed for specifying temporal constraints about compensable transactions. The verification process is further optimized by restricting actions of interest and partitioning property formulae.

References

1. Bocchi, L., Laneve, C., Zavattaro, G.: A calculus for long-running transactions. In: Najm, E., Nestmann, U., Stevens, P. (eds.) FMOODS 2003. LNCS, vol. 2884, pp. 124–138. Springer, Heidelberg (2003)
2. Bruni, R., Melgratti, H., Montanari, U.: Theoretical foundations for compensations in flow composition languages. In: POPL 2005, pp. 209–220. ACM Press, New York (2005)
3. Butler, M., Hoare, T., Ferreira, C.: A trace semantics for long-running transaction. In: Abdallah, A.E., Jones, C.B., Sanders, J.W. (eds.) Communicating Sequential Processes. LNCS, vol. 3525, pp. 133–150. Springer, Heidelberg (2005)
4. Butler, M., Ripon, S.: Executable semantics for compensating CSP. In: Fitzgerald, J.S., Hayes, I.J., Tarlecki, A. (eds.) FM 2005. LNCS, vol. 3582, pp. 243–256. Springer, Heidelberg (2005)
5. Elmagarmid, A.K., Leu, Y., Litwin, W., Rusinkiewicz, M.: A multidatabase transaction model for interbase. In: VLDB 1990, pp. 507–518 (1990)
6. Foster, H., Uchitel, S., Magee, J., Kramer, J.: Model-based verification of Web service compositions. In: ASE 2003, pp. 152–161. IEEE Computer Society, Los Alamitos (2003)
7. Fu, X., Bultan, T., Su, J.: Analysis of interacting BPEL web services. In: Proc. of WWW 2004, pp. 621–630. ACM Press, New York (2004)
8. Garcia-Molina, H., Salem, K.: Sagas. In: Proc. of ACM SIGMOD 1987, pp. 249–259. ACM Press, New York (1987)
9. Geguang, P., Xiangpeng, Z., Shuling, W., Zongyan, Q.: Towards the Semantics and Verification of BPEL4WS. In: WLFM 2005. ENTCS, vol. 151, pp. 33–52. Elsevier, Amsterdam (2006)
10. Laneve, C., Zavattaro, G.: Foundations of web transactions. In: Sassone, V. (ed.) FOSSACS 2005. LNCS, vol. 3441, pp. 282–298. Springer, Heidelberg (2005)
11. Levy, E., Korth, H.F., Silberschatz, A.: A theory of relaxed atomicity. In: PODC 1991, pp. 95–110. ACM Press, New York (1991)
12. Li, J., Zhu, H., He, J.: Algebraic Semantics for Compensable Transactions. In: Jones, C.B., Liu, Z., Woodcock, J. (eds.) ICTAC 2007. LNCS, vol. 4711, pp. 306–321. Springer, Heidelberg (2007)
13. Li, J., Zhu, H., Pu, G., He, J.: A Formal Model for Compensable Transactions. In: Proc. of ICECCS 2007, pp. 64–73. IEEE Computer Society, Los Alamitos (2007)
14. Li, J., Zhu, H., Pu, G., He, J.: Looking into compensable transactions. In: Proc. of SEW-31, pp. 154–166. IEEE Computer Society, Los Alamitos (2007)
15. Mazzara, M., Lucchi, R.: A framework for generic error handling in business processes. In: WS-FM 2004. ENTCS, vol. 105, pp. 133–145. Elsevier, Amsterdam (2004)
16. Nakajima, S.: Model-checking of safety and security aspects in web service flows. In: Koch, N., Fraternali, P., Wirsing, M. (eds.) ICWE 2004. LNCS, vol. 3140, pp. 488–501. Springer, Heidelberg (2004)
17. Ouyang, J., Sahai, A., Machiraju, V.: An approach to optimistic commit and transparent compensation for e-service transactions. HP Laboratories Palo Alto (February 2001)
18. Solanki, M., Cau, A., Zedan, H.: Augmenting semantic web service descriptions with compositional specification. In: WWW 2004, pp. 544–552. ACM Press, New York (2004)

Modelling and Analysing the Contract Net Protocol - Extension Using Coloured Petri Nets

Jonathan Billington, Amar Kumar Gupta, and Guy Edward Gallasch

Computer Systems Engineering Centre
University of South Australia
Mawson Lakes Campus, SA, 5095, Australia
{jonathan.billington, amar.gupta, guy.gallasch}@unisa.edu.au

Abstract. The Contract Net Protocol is a task allocation protocol that facilitates negotiation between bidders and an auctioneer in a Multi-Agent System to form a contract. The extension allows the bidders to interact with more than one auctioneer concurrently, and to update their bids until a bid is granted. This introduces flexibility and ensures better selection of a bid. In this paper, we model the Contract Net Protocol - extension with Coloured Petri Nets and show that it terminates correctly. We analyse the terminal states and prove that the agents have consistent beliefs at the end of the negotiations, and that there is no "dead code" in the procedures. Lastly, we show how the number of terminal states and channel bounds are related to the number of bidders.

Keywords: Contract Net Protocol - extension, Coloured Petri Nets, Verification.

1 Introduction

A Multi-Agent System [4] comprises a set of agents that interact with each other to achieve a goal. Typical agents constitute a service requesting agent, which requests a certain task to be performed, and a service providing agent, which performs the task. These agents undertake negotiations to form contracts. The Contract Net Protocol [7,19] is an elementary protocol that facilitates task allocation between an auctioneer (service requesting agent) and many bidders (service providing agents). This is extended to the Contract Net Protocol - extension [1] that allows the bidders to negotiate with multiple auctioneers simultaneously. This prevents the bidders from losing potential contracts with other auctioneers. Also, the protocol has two different phases of decision making; a provisional and a confirmed decision making phase. This feature allows bidders to submit updated bids and helps ensure that the auctioneers select the best bids. This work is motivated by researchers working on transport logistics [13].

In [3] we modelled the Contract Net Protocol [7,19] using Coloured Petri nets (CPNs) [9,10] and proved a number of properties. In doing so, we demonstrated the effectiveness of CPNs for this task, contrary to the claims made in the literature regarding the inadequacy of CPNs for modelling interaction protocols [11,12].

K. Suzuki et al. (Eds.): FORTE 2008, LNCS 5048, pp. 169–184, 2008.

In this paper, we extend our work to the Contract Net Protocol - extension (CNP-ext), represented using Protocol Flow Diagrams in [13]. The protocol has iterative processes and the work presented in [1] proves that the protocol converges. The importance of the verification of properties of a protocol before implementation [2] has further stimulated this work. To the best of our knowledge, no work has been undertaken on the verification of the properties of this protocol.

This paper has a threefold contribution. Firstly, we present for the first time a model of CNP-ext. We analyse this model using state space techniques for any number of bidders up to 5. Secondly, we show that the protocol terminates correctly and the agents have consistent beliefs regarding the contract at the end of negotiations. Finally, we conjecture relationships between the number of bidders and the number of terminal states and bounds on the underlying channel.

This paper is organised as follows. Section 2 provides an overview of the protocol and its operation. The CPN model of CNP-ext and its operation are presented in Section 3. Section 4 analyses the model and finally Section 5 presents conclusions and avenues for further work.

2   Contract Net Protocol - Extension

In contrast to the Contract Net Protocol that consists of a single auctioneer and multiple bidders, the Contract Net Protocol - extension (CNP-ext) [1] consists of multiple auctioneers negotiating with multiple bidders to form a contract. The auctioneers may negotiate with a number of bidders simultaneously. However, the auctioneers do not interact with each other and their negotiation processes are independent of each other. Similarly, the bidders may interact with multiple auctioneers at the same time, but not with each other. For simplicity, we describe below the CNP-ext in the context of a single auctioneer and multiple bidders.

The auctioneer initiates negotiation by sending a Task Announcement to the bidders, who respond with a Pre Bid (a temporary bid) for the task. When all the Pre Bids have been received the auctioneer selects the one it believes most suitable. This bid is provisionally granted and all others are provisionally rejected. The provisionally granted bidder then prepares and sends a Definitive Bid (a final bid) that may or may not be the same as the Pre Bid. All other bidders have the opportunity to update and re-submit a Pre Bid at this time.

When the auctioneer receives the Definitive Bid and all the updated Pre Bids from the provisionally rejected bidders, it compares the Definitive Bid to the rest of the updated Pre Bids. Two things could then happen. In the first scenario, if the Definitive Bid is still considered superior to all the updated Pre Bids, then the auctioneer sends a Confirm Grant to the corresponding bidder and a Confirm Reject to all other bidders. Negotiation would now be complete. In the second scenario, if an updated Pre Bid exists that is better than the Definitive Bid, then the auctioneer rejects (either Provisional Reject or Confirm Reject) the Definitive Bid. It then provisionally grants the new best Pre Bid and provisionally rejects the rest of the Pre Bids. The provisionally granted bidder then sends a Definitive Bid and the remaining bidders can again submit updated Pre Bids, and the process re-

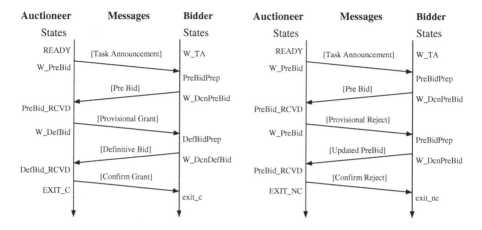

Fig. 1. Confirm Grant of a Definitive Bid   **Fig. 2.** Rejecting an Updated PreBid

peats iteratively. Negotiations will come to an end in one of two ways, either when the auctioneer confirms the grant of a Definitive Bid (and hence firmly rejects the remaining Pre Bids), or when there are no more updated Pre Bids to consider. The latter may arise if the auctioneer progressively terminates negotiations with each bidder that submits a Definitive Bid by sending a Confirm Reject in response, hence terminating negotiations with that bidder.

Multiple auctioneers may interact with the bidders simultaneously. When a Task Announcement is received from more than one auctioneer, a bidder will prioritise the tasks and send Pre Bids to any number of auctioneers. On receipt of a Provisional Grant in return, it prepares and sends a Definitive Bid, while a Provisional Reject causes the bidder to reprioritise its tasks and send updated Pre Bids. A Confirm Grant message commits the bidder to the task, while a Confirm Reject frees the bidder from any further negotiation with that auctioneer. The bidder could however continue negotiating with the other auctioneers.

Examples of interaction between an auctioneer and a single bidder are illustrated in the Time Sequence Diagrams (TSD) in Figs. 1 and 2. In each TSD the auctioneer is represented on the left and the bidder on the right. The changes in state for each are shown down each side. The states of the auctioneers and bidders are defined in Table 1. There are seven possible states for each. READY and W_TA correspond to the initial states of the auctioneers and bidders respectively. The terminal states are EXIT_NC and EXIT_C (uppercase) for the auctioneers and exit_nc and exit_c (lowercase) for the bidders, following the convention of [13].

In Fig. 1, the auctioneer sends a Task Announcement to a bidder, which responds with a Pre Bid. On receipt of the Pre Bid, the auctioneer sends a Provisional Grant, which results in the bidder sending a Definitive Bid for the task. The auctioneer finally confirms this Definitive Bid to end the negotiation with a contract (auctioneer and bidder terminate in the EXIT_C and exit_c states respectively). Figure 2 shows a similar scenario, but this time the auctioneer provisionally rejects the Pre Bid. The bidder sends an Updated Pre Bid in re-

Table 1. Representation of States

Auctioneers	Bidders
READY (READY to send a Task Announcement)	W_TA (Waiting for a Task Announcement)
W_PreBid (Waiting for Pre Bids)	PreBidPrep (Pre Bid Preparation)
PreBid_RCVD (Pre Bid ReCeiVeD)	W_DcnPreBid (Waiting for Decision on Pre Bid)
W_DefBid (Waiting for Definitive Bid)	DefBidPrep (Definitive Bid Preparation)
DefBid_RCVD (Definitive Bid ReCeiVeD)	W_DcnDefBid (Waiting for Decision on Definitive Bid)
EXIT_NC (EXIT with No Contract)	exit_nc (exit with no contract)
EXIT_C (EXIT with Contract)	exit_c (exit with contract)

sponse to the Provisional Reject, which the auctioneer finally rejects. Negotiation ends without a contract.

3   CPN Model of the Contract Net Protocol - Extension

Coloured Petri Nets are a form of High-level Petri net [8] in which tokens are arbitrarily complex data values and places are marked by multisets of such tokens. Each place is typed by a set of values, called a colour set, that specifies allowable values of tokens that can mark that place. In this section we firstly list the assumptions made when creating the model, define the data structures, variables and constants used to annotate the model, and finally describe the structure and operation of the model. We use the software tool, CPN Tools [10], to create and analyse the model. We assume basic familiarity with Petri net concepts, however for a detailed introduction to CPNs the reader is referred to [9,10].

3.1   Assumptions

When creating our CNP-ext model, we made the following assumptions:

1. All bidders are known to the auctioneers before the negotiations take place.
2. All messages (Task Announcement, Pre Bid, Definitive Bid, Provisional Grant, Provisional Reject, Confirm Grant and Confirm Reject) are represented by their name only, as other information contained in these messages does not affect the protocol's procedures.
3. All bidders have enough resources to bid, and will always bid, in response to all Task Announcements.
4. All the bids are received before the process of making a decision takes place, which means that we do not have to model a deadline.
5. The communication channel is lossless but reordering.

3.2   Declarations

Listing 1 shows the declarations for the CNP-ext CPN model. We describe the more significant declarations below. The identity of the auctioneers and bidders are represented by the colour sets AUC (line 3) and BDR (line 8) respectively. The identity of the auctioneers (AUC) and bidders (BDR) ranges from 1 to themaximum number of auctioneers (MaxAucs) and maximum number of bidders (MaxBdrs), respectively. Hence, there are two parameters in the model: MaxAucs (line 2) and MaxBdrs (line 7).

Listing 1. Declarations for the CNP-ext CPN model

```
1  (* ——— Auctioneers ——— *)
2  val MaxAucs = 2;
3  colset AUC = index A with 1..MaxAucs;
4  var auc:AUC;
5
6  (* ——— Bidders ——— *)
7  val MaxBdrs = 2;
8  colset BDR = index B with 1..MaxBdrs;
9  var bdr:BDR;
10
11 (* ——— States ——— *)
12 colset STauc = with READY | W_PreBid | PreBid_RCVD | W_DefBid
13                     | DefBid_RCVD | EXIT_NC | EXIT_C;
14 colset AUC_BDR_STauc = product AUC*BDR*STauc;
15 colset STbdr = with W_TA | PreBidPrep | W_DcnPreBid | DefBidPrep
16                     | W_DcnDefBid | exit_nc | exit_c;
17 colset AUC_BDR_STbdr = product AUC*BDR*STbdr;
18 var st_bdr:STbdr;
19
20 (* ——— Messages ——— *)
21 colset MESauc = with TA | PG | PR | CG | CR;
22 colset ProDcn = subset MESauc with [PG,PR];
23 colset DefBidDcn = subset MESauc with [CG,CR,PR];
24 colset AUC_BDR_MESauc = product AUC*BDR*MESauc;
25 colset MESbdr = with PreBid|DefBid;
26 colset AUC_BDR_MESbdr = product AUC*BDR*MESbdr;
27 var DBdcn:DefBidDcn;
28 var prodcn:ProDcn;
29
30 (* ——— Bids ——— *)
31 colset BIDS = int with 0..MaxBdrs;
32 colset AUC_BIDS = product AUC*BIDS;
33 colset AUC_BOOL = product AUC*BOOL;
34 colset AUC_TB_B2Rcv_W4DefBid = product AUC*BIDS*BIDS*BOOL;
35 var TBids, Bids2Rcv, Bids2Rej:BIDS;
36 var bl:BOOL;
```

The states of the auctioneers and bidders are defined by the colour sets STauc (lines 12-13) and STbdr (lines 15-16) respectively, as defined in Table 1. The colour sets MESauc (line 21) and MESbdr (line 25) define the messages sent from auctioneers to bidders (Task Announcement-TA, Provisional Grant-PG, Provisional Reject-PR, Confirm Grant-CG, Confirm Reject-CR) and bidders to auctioneers (PreBid, DefBid) respectively. In the model we encode multiple auctioneers and bidders within the data structures, rather than in the net structure, thus allowing the number of auctioneers and bidders to be changed without requiring changes to the net structure. Accordingly, we associate the auctioneer's states and messages with the identity of an auctioneer and a bidder in the colour sets AUC_BDR_STauc (line 14) and AUC_BDR_MESauc (line 24), respectively. It is a similar situation for the bidders, thus the colour sets AUC_BDR_STbdr (line 17) and AUC_BDR_MESbdr (line 26) associate the identity of an auctioneer and bidder with the states and messages of a bidder, respectively. The colour set AUC_TB_B2Rcv_W4DefBid (line 34) defines a 4-tuple. It records the identity of the auctioneer, the total number of bidders participating, the number of bids to be received, and if the auctioneer is waiting for a Definitive Bid.

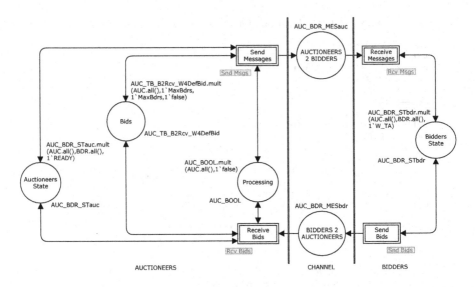

Fig. 3. Main Page of the CPN Model

3.3   Model Structure

The top-level page of the hierarchically constructed CNP-ext CPN model is shown in Fig. 3. It contains 6 places and 4 substitution transitions (double-rectangles, each representing another model page) and provides the main structure for the protocol. The auctioneers are modelled on the left and the bidders on the right. They communicate via two places shown in the middle of the figure, AUCTION-EERS 2 BIDDERS and BIDDERS 2 AUCTIONEERS, that represent a non-lossy but reordering channel for each direction of communication. Typed by the colour sets AUC_BDR_MESauc and AUC_BDR_MESbdr, at any instant, these places may contain the messages of the auctioneers and bidders, each coupled with the identity of an auctioneer and bidder. These two places are initially empty.

The place Auctioneers State is typed by the colour set AUC_BDR_STauc and stores the states of all the auctioneers with respect to all the bidders. It is initially marked by triples consisting of the cartesian product of all auctioneers with all bidders, paired with the READY state. For example for MaxAucs=2 and MaxB-drs=2, the initial marking would be $1'(A(1),B(1),READY)++ 1'(A(1),B(2),$ READY)$++1'(A(2),B(1),READY)++1'(A(2),B(2),READY)$, where $++$ is multiset addition. The place Bidders State that models the states of the bidders can be described in a similar way.

The place Processing, typed by the colour set AUC_BOOL (see Listing. 1), keeps track of the auctioneers that are currently processing bids. In the initial marking, no auctioneers are processing bids.

The place Bids is typed by the colour set AUC_TB_B2Rcv_W4DefBid. It is initially marked with each of the auctioneers negotiating with MaxBdrs bidders, with MaxBdrs bids to be received, with none waiting for a Definitive Bid.

3.4   Model of the Auctioneers

The behaviour of the auctioneers is modelled by the two substitution transitions, Send Messages and Receive Bids, in Fig. 3.

Send Messages. This substitution transition represents the page shown in Fig. 4, which details the procedures for the auctioneers to send messages to the bidders. It consists of 6 executable transitions and 2 additional places. The place Bid Selected, typed by the colour set AUC_BOOL (see Listing 1), shows whether the auctioneers have selected a Definitive Bid in the negotiation process. The initial marking is such that none of the auctioneers have confirmed the grant of a Definitive Bid. The place Bids2Reject, typed by the colour set AUC_BIDS (see Listing 1), records the number of updated Pre Bids to reject after a Definitive Bid has been granted. The initial marking shows that no auctioneers have any bids to reject.

This page operates as follows. Initially, all the auctioneers are in the state READY with respect to all the bidders, and hence are ready to broadcast a Task Announcement to all the bidders. The Broadcasting TAs transition models an auctioneer initiating negotiations by sending a Task Announcement to each of the bidders. Firing this transition causes the selected auctioneer to change state to W_PreBid with respect to all the bidders, and a Task Announcement to be broadcast to each of the bidders. This transition is concurrently enabled for all auctioneers.

At some point, all bidders will respond to the TA with a Pre Bid. When the auctioneer has received all Pre Bids, it would be in the state PreBid_RCVD with respect to all the bidders, the marking of place Bids would indicate that no more bids need to be received, and a true value with respect to this auctioneer on place Processing indicates that the auctioneer can now process the bids. At this instant, the transition Snd Prov Dcns (Send Provisional Decisions) would be enabled. When it fires it sends a provisional decision to each of the bidders. When there is only one bidder, it is sent either a Provisional Grant (PG) or a Provisional Reject (PR), modelled as a non-deterministic choice by the variable prodcn (see Listing 1). Accordingly, the auctioneer changes state to W_DefBid or W_PreBid respectively. When there is more than one bidder (MaxBdrs > 1), then one bidder is sent a PG (also modelled as a non-deterministic choice) and the rest are sent a PR. As before, the auctioneer changes state to W_DefBid with respect to the bidder that it sent the PG, and W_PreBid with respect to rest of the bidders. In either case, a false is returned to the place Processing with respect to this auctioneer, indicating that processing has finished for now.

Later, when the auctioneer receives the Definitive Bid (from the provisionally granted bidder) and all updated Pre Bids (from the provisionally rejected bidders), the transition Snd DefBid Dcn (Send Definitive Bid Decision) becomes enabled. This transition models the auctioneer's decision on the Definitive Bid,

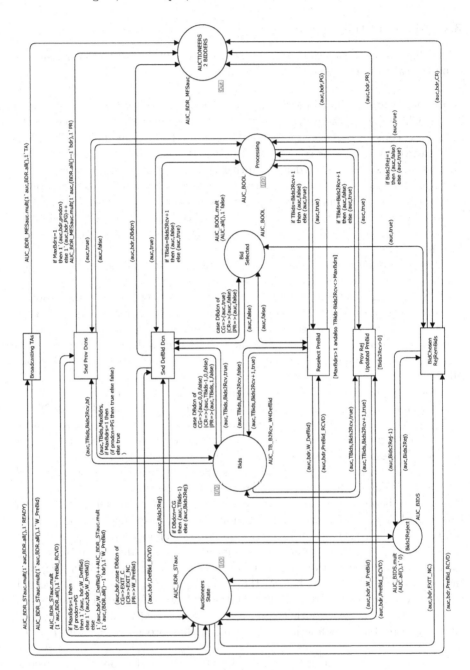

Fig. 4. Send Messages

whether to send a Confirm Grant (CG), Confirm Reject (CR) or Provisional Reject (PR) to the corresponding bidder. In the case of CG, all other bidders are sent a CR and negotiations cease. In the case of either a CR or PR, another Pre Bid is selected, a PG is sent to the corresponding bidder, and the remaining bidders are sent a PR.

The outcome of the Definitive Bid decision is again non-deterministic, modelled by the variable DBdcn (see Listing 1). When the transition Snd DefBid Dcn fires, the auctioneer changes state to EXIT_C, EXIT_NC or W_PreBid depending upon the value of the variable DBdcn (either CG, CR or PR) as can be seen by the expression on the arc joining the transition to the place Auctioneers State. A CG decision deposits a true on the place Bid Selected while a CR or a PR retains the value to false. Also, the number of bidders to be sent a CR (recorded in the Bids2Reject place) is updated accordingly. The expression on the arc joining the transition to the place Bids updates the total bids and the number of bids to be received. In case of a CG decision, both become 0 as the auctioneer would have confirmed a Definitive Bid and hence would not be expecting any more bids. In case of a CR decision, the total bids would be decremented by 1 as the negotiation would with that bidder would cease, and the number of bids to be received would remain 0. Finally, in case of a Provisional Reject (PR) decision, the total bids would remain unchanged as the bidder would still be involved in the negotiation, and the number of bids to be received would be 1. The condition on the arc joining the transition to the place Processing updates the processing status of this auctioneer accordingly.

If the auctioneer sends a CG to the bidder of the Definitive Bid, it then needs to send a CR to the remaining bidders. For this scenario, the transition BidChosen RejRemBids (Bid Chosen Reject Remaining Bids) is enabled, which sends a CR to all the remaining bidders. Its occurrence also causes the auctioneer to change state from PreBid_RCVD to EXIT_NC with respect to each of the rejected bidders. The expression on the arc joining the transition to the place Processing ensures that when the last bid is sent a CR (Bids2Rej=1), the auctioneer is no longer in the processing state.

If the auctioneer sends a CR or a PR to the bidder of the Definitive Bid, then the auctioneer needs to first reselect a Pre Bid (send a PG), and then provisionally reject all the remaining updated Pre Bids. These activities need to occur in sequence and are modelled by the transitions Reselect PreBid and Prov Rej Updated PreBid, where the transition Prov Rej Updated PreBid will only occur after the occurrence of Reselect PreBid.

The firing of Reselect PreBid causes the auctioneer to change state from PreBid_RCVD to W_DefBid and also sends a PG to the bidder. The boolean false is on the place Bid Selected with respect to this auctioneer, indicating that a Definitive Bid has not been selected. Also, the expression on the arc joining the transition to the place Bids increments the value of the bids to be received by 1 (Bids2Rcv+1), and sets the auctioneer to be waiting for a Definitive Bid (shown by the boolean true).

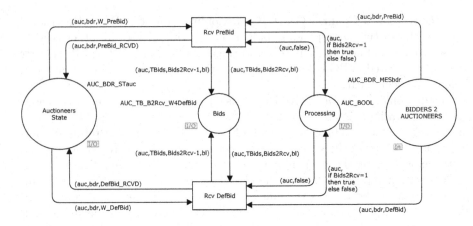

Fig. 5. Receive Bids

The transition Prov Rej Updated PreBid is used to reject the remaining updated Pre Bids only after the process of reselecting a Pre Bid has occurred, which is enforced by its guard. When it occurs, the auctioneer changes state from PreBid_RCVD to W_PreBid with respect to one bidder, and sends a PR message to that bidder. Each time the transition occurs, the number of bids to receive is incremented by 1 (the arc from Prov Rej Updated PreBid to the place Bids). When the auctioneer has finished sending a PR to all the remaining bidders, a boolean false is deposited on the place Processing as evaluated by the expression on the arc joining the transition to the place Processing.

Receive Bids. This substitution transition (see Fig. 5) models the reception of bids and comprises 2 executable transitions: Rcv PreBid (Receive Pre Bid), and Rcv DefBid (Receive Definitive Bid). The firing of Rcv PreBid removes a Pre Bid from the BIDDERS 2 AUCTIONEERS place, causes the auctioneer to change state to PreBid_RCVD with respect to the corresponding bidder, and decrements the number of bids to be received by one (arc from Rcv PreBid to Bids). The Rcv DefBid transition operates in exactly the same way, except that it receives a Definitive Bid from the channel and changes the state of the auctioneer to DefBid_RCVD with respect to the corresponding bidder. When the final bid is received, the processing status of the auctioneer is switched to true (arcs from the transitions to Processing) and the auctioneer can begin to process the bids and send responses.

3.5   Model of the Bidders

The behaviour of the bidders is modelled by the two substitution transitions, Receive Messages and Send Bids, from Fig. 3.

Receive Messages. The page corresponding to this substitution transition is shown in Fig. 6 and comprises five transitions that model the reception of

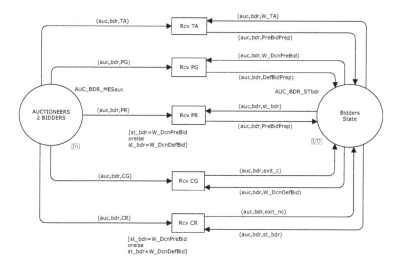

Fig. 6. Receive Messages

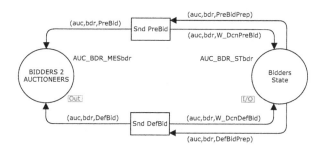

Fig. 7. Send Bids

messages from auctioneers by the bidders. Transition Rcv TA (Receive Task Announcement) models the reception of the Task Announcement, the firing of which causes the TA to be removed from the channel place and the state of the bidder to change from W_TA to PreBidPrep with respect to the corresponding auctioneer (seen in the inscriptions on the arcs between Rcv TA and the Bidders State place). Similarly, the firing of transitions Rcv PG (Receive Provisional Grant), Rcv CG (Receive Confirm Grant), Rcv PR (Receive Provisional Reject) and Rcv CR (Receive Confirm Reject) removes the respective message from the channel place and update the state of the bidder as shown in Fig. 6.

Send Bids. The page corresponding to this substitution transition is given in Fig. 7. It models the procedures for sending a Pre Bid (Snd PreBid) and a Definitive Bid (Snd DefBid).

4   State Space Analysis Results

As all the auctioneers are independent entities and interact with the bidders in a similar way, we analyse the protocol properties for a single auctioneer. Table 2 shows the state space analysis results generated by CPN Tools for different values of MaxBdrs and Fig. 8 shows the reachability graph for one auctioneer and one bidder.

From Table 2, we see that the size of the state space increases as the number of bidders increases. Also, in each case, the number of Strongly Connected Components (Scc's) is less than that in the state space, signifying the presence of cyclic behaviour in the system. This is evident in Fig. 8 and is expected.

4.1   Absence of Deadlocks and Consistency in Beliefs

We can observe from Table 2 that in each case the number of dead markings is one more than MaxBdrs, i.e. No. of Dead Markings = MaxBdrs + 1. This matches the results obtained in [3] for the Contract Net Protocol, which has a single auctioneer dealing with multiple bidders simultaneously. In each case analysed, one of the dead markings corresponds to no contract being established at the end of the negotiations (marking 14 in Fig. 8). This is caused by the auctioneer firmly rejecting each definitive bid, thus ending communication with the corresponding bidder, until no bidders remain. The other MaxBdr dead markings correspond to a contract being formed between the auctioneer and one of the MaxBdr bidders. For MaxBdrs=1, there exists only one such dead marking (marking 15 in Fig. 8). All these MaxBdrs+1 dead markings represent expected termination of the protocol. This is illustrated with the help of Fig. 9, which shows the node descriptors of the dead markings for the case of MaxBdrs=3 and MaxAucs=1.

In each of the dead markings in Fig. 9, the place **Bids** contains a token, (A(1),0,0,false). This records the auctioneer's identity (A(1)), that no bidders are still involved in negotiations (the first 0), that the auctioneer is not expecting any more bids (the second 0), and is not waiting for a definitive bid from a bidder (false). Additionally, all dead markings show that the **Processing** place

Table 2. State space analysis results as a function of the parameter MaxBdrs

Properties/MaxBdrs	1	2	3	4	5
State Space Nodes	15	115	934	7761	63542
State Space Arcs	16	187	2101	22661	228841
Time (hh:mm:ss)	00:00:00	00:00:00	00:00:01	00:00:18	00:21:15
Scc Graph Nodes	7	50	290	1546	7658
Scc Graph Arcs	6	95	853	7153	59221
Dead Markings	2	3	4	5	6
Home Space (Dead Markings)	true	true	true	true	true
Dead Transition Instances	3	1	none	none	none
Channel Bound	1	2	3	4	5

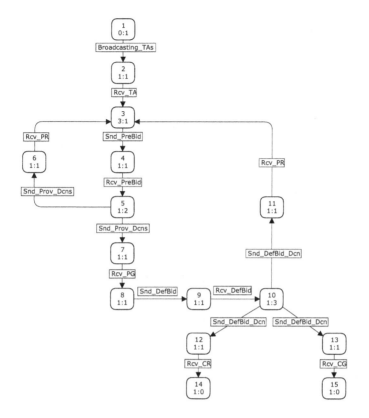

Fig. 8. Reachability Graph (MaxAucs = MaxBdrs = 1)

contains the token (A(1),false), meaning A(1) has replied to all bidders and is no longer processing bids, the Bids2Reject place contains the token (A(1),0), meaning there are no more bids left to be rejected, and both channel places are empty, meaning there are no unprocessed messages or bids. This all represents expected and desirable behaviour.

The markings differ, however, on the Auctioneers State, Bidders State and Bid Selected places. Marking 925 corresponds to the case where no contract is formed at the end of the negotiations. Hence, the marking of these places indicates that the auctioneer exited without a contract with any of the bidders, all bidders exited without a contract with the auctioneer, and no bid was selected, respectively.

The other three dead markings, 572, 547 and 522, correspond to the cases where a contract was awarded to bidder 1, 2 and 3 respectively. The marking of Bid Selected is true for A(1) in all three markings. The marking of Auctioneers State shows that the auctioneer exited with a contract with respect to one of the bidders, and no contract with respect to the other bidders. The marking of Bidders State shows that one bidder exited with a contract while the others did not. In all three markings, the auctioneer exited with a contract with respect to the bidder that exited with a contract. Hence, consistency of belief holds

925:	572:
Bids: 1`(A(1),0,0,false)	Bids: 1`(A(1),0,0,false)
Processing: 1`(A(1),false)	Processing: 1`(A(1),false)
Auctioneers State: 1`(A(1),B(1),EXIT_NC)++	Auctioneers State: 1`(A(1),B(1),EXIT_C)++
1`(A(1),B(2),EXIT_NC)++	1`(A(1),B(2),EXIT_NC)++
1`(A(1),B(3),EXIT_NC)	1`(A(1),B(3),EXIT_NC)
AUCTIONEERS 2 BIDDERS: empty	AUCTIONEERS 2 BIDDERS: empty
Bidders State: 1`(A(1),B(1),exit_nc)++	Bidders State: 1`(A(1),B(1),exit_c)++
1`(A(1),B(2),exit_nc)++	1`(A(1),B(2),exit_nc)++
1`(A(1),B(3),exit_nc)	1`(A(1),B(3),exit_nc)
BIDDERS 2 AUCTIONEERS: empty	BIDDERS 2 AUCTIONEERS: empty
Bid Selected: 1`(A(1),false)	Bid Selected: 1`(A(1),true)
Bids2Reject: 1`(A(1),0)	Bids2Reject: 1`(A(1),0)
547:	522:
Bids: 1`(A(1),0,0,false)	Bids: 1`(A(1),0,0,false)
Processing: 1`(A(1),false)	Processing: 1`(A(1),false)
Auctioneers State: 1`(A(1),B(1),EXIT_NC)++	Auctioneers State: 1`(A(1),B(1),EXIT_NC)++
1`(A(1),B(2),EXIT_C)++	1`(A(1),B(2),EXIT_NC)++
1`(A(1),B(3),EXIT_NC)	1`(A(1),B(3),EXIT_C)
AUCTIONEERS 2 BIDDERS: empty	AUCTIONEERS 2 BIDDERS: empty
Bidders State: 1`(A(1),B(1),exit_nc)++	Bidders State: 1`(A(1),B(1),exit_nc)++
1`(A(1),B(2),exit_c)++	1`(A(1),B(2),exit_nc)++
1`(A(1),B(3),exit_nc)	1`(A(1),B(3),exit_c)
BIDDERS 2 AUCTIONEERS: empty	BIDDERS 2 AUCTIONEERS: empty
Bid Selected: 1`(A(1),true)	Bid Selected: 1`(A(1),true)
Bids2Reject: 1`(A(1),0)	Bids2Reject: 1`(A(1),0)

Fig. 9. Node Descriptors for the dead markings (MaxAucs =1 and MaxBdrs =3)

for these three markings, as it does for marking 925. We conjecture that this property holds for any value of MaxBdrs.

4.2   Absence of Livelocks and Proper Termination

Although the system exhibits cyclic behaviour, it does not livelock. This is shown in Table 2, where we record the result of a state space query that checks whether all dead markings form a home space. A home space is a set of markings with the property that all markings can reach at least one of its members. The results of the query show that all markings can reach at least one dead marking, given suitable fairness assumptions, hence there are no livelocks. We conjecture that this property holds for any value of MaxBdrs. Because the system can always reach at least one dead marking, and that all dead markings are desirable, we conclude that the system terminates correctly.

4.3   Absence of Dead Code

Dead transitions equate to dead code. From Table 2, for $3 \leq \text{MaxBdrs} \leq 5$ we see that there are no dead transitions. We conjecture that this holds for all MaxBdrs ≥ 3. However, for MaxBdrs = 1 we see that there are three dead transitions. These correspond to the transitions Reselect PreBid, Prov Rej Updated PreBid and BidChosen RejRemBids. An auctioneer may reply to a Definitive Bid with either a CG, CR or a PR. If the auctioneer replies with a CG, then there are no other bidders to which CR's need be sent, hence BidChosen RejRemBids is dead. If the auctioneer replies with a CR or PR, there are no Pre Bids for the auctioneer to provisionally grant, hence no other Pre Bids to provisionally reject. Hence Reselect PreBid and Prov Rej Updated PreBid are dead. Therefore, this result is expected. We also see from Table 2 that there is one dead transition when MaxBdrs=2. This corresponds to the transition Prov Rej Updated PreBid. If there are only two bidders, and the auctioneer responds with a CR or PR to a Definitive Bid from one of them, the only Pre Bid is provisionally granted and hence there are no other Pre Bids for the auctioneer to provisionally reject. This is also expected behaviour.

4.4   Channel Bound

Table 2 shows that the channel places are bounded by MaxBdrs for all cases we examined. This can be explained by noting that the single auctioneer interacting with MaxBdrs bidders will, at any instant, send no more than a single message to each of the MaxBdrs bidders, hence a bound of MaxBdrs messages. Similarly, each bidder, at any instant, sends a single message to the auctioneer in reply, hence a bound of MaxBdrs bids.

5   Conclusions and Future Work

In this paper, we have presented, for the first time, an abstract parametric model of the CNP-ext [1] and analysed the protocol using the state space techniques. Our model captures the multithreaded nature of the auctioneers dealing with the bidders concurrently and provides a semantics for the Protocol Flow Diagram representation in [13]. We have proved a number of properties for one auctioneer and a number of bidders from 1 to 5. We have shown that the protocol will always terminate correctly, and that there is consistent belief between the auctioneer and bidders. We have demonstrated that there are no livelocks, and that the only dead transitions are expected. Finally, we have also shown that both the channel bounds are limited to MaxBdrs. We conjecture that these properties hold for all MaxBdrs > 0.

In the future we would like to extend the verification of CNP-ext to any number of bidders, not just 1 to 5. We would then like to relax Assumptions 1 and 4, by extending the model to open multi-agent systems and introducing deadlines, respectively. Finally, we would like to extend this work to the Extended Contract Net Protocol [5,6] and the Provisional Agreement Protocol [14,15,16,17,18] which are more elaborate and complex than CNP-ext.

References

1. Aknine, S., Pinson, S., Shakun, M.F.: An Extended Multi-Agent Negotiation Protocol. Autonomous Agents and Multi-Agent Systems 8(1), 5–45 (2004)
2. Billington, J., Gallasch, G.E., Han, B.: A Coloured Petri Net Approach to Protocol Verification. In: Desel, J., Reisig, W., Rozenberg, G. (eds.) Lectures on Concurrency and Petri Nets 2003. LNCS, vol. 3098, pp. 210–290. Springer, Heidelberg (2004)

3. Billington, J., Gupta, A.K.: Effectiveness of Coloured Petri nets for Modelling and Analysing the Contract Net Protocol. In: Proceedings of 8th Workshop and Tutorial on Practical Use of Coloured Petri Nets and the CPN Tools, Aarhus, Denmark, October 22-24, 2007, pp. 49–65 (2007)
4. Ferber, J.: Multi-Agent Systems: An Introduction to Distributed Artificial Intelligence. Addison-Wesley Longman, Amsterdam (1999)
5. Fischer, K., Kuhn, N.: A DAI Approach to Modelling the Transportation Domain, DFKI Research Report RR-93-25. German Research Centre for Artificial Intelligence (DFKI), Saarbrücken (1993)
6. Fischer, K., Müller, J.P., Heimig, I., Scheer, A.W.: Intelligent Agents in Virtual Enterprises. In: Proceedings of the 1st International Conference on the Practical Application of Intelligent Agents and Multi-Agent Technology, London, UK, pp. 205–223 (1996)
7. Foundation for Intelligent Physical Agents (FIPA), http://www.fipa.org/specs/ fipa00029/SC00029
8. ISO/IEC. Software and Systems Engineering – High-level Petri Nets – Part 1: Concepts, Definitions and Graphical Notation. ISO/IEC 15909-1, 1 (December 2004)
9. Jensen, K.: Coloured Petri Nets: Basic Concepts, Analysis Methods and Practical Use, 2nd edn. Monographs in Theoretical Computer Science, vol. 1 to 3. Springer, Heidelberg (1997)
10. Jensen, K., Kristensen, L.M., Wells, L.: Coloured Petri Nets and CPN Tools for Modelling and Validation of Concurrent Systems. International Journal on Software Tools for Technology Transfer 9(3-4), 213–254 (2007)
11. Paurobally, S.: Rational Agents and the Processes and States of Negotiation. PhD thesis, Imperial College, London, UK (2002)
12. Paurobally, S., Cunningham, J., Jennings, N.R.: Verifying the Contract Net Protocol: A Case Study in Interaction Protocol and Agent Communication Language Semantics. In: Proceedings of 2nd International Workshop on Logic and Communication in Multi-Agent Systems, Nancy, France, pp. 98–117 (2004)
13. Perugini, D.: Agents for Logistics: A Provisional Agreement Approach. PhD thesis, The University of Melbourne, Victoria, Australia (2006)
14. Perugini, D., Lambert, D.: A Distributed Agent Approach to Global Transportation Scheduling. In: Proceedings of IEEE/WIC International Conference on Intelligent Agent Technology (IAT), Halifax, Canada (2003)
15. Perugini, D., Lambert, D.: Distributed Information Fusion Agents. In: Proceedings of the 6th International Conference on Information Fusion, Cairns, Australia (2003)
16. Perugini, D., Lambert, D.: Agent-Based Transport Scheduling in Military Logistics. In: Kudenko, D., Kazakov, D., Alonso, E. (eds.) AAMAS 2004. LNCS (LNAI), vol. 3394. Springer, Heidelberg (2004)
17. Perugini, D., Lambert, D.: Provisional Agreement Protocol for Global Transportation Scheduling. In: Proceedings of International Workshop Agent in Traffic and Transportation as part of AAMAS 2004, New York, U.S (2004)
18. Perugini, D., Lambert, D.: From Single Static to Multiple Dynamic Combinatorial Auctions. In: Proceedings of IEEE/WIC International Conference on Intelligent Agent Technology (IAT), Compiegne University of Technology, France (2005)
19. Smith, R.G.: The Contract Net Protocol: High-Level Communication and Control in a Distributed Problem Solver. IEEE Transactions On Computers C-29(12), 1104–1113 (1980)

Program Repair Suggestions from Graphical State-Transition Specifications

Farn Wang[1,2] and Chih-Hong Cheng[1]

[1] Dept. of Electrical Engineering, National Taiwan University, Taiwan, ROC
[2] Grad. Inst. of Electronic Engineering, National Taiwan University, Taiwan, ROC
farn@cc.ee.ntu.edu.tw

Abstract. In software engineering, graphical formalisms, like state-transition tables and automata, are very often indispensable parts of the specifications. Such a formalism usually leads to specification refinement that maintains the simulation/bisimulation relation between an implementation and a specification. We investigate how to use formal techniques to generate suggestions for repairing a program that breaks the bisimulation relation with a graphical specification. We use state graphs as a unified representation of the program models and specifications. We propose a technique that may evaluate the cost of a repair. We present a PTIME heuristic algorithm that suggests how to repair a model state graph. We then explain how to derive repair suggestions for programs from the repair for state graphs. Finally, we report our experiment that checks the performance of our repair algorithms and the costs of our repairs.

Keywords: state graph, state transition relation, repair, graph theory, cost, evaluation, equivalence, bisimulation.

1 Introduction

The construction of large complex software with quality assurance is becoming more important than ever. In general, quality assurance is achieved with verification techniques, i.e., checking if the behavior of a design meets a specification. Up to now, for program verification, various techniques have been developed, including testing [14] and model checking [5]. Once a bug is reported in the verification process, locating and repairing the bug still rely heavily on human intervention which is costly, time-consuming, and error-prone. In fact, the process of program repair remains to be the least automated in system development. When talking about repairing, the cost is usually taken into account. Thus, without taking repair cost into consideration, research work in program repair is not likely to be useful in practice. This work is to develop techniques for repair suggestions of programs with a cost concept against graphical state-transition specifications.

Graphical specification formalisms have been widely used in software engineering and telecommunication industry. Examples are the state-transition diagrams used in the specification of many protocols, the statecharts of UML, the

K. Suzuki et al. (Eds.): FORTE 2008, LNCS 5048, pp. 185–200, 2008.

abstract machines of SDL, automata, ..., etc. In this work, we adopt such a formalism, called *state graph*, as a unified representation for both program models and state-transition specifications. There are many algorithms and tools that can construct the state graphs of programs automatically [1].

There are many definitions for the verification between two state graphs. For example, we can compare sets of traces of the two state graphs. However, state graphs are usually used as a suggestion for the behavior structures of a program in a state-by-state and transition-by-transition way. Thus we feel that *simulation checking* between state graphs is a better choice in this work. Intuitively, one state graph A_m *is simulated by* another A_s if and only if every transition that A_m can make can also be matched by A_s at a corresponding state. But this framework sometimes is still not good enough for practical verification in the industry. For one thing, a specification state graph could be vacuously satisfied by a faulty program that yields no behavior at all. One way to cope with this problem is to also specify some good behaviors which the program must exhibit. Specifically, we can have a pair of state graphs, $A_s^{(l)}$ and $A_s^{(u)}$ respectively for the lower-bound and the upper-bound specifications. Given the model state graph A_m of a program, we can thus verify whether $A_s^{(1)}$ is simulated by A_m and A_m is simulated by $A_s^{(u)}$.

However, we feel that the framework of simulation-checking with both a lower-bound and an upper-bound specifications is a little complicated and may blur the technical presentation in this article. Instead, we use a less involved framework called *bisimulation checking* [13,15]. Intuitively, two state graphs are *bisimulation equivalent* if and only if for every corresponding state pairs of the two graphs, every transition that the one graph can make at a state can also be matched by the other graph at a corresponding state, and vice versa. In a not very rigorous sense, bisimulation-checking is like simulation-checking when the lower-bound and upper-bound state-transition specifications are the same. The techniques we present in this work for the framework of bisimulation checking should also be applicable to the framework of simulation-checking with lower-bound and upper-bound specifications.

In repairing a program for a specification, engineers usually can evaluate whether a repair is better than another. For example, a better repair might introduce less changes to a program, might run more efficiently, might use less memory, might be more readable, ..., and etc. It is easy to see that there are many dimensions in evaluating how good a repair decision is. Thus it is in general difficult to define a formal approach to evaluate repairs in a way that matches human engineers' intuition. Anyway, we still feel it is important to have the first step in formalizing the evaluation of repairs. In this work, we borrow the graph edit-distance concept in graph theory for the evaluation of the 'cost' of repairs. A *repair* is defined as a sequence of *edit operations* to A_m to make A_m and A_s bisimulation equivalent. We consider several types of *edit operations* to state graphs. The length of an edit operation sequence naturally defines the *cost* of the corresponding repair. In such a context, cost of repairs can help engineers to evaluate the degree of changes to be introduced with a repair. This can be useful in maintaining legacy software when engineers may prefer not to introduce significant changes.

In figure 1, we present our framework of verification and program repair suggestion. We construct the state graphs from a program and a graphical specification of a state transition relation. We then check the bisimulation equivalence

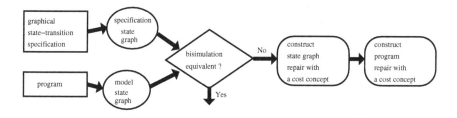

Fig. 1. Framwork of verification and program repair

between the program state graph and the specification state graph. If they are not bisimulation equivalent, then we use the techniques in this work to construct suggestions for repairing the program with a cost concept.

In this work, we establish an upper-bound on the cost to repair a model state graph with respect to a specification one. We also present a logic-based algorithm for the calculation of an upper-bound for the minimum repair cost. We then present a PTIME heuristic algorithm for constructing repairs. We have implemented the heuristic algorithm and compared its performance with a straightforward exploration procedure that searches through the space of repairs. We have experimented against several benchmarks. Our heuristic repair algorithm can sometimes find a repair at a cost lower than the just-mentioned upper-bound. We feel that the heuristic algorithm could be used as a foundation for further investigation in this research direction. Finally, we explain how to convert the repair for state graphs to the repair suggestions for programs.

The rest of the paper is presented as follows. Section 2 reviews related work. Section 3 briefly defines state graphs and bisimulation and explains how programs can be converted to models as state graphs. Section 4 discusses the cost evaluation of repairs. Section 5 establishes an upper-bound of the minimum-cost repair for a given repair task and presents an algorithm for calculating the upper-bound. Section 6 presents algorithms for the construction of repairs with a cost concept and explains how to repair a program based on the repair of the corresponding model state graph. Section 7 reports our experiment. Section 8 is for the conclusion and possible future directions.

2   Related Work

Jobstmann et al. viewed the program repair problem as a game. Given a set of suspicious statements (information from fault localization), they first relax the constraints on those suspicious statements and then look for a further constraint of the statements to make the program satisfy specifications [12]. Thus the possible program repairs are restricted to the original architectures of the models. The work of Griesmayer et al. could be viewed as an extension in this direction [9]. In contrast, our framework does not constrain ourselves to those repairs conforming to the original architectures of the model automata. We allow for any repaired model that can be represented as a state graph. Our framework also enables the analysis of repair costs. Moreover, our framework does not rely on the availability of a fault localizer.

There have been discussions in the Artificial Intelligence (AI) community on repair automation. We discuss two of them in the following. Buccafurri et al. argued, with examples, for the connection between the system repair problem and abductive theory revision problem [3]. They also argued that the repair cost can be estimated with the length of the corresponding edit operation sequence and proposed heuristics to avoid redundancy and optimize in the search of the minimum repair.

Ding and Zhang defined the basic repair steps of Kripke model for specifications in *LTL (linear-time temporal logic)* [6]. To formalize the concept of repair cost, they defined the ordering among repairs and presented theorems in characterizing the minimum repairs for specifications like $F\psi$ and $\psi_1 \wedge \psi_2$. They also presented an algorithm to repair Kripke models for CTL specifications [7].

In this work, we also present a logic-based algorithm for the calculation of MCS between graphs. At this moment, there are many tools that can construct the MCS between two graphs, for instance, *SimPack* [16]. But, to our knowledge, no existing tools support the construction of MCS' of graphs with both arc and vertex labels.

3   State Graphs

For convenience, we have the following notations. Given a set or a sequence V, the size (number of elements) of V is denoted $|V|$. Given a function f, we let f^{-1} be the inverse of f. Also, 'iff' is a shorthand for "if and only if."

Definition 1. (State graphs) A *state graph* A on a set P of atomic propositions and an alphabet Σ is a tuple (Q, P, μ, Σ, E) with the following constraints.
- Q is a finite set of *states*.
- P is a finite set of *atomic propositions*. We assume there is an atomic proposition $ini \in P$ that denotes whether a state is initial.
- $\mu : Q \mapsto (P \mapsto \{false, true\})$ is a labeling function for the states.
- Σ is a finite set of input symbols.
- $E \subseteq (Q \times \Sigma \times Q)$ is a finite set of *transitions*.

Also, we let $ini(A) = \{q \mid \mu(q, ini)\}$ be the set of initial states of A.   ∎

There are many known techniques that allow us to abstract a program into a state graph [1]. Thus state graph can be used as a unified representation for both our program models and our graphical state-transition specifications. For conciseness of presentation, in this work, we use the following *bisimulation relation* [13] to define the verification problem between two state graphs.

Definition 2. (Bisimulation of state graphs) Given a set P of atomic propositions, a set Σ of input symbols, and two state graphs $A_1 = (Q_1, P, \mu_1, \Sigma, E_1)$ and $A_2 = (Q_2, P, \mu_2, \Sigma, E_2)$, a *bisimulation B* between A_1 and A_2 is a relation $B \subseteq Q_1 \times Q_2$ such that for every $(q_1, q_2) \in B$, the following restrictions hold.

- $\mu_1(q_1) = \mu_2(q_2)$.
- For every $(q_1, a, q_1') \in E_1$, there is a $(q_1', q_2') \in B$ with $(q_2, a, q_2') \in E_2$.
- For every $(q_2, a, q_2') \in E_2$, there is a $(q_1', q_2') \in B$ with $(q_1, a, q_1') \in E_1$.

A_1 and A_2 are *bisimulation equivalent*, in symbols $A_1 \equiv A_2$, iff there is a bisimulation B between A_1 and A_2 with the following restrictions.

- For every $q_1 \in ini(A_1)$, there is a $q_2 \in ini(A_2)$ with $(q_1, q_2) \in B$.
- For every $q_2 \in ini(A_2)$, there is a $q_1 \in ini(A_1)$ with $(q_1, q_2) \in B$.   ∎

Bisimulation preserves all properties expressible in the propositional μ-calculus, which subsumes CTL* [8] in expressiveness. The maximal bisimulation between two state graphs can be constructed in deterministic polynomial time [15].

4   Repairs and Their Cost Estimation

As we have said that, there are good repairs and bad repairs. It is in general difficult to evaluate how good a repair is. We first formalize the concept of repairs to state graphs. As in [3,6,7], we may define a repair of a model state graph as a sequence of graph-edit operations that transforms the graph to one that is bisimulation equivalent to a specification. In a repair, we allow the following four types of basic edit operations. Suppose we are given a state graph $A = (Q, P, \mu, \Sigma, E)$.

- **State addition**: Given a state q and a set $L \subseteq P$, $\lambda X.state\_add(X, q, L)$ is an operation that adds state q to X with labels in L. Formally speaking, $state\_add(A, q, L)$ is a new state graph $(Q \cup \{q\}, P, \mu', \Sigma, E)$ such that μ' is identical to μ except that $\mu'(q) = L$. Note that if $q \in Q$, then the addition has no effect.
- **State deletion**: Given a state q, $\lambda X.state\_del(X, q)$ is an operation that takes state q out of state graph X. Formally speaking, $state\_del(A, q)$ is a new state graph $(Q - \{q\}, P, \mu, \Sigma, E)$. Note that if $q \notin Q$, then the operation does not have an effect. Also deleting a state with incoming or outgoing transitions has no effect.
- **Transition addition**: Given two states $q, q' \in Q$ and an $a \in \Sigma$, $\lambda X.xtion\_add(X, q, a, q')$ is an operation that adds transition (q, a, q') to state graph X. Formally speaking, $xtion\_add(A, q, a, q')$ is a new state graph $(Q \cup \{q\}, P, \mu, \Sigma, E \cup \{(q, a, q')\})$. In case $q \notin Q$, $q' \notin Q$, or $a \notin \Sigma$, $xtion\_add(A, q, a, q') = A$.
- **Transition deletion**: Given two states $q, q' \in Q$ and an $a \in \Sigma$, $\lambda X.xtion\_del(X, q, a, q')$ is an operation that takes transition (q, a, q') out of state graph X. Formally, $xtion\_del(A, q, a, q')$ is a new state graph

$(Q \cup \{q\}, P, \mu, \Sigma, E - \{(q, a, q')\})$. In case $q \notin Q$ or $q' \notin Q$, or $a \notin \Sigma$, $xtion\_del(A, q, a, q') = A$.

An *edit sequence* is a sequence of edit operations. Given an edit sequence $e_1 e_2 \ldots e_n$ on a state graph A, the result of the sequence on A, in symbols $A e_1 e_2 \ldots e_n$, is defined inductively as follows.

- $A\epsilon = A$ where ϵ is the null sequence.
- $A(\lambda X.state\_add(X, q, L)) e_2 \ldots e_n = state\_add(A, q, L) e_2 \ldots e_n$.
- $A(\lambda X.state\_del(X, q)) e_2 \ldots e_n = state\_del(A, q) e_2 \ldots e_n$.
- $A(\lambda X.xtion\_add(X, q, a, q')) e_2 \ldots e_n = xtion\_add(A, q, a, q') e_2 \ldots e_n$.
- $A(\lambda X.xtion\_del(X, q, a, q')) e_2 \ldots e_n = xtion\_del(A, q, a, q') e_2 \ldots e_n$.

The *cost* of a repair $\sigma = e_1 \ldots e_n$ is defined as $|\sigma| = n$, i.e., the length of σ. For example, in figure 2, we have (a) for a model graph and (b) for a specification graph. The initial states are with incoming arrows without a source. (c) is the obtained from a repair of (a) for (b) with the minimum repair cost two. A repair is the following edit sequence.

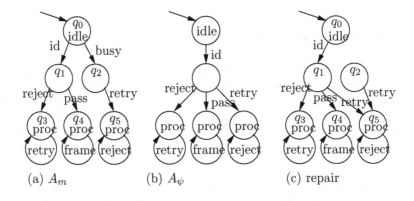

(a) A_m (b) A_ψ (c) repair

Fig. 2. An example of repair

$$(\lambda X.xtion\_del(q_0, busy, q_2))(\lambda X.xtion\_add(q_1, retry, q_5))$$

5   Upper-Bounds for Minimum Repair Cost

State graphs are in fact directed graphs with states and arc labels. In this section, we base on graph theory, specifically the work of Bunke [4], to derive an upper-bound on minimum repair cost for bisimulation equivalence.

5.1   Upper-Bounds from the Graph Theory

We can define the *isomorphism* between state graphs. Two state graphs $A_1 = (Q_1, P, \mu_1, \Sigma, E_1)$ and $A_2 = (Q_2, P, \mu_2, \Sigma, E_2)$ are *isomorphic* if there is a bijective function β from Q_1 to Q_2 such that

- for all $q \in Q_1$, $\mu_1(q) = \mu_2(\beta(q))$;
- for all $(q_1, a, q_2) \in E_1$, $(\beta(q_1), a, \beta(q_2)) \in E_2$;
- for all $(q_1, a, q_2) \in E_2$, $(\beta^{-1}(q_1), a, \beta^{-1}(q_2)) \in E_1$.

We have the following intuitive lemma.

Lemma 1. *Given a model graph A_m, a specification graph A_s, and an edit sequence σ, if $A_m\sigma$ is isomorphic to A_s, then σ is a repair.*

Proof : True since isomorphic state graphs are bisimulation equivalent. ■

Lemma 1 suggests that we can use the length of the shortest edit sequence that changes A_m to A_s as an upper-bound for the minimum repair cost. The upper-bound can be used to bound our exploration in the search for a minimum repair from A_m to A_s.

In the following, since we may use graph theory to handle state graphs, sometimes we conveniently use the terms in graph theory to call the equivalent structures in our state graphs. For example, we may also call a state a *vertex* and a transition an *arc*. The *size* of a graph $A = (Q, P, \mu, \Sigma, E)$, denoted $|A|$, is defined as $|Q| + |E|$. Given a state q, we may write $q \in A$ iff $q \in Q$. Also given a transition (q, a, q'), we may write $(q, a, q') \in A$ iff $(q, a, q') \in E$. A *subgraph* $A' = (Q', P, \mu, \Sigma, E')$ of a state graph $A = (Q, P, \mu, \Sigma, E)$ is a graph such that $Q' \subseteq Q$ and $E' \subseteq E$. Note that we let A and A' share the same state-labeling function for the simplicity of presentation.

Definition 3. (Maximum common subgraph) Let A_1 and A_2 be two graphs and A_1' and A_2' be subgraphs of A_1 and A_2 respectively. We call A_1' (or A_2') a *common subgraph* of A_1 and A_2 if A_1' and A_2' are isomorphic. A graph G is a *maximum common subgraph (MCS)* of A_1 and A_2 if G is a common subgraph of A_1 and A_2 and for all common subgraphs G' of A_1 and A_2, $|G'| \leq |G|$. ■

The relation between edit sequences and MCS was first presented by Bunke in [4]. Bunke's work is based on the assumption that the size of a graph is only relevant to the number of vertices. Moreover, the edit operations of arcs in his work are all free. In contrast, we assume that the cost of an edit operation to an arc (transition) is also one. We have adapted the following lemma from [4] for the relation between edit sequences and MCS.

Lemma 2. *Suppose we are given three state graphs A_1, A_2, and A_c such that A_c is an MCS of A_1 and A_2. Then the shortest edit sequence that changes A_1 to A_2 is of length $|A_1| + |A_2| - 2|A_c|$.* ■

Due to page-limit, we have left the proof to a full version of the paper in our tool website. With lemmas 1 and 2, we can establish the following lemma.

Lemma 3. *Suppose we are given a model state graph A_m and a specification state graph A_s. If A_c is an MCS of A_m and A_s, then the minimum repair cost of A_m for A_s is no greater than $|A_m| + |A_s| - 2|A_c|$.* ■

Due to page-limit, we have left the proof of the lemma to a full version of the paper in our tool website. We use figure 3 to explain lemma 3. The parts circled

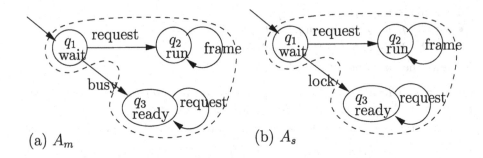

(a) A_m (b) A_s

Fig. 3. Two state graphes

with dashed lines are the MCS, say A_c, of the two state graphs. The minimum repair cost is no greater than $|A_m| + |A_s| - 2|A_c| = 7 + 7 - 2 \times 6 = 2$.

The following lemma shows that the upper-bound established with lemma 3 is actually tight. We can establish the faimily of A_m^i's and A_s^i's in figure 4 that share no MCS.

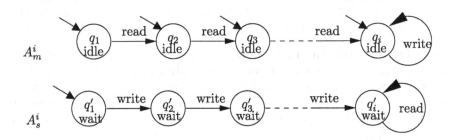

Fig. 4. A family of A_m^i and A_s^i with tight upper-bound repair cost

Lemma 4. *For the family of state graphs in figure 4, for each positive integer i, the minimum cost of repair of A_m^i for A_s^i is $|A_m^i| + |A_s^i|$.*

Proof : As can be seen from figure 4, for each i, there is no common subgraph between A_m^i and A_s^i. Moreover, if any state in A_m^i remains to be initial, A_m^i cannot be repaired to be bisimulation equivalent with A_s^i. To remove states in A_m^i, we first have to remove all transitions in A_m^i. This costs $|A_m^i|$ edit operations. Then we need $|A_s^i|$ edit operations to add A_s^i to A_m^i. In this way, the repaired model becomes isomorphic to A_s^i. According to lemma 1, the repaired model is thus bisimulation equivalent to A_s^i. The cost is thus $|A_m^i| + |A_s^i|$ for each i. ■

5.2   A Logic-Based Algorithm for the MCS

Our algorithm is built on an MCS construction algorithm. Note that the calculation of MCS is an NP-complete problem [10]. Our motivation is that with proper encoding of the logic formulas in advanced data-structures, like BDD [2], we have a better chance to calculate MCS efficiently in the average cases. Specifically, we want to construct a logic formula that characterizes the common subgraphs between two state graphs. A *solution* (satisfying truth assignments) to the formula can be used to help us constructing a common subgraph. An MCS then corresponds to a *maximal* solution that assigns the most number of 1's to the variables.

Given a set V of Boolean variables, a *formula* η of V can be inductively constructed with rule "$\eta ::= v \mid \neg\eta_1 \mid \eta_1 \vee \eta_2$." Standard shorthands like $\eta_1 \wedge \eta_2$, $\eta_1 \rightarrow \eta_2$, and $\eta_1 \leftrightarrow \eta_2$ are also allowed in this work. A *truth value* is either *true* or *false*. An *interpretation* of a formula is a mapping from its set of Boolean variables to truth values. An interpretation I *satisfies* a formula η, in symbols $I \models \eta$, if the following inductive conditions are maintained.

- $I \models v$ iff $I(v) = true$.
- $I \models \neg\eta_1$ iff it is not the case that $I \models \eta_1$.
- $I \models \eta_1 \vee \eta_2$ iff either $I \models \eta_1$ or $I \models \eta_2$.

I is a *solution* to η iff $I \models \eta$. Given two solutions I and I', if for every $v \in V$, $I(v)$ implies $I'(v)$, we say I' is *no smaller than* I. A *maximal* solution is no smaller than any other solutions.

In our formulas, we use the following Boolean variables for the correspondence between states and transitions of two state graphs $A_1 = (Q_1, P, \mu_1, \Sigma, E_1)$ and $A_2 = (Q_2, P, \mu_2, \Sigma, E_2)$.

$$\left\{ c_{q_2}^{q_1} \mid q_1 \in Q_1, q_2 \in Q_2 \right\} \cup \left\{ c_{(q_2,a,q_2')}^{(q_1,a,q_1')} \mid (q_1, a, q_1') \in E_1, (q_2, a, q_2') \in E_2 \right\}.$$

Intuitively, for each $q_1 \in Q_1$ and $q_2 \in Q_2$, $c_{q_2}^{q_1}$ is true iff state q_1 corresponds to state q_2 in the MCS; for each $(q_1, a, q_1') \in E_1$ and $(q_2, a, q_2') \in E_2$, $c_{(q_2,a,q_2')}^{(q_1,a,q_1')}$ is true iff transition (q_1, a, q_1') corresponds to transition (q_2, a, q_2') in the MCS. In the following, we list the restrictions of the correspondence and their respective formulas.

- **State equivalence mutual exclusion**: A state q_1 cannot correspond to more than one state in q_2; and vice versa.

$$\mathrm{VEME}(Q_1, Q_2) \equiv \bigwedge_{q_1 \in Q_1, q_2 \in Q_2} \left(c_{q_2}^{q_1} \rightarrow \left(\begin{array}{c} \bigwedge_{\bar{q}_2 \in Q_2 - \{q_2\}} \neg c_{\bar{q}_2}^{q_1} \\ \wedge \bigwedge_{\bar{q}_1 \in Q_1 - \{q_1\}} \neg c_{q_2}^{\bar{q}_1} \end{array} \right) \right)$$

- **State equivalence structure**: Corresponding states must have the same labels.

$$\mathrm{VES}(Q_1, \mu_1, Q_2, \mu_2) \equiv \bigwedge_{q_1 \in Q_1, q_2 \in Q_2, \mu_1(q_1) \neq \mu_2(q_2)} \neg c_{q_2}^{q_1}$$

- **Transition equivalence mutual exclusion**: A transition in E_1 cannot correspond to more than one transition in E_2; and vice versa.

$$\bigwedge_{\substack{(q_1, a, q_1') \in E_1, \\ (q_2, a, q_2') \in E_2}} \left(c_{(q_2,a,q_2')}^{(q_1,a,q_1')} \rightarrow \left(\begin{array}{c} \bigwedge_{(\bar{q}_2, a, \bar{q}_2') \in Q_2 - \{(q_2,a,q_2')\}} \neg c_{(\bar{q}_2,a,\bar{q}_2')}^{(q_1,a,q_1')} \\ \wedge \bigwedge_{(\bar{q}_1, a, \bar{q}_1') \in Q_1 - \{(q_1,a,q_1')\}} \neg c_{(q_2,a,q_2')}^{(\bar{q}_1,a,\bar{q}_1')} \end{array} \right) \right)$$

- **Transition equivalence structure**: If two transitions correspond to each other, then their sources must correspond to each other, their destinations must correspond to each other, and their transition labels must be the same.

$$\text{AES}(E_1, E_2) \equiv \bigwedge\nolimits_{(q_1,a,q_1')\in E_1, (q_2,a,q_2')\in E_2} \left(c_{(q_2,a,q_2')}^{(q_1,a,q_1')} \to \left(c_{q_2}^{q_1} \wedge c_{q_2'}^{q_1'} \right) \right)$$

We then construct the following formula for *common subgraph restriction:* $\text{CSR}(A_1, A_2)$ as the following conjunction.

$$\text{VEME}(Q_1, Q_2) \wedge \text{VES}(Q_1, \mu_1, Q_2, \mu_2) \wedge \text{AEME}(E_1, E_2) \wedge \text{AES}(E_1, E_2).$$

Given a solution I of $\text{CSR}(A_1, A_2)$, we can construct the common subgraph $\text{CS}(A_1, A_2, I)$ corresponding to I as follows.

$$\left(\left\{ q_2 \mid \exists q_1 (I(c_{q_2}^{q_1})) \right\}, P, \mu_2, \Sigma, \left\{ (q_2, a, q_2') \Big| \exists q_1 \exists a \exists q_1' \left(I \left(c_{(q_2,a,q_2')}^{(q_1,a,q_1')} \right) \right) \right\} \right)$$

Note that we use a subgraph in A_2 to represent the common subgraph. We can also do it the other way around. With the restrictions in the above, we can show that each solution of $\text{CSR}(A_1, A_2)$ fully describes a common subgraph.

Lemma 5. *Given two state graphs* $A_1 = (Q_1, P, \mu_1, \Sigma, E_1)$ *and* $A_2 = (Q_2, P, \mu_2, \Sigma, E_2)$, A_c *is a common subgraph of* A_1 *and* A_2 *iff there is a solution I of* $\text{CSR}(A_1, A_2)$ *such that* A_c *is isomorphic to* $\text{CS}(A_1, A_2, I)$.

Proof : The correctness of the lemma can be established by checking that $\text{CSR}(A_1, A_2)$ correctly encodes all the constraints for MCS construction. ∎

Also a maximal solution encodes an MCS as stated with the following lemma.

Lemma 6. *Given two state graphs* $A_1 = (Q_1, P, \mu_1, \Sigma, E_1)$ *and* $A_2 = (Q_2, P, \mu_2, \Sigma, E_2)$, A_c *is an MCS of* A_1 *and* A_2 *iff there is a maximal solution I of* $\text{CSR}(A_1, A_2)$ *such that* A_c *is isomorphic to* $\text{CS}(A_1, A_2, I)$.

Proof : The lemma follows from lemma 5 and the fact that the number of '1's in a solution actually is equal to the size of the corresponding MCS. ∎

With lemma 6, we have the following algorithm for MCS construction.

MCS(A_1, A_2) {
    Find a maximal solution I for $\text{CSR}(A_1, A_2)$. Return $\text{CS}(A_1, A_2, I)$.
}

Note that we do not elaborate on how to find the maximal solutions. In this work, we use JDD (Java BDD library) [11] to construct $\text{CSR}(A_1, A_2)$. JDD can list all solutions of a formula. A maximal solution has the most number of 1's in the listing. It is also possible to take advantage of the structure-sharing capability of BDDs [2] and design a recursive procedure to efficiently search for the maximal solutions. But due to page-limit, we omit the discussion here.

6   Techniques for Repair Suggestions with a Cost Concept

In a real-world project, minimum cost repairs may be difficult and costly to construct. To improve the performance of automated repair tools, sometimes we may have to settle for quick repairs that may not be of minimum cost. In the following, we present a PTIME heuristic algorithm for constructing repairs of model state graphs. Given a model graph A_m and a specification graph A_s, the algorithm consists of the following three steps.

- Identifying the common structure of A_m and A_s. Here we use the maximal bisimulation between A_m and A_s instead of MCS for the common structure.
- Disabling the difference from A_m to the common structure. The idea is to make all states in the difference from A_m to the common structure unreachable from any initial states.
- Gluing a compact version of the difference from A_s to the common structure to the common structure.

According to lemma 4, these steps do not save time in the worst case. However, according to the experiment, in many cases, they yield repairs with costs lower than the upper-bounds predicted by lemma 3.

At the end, we also discuss how to derive repair suggestions of programs based on the repairs of model state graphs.

6.1   Identifying the Common Structure Between A_m and A_s

Given two state graphs A_1 and A_2, there are classical algorithms that construct the maximal bisimulation, in symbols $B(A_1, A_2)$, between A_1 and A_2. Given a state graph $A = (Q, P, \mu, \Sigma, E)$, $B(A, A)$ is the maximal bisimulation between A and itself. Given a state $q \in Q$, the *bisimulation equivalence class* of q, in symbols $[q]$, is the set of states that are bisimulation equivalent to q in A with respect to $B(A, A)$. Formally speaking, $[q] = \{q' \mid q' \in Q, (q, q') \in B(A, A)\}$. The *bisimulation quotient* of a state graph $A = (Q, P, \mu, \Sigma, E)$, in symbols $[A]$, is a state graph $(\{[q] \mid q \in Q\}, P, \mu', \Sigma, \{([q], a, [q']) \mid (q, a, q') \in E\})$ such that for each $q \in Q$, $\mu'([q]) = \mu(q)$.

Suppose we have two state graphs $A_1 = (Q_1, P, \mu_1, \Sigma, E_1)$ and $A_2 = (Q_2, P, \mu_2, \Sigma, E_2)$. For each $i \in [1, 2]$, we use $\langle A_i \rangle_{B(A_1, A_2)}$ to denote the subgraph of A_i in the maximal bisimulation $B(A_1, A_2)$. That is, $\langle A_i \rangle_{B(A_1, A_2)}$ is a subgraph $(Q, P, \mu_i, \Sigma, \{(q, a, q') \mid q \in Q, q' \in Q, (q, a, q') \in E_i\})$ of A_i such that $Q = \{q \mid q \in Q_i, \exists q' \in Q_{3-i}((q, q') \in B(A_1, A_2) \vee (q', q) \in B(A_1, A_2))\}$. Given a model state graph A_m and a specification state graph A_s, we can view $\langle A_m \rangle_{B(A_m, A_s)}$ and $\langle A_s \rangle_{B(A_m, A_s)}$ as the common structure between A_m and A_s.

6.2   Identifying of the Difference Between A_m and A_s

According to the definition of bisimulation, we know that $\langle A_m \rangle_{B(A_m, A_s)}$ and $\langle A_s \rangle_{B(A_m, A_s)}$ are bisimulation equivalent. They can be viewed as intermediate products in the repair process with all 'unwanted' components removed from A_m. Assume that $A_m = (Q_m, P, \mu_m, \Sigma, E_m)$ and $A_s = (Q_s, P, \mu_s, \Sigma, E_s)$.

Assume that $\langle A_m \rangle_{B(A_m, A_s)} = (Q_b, P, \mu_m, \Sigma, E_b)$. The difference from A_m to $\langle A_m \rangle_{B(A_m, A_s)}$, in symbols $A_m - \langle A_m \rangle_{B(A_m, A_s)}$, can be straightforwardly defined as the following state graph.

$$
\left(\{q \mid q \in Q_m - Q_b\}, P, \mu_m, \Sigma, \left\{ ([q], a, [q']) \,\middle|\, \begin{matrix} (q, a, q') \in E_m, \\ q \in Q_m - Q_b, q' \in Q_m - Q_b \end{matrix} \right\} \right)
$$

We need to disable the effect of $A_m - \langle A_m \rangle_{B(A_m, A_s)}$ for the repair.

Assume that $\langle A_s \rangle_{B(A_m, A_s)} = (Q_b, P, \mu_m, \Sigma, E_b)$. Similarly, we can also define $A_s - \langle A_s \rangle_{B(A_m, A_s)}$ and use it as the difference from A_s to $\langle A_s \rangle_{B(A_m, A_s)}$. However, the 'difference' could still be too big. We propose only to glue the difference from the bisimulation quotient of A_s to $\langle A_s \rangle_{B(A_m, A_s)}$. Specifically, we define this difference, in symbols $[A_s] - \langle A_s \rangle_{B(A_m, A_s)}$, as the following state graph.

$$
\left(\{[q] \mid q \in Q_s - Q_b\}, P, \mu, \Sigma, \left\{ ([q], a, [q']) \,\middle|\, \begin{matrix} (q, a, q') \in E_s, \\ q \in Q_s - Q_b, q' \in Q_s - Q_b \end{matrix} \right\} \right).
$$

We require that for each $q \in Q_s - Q_b$, $\mu([q]) = \mu_s(q)$. This graph captures the behavior of those states in $Q_s - Q_b$ in the bisimulation quotient of A_s.

6.3 Constructing Repair Based on the Common Structure and the Difference

With the concepts defined in the above, we are now ready to present our PTIME algorithm for the repair of A_m for A_s. For convenience, assume that $A_m = (Q_m, P, \mu_m, \Sigma, E_m)$, $A_s = (Q_s, P, \mu_s, \Sigma, E_s)$, $\langle A_m \rangle_{B(A_m, A_s)} = (Q_b, P, \mu_m, \Sigma, E_b)$, and $[A_s] - \langle A_s \rangle_{B(A_m, A_s)} = (Q_d, P, \mu_s, \Sigma, E_d)$. Intuitively, the algorithm consists of the following two steps.

- *Disabling $A_m - \langle A_m \rangle_{B(A_m, A_s)}$ in A_m.* We need to delete all initial states in $A_m - \langle A_m \rangle_{B(A_m, A_s)}$. In addition, we also need to delete all transitions to and from those initial states in $A_m - \langle A_m \rangle_{B(A_m, A_s)}$.
- *Gluing $[A_s] - \langle A_s \rangle_{B(A_m, A_s)}$ to $\langle A_m \rangle_{B(A_m, A_s)}$.* This involves the construction of appropriate transitions between $[A_s] - \langle A_s \rangle_{D(A_m, A_s)}$ and $\langle A_m \rangle_{B(A_m, A_s)}$.

The repair generates a graph $(Q_b \cup Q_d, P, \mu, \Sigma, E)$ with the following constraints.

- $E = E_b \cup E_d$
  $\cup \{(q_1, a, [q_2]) \mid \exists (q_1, q') \in B(A_m, A_s)((q', a, q_2) \in E_s \wedge [q_2] \in Q_d)\}$
  $\cup \{([q_2], a, q_1) \mid \exists (q_1, q') \in B(A_m, A_s)((q_2, a, q') \in E_s \wedge [q_2] \in Q_d)\}$
- For each $q \in Q_b$, $\mu(q) = \mu_m(q)$. For each $[q] \in Q_d$, $\mu([q]) = \mu_s(q)$.

We denote this graph as $\mathrm{Repaired}_B(A_m, A_s)$. Then we can establish the following lemma.

Lemma 7. *For every state graphs A_m and A_s, $\mathrm{Repaired}_B(A_m, A_s)$ is bisimulation equivalent to A_s.*

Proof : Here we sketch a brief proof plan. According to the definition of bisimulation equivalence, we only have to check those states that are reachable from the initial states. This means that we do not need to consider states in $A_m - \langle A_m \rangle_{B(A_m, A_s)}$. We can first assume that for some state q_r in $\mathrm{Repaired}_B(A_m, A_s)$ that is reachable from an initial state, there is no q_s in A_s such that $(q_r, q_s) \in B(\mathrm{Repaired}_B(A_m, A_s), A_s)$. There are two cases to analyze. The first is that there is a transition (q_r, a, q'_r) that $\text{Repaired}_B(A_m, A_s)$ can do at q_r to transit to q'_r but A_s cannot do at any q_s to transit on input a to a state q'_s with $(q'_r, q'_s) \in B(\text{Repaired}_B(A_m, A_s), A_s)$.

- Assume that q_r is in $\langle A_m \rangle_{B(A_m, A_s)}$. According to the definition of $B(A_m, A_s)$, there is a q_s in $\langle A_s \rangle_{B(A_m, A_s)}$ such that $(q_r, q_s) \in B(A_m, A_s)$. There are two more cases to analyze.
    - Assume that q'_r is also in $\langle A_m \rangle_{B(A_m, A_s)}$. According to the definition of $B(A_m, A_s)$, there is a (q_s, a, q'_s) in $\langle A_s \rangle_{B(A_m, A_s)}$ such that $(q_r, q_s) \in B(A_m, A_s)$ and $(q'_r, q'_s) \in B(A_m, A_s)$. This violates our assumptions.
    - Assume that $q'_r = [q'_s]$ is in $[A_s] - \langle A_s \rangle_{B(A_m, A_s)}$. According to the construction of $\text{Repaired}_B(A_m, A_s)$, transition $(q_r, a, [q'_s])$ is there because we have a transition (q_s, a, q'_s) in A_s with $(q_r, q_s) \in B(A_m, A_s)$ and $q'_r = [q'_s]$. This also violates the assumptions.
- The case that q_r is in $[A_s] - \langle A_s \rangle_{B(A_m, A_s)}$ can be proved in a symmetric way.

The "*vice versa*" part is symmetric and is that there is a transition (q_s, a, q'_s) that A_s can do at q_s but $\text{Repaired}_B(A_m, A_s)$ cannot match at any q_r. This case can be proven in a symmetric way. Thus the lemma is proven. ∎

The following lemma shows the complexity of the algorithm.

Lemma 8. $\text{Repaired}_B(A_m, A_s)$ *is constructible in PTIME.*

Proof : According to the classical bisimulation checking algorithm [15], $B(A_m, A_s)$, $\langle A_m \rangle_{B(A_m, A_s)}$, and $\langle A_s \rangle_{B(A_m, A_s)}$ can all be calculated in PTIME. It is easy to see that $[A_s] - \langle A_s \rangle_{B(A_m, A_s)}$ can also be computed in PTIME. Finally, to disable $A_m - \langle A_m \rangle_{B(A_m, A_s)}$ and to glue $[A_s] - \langle A_s \rangle_{B(A_m, A_s)}$ to $\langle A_m \rangle_{B(A_m, A_s)}$, there are at most polynomial number of states and transitions to check and to work on. Thus the lemma is proven. ∎

Suppose $A_m = (Q_m, P, \mu_m, \Sigma, E_m)$, $A_s = (Q_s, P, \mu_s, \Sigma, E_s)$, $\langle A_m \rangle_{B(A_m, A_s)} = (Q_b, P, \mu_b, \Sigma, E_b)$, and $[A_s] - \langle A_s \rangle_{B(A_m, A_s)} = (Q_d, P, \mu_s, \Sigma, E_d)$. By carefully counting the edit operations, we find that the repair cost suggested by $\text{Repaired}_B(A_m, A_s)$ can be computed as follows.

$$
\begin{aligned}
&|ini(A_m)| - |ini(\langle A_m \rangle_{B(A_m, A_s)})| \\
&+ \left| \left\{ (q_1, a, q_2) \,\middle|\, \begin{array}{l} (q_1 \in ini(A_m) - ini(\langle A_m \rangle_{B(A_m, A_s)})) \wedge (q_1, a, q_2) \in E_m) \\ \vee (q_2 \in ini(A_m) - ini(\langle A_m \rangle_{B(A_m, A_s)})) \wedge (q_1, a, q_2) \in E_s) \end{array} \right\} \right| \\
&+ |\{(q_1, a, q_2) \mid q_1 \in Q_b, q_2 \in Q_m - Q_b, (q_1, a, q_2) \in E_m\}| \\
&+ |[A_s] - \langle A_s \rangle_{B(A_m, A_s)}| \\
&+ |\{(q_1, a, [q_2]) \mid \exists (q_1, q') \in B(A_m, A_s)((q', a, q_2) \in E_s \wedge [q_2] \in Q_d)\}| \\
&+ |\{([q_2], a, q_1) \mid \exists (q_1, q') \in B(A_m, A_s)((q_2, a, q') \in E_s \wedge [q_2] \in Q_d)\}|
\end{aligned}
$$

As for the complexity of the algorithm, it is easy to see that this algorithm only incurs polynomial numbers of set subtractions, graph subtractions, bisimulation computations, and graph edit operations. This justifies that the algorithm is in PTIME and only uses polynomial complexity of memory. Due to page limit, we choose to omit the detailed complexity analysis.

6.4   Suggestions for Repairing Programs

The repairs that we may construct in subsection 6.3 are for model state graphs. The engineers still need to know how such repairs can be used as repair suggestions for their programs. Here we give the following rules for deriving repair suggestions for programs. Again, suppose $A_m = (Q_m, P, \mu_m, \Sigma, E_m)$, $A_s = (Q_s, P, \mu_s, \Sigma, E_s)$, $\langle A_m \rangle_{B(A_m, A_s)} = (Q_b, P, \mu_b, \Sigma, E_b)$, and $[A_s] - \langle A_s \rangle_{B(A_m, A_s)} = (Q_d, P, \mu_s, \Sigma, E_d)$. We also assume that for each state in A_m, we still have the information of its entry statements and exit statements in the original program.

- For every initial state in $A_m - \langle A_m \rangle_{B(A_m, A_s)}$, we suggest to the engineers that for such a state, its entry statements should not be the entry points of the program.
- For each transition from a state q_1 in $\langle A_m \rangle_{B(A_m, A_s)}$ to a state q_2 in $A_m - \langle A_m \rangle_{B(A_m, A_s)}$, we suggest to the engineers that the exit statement for the transition from q_1 to q_2 should be disabled.
- We suggest that a program segment that implements $[A_s] - \langle A_s \rangle_{B(A_m, A_s)}$ should be there.
- For each transition from a state q_1 in $\langle A_m \rangle_{B(A_m, A_s)}$ to a state q_2 in $[A_s] - \langle A_s \rangle_{B(A_m, A_s)}$, we suggest to the engineers that we should change a statement of q_1 to a conditional branch statement that may branch to q_2.
- For each transition from a state q_1 in $[A_s] - \langle A_s \rangle_{B(A_m, A_s)}$ to a state q_2 in $\langle A_m \rangle_{B(A_m, A_s)}$, we suggest to the engineers that we should enter an entry statement of q_2 from an exit statement of q_1.

Such suggestions may not lead to the best repair that the engineers may have in mind. But we feel it is certainly a good mechanical support for some initial ideas in repairing a program.

7   Implementation and Experiment

Our experimental tool MODELREPAIR VER.0.1 realizes part of our ideas in finding a minimum repair. The tool supports the construction of MCS, the exploration of a repair space in searching for a repair, and repair construction with the PTIME heuristic algorithm. The tool is available at http://cc.ee.ntu.edu.tw/~val. To visualize the model, we offer interfaces to convert our graph representations into the GOAL format [17]. The users can thus conveniently see the differences between a repaired model and an original model.

To check how well our algorithm performs, we have also implemented an exploration procedure that searches through the space of edit sequences for a minimum cost repair based on the results in section 5. The search strategy of the procedure is breadth-first. Thus it is guaranteed to find a minimum cost repair if enough time and space are allocated. Also we have designed some strategies to speed up the exploration, including partial order among edit operations. The procedure may still run slowly due to the vast repair space. However it can

Table 1. Performance of MODELREPAIR VER.0.1

B	A_m			A_s			UB	exploration algorithm					PTIME algorithm				
	$|A_m|$	$|Q|$	$|E|$	$|A_s|$	$|Q|$	$|E|$		$|A_m\sigma|$	$|Q|$	$|E|$	$|\sigma|$	time	$|A_m\sigma|$	$|Q|$	$|E|$	$|\sigma|$	time
1	11	4	7	14	5	9	5	10	4	6	1	1.79s	14	5	9	5	0.46s
2	9	4	5	15	6	9	10	9	4	5	2	16.6s	9	4	5	4	0.50s
3	4	2	2	7	3	4	3	7	3	4	3	645s	7	3	4	3	0.32s
4	23	9	14	29	11	18	22	$N/A, > 30min$					23	9	14	16	101s
5	18	8	10	20	8	12	18	$N/A, > 30min$					18	8	10	12	11.1s
6	12	4	8	16	5	11	5	Specification inconsistency, 0.53s									
7	12	4	8	15	5	10	5	No repair needed, 0.32s									

B: benchmarks; UB: minimum cost upper-bound predicted with lemma 3;
σ: the corresponding repair; $|Q|$: # states; $|E|$: # transitions; s: seconds;

be used for performance comparison. For interested readers, we have left the procedure to a full version of the paper in our tool website.

We have applied our tool to a few examples. Table 1 summarizes the result of the experiment. All data are collected in Java runtime environment 1.6.0 with Intel Pentium-M 1.6 GHz processor and 512MB RAM. Here 'σ' denotes the repairs we construct. As can be seen, for benchmarks 1 to 5, the PTIME algorithm runs much faster than the repair-space exploration algorithm. For benchmarks 2, 4, and 5, our PTIME algorithm also yields a repair cost lower than the upper-bound predicted by lemma 3 in the column under 'UB.'

For all benchmarks, our heuristic algorithm constructs a repair in less time than the exploration procedure. For benchmarks 1 and 2, our heuristic algorithm constructs repairs with costs greater than the minimum repair costs. But still for benchmarks 2, 4, and 5, the repair costs of our heuristic algorithm are lower than the predicted theoretical upper-bound. In contrast, the exploration procedure did not construct the minimum repairs for benchmarks 3, 4, and 5 in a reasonable amount of time.

8   Conclusion and Future Directions

Our work focuses on the automatic generation of repair suggestions with a cost evaluation that could be useful in controlling the budget for program debugging and preserving the original design intention. We feel that our work could be used as a general foundation for the future research in this direction. One thing is that bisimulation-based repair suggestions may sometimes be based on too strong an assumption. Some program faults may destroy non-trivial bisimulation relations between a model and a specification. In such a case, our algorithm may yield worst-cost repairs. In the future, we may need to investiage what kind of repair suggestions we should make in such a case.

Acknowledgment

We wish to thank Prof. Yih-Kuen Tsay and Mr. Yu-Fang Chen for their helpful suggestions and effort in modifying GOAL to support our implementation and experiments.

References

1. Ball, T., Rajamani, S.K.: Automatically Validating Temporal Safety Properties of Interfaces. In: Dwyer, M.B. (ed.) SPIN 2001. LNCS, vol. 2057, pp. 103–122. Springer, Heidelberg (2001)
2. Bryant, R.E.: Graph-based algorithms for Boolean function manipulation. IEEE Transactions on Computers 35(8), 677–691 (1986)
3. Buccafurri, F., Eiter, T., Gottlob, G., Leone, N.: Enhancing Model Checking in Verification by AI Techniques. Artificial Intelligence 112(1), 55–93 (1999)
4. Bunke, H.: On a Relation between Graph Edit Distance and Maximum Common Subgraph. Pattern Recognition Letters 19, 255–259 (1997)
5. Clarke, E., Emerson, E.A.: Design and Synthesis of Synchronization Skeletons using Branching-Time Temporal Logic. In: Kozen, D. (ed.) Logic of Programs 1981. LNCS, vol. 131. Springer, Heidelberg (1982)
6. Ding, Y., Zhang, Y.: A Logic Approach for LTL System Modification. In: Hacid, M.-S., Murray, N.V., Raś, Z.W., Tsumoto, S. (eds.) ISMIS 2005. LNCS (LNAI), vol. 3488, pp. 435–444. Springer, Heidelberg (2005)
7. Ding, Y., Zhang, Y.: Algorithms for CTL System Modification. In: Khosla, R., Howlett, R.J., Jain, L.C. (eds.) KES 2005. LNCS (LNAI), vol. 3682. Springer, Heidelberg (2005)
8. Fisler, K., Vardi, M.Y.: Bisimulation Minimization in an Automata-Theoretic Verification Framework. In: Gopalakrishnan, G.C., Windley, P. (eds.) FMCAD 1998. LNCS, vol. 1522. Springer, Heidelberg (1998)
9. Griesmayer, A., Bloem, R., Cook, B.: Repair of Boolean Programs with an Application to C. In: Ball, T., Jones, R.B. (eds.) CAV 2006. LNCS, vol. 4144. Springer, Heidelberg (2006)
10. Garey, M.R., Johnson, D.S.: Computers and Intractability: A Guide to the Theory of NP-Completeness. W.H. Freeman, New York (1979)
11. http://javaddlib.sourceforge.net/jdd/
12. Jobstmann, B., Griesmayer, A., Bloem, R.: Program Repair as a Game. In: Etessami, K., Rajamani, S.K. (eds.) CAV 2005. LNCS, vol. 3576. Springer, Heidelberg (2005)
13. Milner, R.: Communication and Concurrency. Prentice-Hall, Englewood Cliffs (1989)
14. Myers, G.J., Sandler, C., Badgett, T., Thomas, T.M.: The Art of Software Testing. Wiley, Chichester (2004)
15. Paige, R., Tarjan, R.E.: Three Partition Refinement Algorithms. SIAM J. 6, 973–989 (1987)
16. http://www.ifi.unizh.ch/ddis/research/semweb/simpack/
17. Tsay, Y.-K., Chen, Y.-F., Tsai, M.-H., Wu, K.-N., Chan, W.-C.: GOAL: A Graphical Tool for Manipulating Buchi Automata and Temporal Formulae. In: Grumberg, O., Huth, M. (eds.) TACAS 2007. LNCS, vol. 4424. Springer, Heidelberg (2007)

Verifying Erlang Telecommunication Systems with the Process Algebra μCRL

Qiang Guo[1], John Derrick[1], and Csaba Hoch[2]

[1] Department of Computer Science,
The University of Sheffield,
Regent Court, 211 Portobello, S1 4DP, UK
{Q.Guo, J.Derrick}@dcs.shef.ac.uk
[2] Faculty of Informatics
Eötvös Loránd Tudományegyetem
Pázmány Péter sétány 1/c., 1117 Budapest, Hungary
hoch@inf.elte.hu

Abstract. Verification is an important process in the development of Erlang systems. A recent strand of work has studied the verification of Erlang applications using the process algebra μCRL. The general idea is that Erlang programs are translated into a μCRL specification, upon which the standard model checkers can be applied for checking the system's properties. In this paper, we pull together some of the existing work and investigate the verification of an Erlang telecommunication system in μCRL. This case study uses a server-client structure and incorporates timing restrictions and is designed and implemented using a number of Erlang/OTP components. We show how this system is translated into a μCRL specification by using the defined rules, after which system properties are checked via the toolset CADP. Through studying the verification of such an application, we aim to validate the effectiveness of the translation rules in an integrated way.

Keywords: Erlang, Telecoms case study, Process Algebras, μCRL, Translation, Verification.

1 Introduction

Erlang [1] is a concurrent functional programming language with explicit support for real-time and fault-tolerant distributed systems. It is available under an Open Source Licence from Ericsson, and since its conception its use and development has widened to a number of sectors such as TCP/IP programming, etc.

A key feature of Erlang is the Open Telecom Platform (OTP) architecture where generic components are encapsulated as design patterns, each of which solves a particular class of problem. These patterns include servers, supervisors, finite state machines etc. This makes Erlang an ideal programming language for the development of fault-tolerant systems containing soft real-time requirements.

Verification is an important part of the Erlang system process. Although Erlang has many high-level features, verification can be still non-trivial. A number

K. Suzuki et al. (Eds.): FORTE 2008, LNCS 5048, pp. 201–217, 2008.

of possible approaches have been explored, including the one we investigate here: abstract an Erlang application into a formal model, upon which model checking [9] techniques can be applied. This approach has recently been applied to the verification of Erlang programs and OTP components [2,3,5,7,14,16] where the process algebra μCRL [13] has been used as the formal language upon which verification is carried out.

Arts *et al.* [2,3] initiated this strand of work and proposed rules for translating Erlang syntax and the OTP components *gen_server*, *supervisor* into μCRL. Benac-Earle [5] continued with the work and developed a toolset, *etomcrl*, to automate the process of translation. Guo *et al.* extended the work by proposing a model for the translation of the OTP finite state machine *gen_fsm* [14] and defining rules for coping with Erlang *timeout* events in μCRL [16].

However, rules for the translation of OTP *gen_server*, *supervisor*, *gen_fsm* and Erlang *timeout* have, so far, only been independently evaluated via some small examples, and no work has evaluated these rules in an application where the above components are integrated as a system. One might argue that if all rules are applied in an integrated way, will they show the similar effects for system verification as they demonstrated in the existing work? Moreover, will a state space explosion mean that effective verification is lost?

In this paper, we attempt to look at these questions by investigating the verification of an Erlang telecommunication system in μCRL. A telecommunication system of server-client structure and timing restriction for operation is developed with Erlang/OTP. The system integrates the use of the *supervisor*, *gen_server*, *gen_fsm* components and uses explicit *timeout* events. We show how the system is then translated into a μCRL specification using the proposed translation rules. We then verify a number of system's properties by using the model checker CADP [8] and investigate the changes of state space when the number of clients increases. The experimental results suggest that when being applied in an integrated system, the translation rules show the similar effect for system verification as being applied independently.

The paper is organized as follows: Section 2 describes a telecommunication system that is used as a case study in this paper; Section 3 implements the system with Erlang programming langauge; Section 4 discusses the translation of the telecoms case study into μCRL; Section 5 looks at the system verification using the standard model checker CADP; conclusions are drawn in Section 6.

2   Telecommunication System

In this section we give an overview of our case study, which is implemented in Erlang in Section 3.

2.1   System Infrastructure

Our telecoms case study uses a client-server structure, and comprises of a database server (DBS) that is used to maintain all client's data and a number of

functional servers (FS) that will process clients' requests. An FS has a capacity
and a user list. The capacity defines the maximum number of clients (mobiles)
that can be connected to a server, while the user list saves all clients (mobiles)
that have been connected to this server. The telecoms system illustrated in Figure 1 is designed with one DBS (named as *DB*), three FSs (named as *SVR_1*,
SVR_2 and *SVR_3*) and five clients (named as *M_1*, *M_2*, *M_3*, *M_4* and *M_5*).

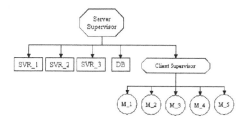

Fig. 1. Telecoms system designed with one DB, three FSs and five clients

Once the system starts up, an FS can communicate with DBS and any other
FSs. A client can communicate with any FSs, and can perform some functional
operations such as *calling* and *top-up*. The behaviour of clients is described in
section 2.2. Each client has an account maintained in the DBS, and in order to
make a phone call, a client needs to save enough money in its account.

Before performing any functional operations, a client needs to connect to an
FS. After being connected to an FS, the client's identity is maintained in the FS'
user list. A client can only be connected to one FS, and if a client has connected
to an FS and tries to connect to another FS, an error message will be returned
and the request is denied. When a client disconnects, the appropriate FS cuts off
the connection and removes this client from the user list to release the resource.
The FS will notify all other FSs about the changes of its clients' state so that
they can correctly respond to the client's requests.

2.2   Client Behaviour Modelling

The behaviour of a client (mobile) is modeled as a finite state machine (FSM),
and the initial design is shown in Figure 2. There are four states: *idle, connected,
calling* and *top_up*, where initially, the system is set to the *idle* state.

The FSM defines the behaviour of a number of operations: *connecting, disconnecting, calling, terminating, top_up* and *cancelling*. Before performing any
operations, a client FSM needs to connect to an FS through sending the *connecting* request. If the FS replies {*ok,connected*}, it indicates that the request is
accepted and the connection is set up. The FSM moves to the state *connected*;
otherwise, if {*error,busy*} arrives, it suggests that the server has reached it maximum capacity. The client will send the *connecting* request to another FS. The

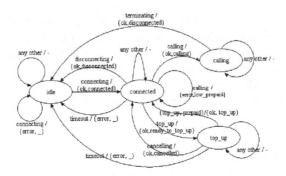

Fig. 2. Client behaviour modelled as an FSM

FSM remains in the state *idle*. The client will iteratively send the *connecting* request to each FS until the connection is approved and set up by an FS.

A client can stop the connection by sending the *disconnecting* request to the FS. Once the *disconnecting* request being received, the FS will cut off the connection and remove the client from its user list to release the resource. A reply message {*ok,disconnected*} will be sent to the client, and upon receiving this reply, the FSM will be reset to the state *idle*.

When in the state *connected*, a client can make a phone call through *calling* operation or top up it account through *top_up* operation. When the *calling* request is sent, if its account has enough money, a client will receive {*ok,calling*} from the appropriate FS, enabling the calling process. The FSM then moves to the state *calling*; otherwise, {*error, low_prepaid*} will be received, asking the client to top up its account. The FSM remains in the state *connected*.

When in the state *calling*, only the *terminating* operation can terminate a calling process. This prevents the calling process from being disrupted by some unintended actions. When the *terminating* request is sent, the DBS will reduce the amount of money from this client's account. The FS then cuts off the client's connection and releases the resource from its user list. Meanwhile, a message {ok,*disconnected*} is sent to the client, and on receiving the reply, the FSM is reset to the state *idle*.

After being connected to an FS, a client can ask to top up its account by sending the *top_up* request. If {*ok, ready_to_top_up*} is received, it indicates that the top up process is accepted by the FS, and the FSM moves to the state *top_up*. The client can then transfer money to its account through {*top_up, Prepaid*} operation where *Prepaid* is the amount of money that is about to be transfered. When the transaction succeeds, the FS replies the client with {*ok, top_up*} and when receiving such a reply, the FSM returns to the state *connected*.

A client FSM has a timing restriction applicable when in states *connected* or *top_up*. Specifically, when the FSM is directed to the state *connected* or *top_up*, a timer will be instantiated which enables the timing process. If, within the predefined time period, no action is performed by the client, a *timeout* event will be generated and sent to the FS. By receiving *timeout* event, the FS cuts off the connection and releases the resource from its user list. The FSM is then reset to the state *idle*.

3   Erlang Implementation

Erlang is used to implement the telecoms system, making use of the OTP design patterns as is common practice.

3.1   Functional Server Implementation

The functional server (FS) is implemented using the Erlang/OTP *gen_server* module. A generic server is implemented by providing a *callback module* where (*callback*) functions are defined specifying the concrete actions of the server such as server state handling and response to messages.

In this work, the callback function *handle_call* in the FS module is comprised of two parts. One (using keyword *request*) processes client's requests; the other (using keyword *notify*) deals with the notification sent from FSs:

```
handle_call({request,R,M},Fr,Chs)→      :   case Request of
   {Reply,State}= handle_request(R,M,Chs), :      connecting →
   {reply,Reply,State};                  :         do_connecting(M,Chs);
handle_call({notify,M,F},Fr,Chs)→        :      disconnecting →
   {C,N,MList,SVRList} = Chs,            :         do_disconnecting(M,Chs);
   case F of                            :      cancelling →
      add →                             :         do_cancelling(M,Chs);
         {reply,ok,{C,N,               :      calling →
            MList++[M],SVRList}};      :         do_calling(M,Chs);
      remove →                          :      terminating →
         {reply,ok,                     :         do_terminating(M,Chs);
            {C,N,delete(M,MList),SVRList}}: top_up →
   end.                                  :         do_top_up(M,Chs);
handle_request(timeout,M,Chs)→          :      {top_up, Prepaid} →
   do_timeout(Mobile,Chs);              :         top_up_tranfer(M,Chs)
handle_request(Request,M,Chs)→          :   end.
```

The internal variable *Chs* (defined by the Erlang system for saving values) is defined with the form of $\{C, N, MList, SVRList\}$ where C defines the FS' capacity, N counts for the number of clients that has been connected to this FS, *MList* saves clients that have connected to this FS and *SVRList* saves all FS servers running in the system.

The function *handle_request(Request,Mobile,Chs)* is defined where a list of *do* functions is called to process client's requests. The function *do_connecting* is defined to set up connection between the FS and a client. It first examines whether the FS reaches its maximum capacity. If the FS is full, $\{error, busy\}$ will be returned to the client; otherwise, the connection is set up. The client is then registered in *MList* and N is increased by 1. The function *do_disconnecting* is defined to disconnect a client from the FS. When the *disconnecting* request arrives, the FS cuts off the connection and then, by calling the function *notify_servers*, notifies other FSs (saved in *SVRList*) to release the resource (removes the client from *MList*).

The *do_calling* function monitors the calling process. When the *calling* request is received, the function reads the client's data from the DBS and checks whether it has enough money for making a call. If so, the calling process is enabled; otherwise, {*error, low_prepaid*} is replied, asking the client to top up its account. When the client finishes calling, it sends the *terminating* request to the FS. Upon receiving the request, the FS enables the *do_terminating* function to subtract amount of money from the client's account, and then cut off the connection through *disconnecting* operation. The function *do_top_up* and *top_up_tranfer* are defined to top up client's account. When the *top_up* request is received, the FS enables the process by replying the client with {*ok,ready_to_top_up*}. Once the client's money is received, the *top_up_tranfer* function is enabled to complete the transaction.

3.2   Client Implementation

The client behaviour is implemented using the OTP *gen_fsm* module, and the state transition rules are defined conforming to the following convention:

$$StateName(Event,\ StateData) \rightarrow$$
$$... \text{ code for actions } ...;$$
$$\{next\_state, StateName', StateData', Timer\}.$$

where the state function returns a tuple that contains the name of the next state, *StateName'*, and an updated state data, *StateData'*. *Timer* is an optional element, if it is set to a value, a timer is instantiated, and a *timeout* event will be generated when the time-up occurs. The function *send_event* is defined to trigger a transition. When *send_event* is executed, the *gen_fsm* module automatically calls the *current state* function.

In accordance with the design given above, four state functions are defined in the client module: *idle, connected, calling* and *top_up*. The state function *idle* initiates a *connecting* request to the FS *SVR*. If the FS *SVR* replies the FSM with {*ok,connected*}, the request is accepted and the connection is set up. The FSM moves to the state *connected*; otherwise, the request is denied and the FSM remains unchanged.

```
idle([Act,SVR],{M,_RSVR,SVRList})→          :      {error,busy}→
   case member(SVR,SVRList) of              :         display(server,busy),
      true →                                :         {next_state,idle,
         F=gen_server:call(SVR,{request,Act,M}),: {M,nil,SVRList}}
         case F of                          :      end;
            {ok,connected}→                 :   false →
               display(connected),          :      display(server,invalid)
               {next_state,connected,       :      {next_state,idle,{M,nil,SVRList}}
                  {M,SVR,SVRList},20000};   :end.
```

Once the client is connected to an FS, an event will trigger the state function *connected*, which evaluates the request and then makes decisions for the consequent actions. For example, if a *calling* request is made, the function will call the FS to evaluate the client's state. If the client has enough money in its account, {*ok,calling*} will be returned to approve the calling process, and upon receiving the reply, the FSM moves to the state *calling*.

```
connected(timeout,{M,SVR,SVRList})→
    gen_server:call(SVR,{request,timeout,M}),
    display(M,timeout),
    {next_state,idle,{M,nil,SVRList}};
connected([Act,_SVR],{M,SVR,SVRList})→
    case Act==terminating of
        true →
            display(action,invalid),
            {next_state,connected,
                {M,SVR,SVRList},20000};
        false →
            F=gen_server:call(SVR,{request,Act,M}):
            case F of
                {ok,disconnected}→
                    display(disconnected),
                    {next_state,idle,
                        {M,SVR,SVRList}};
                {ok,calling}→
                    display(client,calling),
                    {next_state,calling,
                        {M,SVR,SVRList}};
                {error,low_prepaid}→
                    display(low_prepaid),
                    {next_state,connected,
                        {M,SVR,SVRList},20000};
                {ok,ready_to_top_up}→
                    display(ready_to_top_up),
                    {next_state,top_up,
                        {M,SVR,SVRList},20000};
                _Other →
                    display(action,invalid),
                    {next_state,connected,
                        {M,SVR,SVRList},20000}
            end
    end.
```

When in the state *calling*, only the *terminating* action can stop the calling process. This prevents the calling process from being disrupted by any unintended actions.

```
calling([Act,_SVR],{M,SVR,SVRList})→
    case Act of
        terminating →
            gen_server:call(SVR,{request,Act,M}),
            display(call,terminating),
            {next_state,idle,
                {M,nil,SVRList}};
        false →
            display(server,invalid),
            {next_state,calling,
                {M,SVR,SVRList}}
    end.
```

When being connected to an FS, the client can ask to top up its account by sending the *top_up* request to the FS. If {*ok,ready_to_top_up*} is replied, the top up process is enabled, and the FSM moves to the state *top_up*. An action will trigger the state function *top_up* to either start the transaction by {*top_up, Prepaid*} operation (*Prepaid* is the amount of money the client is about to transfer), or cancel the process by sending the *cancelling* request.

```
top_up(timeout,{M,SVR,SVRList})→
    gen_server:call(SVR,{request,timeout,M}),
    display(M,timeout),
    {next_state,idle,{M,nil,SVRList}};
top_up([Act,_SVR],{M,SVR,SVRList})→
    case gen_server:call(SVR,{request,Act,M}) of:
        {ok,top_up} →
            display(top_up,ok),
            {next_state,connected,
                {M,SVR,SVRList},20000};
        {ok,cancelled} →
            display(top_up,cancelled),
            {next_state,connected,
                {M,SVR,SVRList},20000};
        _Other →
            display(action,invalid),
            {next_state,top_up,
                {M,SVR,SVRList},20000}
    end.
```

When the FSM moves to the state *connected* and *top_up*, a timer is initiated. The timer is set to 20,000ms. If within the time period, no action is performed, a *timeout* event will be generated and sent to the FS. The FSM is reset to the state *idle*. A function *command* is defined to simulate the receiving of external actions. It calls *gen_server:send_event* to triggers the state functions.

4 Translating Our Case Study into μCRL

In this section we describe the verification methodology used in this project. It uses the process algebra μCRL (micro Common Representation Language) [13] which is an extension of the process algebra ACP [4], where equational *abstract data types* have been integrated into the process specification to enable the specification of both data and process behaviour. We assume the reader is familiar with μCRL.

4.1 Pre-processing

Before the translation begins, the Erlang input is pre-processed which transforms the Erlang code into an optimized format, but has identical behaviour. For example, Erlang makes extensive use of pattern matching in its function definitions, and overlapping between patterns could lead to the system being represented by a faulty model in μCRL. This work transforms Erlang programs using the techniques discussed in [15] where pattern matching clauses in a function are replaced with a series of calling functions, each of which being guarded by the function *patterns_match*.

For example, the function *handle_request* is transformed as shown above. A data structure, called a *Structure Splitting Tree (SST)* [15], is applied for pattern evaluation, and the use of such an SST for pattern evaluation guarantees the elimination of overlapping between patterns in the transformed program.

```
handle_request(R,M,Chs) →              : hr_case_6(true,R,M,Chs,Vars) →
    hr_case_1(eval:pattern_match([R],   :    do_top_up(M,Chs,Vars);
        [connecting]),R,M,Chs,[]).      : hr_case_6(false,R,M,Chs,Vars) →
                                        :    hr_case_7(eval:pattern_match([R],
                                        :      [{top_up,Prepaid}]),R,M,
hr_case_1(true,R,M,Chs,Vars) →          :      Chs,Vars++[Prepaid]).
    do_connecting(M,Chs,Vars);          : hr_case_7(true,R,M,Chs,Vars) →
hr_case_1(false,R,M,Chs,Vars) →         :    top_up_transfer(M,Chs,Vars);
    hr_case_2(eval:pattern_match([R],   : hr_case_7(false,R,M,Chs,Vars) →
        [disconnecting]),R,M,Chs,Vars).: {error, action}
    ...
```

4.2 Translating the Server Component

Erlang performs synchronous and asynchronous communications using the generic server primitives *gen_sever:call* / *handle_call* and *gen_sever:cast* / *handle_cast* respectively. One then has to model both synchronous and a synchronous communication in μ CRL, and to do so we use a *Server_Buffer* process (described in [5]). A data type *GSBuffer* is defined to contain the data for the process *Server_Buffer*. The actions *gen_server_call* and *gscall* are defined to write a message to the buffer while, *gshall* and *handle_call* to read a message from the buffer.

The database server is translated into a process *SDB*, and it maintains a number of clients, each in the form *{CName,Prepaid,State}* where *CName* is the client's name, *Prepaid* shows the amount of money saved in the client's account and *State* indicates whether the client is connected to an FS or not. The actions *server_read_db* and *db_send_data* are defined to read a client's data out from the process, *server_read_db* | *db_send_data* = *read_db*. The actions *servr_update_db* and *db_ack_request* are used to update the client's data in the process, *servr_update_db* | *db_ack_request* = *update_db*.

The functional server (FS) is translated into a process *server*. The process contains a server ID *SVRID*, a capacity C and a client list *CLs*. It uses the action *handle_call* to receive the client's requests: when a request is received, the *server* process first checks whether the request is made for itself. If so, the process calls the process *handle_request* to tackle the request; otherwise, its returns without changing anything.

$$\begin{aligned}
&\text{proc server(SVRID:Term,C:Term,CLs:Term)} = \\
&\quad \text{sum(SVR:Term,sum(Request:Term,sum(Client:Ter,} \\
&\qquad \text{handle\_call(SVR,Request,Client).} \\
&\qquad \text{handle\_request(SVR,Client,Request,C,CLs))))} \\
&\qquad \quad \triangleleft \text{eq(SVRID,SVR)} \triangleright \text{server(SVRID,C,CLs)}
\end{aligned}$$

For each client's request, a request process is defined. Once the *handle_request* is enabled, it selects the corresponding request process. The selected process first performs all pre-defined actions and then replies the client with a message through the action *gen_server_reply*. For example, when the *connecting* request is received, the process *handle_request_ connecting* is activated. It first checks whether the server reaches its maximum capacity. If the server is full, the process goes back to the process *server* without changing anything; otherwise, if the client has not been connected to a server before, the process sets up the connection and replies the client with {*ok, connected*}.

$$\begin{aligned}
&\text{handle\_request\_connecting(SVRID:Term,CL:Term,C:Term,CLs:Term)} = \\
&\quad \text{sum(Vals:Term, server\_read\_db(Vals).} \\
&\quad \text{(gen\_server\_reply(SVRID,tuple(error,tuplenil(unregister\_user)),CL).} \\
&\quad \text{server(SVRID,C,CLs)} \\
&\qquad \triangleleft \text{is\_nil(find\_client(CL,Vals))} \triangleright \\
&\qquad \text{(gen\_server\_reply(SVRID,tuple(error,tuplenil(already\_connected)),CL).} \\
&\qquad \text{server(SVRID,C,CLs)} \\
&\qquad \quad \triangleleft \text{eq(find\_client(CL,Vals),CL)} \triangleright \\
&\qquad \quad \text{(server\_update\_db(CL,find\_client(CL,Vals),CL),true).} \\
&\qquad \quad \text{gen\_server\_reply(SVRID,tuple(ok,tuplenil(connected)),CL).} \\
&\qquad \quad \text{server(SVRID,C,list\_append(CL,CLs))} \\
&\qquad \triangleleft \text{mcrl\_less(list\_number(CLs),C)} \triangleright \\
&\qquad \text{gen\_server\_reply(SVRID,tuple(error,tuplenil(busy)),CL).} \\
&\qquad \text{server(SVRID,C,CLS)))))}
\end{aligned}$$

The process *handle_timeout* is defined to deal with *timeout* event. Once the *timeout* event is generated from a client, the process *handle_timeout* will be activated. It cuts off the connection between the server and the client and removes the client from its user list to release the resource.

4.3 Translating the Client Component

The client was initially modelled as an FSM and implemented using the OTP *gen_fsm*. This is then translated into μCRL using techniques defined in [14], where the translation process is comprised of two parts, *simulating state management* (SSM) and *state function translation* (SFT).

In this work, a (one place) stack is used to perform the SSM which is modified by using a global variable (GV) process. A GV process contains a list of indexed GVs, where each GV is of the format {*VName, Val*} where the *VName* gives the variable's name and the *Val* the value. A GV process with three GVs, V_1, V_2 and V_3, is defined as follows:

proc
  GVs(V1:Term,V2:Term,Var3:Term) =
    sum(V:Term,receive_val(V).
      (GVs(V,V2,V3) ◁ eq(element(int(1),V),element(int(1),V1)) ▷
        (GVs(V1,V,V3) ◁ eq(element(int(1),V),element(int(1),V2)) ▷
          (GVs(V1,V2,V) ◁ eq(element(int(1),V),element(int(1),V3)) ▷ delta))))
+
  send_val(V1,V2,V3).GVs(V1,V2,V3)

A GV can be read out through the actions *read_val send_val, write_val | receive_val = write*, and be modified through the actions *write_val / receive_val, write_val | receive_val = write*. We use a GV to stand for a client where *VName* and *Val* are used to save the client FSM's *current state* and the *state data* respectively. We found that, by applying such a modification, the state space is largely reduced.

The process *receive_cmd* is defined to receive commands generated from the external actions. For each client, a unique ID *CLID* is associated with all its FSM processes. Once a command is received, the process *receive_cmd* calls the process *read_clients*. According to the *CLID*, the designated FSM's *current* state and the *state data* are read out. The corresponding state process is then selected for performing all defined actions. Once the execution of the state process finishes, the FSM moves to the process *fsm_update_state* to update the *current* state and the *state data*.

For example, when the FSM is in the state *idle* and the *connecting* command is received, the state process *fsm_idle* is activated. The process *fsm_idle* sends the request to an FS and then waits for reply. If the FS returns *busy*, the process will calls for another FS; otherwise, the connection is set up. The process then calls for the process *fsm_update_state* to update the state *connected* as the current state. Thus we have the following:

  fsm_idle(CLID:Term,Data:Term,Cmd:Term,SList:Term,SMList:Term) =
    gen_server_call(hd(SList),Cmd,ClID).
    wait_for_reply(hd(SList),CLID,Data,Cmd,SList,SMList)

  wait_for_reply(SVRID:Term,CLID:Term,Data:Term,Cmd:Term,) =
    sum(S:Term,sum(R:Term,sum(CL:Term,
      gen_server_replied(S,R,CL).
      ((client_info(S,R,CL).
       (fsm_idle(CLID,Data,Cmd,SMList,SMList)
        ◁ is_nil(SList) ▷ fsm_idle(CLID,Data,Cmd,tl(SMList),SMList))
        ◁ is_busy(element(int(2),R)) ▷
          (fsm_update_state(CLID,connected,Data,SList,SMList,true,false)
            ◁ is_connected(element(int(2),R))▷
              fsm_update_state(CLID,idle,Data,SList,SMList,false,false,2))))
        ◁ eq(CL,CLID) ▷ wait_for_reply(SVRID,CLID,Data,Cmd)))))

The process *fsm_update_state* is parameterized with two arguments, *FT* and *FTM*. The *FT* determines whether the updated current state has timing restrictions on it; the *FTM* decides whether the process will be terminated due to some unexpected events. If the newly updated current state process has timing restrictions, the *FT* will be set to *true*, which enables the process *fsm_timing* to count down the time. If, within the predefined time period, no external action is performed, a *timeout* event will be generated and sent to the FS. Afterwards, the process is terminated by setting the *FTM* to *true*. Thus we have the following output from the translation process:

fsm_update_state(CLID:Term,SNext:Term,Data:Term,Cmd:Term,
                SList:Term,SMList:Term,FT:Term,FTM:Term,TR:Nat) =
write_val(tuple(CLID,tuplenil(tuple(SNext,tuplenil(Data))))).
(delta ◁ eq(FTM,true) ▷
        (fsm_timing(CLID,SNext,Data,SList,SMList,on(TR))
                ◁eq(FT,true)▷ receive_cmd(SList,SMList)))

The process *fsm_timing* and the process *count_down* are parameterized with a *timer* [16]. By using an explicit *tick* action in the process *count_down*, we apply a discrete-time timing model to support the translation of *timeout* event. When the process *fsm_timing* is called at the first time, the timer t is initiated and initialized. The process will either call for the process *count_down* to start the timing process or the *receive_cmd* process to continue with another external command.

fsm_timing(CLID:Term,SNext:Term,Data:Term,SList:Term,SMList:Term,t:Timer) =
    count_down(CLID,SNext,Data,SList,t) + receive_cmd(SList,SMList)

When the *count_down* process is activated, it checks whether the *timer* expires (using the function *expire(t:Timer)*). If not, the process will first perform the *tick* action once, standing for the passing of one time unit. The process then moves back to the process *fsm_timing*, counting down the timer t by one unit (*pred(t)*); otherwise, if the timer expires, the process *fsm_update_state* is called, with the next state *SNext* being reset to *idle* and the *FTM* to *true*.

count_down(CLID:Term,SNext:Term,Data:Term,SList:Term,SMList:Term,t:Timer) =
    tick.fsm_timing(CLID,SNext,Data,SList,SMList,pred(t))
        ◁ not(expire(t)) ▷
            gen_server_call(hd(SList),timeout,CLID).
            fsm_update_state(CLID,idle,nil,nil,SList,SMList,false,true)

4.4   System Translation

By considering the translation of server section and client section together, the system is translated into a complete μCRL specification. In the specification, every server and client are initialized with a unique client ID. For each client, the process *client_cmds(CLID, CmdList)* is applied to initialize a list of external actions where *CLID* indicates the client's ID and *CmdList* saves the sequence of commands. A client receives a command through the action *r_cmd(CLID, Cmd)*.

A client sends a request to an FS through the action *gen_server_call(SVRID, Cmd, CLID)* where *SVRID* indicates the target server ID while *CLID* the sender's ID. A client receives a reply through the action *gen_server_replied(SVRID, Reply, CLID)* where *SVRID* shows from which server the reply comes and *CLID* indicates to which client the reply is sent.

When receiving a request, an FS process compares its ID with the received *SVRID* to examine whether the request is made for the server itself. If so, the request is accepted and the consequential actions will be performed; otherwise, the FS process ignores the request and returns without changing anything. Similarly, when receiving a reply, a client process compares its ID with the received *CLID* to check whether the message is replied to the client itself. If so, the client process performs the actions extracted from the reply; otherwise, the process ignores the message. Through ID checking, a peer-to-peer communication structure is defined in the μCRL specification.

We have now reached a point whereby the design, as implemented in Erlang/OTP has been translated (in fact, abstracted) to a μ CRL specification, and we now described how properties of the initial design can be checked on this model.

5   Verifying the Telecommunication System with μCRL

In this section, a number of system properties are abstracted and verified. In our experiments, the property under verification (PUV) is devised in a way where the behaviour of FS(s), the behaviour of client(s) and the communication between the FS and the client are considered as an integrated whole. Thus, instead of focusing on particular individual components, the properties we are concerned with in this case study are defined across the whole system.

5.1   Property Verification

The system used for simulation is constructed as shown in Figure 1 where three functional servers (svr_1, svr_2 and svr_3) and five clients (m_1, m_2, m_3, m_4 and m_5) are used. We initialize the capacity of every server to 1. The clients m_1, m_3, m_5 are preset with £1 in their accounts, while m_2, m_4 with £0. We define that the minimum cost of making a phone call to be £1. The timer for the functions with timing restriction is set to 20,000ms, and we define the passing of one time unit as 10,000ms, represented by one *tick* action. As discussed in Section 3.2, the *gen_fsm:send_event* is often called through external actions. Therefore, before starting a simulation process, for each client FSM, a sequence of actions needs to be initialized in the process *Client_Cmds* to simulate the external behaviour.

We first devise two experiments to verify the system's client-server property. In the first experiment, the client m_1 attempts to make a phone call while m_2, m_3, m_4 and m_5 are idle; in the second, the client m_2 tries to make a phone call while m_1, m_3, m_4 and m_5 are idle. Thus, for both these initial experiments, only one client is active. Through these two experiments we want to check whether the FS(s) and the client act as defined in design, and whether the communication between the FS and the client is correctly running.

The commands for the two experiments are coded in the list $Cmd = cons(connecting, cons(calling, nil))$ and initialized in the process *client_cmds* respectively. The Labelled Transition Systems (LTSs) derived from the toolset CADP [8] are shown in Figure 3 and 4. Here, we hide the actions *update_db* and *read_db* as internal actions, denoted by i in the LTSs.

Verification of the properties can be performed by using the model checker CADP, where the system properties are formalized by a set of temporal logic formulae. For example, in the first experiment, to check "without being connected to svr_1, m_1 cannot make a phone call.". This property can be formalized as:

[not(client_info(m_1, connected, svr_1))*. client_info(m_1, calling, svr_1))] false

Similarly, to check "when m_1 is connected to svr_1, without delaying enough time (two *tick* actions being consecutively performed), a *timeout* event cannot be generated.", the property is formalized as:

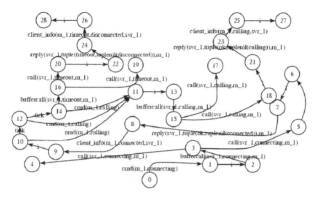

Fig. 3. LTS: The client m_1 makes a phone call

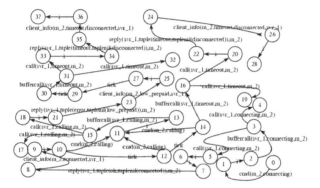

Fig. 4. LTS: The client m_2 makes a phone call

[true*. client_info(m_1, connected, svr_1)*]
<not('tick.tick')*. client_info(m_1, timeout, disconnected, svr_1)> false

In the second experiment, to check "when m_2 is connected to svr_1, if m_2 has not preset enough money in its account, the calling process cannot be accepted.", the property is formalized as:

<true*. client_info(m_1, connected, svr_1) *. client_info(m_2, low_prepaid, svr_1) *. client_info(m_1, calling, svr_1)> false

Next, we construct an experiment to examine the system's behaviour where more than one clients are active. Two clients m_1 and m_2 request to connect to a server simultaneously. Since the capacity of the FS is set to 1, according to the design, when an FS, for example svr_1, accepts the request of a client, say m_1, it should reply the other m_2 with *busy*; the client m_2 should afterwards request a connection to svr_2. Similar to the previous experiments, we want to check the behaviour of FSs and the clients in an integrated way, but use more complicated system structure. Figure 5 illustrates the derived LTS. Here, the actions *call*, *buffercall* and *reply* are hidden as internal actions as well.

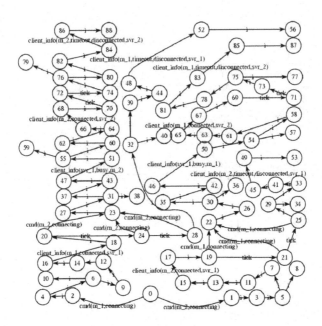

Fig. 5. m_1 and m_2 make requests to connect

A number of properties can then be automatically verified via CADP. For example, to check "when m_1 is connected to svr_1 and m_2 requests to svr_1, svr_1 will reply m_2 with *busy*.". The property is formalized as:

<true*. client_info(m_1, connected, svr_1) *. cmd(m_2, connecting) *. client_info(m_2, busy, svr_1)> true

Another property we want to check is formalized as:

<true*. cmd(m_2, connecting) *. client_info(m_2, busy, svr_1) *. cmd(m_2, connecting) *. client_info(m_2, connected, svr_2)> true

stating that "when m_2 requests to connect to svr_1 and receives the reply of *busy*, it will request to connect to svr_2 and its request will be accepted by svr_2."

We also devise an experiment to show how the methodology can be used for fault detection. A system with two FSs (svr_1 and svr_2) and four clients (m_1, m_2, m_3 and m_4) is constructed, where four clients simultaneously request a connection to an FS. Both svr_1 and svr_2 are meant to be designed with a capacity of 2, and we assume that one (say svr_2) by mistakenly implemented with a capacity of 1. This could cause serious problems as one client will iteratively make a request to connect to the system without knowing whether he/she will ever get through.

The erroneous implementation is then translated into a μCRL specification from which we derive its LTS, however, since it has a total of 354 states and 407 transitions it cannot be clearly presented here. As usual we use the toolset CADP to verify the properties.

One way to detect such a problem is to check whether the four clients are successfully connected to the FSs. Since the system is designed with the capacity of 4, all four clients should have connected to an FS. Thus, for each client, we define the following property:

[true*. "cmd(m_i, connecting)" *]
(<true* "client_info(m_i, connected, svr_1))"> or
<true* "client_info(m_i, connected, svr_2))">) true

stating "when client m_i sends connecting request to the system, its request should
be either accepted by $sver\_1$ or by $sver\_2$". Using these properties, the CADP model
checker can correctly distinguish the correct and faulty implementations based upon
the design we wish to check against.

5.2   State Space Investigation

In addition to system wide property checking, we were interested in whether the integrated system had a tractable state space as the size of its components grew, thus we
also investigated the state space generated from the μCRL specification by using the
toolset CADP.

Table 1. One FS with capacity of 5

Table 2. Three FSs with capacity
of 1,2 and 3 respectively

Clients	States	Transitions
1	39	40
2	413	456
3	4381	5055
4	4845	5681
5	5309	6307

Clients	States	Transitions
1	49	50
2	867	932
3	12307	14073
4	13449	15917
5	14591	17761

We first construct a system where only one FS is applied. The FS' capacity is set to 5.
A number of clients simultaneously request a phone connection. Before the simulation
starts, all clients have preset enough money in their account. We incrementally increase
the number of clients from 1 to 5, and Table 1 illustrates the changes of the state space
that result. It can be seen that when the second and third client are connected to the
FS, the state space increases rapidly: by a factor of almost 10. However, after this the
subsequent increases level off, and the size is increased by roughly 20% when one new
client is added to the system.

The same phenomenon is noticed as well when we apply three FSs to the system.
The server capacities are set to 1, 2 and 3 respectively, and the resultant state space
is shown in Table 2. This seems to suggest that, with the number of clients being
increased, the state space will fairly reach a saturated point where the state space
is slowly increased by a stable pace. We are currently investigating whether this is a
general phenomenon or one peculiar to this particular example.

6   Conclusions and Future Work

Verification is an important process in the development of Erlang applications. This paper contributes to the recent strand of work which has studied the verification of Erlang
applications using the process algebra μCRL. The basic methodology in this approach

is for an Erlang application to be translated (abstracted) into a μCRL specification, upon which the standard model checker CADP can be applied.

The study of how best to translate Erlang into μCRL contains many open research issues and is still in its early stage. Recent results had shown how components such as *supervisor*, *gen_server*, *gen_fsm* and the Erlang *timeout* event could be translated into μCRL, but the translation rules for each component had been evaluated independently. At FORTE'07 we defined the rules for translating *gen_fsm* into μCRL, and evaluated the rules with two case studies. This was extended in [16] by defining the rules for coping with Erlang *timeout* events and evaluated the work with some case studies. The experimental results show quite a promising effect for system verification.

However, no work had investigated the translation rules in an application where the *gen_server*, *supervisor*, *gen_fsm* and *timeout* events were incorporated in an integrated system. This forces us to face a challenge. If we apply all rules in an integrated way, will these rules show the similar effects for system verification as they independently demonstrated? Moreover, will a state space explosion mean that effective verification is lost? These questions are important to us since we want to make sure (or at least be confident) that all the defined rules can work in an integrated way, or that this requirement could be achieved through modifying some rules before we looked at the translation of other OTP components (such as *applications*).

In this paper, we have attempted to look at these questions by investigating the verification of an Erlang telecommunication system in μCRL. The system integrates the use of the *supervisor*, *gen_server*, *gen_fsm* components and uses explicit *timeout* events. We have shown how the system is translated into a μCRL specification using the proposed translation rules, and verified a number of system properties by using CADP and investigated the changes of state space when the number of clients increases. In our experiments, a property under verification (PUV) is defined in a way where the behaviour of the functional servers (FSs), the behavior of the clients and the communication between the FSs and the clients should be verified simultaneously. Thus, each PUV looks at a property in the view of complete system. A faulty implementation was also used to test the capability of fault detection, and based upon the design the faulty implementation was correctly distinguished by CADP.

The experimental results suggest that when being applied in an integrated system, the translation rules show the similar effect for system verification as being applied independently. The study of the changes in state space suggests, with the number of clients being increased, the state space is slowly increased by a stable pace. All experimental evidence gives us confidence that we are working in the correct direction, and thus we can continue with the study of some other OTP components.

There remains much to be done. Work continues on the automation of the translation of additional OTP components, as does work on verifying the correctness of the translation against the Erlang semantics [10,11]. This latter aspect remains a challenging task, for the full semantics for distributed nodes in an Erlang application can have, semantically, some very subtle behaviour, as discussed in, for example, [18].

Acknowledgements

This work is supported by the UK Engineering and Physical Sciences Research Council (EPSRC) grant EP/C525000/1. We would like to thank the developers of the tool sets of μCRL and CADP for permitting the use of tools for system verification.

References

1. Armstrong, J., Virding, R., Wikström, C., Williams, M.: Concurrent Programming in Erlang, 2nd edn. Prentice-Hall, Englewood Cliffs (1996)
2. Arts, T., Benac-Earle, C., Derrick, J.: Verifying Erlang code: a resource locker case-study. In: Eriksson, L.-H., Lindsay, P.A. (eds.) FME 2002. LNCS, vol. 2391, pp. 184–203. Springer, Heidelberg (2002)
3. Arts, T., Benac-Earle, C., Penas, J.J.S.: Translating Erlang to μCRL. In: The Fourth International Conference on Application of Concurrency to System Design (ACSD 2004), June 2004, pp. 135–144. IEEE Computer Society, Los Alamitos (2004)
4. Baeten, J.C.M., Weijland, W.P.: Process Algebra. Cambridge University Press, Cambridge (1990)
5. Benac-Earle, C.: Model checking the interaction of Erlang components. PhD thesis, The University of Kent, Canterbury, Department of Computer Science (2006)
6. Benac-Earle, C., Fredlund, L.-Å.: Verification of Language Based Fault-Tolerance. In: Moreno Díaz, R., Pichler, F., Quesada Arencibia, A. (eds.) EUROCAST 2005. LNCS, vol. 3643, pp. 140–149. Springer, Heidelberg (2005)
7. Benac-Earle, C., Fredlund, L.-Å., Derrick, J.: Verifying Fault-Tolerant Erlang Programs. In: Sagonas, K., Armstrong, J. (eds.) Proceedings of ACM SigPlan Erlang 2005 Workshop, pp. 26–34. ACM Press, New York (2005)
8. CADP, http://www.inrialpes.fr/vasy/cadp/
9. Clarke, E., Grumberg, O., Long, D.: Model Checking. MIT Press, Cambridge (1999)
10. Fredlund, L.Å: Towards a sematics for Erlang. In: Foundatins of Mobile Computation: A Post-Conference Satellite Workshop of FST and TCS (1999)
11. Fredlund, L.-Å.: A Framework for Reasoning about Erlang Code. PhD thesis, Roral Institute of Technology, Stockholm, Sweden (2001)
12. Fredlund, L.-Å., Gurov, D., Noll, T., Dam, M., Arts, T., Chugunov, G.: A verification tool for Erlang. International Journal on Software Tools for Technology Transfer 4(4), 405–420 (2003)
13. Groote, J.F., Ponse, A.: The syntax and sematics of μCRL. In: Algebra of Communicating Processes 1994, Workshop in Computing, pp. 26–62 (1995)
14. Guo, Q.: Verifying Erlang/OTP Components in μCRL. In: Derrick, J., Vain, J. (eds.) FORTE 2007. LNCS, vol. 4574. pp. 227–246. Springer, Heidelberg (2007)
15. Guo, Q., Derrick, J.: Eliminating overlapping of pattern matching when verifying Erlang programs in μCRL. In: Sha, E., Han, S.-K., Xu, C.-Z., Kim, M.-H., Yang, L.T., Xiao, B. (eds.) EUC 2006. LNCS, vol. 4096, Springer, Heidelberg (2006)
16. Guo, Q., Derrick, J.: Verification of Timed Erlang/OTP Components Using the Process Algebra μCRL. In: Thompson, S., Fredlund, L.-A. (eds.) 6th ACM SIGPLAN Erlang Workshop, pp. 55–64. ACM Press, New York (2007)
17. Huch, F.: Verification of Erlang programs using abstract interpretation and model checking. ACM SIGPLAN Notices 34(9), 261–272 (1999)
18. Svensson, H., Fredlund, L.-ÅA.: A More Accurate Semantics for Distributed Erlang. In: Thompson, S., Fredlund, L.-A. (eds) 6th ACM SIGPLAN Erlang Workshop, pp. 43–54. ACM Press, New York (2007)

NQSL - Formal Language and Tool Support for Network Quality-of-Service Requirements

Christian Webel, Reinhard Gotzhein, and Joachim Nicolay

Department of Computer Sciences, University of Kaiserslautern,
Kaiserslautern, Germany
{webel, gotzhein, j_nicola}@cs.uni-kl.de

Abstract. Network Quality-of-Service (QoS) is a central characteristic of the design of modern communication systems. Before designing and implementing communication systems, network QoS requirements and QoS mappings have to be specified and analyzed. In this paper, we provide language and tool support for this purpose. To specify network QoS requirements and QoS mappings, we define a formal description technique called *NQSL*, the *Network QoS Specification Language*. To support the efficient handling of NQSL specifications, we present a tool chain consisting of the Graphical NQSL Editor (GNE), the NQSL Analyzer (NA) for QoS domain reduction, and the NQSL-to-SDL Compiler (NSC) for the generation of SDL data and process types.

1   Introduction

The provision of *network Quality-of-Service* (*network QoS*) is one of the major challenges in the development of future communication systems. Network QoS comprises performance, reliability, guarantee, and scalability aspects on different levels of abstraction, as well as mappings between these levels. During *requirements analysis*, network QoS requirements are to be specified formally. In particular, the relevant network QoS aspects of a system are to be identified by defining QoS domains, QoS domains of adjacent levels are to be mapped, and subsets of QoS domains are to be selected. During *system design*, a QoS architecture has to be devised, QoS functionalities are to be identified, and QoS mechanisms to realize these functionalities must be supplied. Since QoS functionalities are placed on different system levels and have high interdependencies, and since the QoS status of a networked system may be subject to frequent changes both on application level and on resource level, the provision of network QoS is a highly complex task that requires a cross-layer approach in all development phases.

In previous work [1], we have introduced a formalization of network QoS. In particular, we have formalized the notions of QoS domain, QoS scalability, QoS mapping, and QoS requirements. Moreover, we have identified formal criteria to reduce QoS domains for consistency and tractability, based on utility and cost. In this paper, we build on and extend these results by providing language and

K. Suzuki et al. (Eds.): FORTE 2008, LNCS 5048, pp. 218–233, 2008.

tool support. To specify network QoS requirements and QoS mappings, we define a formal description technique called *NQSL*, the *Network QoS Specification Language*. To support the efficient handling of NQSL specifications, we present a tool chain consisting of the Graphical NQSL Editor (GNE), the NQSL Analyzer (NA), and the NQSL-to-SDL Compiler (NSC). These tools relieve the system developer from several tedious and error-prone tasks, such as applying QoS mappings by hand or reducing QoS domains based on the definitions of utility and cost functions. Both tasks are required to evaluate and assess QoS mappings and the set of relevant QoS domain values on different levels of abstraction, and have to be repeated after each modification of the QoS requirements specification.

The remaining part of this paper is organized as follows: In Section 2, we survey related work. In Section 3, we summarize our formalization of network QoS requirements (cf. [1]). Section 4 introduces NQSL, the Network QoS Specification Language. In Section 5, the NQSL tools GNE, NA, and NSC are presented. Conclusions are drawn in Section 6.

2   Related Work

To cope with various requirements of system designs, user preferences, middleware, hardware, networks, operating systems, and applications, several QoS specification techniques have been proposed (see [2] for a classification):

- QML (Quality Modelling Language) [3] is focused on the specification of application layer QoS requirements. QoS requirements of lower layers, QoS scaling, and QoS mappings are not addressed.
- CQML (Component Quality Modeling Language) [4] adopts some of the fundamental concepts of QML, and also addresses dynamic QoS scaling. As QML, it is focused on the application layer. Since CQML is widely used, several tool kits exist, including front-end tools and parsers, *e.g.* [5].
- QDL (Quality Description Language) has been proposed as a part of the QuO (Quality Objects) framework [6] that supports QoS on the CORBA object layer. With QDL, it is possible to specify QoS requirements on application layer and on resource layer, and to define QoS scaling.
- The Quality Assurance Language (QuAL) is part of the Quality of Service Management Environment (QoSME) [7]. With QuAL, QoS requirements are specified in a process-oriented way. QoS-A (Quality-of-Service Architecture) [8] uses a parameter-based specification approach, including QoS adaptation and QoS mappings.

In summary, it can be stated that previous formal treatments of QoS address only some aspects of QoS requirement specification, focusing, for instance, on a subset of abstraction layers, or leaving out QoS mappings. Our work comprises the aforementioned issues and therefore provides a holistic, comprehensive formalization of network QoS requirements, across layers. Furthermore, we provide QoS tools beyond front-end tools, in particular, an analysis tool and a compiler.

3   Formalization of Quality-of-Service

In previous work [1], we have introduced a formalization of network QoS. In particular, we have formalized the notions of QoS domain, QoS scalability, QoS mapping, and QoS requirements. In this paper, we build on and extend these results. Therefore, we provide a survey of the formalization of network QoS in this section.

3.1   Formalization of Network QoS Requirements

The need for formalization of network QoS requirements arises from the fact that a precise description of network QoS between service user and service provider is needed to police, control, and maintain the data flow a user emits to the communication system. Further on, the mechanisms realizing these functionalities need a precise and well-defined description of QoS. Formalization of network QoS is done by firstly identifying the QoS domain, and secondly by describing the QoS scalability.

The *QoS domain* Q captures the QoS characteristics of a class of data flows, i.e. performance, reliability, and guarantee and is therefore defined as $Q = P \times R \times G$, where P is the performance domain, R is the reliability domain, and G is the guarantee domain. An element $q = (p, r, g)$ of Q is called *QoS domain value*. *QoS performance* describes efficiency aspects characterizing the required amount of resources and the timeliness of the service. The relevant efficiency parameters are included in the *QoS performance domain* P with $P = P_1 \times \ldots \times P_n = \prod_{i=1}^{n} P_i$, where $P_1, \ldots, P_n$ are performance subdomains. The *QoS reliability* describes the safety-of-operation aspects characterizing the fault behaviour (e.g., loss rate and distribution, corruption rate and distribution, error burstiness) and is defined as $R = Loss \times Period \times Burstiness \times Corruption$, with $Loss = \mathbb{N}_0$, $Period = \mathbb{R}_+$, $Burstiness = \mathbb{R}_+$, and $CorruptionRate = \{cr \in \mathbb{R} \mid 0 \leq cr < 100\}$. The *QoS guarantee* describes the degree of commitment characterizing the binding character of the service. QoS guarantee is formalized by the *QoS guarantee* domain as $G = DoC \times Stat \times Prio$, where $Stat = \{p \in \mathbb{R} \mid 0 < p \leq 1\}$, $Prio = \mathbb{N}$, and $DoC = \{bestEffort, enhancedBestEffort, statistical, deterministic\}$.

Varying communication resources require adaptive mechanisms to avoid network overload, and to scale the application service. The *QoS scalability* S describes the control aspects characterizing the scope for dynamic adaptation of the QoS aspects of a data flow (described by a QoS domain) to a certain granted network QoS. The *QoS scalability domain* S is defined as $S = Util \times Cost \times Up \times Down$, where $Util = \{u \mid u : Q \rightarrow [0,1]\}$, $Cost = \{c \mid c : Q \rightarrow \mathbb{R}_+\}$, and $Up, Down \in \{x \in \mathbb{R}_+ \mid 0 \leq x \leq 1\}$. The elements of *Util* and *Cost* are called *utility functions* and *cost functions*, respectively. A utility function determines the usefulness of QoS domain values, a cost function c expresses the amount of needed resources, associating higher costs with scarcer resources. QoS domain values with the same utility (cost) ($\sim_{u(c)}$) are assigned to the same so-called $u(c)$-equivalence class of Q: $[x]_{u(c)} = \{q \in Q \mid q \sim_{u(c)} x\}$.

The *QoS requirements qosReq* define the set of valid QoS domain values and a QoS scalability value, and are formally stated as a triple (q_{min}, q_{opt}, s), where $q_{min}, q_{opt} \in Q$ and $s \in S$. The QoS domain values q_{min} and q_{opt} specify a set $Q' \subseteq Q$ of valid QoS domain values. To obtain Q', a preorder $\precsim_u$ induced by the utility function is applied: $Q' = \{q \in Q \mid q_{min} \precsim_u q \precsim_u q_{opt}\}$.

For consistency and tractability, we stepwise reduce the QoS domain Q. In a first step, we define the *reduced* QoS domain Q^u by selecting the best element of each u-equivalence class of Q regarding c, and by considering values from Q' only. Let m be the cardinality of $Q/\sim_u$, the quotient set of Q w.r.t. $\sim_u$, and let $[x]_u^i$ denote the ith element of $Q/\sim_u$ regarding $\precsim_u$ (ith u-equivalence class). Then, $Q^u = \{q_1, \ldots, q_m\} \cap Q'$, $\quad q_i = q \in [x]_u^i \mid \forall y \in [x]_u^i . q \precsim_c y$, $\quad 1 \leq i \leq m$. A further reduction induces a derived QoS domain $Q^{u,c}$, discarding QoS domain values with higher cost, but less utility, $Q^{u,c} = \{q \in Q^u \mid \forall y \in Q^u . c(q) > c(y) \Rightarrow u(q) > u(y)\}$ [1].

3.2 Formal QoS Mappings

The mechanisms realizing QoS management tasks are typically embedded in the communication system, prevalent across layers, hiding complex tasks from the application. This leads to abstract QoS requirements on higher system layers, whereas on lower system layers, the level of detail increases. To rigorously relate the different viewpoints on network QoS, a well-defined translation of the requirements is needed, called *QoS mapping*. The QoS mapping can be decomposed into QoS domain mapping and QoS scalability mapping.

The QoS domain mapping $dm : Q_h \rightarrow Q_l$ is a function from a (higher layer) QoS domain Q_h to a (lower layer) QoS domain Q_l. The domain mapping dm may be defined using the auxiliary functions $dm_P : Q_h \rightarrow P_l$ (performance mapping), $dm_R : Q_h \rightarrow R_l$ (reliability mapping) and $dm_G : Q_h \rightarrow G_l$ (guarantee mapping). A detailed description of the three mapping subfunctions is given in [1]. In general, the QoS mappings are neither injective nor surjective.

The QoS scalability mapping is needed to apply control aspects characterizing the dynamic adaptation of QoS parameters on different system levels. A QoS scalability mapping sm is a set of four mapping functions sm_{Util}, sm_{Cost}, sm_{Up} and sm_{Down}, translating the different scalability domains into each other [1].

4 The Network Quality-of-Service Specification Language

In this section, we introduce *NQSL*, the *Network Quality-of-Service Specification Language* for the formal specification of QoS requirements. NQSL is directly derived from the formalization of network QoS in [1], which we have outlined in Section 3. It supports the specification of QoS domains and subdomains, QoS scalability, QoS mappings, and QoS requirements. The syntax of NQSL mainly adds keywords identifying concepts of network QoS, notation to specify

---

[1] For examples, see Section 5.2.

functions, and a set of basic data types. Due to this direct correspondance of the formalization of network QoS, which uses basic mathematical notation, and NQSL language elements, it is straightforward to associate a formal semantics with NQSL specifications.

To give a flavour of NQSL, we briefly present the language elements for the specification of QoS domains and subdomains. The complete definition of NQSL can be found in [9]. The syntax of NQSL is defined in Extended BNF (EBNF), using the usual notational conventions: non-terminals are written in angle-brackets `<non-terminal>`, terminals are enclosed by single quotes `'terminal'`, productions are declared in the form `<non-terminal> = expansion;`, square brackets enclose optional parts `[optional]`, and alternatives are separated by |.

As stated in Section 3.1, a QoS domain captures the QoS characteristics of a class of data flows, i.e. performance, reliability, and guarantee. A QoS domain (see List. 1.1) is identified by its *domain_ name* and defined by a *domain_ body* consisting of declarations of performance, reliability, and guarantee domains. A QoS subdomain is identified by a unique *name* and defined by a type, using basic data types (**Integer**, **Real**, **Enum**), tuples of data types (**Integer** × **Real**), or previously defined subdomains. Optionally, the domain of the data type can be restricted to a set of possible values.

Listing 1.1. NQSL: QoS domain and subdomain definition (excerpt)

```
<qosdomain_decl>       = 'QoSDomain' <domain_name> '{' <domain_body> '}';
<domain_body>          = <performance_domain> <reliability_domain>
                                                <guarantee_domain>;
<performance_domain>   = 'Performance' '{' <partdomain_body> '}';
<reliability_domain>   = 'Reliability' '{' <partdomain_body> '}';
<guarantee_domain>     = 'Guarantee'   '{' <partdomain_body> '}';
(...)
<subdomain_decl>       = 'Subdomain' <subdomain_body>;
                                       | 'Subdomain' <identifier>;
<subdomain_body>       = '{' <name_decl> <type_decl> [<typedomain_decl>] '}';
<name_decl>            = 'name'   ':' <identifier> ';';
<type_decl>            = 'type'   ':' <datatype_body> ';';
<typedomain_decl>      = 'domain' ':' <typedomain_body> ';';
```

In Listing 1.2, an excerpt of the QoS domain *Video* is specified in NQSL. The performance domain consists of three subdomains. The first subdomain *Resolution* is defined as a tuple of integers, with the values restricted to the pairs $(320, 240)$, $(480, 360)$, and $(640, 480)$. The subdomains *Quality* and *FrameRate* have already been defined, and therefore are referenced.

Listing 1.2. NQSL specification: QoS domain *Video* (excerpt)

```
QoSDomain Video{
     Performance{
          Subdomain {
               name:    Resolution;
               type:    (Integer,Integer);
               domain:  {(320,240),(480,360),(640,480)}; }
          Subdomain Quality;
          Subdomain FrameRate;
     }
     Reliability{    (...)        }
     Guarantee{      (...)        }
}
```

A QoS requirements specification is identified by a unique name and uses a QoS domain defined beforehand. It consists of a set of QoS requirement profiles qosReq, which are subdivided into a description of minimum and optimum QoS as well as scalability. Listing 1.3 gives an excerpt of the QoS requirement specification *VideoTransmission*. The specification consists of two QoS requirement profiles *Surveillance* and *Panorama*. In the example, the scalability aspect is shown, with utility and cost functions restricted to the performance domain. For instance, utility is defined by refering to performance subdomains *Resolution*, *Quality*, and *FrameRate*, with Resolution.1 denoting the first tuple element. W.l.o.g. we assume that the needed transmission rate on *Hardware* layer would provide a good metric for the needed resources. The specification of optimum QoS can be found below (see Fig. 4).

Listing 1.3. NQSL specification: QoS scalability of *Video* (excerpt)

```
specification VideoTransmission uses Video {
        qosreq Surveillance {
            minimum{ (...) }
            optimum{ (...) }
            scalability {
                util = 0.1*((Resolution.1−160)/480) + 0.1*(Quality/75) +
                            0.8*(FrameRate/25);
                cost Hardware = TransmissionRate;
                up = 0.2;
                down = 0.1; }
        }
        qosreq Panorama { (...)}
}
```

To determine the costs of a video data flow configuration on application level from the costs specified on hardware level, QoS domain mappings are used. In Listing 1.4, two domain mappings are specified, mapping the QoS domain *Video* to *Hardware* via *Middleware*. Note that for the subdomains *reliability* and *guarantee*, we assume identical mappings, therefore, no explicit QoS mappings are provided.

Listing 1.4. NQSL specification: QoS domain mappings

```
domainmapping from Video to Middleware{
    performance:
        NoOfFrames=ceil((160*Quality+3000)*(Resolution.1−160)/(160*1420));
        Period=1/FrameRate;
    reliability;
    guarantee; }
domainmapping from Middleware to Hardware{
    performance:
        TransmissionRate = NoOfFrames/Period*1512;
    reliability;
    guarantee; }
```

5   Tool Support for NQSL

In this section, we present our tool support for NQSL, consisting of the Graphical NQSL Editor (GNE), the NQSL Analyzer (NA), and the NQSL-to-SDL Compiler (NSC).

5.1   Graphical NQSL Editor

The *Graphical NQSL Editor (GNE)* is generated from a metamodel for network
QoS, and implemented as a plugin for Eclipse IDE, using the *Eclipse Modeling Framework (EMF)* [10] and the *Graphical Modeling Framework (GMF)* [11].
Starting point is the *domain model* defined as a metamodel that is described
in *ECore*, a UML-dialect and part of the Meta Object Facility (MOF) [12] that
is limited to class diagrams. Based on this metamodel, EMF generates a rudi-
mentary editor with basic functionalities such as creating or modifying objects.
In the next step, GMF is used to generate a more sophisticated editor. Based
on the Java classes generated by EMF and the domain model, GMF creates a
graphical editor that is much more comfortable and intuitive to use. To this,
the *graphical definition model* identifying graphical elements, *e.g.* figures, nodes,
links etc., and the *tooling definition model* specifying the palette, creation tools,
actions, etc. of the graphical elements are needed. These three models are bound
by the *mapping definition model*. Based on this model, the *generation model* is
obtained by a transformation step.

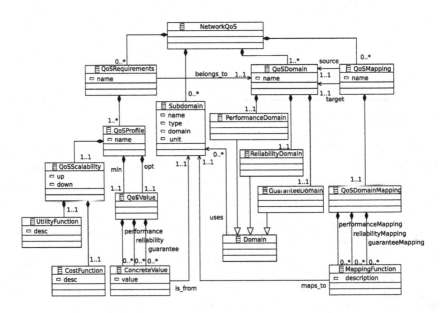

Fig. 1. Domain Model for the Graphical NQSL Editor

Starting point for the development of the graphical editor for NQSL is the domain model in Fig. 1. This metamodel is based on the formalization of network
QoS surveyed in Section 3. The metamodel introduces a class *NetworkQoS*, which
encapsulates QoS requirements and QoS mappings. Additionally, QoS domains
and QoS subdomains are aggregated in this class; this way, a QoS subdomain
can be used in different QoS domains, which is modeled by references. A QoS requirement specification is modeled by the class *QoSRequirements*, which in turn

consists of a set of QoS profiles capturing different application scenarios. The relation between QoS requirements and QoS domain is modeled by a reference. To simplify the implementation, the domains of QoS performance, QoS reliability and QoS guarantee are collected in a superclass *Domain*. The *QoSScalabiliy* is modelled as described in the formalization. QoS scalability consists of *UtilityFunction*, *CostFunction*, and two thresholds *up* and *down*. The mappings for performance, reliability and guarantee are collected in *MappingFunction*. The QoS scalability mapping is not be explicitly modeled, as it is identical for all QoS specifications.

Following the formalization of network QoS, the Graphical NQSL Editor (GNE) consists of three parts: an editor for QoS domains and subdomains, an editor for QoS mappings between QoS domains, and an editor for QoS requirements. Fig. 2 shows the user interface of the *GNE domain editor*. A QoS domain is created by referencing previously built QoS subdomains. Notice that QoS subdomains can be used in several QoS domains.

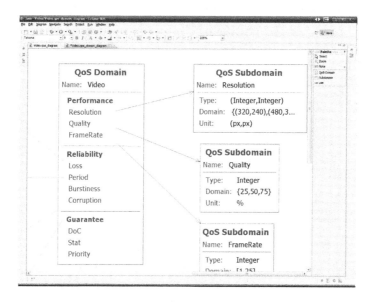

Fig. 2. GNE Domain Editor

The user interface of the *GNE Mapping Editor* is shown in Fig. 3. Two previously defined QoS domains *Video* and *Middleware* are related by specifying the QoS mapping *Video2Middleware*. If QoS subdomains of source and target domain are different, a customized mapping function has to be supplied. If some QoS subdomains are identical, *e.g.* priority or loss, a default mapping is generated. In addition, the direction of the mapping can be controlled by relations *map from* and *map to*.

Finally, the *GNE Requirements Editor* is used to define QoS requirements, consisting of a set of QoS profiles, on application level (see Fig. 4). First, a new

Fig. 3. GNE Mapping Editor

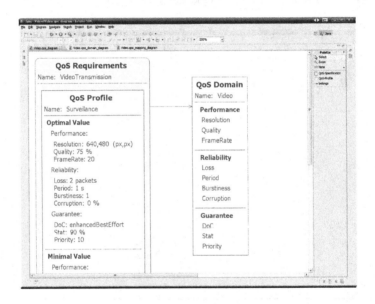

Fig. 4. GNE Requirements Editor

QoS requirements specification is created and associated with a QoS domain. Then, QoS profiles can be added by specifying concrete minimum and optimum QoS, and a QoS scalability value. In the example, the QoS requirements specification *VideoTransmission* is associated with the QoS domain *Video* and consists of the QoS profile *Surveillance*.

For further processing, GNE supports the transformation of QoS domains, QoS requirements, and QoS mappings from XMI [13], which is the default data format, to NQSL. Since the data is available in a XML-based format, we used XSLT [14] for this transformation.Figure 5 shows the transformation of subdomain *Resolution* to the corresponding NQSL description.

QoS Subdomain	
Name: Resolution	
Type:	(Integer,Integer)
Domain:	{(320,240),(480,360),(640,480)}
Unit:	(px,px)

```
Subdomain {
  name:   Resolution;
  type:   (Integer, Integer);
  domain: {(320, 240),(480,360),(640, 480)};
}
```

(a) Subdomain *Resolution*   (b) Result in NQSL

```
<xsl:for-each select="/qos:NetworkQoSDescription/subdomains">
  subdomain {
     name: <xsl:value-of select="@name" />;
     type: <xsl:value-of select="@type" />;
     domain: <xsl:value-of select="@domain" />;
  }
</xsl:for-each>
```

(c) Transformation in XSLT

Fig. 5. Transformation Process

5.2 NSQL Analyzer

Based on the definition of QoS domains on all abstraction levels, QoS mappings between them, and the QoS requirements on application level (see Section 5.1), the *NQSL Analyzer (NA)* performs QoS domain reductions and derives QoS requirements on communication level and on resource level. This relieves the system developer from filling in QoS requirements on lower levels and checking their consistency. Moreover, the analysis results provide feedback on QoS mappings, and support the assessment of utility and cost functions. Finally, they serve as input for generating fragments of the system design, e.g. QoS data structures and QoS scaling functionality based on QoS scaling tables.

To perform *QoS domain reductions*, the NQSL analyzer works in three steps, which are performed subsequently on all abstraction levels and for each QoS profile:

– In Step 1, the QoS domain is reduced to a set of u-equivalence class representatives. Here, the NQSL analyzer determines the u-equivalence classes of the QoS domain as induced by the utility function u of a QoS requirement profile (see Section 3.1). For each equivalence class, the QoS domain value with minimum cost according to the cost function c is kept as representative for that class, i.e. all other QoS domain values of that class are discarded. To limit memory needs of the system implementation later on, an upper bound for the number of equivalence classes can be set. At this point, the system developer obtains feedback about the distribution of the corresponding utility values in the interval $[0, 1]$. An example is given in Table 1. Note that to keep the presentation concise, we consider a very small QoS domain, comprising 9 values only (see Table 1(a)). A more realistic cardinality would be in the order of 10^3 to 10^5. Each QoS domain value consists of a tuple for resolution and values denoting JPEG quality and frame rate. Furthermore, the corresponding utilities and costs are shown. In the example, the utility of each QoS value is defined by the user, whereas the costs are calculated by means of the QoS performance mappings and cost function shown in Listings 1.3 and 1.4. Based on the utility, 5 equivalence classes $[x]_u$ are obtained. Selecting the QoS domain value with minimum cost in each equivalence class leads to a reduced QoS domain Q^u, as shown in Table 1(b).

Table 1. QoS Domain Q_{Video}

(a) *QoS domain values q_{Video} of QoS domain Q_{Video}*

value	utility	cost[10^3]	value	utility	cost[10^3]
((320,240),25,25)	0.1	175	((480,360),75,25)	0.5	750
((320,240),50,25)	0.1	275	((640,480),25,25)	0.7	525
((320,240),75,25)	0.3	375	((640,480),50,25)	0.7	825
((480,360),25,25)	0.3	350	((640,480),75,25)	0.9	1125
((480,360),50,25)	0.5	550			

(b) *equivalence partitioning* into 5 classes and keeping cost-optimal QoS domain values

$[x]_u$	value	cost[10^3]	$[x]_u$	value	cost[10^3]
$[0.1]_u$	((320,240),25,25)	175	$[0.7]_u$	((640,480),25,25)	525
$[0.3]_u$	((480,360),25,25)	350	$[0.9]_u$	((640,480),75,25)	1125
$[0.5]_u$	((480,360),50,25)	550			

- In Step 2, the number of QoS domain values is further reduced by applying the *cost criterion* (see also [1]). In general, it is possible that for QoS domain values q and q', $u(q) > u(q')$, while $c(q) \leq c(q')$. If this is the case, the QoS domain value q' can be discarded, as it is associated with higher or equal cost, but less utility. Discarding of QoS domain values is continued until for all remaining QoS domain values q and q', $u(q) > u(q')$ implies $c(q) > c(q')$. In the example, the QoS domain value $((480, 360), 50, 25)$ is discarded since $((640, 480), 25, 25)$ provides better utility at lower cost.

Table 2. Reduced Equivalence Classes

$[x]_u$	value	cost[10^3]	$[x]_u$	value	cost[10^3]
$[0.1]_u$	((320,240),25,25)	175	$[0.7]_u$	((640,480),25,25)	525
$[0.3]_u$	((480,360),25,25)	250	$[0.9]_u$	((640,480),75,25)	1125
~~$[0.5]_u$~~	~~((480,360),50,25)~~	~~550~~			

- In Step 3, the QoS domain values are further reduced by keeping only those QoS domain values that satisfy the QoS profiles of the QoS requirements, i.e. q_{min} and q_{opt}. First, the equivalence class representatives of q_{min} and q_{opt} are determined. From these representatives, the utility interval corresponding to the QoS requirements are obtained. Finally, all QoS domain values with a utility outside this interval are discarded. The remaining QoS domain values constitute entries of the QoS scaling table. In the example, we assume that we have only one QoS profile with q_{min} in $[0.3]_u$ and q_{opt} in $[0.9]_u$. This leads to the QoS scaling table shown in Tab. 3.

Table 3. QoS Scaling Table

$[\mathbf{x}]_u$	value	cost	$[\mathbf{x}]_u$	value	cost
$[0.3]_u$	((480,360),25,25)	350	$[0.9]_u$	((640,480),75,25)	1125
$[0.7]_u$	((640,480),25,25)	525			

Thus, for every QoS profile of a QoS requirements specification, a QoS scaling table is generated. To derive *QoS requirements* on communication level and on resource level, the NQSL analyzer applies the corresponding QoS mappings to the set of QoS domain values remaining after QoS domain reduction. For each layer, the QoS requirement specification is derived by determining the utility of the resulting QoS domain values, and by selecting the QoS domain values with minimum and optimum utility. In the example shown in Tab. 4, the QoS profile is mapped to a corresponding QoS profile on middleware layer, described by the number of data frames required for the transmission of one picture frame, and the period between two picture frames, i.e. $Q_{Middleware} = NoFrames \times Period$ [s]. To obtain the corresponding QoS domain values on middleware layer, the QoS mapping defined in Listing 1.3 has been applied. From these results, it follows that the minimum and maximum QoS domain values on middleware layer are $(10, 0.04)$ and $(32, 0.04)$, respectively.

Table 4. Results of QoS Mapping

application layer			middleware layer		
$[\mathbf{x}]_u$	value	cost	$[\mathbf{x}]_u$	value	cost
$[0.3]_u$	((480,360),25,25)	350	$[0.3]_u$	(10, 0.04)	350
$[0.7]_u$	((640,480),25,25)	525	$[0.7]_u$	(15, 0.04)	525
$[0.9]_u$	((640,480),75,25)	1125	$[0.9]_u$	(32, 0.04)	1125

We have implemented the NQSL analyzer in Java. Currently, performance and guarantee mappings are supported by the tool.

5.3   NQSL-to-SDL Compiler

After finalizing the QoS requirements specification in NQSL, the developer turns to the specification of the system design. For the design, a QoS architecture has to be devised, required QoS functionalities such as access tests, resource reservation, traffic control, and scaling strategies are to be identified, and corresponding mechanisms to realize these functionalities must be provided. Furthermore, it has to be shown that the design satisfies the abstract QoS requirements.

Certainly, the design decisions that are to be taken here are far too complex to be automated entirely. However, it is feasible to generate fragments of the design. To start with, we have developed the *NQSL-to-SDL Compiler (NSC)* that translates QoS domains and QoS requirements specified in NQSL to corresponding data type definitions and QoS scaling process types based on QoS domain tables in SDL [15]. SDL, ITU-T's Specification and Description Language, is a formal design language for telecommunication systems that is widely used in industry and academia, with commercial tool support including graphical editors, analyzers, simulators, and SDL-to-C compilers. Fig. 6(a) shows a screen dump of the user interface of the NSC. As input, the tool accepts the NQSL output of the Graphical NQSL Editor. One output of the NSC are layer specific SDL packages, containing the according SDL data type definitions of the QoS domain. The NSC has been integrated into Telelogic TAU [16], the SDL tool suite of a commercial provider of SDL tools. It has been written in Java, using JFlex [17] for lexical analysis and CUP [18] for parsing. For better usability, we have integrated the NQSL Analyzer into the NSC user interface.

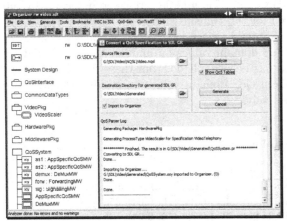

(a) User Interface integrated in Telelogic TAU

(b) Generated SDL data types

Fig. 6. NQSL-to-SDL Compiler

For a given QoS domain, the NSC generates an SDL package, *i.e.* a library that can be imported by SDL system specifications. The generated SDL package contains SDL data type definitions of all problem-specific QoS subdomains of the NQSL specification. QoS subdomains that are not problem-specific, such as *degree of commmitment* or *priority* of the QoS guarantee domain, are collected in the predefined SDL package *CommonDataTypes*, which s imported by every other SDL package generated by the NSC.

QoS domains and subdomains are mapped to SDL syntypes or newtypes, depending on their complexity. Fig. 6(b) shows the SDL data types generated

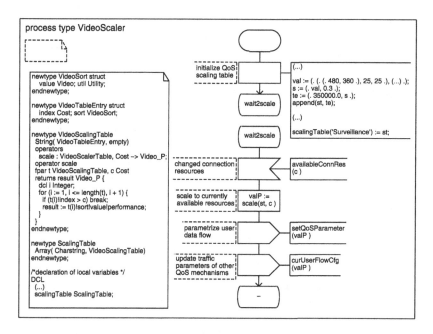

Fig. 7. Generated Process Type *VideoScaler* (excerpt)

for the QoS domain Q_{Video}, which are contained in the new SDL package *VideoPkg*. For the QoS domain Q_{Video}, the SDL data type *Video* (see bottom of Fig. 6(b)) is derived. This data type is structured into the performance data type *Video_P*, the reliability data type *Video_R*, and the guarantee data type *Video_G*. The subdomains *Resolution*, *Quality* and *FrameRate* of the performance domain *Video_P* are also defined within this package; the subdomains of the reliability and performance domain are imported from in the predefined SDL package *CommonDataTypes*.

Starting point for the translation of a QoS requirements specification to SDL is a reduced and optimized QoS domain as described in Sections 3.1 and 5.2. For this reason, a preceding NQSL analyzer run is mandatory. For every QoS requirements specification, an SDL scaling process type is automatically generated, consisting of a scaling algorithm and a scaling table. The scaling table aggregates the reduced QoS domain tables containing the optimal QoS domain values created for every QoS profile of a QoS requirements specification. The scaling algorithm selects the currently best QoS domain value under a given resource situation.

Figure 7 shows the process type *VideoScaler* generated by the NSC. The scaling algorithm is realized by an operator *scale* defined on the SDL data type *VideoScalingTable*. During the startup phase of the process, the tables for the QoS profiles of a specification are initialised according the output of the NQSL analyzer. If the resource situation changes as indicated by the input signal *availableConnRes*, the scaling operation is performed, and the user data flow configuration is updated. Further, the current application scenario can be chosen by another input signal (not shown in the figure).

6   Conclusions and Future Work

In this paper, we have presented NQSL, the Network QoS Specification Language, to formally specify network QoS. NQSL is derived from our previous formalization of network QoS with specific emphasis of scalability and cross-layer development. It provides language elements for specifying QoS domains, QoS subdomains, and QoS mappings. Further, QoS requirements can be defined by specifying QoS profiles, expressed by minimum and optimum QoS domain values and a QoS scalability value that consists of utility function, cost function, and two thresholds. To support the efficient handling of NQSL specifications, we have presented a tool chain consisting of the Graphical NQSL Editor (GNE), the NQSL Analyzer (NA), and the NQSL-to-SDL Compiler (NSC).

The work presented in this paper solves a number of problems of practical relevance. First, it is very important that network QoS requirements be specified formally. While there are several languages reported in the literature already, NQSL goes one step further by supporting the specification of network QoS requirements on all system layers, by including QoS scalability, and by supporting QoS mappings. Second, for practical usage, tool support is mandatory. Here, our tool chain supports editing, analyzing, and transforming NQSL specifications, relieving the system developer from several tedious and error-prone tasks, such as applying QoS mappings by hand or reducing QoS domains based on the definitions of utility and cost functions. To further increase usability, the SDL generator has been integrated into Telelogic SDL Suite. We are currently not aware of QoS tools with comparable functionality.

Our future work aims at extensions of our tool chain for QoS system development, and at SDL system designs satisfying formally specified network QoS requirements. The next step will be the extension of the NQSL-to-SDL compiler by architectural QoS concepts. Thereby, it will be possible to automatically generate a complete SDL system structure with QoS functionalities. Another step is the formal definition of a distributed resource management and scalability model for multiple data flows. This model will use the derived QoS profiles across layers to provide and manage QoS for different user data flows in a correct and efficient manner.

Acknowledgments. The work presented in this paper was in part carried out in the BelAmI (Bilateral German-Hungarian Research Collaboration on Ambient Intelligence Systems) project, funded by German Federal Ministry of Education and Research (BMBF), Fraunhofer-Gesellschaft and the Ministry for Science, Education, Research and Culture (MWWFK) of Rheinland-Pfalz.

References

1. Webel, C., Gotzhein, R.: Formalization of Network Quality-of-Service Requirements. In: Derrick, J., Vain, J. (eds.) FORTE 2007. LNCS, vol. 4574, pp. 309–324. Springer, Heidelberg (2007)
2. Jin, J., Nahrstedt, K.: QoS Specification Languages for Distributed Multimedia Applications: A Survey and Taxonomy. IEEE MultiMedia 11(3), 74–87 (2004)
3. Frølund, S., Koistinen, J.: QML: A Language for Quality of Service Specification. Technical Report HPL-98-10, p. 63, Software Technology Laboratory, Hewlett-Packard Company (1998)
4. Aagedal, J.Ø.: Quality of Service Support in Development of Distributed Systems. PhD thesis, University of Oslo, Oslo, Norway (2001)
5. Röttger, S., Zschaler, S.: Tool support for refinement of non-functional specifications. Software and Systems Modelling journal (SoSyM) 6(2) (June 2007)
6. Vanegas, R., Zinky, J.A., Loyall, J.P., Karr, D., Schantz, R.E., Bakken, D.E.: QuO's Runtime Support for Quality of Service in Distributed Objects. In: Proceedings of the IFIP International Conference on Distributed Systems Platforms and Open Distributed Processing (Middleware 1998), The Lake District, UK, pp. 207–222 (1998)
7. Florissi, P.G.S.: QoSME: QoS Management Environment. PhD thesis, Columbia University (1996)
8. Campbell, A.T.: A Quality of Service Architecture. PhD thesis, Computing Department, Lancaster University (1996)
9. Webel, C.: NQSL - A Specification Language for Network Quality of Service. Technical Report 368/07, Department of Computer Science, University of Kaiserslautern (2007)
10. Eclipse Foundation: Eclipse Modeling Framework Project (EMF) (2007), http://www.eclipse.org/modeling/emf/
11. Eclipse Foundation: The Eclipse Graphical Modeling Framework (GMF) (2007), http://www.eclipse.org/gmf/
12. Object Management Group, Inc.: Meta Object Facility (MOF) Specification (2000), http://www.omg.org/mof/
13. Object Management Group, Inc.: Xml metadata interchange (xmi) specification (2007), http://www.omg.org/technology/documents/formal/xmi.htm
14. World Wide Web Consortium: XSL Transformations (XSLT). W3C Recommendation (1999), http://www.w3.org/TR/xslt
15. International Telecommunications Union: Specification and Description Language (SDL). ITU-T Recommendation Z.100 (August 2002)
16. Telelogic AB: Telelogic SDL Suite and TTCN Suite (2007), http://www.telelogic.com/products/tau/sdl/index.cfm
17. JFlex: JFlex - The Fast Scanner Generator for Java (2007), http://jflex.de/
18. CUP: CUP – LALR Parser Generator in Java (2006), http://www2.cs.tum.edu/projects/cup/

Timed Mobile Ambients for Network Protocols

Bogdan Aman[2] and Gabriel Ciobanu[1,2]

[1] "A.I.Cuza" University, Faculty of Computer Science
Blvd. Carol I no.11, 700506 Iaşi, Romania
[2] Romanian, Academy, Institute of Computer Science
Blvd. Carol I no.8, 700505 Iaşi, Romania
baman@iit.tuiasi.ro, gabriel@info.uaic.ro

Abstract. Ambient calculus is a calculus for mobile computing able to express local communications inside hierarchical domains. So far the timing properties have not been considered in the framework of mobile ambients. We add timers to capabilities and ambients, and provide an operational semantics of the new calculus. Certain results are related to the passage of time, and some new behavioural equivalences over timed mobile ambients are defined. Timeout for network communication (TTL) can be naturally modelled by the time constraints over capabilities and ambients. The new formalism can be used to describe network protocols; Simple Network Management Protocol (SNMP) may implement its own strategy for timeout and retransmission in TCP/IP.

1   Introduction

Ambient calculus is a formalism for describing distributed and mobile computation introduced in [6]. In contrast with other formalisms for mobile processes such as the π-calculus [19] whose computational model is based on the notion of *communication*, the ambient calculus is based on the notion of *movement*. An ambient represents a unit of movement. Ambient mobility is controlled by the capabilities *in*, *out*, and *open*. Capabilities are similar to prefixes in CCS [18] and π-calculus. Several variants of the ambient calculus have been proposed by adding and/or removing features of the original calculus [5,15,17].

The definition of mobile ambients is related in [6] to the network communication. Ambient calculus can model communication protocols. Timing properties are important in network communication. For instance, a *Time to Live* (TTL) value is used to indicate the timeout for a communication unit before it should be discarded. Servers do not apply a single fixed timeout for all communication units. Simple Network Management Protocol (SNMP) could implement its own strategy for timeout and retransmission in TCP/IP communication protocol. TTL and retransmission in TCP/IP protocol provide a good motivation to add timers to ambients. So far the timing properties have not been considered in the framework of mobile ambients. In this paper we associate timers not only to ambients, but also to capabilities. The resulting formalism is called timed mobile ambients (tMA), and represents a conservative extension of the ambient calculus.

K. Suzuki et al. (Eds.): FORTE 2008, LNCS 5048, pp. 234–250, 2008.

We use a clock just for the sake of uniformity; all the clocks work in the same way. In fact, working with located processes and a migration primitive *go*, we use only local clocks, and the change from one local clock to another one is possible by the migration primitive *go*. This is sound because we use relative time given by timers, and not an absolute time.

The structure of the paper is as follows. Section 2 introduces the pure mobile ambients followed by the description of the timed mobile ambients (tMA). The passage of time is given by a discrete time progress function. We provide an operational semantics of the new calculus given by a reduction relation. In Section 3 we use tMA to describe the Transmission Control Protocol (TCP). In Section 4 we introduce and study some behavioural equivalences over timed mobile ambients. Other results are related to the passage of time. Conclusion and references end the paper.

2   Mobile Ambients with Time Constraints

We provide a short description of the pure mobile ambients, an algebraic formalism which studies the distributed concurrent systems; more information can be found in [6]. The following table describes the syntax of mobile ambients.

Table 1. *Mobile Ambients Syntax*

n, m, p		ambient names	P, Q	$::=$	processes
C	$::=$	capabilities		$\mathbf{0}$	inactivity
	$in\ n$	can enter n		$C.P$	movement
	$out\ n$	can exit n		$n[P]$	ambient
	$open\ n$	can open n		$P\mid Q$	composition
				$(\nu n)P$	restriction
				$*P$	replication

Process $\mathbf{0}$ is an inactive process (it does nothing). A movement $C.P$ is provided by the capability C, followed by the execution of P. An ambient $n[P]$ represents a bounded place labelled by n in which a process P is executed. $P\mid Q$ is a parallel composition of processes P and Q. $(\nu n)P$ creates a new unique name n within the scope of P. $*P$ denotes the unbounded replication of a process P, producing as many parallel replicas of P as needed.

The semantic of the ambient calculus is given by two relations: structural congruence and reduction. The *structural congruence* $P \equiv Q$ relates different syntactic representations of the same process; it is used to define the reduction relation. The *reduction relation* $P \rightarrow Q$ describes the system evolution. We denote by $\rightarrow^*$ the reflexive and transitive closure of $\rightarrow$.

The structural congruence is defined as the least relation over processes satisfying the axioms from the table below:

Table 2. *Structural congruence*

$(P \mid Q) \mid R \equiv P \mid (Q \mid R)$	$P \equiv Q$ implies $Q \equiv P$
$P \mid Q \equiv Q \mid P$, $\quad *P \equiv P \mid *P$	$P \equiv Q$, $Q \equiv R$ implies $P \equiv R$
$(\nu n)(\nu m)P \equiv (\nu m)(\nu n)P$ if $n \neq m$	$P \equiv Q$ implies $(\nu n)P \equiv (\nu n)Q$
$(\nu n)(P \mid Q) \equiv P \mid (\nu n)Q$ if $n \notin fnAmb(P)$	$P \equiv Q$ implies $P \mid R \equiv Q \mid R$
$(\nu n)m[P] \equiv m[(\nu n)P]$ if $n \neq m$	$P \equiv Q$ implies $*P \equiv *Q$
$P \equiv P$, $\quad P \mid 0 \equiv P$	$P \equiv Q$ implies $n[P] \equiv n[Q]$
$(\nu n)0 \equiv 0$; $\quad *0 \equiv 0$	$P \equiv Q$ implies $C.P \equiv C.Q$

The rules from the left side of the table describe the commutativity/ associativity of composition, unfolding recursion, changing the restriction scope. The rules from the right side describe how structural congruence is propagated across processes. The set of free names for a process is defined as follows:

$$fnAmb(P) = \begin{cases} \emptyset & \text{if } P = 0 \\ fnAmb(R) \cup \{n\} & \text{if } P = cap\ n.R, \text{ with } cap \in \{in, out, open\} \\ fnAmb(R) \cup \{n\} & \text{if } P = n[R] \\ fnAmb(R) \cup fnAmb(Q) & \text{if } P = R \mid Q \\ fnAmb(R) - \{n\} & \text{if } P = (\nu n)R \\ fnAmb(R) & \text{if } P = *R \end{cases}$$

The reduction relation is defined as the least relation over processes satisfying the following set of axioms and rules:

Table 3. *Reduction Rules*

(In)	$n[in\ m.\ P \mid Q] \mid m[R] \to m[n[P \mid Q] \mid R]$
(Out)	$m[n[out\ m.\ P \mid Q] \mid R] \to n[P \mid Q] \mid m[R]$
(Open)	$open\ n.\ P \mid n[Q] \to P \mid Q$
(Res)	$P \to Q$ implies $(\nu n)P \to (\nu n)Q$
(Amb)	$P \to Q$ implies $n[P] \to n[Q]$
(Par)	$P \to Q$ implies $P \mid R \to Q \mid R$
(Struct)	$\dfrac{P' \equiv P,\ P \to Q,\ Q \equiv Q'}{P' \to Q'}$

The first three rules are the reductions for *in, out, open*. The next three rules propagate reductions across scopes, ambient nesting and parallel composition. The final rule allows the use of structural congruence during reduction.

We ignore the communications inside ambients and use pure mobile ambients to express the time and space constraints. We can also easily introduce channels and study the aspects related to them, with no difference in expressing the network protocols.

In order to identify an entity, TCP/IP protocols use the IP address, which uniquely identifies the connection of a host to the Internet. However, people prefer to use names instead of numeric addresses. A system that can map a

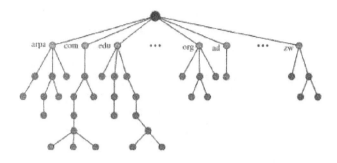

Fig. 1. Domain Name System(DNS)

name to an address or an address to a name is the domain name system, which
is represented hierarchically in what follows:

The information contained in DNS must be stored. One way to do this is to
divide the whole space into many domains based on the first level.

Inspired from the domain name system, we also consider a distribution of
parallel locations between which the ambients can migrate, each location being the place where the nested ambients interact. In our model the root node,
represented in the above picture, disappears and its function is supplied by the
execution of the migration primitive *go*. Thus we get a more realistic description
of the distributed computation and mobility. A natural example motivating an
extension from timed distributed π-calculus to timed mobile ambients is presented in [7].

The syntax of the timed mobile ambients is defined in Table 4.

Table 4. *Syntax of tMA*

$a, b, \ldots$	names	$P, Q ::=$	processes
$C \quad ::=$	capabilities	$\mathbf{0}$	inactivity
in n	can enter an ambient n	$C^{\Delta t}.(P, Q)$	movement
out n	can exit an ambient n	$(n^{\Delta t}[P]^\mu, Q)$	ambient
open n	can open an ambient n	$P \mid Q$	composition
go k	migration	$(\nu n)P$	restriction
M, N $::=$	located processes	$*P$	replication
$l[[P]]$	location		
$(\nu k)M$	restriction		
$M \mid N$	composition		

We use m, n for *ambient names*; k, l for *physical locations*; a, p for *ambient tags*
- a stands for *active* ambients, while p stands for *passive* ambients - we use μ to
stand for both ambient tags.

In timed Mobile Ambients (tMA) capabilities and ambients are used as temporal resources; if nothing happens in a predefined interval of time, the waiting
process goes to another state. Since the expiration of a timer offers an alternative,

we shall not use the choice operator as in other process calculi. The timer Δt of each temporal resource indicates that the resource is available only for a determined period of time t. We add timers to both ambients and capabilities. A process can be executed only if it is inside a location. When an ambient migrates between locations, all the processes running inside suspend their execution until the ambient reaches its destination.

We write $n^{\Delta t}[P]^{\mu}$ to denote an ambient having the timer Δt and the tag μ. The tag μ is a neutral tag that indicates if an ambient is active or passive. The novelty comes from the fact that an ambient can disappear. If $t > 0$ the ambient behaves exactly as in untimed mobile ambients. Since the timer Δt can expire ($t = 0$) we use a pair $(n^{\Delta t}[P]^{\mu}, Q)$ to denote a timed ambient, where Q is a *safety process*. If nothing happens in t units of time, the ambient n is dissolved, the process P running inside the ambient is reduced to $\mathbf{0}$, and the process Q is executed. If $Q = \mathbf{0}$ we can simply write $n^{\Delta t}[P]^{\mu}$ instead of $(n^{\Delta t}[P]^{\mu}, Q)$. Similarly, for movement, we use a pair of processes. The process $open^{\Delta t}n.(P, Q)$ evolves to P whenever, in the period of time Δt, the process becomes sibling to an ambient n; otherwise it evolves to Q.

When we describe initially the ambients, we consider that all ambients are active, and we associate the tag a to them. From Table 4 it can be seen that we consider only ambients to be placed at some locations.

2.1 Semantics

The main feature of tMA is given by the explicit use of time. The passage of time is described by two discrete time progress functions: Φ_{Δ} defined over the set $\mathcal{L}$ of located processes, and ϕ_{Δ} defined over the set $\mathcal{P}$ of timed processes. The possible actions are performed at every tick of a universal clock. The function ϕ_{Δ}, inspired from [3], affects the ambients, and the capabilities which are not consumed. The consumed capabilities and ambients disappear together with their timers. If a capability or ambient has the timer equal to ∞, thus simulating the behaviour of an untimed capability or ambient, we use the equality $\infty - 1 = \infty$ when applying the function ϕ_{Δ}. This function modifies a process accordingly with the passage of time. Another property of the time progress function ϕ_{Δ} is that the passive ambients can become active in the next unit of time in order to participate in other reductions.

For the process $C^{\Delta t}.(P, Q)$ the timer of P is activated only after the consumption of capability $C^{\Delta t}$ (in at most t units of time). Reduction rules (Table 6) show how the time function Φ_{Δ} is used.

Definition 1. *(Global time progress function) We define* $\Phi_{\Delta} : \mathcal{L} \to \mathcal{L}$, *by:*

$$\Phi_{\Delta}(M) = \begin{cases} \Phi_{\Delta}(M_1) \mid \Phi_{\Delta}(M_2) & \text{if } M = M_1 \mid M_2 \\ (\nu k)\Phi_{\Delta}(N) & \text{if } M = (\nu k)N \\ l[[\phi_{\Delta}(P)]] & \text{if } M = l[[P]] \end{cases}$$

where the function $\phi_{\Delta} : \mathcal{P} \to \mathcal{P}$ *has the following definition:*

$$\phi_\Delta(P) = \begin{cases} C^{\Delta(t-1)}.(R,Q) & \text{if } P = C^{\Delta t}.(R,Q),\ t > 0 \\ Q & \text{if } P = C^{\Delta t}.(R,Q),\ t = 0 \\ \phi_\Delta(R) \mid \phi_\Delta(Q) & \text{if } P = R \mid Q \\ (\nu n)\phi_\Delta(R) & \text{if } P = (\nu n)R \\ (n^{\Delta(t-1)}[\phi_\Delta(R)]^a, Q) & \text{if } P = (n^{\Delta t}[R]^\mu, Q),\ t > 0 \\ Q & \text{if } P = (n^{\Delta t}[R]^\mu, Q),\ t = 0 \\ P & \text{if } P = *R \text{ or } P = \mathbf{0} \end{cases}$$

Processes are grouped into equivalence classes by the following equivalence relation, Ξ, called structural congruence. This relation provides a way of rearranging expressions so that interacting parts can be brought together.

Table 5. *Structural Congruence in tMA*

(S-Sym)	$P \Xi Q$ implies $Q \Xi P$	**(S-Refl)**	$P \Xi P$
(S-Trans)	$P \Xi R,\ R \Xi Q$ implies $P \Xi Q$	**(S-Par Assoc)**	$(P \mid Q) \mid R \Xi P \mid (Q \mid R)$
(S-Res)	$P \Xi Q$ implies $(\nu n)P \Xi (\nu n)Q$	**(S-Repl Par)**	$*P \Xi P \mid *P$
(S-Par)	$P \Xi Q$ implies $R \mid P \Xi R \mid Q$	**(S-Zero Par)**	$P \mid \mathbf{0} \Xi P$
(S-Par Com)	$P \mid Q \Xi Q \mid P$	**(S-Zero Res)**	$(\nu n)\mathbf{0} \Xi \mathbf{0}$
(S-Repl)	$P \Xi Q$ implies $*P \Xi *Q$	**(S-Zero Repl)**	$*\mathbf{0} \Xi \mathbf{0}$
(S-Amb)	$P \Xi Q$ and $R \Xi R'$ implies $(n^{\Delta t}[P]^\mu, R) \Xi (n^{\Delta t}[Q]^\mu, R')$		
(S-Loc)	$P \Xi Q$ implies $k[[P]] \Xi k[[Q]]$		
(S-Par Loc)	$k[[P \mid Q]] \Xi k[[P]] \mid k[[Q]]$		
(S-Cap)	$P \Xi Q$ and $R \Xi R'$ implies $C^{\Delta t}.(P,R) \Xi C^{\Delta t}.(Q,R')$		
(S-Res Res)	$(\nu n)(\nu m)P \Xi (\nu m)(\nu n)P$ if $n \neq m$		
(S-Res Par)	$(\nu n)(P \mid Q) \Xi P \mid (\nu n)Q$ if $n \notin fnAmb(P)$		
(S-Res Par Loc)	$(\nu k)(M \mid N) \Xi M \mid (\nu k)N$ if $k \notin fnLoc(M)$		
(S-Res Amb)	$(\nu n)(m^{\Delta t}[P]^\mu, Q) \Xi (m^{\Delta t}[(\nu n)P]^\mu, Q)$ if $m \neq n$ and $n \notin fnAmb(Q)$		

The set of free names for a located process is defined as follow:

$$fnLoc(M) = \begin{cases} fnLoc(P) \cup \{k\} & \text{if } M = k[[P]] \\ fnLoc(N_1) \cup fnLoc(N_2) & \text{if } M = N_1 \mid N_2 \\ fnLoc(N) - \{k\} & \text{if } M = (\nu k)N \end{cases} \text{, where}$$

$$fnLoc(P) = \begin{cases} \emptyset & \text{if } P = \mathbf{0} \\ fnLoc(R) \cup \{k\} & \text{if } P = go^{\Delta t}k.(R.R') \\ fnLoc(R) \cup fnLoc(Q) & \text{otherwise} \end{cases}$$

We denote by $-\not\rightarrow$ the fact that none of the rules from the following Table, except the rule **(R-TimePass)** can be applied. The behaviour of processes is given by the following reduction rules:

Table 6. *Reduction rules*

(R-Migrate)	$\dfrac{t' = 1}{l[[(n^{\Delta t}[go^{\Delta t'}k.(P,P')]^a, Q)]] \dashrightarrow k[[(n^{\Delta t}[P]^p, Q)]]}$

$$(\text{R-In}) \quad \frac{-}{\substack{(n^{\Delta t'}[in^{\Delta t}m.(P,P') \mid Q]^a, S') \mid (m^{\Delta t''}[R]^\mu, S'') \dashrightarrow \\ (m^{\Delta t''}[(n^{\Delta t'}[P \mid Q]^p, S') \mid R]^\mu, S'')}}$$

$$(\text{R-Out}) \quad \frac{-}{\substack{(m^{\Delta t'}[(n^{\Delta t''}[out^{\Delta t}m.(P,P') \mid Q]^a, S'') \mid R]^\mu, S') \dashrightarrow \\ (n^{\Delta t''}[P \mid Q]^p, S'') \mid (m^{\Delta t'}[R]^\mu, S')}}$$

$$(\text{R-Open}) \quad \frac{-}{open^{\Delta t}m.\,(P,P') \mid (m^{\Delta t'}[Q]^\mu, S') \dashrightarrow P \mid Q}$$

(R-Amb)	$\dfrac{P \dashrightarrow Q}{(n^{\Delta t}[P]^\mu, R) \dashrightarrow (n^{\Delta t}[Q]^\mu, R)}$	(R-Par1)	$\dfrac{P \dashrightarrow Q}{P \mid R \dashrightarrow Q \mid R}$
(R-Par2)	$\dfrac{P \dashrightarrow Q,\ P' \dashrightarrow Q'}{P \mid P' \dashrightarrow Q \mid Q'}$	(R-Res)	$\dfrac{P \to Q}{(\nu n)P \dashrightarrow (\nu n)Q}$
(R-Struct)	$\dfrac{M' \equiv M,\ M \dashrightarrow N,\ N \equiv N'}{M' \dashrightarrow N'}$	(R-Loc)	$\dfrac{P \dashrightarrow Q}{l[[P]] \dashrightarrow l[[Q]]}$
(R-LocPar1)	$\dfrac{M \dashrightarrow M'}{M \mid N \dashrightarrow M' \mid N}$	(R-LocPar2)	$\dfrac{M \dashrightarrow M',\ N \dashrightarrow N'}{M \mid N \dashrightarrow M' \mid N'}$
(R-LocRes)	$\dfrac{M \dashrightarrow M'}{(\nu k)M \dashrightarrow (\nu k)M}$	(R-TimePass)	$\dfrac{M \not\dashrightarrow}{M \dashrightarrow \Phi_\Delta(M)}$

In the rules **(R-In)**, **(R-Out)**, **(R-Open)** ambient m can be *passive* or *active*, while in the rules **(R-Migrate)**, **(R-In)**, **(R-Out)** ambient n is *active*. The difference between *passive* and *active* ambients is that the *passive* ambients can be used in several reductions in a unit of time, while the *active* ambients can be used in at most one reduction in a unit of time, by consuming their capabilities. In the rules **(R-In)**, **(R-Out)** the *active* ambient n becomes *passive*, forcing it to consume only one capability in one unit of time. The ambients which are tagged as *passive*, become *active* again by applying the global time-stepping function **(R-TimePass)**. We use the tag μ in these rules because it does not matter whether or not the ambient is passive or active.

In the rules **(R-Migrate)** if the physical location k does not exist then it is created. Rule **(R-Migrate)** simulates the movement of an *active* ambient n from location l to location k in order to interact with some ambient located at k; notice that the ambient tag changes to p, meaning that the ambient becomes *passive*.

In timed mobile ambients, if a process evolves by one of the rules **(R-In)**, **(R-Out)**, **(R-Open)**, **(R-Migrate)**, while another one does not perform any reduction, then rule **(R-Par1)** should be applied. If more than one process evolve in parallel by applying one of the rules **(R-In)**, **(R-Out)**, **(R-Open)**, **(R-Migrate)**, then the rule **(R-Par2)** should be applied. We use the rule **(R-Par2)** to compose processes that are active, and the rule **(R-Par1)** to compose

processes that are active and passive. An example for the usage of the rule
(**R-Par1**) is given by:

$$\frac{m^{\Delta t_1}[Q]^{\mu} \mid open^{\Delta t_2} m \to Q}{m^{\Delta t_1}[Q]^{\mu} \mid open^{\Delta t_2} m \mid in^{\Delta t_3} t \to Q \mid in^{\Delta t_3} t}$$

A similar argument can be used for arguing in case of the rules (**R-LocPar1**)
and (**R-LocPar2**). The rule (**R-LocRes**) propagate reductions across location
scopes. In Section 3 illustrate how some of the rules from Table 6 are working.

We can say that a system described with tMA satisfies the properties [13]:

- **Time Determinism**: at each time only one reduction rule can be applied.
  A possible problem could appear only if we apply (**R-TimePass**) when we
  can apply another rule. However this is not possible because (**R-TimePass**)
  is applied only if the process does not evolve $(\nrightarrow)$.
- **Maximal Progress**: a process cannot delay if it can evolve.
- **Time Continuity**: to go from a process P at time t, to a process P_0 at time
  $t + \Delta t$, we must go through all the intermediate time steps of the interval
  $[t, t + \Delta t]$.

3   Transmission Control Protocol

Transmission Control Protocol (TCP) is a connection-oriented protocol. Using
TCP applications on networked hosts can establish connections to one another,
over which they can exchange data. The protocol is reliable and delivers the
data from sender to receiver in the order it has been sent. TCP distinguishes
data from multiple connections made by concurrent applications running on the
same host.

TCP needs to establish a connection before sending data. To establish a connection, TCP uses a *three-way handshake*. In order for a client to connect to
a server, the server must first open a port for the connection: this is called a
passive open. A client can initiate an *active open*, only after the passive open is
established. TCP connections have three phases:

1. the active open is performed by sending a synchronization packet (SYN flag
   set) to the server;
2. the server replies with a packet (SYN and ACK flag set);
3. the client sends a packet (ACK flag set) back to the server.

After all these steps are performed, both the client and the server have received
an acknowledgement of the connection and the data transfer can begin.

The connection termination phase uses, at most, a *four-way handshake*. This
is caused by TCP's *half closed*. Since a TCP connection is full-duplex (data can
flow in each direction independently of the other direction), each direction must
be shut down independently. When an endpoint wishes to stop its half of the
connection, it transmits a FIN packet, which the other end acknowledges with an
ACK. The receipt of a FIN only means that there can be no more data flowing
in that direction. A TCP can still send data after receiving a FIN. Therefore,
a connection termination requires a pair of FIN and ACK segments from each
TCP endpoint.

It is also possible to terminate the connection by a 3-way handshake, when a process sends a FIN and the other host replies with a FIN & ACK (merely combines 2 steps into one) and first host replies with an ACK. This is perhaps the most common method.

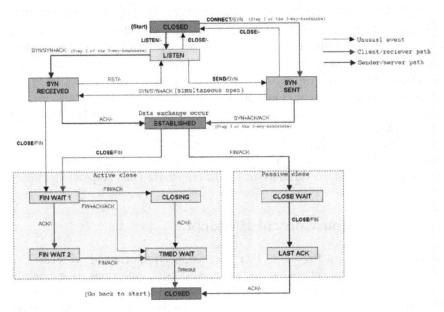

Fig 2. TCP State Diagram

Every implementation must choose a value for its *maximum segment lifetime*. It is the maximum amount of time any segment can exist in the network before being discarded; this justifies why we have added timers to ambients. We know this time limit is bounded, since TCP segments are transmitted as IP datagrams, and the IP datagram has the TTL field that limits its lifetime. (RFC 793 specifies the MSL as 2 minutes. Common implementation values, however, are 30 seconds, 1 minute, or 2 minutes. [21])

In what follows, we represent TCP in tMA, when only a client and a server are involved. For simplicity, we do not add the safety process to the capabilities which we know for sure that they are going to be consumed, and for the ambients which have the timer ∞.

Table 7. *Transmission Control Protocol represented in tMA*

$system := l_1[[client^\infty[send \mid send\_ack]^{\mu_1}]] \mid l_2[[server^\infty[receive]^{\mu_2}]]$

$send =$
$\quad SYN^{\Delta t_1}[out^{\Delta t_2} client.go^{\Delta t_3} l_2.in^{\Delta t_3} server]^{\mu_3}$

$send\_ack =$
$\quad open^{\Delta t_4} SYNACK. (ACK^{\Delta t_5}[out^{\Delta t_6} client.go^{\Delta t_7} l_2.in^{\Delta t_7} server]^{\mu_4}, send \mid send\_ack)$

$receive =$
$\quad open^{\Delta t_8} SYN. (SYNACK^{\Delta t_9}[out^{\Delta t_{10}} server.go^{\Delta t_{11}} l_1.in^{\Delta t_{11}} client]^{\mu_5} \mid receive)$

We write *send*, *send_ack* and *receive* processes to simulate the *three-way handshake* for establishing the connection. The transmission of data and the end of the connection could be represented in a similar way.

The *client* tries to connect to the *server* by sending an ambient SYN. If $\mu_3 = a$, then the capability $out^{\Delta t_2} client$ can be executed immediately such that we do not use a safety process. This is realized by applying a rule **(R-Out)**

$$client^{\infty}[(SYN^{\Delta t_1}[out^{\Delta t_2} client.go^{\Delta t} l_2....]^a,...) | ...]^{\mu_1}$$
$$\dashrightarrow client^{\infty}[...]^{\mu_1} | (SYN^{\Delta t_1}[go^{\Delta t} l_2....]^p,...)$$

If the timer Δt_4 representing the units of time the client is willing to wait for the $SYNACK$ ambient expires, then the client sends another SYN ambient. If $t_4 = 0$ then the rule **(R-TimePass)** is applied and the safety process is launched:

$$open^{\Delta 0} SYNACK.(ACK^{\Delta t_5}[out^{\Delta t_6} client.in^{\Delta t_7} server]^{\mu_4}, send | send\_ack)$$
$$\dashrightarrow send | send\_ack$$

At this moment the process of establishing the connection could begin again. Suppose that before the timer Δt expires the ambient SYN with $\mu_3 = a$ migrates to location l_2 by applying a **(R-Migrate)** rule:

$$l_1[[SYN^{\Delta t_1}[go^{\Delta t} l_2.in^{\Delta t_3} server]^a]] \dashrightarrow l_2[[SYN^{\Delta t_1}[in^{\Delta t_3} server]^p]]$$

Then by applying the rule **(R-In)** for $\mu_3 = a$ we obtain:

$$SYN^{\Delta t_1}[in^{\Delta t_3} server : l_4]^a]] | l_2[[server^{\infty}[...]^{\mu_2} \dashrightarrow server^{\infty}[SYN^{\Delta t_1}[ ]^p]^{\mu_2}$$

Here the ambient SYN is dissolved and a new $SYNACK$ ambient is created. This is realized by applying a rule **(R-Open)**:

$$SYN^{\Delta t_1}[ ]^{\mu_3} | open^{\Delta t_8} SYN.(SYNACK^{\Delta t_9}[...]^{\mu_5},...) \dashrightarrow SYNACK^{\Delta t_9}[...]^{\mu_5}$$

If the timer Δt_1 expires the client still waits for the timer Δt_4 to expire in order to send another ambient SYN. If the SYN ambient reaches the *server* ambient and an ambient $SYNACK$ is received from the server, then the *client* sends an ambient ACK. Once the server receives with success the ambient SYN it tries to sends an ambient $SYNACK$ to confirm that is agrees with the connection.

4   Timed Mobile Ambients Behaviour

In this section we provide some bisimulation relations with respect to the passage of time and locations inspired from domain name system. In process algebra two terms are said to be equivalent if they have the same behaviour in all possible contexts.

One of the most important scenario in which the services of ARP can be used is the following one: the sender is a router that has received a datagram destined for a host on another network. It checks its routing table and finds the IP address of the next router. The IP address of the next router becomes the logical address that must be mapped to a physical address.

The routing table consists of all the names of the routers from the first level, which in our cases are represented by top ambients. Also, DNS requires that each server keep a TTL counter for each mapping it caches. This two cases are treated in the following two subsections.

4.1 Location Bisimulation

Instead of comparing the behaviour of two ambients in all possible contexts, we compare the two ambients with respect to an observer placed at a given location k. That is, two ambients are equivalent with respect to an observer placed at a location k if they have the same observable behaviour at location k. We consider that an observer placed at the physical location k can only observe the top ambients from the physical location k.

Definition 2. *i)* *A k-barb predicate* $\downarrow_{n@k}$ *over ambients is defined inductively by the following system of rules:*

$$\frac{-}{k[[(n^{\Delta t}[P]^{\mu}, R)]] \downarrow_{n@k}} \quad \frac{k[[P]] \downarrow_{n@k}}{k[[P \mid Q]] \downarrow_{n@k}} \quad \frac{M \downarrow_{n@k}}{M \mid N \downarrow_{n@k}} \quad \frac{M \downarrow_{n@k} \text{ and } l \neq k}{(\nu l)M \downarrow_{n@k}}$$

ii) *A k-barbed bisimulation* $\mathcal{R}$ *over ambients is a symmetric binary relation over processes which for all* $(M, N) \in \mathcal{R}$ *implies*

1. *if* $M \downarrow_{n@k}$*, then* $N \downarrow_{n@k}$ *for any barb* $\downarrow_{n@k}$*;*
2. *if* $M \dashrightarrow M'$*, then* $N \dashrightarrow N'$ *and* $(M', N') \in \mathcal{R}$*.*

Two processes are k-barbed bisimilar over ambients with respect to a location k, denoted $M \sim_k N$*, if and only if* $(M, N) \in \mathcal{R}$ *for some k-barbed bisimulation over ambients* $\mathcal{R}$*.*

Instead of considering observers placed at given physical locations, we say that two ambients are similar if they contain the same top ambients. A global observer has a global view of the system, while a local observer has a local view of the system.

Definition 3. *i)* *A global barb predicate* $\downarrow_n$ *over ambients is defined inductively by the following system of rules:*

$$\frac{-}{k[[(n^{\Delta t}[P]^{\mu}, R)]] \downarrow_n} \quad \frac{k[[P]] \downarrow_n}{k[[P \mid Q]] \downarrow_n} \quad \frac{M \downarrow_n}{M \mid N \downarrow_n} \quad \frac{M \downarrow_n \text{ and } l \neq k}{(\nu l)M \downarrow_n}$$

ii) *A global barbed bisimulation* $\mathcal{R}$ *over ambients is a symmetric binary relation over processes which for all* $(M, N) \in \mathcal{R}$ *implies*

1. *if* $M \downarrow_n$*, then* $N \downarrow_n$ *for any barb* $\downarrow_n$*;*
2. *if* $M \dashrightarrow M'$*, then* $N \dashrightarrow N'$ *and* $(M', N') \in \mathcal{R}$*.*

Two processes are global barbed bisimilar over ambients, denoted $M \overset{\cdot}{\sim} N$*, if and only if* $(M, N) \in \mathcal{R}$ *for some global barbed bisimulation over ambients* $\mathcal{R}$*.*

The following proposition states that if two ambients are equivalent with respect to observers placed at all locations, then they are equivalent with respect to a global observer. The reverse of the proposition it is not true because in $M \overset{\cdot}{\sim} N$ there is no mention of any locations, so two ambients placed at different locations can contain the same top ambients, but they can contain different top ambients with respect to observers placed at all the possible locations.

Proposition 1. *If $M \overset{.}{\sim}_k N$ for all the locations k, then $M \overset{.}{\sim} N$.*

Proof (Sketch). From the definition of $\overset{.}{\sim}_k$ it results that the processes perform the same reductions and contain the same top ambients related to an observer placed at physical location k. By considering observers placed at all the possible locations k, the processes execute the same reductions and contain the same top ambients after every reduction. Because they perform the same reductions related to every location k, it means that they have the same movement through space and time. From the definition of $\overset{.}{\sim}$ it results that $M \overset{.}{\sim} N$.

In both local and global bisimulations, the observer is restricted to observe only top ambients. In a similar way we can replace the power to observe ambients with the power to observe capabilities. Having locations, ambients and capabilities, it is rather natural to strengthen the observing power of the observer by combining these observation possibilities.

4.2   Timed Location Bisimulation

Since we also deal with timed features, we may consider the observer able to check the value of different timers. We consider that an observer placed at the physical location k can only observe the top ambients together with their timers placed at the physical location k.

Definition 4. *i) A timed k-barb predicate $\downarrow^t_{n@k}$ over ambients is defined inductively by the following system of rules:*

$$\frac{-}{k[[(n^{\Delta t}[P]^\mu, R)]] \downarrow^t_{n@k}} \quad \frac{k[[P]] \downarrow^t_{n@k}}{k[[P \mid Q]] \downarrow^t_{n@k}} \quad \frac{M \downarrow^t_{n@k}}{M \mid N \downarrow^t_{n@k}} \quad \frac{M \downarrow^t_{n@k} \text{ and } l \neq k}{(\nu l)M \downarrow^t_{n@k}}$$

ii) A timed k-barbed bisimulation $\mathcal{R}$ over ambients is a symmetric binary relation over processes which for all $(M, N) \in \mathcal{R}$ implies

1. *if $M \downarrow^t_{n@k}$, then $N \downarrow^t_{n@k}$ for any barb $\downarrow^t_{n@k}$;*
2. *if $M \dashrightarrow M'$, then $N \dashrightarrow N'$ and $(M', N') \in \mathcal{R}$.*

Two processes are timed k-barbed bisimilar over ambients related to location k, denoted $M \overset{.}{\sim}^t_k N$, if and only if $(M, N) \in \mathcal{R}$ for some timed k-barbed bisimulation over ambients $\mathcal{R}$.

Instead of considering observers placed at given physical locations, we may say that two ambients are similar if they contain the same top ambients with the same timers.

Definition 5. *i) A timed global barb predicate $\downarrow^t_n$ over ambients is defined inductively by the following system of rules:*

$$\frac{-}{k[[(n^{\Delta t}[P]^\mu, R)]] \downarrow^t_n} \quad \frac{k[[P]] \downarrow^t_n}{k[[P \mid Q]] \downarrow^t_n} \quad \frac{M \downarrow^t_n}{M \mid N \downarrow^t_n} \quad \frac{M \downarrow^t_n \text{ and } l \neq k}{(\nu l)M \downarrow^t_n}$$

ii) A timed global barbed bisimulation $\mathcal{R}$ over ambients is a symmetric binary relation over processes which for all $(M, N) \in \mathcal{R}$ implies

1. *if $M \downarrow_n^t$ then $N \downarrow_n^t$ for any barb $\downarrow_n^t$;*
2. *if $M \dashrightarrow M'$, then $N \dashrightarrow N'$ and $(M', N') \in \mathcal{R}$.*

Two processes are timed global barbed bisimilar over ambients, denoted $M \overset{.}{\sim}^t N$, if and only if $(M, N) \in \mathcal{R}$ for some timed global barbed bisimulation over ambients $\mathcal{R}$.

The following proposition is similar to Proposition 1, the main difference being the fact that the observers work also with the timers of the ambients.

Proposition 2. *If $M \overset{.}{\sim}_k^t N$ for all the locations k, then $M \overset{.}{\sim}^t N$.*

Proof (Sketch). The same reasoning as at Proposition 1.

Proposition 3. *The timed barbed bisimulation over ambients is strictly finer than the barbed bisimulation over ambients:*

1. *$\forall M, N$, if $M \overset{.}{\sim}_k^t N$ then $M \overset{.}{\sim}_k N$*
2. *$\exists M, N$ such that $M \overset{.}{\sim}_k N$ and $M \overset{.}{\not\sim}_k^t N$.*

Proof. It is easy to see that $M \downarrow_{n@k}^t$ implies $M \downarrow_{n@k}$. If the observer can observe the same top ambients and ambient timers at location k, then the observer can observe just the top ambients at location k while ignoring the timers of the ambients. For the second part we give a counterexample.
Counterexample: let us consider the processes M, N defined as follows:
$$M = k[[n^{\Delta t_1}[P]^{\mu_1}]] \text{ and } N = k[[n^{\Delta t_2}[P]^{\mu_2}]] \text{ with } t_1 \neq t_2$$
It holds that $M \downarrow_{n@k}$ and $N \downarrow_{n@k}$, and thus $M \overset{.}{\sim}_k Q$. Following the definition of timed barbed bisimulation over ambients, it holds that $M \downarrow_{n@k}^{t_1}$ and $N \downarrow_{n@k}^{t_2}$, and since $t_1 \neq t_2$ we have $M \overset{.}{\not\sim}_k^t N$.

Similar results can be obtained between various bisimulations by considering observers with power of observing any combination of ambients, capabilities, timers over ambients and capabilities, located or not.

Example 1. Let us consider the following two mobile ambients: $M = k[[n^{\Delta 4}[\ ]^{\mu} \mid out^{\Delta 1}n.(m^{\Delta 6}[P]^{\mu}, Q)]]$ and $N = k[[n^{\Delta 4}[(m^{\Delta 7}[out^{\Delta 1}n.P]^{\mu}, Q)]]^{\mu}]]$.
We have that $M \downarrow_{n@k}^4$ and also $N \downarrow_{n@k}^4$. After one reduction step we obtain: $M \dashrightarrow M'$, with $M' = k[[n^{\Delta 4}[\ ]^{\mu} \mid (m^{\Delta 6}[P]^{\mu}, Q)]]$ and $N \dashrightarrow N'$, with $N' = k[[n^{\Delta 4}[\ ]^{\mu} \mid (m^{\Delta 6}[P]^{\mu}, Q)]]$. We observe that $M' = N'$ so $M' \overset{.}{\sim}_k^t N'$, from where it results that $M \overset{.}{\sim}_k^t N$.

4.3   Properties Related to the Passage of Time

We denote by $M \overset{t}{\dashrightarrow} N$ the fact that process P evolves to process Q after applying the rule **(R-TimePass)** for $t \geq 0$ times. We denote by $\cong$ the relation which respects all the rules of Table 5 except the rule **(S-Repl Par)**.
We claim that the passage of time cannot cause a nondeterministic behaviour.

Proposition 4. *If $M \cong N$, $M \xrightarrow{t} M'$ and $N \xrightarrow{t} N'$ then $M' \cong N'$.*

Proof. The proof proceeds by structural induction, by studying all the cases from Table 5 except the rule (**S-Repl Par**).

The following example motivates why we have removed the rule (**S-Repl Par**). Let $P = in^{\Delta 5}n$. Then we have $k[[*P]] \Xi k[[P \mid *P]]$. By applying the time-progress function Φ_Δ, we obtain $\Phi_\Delta(k[[P \mid *P]]) = k[[in^{\Delta 4}n \mid *P]] \not\Xi k[[*P]] = \Phi_\Delta(k[[*P]])$.

We say that a process M simulates another process N if whenever N reduces, M may mimic this reduction and evolves into a new state which continues to be in the same simulation relation with the new state of N. Bisimilarity of two processes is defined by requiring that the simulation relation is symmetric, that is, each process can mimic any event of the other while remaining in the bisimulation relation with the new state of the former process. Since we have a clock, it is possible to define a bisimulation in tMA which requires processes to match their time passages.

Definition 6. *A binary relation $\mathcal{R}$ over processes is a strong simulation if whenever $(M, N) \in \mathcal{R}$, if $M \xrightarrow{t} M'$ then there exists N' such that $N \xrightarrow{t} N'$ and $(M', N') \in \mathcal{R}$. A binary relation $\mathcal{R}$ is said to be a strong bisimulation if both $\mathcal{R}$ and its converse are strong simulations. We say that M and N are strongly bisimilar, written $M \sim_t N$, if there exists a strong bisimulation $\mathcal{R}$ such that $M\mathcal{R}N$.*

Proposition 5. *If $M \sim_t N$, then $M \sim_{kt} N$ for any $k \in \mathbb{N}^*$.*

Proposition 6. *If $M \sim_t N$ and $M \sim_{t'} N$, then $M \sim_{[t,t']} N$ where by $[t, t']$ we have denoted the least common multiple.*

Proposition 7. *$\sim_t$ is an equivalence relation.*

Proof. To demonstrate that $\sim_t$ is an equivalence relation we must show that:
1. *$M \sim_t M$*
2. *if $M \sim_t N$ then $N \sim_t M$*
3. *if $M \sim_t N$ and $N \sim_t N_1$ then $M \sim_t N_1$*

1. *Obvious.*
2. *It results from the definition.*
3. *To demonstrate that $M \sim_t N_1$ we must show that if $M \xrightarrow{t} M'$ then there exist N_1' such that $N_1 \xrightarrow{t} N_1'$ with $M' \sim_t N_1'$. $M \sim_t N$ implies that if $M \xrightarrow{t} M'$ then there exists N' such that $N \xrightarrow{t} N'$ and $M' \sim_t N'$. Similarly, $N \sim_t N_1$ implies that if $N \xrightarrow{t} N'$ then there exists N_1' such that $N_1 \xrightarrow{t} N_1'$ and $N' \sim_t N_1'$. It results that if $M \xrightarrow{t} M'$ then there exists N_1' such that $N_1 \xrightarrow{t} N_1'$, and by induction and using the symmetry expressed by 2 we have that $M' \sim_t N_1'$. From Definition 6, it results that $M \sim_t N_1$.*

Definition 7. *A process context $\mathcal{C}$ is a process containing a hole, represented by $[\,]$. The elementary process contexts are given by the following syntax:*
$$\mathcal{C} ::= [\,] \mid (\nu n)\mathcal{C} \mid P \mid \mathcal{C} \mid \mathcal{C} \mid P \mid (n^{\Delta t}[\mathcal{C}]^\mu, Q), (n^{\Delta t}[\mathcal{P}]^\mu, \mathcal{C})$$

Let $\mathcal{C}(P)$ be the process obtained by filling the hole in $\mathcal{C}$ with a copy of P; we note that certain names free in P may become bound. We say that an equivalence relation is a *congruence* if it is preserved by all elementary contexts, namely the ones from the above definition.

Proposition 8. $\sim_t$ *is a congruence.*

Proof. We know that $\sim_t$ is an equivalence relation (Proposition 7), and we should prove that if $k[[P]] \sim_t k[[Q]]$ then the following relations hold:

1. $k[[(\nu n)P]] \sim_t k[[(\nu n)Q]]$
2. $k[[P \mid R]] \sim_t k[[Q \mid R]]$
3. $k[[R \mid P]] \sim_t k[[R \mid Q]]$
4. $k[[(n^{\Delta t}[P]^{\mu}, R)]] \sim_t k[[(n^{\Delta t}[Q]^{\mu}, R)]]$
5. $k[[(n^{\Delta t}[R]^{\mu'}, P)]] \sim_t k[[(n^{\Delta t}[R]^{\mu'}, Q)]]$

We consider only the second relationship; the others are similar. We prove that
$$\mathcal{R} = \{(k[[P \mid R]], k[[Q \mid R]]) \mid k[[P]] \sim_t k[[Q]]\}$$
is a strong bisimulation. Let $k[[P \mid R]] \overset{t}{\dashrightarrow} U$. We must find V such that
$k[[Q \mid R]] \overset{t}{\dashrightarrow} V$ *and* $(U, V) \in \mathcal{R}$. *We have that* $U = k[[P' \mid R']]$ *and* $V = k[[Q' \mid R']]$, *where* $k[[P]] \overset{t}{\dashrightarrow} k[[P']]$, $k[[Q]] \overset{t}{\dashrightarrow} k[[Q']]$ *and* $k[[R]] \overset{t}{\dashrightarrow} k[[R']]$. *From* $k[[P]] \sim_t k[[Q]]$ *we have that* $k[[P']] \sim_t k[[Q']]$, *which means that* $(U, V) \in \mathcal{R}$.

Definition 8. *A binary relation $\mathcal{R}$ over processes is a weak timed simulation if whenever $(M, N) \in \mathcal{R}$, if $M \overset{t}{\dashrightarrow} M'$ then there exists N' and $t' \geq t$ such that $N \overset{t'}{\dashrightarrow} N'$ and $(M', N') \in \mathcal{R}$. We say that M can simulate in time N, written $M \rhd_t N$, if there exists a weak timed simulation $\mathcal{R}$ such that $M\mathcal{R}N$.*

Proposition 9. $M \sim_t N$ *iff* $M \rhd_t N$ *and* $M \rhd_t M$.

Proof (Sketch).

If $M \sim_t N$ then it is obvious that exists $t' = t$ such that $M \rhd_t N$ and $N \rhd_t M$.

If $M \rhd_t N$ and $N \rhd_t M$ it results that there exists t' in both cases such that $t = t'$, which implies that $M \sim_t N$.

5   Conclusion

Process algebra is the general study of distributed concurrent systems in an algebraic framework. In the past few years, some successful models have been formulated within this framework: ACP [4], CCS [18], CSP [16], distributed π-calculus [14], MA [6]. None of these approaches is able to naturally describe properties of timing. Process algebra with timing features are presented in [1,9,10,11,12,20]. We have extended the pure mobile ambients by adding time constraints to capabilities and ambients. Two formalisms called timed π-calculus and timed distributed π-calculus are presented in [2], respectively [8]; it also uses a relative time given by timers, and a clock whose tick decreases the timers. Timers are used to restrict the interaction between components, and both types and timers are used to control the resource availability. In timed distributed π-calculus the notion of space is flat. A more realistic account of physical distribution is obtained using a hierarchical representation of space, and this is given in timed mobile ambients. Thus we get a more realistic description of the distributed computation and mobility. A natural example motivating an extension from timed distributed π-calculus to timed mobile ambients is presented in [7].

The formalism defined in this paper does not follow any of the other process algebra mentioned above. It is well motivated by the existence of timers in TCP/IP communication protocols; the timers fit very well to the description of messages as mobile ambients. Another motivation for our work is given by the Real-time Transport Protocol (or RTP) which defines a standardized packet format for delivering audio and video over the Internet. RTP can carry any data with real-time characteristics, such as interactive audio and video. It goes along with the RTCP and it is built on top of the User Datagram Protocol (UDP). Applications using RTP are less sensitive to packet loss, but typically very sensitive to delays, so UDP is a better choice than TCP for such applications. The protocols themselves do not provide mechanisms to ensure timely delivery. They also do not give any Quality of Service (QoS) guarantees. These things have to be provided by some other mechanism.

Starting from such motivations, we extend with time restrictions a formalism designed for mobility in order to study various aspects related to time. The formalism used is the basic ambient calculus, which means that we have not taken into account the primitives for communication. The novelty comes from the fact that the ambients can also expire, simulating in this way the maximum amount of time any package can exist in a network before being discarded. We have provided an operational semantics by a structural equivalence and a reduction relation. The structural relation introduced in this paper is different from the structural congruence for mobile ambients because it does not allow sibling ambients to commute their position. The reduction relation is intuitive, and we have shown in Section 4 how some of the reduction rules are used, namely **(R-In)**, **(R-Out)**, **(R-Open)**, **(R-Migrate)** and **(R-TimePass)**. To describe thes passage of time we have given a discrete time progress function. We have introduced and studied some behavioural equivalences over timed mobile ambients. After introducing the aspects of time and locations over mobile ambients, we have established some bisimulations between processes by defining different barbs.

References

1. Aceto, L., Murphy, D.: Timing and Causality in Process Algebra. Acta Informatica 33(4), 317–350 (1996)
2. Berger, M.: Basic Theory of Reduction Congruence for Two Timed Asynchronous pi-Calculi. In: Gardner, P., Yoshida, N. (eds.) CONCUR 2004. LNCS, vol. 3170, pp. 115–130. Springer, Heidelberg (2004)
3. Berger, M.: Towards Abstractions for Distributed Systems PhD thesis, Imperial College, Department of Computing (2002)

4. Bergstra, J.A., Klop, J.W.: Process Theory based on Bisimulation Semantics. In: de Bakker, J.W., de Roever, W.-P., Rozenberg, G. (eds.) Linear Time, Branching Time and Partial Order in Logics and Models for Concurrency. LNCS, vol. 354, pp. 50–122. Springer, Heidelberg (1989)
5. Bugliesi, M., Castagna, G., Crafa, S.: Boxed Ambients. In: Kobayashi, N., Pierce, B.C. (eds.) TACS 2001. LNCS, vol. 2215, pp. 38–63. Springer, Heidelberg (2001)
6. Cardelli, L., Gordon, A.: Mobile Ambients. Theoretical Computer Science 240(1), 170–213 (2000)
7. Ciobanu, G.: Interaction in time and space. In: Proceedings of Foundations of Interactive Computation. Electronic Notes in Theoretical Computer Science, pp. 45–61 (to appear, 2007)
8. Ciobanu, G., Prisacariu, C.: Timers for Distributed Systems. In: International Workshop on Quantitative Aspects of Programming Languages. Electronic Notes in Theoretical Computer Science, vol. 164(3), pp. 81–99 (2006)
9. Cleveland, R., Zwarico, A.: A theory of testing for real-time. Logic in Computer Science, 110–119 (1991)
10. Corradini, F.: On performance Congruences for Process Algebras. Information and Computation 145(2), 191–230 (1998)
11. Corradini, F.: Absolute versus relative time in process algebras. Information and Computation 156(1), 122–172 (2000)
12. Gorrieri, R., Roccetti, M., Stancampiano, E.: A Theory of Processes with Durational Actions. Theoretical Computer Science 140(1), 73–94 (1995)
13. Hennessy, M., Regan, T.: A process algebra for timed systems. Information and Computation 117, 221–239 (1995)
14. Hennessy, M., Riely, J.: Resource access control in systems of mobile agents. Information and Computation 173(1), 82–120 (2002)
15. Hirschkoff, D., Teller, D., Zimmer, P.: Using ambients to control resources. In: Brim, L., Jančar, P., Křetínský, M., Kucera, A. (eds.) CONCUR 2002. LNCS, vol. 2421, pp. 288–303. Springer, Heidelberg (2002)
16. Hoare, C.A.R.: Communicating Sequential Processes. Prentice Hall International, Englewood Cliffs (1985)
17. Levi, F., Sangiorgi, D.: Controlling interference in ambients. Principles of Programming Languages, 352–364 (2000)
18. Milner, R.: Communication and Concurrency. Prentice Hall International, Englewood Cliffs (1989)
19. Milner, R.: Communicating and mobile systems: the π-calculus. Cambridge University Press, Cambridge (1999)
20. Moller, F., Tofts, C.: A temporal Calculus of Communicating Systems. In: Groote, J.F., Baeten, J.C.M. (eds.) CONCUR 1991. LNCS, vol. 527, pp. 401–415. Springer, Heidelberg (1991)
21. Stevens, W.R.: TCP/IP Illustrated, Volume 1 - The Protocols, vol. 1. Addison-Wesley, Reading (1993)

A Specification Framework for Earth-Friendly Logistics

Ichiro Satoh

National Institute of Informatics
2-1-2 Hitotsubashi, Chiyoda-ku, Tokyo 101-8430, Japan
ichiro@nii.ac.jp

Abstract. This paper describes the use of a formal approach to logistics management systems to reduce the environmental impact of logistics operations. Trucks play an essential role as carriers in modern logistics services, but collectively they emit a huge quantity of carbon dioxide. To reduce fossil fuel consumption and carbon dioxide emissions resulting from transport, we must enhance the transport efficiency of trucks. The milk-run approach is one of the most effective and popular solutions to this problem. However, it tends to be too complicated to implement in a logistics management system. The framework described in this paper provides a language for specifying the routes of trucks and an order relation as a route selection mechanism. The former is formulated as process calculus and the latter selects suitable trucks according to their routes. This paper also describes a prototype implementation of the framework as a distributed logistics management system based on the use of RFID tags.

1 Introduction

Most transport logistics operations involve huge numbers of trucks, with each truck consuming large quantities of fossil fuel and discharging a large quantity of carbon dioxide (CO_2) into the atmosphere. To reduce fossil-fuel consumption and CO_2 emissions from transport, we need to enhance the efficiency of trucks. The *milk-run* approach, which is one of the most efficient and popular ways of improving truck-load ratios, refers to a means of transportation in which a single truck cycles around multiple suppliers to collect or deliver freight. The name is derived from the milk-runs carried out by farmers collecting milk from dairy cows spread out over pastures. For example, suppose five suppliers, e.g., dairy farmers, send their products to the processing plant every weekday. Using the milk-run approach, one truck calls at each of the suppliers on a daily basis before delivering the collected milk to the customer's plant. In a more traditional approach, e.g., the *Just-In-Time* approach, all suppliers have their own trucks and send one truckload per day to the customer (Figure 1).

Recently, a variety of industries, e.g., food and automobile manufacturers, in addition to the dairy industry, have attempted to use the milk-run approach to reduce the environmental impact of their logistics operations. However, in the milk-run approach, they have to provide multiple trucks using varied routes to satisfy the needs of customers and cater for the requirements of the products. Therefore, the customers and suppliers are confronted by another problem: they need to design truck routes and select suitable trucks with routes that satisfy their requirements.

K. Suzuki et al. (Eds.): FORTE 2008, LNCS 5048, pp. 251–266, 2008.
© IFIP International Federation for Information Processing 2008

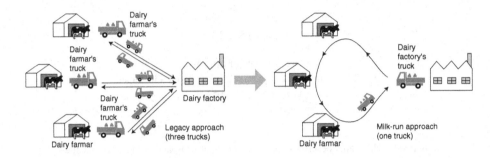

Fig. 1. Legacy approach vs. Milk-run approach

This paper proposes a novel framework for specifying truck routes and selecting appropriate trucks. The framework introduces a specification language that describes truck routes and a mechanism for selecting suitable milk-run trucks. Since the language is formulated based on an extended process calculus for specifying and reasoning on the routes of trucks, we can determine whether a truck can visit various points, e.g., farmers and manufacturers, along its route to collect or deliver items. The mechanism enables collection/delivery points to select trucks according to the truck route because the route a truck takes is critical in determining its efficiency. The framework was inspired by our experience of real logistics systems. We implemented a prototype of the framework in a distributed logistics management system. We believe that this framework provides a novel and practical application of process calculi in the real world. However, we leave the theoretical aspects of the framework to our future papers because this paper addresses a fundamental platform for managing a milk-run logistics operation.

This paper is organized as follows: Section 2 presents the basic ideas behind the framework. Section 3 defines a process calculus for specifying the routes of trucks for a milk-run logistics-operation, and Section 4 presents an order relation over terms of the languages as a mechanism for selecting routes. Section 5 describes a prototype implementation of the framework and a typical application scenario and Section 6 includes a survey of related work. Section 7 discusses our future work and Section 8 has concluding remarks.

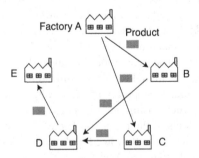

Fig. 2. Five factories with dependencies

2 Background

This paper describes a formal method for specifying the routes of trucks and selecting appropriate trucks to support milk-run operations in transport logistics.

2.1 Example Scenario

Before discussing the framework proposed in this paper, we describe our basic example scenario. Figure 2 shows five factories, A, B, C, D, and E, that have the following dependencies:

- Factory A manufactures products and ships the products to factories B and C.
- Factory B manufactures products and ships the products to factory D.
- Factory C manufactures products and ships the products to factory D.
- Factory D manufactures products and ships the products to factory E.

We assume that a truck has sufficient carrying capacity. It starts at factory A and may visit factory A again. Figure 3 shows four trucks carrying out milk-runs on different routes. The first, second, and third trucks can satisfy the above requirements but the fourth cannot. The third is less efficient than the first and second on their rounds. The framework proposed in this paper was inspired by our real experiences. Although the milk-run approach is effective in reducing the amount of CO_2 emitted by trucks, its management tends to be complicated, which is one of the most significant barriers preventing wider adoption of the approach in real logistics.

2.2 Requirements

This paper assumes that one or more trucks involved in milk-run logistics operations call at multiple points along their routes. Customers and suppliers have to decide which truck and which route will best satisfy their requirements, and this decision is not an easy one. The framework must therefore satisfy the following demands of real logistics systems.

- One or more trucks are available for a milk-run, but their routes may be different. Therefore, points, i.e., suppliers and customers, need to select appropriate trucks according to truck routes. This framework therefore needs to provide a mechanism for selecting truck routes.
- Trucks may be shared by multiple suppliers and customers, so that they collect products at one or more source points and deliver the products at one or more destination points on their way. The trucks need to visit the source points before they visit the destination points. The framework therefore needs to specify the order in which trucks call at various points.
- The routes taken by trucks may also affect product quality. For example, foods should be transported by the shortest route possible to keep their freshness, and perishable foodstuffs should be picked up later than preservable foodstuffs and taken to a food processor or consumer.

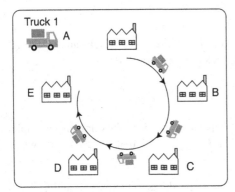
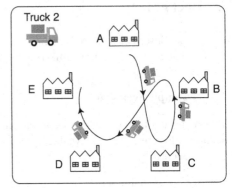
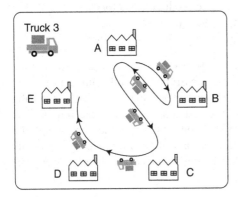
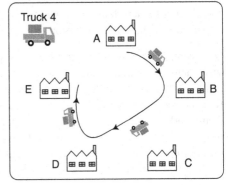

Fig. 3. Four trucks for milk-run operation

- Some products may be collected/delivered at points by trucks without any need for a specific order of arrival at collection/delivery points. That is, the order of the movement of trucks between points does not affect the efficiency of the trucks' operations. Suppliers or customers should select a truck according to the number of movements between the points that the trucks visit.
- Truck routes tend to be regular and static, although they may be changed weekly or monthly. Nevertheless, trucks may bypass some points or take shortcuts without stopping at specified points if they have no freight to deliver to the points or products to pick up.
- Pallets or boxes that contain multiple products are considered as transport units in many current logistics systems, rather than as individual products. These types of containers may have multiple destinations and the receivers may take only some of the products in the container when it arrives at their point.
- In real logistics systems, most points, i.e., suppliers and customers, involve small to medium enterprises or individual operators. They do not want to invest in any additional equipment to support milk-run logistics.
- Current logistics management systems rely heavily on barcodes or RFID tags attached to products or containers. The framework should therefore be compatible

with existing infrastructure and equipment for reading barcodes or tags. However, two-dimensional barcodes or RFID tags do not hold a large amount of data, e.g., up to 128 bytes.[1] The time required to read data from an RFID tag tends to be proportional to the size of the data. The length of route specification should be compact.

2.3 Basic Approach

Truck routes and the requirements of suppliers and customers are various and complex. The selection of trucks for milk-run operations is critical for industrial efficiency and for minimizing carbon dioxide emissions. Careful consideration must be given to selecting suitable trucks with routes that satisfy the requirements of customers and suppliers. Therefore, we need a formal method to solve this problem. To satisfy the above requirements, the framework has two parts.

- It provides a specification language for describing and analyzing truck routes. The language is aimed at specifying only the routes of trucks formulated as an extended process calculus with the expressiveness of truck routes between collection/delivery points.
- It framework defines an algebraic order relation over the terms of the language. The relation is defined based on the notion of bisimulation and compares possible truck routes and the routes required by its specifications. This allows us to accurately determine whether the former satisfies the latter.

Note that the order relation is not intended to generate the most efficient route. Thus, the computational complexity for this relation is not large. Since our goal is to develop a suitable mechanism for selecting trucks for milk-run logistics operations, this paper does not limit the types of products that the trucks carry.

2.4 Remarks

- The framework does not assume any particular logistics system and the specifications of all trucks are independent of any particular logistics service.
- The current implementation does not support any real-time constraints. However, the timing of a truck's arrival at various points tends to depend on external factors, e.g., traffic congestion and the cost of the shipment, in real logistics systems. The milk-run approach is, by its nature, suitable for earth-friendly logistics systems, but not for just-in-time ones.
- The framework is not intended to provide route optimization because truck routes tend to be designed according to external factors.
- Some readers may think that simple executable languages, such as Lisp and Prolog, should be used to specify routes, but it is difficult to verify whether or not routes written in such languages will satisfy the requirements of customers and suppliers because these languages have many primitives that are not used in describing routes.

---

[1] The amount of data held by barcodes and RFID tags depends on individual systems.

3 Specification Language for Milk-Run Truck Routes

This section defines a language for specifying and reasoning about truck routes. The language consists of two classes. The first is designed to specify truck routes and the second is designed to specify the routes required by products or customers.

Definition 1. it The set $\mathcal{E}$ of expressions of the language, ranged over by $E, E_1, E_2, \ldots$ is defined recursively by the following abstract syntax:

$$E ::= 0 \quad | \quad \ell \quad | \quad E_1 ; E_2 \quad | \quad E_1 + E_2$$
$$| \quad E_1 \# E_2 \quad | \quad E_1 \,\%\, E_2 \quad | \quad E_1 \,\&\, E_2 \quad | \quad E^*$$

where $\mathcal{L}$ is the set of location names ranged over by $\ell, \ell_1, \ell_2, \ldots$, and where points correspond to the locations of suppliers and customers. We often omit 0. We describe a subset language of $\mathcal{E}$ as $\mathcal{S}$, when eliminating $E_1 \# E_2$, $E_1 \,\%\, E_2$, $E_1 \,\&\, E_2$, and E^* from $\mathcal{E}$. Let $S, S_1, S_2, \ldots$ be elements of $\mathcal{S}$. □

This framework assumes that each truck has its own route written in $\mathcal{S}$ and that its driver visits points along the route, i.e., intuitively, the meaning of the terms is as follows:

- 0 represents a terminated route.
- ℓ represents that a truck moves to a point called ℓ.
- $E_1 ; E_2$ denotes the sequential composition of two routes E_1 and E_2. If the route of E_1 terminates, then the route of E_2 follows that of E_1.
- $E_1 + E_2$ represents the route of a truck according to either E_1 or E_2, where the selection is done by the truck.
- $E_1 \# E_2$ means that a truck itself can go through either E_1 or E_2.
- $E_1 \,\%\, E_2$ means that a truck can follow either E_1 before E_2 or E_2 before E_1 on its route.
- $E_1 \,\&\, E_2$ means that two routes, E_1 and E_2, may be executed asynchronously.
- E^* is a transitive closure of E and means that a truck may move along E an arbitrary number of times.

where in $E_1 + E_2$ the truck can select the E_1 (or E_2) route when the E_1 route is available. For example, if the E_1 route is available and the E_2 route is congested, the truck goes through the E_1 route. $E_1 \# E_2$ means that a truck can go through either E_1 or E_2. $E_1 \,\%\, E_2$, $E_1 \,\&\, E_2$, and E^* are used to specify possible routes. For example, $E_1 \# E_2$ permits the truck to go through one of the E_1 or E_2 routes.

To accurately express such routes, we need to define a specification language based on a process calculus approach such as CCS [6]. The semantics of the language are defined by the following labeled transition rules:

Definition 2. it The language is a labeled transition system $\langle\, \mathcal{E}, \mathcal{L} \cup \{\tau\} \,\{\, \xrightarrow{\alpha} \subseteq \mathcal{E} \times \mathcal{E} \,|\, \alpha \in \mathcal{E} \cup \{\tau\} \,\} \,\rangle$ is defined as the induction rules below:

$$\frac{-}{\ell \xrightarrow{\ell} 0} \qquad \frac{E_1 \xrightarrow{\ell} E_1'}{E_1 \; ; \; E_2 \xrightarrow{\ell} E_1' \; ; \; E_2} \qquad \frac{E_1 \xrightarrow{\ell} E_1'}{E_1 + E_2 \xrightarrow{\ell} E_1'} \qquad \frac{E_2 \xrightarrow{\ell} E_2'}{E_1 + E_2 \xrightarrow{\ell} E_2'}$$

$$\frac{E_1 \xrightarrow{\ell} E_1'}{E_1 \,\&\, E_2 \xrightarrow{\ell} E_1' \,\&\, E_2} \qquad \frac{E_2 \xrightarrow{\ell} E_2'}{E_1 \,\&\, E_2 \xrightarrow{\ell} E_1 \,\&\, E_2'}$$

$$\frac{E_1 \xrightarrow{\tau} E_1'}{E_1 \; ; \; E_2 \xrightarrow{\tau} E_1' \; ; \; E_2} \qquad \frac{-}{E_1 \,\#\, E_2 \xrightarrow{\tau} E_1} \qquad \frac{-}{E_1 \,\#\, E_2 \xrightarrow{\tau} E_2} \qquad \frac{-}{E_1 \,\%\, E_2 \xrightarrow{\tau} E_1 \; ; \; E_2}$$

$$\frac{-}{E_1 \,\%\, E_2 \xrightarrow{\tau} E_2 \; ; \; E_1} \qquad \frac{E_1 \xrightarrow{\tau} E_1'}{E_1 + E_2 \xrightarrow{\tau} E_1' + E_2} \qquad \frac{E_2 \xrightarrow{\tau} E_2'}{E_1 + E_2 \xrightarrow{\tau} E_1 + E_2'}$$

$$\frac{E_1 \xrightarrow{\tau} E_1'}{E_1 \,\&\, E_2 \xrightarrow{\tau} E_1' \,\&\, E_2} \qquad \frac{E_2 \xrightarrow{\tau} E_2'}{E_1 \,\&\, E_2 \xrightarrow{\tau} E_1 \,\&\, E_2'}$$

where $0 \; ; \; E$ is treated as being syntactically equal to E. $E^\star$ is recursively defined as $0 \,\#\, (E \; ; \; E^\star)$. We often abbreviate $E_0 \xrightarrow{\tau} \cdots \xrightarrow{\tau} E_n$ to $E_0 (\xrightarrow{\tau})^n E_n$. $\qquad\square$

In Definition 2, the ℓ-transition defines the semantics of a trucks movement. For example $E \xrightarrow{\ell} E'$ means that the truck moves to a point named ℓ and then behaves as E'. Also, if there are two possible transitions $E \xrightarrow{\ell_1} E_1$ and $E \xrightarrow{\ell_2} E_2$ for a truck, the processing by the truck chooses one of the destinations, ℓ_1 or ℓ_2. In contrast, the τ-transition corresponds to a non-deterministic choice of a truck's routes .

Readers may think that the above operational semantics could be more compact. However, the aim is to design a system that can be easily implemented because the purpose of the framework is not to provide just a theoretical foundation for determining truck-route logistics, but a practical mechanism for selecting suitable trucks for milk-run operations. The language does not needs recursive or loop notations, because each truck does not continue to run for 24 hours everyday.

We show several basic examples of the language as shown in Figure 4.

– Route specification, $a \; ; \; b \; ; \; c \; ; \; d$, in $\mathcal{S}$ is interpreted as follows:

$$\begin{aligned} a \; ; \; b \; ; \; c \; ; \; d &\xrightarrow{a} b \; ; \; c \; ; \; d \\ &\xrightarrow{b} c \; ; \; d \\ &\xrightarrow{c} d \\ &\xrightarrow{d} \end{aligned}$$

The first diagram in Figure 4 illustrates the above derivation.

– Next, we show an example of a specification in $\mathcal{E}$. This is a route requirement.

$$\begin{aligned} a \; ; \; (b \,\#\, c) \; ; \; d \; ; \; e &\xrightarrow{a} (b \,\#\, c) \; ; \; d \; ; \; e \\ &\xrightarrow{\tau} b \; ; \; d \; ; \; e \quad \text{or} \quad c \; ; \; d \; ; \; e \end{aligned}$$

where $\#$ corresponds to a combination of two required routes so that trucks are required to follow both routes as shown in the third diagram in Figure 4. That is, a truck needs to call at point a and then at either b or c. Next, it calls at d and then e.

– We show another route requirement specification, $a \; ; \; (b \,\%\, c) \; ; \; d \; ; \; e$, in $\mathcal{E}$. It has two derivations as follows:

$$\begin{aligned} a \; ; \; (b \,\%\, c) \; ; \; d \; ; \; e &\xrightarrow{a} (b \,\%\, c) \; ; \; d \; ; \; e \\ &\xrightarrow{\tau} b \; ; \; c \; ; \; d \; ; \; e \quad \text{or} \quad c \; ; \; b \; ; \; d \; ; \; e \end{aligned}$$

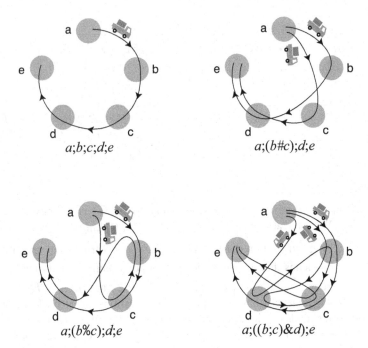

Fig. 4. Examples of specification

where % means that trucks can take either one of the two routes before they take the other. The second diagram in Figure 4 shows possible routes that could satisfy this requirement specification.

- $a ; ((b ; c) \& d) ; e$ in $\mathcal{E}$ is an example of $\&$.

$$a ; ((b ; c) \& d) ; e \xrightarrow{a} ((b ; c) \& d) ; e$$
$$\xrightarrow{b} (c \& d) ; e$$
$$\xrightarrow{c} d ; e$$
$$\xrightarrow{d} e$$

where $\&$ corresponds to asynchronous reduction. Thus, this permits a truck to move to d while moving along $c ; b$. As shown in the fourth diagram in Figure 4, the following two derivations are possible in addition to the above derivation.

$$a ; ((b ; c) \& d) ; e \xrightarrow{a} ((b ; c) \& d) ; e$$
$$\xrightarrow{b} (c \& d) ; e$$
$$\xrightarrow{d} c ; e$$
$$\xrightarrow{c} e$$

or

$$a ; ((b ; c) \& d) ; e \xrightarrow{a} ((b ; c) \& d) ; e$$
$$\xrightarrow{d} (b ; c) ; e$$
$$\xrightarrow{b} c ; e$$
$$\xrightarrow{c} e$$

– The first requirement presented in the previous section is described as specification $(a \; ; \; (b \, \% \, c)) \, \& \, d^* \, \& \, e^*$. We show one of the possible derivations from the specification as follows:

$$(a \; ; \; (b \, \% \, c)) \, \& \, d^* \, \& \, e^* \; \xrightarrow{a} \; (b \, \% \, c)) \, \& \, d^* \, \& \, e^*$$
$$\xrightarrow{b} \; c \, \& \, d^* \, \& \, e^*$$

We can also have another derivation from the specification as follows:

$$(a \; ; \; (b \, \% \, c)) \, \& \, d^* \, \& \, e^* \; \xrightarrow{a} \; (b \, \% \, c)) \, \& \, d^* \, \& \, e^*$$
$$\xrightarrow{c} \; b \, \& \, d^* \, \& \, e^*$$

where $E \, \& \, d^*$ means that the truck can visit d more than zero times while it moves along E.

$$(a \; ; \; (b \, \% \, c)) \, \& \, d^* \, \& \, e^* \; \overset{\text{def}}{=} \; (a \; ; \; (b \, \% \, c)) \, \& \, (0 \, \# \, d \; ; \; d^*) \, \& \, e^*$$
$$\xrightarrow{tau} \; (a \; ; \; (b \, \% \, c)) \, \& \, (d \; ; \; d^*) \, \& \, e^*$$
$$\xrightarrow{d} \; (a \; ; \; (b \, \% \, c)) \, \& \, d^* \, \& \, e^*$$

To describe routes in a compact notation, we define several macro notations for specifying the typical routes of trucks in a logistics operation. We describe a list of point names as $[\ell_1, \ell_2, \ldots, \ell_n]$, where $\ell_1, \ell_2, \ldots, \ell_n \in \mathcal{L}$. Let $[]$ be an empty list, $car(X)$ be the top element of list X, i.e., ℓ_1, and $cdr(X)$ be the remaining list of X except for the top element, i.e., $[\ell_2, \ldots, \ell_n]$. Each point list is often written as $\$(H)$ in terms of the language, where H is the name of a list, to avoid confusion between the name of a point and the name of the list. These macros do not extend the language because they are mapped into $\mathcal{E}$.

$$Cycle(\$(X)) \overset{\text{def}}{=} car(\$(X)) \; ; \; Cycle(cdr(\$(X)))$$
$$Cycle([]) \overset{\text{def}}{=} 0$$
$$Star(\$(X)|\ell) \overset{\text{def}}{=} (car(\$(X)) \; ; \; \ell) \; ; \; Star(cdr(\$(X))|\ell)$$
$$Star([]|\ell) \overset{\text{def}}{=} 0$$

Figure 5 illustrates $Cycle$ and $Star$ notations. Let ℓ be an element of $\mathcal{L}$ and X be a list of node names in $\mathcal{L}$. For example, $Cycle(\$(\text{DAIRY-FARMERS}))$ allows a truck to travel around the points specified in the DAIRY- FARMERS list consisting of the names of dairy farmers that produce milk; and f is a processing plant for dairy products. $Star(\$(\text{DAIRY-FARMERS})|f)$ corresponds to a star-shaped route, which allows a truck to go back and forth between the destinations specified in the DAIRY-FARMERS list and a given base point, e.g., a dairy factory, specified as f as the order of the list. To illustrate the transition defined in Definition 2, we show the transition of $Star$

($(DARY-FARMERS)|$f$) in $(DAIRY-FARMERS) = [a, b, c, d]$, where a, b, c, and d are the locations of dairy farmers as follows:

$$
\begin{aligned}
Star(\$(\text{DAIRY-FARMERS})|f) \;\; &is \;\; Star([a,b,c,d]|f) \\
&\overset{\text{def}}{=} (a \; ; \; f) \; ; \; Star([b,c,d]|f) \\
&\overset{a}{\longrightarrow} f \; ; \; Star([b,c,d]|f) \\
&\overset{f}{\longrightarrow} Star([b,c,d]|f) \\
&\overset{\text{def}}{=} (b \; ; \; f) \; ; \; Star([c,d]|f) \\
&\overset{b}{\longrightarrow} f \; ; \; Star([c,d]|f) \\
&\overset{f}{\longrightarrow} Star([c,d]|f)
\end{aligned}
$$

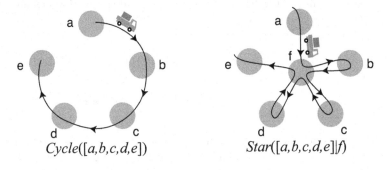

$Cycle([a,b,c,d,e])$ $Star([a,b,c,d,e]|f)$

Fig. 5. Cycle and Star macros for routes

4   Order Relation for Route Selection

This section defines an order relation for selecting trucks according to their routes based on the concept of bisimulation [6]. The relation is suitable for selecting a truck for a milk-run operation with a route that satisfies the requirements of suppliers and customers.

Definition 3. it A binary relation $\mathcal{R}^n$ ($\mathcal{R} \subseteq (\mathcal{E} \times \mathcal{S}) \times \mathcal{N}$) is an *n-route* prebisimulation, where $\mathcal{N}$ is the set of natural numbers, if whenever $(E, S) \in \mathcal{R}^n$ where $n \geq 0$, then, the following holds for all $\ell \in \mathcal{L}$ or τ.

i) if $E \overset{\ell}{\longrightarrow} E'$ then there is an S' such that $S \overset{\ell}{\longrightarrow} S'$ and $(E', S') \in \mathcal{R}^{n-1}$

ii) $E (\overset{\tau}{\longrightarrow})^* E'$ and $(E', S) \in \mathcal{R}^n$

iii) if $S \overset{\ell}{\longrightarrow} S'$ then there exist E', E'' such that $E (\overset{\tau}{\longrightarrow})^* E' \overset{\ell}{\longrightarrow} E''$ and $(E', S') \in \mathcal{R}^{n-1}$

where $E \sqsupseteq_n S$ if there exist some n-route prebisimulations such that $(E, S) \in \mathcal{R}^n$. We call the $\sqsupseteq_n$ *n-route* order. We often abbreviate $\sqsupseteq_n$ to $\sqsupseteq$.   □

The informal meaning of $E \sqsupseteq_n S$ is that S is included in one of the permissible routes specified in E and n corresponds to the number of movements of a truck that can satisfy E. We show several basic properties of the order relation below. Let us look at some basic examples.

- $(a \% b \% c) ; d \sqsupseteq_4 c ; a ; b ; d$
  where the left-hand-side requires a truck to carry products to three points, a, b, and c in an indefinite order and then return to point d; the right-hand-side requires a truck to carry products to three points, c, a, and b, sequentially. When the left-hand-side is changed to $a ; b ; c ; d$, the relation is still preserved, but when the left-hand-side becomes $a ; d ; b ; d ; c ; d$ or $a ; b ; d$, the relation is not preserved.
- $((a ; b ; c) \& d^*) ; d \sqsupseteq_6 a ; d ; b ; d ; c ; d$
  where the left-hand-side allows a truck to drop in at point d an arbitrary number of times on route $a ; b ; c$ and then finish its movement at point d. The right-hand-side is a star-shaped route between three destinations, a, b, c, and point d satisfies the left-hand-side.
- $((a ; b) \& c^*) \# ((b ; c) \& a^*) \sqsupseteq_3 a ; b ; c$
  where $((a ; b) \& c^*)$ and $((b ; c) \& a^*)$ on the left-hand-side are the required routes of two products, respectively. The first product is collected from point a and is then delivered to point b. The second product is collected from point b and is then delivered to point c. Both products permit trucks to visit c or a more then zero times. $\#$ on the left-hand-side means that trucks must satisfy both required routes. $a ; b ; c$ can satisfy the requirement specified on the left-hand-side. $b ; c ; a ; b$ still satisfies the left-hand-side, but the number of truck movements is greater than the $a ; b ; c$.

5   Implementation

This section describes a prototype implementation of our framework and a preliminary experiment using an RFID tag system. The experiment was constructed as a distributed logistics management system consisting of six supplier points in addition to a customer point with a route-selection server. Figure 6 shows the basic structure of the system. The server was responsible for receiving route requirements from suppliers and customers through a network and selecting suitable trucks with routes that satisfied these requirements.

5.1   Route Selection Algorithm

Here, let us explain the selection algorithm used for the current implementation, which we tried to make as faithful to Definition 3 as possible. The server maintains its own repository database containing the routes of trucks. To reduce the cost of the selection algorithm, the possible routes written in $\mathcal{E}$ are transformed into tree structures before they are stored in the database. These are called `transition trees` or `derivation trees` in the literature on process calculus [6]. Each tree is derived from a route in $\mathcal{E}$ according to Definition 2 and consists of arcs corresponding to ℓ-transitions or τ-transitions in the route. When a route selection server receives a required route from suppliers or customers, it extracts the required route written in S and

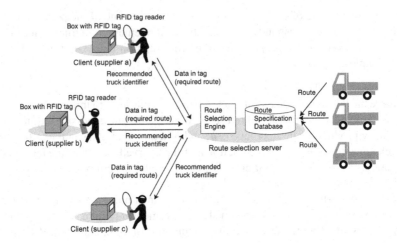

Fig. 6. Basic structure of logistics management system

then transforms the route into a transition tree. It next determines whether or not the trees derived from the routes stored in the database system can satisfy the tree derived from the required route by matching the two trees according to the definition of the order relation ($\sqsupseteq_n \subseteq \mathcal{E} \times \mathcal{S}$) as in the following.

(1) If each node in one of the two trees has arcs corresponding to ℓ-transitions, then the corresponding node in the other tree can have the same arcs, and the sub-nodes derived through the matching arcs of the two trees can still satisfy either (1) or (2).

(2) If each node in the tree derived from the required route has one or more arcs corresponding to τ-transitions, then at least one of the nodes derived through the arcs and the corresponding node in the tree derived from the truck's route can still satisfy (1) or (2).

(3) If neither (1) nor (2) is satisfied, the route selection server backtracks from the current nodes in the two trees and tries to apply (1) or (2) to their two backtracked nodes.

Figure 7 illustrates the matching of two transition trees in the above algorithm. If one or more truck routes in the database satisfy the required route, it selects the truck with the least number of truck movement between points, which is n of $\sqsubseteq_n$ in Definition 3. Although the cost of selecting a route is dependent on the number of trucks and the length of their routes, the system can handle each of the routes presented in this paper within a few milliseconds.

Non-deterministic operators, e.g., # and % , tend to cause the exposition of a number of sub-trees in transition trees. Nevertheless, our algorithm can easily restrain the number of sub-trees resulting from non-deterministic operators because the expansion rules of expressions, i.e., the operational semantics of the language, distinguish between derivations resulting from deterministic operators and those resulting from non-deterministic operators. Readers may wonder why E^* operator creates an infinite number of sub-trees, but the current implementation interprets the operator in a lazy evaluation manner.

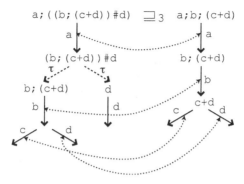

Fig. 7. Matching transition trees in route-order relation algorithm

5.2   Route Specification in RFID Tags

The current implementation assumes that the routes required for products or pallets are stored in RFID tags attached to the products or pallets because they may have their own delivery requirements. The current implementation supported three commercial passive RFID tags systems: OMRON V700 RFID system (125 kHz), Phillips i-Code system (13.56 MHz), and Texas Instruments Tag-It systems (13.56 MHz). The first system provides each tag with 240 bytes, the second with 112 bytes, and the third with 32 bytes. We were able to maintain each of the example routes presented in these papers in the first and second tag systems, where the length of the identifier for each point was 4 bytes. Tags in the third system may not be able to store route specifications internally, but can maintain references to route specifications stored in a database server.

Fig. 8. RFID tag reader scans route specification from tag

5.3   Early Experience

Our prototype implementation assumes that each client-side system at a supplier or customer point has more than one RFID tag reader. The reader periodically or explicitly tries to detect the presence of tags within its coverage area. Figure 8 shows a 13.56-MHz-based RFID tag reader embedded with a WiFi network interface scanning a tag attached to a pallet in a warehouse The tag specifies the route required to deliver the pallet. When it reads the data from a tag, it sends the route stored in the tag to the route-selection server via WiFi and waits for a response from the server. When it receives a truck identifier from the server, it displays the identifier on its screen.

The current implementation of the algorithm was not optimized for performance. Nevertheless, we describe the basic performance of the implementation. The cost of reading the route specification in a tag depends on the length of the specification, e.g., the cost of reading a specification with a length of less than 40 bytes is within 0.2 sec. When the routes of five trucks were registered in the server running on a computer (Intel Core 2 Duo 2 GHz and Windows XP), the cost of selecting a truck after the reader had detected a tag, including the cost of communication between the server and client via a TCP/IP session, was less than 1.2 sec. Client-side systems for suppliers and customers can be operated using only RFID readers, which connect to a server through either wired or wireless networks. This means they do not need any special equipment to use the logistics management system. This is important because in milk-run logistics, most suppliers are small to medium enterprises that do not want to have to invest in additional equipment for milk-run logistics.

6 Related Work

There have been many attempts to use process calculi, e.g., as formal methods for various business enterprise processes. Several researchers have used process calculi, e.g., π-calculus, as business-process modeling languages, such as BPEL, [13,4,8,12]. π-calculus has been used as a formal composition language for software composition and Web service composition, e.g., Orc [7] and SCC [1]. Process calculi are theoretically sound and support bisimulation analysis and model checking. They are also gaining increasing acceptance as a support tool in industry. However, there have been no process-calculus-based formal methods for logistics, in particular for improving the transport efficiency of trucks.

Several papers have explored formal models for specifying and reasoning about mobile agents, e.g., Mobile UNITY [5], Ambient calculus [2], and Join-calculus [3]. Ambient calculus [2] allows mobile agents (called ambients in the calculus) to contain other agents and to move with all inner ambients. The calculus must always model the mobility of agents as navigation along a hierarchy of agents, whereas the itineraries of real mobile agents may be more complicated. Join-calculus [3] also introduces the notion of named locations that form a tree. The mobility of an agent is modeled as a transformation of sub-trees from one part of the tree to another. The author presented a formal method for using mobile agents in network management systems [11]. However, this method was aimed only at mobile agents and assumed the notion of two-layer mobile agents.

7 Future Work

This section discusses further issues that need to be resolved. This paper assumes that trucks are independent, but coordination of multiple trucks is often necessary to ensure efficient transportation. In future research, we are interested in developing a mechanism for dividing single routes into multiple sub-routes and assigning these subtasks to one or more trucks. The order relation proposed in this paper can select truck routes according to the number of movements between points as well as the order in which the trucks visit each point. The amount of CO_2 emissions resulting from transport depends on the distance covered by trucks. We need to introduce the notion of distance into the framework. Although the milk-run approach is useful for non-just-in-time logistics, we are interesting in extending the framework by incorporating the ability to reason about time constraints. The language itself is general. We developed a methodology for testing software for mobile terminals that can be carried between networks and reconnected to current networks [9]. We plan to use the language as a control language for testing software in the methodology. As mentioned previously, the goal of the proposed framework is to establish both a theoretical and practical foundation for earth-friendly logistics. In fact, we have already started some large-scale experiments with logistics and warehouse companies in collaboration with the Ministry of Land, Infrastructure and Transport in Japan, to demonstrate the effectiveness of the proposed framework. The author is a member of the ISO/IEC standardization committee (SC31) for RFID tags and barcodes and supported several logistic services, including milk-run based logistic operations. We believe the the language can provide a foundation for tags and barcodes for earth-friendly logistic systems.

8 Conclusion

We presented a formal method for improving transport efficiency, using the example of milk-run logistics, to reduce the environmental impacts of transport operations. The method was formulated based on a process calculus-based language and an order relation over two terms corresponding to truck routes and the required routes in the language. The language can specify truck routes for milk-run operations and the required routes for shipping. The relation can be used to accurately determine whether a truck route satisfies the requirements of customers and suppliers. A prototype implementation system based on the framework was constructed using Java language and RFID tag systems and applied to our experimental distributed logistics management system.

References

1. Boreale, M., Bruni, R., Caires, L., De Nicola, R., Lanese, I., Loreti, M., Martins, F., Montanari, U., Ravara, A., Sangiorgi, D., Vasconcelos, V.T., Zavattaro, G.: SCC: a Service Centered Calculus. In: Bravetti, M., Núñez, M., Zavattaro, G. (eds.) WS-FM 2006. LNCS, vol. 4184, pp. 38–57. Springer, Heidelberg (2006)
2. Cardelli, L., Gordon, A.D.: Mobile Ambients. In: Nivat, M. (ed.) ETAPS 1998 and FOS-SACS 1998. LNCS, vol. 1378, pp. 140–155. Springer, Heidelberg (1998)
3. Fournet, C., Gonthier, G., Levy, J., Marnaget, L., Remy, D.: A Calculus of Mobile Agents. In: Sassone, V., Montanari, U. (eds.) CONCUR 1996. LNCS, vol. 1119, pp. 406–421. Springer, Heidelberg (1996)
4. Mazzara, M., Lucchi, R.: A pi-calculus based semantics for WS-BPEL. Journal of Logic and Algebraic Programming 70(1), 96–118 (2006)

5. McCann, P.J., Roman, G.-C.: Compositional Programming Abstractions for Mobile Computing. IEEE Transaction on Software Engineering 24(2) (1998)
6. Milner, R.: Communication and Concurrency. Prentice-Hall, Englewood Cliffs (1989)
7. Misra, J., Cook, W.R.: Computation orchestration: A basis for wide-area computing. Journal of Software and Systems Modeling (2006); A preliminary version of this paper appeared in the Lecture Notes for NATO summer school (August 2004)
8. Puhlmann, F., Weske, M.: Using the Pi-Calculus for Formalizing Workflow Patterns. In: Proceedings of the International Conference on Business Process Management, pp. 153–168 (2005)
9. Satoh, I.: A Testing Framework for Mobile Computing Software. IEEE Transactions on Software Engineering 29(12), 1112–1121 (2003)
10. Satoh, I.: A Location Model for Pervasive Computing Environments. In: Proceedings of IEEE 3rd International Conference on Pervasive Computing and Communications (PerCom 2005), pp. 215–224. IEEE Computer Society, Los Alamitos (2005)
11. Satoh, I.: Building and Selecting Mobile Agents for Network Management. Journal of Network and Systems Management 14(1), 147–169 (2006)
12. Smith, H.: Business Process Management-The Third Wave: Business Process Modeling Language (BPML) and Its Pi-Calculus Foundations. Information and Software Technology 45(15), 1065–1069 (2003)
13. Xu, K., Liu, Y., Zhu, J., Wu, C.: Pi-Calculus Based Bi-transformation of State-Driven Model and Flow-Driven Model. International Journal of Business Process Integration and Management (2006)

A Hierarchy of Equivalences for Probabilistic Processes[*]

Manuel Núñez and Luis Llana

Dept. Sistemas Informáticos y Computación
Facultad de Informática
Universidad Complutense de Madrid, 28040 Madrid, Spain
{mn,llana}@sip.ucm.es

Abstract. We study several process equivalences on a probabilistic process algebra. First, we define an operational semantics. Afterwards we introduce the notion of *passing* a test with a probability. We consider three families of tests according to the intended behavior of an external observer: *Reactive* (sequential tests), *generative* (branching tests), and *limited generative* (equitable branching tests). For each of these families we define three predicates over processes and tests (*may-pass*, *must-pass*, $pass_p$) which induce three equivalences. Finally, we relate these nine equivalences and provide either alternative characterizations or fully abstract denotational semantics. These semantic frameworks cover from simple traces to probabilistic acceptance trees.

1 Introduction

Process algebras [16,24,1,25,2] are an adequate mechanism to formally specify and analyze networked and distributed systems. The process algebra literature includes numerous semantic models. These semantic frameworks are used to describe the behavior of processes as well as to define relations on them. Testing semantics [7,15] represents one of these semantic frameworks. Intuitively, two processes are *testing equivalent* if they have the same *responses* for all the *tests* belonging to a certain set. Depending on how these responses are analyzed, several testing semantics can be defined: May, must, refusal, fair, etc. We consider that this semantic framework is very suitable because it is easy to understand and allows us to give different equivalences just by modifying the idea of what a test is or when a test is successfully passed.

Once the *basic* frameworks were studied, research in process algebras has tried to close the gap between formal models and real systems. Thus, features which were initially abstracted have been introduced later. This is the case of probabilistic information. In particular, if we concentrate only on probabilistic testing, regardless whether the underlying model is a process algebra or another formalism, several semantics have been defined. This area of research was very active

---

[*] This research was partially supported by the Spanish MEC project WEST/FAST TIN2006-15578-C02-01 and the Marie Curie project MRTN-CT-2003-505121/ TAROT.

in the previous decade (we can mention [5,35,18,30,29,33,26,12,21,6,31]). Moreover, there also exists recent work on the topic (see, for example [19,3,28,34,4,8]). Despite the myriad of papers on the subject, there is a lack of papers comparing several testing approaches under the same umbrella. In fact, most work in this direction is limited to compare a may and a must variants in a given probabilistic setting. That is, we miss a classification in the probabilistic setting similar to the ones provided in [9,10] for nonprobabilistic processes. This paper represents a first step towards such a complete study.

In this paper we study different testing semantics for the probabilistic process algebra PPA defined in [30,28]. This process algebra has two choice operators (external and internal), which are extended with a probability. In addition, it allows the definition of recursive behaviors. The study of the different semantics is performed in a testing framework. We propose three families of tests according to the capabilities of an external observer:

- In the *reactive* model [22] the environment can offer only one action at a given time. Intuitively, an entity interacting with a system *can press only one button at a given time.*
- In the *generative* model [11] the environment can offer more than an action and with different probabilities. So, *more than one button can be pressed at a given time and they can be pressed with different strengths.*
- In the *limited generative* model [29] the environment can offer several actions at a given time, but the probabilities associated with these actions are the same. So, *more than one button can be pressed at a given time, but they have to be pressed with the same strength.*

For each of the above families of tests we consider three different definitions of successfully passing a test:

- P *may-pass* T if the probability with which P *passes* T is greater than zero.
- P *muss-pass* T if the probability with which P *passes* T is equal to one.
- P $pass_p$ T if the probability with which P *passes* T is equal to p.

The combination of these two ideas (the different families of tests and the different interpretations of successfully passing a test) induce nine equivalence relations. In order to provide real usefulness to these equivalences, we relate them and provide either alternative characterizations or fully abstract denotational semantics.

We will show that the *may* interpretation coincides in the three families of tests. We define a fully abstract denotational semantics, based on traces, for the induced equivalence. For the *must-reactive* interpretation, we show that a fully abstract denotational semantics cannot be defined by using the usual least fixpoint techniques. Thus, we give an alternative characterization based on *must* traces. The *must* interpretation coincides for the *generative* and *limited generative* models, and we give an alternative characterization based on acceptance sets [15]. We show that the reactive testing equivalence is not a congruence and we define an alternative characterization based on *probabilistic traces*. For the

$$\approx^{\mathcal{R}}_{\text{must}} \;\sqsubseteq\; \approx^{\mathcal{LG}}_{\text{must}} \;=\; \approx^{\mathcal{G}}_{\text{must}}$$

$$\sqcap \qquad\qquad \sqcap \qquad\qquad \sqcap$$

$$\approx^{\mathcal{R}} \;\sqsubseteq\; \approx^{\mathcal{LG}} \;\sqsubseteq\; \approx^{\mathcal{G}}$$

$$\sqcup \qquad\qquad \sqcup \qquad\qquad \sqcup$$

$$\approx^{\mathcal{R}}_{\text{may}} \;=\; \approx^{\mathcal{LG}}_{\text{may}} \;=\; \approx^{\mathcal{G}}_{\text{may}}$$

Fig. 1. Hierarchy of testing equivalences for PPA

generative model we have a fully abstract denotational semantics based on probabilistic acceptance trees [28]. Finally, we provide an alternative characterization, based on a set of *essential* tests, for the limited generative model. In Figure 1 we show how the different equivalences studied in this paper are related.

As a derived result, our testing equivalences appropriately deal with *unfair divergences* caused by unguarded recursive definitions in the context of an internal choice. In fact, our results about fairness can be compared with those in [27,32], while they are not so similar to those in [14] where fairness is only considered in the context of parallel compositions. A study on the relation between probabilistic testing and fairness can be found in [31].

In terms of related work, our reactive and generative models follow the same intuitive ideas as those in [11], but we do not need to give different operational semantics for each of the models. We have just an operational semantics and the differences between the models come from the considered families of tests. The model described in [35], and other testing frameworks based on it, can be compared to our generative point of view. They define a probabilistic process algebra with two choice operators but, unlike PPA, the external choice does not have an associated probability. This fact simplifies the operational semantics but complicates the definition of a testing semantics: A process passes a test with a set of probabilities. They adapt the notions of *may* and *must* equivalences by computing the infimum and supremum of sets of probabilities. For these equivalences, compositional characterizations are defined in [18] and characterized as simulations in [19]. We think that these characterizations are so complicated because of the absence of probabilities in external choices. In contrast, our operational semantics is slightly harder, because we have to deal with probabilities in the scope of the external choice, but testing equivalences are simpler and more intuitive. Thus, the alternative characterizations for the *may* and *must* interpretations are clearer and more similar to the nonprobabilistic model.

In [20,17,23] several equivalence relations for probabilistic processes are given by adapting nonprobabilistic relations to the probabilistic setting. In spite of being interesting, they relate probabilistic equivalence relations which are not in a common framework. We address our work in a rather different way: We begin by settling a testing framework, then we define natural semantic equivalences in this framework, and, finally, we provide alternative characterizations for these equivalences and relate them.

The rest of the paper is organized as follows. Section 2 presents the syntax, operational and testing semantics for PPA. In Sections 3, 4, and 5 we study testing semantics and alternative characterizations for the reactive, generative, and limited generative models, respectively. Finally, in Section 6 we present our conclusions.

2   An Overwiew of PPA

In this section, we briefly review the basic concepts of our probabilistic process algebra: Syntax, operational semantics and testing semantics. This process algebra was used in [28], so more details can be found there (in particular, intuitive explanations of the operational semantics rules and the intended meaning of the rules defining the interaction between a process and a test). In addition, in this section we also define the interaction between a process and a test and adapt the *must* and *may* equivalences to our probabilistic framework.

2.1   Syntax and Operational Semantics of PPA

Definition 1. Given a finite set of actions *Act* and a set of identifiers *Id*, the set of PPA processes is defined by the following BNF expression:

$$P ::= Nil \mid \Omega \mid X \mid a; P \mid P \oplus_p P \mid P +_p P \mid recX.P$$

where $p \in (0,1)$, $a \in Act$, and $X \in Id$. □

From now on, except as noted, we only consider closed processes, that is processes without free occurrences of variables. In this process algebra, *Nil* is a deadlocked process, Ω is a divergent process, $a; P$ denotes the action a prefixing the process P, $P \oplus_p Q$ denotes an internal choice between P and Q with associated probability p, $P +_p Q$ is an external choice between P and Q with associated probability p, and *recX.P* is used to define recursive processes. We can extend the external choice operator to an n-ary one.

Definition 2. Let $P_1, \ldots, P_n$ be processes and $p_1, \ldots, p_n > 0$ such that $\sum p_i = 1$. We define the *generalized external choice* as:

1. $\sum_{i=1}^{1}[1] P = P$.
2. $\sum_{i=1}^{n}[p_i] P_i = P_1 +_{p_1} (\sum_{i=1}^{n-1}[\frac{p_{i+1}}{1-p_1}] P_{i+1})$. □

Next we give a syntactic definition for the *stability* of a process. It expresses that a process does not have unguarded internal choices, or equivalently that a process will not be able to (immediately) perform an internal transition. We also define a function *live* computing whether a stable process is operationally equivalent to *Nil*.

$$(PRE)\frac{}{a;P\stackrel{a}{\longrightarrow}_1 P} \qquad (INT1)\frac{}{P\oplus_p Q\succ\!\!\!\longrightarrow_p P} \qquad (INT2)\frac{}{P\oplus_p Q\succ\!\!\!\longrightarrow_{1-p} Q}$$

$$(EXT1)\frac{P\succ\!\!\!\longrightarrow_q P' \wedge \texttt{stable}(Q)}{P+_p Q\succ\!\!\!\longrightarrow_q P'+_p Q} \qquad\qquad (EXT2)\frac{Q\succ\!\!\!\longrightarrow_q Q' \wedge \texttt{stable}(P)}{P+_p Q\succ\!\!\!\longrightarrow_q P+_p Q'}$$

$$(EXT3)\frac{P\succ\!\!\!\longrightarrow_{q_1} P' \wedge Q\succ\!\!\!\longrightarrow_{q_2} Q'}{P+_p Q\succ\!\!\!\longrightarrow_{q_1\cdot q_2} P'+_p Q'}$$

$$(EXT4)\frac{P\stackrel{a}{\longrightarrow}_q P' \wedge \texttt{stable}(Q)}{P+_p Q\stackrel{a}{\longrightarrow}_{p\cdot\hat{q}} P'} \qquad\qquad (EXT5)\frac{Q\stackrel{a}{\longrightarrow}_q Q' \wedge \texttt{stable}(P)}{P+_p Q\stackrel{a}{\longrightarrow}_{(1-p)\cdot\hat{q}} Q'}$$

$$(REC)\frac{}{\texttt{rec } X.P\succ\!\!\!\longrightarrow_1 P\{\texttt{rec } X.P/X\}} \qquad (DIV)\frac{}{\Omega\succ\!\!\!\longrightarrow_1 \Omega}$$

where $\hat{q} = \frac{q}{p\cdot\texttt{live}(P)+(1-p)\cdot\texttt{live}(Q)}$.

Fig. 2. Operational Semantics of PPA

Definition 3. We define the predicate $\texttt{stable}(P)$ over PPA processes as:

- $\texttt{stable}(Nil) = \texttt{stable}(a;P) = \texttt{true}$
- $\texttt{stable}(\Omega) = \texttt{stable}(X) = \texttt{stable}(P_1 \oplus_p P_2) = \texttt{stable}(recX.P) = \texttt{false}$
- $\texttt{stable}(P_1 +_p P_2) = \texttt{stable}(P_1) \wedge \texttt{stable}(P_2)$

We define the function $\texttt{live}(P)$ over PPA processes as:

- $\texttt{live}(Nil) = 0$
- $\texttt{live}(a;P) = 1$
- $\texttt{live}(P_1 +_p P_2) = \max(\texttt{live}(P_1), \texttt{live}(P_2))$ □

Even though the function $\texttt{live}(\_)$ is not defined for unstable processes, this fact does not represent a problem since we will apply it only to stable processes. The set of rules that define the operational semantics is given in Figure 2. There are two types of transitions. The intuitive meaning of a transition $P \stackrel{a}{\longrightarrow}_p Q$ (external transitions) is that if the environment offers all the actions in Act then the probability with which P performs a and then behaves as Q is equal to p; the meaning of $P \succ\!\!\!\longrightarrow_p Q$ (internal transitions) is that the process P evolves to Q with probability p without interaction with the environment.

For the sake of simplicity, we use multisets of transitions in order to get sets of transitions. So, if a transition can be derived in several ways, each derivation generates a different instance of this transition. For example, let us consider the process $P = a +_{\frac{1}{2}} a$, where trailing occurrences of Nil have been omitted. If we were not careful, we would have the transition $P \stackrel{a}{\longrightarrow}_{\frac{1}{2}} Nil$ only once, while we should have this transition twice. This problem is similar for the $\oplus_p$ operator. So, if a transition can be derived in several ways, we consider that each derivation generates a different instance. In particular, when we define the testing semantics we will consider multisets of computations as well. We will use the delimiters { and } to denote multisets.

As shown in [28], this operational semantics separates between internal and external transitions. So, a process can perform an external transition only if this process is stable (that is, it cannot perform internal transitions).

$$\frac{P \succ\!\!\longrightarrow_p P' \wedge T_\oplus = 0}{P \mid T \longmapsto_p P' \mid T} \qquad \frac{T \succ\!\!\longrightarrow_p T' \wedge P_\oplus = 0}{P \mid T \longmapsto_p P \mid T'} \qquad \frac{P \succ\!\!\longrightarrow_p P' \wedge T \succ\!\!\longrightarrow_q T'}{P \mid T \longmapsto_{p \cdot q} P' \mid T'}$$

$$\frac{P \xrightarrow{a}_p P' \wedge T \xrightarrow{a}_q T'}{P \mid T \longmapsto_{r_1} P' \mid T'} \qquad \frac{T \xrightarrow{\omega}_p T' \wedge P_\oplus = 0}{P \mid T \xmapsto{\omega}_{r_2} Nil}$$

where $r_1 = \dfrac{f_1^{P,T}(p) \cdot f_2^{P,T}(q)}{\mu(P,T)}$ and $r_2 = \dfrac{f_2^{P,T}(p)}{\mu(P,T)}$.

$$f_1^{P,T}(p) = \frac{p}{\sum_a \left\{ r \mid \exists P', T', p' : P \xrightarrow{a}_r P' \wedge T \xrightarrow{a}_{p'} T' \right\}}$$

$$f_2^{P,T}(q) = \frac{q}{\sum_a \left\{ r \mid \exists P', T', p' : T \xrightarrow{a}_r T' \wedge P \xrightarrow{a}_{p'} P' \right\} + \sum \left\{ r \mid \exists T' : T \xrightarrow{\omega}_r T' \right\}}$$

$$\mu(P,T) = \sum_a \{ f_1^{P,T}(p) \cdot f_2^{P,T}(q) \mid \exists P', T' : P \xrightarrow{a}_p P' \wedge T \xrightarrow{a}_q T' \}$$
$$+ \sum \{ f_2^{P,T}(p) \mid \exists T' : T \xrightarrow{\omega}_p T' \}$$

Fig. 3. Rules for the parallel composition

Lemma 1. Let P be a process. If there exist p and P' such that $P \succ\!\!\longrightarrow_p P'$ then there do not exist q, a, P'' such that $P \xrightarrow{a}_q P''$. Equivalently, if there exist p, a, P' such that $P \xrightarrow{a}_p P'$ then there do not exist q and P'' such that $P \succ\!\!\longrightarrow_q P''$.

2.2 Testing Semantics

As usual, tests are processes where the alphabet Act is extended with a new action ω indicating successful termination. The operational semantics of tests is the same as that of processes (considering ω as an ordinary action). The rules defining the interaction between a process and a test (modelled by their parallel composition) are given in Figure 3. In these rules we use a *normalization factor* $\mu(P,T)$ similar to that in [6]. In addition, we also use two *prenormalization factors* ($f_1^{P,T}$ and $f_2^{P,T}$) in order to *distribute* the probability associated with those actions which cannot be performed by both sides of the parallel composition among the actions which can be performed by both sides. This represents a small change with respect to the definition given in [28], but it does not change the induced testing equivalence (even though it changes the probability with which processes pass tests).

Example 1. Let $P = (a; Nil) +_{\frac{1}{4}} (b; Nil)$ and $T = (a; Nil) +_{\frac{1}{2}} \omega$. If we would not use prenormalization factors we would have P passes the test T with a probability $\frac{1}{5} = \frac{\frac{1}{4} \cdot \frac{1}{2}}{\frac{1}{4} \cdot \frac{1}{2} + \frac{1}{2}}$ while using prenormalization factors we obtain a probability of $\frac{1}{2} = \frac{\frac{1}{2}}{\frac{1}{2} + \frac{1}{2}}$. This is a more intuitive result because the action b should not *subtract* probability from a.

Definition 4. Let P be a process and T be a test. A *computation* is a *maximal* sequence of transitions of the form

$$C = P \mid T \longmapsto_{p_1} P_1 \mid T_1 \longmapsto_{p_2} \cdots P_{n-1} \mid T_{n-1} \overset{?}{\longmapsto}_{p_n} R$$

where ? denotes either an empty label or the special action ω. A sequence is said to be *maximal* when there do not exist $p > 0$ and R' such that $R \overset{?}{\longmapsto}_p R'$.

When the last transition is of the form $P_{n-1} \mid T_{n-1} \overset{\omega}{\longmapsto}_{p_n} Nil$ we say that the computation is *successful*. We denote by $\tilde{C}$ the *set of successful computations* from C. The probability of a successful computation S, denoted by $Pr(S)$, is inductively defined as

$$Pr(Nil) = 1 \text{ (i.e. } T \text{ has succeeded)}$$
$$Pr(P \mid T \overset{*}{\longmapsto}_p C) = p \cdot Pr(C)$$

We write P *may-pass* T if $\sum_{S \in \tilde{C}} Pr(S) > 0$. We write P *muss-pass* T if $\sum_{S \in \tilde{C}} Pr(S) = 1$. We write P *pass$_p$* T if $\sum_{S \in \tilde{C}} Pr(S) = p$.   □

In the previous definition, by *maximal* we mean that it cannot be extended, that is, from the reached point on, the composition of process and test cannot perform any action. Given a family of tests we can define the corresponding notions of testing, *may*, and *must* equivalences with respect to this family.

Definition 5. Given a family of probabilistic tests $\mathcal{T}$ and two processes P and Q we say:

- P and Q are *probabilistic testing equivalent* with respect to $\mathcal{T}$, denoted by $P \approx^{\mathcal{T}} Q$, iff for all $T \in \mathcal{T}$ we have $P \text{ pass}_p T \iff Q \text{ pass}_p T$.
- P and Q are *probabilistic may-testing equivalent* with respect to $\mathcal{T}$, denoted by $P \approx^{\mathcal{T}}_{may} Q$, iff for all $T \in \mathcal{T}$ we have $P \text{ may-pass } T \iff Q \text{ may-pass } T$.
- P and Q are *probabilistic must-testing equivalent* with respect to $\mathcal{T}$, denoted by $P \approx^{\mathcal{T}}_{must} Q$, iff for all $T \in \mathcal{T}$ we have $P \text{ muss-pass } T \iff Q \text{ muss-pass } T$.

□

As shown in [28], the set of tests can be reduced by considering tests without internal choices and without nondeterminism caused by prefixing by the same action in an external choice.

Lemma 2. Let P be a process, T and T' be tests, and $a \in Act$. We have:

1. $P \text{ pass}_q (T \oplus_p T')$ iff $P \text{ pass}_{q_1} T \wedge P \text{ pass}_{q_2} T' \wedge p \cdot q_1 + (1 - p) \cdot q_2 = q$
2. $P \text{ pass}_q (a; T) +_p (a; T')$ iff $P \text{ pass}_q a; (T \oplus_p T')$

3   The Reactive Model

In the reactive model the environment can offer only one action each time, that is, *only one button can be pressed at a given time*. In a testing framework, this interpretation gives rise to tests being just traces finishing with the acceptance action ω.

Definition 6. (Reactive Tests) The set of *reactive tests*, denoted by $\mathcal{R}$, is defined by the BNF expression $T = \omega \mid a; T$. ☐

3.1 Alternative Characterization for $\approx^{\mathcal{R}}$

The next example shows that $\approx^{\mathcal{R}}$, that is, the test equivalence induced by considering $\mathcal{R}$ as set of tests, is not a congruence. So, we cannot define a fully abstract (compositional) denotational semantics for this equivalence.

Example 2. Consider $P = (a; c) +_{\frac{1}{3}} b$ and $P' = (a; c) +_{\frac{1}{3}} b$. Obviously, $P \approx^{\mathcal{R}} P'$, but if we consider $Q = a; b$, we have $P +_{\frac{1}{2}} Q \not\approx^{\mathcal{R}} P' +_{\frac{1}{2}} Q$. For example, if $T = a; b; \omega$ then we have $P +_{\frac{1}{2}} Q \, pass_{\frac{2}{3}} \, T$ while $P' +_{\frac{1}{2}} Q \, pass_{\frac{3}{4}} \, T$.

However, the rest of the operators are congruent for $\approx^{\mathcal{R}}$.

Proposition 1. Let P and P' be processes such that $P \approx^{\mathcal{R}} P'$. Then,

- For all action $a \in Act$ we have $a; P \approx^{\mathcal{R}} a; P'$.
- For all process Q and probability $p \in (0, 1)$ we have $P \oplus_p Q \approx^{\mathcal{R}} P' \oplus_p Q$ and $Q \oplus_p P \approx^{\mathcal{R}} Q \oplus_p P'$.

Let $P(X)$ and $P'(X)$ be two terms with the free occurrence of the identifier X (that is, processes but with a free variable). If for all process Q we have $P(Q) \approx^{\mathcal{R}} P'(Q)$ then $recX.P \approx^{\mathcal{R}} recX.P'$.

We will define an alternative characterization of this equivalence based on the operational behavior of processes, considering *probabilistic traces*. First we extend $\longrightarrow$ to sequences of actions and $\succ\!\!\longrightarrow$ to sequences of internal transitions.

Definition 7. Let P and P' be processes. We write $P \succ\!\!\longrightarrow_p^* P'$ if this transition can be derived from the following rules:

$$P \succ\!\!\longrightarrow_1^* P \quad \text{if } \texttt{stable}(P)$$
$$P \succ\!\!\longrightarrow_p^* P' \quad \text{if } \exists q, q', Q : \ P \succ\!\!\longrightarrow_q Q \succ\!\!\longrightarrow_{q'}^* P' \wedge p = q \cdot q'$$

We write $P \xrightarrow{s}_p P'$ if this transition can be derived from the following rules:

$$P \xrightarrow{\epsilon}_p P' \quad \text{if } P \succ\!\!\longrightarrow_p^* P'$$
$$P \xrightarrow{\langle a \rangle \circ s'}_p P' \quad \text{if } \exists P_1, P_2, p_1, p_2, p_3 : \ P \succ\!\!\longrightarrow_{p_1}^* P_1 \wedge P_1 \xrightarrow{a}_{p_2} P_2 \wedge P_2 \xrightarrow{s'}_{p_3} P'$$

where $p = p_1 \cdot \dfrac{p_2}{\sum_{P'}\left\{ q \mid P_1 \xrightarrow{a}_q P' \right\}} \cdot p_3$ and $s \circ s'$ denotes the concatenation of s and s'. We write $P \xrightarrow{s}_0 P'$ if $P \xrightarrow{s}_p P'$ cannot be derived from the previous rules. ☐

Let us note that if $P \succ\!\!\longrightarrow_p^* P'$ then P' must be stable. So, $\succ\!\!\longrightarrow^*$ is not *exactly* the reflexive and transitive closure of $\succ\!\!\longrightarrow$. Let us also note that the value p appearing in $P \xrightarrow{s}_p P'$ indicates the product of the probabilities associated with the nondeterministic choices involved in the execution of the sequence s. This nondeterminism can be produced by internal transitions but also by external transitions labelled with the same action. As in the case of $\rightarrowtail$ and $\longrightarrow$, we must consider the possible repetitions of *generalized* transitions of the form $P \xrightarrow{s}_p P'$ and $P \rightarrowtail^*_p P'$.

Definition 8. Let P be a process. We define the *set of probabilistic traces* of P as $ptraces(P) = \{(s,p) \mid p = \sum_{P'} \{\mid q \mid P \xrightarrow{s}_q P' \mid\} \land p > 0\}$. Given a trace s, we define the function $prob(P, s)$ as p if $(s,p) \in ptraces(P)$ and as 0, otherwise.
□

Lemma 3. Let P be a process. We have $prob(P, s) = p$ iff $P\ pass_p\ \tilde{s}$, where $\tilde{s}$ denotes the reactive test conformed by the actions of the sequence s finishing with ω.

Theorem 1. Let P and P' be processes. We have $P \approx^{\mathcal{R}} P'$ iff $ptraces(P) = ptraces(P')$.

3.2   The *must* Reactive Equivalence

The next example shows that we cannot define a fully abstract denotational semantics using the usual least fixpoint technique. Instead, we will define an alternative characterization from the probabilistic traces of a process.

Example 3. Let $Q = recX.P(X)$, where $P(X) = (a; Nil) \oplus_p X$. We have that $Q \approx^{\mathcal{R}}_{must} a; Nil$. However, Ω is fixpoint of the equation $X = P(X)$ because $\Omega \approx^{\mathcal{R}}_{must} (a; Nil) \oplus_p \Omega$. Obviously, Ω is the least fixpoint. So, if we define the semantics of a recursive process with the usual technique we do not obtain the desired results.

Definition 9. Let P be a process. We define the *set of must probabilistic traces* of P as $must\text{-}traces(P) = \{s \mid (s,1) \in ptraces(P)\}$.
□

That is, given a process, we consider its probabilistic traces which have 1 as associated probability. The induced equivalence coincides with $\approx^{\mathcal{R}}_{must}$ as it is stated in the next result.

Theorem 2. Let P, P' be processes. We have $P \approx^{\mathcal{R}}_{must} P'$ iff $must\text{-}traces(P) = must\text{-}traces(P')$.

3.3   The *may* Reactive Equivalence

Following a similar reasoning to that used for the *must* reactive equivalence, we can define an alternative characterization for $\approx^{\mathcal{R}}_{may}$, considering the traces of a process and *forgetting* the probabilistic information.

Definition 10. Let P be a process. We define the *set of may probabilistic traces* of P as $may\text{-}traces(P) = \{s \mid (s,p) \in ptraces(P)\}$.
□

Theorem 3. Let P and P' be processes. We have $P \approx^{\mathcal{R}}_{\text{may}} P'$ iff $\textit{may-traces}(P) = \textit{may-traces}(P')$.

But in this equivalence we can go further because a fully abstract denotational semantics for $\approx^{\mathcal{R}}_{\text{may}}$ can be given in terms of traces. The semantic domain, denoted by $\textbf{TRA}_{Act}$, will be the sets of traces. We denote by $R, R_1, \ldots$ the elements of $\textbf{TRA}_{Act}$ and by $[\![P]\!]^{\mathcal{R}}_{\text{may}}$ the semantics of process P.

Definition 11. Let $R_1, R_2 \in \textbf{TRA}_{Act}$. We write $R_1 \sqsubseteq_{\textbf{TRA}} R_2$ if for all $s \in Act^*$ we have $s \in R_1$ implies $s \in R_2$. We write $R_1 =_{\textbf{TRA}} R_2$ if for all $s \in Act^*$ we have $s \in R_1$ iff $s \in R_2$.   □

Lemma 4. $(\textbf{TRA}_{Act}, \sqsubseteq_{\textbf{TRA}})$ is a cpo.

Nil only has the empty trace. So, $[\![Nil]\!]^{\mathcal{R}}_{\text{may}} = \{\epsilon\}$. Ω can execute no trace because the only transition which Ω can perform is $\Omega \succ\!\!\longrightarrow_1 \Omega$. So, this process cannot be stable. Thus, $[\![\Omega]\!]^{\mathcal{R}}_{\text{may}} = \emptyset$.

For all $a \in Act$ we define the semantic function $a; \_ :: \textbf{TRA}_{Act} \longrightarrow \textbf{TRA}_{Act}$. The element $a; R \in \textbf{TRA}_{Act}$ has the same traces as R but prefixed by the action a. So, $a; R = \{(a \circ s) \mid s \in R\} \cup \{\epsilon\}$. We add the empty trace because the syntactic process *associated* with this semantic process is stable.

For all $p \in (0,1)$ the functions $\oplus_p :: \textbf{TRA}_{Act} \times \textbf{TRA}_{Act} \longrightarrow \textbf{TRA}_{Act}$ return the union of the corresponding sets of traces. That is, $R_1 \oplus_p R_2 = R_1 \cup R_2$.

In the case of the external choice we must consider if any of the processes is *equivalent* to Ω. For all $p \in (0,1)$ the function $+_p :: \textbf{TRA}_{Act} \times \textbf{TRA}_{Act} \longrightarrow \textbf{TRA}_{Act}$ is defined as

$$R_1 +_p R_2 = \begin{cases} \emptyset & \text{if } R_1 =_{\textbf{TRA}} \emptyset \lor R_2 =_{\textbf{TRA}} \emptyset \\ R_1 \cup R_2 & \text{otherwise} \end{cases}$$

Proposition 2. For all $a \in Act$ the semantic function $a; \_$ is continuous. For all $p \in (0,1)$ the semantic functions $\oplus_p$ and $+_p$ are continuous.

As usual when defining a denotational semantics, the meaning of recursive expressions $recX.P(X)$ is given by the limit of its finite approximations

$$P_0 = \Omega, P_1 = P(\Omega), \ldots, P_n = P^n(\Omega)$$

Since all the operators of the language are continuous, this limit is the least fixpoint of the equation $X = P(X)$. That is, $[\![recX.\ P(X)]\!]^{\mathcal{R}}_{\text{may}} = \bigsqcup_{n=0}^{\infty} [\![P_n]\!]^{\mathcal{R}}_{\text{may}}$.

Lemma 5. Let P be a process. We have $s \in [\![P]\!]^{\mathcal{R}}_{\text{may}}$ iff P *may-pass* $\tilde{s}$, where $\tilde{s}$ denotes the reactive test conformed by the actions of the sequence s finishing with ω.

Theorem 4. Let P, P' be processes. We have $[\![P]\!]^{\mathcal{R}}_{\text{may}} =_{\textbf{TRA}} [\![P']\!]^{\mathcal{R}}_{\text{may}}$ iff $P \approx^{\mathcal{R}}_{\text{may}} P'$.

Let us remark that a fully abstract denotational semantics can be easily defined, from this one, for $\approx^{\mathcal{R}}$ (reactive testing equivalence) if we consider the subset of PPA without external choices. It is enough to modify the semantic functions adding a probability equal to 1 to the empty trace, taking into account the probability associated with the traces of R, when defining $a; R$, and considering the probability associated with internal choices (see [28]).

As a concluding remark, we have that *may* and *must* reactive equivalences do not imply reactive equivalence (obviously, reactive equivalence implies *may* and *must* equivalences). For example, let us consider $P = a \oplus_{\frac{1}{3}} b$ and $Q = a \oplus_{\frac{1}{2}} b$, where trailing occurrences of *Nil* have been removed. We have $P \approx^{\mathcal{R}}_{\text{may}} Q$ and $P \approx^{\mathcal{R}}_{\text{must}} Q$ but $P \not\approx^{\mathcal{R}} Q$, because, for example, $P \, pass_{\frac{1}{3}} \, a; \omega$ while $Q \, pass_{\frac{1}{2}} \, a; \omega$.

Finally, let us mention that reactive equivalences are in general too weak. For example, they cannot distinguish between $a +_p b$ and $a +_q b$. Also, these equivalences identify processes which will be divergent in the next step. For example, reactive equivalences identify the processes $a; \Omega$ and $b; \Omega$ (and both are equivalent to *Nil*).

4   The Generative Model

In the generative model the environment can offer several actions each time, and with different probabilities. That is, *several buttons can be pressed at the same time and with different strengths.* So, in this model the family of tests, denoted by $\mathcal{G}$, is the whole set of probabilistic tests. Nevertheless, the set of tests can be reduced by applying Lemma 2 and by considering that recursive tests do not increase the distinguishing power of tests.

For the generative testing equivalence $(\approx^{\mathcal{G}})$ a fully abstract denotational semantics was defined in [28] and extensively studied. This denotational semantics is based on the notion of *probabilistic acceptance trees* which are a natural extension of acceptance trees [13]. These trees have two kinds of nodes: *Internal* and *external.* The root is an internal node. Arcs outgoing from internal nodes are labelled with different *states* (sets of pairs ⟨action, probability⟩ where the actions are different, and if the state is not empty then the probabilities sum up to one), with an associated probability. The sum of these probabilities is less than or equal to 1, and the difference between one and this sum denotes the probability of divergence at this point. These arcs go to external nodes. The arcs outgoing from external nodes are labelled with the actions belonging to the state labelling the ingoing arc. For any action in that state, there is a (unique) arc labelled with this action. These arcs go to internal nodes. An example is shown in Figure 4.

There are two important differences with respect to nonprobabilistic acceptance trees (of course, out of probabilities). First, there can be more than one state with the same actions. For example, a process may have the states: $\{(a, \frac{1}{3}), (b, \frac{2}{3})\}$ and $\{(a, \frac{1}{4}), (b, \frac{3}{4})\}$. Second, the *continuations* after the same action are not joined. So the process $(a; P) \oplus_p ((a; P') +_q (b; Q))$ is not necessarily equivalent to the process $(a; (P \oplus_{q'} P')) \oplus_p ((a; (P \oplus_{q''} P')) +_q (b; Q))$.

Due to lack of space, we do not present the semantic functions corresponding to the syntactic operators (they can be found in [28]) and we just repeat the final result.

Theorem 5. Let P, P' be processes. We have $P \approx^{\mathcal{G}} P'$ iff $[\![P]\!]^{\mathcal{G}} = [\![P']\!]^{\mathcal{G}}$.

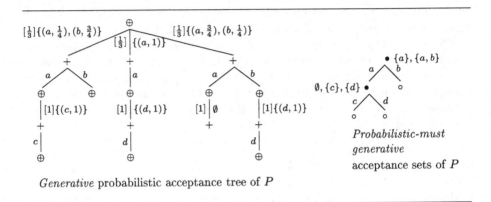

Generative probabilistic acceptance tree of P

Fig. 4. Semantics of $P = (a; d; \Omega) \oplus_{\frac{1}{3}} (((a; c; \Omega) +_{\frac{1}{4}} b; \Omega) \oplus_{\frac{1}{2}} ((a; Nil) +_{\frac{3}{4}} b; d; \Omega))$

Even though we have increased the set of tests, this fact does not influence the *may* interpretation, that is, as in the nonprobabilistic case, it is enough to consider *sequential* tests to characterize a *may* equivalence. Thus, if two processes are *may* reactive equivalent, they will be *may* generative equivalent. This is so because if one process passes a generative test with a probability greater than zero then each successful computation generates a sequential test conformed by the actions taking part in the computation. Because they are *may* reactive equivalent, this computation is also successful for the other process, and so it passes the generative test with a probability greater than 0.

Theorem 6. Let P and P' be processes. We have $P \approx^{\mathcal{R}}_{\text{may}} P'$ iff $P \approx^{\mathcal{G}}_{\text{may}} P'$.

4.1   The *must* Generative Equivalence

Using a similar argument to that of Example 3, we cannot define a fully abstract denotational semantics using the usual least fixpoint techniques for this equivalence. Instead, we will define an alternative characterization, in the same way that for the nonprobabilistic case, based on *acceptance sets* [7,15].

Definition 12. Given a stable process P, the set of actions that can be (immediately) performed by P is given by $S(P) = \{a \mid \exists P', p : P \xrightarrow{a}_p P'\}$. Given a process P and a sequence of actions $s \in Act^*$, we define the *acceptance sets* of P *after* s as:

$$A(P, s) = \begin{cases} \emptyset & \text{if } \sum_Q \{ p \mid P \xrightarrow{s}_p Q \} < 1 \\ \{ S(P') \mid \exists P', p : P \xrightarrow{s}_p P' \wedge p > 0 \} & \text{otherwise} \end{cases}$$

□

The previous definition needs some explanation. In order to compute the acceptance sets of a process after a sequence s, first we compute the processes to which the process may evolve by performing the generalized external transition corresponding to s. If the sum of the probabilities associated with these transitions is less than one, then there exists a *computation* reaching a divergent process. In this case, as in the nonprobabilistic case, we consider that from this point on the process is divergent, and we return $\emptyset$ as acceptance set.[1] For example, let us consider $P = (a; \Omega) +_{\frac{1}{2}} (a; b; Nil)$. We have $\sum \{ p \mid P \xrightarrow{\langle a \rangle}_p Q \} = \frac{1}{2}$ because we only can derive $P \xrightarrow{\langle a \rangle}_{\frac{1}{2}} b; Nil$ (we cannot derive $P \xrightarrow{\langle a \rangle}_{\frac{1}{2}} \Omega$ because Ω is not stable). Thus, $A(P, \langle a \rangle) = \emptyset$ (as in the nonprobabilistic case, this process is *must equivalent* to $a; \Omega$). If the sum of these probabilities is equal to 1 then we compute the acceptance sets as in the nonprobabilistic setting (an example is shown in Figure 4).

Let us note that, as in the *must-reactive* case, this alternative characterization considers *unfair divergences* caused by unguarded recursive definitions in internal choices. For example, let $P = recX.(a; Nil) \oplus_{\frac{1}{3}} X$. We have

$$P \succ\!\!\longrightarrow^*_{\frac{1}{3}} a; Nil, \ P \succ\!\!\longrightarrow^*_{\frac{2}{9}} a; Nil, \ P \succ\!\!\longrightarrow^*_{\frac{4}{27}} a; Nil \ \ldots$$

and the probabilities associated with these transitions sum up to 1 since we have $\frac{1}{3} \sum_{i=0}^{\infty} (1 - \frac{1}{3})^i = 1$. So, $A(P, \epsilon) = \{\{a\}\}$ and then P is equivalent to $a; Nil$.

Next, we define an equivalence relation which coincides with $\approx^{\mathcal{G}}_{must}$.

Definition 13. Let $\mathcal{A}$ and $\mathcal{B}$ be acceptance sets. We write $\mathcal{A} \simeq \mathcal{B}$ if for every $A \in \mathcal{A}$ there exists $B \in \mathcal{B}$ such that $B \subseteq A$, and for every $B \in \mathcal{B}$ there exists $A \in \mathcal{A}$ such that $A \subseteq B$.

Let P and P' be processes. We write $P =_{must} P'$ if for all $s \in Act^*$ we have $A(P, s) \simeq A(P', s)$. □

Theorem 7. Let P and P' be processes. We have $P \approx^{\mathcal{G}}_{must} P'$ iff $P =_{must} P'$.

5   The Limited Generative Model

In the limited generative model we consider deterministic[2] tests and such that there is an equitable distribution of probabilities among the offered actions at

---

[1] Let us remark that $A(P, s) = \emptyset$ is not the same as $A(P, s) = \{\emptyset\}$. The former corresponds to a divergent process (i.e. equivalent to Ω) while the latter corresponds to a deadlocked process (i.e. equivalent to Nil).

[2] This is not a real constraint because, by Lemma 2, nondeterministic tests do not increase the distinguishing power.

a given time. This means that *several buttons can be simultaneously pressed but all of them with the same strength.*

Definition 14. The set of *limited generative tests*, denoted by $\mathcal{LG}$, is defined by the BNF expression $T = Nil \mid \sum_{i=1}^{n}[\frac{1}{n}]b_i; T_i$, where $b_i \in Act \cup \omega$ are different actions.   □

The *may* interpretation in this model coincides with that of the reactive model. In the case of the *must* interpretation, we have that $\approx^{\mathcal{LG}}_{\text{must}}$ coincides with $\approx^{\mathcal{G}}_{\text{must}}$. Intuitively, if a process passes a test with probability 1 it does not matter the possible distribution of probabilities among the offered actions.

Theorem 8. Let P and P' be processes. We have $P \approx^{\mathcal{LG}}_{\text{may}} P'$ iff $P \approx^{\mathcal{G}}_{\text{may}} P'$. We have $P \approx^{\mathcal{LG}}_{\text{must}} P'$ iff $P \approx^{\mathcal{G}}_{\text{must}} P'$.

In [29], an alternative characterization based on limited probabilistic barbs was given for the limited generative testing equivalence ($\approx^{\mathcal{LG}}$), for a probabilistic version of LOTOS. These results can be adapted to our framework. First, we precisely define the new set of tests.

Definition 15. The set of *limited probabilistic barbs*, denoted by $\mathcal{LPB}$, is defined by the BNF expression: $T = \omega \mid \sum_{i=1}^{n}[\frac{1}{n}]b_i; R_i$, where $b_i \in Act \cup \omega$ are different actions, and $R_i = Nil$ for all $1 \leq i < n$ while $R_n = T$.

We write $P \approx^{\mathcal{LGB}} P'$ if for all $T \in \mathcal{LGB}$ we have $P \, pass_p \, T$ iff $P' \, pass_p \, T$.   □

That is, a limited probabilistic barb is a limited probabilistic test such that at most only one of the offered actions at each time has a continuation (the rest of actions are prefixing the process *Nil*). This family of tests has the same distinguishing power as the whole family, as it is stated in the next result.

Theorem 9. Let P and P' be processes. We have $P \approx^{\mathcal{LG}} P'$ iff $P \approx^{\mathcal{LGB}} P'$.

But this alternative characterization is not suitable to be extended to a denotational semantics. A fully abstract denotational semantics could be given for this equivalence by modifying the probabilistic acceptance trees model, but the definitions are too involved since several states must be joined into one. For example, we have $(a +_{\frac{1}{4}} b) \oplus_{\frac{1}{2}} (a +_{\frac{3}{4}} b) \approx^{\mathcal{LG}} a +_{\frac{1}{2}} b$ (*Nil*'s have been omitted), while these two processes are not equivalent in the generative model (the test $T = (a; \omega) +_{\frac{1}{3}} (b; Nil)$ distinguishes them).

6   Conclusion

In this paper we have proposed a number of testing equivalences on PPA. Since we use a testing framework, the definitions of these equivalences are very natural and easy to understand. Testing equivalences are intuitive but they are not suitable for a practical use since they are based on the behavior of a process with respect to an infinite set of tests. So, we have given alternative characterizations and fully abstract denotational semantics. The hierarchy we have settled brings up both useful information about different probabilistic testing equivalences and relationships between denotational models.

References

1. Baeten, J.C.M., Weijland, W.P.: Process Algebra. In: Cambridge Tracts in Computer Science 18, Cambridge University Press, Cambridge (1990)
2. Bergstra, J.A., Ponse, A., Smolka, S.A. (eds.): Handbook of Process Algebra. North-Holland, Amsterdam (2001)
3. Cazorla, D., Cuartero, F., Valero, V., Pelayo, F.L., Pardo, J.J.: Algebraic theory of probabilistic and non-deterministic processes. Journal of Logic and Algebraic Programming 55(1–2), 57–103 (2003)
4. Cheung, L., Stoelinga, M., Vaandrager, F.: A testing scenario for probabilistic processes. Journal of the ACM 54(6), Article 29 (2007)
5. Christoff, I.: Testing equivalences and fully abstract models for probabilistic processes. In: Baeten, J.C.M., Klop, J.W. (eds.) CONCUR 1990. LNCS, vol. 458, pp. 126–140. Springer, Heidelberg (1990)
6. Cleaveland, R., Dayar, Z., Smolka, S.A., Yuen, S.: Testing preorders for probabilistic processes. Information and Computation 154(2), 93–148 (1999)
7. de Nicola, R., Hennessy, M.C.B.: Testing equivalences for processes. Theoretical Computer Science 34, 83–133 (1984)
8. Deng, Y., van Glabbeek, R., Hennessy, M., Morgan, C., Zhang, C.: Characterising testing preorders for finite probabilistic processes. In: 22nd Annual IEEE Symposium on Logic in Computer Science, LICS 2007, pp. 313–325. IEEE Computer Society Press, Los Alamitos (2007)
9. van Glabbeek, R.: The linear time-branching time spectrum II. In: Best, E. (ed.) CONCUR 1993. LNCS, vol. 715, pp. 66–81. Springer, Heidelberg (1993)
10. van Glabbeek, R.: The linear time-branching time spectrum I. The semantics of concrete, sequential processes. In: Bergstra, J.A., Ponse, A., Smolka, S.A. (eds.) Handbook of process algebra, ch. 1, North-Holland, Amsterdam (2001)
11. van Glabbeek, R., Smolka, S.A., Steffen, B.: Reactive, generative and stratified models of probabilistic processes. Information and Computation 121(1), 59–80 (1995)
12. Gregorio, C., Núñez, M.: Denotational semantics for probabilistic refusal testing. In: PROBMIV 1998. Electronic Notes in Theoretical Computer Science, vol. 22. Elsevier, Amsterdam (1999)
13. Hennessy, M.: Acceptance trees. Journal of the ACM 32(4), 896–928 (1985)
14. Hennessy, M.: An algebraic theory of fair asynchronous communicating processes. Theoretical Computer Science 49, 121–143 (1987)
15. Hennessy, M.: Algebraic Theory of Processes. MIT Press, Cambridge (1988)
16. Hoare, C.A.R.: Communicating Sequential Processes. Prentice-Hall, Englewood Cliffs (1985)
17. Huynh, D.T., Tian, L.: On some equivalence relations for probabilistic processes. Fundamenta Informaticae 17, 211–234 (1992)
18. Jonsson, B., Yi, W.: Compositional testing preorders for probabilistic processes. In: 10th IEEE Symposium on Logic In Computer Science, pp. 431–443. IEEE Computer Society Press, Los Alamitos (1995)
19. Jonsson, B., Yi, W.: Testing preorders for probabilistic processes can be characterized by simulations. Theoretical Computer Science 282, 33–51 (2002)
20. Jou, C.-C., Smolka, S.A.: Equivalences, congruences and complete axiomatizations for probabilistic processes. In: Baeten, J.C.M., Klop, J.W. (eds.) CONCUR 1990. LNCS, vol. 458, pp. 367–383. Springer, Heidelberg (1990)

21. Kwiatkowska, M., Norman, G.J.: A testing equivalence for reactive probabilistic processes. In: EXPRESS 1998. Electronic Notes in Theoretical Computer Science, vol. 16. Elsevier, Amsterdam (1998)

22. Larsen, K., Skou, A.: Bisimulation through probabilistic testing. Information and Computation 94(1), 1–28 (1991)

23. López, N., Núñez, M.: An overview of probabilistic process algebras and their equivalences. In: Baier, C., Haverkort, B.R., Hermanns, H., Katoen, J.-P., Siegle, M. (eds.) Validation of Stochastic Systems. LNCS, vol. 2925, pp. 89–123. Springer, Heidelberg (2004)

24. Milner, R.: Communication and Concurrency. Prentice-Hall, Englewood Cliffs (1989)

25. Milner, R.: Communicating and Mobile Systems: the π-Calculus. Cambridge University Press, Cambridge (1999)

26. Narayan Kumar, K., Cleaveland, R., Smolka, S.A.: Infinite probabilistic and nonprobabilistic testing. In: Arvind, V., Ramanujam, R. (eds.) FST TCS 1998. LNCS, vol. 1530, pp. 209–220. Springer, Heidelberg (1998)

27. Natarajan, V., Cleaveland, R.: Divergence and fair testing. In: Fülöp, Z., Gecseg, F. (eds.) ICALP 1995. LNCS, vol. 944, pp. 648–659. Springer, Heidelberg (1995)

28. Núñez, M.: Algebraic theory of probabilistic processes. Journal of Logic and Algebraic Programming 56(1–2), 117–177 (2003)

29. Núñez, M., de Frutos, D.: Testing semantics for probabilistic LOTOS. In: 8th IFIP WG6.1 Int. Conf. on Formal Description Techniques, FORTE 1995, pp. 365–380. Chapman & Hall, Boca Raton (1995)

30. Núñez, M., de Frutos, D., Llana, L.: Acceptance trees for probabilistic processes. In: Lee, I., Smolka, S.A. (eds.) CONCUR 1995. LNCS, vol. 962, pp. 249–263. Springer, Heidelberg (1995)

31. Núñez, M., Rupérez, D.: Fair testing through probabilistic testing. In: Formal Description Techniques for Distributed Systems and Communication Protocols (XII), and Protocol Specification, Testing, and Verification (XIX), pp. 135–150. Kluwer Academic Publishers, Dordrecht (1999)

32. Rensink, A., Vogler, W.: Fair testing. Information and Computation 205(2), 125–198 (2007)

33. Segala, R.: Testing probabilistic automata. In: Sassone, V., Montanari, U. (eds.) CONCUR 1996. LNCS, vol. 1119, pp. 299–314. Springer, Heidelberg (1996)

34. Stoelinga, M., Vaandrager, F.: A testing scenario for probabilistic automata. In: Baeten, J.C.M., Lenstra, J.K., Parrow, J., Woeginger, G.J. (eds.) ICALP 2003. LNCS, vol. 2719, pp. 464–477. Springer, Heidelberg (2003)

35. Yi, W., Larsen, K.G.: Testing probabilistic and nondeterministic processes. In: 12th IFIP/WG6.1 Int. Symposium on Protocol Specification, Testing and Verification, PSTV 1992, pp. 47–61. North-Holland, Amsterdam (1992)

Multiset Bisimulations as a Common Framework for Ordinary and Probabilistic Bisimulations[*]

David de Frutos Escrig, Miguel Palomino, and Ignacio Fábregas

Departamento de Sistemas Informáticos y Computación
Universidad Complutense de Madrid
{defrutos,miguelpt}@sip.ucm.es, fabregas@fdi.ucm.es

Abstract. Our concrete objective is to present both ordinary bisimulations and probabilistic bisimulations in a common coalgebraic framework based on multiset bisimulations. For that we show how to relate the underlying powerset and probabilistic distributions functors with the multiset functor by means of adequate natural transformations. This leads us to the general topic that we investigate in the paper: a natural transformation from a functor F to another G transforms F-bisimulations into G-bisimulations but, in general, it is not possible to express G-bisimulations in terms of F-bisimulations. However, they can be characterized by considering Hughes and Jacobs' notion of simulation, taking as the order on the functor F the equivalence induced by the epi-mono decomposition of the natural transformation relating F and G. We also consider the case of alternating probabilistic systems where non-deterministic and probabilistic choices are mixed, although only in a partial way, and extend all these results to categorical simulations.

1 Introduction

Bisimulations are the adequate way to capture behavioural indistinguishability of states of systems. Ordinary bisimulations were introduced [11] to cope with labelled transition systems and other similar models and have been used to define the formal observational semantics of many popular languages and formalisms, such as CCS. Bisimilarity is also the natural way to express equivalence of states in any system described by means of a coalgebra over an arbitrary functor F. The general categorical definition can be presented in a more concrete way for the class of polynomial functors, that are defined by means of a simple signature of constructors and whose properties, including the definition of relation lifting, can be studied by means of structural induction. In particular, the powerset constructor is one of them, and therefore the class of labelled transition systems can be studied as a simple and illustrative example of the categorical framework.

The simplicity and richness of the theory of bisimulations made it interesting to define several extensions in which the structure on the set of labels of

---

[*] Research supported by the Spanish projects DESAFIOS TIN2006-15660-C02-01, WEST TIN2006-15578-C02-01 and PROMESAS S-0505/TIC/0407.

K. Suzuki et al. (Eds.): FORTE 2008, LNCS 5048, pp. 283–298, 2008.

the considered systems was taken into account, instead of the plain approach made by simple (strong) bisimulations. For instance, weak bisimulation takes into account the existence of non-observable actions, while timed and probabilistic bisimulation introduce timed or probabilistic features. In particular, the original definition of probabilistic bisimulation for probabilistic transition systems had to capture the fact that one should be able to accumulate the probabilities of several transitions arriving at equivalent (bisimilar) states in order to simulate some transition or, conversely, that one should be able to distribute the probability of a transition among several others connecting the same states.

The classical definition by Larsen and Skou [9] certainly generalizes the definition of ordinary bisimulation in a nice way, although at the cost of leaving out the categorical scenario discussed above. However, Vink and Rutten proved in [17] that the definition can be reformulated in a coalgebraic way. For that, they considered a functor $\mathcal{D}$ defining probabilistic distributions, that appears as the primitive construction in the definition of the corresponding probabilistic systems. Even though this is quite an elegant characterization, it forces us to leave the realm of (probabilistic) transition systems, moving into the more abstract one of probabilistic distributions.

We would like to directly manage probabilistic transition systems in order to compare the results about ordinary transition systems and those on probabilistic systems as much as possible. We have found that multi-transition systems, where we can have several identical transitions and the number of times they appear matters, constitute the adequate framework to establish the relation between those two kinds of transition systems. As a matter of fact, we will see that the use of multisets instead of just plain sets leads us to a natural presentation of relation lifting for that construction; besides, we can add the corresponding functor to the collection defining polynomial functors, thus obtaining an enlarged class with nice properties similar to those in the original class.

Although a general theory combining non-deterministic and probabilistic choices seems quite hard to develop, since it is difficult to combine both functors in a smooth way [16], we will present the case of *alternating*[1] probabilistic systems. In those systems, the classical definitions of ordinary and probabilistic bisimulation can be combined to obtain the natural definition of alternating probabilistic bisimulation, that perfectly fits into our framework based on categorical simulations on our multi-transition systems.

The functors defining ordinary transition systems and probabilistic systems can be obtained by applying an adequate *natural transformation* to a functor defining multiset transition systems. In both cases bisimulations are preserved in both directions when applying those transformations. This leads us to the general theory that we investigate in this paper: as is well-known, any natural transformation between two functors F and G transforms F-bisimulations into G-bisimulations; in addition, and more interesting, whenever the natural transformation relating F

---

[1] Although we call alternating to our systems, we do not need the strict alternation between non-deterministic and probabilistic states as appears in [4], but only that these two kind of choices do not appear mixed after the same state.

and G is an epi, we can reflect G-bisimulations and express them at the level of the functor F, though this cannot be done in general just by means of F-bisimulations. However, they can be characterized by using Hughes and Jacobs' notion of simulation [6], when we consider as the order on the functor F the equivalence induced by the epi-mono decomposition of the natural transformation relating F and G. Once categorical simulations have come into play, it is nice to find that we can extend all our results to simulations based on any order. These extensions can be considered to be the main results in the paper, since all our previous results on bisimulations could be presented as particular cases of them, using the fact that bisimulations are a particular case of categorical simulations.

Although in a different direction, namely, that of exploring the relation between non-deterministic and probabilistic choices instead of the different notions of distributed bisimulations, in this paper we continue the work initiated in FORTE 2007 [3]. The goal is the exploration of ways in which the general theory of categorical bisimulations and simulations can be applied to obtain almost for free interesting results on concrete cases that, without the support of that general theory, would need different non-trivial proofs. Therefore, our work has a mixed flavour: on the one hand we develop new abstract results that extend the general theory; on the other hand we apply these results to simple but important concrete concepts, that therefore are proved to be particular cases of the rich general theory. These are only concrete examples that we hope to extend and generalize in the near future.

2   Basic Definitions

We review in this section standard material on coalgebras and bisimulations, as can be found for example in [8,12,7]. Besides, we introduce some notations on multisets and the corresponding functor $\mathcal{M}$, as well as for the functor $\mathcal{D}$ defining discrete probabilistic distributions.

An arbitrary endofunctor $F : \mathbf{Sets} \longrightarrow \mathbf{Sets}$ can be lifted to a functor in the category $\mathbf{Rel}$ of relations $\mathrm{Rel}(F) : \mathbf{Rel} \longrightarrow \mathbf{Rel}$. In set-theoretic terms, for a relation $R \subseteq X_1 \times X_2$,

$$\mathrm{Rel}(F)(R) = \{\langle u, v \rangle \in FX_1 \times FX_2 \mid \exists w \in F(R).\, F(r_1)(w) = u, F(r_2)(w) = v\}.$$

It is well-known that for polynomial functors F, $\mathrm{Rel}(F)$ can be equivalently defined by induction on the structure of F. Since we will be making extensive use of the powerset functor, we next present how the definition particularizes to it:

$$\begin{aligned}
\mathrm{Rel}(\mathcal{P}G)(R) = \{(U, V) \mid &\forall u \in U.\, \exists v \in V.\, \mathrm{Rel}(G)(R)(u, v) \wedge \\
&\forall v \in V.\, \exists u \in U.\, \mathrm{Rel}(G)(R)(u, v)\}.
\end{aligned}$$

Multisets will be represented by considering their characteristic function $\chi_M : X \longrightarrow \mathbb{N}$; similarly, discrete probabilistic distributions are represented by discrete measures $p_D : X \longrightarrow [0, 1]$, with $\sum_{x \in X} p_D(x) = 1$.

We will use along the paper several different ways to enumerate the "elements" of a multiset. We define the support of a multiset M as the set of elements that appear in it: $\{M\}_X = \{x \in X \mid \chi_M(x) > 0\}$. We are only interested in multisets having a finite support, so that in the following we will assume that every multiset is finite. Given a finite subset Y of X and an enumeration of its elements $\{y_1, \ldots y_m\}$, for each tuple of natural weights $\langle n_1, \ldots, n_m \rangle$ we will denote by $\sum_{y_i \in Y} n_i \cdot y_i$ the multiset M given by $\chi_M(y_i) = n_i$ and $\chi_M(y) = 0$ for $y \notin Y$. By abuse of notation we will sometimes consider sets as a particular case of multisets, by taking for each finite set $Y = \{y_1, \ldots y_n\}$ the canonical associated multiset $\sum_{y_i \in Y} 1 \cdot y_i$. Finally, we also enumerate the elements of a multiset by means of a generating function: given a finite set I and $x : I \longrightarrow X$, we denote by $\{x_i \mid i \in I\}$ the multiset M_I given by $\chi_{M_I}(y) = |\{i \in I \mid x_i = y\}|$. Note that in this case sets are just the multisets generated by an injective generating function.

We will denote by $\mathcal{M}(X)$ the set of multisets on X, while $\mathcal{D}(X)$ represents the set of probabilistic distributions on X. Both constructions can be naturally extended to functions, thus getting the desired functors: for $f : X \longrightarrow Y$ we define $\mathcal{M}(f) : \mathcal{M}(X) \longrightarrow \mathcal{M}(Y)$ by $\mathcal{M}(f)(\chi)(y) = \sum_{f(x)=y} \chi(x)$, and $\mathcal{D}(f) : \mathcal{D}(X) \longrightarrow \mathcal{D}(Y)$ by $\mathcal{D}(f)(p)(y) = \sum_{f(x)=y} p(x)$.

Although the multiset and the probabilistic distributions functors are not polynomial, this class can be enlarged by incorporating them since their liftings can be defined with the following equations:

$$\mathrm{Rel}(\mathcal{M}G)(R) = \{(M, N) \mid \exists f : I \longrightarrow GX, g : I \longrightarrow GY, \text{generating functions of} \\ M \text{ and } N \text{ s.t. } \forall i \in I. (f(i), g(i)) \in \mathrm{Rel}(G)(R)\};$$

$$\mathrm{Rel}(\mathcal{D}G)(R) = \{(d^x, d^y) \in \mathcal{D}(G(X)) \times \mathcal{D}(G(Y)) \mid \forall U \subseteq G(X). \forall V \subseteq G(Y). \\ \Pi_1^{-1}(U) = \Pi_2^{-1}(V) \Rightarrow \sum_{x \in U} d^x(x) = \sum_{y \in V} d^y(y)\},$$

where Π_1 and Π_2 are the projections of $\mathrm{Rel}(G)(R)$ into GX and GY, respectively.

F-coalgebras are just functions $\alpha : X \longrightarrow FX$. For instance, plain labelled transition systems arise as coalgebras for the functor $\mathcal{P}(A \times X)$. We will also consider multitransition systems, which correspond to the functor $\mathcal{M}(A \times X)$, and probabilistic transition systems, corresponding to $\mathcal{M}_1([0,1] \times A \times X)$, where we only allow multisets in which the sum of its associated probabilities is 1.

Then, the lifting of the functor $\mathcal{M}_1([0,1] \times \cdot)$ is defined as a particular case of that of $\mathcal{M}$ by:

$$\mathrm{Rel}(\mathcal{M}_1([0,1] \times \cdot)G)(R) = \\ \{(M, N) \in \mathcal{M}_1([0,1] \times GX) \times \mathcal{M}_1([0,1] \times GY) \mid \\ \exists f : I \to [0,1] \times GX, g : I \to [0,1] \times GY, \text{generating functions of } M \text{ and} \\ N \text{ s.t. } \forall i \in I. \Pi_1(f(i)) = \Pi_1(g(i)) \wedge (\Pi_2(f(i)), \Pi_2(g(i))) \in \mathrm{Rel}(G)(R)\}.$$

A bisimulation for coalgebras $c : X \longrightarrow FX$ and $d : Y \longrightarrow FY$ is a relation $R \subseteq X \times Y$ which is "closed under c and d": if $(x, y) \in R$ then $(c(x), d(y)) \in \mathrm{Rel}(F)(R)$. We shall use the term F-bisimulation sometimes to emphasize the functor we are working with.

Bisimulations can also be characterized by means of spans, using the general categorical definition by Aczel and Mendler [1]:

$$\begin{array}{ccccc}
X & \xleftarrow{\;r_1\;} & R & \xrightarrow{\;r_2\;} & Y \\
\downarrow{\scriptstyle c} & & \downarrow{\scriptstyle e} & & \downarrow{\scriptstyle d} \\
FX & \xleftarrow{\;Fr_1\;} & FR & \xrightarrow{\;Fr_2\;} & FY
\end{array}$$

R is a bisimulation iff it is the carrier of some coalgebra e making the above diagram commute, where the r_i are the projections of R into X and Y.

We will also need the general concept of simulation introduced by Hughes and Jacobs [6] using orders on functors. Let $F : \mathbf{Sets} \longrightarrow \mathbf{Sets}$ be a functor. An order on F is defined by means of a functorial collection of preorders $\sqsubseteq_X \subseteq FX \times FX$ that must be preserved by renaming: for every $f : X \longrightarrow Y$, if $u \sqsubseteq_X u'$ then $Ff(u) \sqsubseteq_Y Ff(u')$.

Given an order $\sqsubseteq$ on F, a $\sqsubseteq$-simulation for coalgebras $c : X \longrightarrow FX$ and $d : Y \longrightarrow FY$ is a relation $R \subseteq X \times Y$ such that

$$\text{if } (x, y) \in R \text{ then } (c(x), d(y)) \in \mathrm{Rel}(F)_{\sqsubseteq}(R),$$

where $\mathrm{Rel}(F)_{\sqsubseteq}(R)$ is $\sqsubseteq \circ \mathrm{Rel}(F)(R) \circ \sqsubseteq$, which can be expanded to

$$\mathrm{Rel}(F)_{\sqsubseteq}(R) = \{(u, v) \mid \exists w \in F(\mathcal{R}). \; u \sqsubseteq Fr_1(w) \wedge Fr_2(w) \sqsubseteq v\}.$$

One of the cases under this general notion of coalgebraic simulation is that of ordinary simulation. Also, equivalence (functorial) relations, represented by $\equiv$, are a particular class of orders on F, thus generating the corresponding class of $\equiv$-simulations. As is the case for ordinary bisimulations, $\equiv$-simulations themselves need not be equivalence relations, but once we impose to the equivalence $\equiv$ the technical condition of being stable [6] then the induced notion of $\equiv$-similarity becomes an equivalence itself.

Proposition 1. *For any stable functorial equivalence relation $\equiv_X \subseteq FX \times FX$, the induced notion of $\equiv_a$-similarity relating elements of X for a coalgebra $a : X \longrightarrow FX$ is an equivalence relation. In particular, for the plain equality relation $=_X \subseteq FX \times FX$, $=_X$-similarity coincides with plain F-bisimulation.*

3   Natural Transformations and Bisimulations

Natural transformations are the natural way to relate two functors. Given F and G, two functors on $\mathbf{Sets}$, a natural transformation $\alpha : F \Rightarrow G$ is defined as a family of functions $\alpha_X : FX \to GX$ such that, for all $f : X \longrightarrow Y$, $Gf \circ \alpha_X = \alpha_Y \circ Ff$. We are particularly interested in the natural transformations relating $\mathcal{M}$ and $\mathcal{P}$, and those between the functors defining probabilistic transition systems and probabilistic distributions. For the sake of conciseness we will often omit the action component A when working with these functors; this does not affect the validity of the definitions nor the results.

Proposition 2. *The support of multisets,* $\{\cdot\}_X : \mathcal{M}(X) \longrightarrow \mathcal{P}(X)$, *gives rise to a natural transformation* $\{\cdot\} : \mathcal{M} \Rightarrow \mathcal{P}$.
Similarly, $\mathcal{D}_{M_X} : \mathcal{M}_1([0,1] \times X) \longrightarrow \mathcal{D}(X)$ *given by*

$$\mathcal{D}_M(\sum n_i \cdot (p_i, x_i))(x) = \sum_{x_i = x} n_i p_i$$

induces a natural transformation $\mathcal{D}_M : \mathcal{M}_1([0,1] \times \cdot) \Rightarrow \mathcal{D}(\cdot)$.

Proof. Let $f : X \longrightarrow Y$. We have $(\mathcal{P}f \circ \{\cdot\}_X)(\sum n_i \cdot x_i) = \mathcal{P}f(\{x_i\}) = \{f(x_i)\} = \{\cdot\}_Y(\sum n_i \cdot f(x_i)) = (\{\cdot\}_Y \circ \mathcal{M}f)(\sum n_i \cdot x_i)$, which proves that $\{\cdot\}$ is a natural transformation.

In the case of $\mathcal{D}_M$: $(\mathcal{D}f \circ \mathcal{D}_{M_X})(\sum n_i \cdot (p_i, x_i)) = \mathcal{D}f(\sum n_i p_i \cdot x_i)$, which is $\sum_{f(x_i) = y} n_i p_i \cdot y = \mathcal{D}_{M_Y}(\sum n_i \cdot (p_i, f(x_i))) = (\mathcal{D}_{M_Y} \circ \mathcal{M}_1 f)(\sum n_i \cdot (p_i, x_i))$; this proves that $\mathcal{D}_M$ is a natural transformation. □

Probabilistic transition systems were defined in [9] as $\mathcal{P} = (Pr, Act, Can, \mu)$, where Pr is a set of processes, Act the set of actions, $Can : Pr \longrightarrow \mathcal{P}(Act)$ indicates the initial offer of each process, and $\mu_{p,a} \in \mathcal{D}(Pr)$ for all $p \in Pr$, $a \in Can(p)$. Under this definition we cannot talk about "different probabilistic transitions" reaching the same process, that is, whenever we have a transition $p \xrightarrow{a}_\mu p'$ it "accumulates" all possible ways to go from p to p' executing a.

In our opinion this is not a purely operational way to present probabilistic systems. For instance, if we are defining the operational semantics of a process such as $p = \frac{1}{2}a + \frac{1}{2}a$, then we would intuitively have two different transitions reaching the same final state *stop*, but if we were using Larsen and Skou's original definition, we should mix them both into a single $p \xrightarrow{a}_1 stop$. Certainly, we could keep these two transitions separated under that definition if, for some reason, we decided to introduce in the set Pr two different states $stop_1$ and $stop_2$, thus obtaining $p \xrightarrow{a}_{1/2} stop_1$ and $p \xrightarrow{a}_{1/2} stop_2$. But then we observe that whether our model captures or not the existence of two different transitions depends on the way we define our set of processes Pr.

In order to get a more natural operational representation of probabilistic systems we define them[2] as $\mathcal{M}_1([0,1] \times A \times \cdot)$-coalgebras. Once we use "ordinary" transitions labelled by pairs (q, a) to represent the probabilistic transitions we have no problem to distinguish two "different" transitions $p \xrightarrow{a}_{q'} p'$, $p \xrightarrow{a}_{q''} p''$, if $p' \neq p''$. However, in such a case it would not be adequate to treat the case $p' = p''$ in a different way. This is why we use $\mathcal{M}_1$ instead of $\mathcal{P}_1$ to define our probabilistic multi-transition systems (abbreviated as pmts).

We can easily translate the classical definition of probabilistic bisimulation between probabilistic transition systems in [9], to our own pmts's as follows.

---

[2] Although Larsen and Skou defined their systems following the reactive aproach [4], and therefore the sum of their probabilities is 1 for each action a, we prefer to follow in this paper the generative aproach, so that the total addition of all the probabilities is 1. This is done to simplify the notation, since all the results in this paper are equally valid for the reactive model.

Definition 1. *A probabilistic bisimulation on a coalgebra $p : X \rightarrow \mathcal{M}_1([0, 1] \times A \times X)$ is an equivalence relation $\equiv_p$ on X such that, whenever $x_1 \equiv_p x_2$, taking $p(x_i) = \sum t_j^i \cdot (p_j^i, a_j^i, x_j^i)$, we also have $\sum\{t_j^1 \cdot p_j^1 \mid a_j^1 = a, x_j^1 \in E\} = \sum\{t_j^2 \cdot p_j^2 \mid a_j^2 = a, x_j^2 \in E\}$, for all $a \in A$ and every equivalence class E in $X/\equiv_p$.*

In [17] it is proved that probabilistic bisimilarity defined by probabilistic bisimulations coincides with categorical $\mathcal{D}$-bisimilarity. By applying the functor $\mathcal{D}_M$ we can transform our pmts's into their presentation as Larsen and Skou's pts's. Then it is trivial to check that the corresponding notions of probabilistc bisimulation coincide, and therefore they also coincide with categorical $\mathcal{D}$-bisimilarity.

However, that is clearly not the case for plain categorical $\mathcal{M}_1([0, 1] \times A \times \cdot)$-bisimulations. This is so because when we consider the functor $\mathcal{M}_1([0, 1] \times A \times \cdot)$, probabilistic transitions are considered as plain transitions labelled with pairs over $[0, 1] \times A$, whose first component has no special meaning. As a result, we have, for instance, no bisimulation relating x and y if we consider $X = \{x\}$, $Y = \{y\}$, $p_a : X \rightarrow \mathcal{M}_1([0, 1] \times A \times X)$ with $p_a(x) = 1 \cdot (1, a, x)$ and $p_b : Y \rightarrow \mathcal{M}_1([0, 1] \times A \times Y)$ with $p_b(y) = 2 \cdot (\frac{1}{2}, a, y)$.

All these facts prove that our probabilistic multi-transition systems are too concrete a representation of probabilistic distributions, which is formally captured by the fact that the components of the natural transformation $\mathcal{D}_M$ are not injective. As a consequence, by using them we do not have a pure coalgebraic characterization of probabilistic bisimulations. By contrast, the original definition of pts's stands apart from the operational way, mixing different transitions into a single distribution. Besides it has to consider the quotient set $X/\equiv_p$ when defining probabilistic bisimulations. Our goal will be to obtain a characterization of the notion of probabilistic bisimilarity in terms of our pmts's, and this will be done using the notion of categorical simulation, as we will see in Section 4. Next, we present a collection of general interesting results. First we will see that bisimulations are preserved by natural transformations.

Theorem 1 ([12]). *If $R \subseteq X \times Y$ is a bisimulation relating $a : X \longrightarrow FX$ and $b : Y \longrightarrow FY$, then R is also a bisimulation relating $a' : X \longrightarrow GX$, given by $a' = \alpha_X \circ a$, and $b' : Y \longrightarrow GY$, given by $b' = \alpha_Y \circ b$.*

Corollary 1. *For a and $a' = \alpha_X \circ a$, bisimulation equivalence in a is included in bisimulation equivalence in a', that is, $x_1 \equiv_a x_2$ implies $x_1 \equiv_{a'} x_2$.*

A general converse result cannot be expected because in general there is no canonical way to transform G into F. Since the main objective in this paper is to relate $\mathcal{M}$-bisimulations with $\mathcal{P}$ and $\mathcal{D}$-bisimulations, we searched for particular properties of the natural transformations relating these functors which could help us to get the desired general results covering in particular these two cases. This is how we have obtained the concept of quotient functors that we develop in the following.

Definition 2. *Let F be an endofunctor on* **Sets** *and $\equiv$ a functorial equivalence relation $\equiv_X \subseteq FX \times FX$. We define the* quotient functor $F/\equiv$ *by $(F/\equiv)(X) = FX/\equiv_X$, and for any $f : X \longrightarrow Y$, $u \in FX$, and $\bar{u}$ its equivalence class, $(F/\equiv)(f)(\bar{u}) = \overline{F(f)(u)}$, that is well defined since $\equiv$ is functorial.*

Definition 3. *1. We say that a functor G is the* quotient *of F under a functorial equivalence relation $\equiv$ whenever $F/\equiv$ and G are isomorphic, which means that there is a pair of natural transformations $\alpha : F/\equiv \Rightarrow G$ and $\beta : G \Rightarrow F/\equiv$ such that $\beta \circ \alpha = Id_{F/\equiv}$ and $\alpha \circ \beta = Id_G$.*
2. Given a natural transformation $\alpha : F \Rightarrow G$, we write $\equiv^\alpha$ for the family of equivalence relations $\equiv^\alpha_X \subseteq FX \times FX$ defined by the kernel of α: $u_1 \equiv^\alpha_X u_2 \iff \alpha_X(u_1) = \alpha_X(u_2)$.

Proposition 3. *For every natural transformation $\alpha : F \Rightarrow G$, $\equiv^\alpha$ is functorial.*

Proof. We need to show that, for any $f : X \longrightarrow Y$, whenever $u_1 \equiv^\alpha_X u_2$, that is, $\alpha_X(u_1) = \alpha_X(u_2)$, we also have $Ff(u_1) \equiv^\alpha_Y Ff(u_2)$, that is $\alpha_Y(F(f)(u_1)) = \alpha_Y(F(f)(u_2))$; this follows because $\alpha_Y \circ F(f) = G(f) \circ \alpha_X$.   □

If every component α_X of a natural transformation is surjective, α is said to be epi.

Proposition 4. *Whenever α is epi, G is the quotient of F under $\equiv^\alpha$, just considering the inverse natural transformation $\alpha^{-1} : G \Rightarrow F/\equiv$ given by $\alpha_X^{-1} : G(X) \longrightarrow (F/\equiv^\alpha)(X)$ with $\alpha_X^{-1}(v) = \bar{u}$ where $\alpha_X(u) = v$.*

Corollary 2. *$\mathcal{P}$ is the quotient of $\mathcal{M}$ under the kernel of the natural transformation $\{\cdot\} : \mathcal{M} \Rightarrow \mathcal{P}$.*

Corollary 3. *$\mathcal{D}$ is the quotient of $\mathcal{M}_1([0,1] \times \cdot)$ under the kernel of the natural transformation $\mathcal{D}_\mathcal{M} : \mathcal{M}_1([0,1] \times \cdot) \Rightarrow \mathcal{D}$.*

4 $\equiv^\alpha$-simulations Through Quotients of Bisimulations

Let us start by studying the relationships between coalgebras corresponding to functors related by an epi natural transformation.

Definition 4. *Let $\alpha : F \Rightarrow G$ be a natural transformation and $a : X \longrightarrow FX$ an F-coalgebra. We define the α-image of a as the coalgebra $a_\alpha : X \longrightarrow GX$ given by $a_\alpha = \alpha_X \circ a$.*

Definition 5. *Given a natural transformation $\alpha : F \Rightarrow G$ and a G-coalgebra $b : X \longrightarrow GX$, we say that $a : X \longrightarrow FX$ is a concrete F-representation of b iff $b = \alpha_X \circ a$.*

The following result follows immediately from the previous definitions.

Proposition 5. *If α is epi then every G-coalgebra has an F-representation.*

Next we relate G-bisimulations with $\equiv^\alpha$-simulations:

Theorem 2. *Let $\alpha : F \Rightarrow G$ be an epi natural transformation and $b_1 : X_1 \longrightarrow GX_1$, $b_2 : X_2 \longrightarrow GX_2$ two G-coalgebras, with concrete F-representations $a_1 : X_1 \longrightarrow FX_1$ and $a_2 : X_2 \longrightarrow FX_2$. Then, the G-bisimulations relating b_1 and b_2 are precisely the $\equiv^\alpha$-simulations relating a_1 and a_2.*

Proof. Let us show[3] that, for every relation $R \subseteq X_1 \times X_2$,

$$\mathrm{Rel}(F)_{\equiv^\alpha}(R) = \{(u,v) \in FX_1 \times FX_2 \mid (\alpha_{X_1}(u), \alpha_{X_2}(v)) \in \mathrm{Rel}(G)(R)\}.$$

We have, unfolding the definition of $\mathrm{Rel}(F)_{\equiv^\alpha}(R)$ and using the fact that α is a natural transformation:

$$
\begin{aligned}
\mathrm{Rel}(F)_{\equiv^\alpha}(R) &= \{(u,v) \in FX_1 \times FX_2 \mid \exists w \in FR.\, u \equiv^\alpha Fr_1(w) \wedge Fr_2(w) \equiv^\alpha v\} \\
&= \{(u,v) \in FX_1 \times FX_2 \mid \exists w \in FR.\, \alpha_{X_1}(u) = \alpha_{X_1}(Fr_1(w)) \wedge \\
&\qquad\qquad\qquad\qquad\qquad\qquad\qquad \alpha_{X_2}(v) = \alpha_{X_2}(Fr_2(w))\} \\
&= \{(u,v) \in FX_1 \times FX_2 \mid \exists w \in FR.\, \alpha_{X_1}(u) = Gr_1(\alpha_R(w)) \wedge \\
&\qquad\qquad\qquad\qquad\qquad\qquad\qquad \alpha_{X_2}(v) = Gr_2(\alpha_R(w))\}.
\end{aligned}
$$

On the other hand,

$$\mathrm{Rel}(G)(R) = \{(x,y) \in GX_1 \times GX_2 \mid \exists z \in GR.\, Gr_1(z) = x \wedge Gr_2(z) = y\}.$$

Now, if $(u,v) \in \mathrm{Rel}(F)_{\equiv^\alpha}(R)$, by taking $\alpha_R(w)$ as the value of $z \in GR$ we have that $(\alpha_{X_1}(u), \alpha_{X_2}(v)) \in \mathrm{Rel}(G)(R)$. Conversely, if $(\alpha_{X_1}(u), \alpha_{X_2}(v)) \in \mathrm{Rel}(G)(R)$ is witnessed by z, let $w \in FR$ be such that $\alpha_R(w) = z$, which must exists because α is epi; it follows that $(u,v) \in \mathrm{Rel}(F)_{\equiv^\alpha}(R)$.

Then, $(b_1(x), b_2(y)) \in \mathrm{Rel}(G)(R)$ if and only if $(a_1(x), a_2(x)) \in \mathrm{Rel}(F)_{\equiv^\alpha}(R)$, from where it follows that R is a G-bisimulation if and only if it is a $\equiv^\alpha$-simulation. $\square$

Corollary 4. *(i) Bisimulations between labelled transition systems are $\equiv^{\{\cdot\}}$-simulations between multi-transition systems. (ii) Bisimulations between probabilistic systems are just $\equiv^{\mathcal{D}M}$-simulations between (an appropriate class of) multi-transition systems.*

Example 1. Let us illustrate this result by means of some simple examples using the natural transformation $\{\cdot\} : \mathcal{M} \to \mathcal{P}$.

1. If we consider the ordinary transition systems $s_X : \{x, x'\} \longrightarrow \mathcal{P}(\{x, x'\})$, with $s_X(x) = \{x'\}$, $s_X(x') = \emptyset$, and $s_Y : \{y, y_1', y_2'\} \longrightarrow \mathcal{P}(\{y, y_1', y_2'\})$ with $s_Y(y) = \{y_1', y_2'\}$, $s_Y(y_1') = \emptyset$, and $s_Y(y_2') = \emptyset$, we have a simple $\mathcal{P}$-bisimulation relating the initial states x and y, given by $R = \{(x, y), (x', y_1'), (x', y_2')\}$.

---

[3] It is not difficult to present this proof as a commutative diagram. Then one has to check that all the "small squares" in the diagram are indeed commutative, in order to be able to conclude commutativity of the full diagram. This is what we have carefully done in our proof above.

Denoting by s_X^1 and s_Y^1 the canonical $\mathcal{M}$-representations of s_X and s_Y, obtained by the embedding of sets into multisets, it is obvious that there is no $\mathcal{M}$-bisimulation relating x and y. But if we consider $s_X^2(x) = \{2 \cdot x'\}$, $s_X^2(x') = \emptyset$, we have now an $\mathcal{M}$-bisimulation between the multi-transition systems s_X^2 and s_Y^1 relating x and y. And, by Theorem 2, we have that s_X^1 is also $\equiv^{\{\cdot\}}$-simulated by s_Y^1, since $\{s_X^1\}_{\mathcal{M}} = \{s_X^2\}_{\mathcal{M}} = s_X$ and s_X and s_Y are $\mathcal{P}$-bisimilar. Obviously, the same happens for any $\{\cdot\}$-representation of s_X, s_X^k with $s_X^k = \{k \cdot x'\}$ and $s_X^k(x') = \emptyset$.

2. In the example above we got the $\equiv^{\{\cdot\}}$-simulation by proving that there are $\mathcal{M}$-representations of the considered coalgebras for which the given relation is also an $\mathcal{M}$-bisimulation. However, this is not necessary as the following shows. Let us consider $t_X : \{x\} \longrightarrow \mathcal{P}(\{x\})$ with $t_X(x) = \{x\}$ and $Y = \{\beta \mid \beta \in \mathbb{N}^*, \beta_i \leq i\}$ with $t_Y(\beta) = \{\beta \circ \langle j \rangle \mid \beta \circ \langle j \rangle \in Y\}$. It is clear that $R = \{(x, \beta) \mid \beta \in Y\}$ is the (only) $\mathcal{P}$-bisimulation relating x and ϵ, the initial states of t_X and t_Y. However, in this case there exists no $\mathcal{M}$-bisimulation relating two $\mathcal{M}$-representations of t_X and t_Y, because $|t_Y(\beta)| = |\beta| + 1$ and therefore we would need a representation t_X^k with $t_X^k(x) = \{k \cdot x\}$ such that $k \geq l$ for all $l \in \mathbb{N}$, which is not possible because the definition of multiset does not allow the infinite repetition of any of its members. Instead, Theorem 2 shows that any two $\mathcal{M}$-representations of t_X and t_Y are $\equiv^{\{\cdot\}}$-similar.

The reason why we had an $\mathcal{M}$-bisimulation relating the appropriate $\mathcal{M}$-representations of the compared $\mathcal{P}$-coalgebras in our first example was because we were under the hypothesis of the following proposition.

Proposition 6. *Let $\alpha : F \Rightarrow G$ be an epi natural transformation. Whenever a G-bisimulation R relating $b_1 : X \longrightarrow GX$ and $b_2 : Y \longrightarrow GY$ is near injective, which means that $|\{b_2(y) \mid (x, y) \in R\}| \leq 1$ for all $x \in X$ and $|\{b_1(x) \mid (x, y) \in R\}| \leq 1$ for all $y \in Y$, there exist some F-representations of b_1 and b_2, $a_1 : X \longrightarrow FX$ and $a_2 : Y \longrightarrow FY$, respectively, such that R is also a bisimulation relating a_1 and a_2.*

Proof. By Theorem 2, R is also a $\equiv^\alpha$-simulation for any pair of F-representations of b_1 and b_2; let a_1, a_2 be any such pair. Then, for all $(x, y) \in R$ we have $(a_1(x), a_2(y)) \in (\equiv^\alpha \circ \mathrm{Rel}(F) \circ \equiv^\alpha)(R)$, and hence there exist $a_1'(x, y) \in FX$, $a_2'(x, y) \in FY$ such that

$$a_1(x) \equiv^\alpha a_1'(x, y), \quad a_2'(x, y) \equiv^\alpha a_2(y) \quad \text{and} \quad (a_1'(x, y), a_2'(x, y)) \in \mathrm{Rel}(F)(R).$$

We now define an equivalence relation $\equiv$ on R by considering the transitive closure of:

- $(x, y_1) \equiv (x, y_2)$ for all $(x, y_1), (x, y_2) \in R$.
- $(x_1, y) \equiv (x_2, y)$ for all $(x_1, y), (x_2, y) \in R$.

Since R is near injective, it follows that if $(x_1, y_1) \equiv (x_2, y_2)$ then $b_1(x_1) = b_1(x_2)$ and $b_2(y_1) = b_2(y_2)$, and thus $a_1'(x_1, y_1) \equiv^\alpha a_1'(x_2, y_2)$ and $a_2'(x_1, y_1) \equiv^\alpha a_2'(x_2, y_2)$.

We consider $R/\equiv$ and for each equivalence class of the quotient set we choose a canonical representative $\overline{(x,y)}$. Obviously we have that $(x,y_1),(x,y_2) \in R$ implies $\overline{(x,y_1)} = \overline{(x,y_2)}$ and that $(x_1,y),(x_2,y) \in R$ implies $\overline{(x_1,y)} = \overline{(x_2,y)}$.

Let us now define two coalgebras $a_1' : X \longrightarrow FX$ and $a_2' : Y \longrightarrow FY$ as follows:

- If there exists some y such that $(x,y) \in R$ we take $a_1'(x) = a_1'\overline{(x,y)}$ for any such y; otherwise, we define $a_1'(x)$ as $a_1(x)$.
- If there exists some x such that $(x,y) \in R$ we take $a_2'(y) = a_2'\overline{(x,y)}$ for any such x; otherwise, $a_2'(y)$ is $a_2(y)$.

With the above definitions,

$$a_1'(x) = a_1'\overline{(x,y)} \equiv^\alpha a_1'(x,y) \equiv^\alpha a_1(x),$$

and similarly $a_2'(y) \equiv^\alpha a_2(y)$, so that a_1', a_2' are F-representations of b_1 and b_2. Besides,

$$\text{if } (x,y) \in R \text{ then } (a_1'(x), a_2'(y)) \in \text{Rel}(F)(R)$$

and R is an F-bisimulation relating them.   □

Let us conclude this illustration of our main theorem by explaining why we needed an infinite coalgebra to get a counterexample of the result between bisimulations relating G-coalgebras and those relating their F-representations. As a matter of fact, in the case of the multiset and the powerset functors we could prove the result in Proposition 6 not only for near injective bisimulations but for any relation where no element is related with infinitely many others. However, we will not prove this fact here since it does not seem to generalize to arbitrary natural transformations relating two functors.

Example 2. Next we present an example for the natural transformation $\mathcal{D}_M :$ $\mathcal{M}_1([0,1] \times X) \Rightarrow \mathcal{D}(X)$. If we consider the two probabilistic transition systems s_X and s_Y given by their multisets of probabilistic transitions: $s_X = \{(\frac{1}{2}, x, x_1'), (\frac{1}{2}, x, x_2')\}$, $s_Y = \{(\frac{1}{3}, y, y_1'), (\frac{1}{3}, y, y_2'), (\frac{1}{3}, y, y_3')\}$, where each triple (p, x, x') represents the probabilistic transition $x \xrightarrow{p} x'$, we have the following $\mathcal{D}$-bisimulation relating the initial states x and y: $R = \{(x,y)\} \cup \{(x_i', y_j') \mid i = 1,2, j = 1,2,3\}$. It is easy to see that for the two $\mathcal{M}_1$-representations $s_X^3 = \{3 \cdot (\frac{1}{6}, x, x_1'), 3 \cdot (\frac{1}{6}, x, x_2')\}$ and $s_Y^2 = \{2 \cdot (\frac{1}{6}, y, y_1'), 2 \cdot (\frac{1}{6}, y, y_2'), 2 \cdot (\frac{1}{6}, y, y_3')\}$, R is also an $\mathcal{M}_1$-bisimulation between them, using the facts that $(x_1', y_1') \in R$, $(x_2', y_2') \in R$ and $(x_1', y_3') \in R$, $(x_2', y_3') \in R$. From this result we immediately conclude that any two $\mathcal{M}_1$-representations of s_X and s_Y are $\equiv^{\mathcal{D}_M}$-similar.

5   Natural Transformations and Simulations

In this section we will see that all our results about bisimulations in the previous sections can be extended to categorical simulations defined by means of an order on the corresponding functors. Therefore, our first result concerns the preservation of functorial orders by means of natural transformations.

Definition 6. *Given a natural transformation* $\alpha : F \Rightarrow G$ *and* $\sqsubseteq_G$ *an order on* G, *we define the induced order* $\sqsubseteq_G^{\alpha-}$ *on* F *by:* $x \sqsubseteq_G^{\alpha-} x' \iff \alpha_X(x) \sqsubseteq_G \alpha_X(x')$.

It is immediate that $\sqsubseteq_G^{\alpha-}$ is indeed an order on F; given $f : X \longrightarrow Y$ and $x, x' \in X$:

$$x \sqsubseteq_G^{\alpha-} x' \iff \alpha_X(x) \sqsubseteq_G \alpha_X(x')$$
$$\implies Gf(\alpha_X(x)) \sqsubseteq_G Gf(\alpha_X(x'))$$
$$\iff \alpha_Y(Ff(x)) \sqsubseteq_G \alpha_Y(Ff(x'))$$
$$\iff Ff(x) \sqsubseteq_G^{\alpha-} Ff(x'),$$

where the implication follows because $\sqsubseteq_G$ is functorial.

Example 3. Taking $\{\cdot\} : \mathcal{M} \Rightarrow \mathcal{P}$ and $\sqsubseteq_{\mathcal{P}} = \subseteq$, then the induced order $\sqsubseteq_{\mathcal{P}}^{\{\cdot\}-}$ on $\mathcal{M}$ is defined as $u \sqsubseteq_{\mathcal{P}}^{\{\cdot\}-} v$ iff $\{u\} \subseteq \{v\}$: that is, it coincides with multiset inclusion.

Another example corresponds to the equality relation on G.

Proposition 7. *The induced order* $=_G^{\alpha-}$ *on* F *is just the relation* $\equiv^\alpha$.

Proof. The definition of $\equiv^\alpha$ is just the particular case of our definition of $\sqsubseteq_G^{\alpha-}$ for the equality relation on G as an order on it. $\square$

Orders on F can be also translated to G through a natural transformation $\alpha : F \Rightarrow G$.

Definition 7. *Given a natural transformation* $\alpha : F \Rightarrow G$ *and* $\sqsubseteq_F$ *an order on* F, *we define the projected order* $\sqsubseteq_F^\alpha$ *on* G *as the transitive closure of the relation* $x \sqsubseteq_F^\alpha x'$, *which holds if:*

there exist x_1, x_1' *such that* $x = \alpha_X(x_1)$, $x' = \alpha_X(x_1')$ *and* $x_1 \sqsubseteq_F x_1'$, *or* $x = x'$.

We need to add the last condition in the definition above in order to cover the case in which α is not an epi. Obviously, we can remove it whenever α is indeed an epi, and in the following we will see that we only need that condition in order to guarantee reflexivity of $\sqsubseteq_F^\alpha$ in the whole of GX, because all of our results concerning this order will be based on its restriction to the images of the components of the natural transformation α_X.

Again, it is easy to prove that $\sqsubseteq_F^\alpha$ is indeed an order on G. By definition, it is reflexive and transitive. It is also functorial: given $f : X \longrightarrow Y$ and $x \sqsubseteq_F^\alpha x'$, with $x = \alpha_X(x_1)$ and $x' = \alpha(x_1')$ such that $x_1 \sqsubseteq_F x_1'$, we need to show $Gf(x) \sqsubseteq_F^\alpha Gf(x')$. Since $Gf(x) = Gf(\alpha(x_1)) = \alpha(Ff(x_1))$, $Gf(x') = Gf(\alpha(x_1')) = \alpha(Ff(x_1'))$, and $Ff(x_1) \sqsubseteq_F Ff(x_1')$, the result follows by the definition of $\sqsubseteq_F^\alpha$.

Theorem 3 (Simulations are preserved by natural transformations). *If* $R \subseteq X \times Y$ *is a* $\sqsubseteq_F$-*simulation relating* $a : X \longrightarrow FX$ *and* $b : Y \longrightarrow FY$, *and* $\alpha : F \Rightarrow G$ *is a natural transformation, then* R *is also a* $\sqsubseteq_F^\alpha$-*simulation relating* $a' = \alpha_X \circ a$ *and* $b' = \alpha_Y \circ b$.

Proof. Let $(x, y) \in R$: we need to show that $(a'(x), b'(y)) \in \mathrm{Rel}(G)_{\sqsubseteq_F^\alpha}(R)$. Since R is a $\sqsubseteq_F$-simulation, $(a(x), b(x)) \in \mathrm{Rel}(F)_{\sqsubseteq_F}(R)$. This means that there exists $w \in FR$ such that $a(x) \sqsubseteq_F Fr_1(w)$ and $Fr_2(w) \sqsubseteq_F b(x)$, and hence that there exists $z = \alpha_R(w) \in GR$ such that $a'(x) \sqsubseteq_F^\alpha \alpha_X(Fr_1(w)) = Gr_1(z)$ and $Gr_2(z) = \alpha_Y(Fr_2(w)) \sqsubseteq_F^\alpha b'(x)$; therefore, $(a'(x), b'(x)) \in \mathrm{Rel}(G)_{\sqsubseteq_F^\alpha}(R)$. $\square$

As said before, bisimulations are just the particular case of simulations corresponding to the equality relation. Obviously we have that $=_F^\alpha$ is $=_G$ and therefore Theorem 1 about the preservation of bisimulations by natural transformations is a particular case of our new preservation theorem covering arbitrary $\sqsubseteq_F$-simulations.

Analogously, we now generalized Theorem 2 to arbitrary $\sqsubseteq_G$-simulations.

Theorem 4. *Let $\alpha : F \Rightarrow G$ be an epi natural transformation, $\sqsubseteq_G$ an order on G and $b_1 : X_1 \longrightarrow GX_1$, $b_2 : X_2 \longrightarrow GX_2$ two coalgebras, with $a_1 : X_1 \longrightarrow FX_1$, $a_2 : X_2 \longrightarrow FX_2$ arbitrary concrete F-representations. Then, the $\sqsubseteq_G$-simulations relating b_1 and b_2 are precisely the $\sqsubseteq_G^{\alpha^-}$-simulations relating a_1 and a_2.*

Proof. Just like Theorem 2, the result follows from showing that, for every relation $R \subseteq X_1 \times X_2$,

$$\mathrm{Rel}(F)_{\sqsubseteq_G^{\alpha^-}}(R) = \{(u, v) \in FX_1 \times FX_2 \mid (\alpha_{X_1}(u), \alpha_{X_2}(v)) \in \mathrm{Rel}(G)_{\sqsubseteq_G}(R)\}.$$

Unfolding the definition of $\mathrm{Rel}(F)_{\sqsubseteq_G^{\alpha^-}}(R)$ and using the fact that α is a natural transformation:

$$\mathrm{Rel}(F)_{\sqsubseteq_G^{\alpha^-}}(R) = \{(u, v) \in FX_1 \times FX_2 \mid \exists w \in FR.\, u \sqsubseteq_G^{\alpha^-} Fr_1(w) \wedge$$
$$Fr_2(w) \sqsubseteq_G^{\alpha^-} v\}$$
$$= \{(u, v) \in FX_1 \times FX_2 \mid \exists w \in FR.\, \alpha_{X_1}(u) \sqsubseteq_G \alpha_{X_1}(Fr_1(w)) \wedge$$
$$\alpha_{X_2}(Fr_2(w)) \sqsubseteq_G \alpha_{X_2}(v)\}$$
$$= \{(u, v) \in FX_1 \times FX_2 \mid \exists w \in FR.\, \alpha_{X_1}(u) \sqsubseteq_G Gr_1(\alpha_R(w)) \wedge$$
$$Gr_2(\alpha_R(w)) \sqsubseteq_G \alpha_{X_2}(v)\}.$$

On the other hand,

$$\mathrm{Rel}(G)_{\sqsubseteq_G}(R) = \{(x, y) \in GX_1 \times GX_2 \mid \exists z \in GR.\, x \sqsubseteq_G Gr_1(z) \wedge Gr_2(z) \sqsubseteq_G y\}.$$

Now, if $(u, v) \in \mathrm{Rel}(F)_{\sqsubseteq_G^{\alpha^-}}(R)$, by taking $\alpha_R(w)$ as the value of $z \in GR$ we have that $(\alpha_{X_1}(u), \alpha_{X_2}(v)) \in \mathrm{Rel}(G)_{\sqsubseteq_G}(R)$. Conversely, if $(\alpha_{X_1}(u), \alpha_{X_2}(v)) \in \mathrm{Rel}(G)_{\sqsubseteq_G}(R)$ is witnessed by z, let $w \in FR$ be such that $\alpha_R(w) = z$, which must exist because α is epi; it follows that $(u, v) \in \mathrm{Rel}(F)_{\sqsubseteq_G^{\alpha^-}}(R)$. $\square$

6   Combining Non-determinism and Probabilistic Choices

Probabilistic choice appears as a quantitative counterpart of non-deterministic choice. However, it has been also argued that the motivations supporting the use of these two constructions are different, so that it is also interesting to be able to manage both together. The literature on the subject is full of proposals in this direction [13,10,14], but it has been proved in [16] that there is no distributive law of the probabilistic monad V over the powerset monad P. As a consequence, if we want to combine the two categorical theories to obtain a common framework, we have to sacrifice some of the properties of one of those monads. Varacca and Winskel have followed this idea by relaxing the definition of the monad V, removing the axiom $A \oplus_p A = A$, so that they are aware of the probabilistic choices taken along a computation even if they are superfluous.

We have not yet studied that general case, whose solution in [16] is technically correct, but could be considered intuitively not too satisfactory since one would like to maintain the idempotent law $A \oplus_p A = A$, even if this means that only some practical cases can be considered.

As a first step in this direction we will present here the simple case of alternating probabilistic systems, which in our multi-transition system framework can be defined as follows:

Definition 8. *Alternating multi-transition systems are defined as $(\mathcal{M}(A \times \cdot) \cup \mathcal{M}_1([0,1] \times A \times \cdot))$-coalgebras: any state of a system represents either a non-deterministic choice or a probabilistic choice; however, probabilistic and non-deterministic choices cannot be mixed together.*

By combining the two natural transformations $\{\cdot\}$ and $\mathcal{D}_M$ we obtain the natural transformation $\mathcal{D}_M^a$, that captures the behaviour of alternating transition systems.

Definition 9. *We use the term* alternating probabilistic systems *to refer to the $(\mathcal{P}(A \times \cdot) \cup \mathcal{D}(A \times \cdot))$-coalgebras. By combining the classical definition of bisimulation and that of probabilistic bisimulations we obtain the natural definition of probabilistic bisimulation for alternating probabilistic systems.*
We define $\mathcal{D}_{M_X}^a : \mathcal{M}(A \times \cdot) \cup \mathcal{M}_1([0,1] \times A \times \cdot) \Rightarrow \mathcal{P}(A \times \cdot) \cup \mathcal{D}(A \times \cdot)$ as $\mathcal{D}_{M_X}^a(M) = \{\cdot\}(M)$, $\mathcal{D}_{M_X}^a(M_1) = \mathcal{D}_M(M_1)$, where $M \in \mathcal{M}(A \times X)$, $M_1 \in \mathcal{M}_1([0,1] \times A \times X)$.

Then we can consider the induced functorial equivalence $\equiv^{\mathcal{D}_M^a}$ which roughly corresponds to the application of $\equiv^{\{\cdot\}}$ in the non-deterministic states, and the application of $\equiv^{\mathcal{D}_M}$ in the probabilistic states. As a consequence of Theorem 2 we obtain the following corollary.

Corollary 5. *Bisimulations between alternating probabilistic systems are just $\equiv^{\mathcal{D}_M^a}$-simulations between alternating multi-transition systems.*

Example 4. Let $X = \{x, x_1', x_2', x_3', x_4'\}$, $Y = \{y, y_1', y_2', y_3', y_4'\}$ and let us define (disregarding actions) the alternating multi-transition systems $a_X : X \longrightarrow \mathcal{M}(X) \cup \mathcal{M}_1([0,1] \times X)$ and $a_Y : Y \longrightarrow \mathcal{M}(Y) \cup \mathcal{M}_1([0,1] \times Y)$ as $a_X(x) = \{1 \cdot (\frac{1}{2}, x_1'), 1 \cdot (\frac{1}{2}, x_2')\}$, $a_X(x_1') = \{1 \cdot x_3'\}$, $a_X(x_2') = \{1 \cdot x_4'\}$, $a_X(x_3') = a_X(x_4') = \emptyset$, $a_Y(y) = \{1 \cdot (\frac{1}{3}, y_1'), 1 \cdot (\frac{1}{3}, y_2'), 1 \cdot (\frac{1}{3}, y_3')\}$, $a_Y(y_1') = a_Y(y_2') = a_Y(y_3') = \{1 \cdot y_4'\}$,

$a_Y(y_4') = \emptyset$. a_X and a_Y induce the canonical alternating probabilistic systems $b_X : X \longrightarrow \mathcal{P}(X) \cup \mathcal{D}(X)$ and $b_Y : Y \longrightarrow \mathcal{P}(Y) \cup \mathcal{D}(Y)$ (for example, $b_X(x) = \frac{1}{2}x_1' + \frac{1}{2}x_2'$ and $b_Y(y_3') = \{y_4'\}$).

Now, if we want to know if there is a bisimulation between b_X and b_Y we can use the fact that $R = \{(x,y)\} \cup \{(x_i', y_j') \mid i = 1, 2, j = 1, 2, 3\} \cup \{(x_i', y_4') \mid i = 3, 4\}$ is a $\equiv^{\mathcal{D}_M^a}$-bisimulation between a_X and a_Y (using a similar argument to that in Example 2), and apply Corollary 5 to conclude that there is a $(\mathcal{P} \cup \mathcal{D})$-bisimulation between b_X and b_Y.

7   Conclusion

In this paper we have shown that multitransition systems are a common framework wherein bisimulation of ordinary and probabilistic transition systems almost collapse into the same concept of multiset (bi)simulation. Indeed, the definition of bisimulation for the multiset functor is extremely simple, which supports the idea that multisets are the natural framework in which to justify the use of bisimulation as the canonical notion of equivalence between (states of) systems.

These results have been obtained by exploiting the fact that natural transformations between two functors relate in a nice way bisimulations over their corresponding coalgebras. We have illustrated these general results by means of the natural transformations that connect the powerset and the probabilistic distributions functors with the multiset functor.

The categorical notion of simulation proposed by Hughes and Jacobs has played a very important role in our work; this fact, in our opinion, is far from being casual. In particular, categorical simulations based on equivalence relations always define equivalence relations weaker than bisimulation equivalence. Besides, as illustrated by their use in this paper, they can be used to relate the bisimulation equivalence corresponding to functors connected by a natural transformation.

Related to our work is [2], where probabilistic bisimulations are studied in connection with natural transformations and other categorical notions. Even though some connections can be found, there are very important differences; in particular they do not consider categorical simulations nor use the multiset functor as a general framework in which to study both ordinary and probabilistic bisimulations. We can also mention [15], where the functor $\mathcal{D}$ is replaced with a functor of indexed valuations so that it can be combined with the powerset functor.

A direction for further study that we intend to explore concerns other classes of bisimulations, like the forward-backward ones estudied in [5]. Besides we will study more general combinations of non-deterministic and probabilistic choices, comparing in detail our approach with the use of indexed valuations in [15,16] to combine the monads defining the corresponding functors.

We are confident we will be able to study them in a common setting by generalizing and adapting all the appropriate notions on categorical simulations.

References

1. Aczel, P., Mendler, N.P.: A final coalgebra theorem. In: Pitt, D.H., Rydeheard, D.E., Dybjer, P., Pitts, A.M., Poigné, A. (eds.) Category Theory and Computer Science. LNCS, vol. 389, pp. 357–365. Springer, Heidelberg (1989)
2. Bartels, F., Sokolova, A., de Vink, E.P.: A hierarchy of probabilistic system types. Theoretical Computer Science 327(1-2), 3–22 (2004)
3. de Frutos-Escrig, D., Rosa-Velardo, F., Gregorio-Rodríguez, C.: New Bisimulation Semantics for Distributed Systems. In: Derrick, J., Vain, J. (eds.) FORTE 2007. LNCS, vol. 4574, pp. 143–159. Springer, Heidelberg (2007)
4. van Glabbeek, R.J., Smolka, S.A., Steffen, B.: Reactive, Generative and Stratified Models of Probabilistic Processes. Information and Computation 121(1), 59–80 (1995)
5. Hasuo, I.: Generic forward and backward simulations. In: Baier, C., Hermanns, H. (eds.) CONCUR 2006. LNCS, vol. 4137, pp. 406–420. Springer, Heidelberg (2006)
6. Hughes, J., Jacobs, B.: Simulations in coalgebra. Theoretical Computer Science 327(1-2), 71–108 (2004)
7. Jacobs, B.: Introduction to coalgebra. towards mathematics of states and observations. Book in preparation, Available at: http://www.cs.ru.nl/B.Jacobs/CLG/JacobsCoalgebraIntro.pdf
8. Jacobs, B., Rutten, J.: A tutorial on (co)algebras and (co)induction. Bulletin of the European Association for Theoretical Computer Science 62, 222–259 (1997)
9. Larsen, K.G., Skou, A.: Bisimulation through probabilistic testing. Information and Computation 94(1), 1–28 (1991)
10. Mislove, M.W.: Nondeterminism and Probabilistic Choice: Obeying the Laws. In: Palamidessi, C. (ed.) CONCUR 2000. LNCS, vol. 1877, pp. 350–364. Springer, Heidelberg (2000)
11. Park, D.: Concurrency and automata on infinite sequences. In: Deussen, P. (ed.) GI-TCS 1981. LNCS, vol. 104, pp. 167–183. Springer, Heidelberg (1981)
12. Rutten, J.J.M.M.: Universal coalgebra: a theory of systems. Theoretical Computer Science 249(1), 3–80 (2000)
13. Segala, R., Lynch, N.A.: Probabilistic Simulations for Probabilistic Processes. Nordic Journal on Computing 2(2), 250–273 (1995)
14. Tix, R., Keimel, K., Plotkin, G.: Semantic Domains for Combining Probability and Non-Determinism. ENTCS, vol. 129, pp. 1–104. Elsevier, Amsterdam (2005)
15. Varacca, D.: The powerdomain of indexed valuations. In: LICS 2002: Proceedings of the 17th Annual IEEE Symposium on Logic in Computer Science, pp. 299–310. IEEE Computer Society, Los Alamitos (2002)
16. Varacca, D., Winskel, G.: Distributing Probabililty over Nondeterminism. Mathematical Structures in Computer Science 16(1), 87–113 (2006)
17. de Vink, E.P., Rutten, J.J.M.M.: Bisimulation for probabilistic transition systems: A coalgebraic approach. Theoretical Computer Science 221(1-2), 271–293 (1999)

Detecting Communication Protocol Security Flaws by Formal Fuzz Testing and Machine Learning

Guoqiang Shu, Yating Hsu, and David Lee

Department of Computer Science and Engineering, the Ohio State University
Columbus, OH 43210, USA
{shug, hsuya, lee}@cse.ohio-state.edu

Abstract. Network-based fuzz testing has become an effective mechanism to ensure the security and reliability of communication protocol systems. However, fuzz testing is still conducted in an ad-hoc manner with considerable manual effort, which is mainly due to the unavailability of protocol model. In this paper we present our on-going work of developing an automated and measurable protocol fuzz testing approach that uses a formally synthesized approximate formal protocol specification to guide the testing process. We adopt the Finite State Machine protocol model and study two formal methods for protocol synthesis: an active black-box checking algorithm that has provable optimality and a passive trace minimization algorithm that is less accurate but much more efficient. We also present our preliminary results of using this method to implementations of the MSN instant messaging protocol: MSN clients Gaim (pidgin) and aMSN. Our testing reveals some serious reliability and security flaws by automatically crashing both of them.

Keywords: Fuzz testing, Security Testing, Protocol Synthesis.

1 Motivation

Network-based fuzz testing is a very effective approach to improve the security and reliability of protocol system implementations [7, 9]. It works by mutating the normal traffic at the ingress interface of a component in order to reveal unwanted behavior such as crashing or confidentiality violation [3]. Identifying such flaws is extremely important since they might be exploited by malicious parties to launch attacks. On the other hand, it has been reported that for today's complicated system these flaws are ubiquitous due to incorrect assumptions on the input data. However, unlike software fuzz testing where white-box approach [4, 5] is widely used, protocol fuzz testing is usually conducted in an ad-hoc manner with input selected either randomly or manually [5]. With such restrictions it is very difficult to measure the comprehensiveness of testing and the level of test automation is low. With knowledge of the protocol message format, some preliminary systematic approaches such as message type covering become feasible. However they are in general inaccurate for various reasons. For example, messages of same type could serve very different roles in a protocol session and therefore should be distinguished in testing.

In this work we propose an automated solution to improve the quality and measurability of black-box fuzz testing using a formal protocol specification synthesis

K. Suzuki et al. (Eds.): FORTE 2008, LNCS 5048, pp. 299–304, 2008.

approach. The key idea is to obtain an approximate formal model of the component under test and use it to automatically guide test selection for better fault coverage. Such model is based on presumed knowledge of protocol messages [2] while its primary function is to describe the states and transitions in a session. Note that formal specifications are usually not available in practice for real protocol systems. Construction of such a specification model endows significant guidance to systematic black-box testing which is otherwise impossible. Specifically, we can design test sequences to achieve formally defined fault coverage criteria with regard to the specification, and meanwhile to intelligently choose mutated inputs based on special context in the model. Note that the specification synthesis problem we study has fundamental difference with the protocol design and implementation synthesis problems extensively studied in the literature, which aim at using formal models to facilitate developing error-free protocol instead of recovering the specification for given implementation.

In this paper we discuss two alternative formal methods for Finite State Machine (FSM) based specification synthesis which we applied in fuzz testing of real world network applications. Our experiments show that this approach is promising in automatic discovery of new bugs in protocol implementations of real internet applications.

2   Formal Protocol Synthesis

We adopt a variant of classic Communicating Extended Finite State Machine (CEFSM) to model a communication protocol. The behavior of each protocol principal is described by a deterministic EFSM that has state variables and input/output message parameters with symbolic value domain. The detailed modeling is in [8, 11]. In this work we focus on one principal and use its reachability graph (an FSM) representation. An *FSM* is a 5-tuple $<S, s_0, I, O, f_{next}, f_{output}>$, where S and s_0 are state (configuration in EFSM) set and initial state, I and O are input and output alphabet, $f_{next} : S \times I \rightarrow S$ is the transition function and $f_{output} : S \times I \rightarrow O$ is the output function. Both f_{next} and f_{output} might be partial function. We call an FSM a tree FSM if its state transition graph is a tree. A trace of FSM is a sequence of input/output pairs, $tr = \{<I_1,O_1>,<I_2,O_2>,...,<I_k,O_k>\}$, and a test case is simply a sequence of inputs.

Given a black box protocol component implementation B, our objective is to synthesize a deterministic FSM model M_x that later guides our fuzz testing algorithm. M_x should ideally be an abstraction of all observed behavior of B, and its input (output) alphabet I_x is a subset of B's input alphabet I_B. The ultimate goal of testing then is to find a sequence of any length L: $\{<I_k,O_k>, 0 \leq k \leq L, I_k \subseteq I_B, O_k \subseteq O_B\}$ that will lead B to an observable failure state. Below we discuss two approaches to construct M_x – an active learning algorithm and a passive machine minimization algorithm.

2.1   FSM Learning Algorithm

Since the tester has full control of the input and output of B, an obvious way to get its model is through active learning. Following the theoretical insights of [1,10] on automata learning, we design the following procedure. An estimation model B^* of the implementation B is maintained and initialized as an FSM with an initial state only. B^* is updated as more traces are discovered according to the supervised FSM learning algorithm L^*_{fsm} (based on Angluin's L^* algorithm with details omitted due to space limit; see [1]). A conformance test generator serves the role of "teacher" in learning process that provides traces as counter-example – showing the difference between B^* and B. The counter-example is used to prepare for the next estimation that becomes supposedly more accurate: containing more input types or more states.

This iterative process starts with a small subset of input alphabet and terminates when the teacher is not able to find any counter-examples to help learning. We can prove this strategy is always "promising" in the following sense: if B contains N states and P inputs, at most $(N+P)$ guesses will be made before we get $M_x=B^*=B$. The cost of this process is determined by both the strategy used by the teacher and the L^*_{fsm} learning algorithm itself. We could prove that it takes $O(P^* \cdot N^{*2})$ to update B^* with P^* inputs and N^* states, and the total cost of learning B in worst case is $O(T \cdot P^2 \cdot N^2 + T \cdot P \cdot N^3)$ where T denotes the cost of calculating the counter-example at each round. In practice due to this high cost we usually stop after several iterations with an approximate model.

2.2 Partial FSM Minimization Algorithm

We also study an alternative that requires more observation but potentially less computation. The idea is to first gather a large number of traces from B by *passive* monitoring, compute a tree FSM, and minimize it. Given a set of traces, the synthesis of tree FSM is quite straightforward. Starting with empty FSM we add one trace at a time. We find the longest prefix of a trace that is already in the current FSM, presumably ending at state s, then create a new branch from s with the rest of the trace. One practical issue in this step is handling session related fields. We want to identify data fields in an input/output message whose value does not affect the state transition of this session and therefore could be symbolized. Typical examples of such fields include username, nonce and session ID. Identification of these fields reduces the redundancy of the tree FSM; however it is nontrivial and sometimes requires manual effort. In our on-going work we are investigating efficient and automated solutions.

After the tree FSM is constructed, we want to minimize the number of states by merging compatible sets. Minimization problem for partial FSM is a well studied NP-hard problem and many heuristic solutions have been proposed [6]. A simple optimistic algorithm is Bierman's algorithm also described in [6]: first a set of constraints of merging is calculated dictating which pair of states can be merged and which two pairs must be both merged or both unmerged; after that new state IDs are given to the states and whenever a constraint is violated the assignment is modified. The complexity of this algorithm in worst case is obviously exponential but we can modify it by limiting backtracking to get a polynomial suboptimal algorithm. As an extreme case, we might choose not to backtrack at all (i.e. always assign new state ID) to achieve linear time.

3 Fuzz Testing Strategy

Once we have synthesized the approximate protocol specification M_x, it is used to guide fuzz testing experiments. Coverage metrics can be formally defined to measure the comprehensiveness of a set of tests. Let $I_0 I_1 \ldots I_L$ be a sequence in M_x, and a fuzz testing sequence has the general form of $I_0 I_1 \ldots I_k f_{fuzz}(I_{k+1} \ldots I_L)$, where the prefix of length k is a leading sequence that takes B to a certain state and the rest is the result of applying a fuzz function $f_{fuzz}: I^* \to I_B^*$ to the original postfix. Let us consider a special function that modifies the format of last input message only, and we want to test this function for all transitions in M_x. Given a set of K test sequences $\{SEQ_i = PREFIX_i\ f(LAST_i)\mid 0 \leq i \leq K, PREFIX_i \in I^*, LAST_i \in I\}$, the formula below computes its transition coverage as the number of transitions covered by the last input of a message divided by the total transitions in M_x.

$$TR\_Coverage = \frac{\left|\{<s', LAST_i>\mid s'=f_{next}(s_0, PREFIX_i) \wedge f_{next}(s', LAST_i) \downarrow, 0 \leq i \leq K\}\right|}{\left|\{<s,i>\mid f_{next}(s,i) \downarrow, s \in S, i \in I\}\right|}$$

Other metrics could be similarly developed corresponding to popular fuzz functions on input sequence such as repetition, stealing, replay and pre-play. The actual test generator should be designed to give preference to sequences that increase the metric.

4 Experiments and Evaluation

We have implemented both of the synthesis strategies as well as several typical fuzz functions and applied them to evaluate two popular alternatives of MSN instant messaging clients Gaim (pidgin) and aMSN. In order to take over the I/O of the client we developed a proxy through which the client is connected to the server (shown in Figure 1). We also implement a simple encoder and decoder for MSN protocol messages. The goal of fuzz testing is to find input sequences that will crash the client process (a behavior that is definitely unwanted). We synthesize a model for the login phase of MSN protocol containing around 50 states and 70 transitions. Several typical fuzz functions on single transition are manually developed, after which testing is done automatically toward 100% transition coverage for each function.

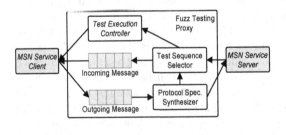

Fig. 1. An MSN Client Fuzz Testing Tool

Table 1. Testing two MSN Clients with synthesized model

Size of tree FSM	450
#states/#transitions of synthesized FSM	50/ 70
Fuzz functions used	5
Bugs found in Gaim	3
Bugs found in aMSN	8

As summarized by Table 1, we found many previously unknown bugs of both clients and we are continuously uncovering more. Our fuzz functions fall into two categories: (1) changing the data field of a message to form an invalid input from I_B-I_{Mx}; and (2) changing the message type to form an undefined transition with respect to the current state. Below we report instances of bugs from each category.

- **Invalid Status Code:** ILN message type is used for buddy presence notification; the syntax of the command is *"ILN TrID status_code Account Display ClientID"* where the *status_code* field is used to indicate the presence of a contact such as available, busy, or away. MSN protocol gives a list of legitimate status codes but if we change it to an invalid value, aMSN crashes immediately after receiving the message.
- **Elimination of E-Mail Address Field:** a simple fuzz function that eliminates every field from an input message that is in the form of an email address (used as account name) will cause both Gaim and aMSN to crash.
- **Skipping Contact List Message:** in order to obtain the buddy list of a user, a sequence of messages is exchanged between the server and client including an *LST* message to download the contact list followed by a sequence of *ILN* messages to obtain presence information. We found that if the LST message is skipped (i.e. dropped); aMSN will crash when receiving the *ILN* message.
- **Random Message Type Mutation:** we could simply modify the input message type to a random message type that is undefined in the current state. For instance, when we change *CVR* or *VER* message (both used to negotiate protocol version) to *LST* type, both clients will crash. A variant of this operation is random message type swapping of two adjacent transitions, and aMSN crashes when this is applied to *LST* and *UBX* messages.

5 Conclusion

We investigate the proposed fuzz testing approach that has shown great potential and practicality. A key problem to tackle is how to improve the quality of the synthesized specification. For instance, our current tool does not recover the dependency relationship among message fields, which gives valuable insights regarding what input might be destructive. Toward this goal analysis for both control plane and data plane of the protocol traces are to be integrated. On the other hand, we envision that formal protocol synthesis techniques could be useful in other domains, such as protocol reverse engineering [2] and network testbed development [12].

References

1. Angulin, D.: Learning regular sets from queries and counterexamples. Information and Computation 75, 87–106 (1987)
2. Cui, W., Kannan, J., Wang, H.: Discoverer: Automatic Protocol Reverse Engineering from Network Traces. In: The 16th USENIX Security Symposium (2007)
3. Dolev, D., Yao, A.: On the security of public-key protocols. IEEE Transaction on Information Theory 29, 198–208 (1983)
4. Godefroid, P., Klarlund, N., Sen, K.: DART: Directed Automated Random Testing. In: Proceedings of PLDI 2005 (ACM SIGPLAN 2005 Conference on Programming Language Design and Implementation), pp. 213–223 (2005)
5. Godefroid, P., Levin, M.Y., Molnar, D.: Automated Whitebox Fuzz Testing. Technical Report MS-TR-2007-58, Microsoft (May 2007)
6. Gören, S., Ferguson, F.J.: On state reduction of incompletely specified finite state machines. Computers and Electrical Engineering 33(1), 58–69 (2007)
7. Howard, M.: Inside the Windows Security Push. IEEE Security & Privacy, 57–61 (2003)

8. Lee, D., Yannakakis, M.: Principles and methods of testing finite state machines - A survey. In: Proceedings of the IEEE, 1090–1123 (1996)
9. Oehlert, P.: Violating Assumptions with Fuzzing. IEEE Security & Privacy, pp. 58-62 (2005)
10. Peled, D., Vardi, M.Y., Yannakakis, M.: Black-box checking. In: Proceedings of IFIP FORTE/PSTV (1999)
11. Shu, G., Lee, D.: Testing Security Properties of protocol implementations – a machine learning based approach. In: Proceedings of IEEE ICDCS (2007)
12. Wang, L., Ellis, C., Yin, W., Luong, D.D.: Hercules: An Environment for Large-Scale Enterprise Infrastructure Testing. In: Proceedings of the Workshop on Advances and Innovations in Systems Testing (2007)

Using SPIN to Detect Vulnerabilities in the AACS Drive-Host Authentication Protocol

Wei Wang and Dongyao Ji

The State Key Laboratory of Information Security,
Graduate University of Chinese Academy of Science,
No.19 Yuquan Road, Shijingshan District, Beijing, 100049, P.R. China
bessie19831109@163.com

Abstract. In this paper, we use SPIN, a model checker for LTL, to detect vulnerabilities in the AACS drive-host authentication protocol. Before the detection, we propose a variant of the Dolev-Yao attacker model [4] and incorporate the synthesis and analysis rules [7] to formalize the protocol and the intruder capabilities. During the detection, we check the authenticity of the protocol and identify a few weaknesses. Besides, we propose a novel collusion attack that seriously threaten the security of the protocol, and build a corresponding LTL formula. Based on the formula, SPIN detects a few relevant attack instances in the original scheme of the authentication protocol and a modified scheme advanced in [5].

Keywords: AACS, SPIN, Model Checker, LTL, Authenticity, Collusion Attack.

1 Introduction

Nowadays, in the field of protocol verification, the formal verification techniques appear to be a popular method for analyzing the vulnerabilities of protocols. There are two major approaches: theorem-proving and model-checking. Compared with theorem-proving, model-checking seems to be more suitable to detect errors and find corresponding attack modes of the target protocols [3].

So far, some researchers have developed specific model checkers for particular properties verification, whereas others have shown the ability of the general purpose tools such as FDR and SMV to achieve the same purpose. In this paper, we would like to implement our protocol verification using the general purpose tool of SPIN, which is one of the most powerful general purpose model checkers. Until now, some researchers have already shown how it can be used to check the security properties such as secrecy and authenticity, and successfully found the known attack in the Needham-Schroeder Public Key Authentication Protocol [2,8].

In this paper, we will use SPIN to verify the AACS drive-host authentication protocol. The Advanced Access Content System (AACS) is a content distribution system for recordable and pre-recorded media. This system consists of three entities: a drive, PC host and the AACS protected optical media. The AACS drive-host authentication protocol, a part of the AACS protection scheme, plays the role of practicing the mutual authentication between the PC host and the drive and letting them negotiate a shared

K. Suzuki et al. (Eds.): FORTE 2008, LNCS 5048, pp. 305–323, 2008.
© IFIP International Federation for Information Processing 2008

key which is used for message authentication in the subsequent interaction between the PC host and the drive [1].

In the whole process of verifying the AACS drive-host authentication protocol, we not only make use of the technique of model-checking, but also adopt the method of static analysis. And according to the variant of the Dolev-Yao attacker model [4] advanced by us in order to match the specific scheme of the target protocol, we make the formalization of the protocol and the intruder's behavior. Besides checking the property of authenticity, we also define a novel collusion attack which poses a threat to the security of the AACS protection scheme. Through the verification, we have discovered several relevant attack instances in the original AACS drive-host authentication scheme. In addition, a modified AACS drive-host authentication scheme, proposed in [5], also reveals its vulnerability to the novel collusion attack in our further verification.

This paper is organized as follows. In section 2, we construct the formal model of the target protocol, which includes the description of a variant of Dolev-Yao attacker model. In section 3, we briefly describe the general process of verifying the target protocol using SPIN. In section 4 and section 5, we present the process of checking the authenticity and verifying the feasibility of the newly-defined collusion attack in SPIN.

2   A Formal Model for Security Protocols

In this section, we present a formal model of the AACS drive-host authentication protocol and describe a variant of Dolev-Yao attacker model [4]. Besides, we have made some modifications of the semantics of security protocols built in [9] to simplify the process of modeling the target protocol. More detailed description can be found in [10].

First, we would like to discuss the occasion of generating a fresh nonce in the AACS drive-host authentication scheme: when finish one session no matter whether it is succeed or not, both the host and the drive would call the random number generator to acquire a fresh nonce used in a next session. But in this paper, our concern is only about a single session. Therefore, for the purpose of simplifying the model of the AACS drive-host authentication protocol, we define nonces as constants.

Next, we describe the definitions of several necessary terms used in the following discussion. We start with the set of *agents* – Ag, which includes the *intruder I* and other agents who are called *honest agents*. K, denotes the set of *private keys* which are owned by corresponding agents, and we use k_p to denote the *private key* belongs to agent p. *Cert*, denotes the set of *certificates* which represent the identities of corresponding agents, and we use $Cert_p$ to denote the *certificate* of p. N, denotes the set of *nonces*. P, the set of *parameters*, is used for some particular purposes. $\mathcal{T}_0$, the set of *basic terms*, is defined to be $Ag \cup K \cup Cert \cup N \cup P$. $\mathcal{T}$, the set of *information terms*, is defined to be:

$$\mathcal{T} ::= m \mid (t, t') \mid \{t\}_k . \tag{1}$$

where m ranges over $\mathcal{T}_0$, k ranges over K, t and t' range over $\mathcal{T}$; and (t, t') denotes the concatenation of t and t', and $\{t\}_k$ denotes using k to encrypt the term t.

In addition, we define a set of actions:

$$\Sigma = \{A!B{:}t, A?B{:}t \mid A, B \in Ag, A \neq B, t \in \mathcal{T}\} . \tag{2}$$

analz-rules:

$$\frac{}{T \cup \{t\} \vdash t}\ \mathsf{Ax_a} \qquad \frac{T \vdash (t_1, t_2)}{T \vdash t_i}\ \mathsf{split}_i\ (i=1, 2) \qquad \frac{T \vdash \{t\}_{k_p} \quad T \vdash Cert_p \quad T \vdash t}{T \vdash true}\ \mathsf{verify}$$

synth-rules:

$$\frac{}{T \cup \{t\} \vdash t}\ \mathsf{Ax_s} \qquad \frac{T \vdash t_1 \quad T \vdash t_2}{T \vdash (t_1, t_2)}\ \mathsf{pair} \qquad \frac{T \vdash t \quad T \vdash k_p}{T \vdash \{t\}_{k_p}}\ \mathsf{sign}$$

Fig. 1. The Modified Analz and Synth Rules

As we can see, there are two actions which are denoted as "Send" and "Receive":

- Send: *A*!*B*:*t*, *A* is the sender, *B* is the intended receiver, and *t* is the message.
- Receive: *A*?*B*:*t*, *A* is the receiver, *B* is the purported sender, and *t* is the message.

Definition 1. *A* protocol *is a pair* Pr = (C, R), *where* C $\subseteq \mathcal{T}_0$ *is the set of constants of* Pr, *and* R *is the set of roles of* Pr.

Definition 2. *A* sequent *is of the form* $T \vdash t$ *where* $T \subseteq \mathcal{T}$ *and* $t \in \mathcal{T}$. *An* analz-*proof* (synth-*proof*) π *of* $T \vdash t$ *is an inverted tree whose nodes are labeled by sequents and connected by one of the* analz-*rules* (synth-*rules*) *in Fig. 1, whose root is labeled* $T \vdash t$, *and whose leaves are labeled by instances of the* Ax_a *rule* (Ax_s *rule*). *For a set of terms* T, analz(T) (synth(T)) *is the set of terms t such that there is an* analz-*proof* (*a* synth-*proof*) *of* $T \vdash t$. *For ease of notation,* synth(analz(T)) *is denoted by* $\overline{T}$.

The definitions of analz and synth are due to [7].

As we can see, Fig. 1 shows the modified analz and synth rules, which are based on the variant of the Dolev-Yao model [4], consist of split, pair, verify and sign. Specifically, the verify rule has its practical significance: if one knows three items – the signature $\{t\}_{k_p}$ (denoting using k_p, the private key of p, to sign the term t), $Cert_p$ (the certificate of p), and the term t, it can confirm the validity of the signature, which means that the signature $\{t\}_{k_p}$ would be successfully decrypted by the public key extracted from $Cert_p$, and the decrypted term is the same with t.

Definition 3. *An* information state *s is a tuple* $(s_A)_{A \in Ag}$ *where* $s_A \subseteq \mathcal{T}$ *for each agent A. The notions of an action enabled at a state and update of a state on an action are defined as follows:*

- *A*!*B*:*t is* enabled *at s iff* $t \in \overline{s_A}$.
- *A*?*B*:*t is* enabled *at s iff* $t \in \overline{s_I}$.
- $update(s, A!B{:}t) \stackrel{\text{def}}{=} s'$ *where* $s'_A = s_A$, $s'_I = s_I \cup \{t\}$, *and for all agents C distinct from A and I,* $s'_C = s_C$.
- $update(s, A?B{:}t) \stackrel{\text{def}}{=} s'$ *where* $s'_A = s_A \cup \{t\}$ *and for all agents C distinct from A,* $s'_C = s_C$.

3   Protocol Verification Using Spin

Spin is designed to validate the logical consistency of concurrent and distributed systems, such as data communications protocols, and trace the logical design errors [11]. By constructing a LTL formula of a desired property and simulating a correct model of the target protocol, one could easily carry out the verification on SPIN; and when detecting a violation of the target property, SPIN could provide the counterexample run. In this fragment, we will discuss the model construction process, which amounts to two steps: the formalization of the protocol and the formalization of the intruder's behavior.

3.1   Formalization of the Protocol

First of all, we want to simplify the original flow representation of the drive-host authentication scheme [1] by abstracting the core steps. The simplified scheme is represented in Fig. 2.

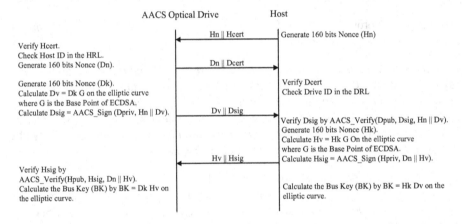

Fig. 2. The Simplified AACS Drive-Host Authentication Protocol

In the model-checking approach, protocols can be described as patterns of messages exchanged between different agents, and each agent is described as a proctype in SPIN. In the init process, we would provide a fresh instance to each proctype. Sometimes an agent may play multiple roles in the practical operation of the protocol, thus, we need to construct multiple instances of it. In the init process of the model built for the AACS drive-host authentication protocol, we construct four instances in all: PHost(host, intruder, Hn, Hv, Hcert, Hsk), PHost(host, drive, Hn, Hv, Hcert, Hsk) for the host; PDrive(drive, Dn, Dv, Dcert, Dsk) for the drive; PIntruder() for the intruder.

```
init{
    ...
    atomic{
        if
        :: run PHost(host, intruder, Hn, Hv, Hcert, Hsk)
```

```
:: run PHost(host, drive, Hn, Hv, Hcert, Hsk)
fi;
run PDrive(drive, Dn, Dv, Dcert, Dsk);
run PIntruder();
}
}
```

In addition, we need to model the certificate used in the protocol. Instead of introducing the widely accepted format of the X.509 digital certificate, we define a new data type – Cert. In the X.509 digital certificate, there are various fields storing necessary information; but, among them, what matters to us are merely "Subject Distinguished Name" and "Public Key". So, in this model, the structure of the digital certificate is redefined like this:

```
typedef Cert {
    mtype identifier;
    byte pk
};
```

We also need to model the private key. Actually, private key is the value of number that could be worked with the corresponding public key to sign and verify a message in order to achieve authentication: if one receives a message encrypted with a private key and such message can be decrypted using the public key acquired from the certificate of a particular agent – P, it could confirm that the message is sent by agent P. So the match relation between the certificate and the private key is the key to the overall authentication procedure, and thus it is also the focus of our modeling. In our model, we choose to expand the data structure of the private key to abstract the match relation.

```
typedef Private_Key {
    mtype identifier;
    byte sk
};
```

As we can see, there are two fields in the structure of Private_Key. Obviously, the first one, Private_Key.identifier, represents the identity of the owner. By comparing it with the first field of Cert, we can verify the match relation and then carry out the signature verification process. The following is the core part of the process simulating the host, from which we can see the signature verification process more specifically.

```
Proctype PHost(mtype self; mtype party; mtype nonce; mtype v; Cert
cert; Private_Key hk){
    mtype g1, g2, g3;  Cert c;  Private_Key k;
    atomic{
        HostRunning(self, party);
        //Host initiates a session with the corresponding party
        ca! self, nonce, cert; //Host sends "Hn||Hcert"
    }
    atomic{
```

```
ca? eval(self), g1, c;//Host receives "Dn||Dcert"
cb? eval(self), eval(nonce), g2, k, g3;
//Host receives "(Hn||Dv)SK(Dsk)||Dv"
if
::(g2 == g3 && c.identifier == k.identifier)
->HostCommit(self, c.identifier);
//Host commits the session with the corresponding party
cb! self, g1, v, hk, v;//Host sends "(Dn||Hv)SK(Hsk)||Hv"
::else skip
fi;
    }
}
```

Besides, SPIN also provides a data type – chan, to simulate the synchronous channels in the system. According to the different message modes used in the protocol, we build corresponding structure for each of them. In this protocol, there are two message modes: $x_1 \| x_2$ and $(x_1 \| x_2)SK(x_3) \| x_4$. So the channel structures are defined as follows:

```
chan ca = [0] of {mtype, mtype, Cert};//Message mode x1||x2
chan cb = [0] of {mtype, mtype, mtype, Private_Key, mtype};
//Message mode (x1||x2)SK(x3)||x4
```

3.2   Formalization of the Intruder

Based on Dolev-Yao attacker model [4], the intruder could non-deterministically intercept a message on some channel to update its knowledge, and generate a new message on some channel using the known information. The intruder updates its knowledge by using analz-rules and generates messages by using synth-rules.

In the subsequent discussion, we will describe the whole process of formalizing the intruder's behavior concretely, which consists of three parts: the initial knowledge, the analz-phase and the synth-phase. We need to note that, in this model, the intruder is a legitimate agent; in other words, the intruder is not a revoked device, and it has a valid certificate signed by AACS LA and can thus sign and verify the digital signatures specified in the AACS drive-host authentication protocol.

Before the commencement of the protocol, the intruder has its initial knowledge which is the basis of the later analz-phase and synth-phase. The intruder's initial knowledge is made up of the identities of all the principles in the system, i.e. host, drive, and intruder; moreover, the intruder also holds its private key Isk, its certificate Icert and the generic data gD. After the protocol begins running, the intruder would start on intercepting and generating messages.

In the analz-phase, the intruder breaks up a message into constituent parts and stores them; furthermore, it also verifies the signatures included in the messages using the certificates contained in its knowledge. And by doing these jobs, the intruder could increase its knowledge. For instance, if the intruder intercepts the message Hn||Hcert, it could acquire and store the nonce Hn and the certificate Hcert. In order to avoid storing redundant knowledge elements, we assume that the intruder always records the learned items in their most elementary forms. For example, if message Hn||Icert is intercepted, what the intruder records is Hn, rather than Icert or the whole message Hn‖Icert; because Icert is not fresh to it, and message Hn‖Icert can be built from Hn and Icert, which is not in the most elementary form. We also assume that the intruder records a complex message in its knowledge only if it cannot build that message. Taking another case for example, if the intruder intercepts the message (Dn‖Hv)SK(Hsk)‖Hv, besides recording the parameter Hv, it also needs to record the complex part (Dn‖Hv)SK(Hsk). Since the intruder cannot get private key of the host – Hsk, and thus cannot generate the signature, though it might know the certificate of the host – Hcert, and decrypt that signature.

In the synth-phase, based on the synth-rules, the intruder can generate a message by choosing the recipient and the message type and filling in each field with the appropriate data item which is known to it; besides, the intruder also can simply replay an entire stored message. For example, if the intruder possesses the data items Hn and Hcert, it can concatenate them into Hn‖Hcert and send it to the drive. Theoretically, the intruder can generate whatever it wants; but, to improve the efficiency of our model, we build a restriction in the synth-phase: the message the intruder generates should be valid and in accordance with the corresponding message mode. Obviously, the purpose of making this restriction is to prevent the intruder from generating invalid message. For instance, if the intruder generates and sends a message (Hn‖Hv)SK(Hsk)‖Dv, none of the agents in the system would accept it, since this message does not comply with the message mode which requires the second parameter should be identical with the fourth parameter (but Hv≠Dv).

4 Formalization of the Authenticity Property

4.1 Formalization of the Authenticity Property

Property formalization is another essential part of verifying security protocols with model checkers. In general, secrecy and authenticity are the properties often be checked when analyzing security protocols, but in this paper, secrecy does not need to be considered. Since in the AACS drive-host authentication protocol, data items contained in messages are transferred in two forms – plain text and cipher text. The plain text data could be seen by any agent. The cipher text data, encrypted with someone's private key, could be decrypted by anyone who possesses the corresponding certificate; and other agents without the proper certificate also could acquire the corresponding plain text of all the cipher text data, since in this protocol all the cipher text data has another copy which is transferred in the plain text. So secrecy is not the property worth verification in this protocol. The property we choose to verify here is authenticity.

During the verification, we firstly build three roles involved – Host, Drive and Intruder; then, we define six global Boolean variables:

```
bit HostRunningHD = 0,  HostCommitHD = 0,  HostKnowDv = 0;
bit DriveRunningHD = 0, DriveCommitHD = 0, DriveKnowHv = 0;
```

HostRunningHD is true iff Host takes apart in a session with Drive. DriveRunningHD is true iff Drive takes apart in a session with Host. HostCommitHD is true iff

Host commits to a session with Drive. DriveCommitHD is true iff Drive commits to a session with Host. HostKnowDv is true iff Host knows the parameter Dv. DriveKnowHv is true iff Drive knows the parameter Hv.

The authentication of Host to Drive can be expressed as that HostRunningHD must become true before the DriveCommitHD becomes true, whereas the converse authentication of Drive to Host is that DriveRunningHD must become true before the Host-CommitHD becomes true. These properties can be expressed in the LTL formalism:

$$\Box((\Box !DriveCommitHD) \;||\; (!DriveCommitHD \cup HostRunningHD)) \; . \tag{3}$$

$$\Box((\Box !HostCommitHD) \;||\; (!HostCommitHD \cup DriveRunningHD)) \; . \tag{4}$$

Equation (3) means that the protocol suffices to the authentication of Host to Drive; (4) means that the protocol suffices to the authentication of Drive to Host.

4.2   The Experimental Result

After the verification on SPIN, we discover two attack instances (Attack 1 & Attack 2) violating (3) and two attack instances (Attack 3 & Attack 4) violating (4). Those instances are shown in Fig. 3, and the relevant experimental data is list in Table 1.

Table 1. Attack and Relevant Data

Attack	Attack 1	Attack 2	Attack 3	Attack 4
HostRunningHD	0	0	1	1
HostCommitHD	0	0	1	1
DriveRunningHD	1	1	0	0
DriveCommitHD	1	1	0	0
HostKnowDv	1	0	1	1
DriveKnowHv	1	1	0	1

Here, we want to make some notations about those attacks shown in Fig. 3. In Attack 1 and Attack 2, Host initially sends its random nonce Hn and certificate Hcert to Intruder rather than Drive, in order to initiate a session with Intruder; in Attack 3 and Attack 4, Host intends to send its random nonce Hn and certificate Hcert to Drive to initiate a session with Drive, but this message is intercepted by Intruder. In addition, in Attack 1 and Attack 4, Host and Drive can negotiate a shared Bus Key when the session finished; however, they cannot get the shared Bus Key in Attack 2 and Attack 3, since Host has no way to get Drive's parameter Dv in Attack 2 and Drive cannot get Host's parameter Hv in Attack 3 during the whole session.

5   Formalization of the Collusion Attack

5.1   Introduction of the Collusion Attack

AACS is applicable to a PC-based system. In such a system, a drive and PC host act together as the Recording Device and/or Playback Device for AACS protected content.

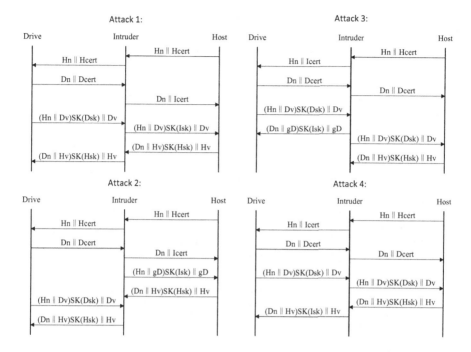

Fig. 3. The Attack Instances

Mutual authentication is the initial procedure in the whole system, by which the drive and the PC host verify each counterpart is an AACS compliant device which has a valid certificate signed by the AACS LA and can sign and verify digital signatures specified in the AACS drive-host authentication protocol.

In the AACS drive-host authentication scheme, the host's process of verifying the drive's legitimacy consists of three steps: first, the host verifies the signature of the Drive Certificate using the AACS LA Public Key; next, it checks the Drive Revocation List to ensure that the Drive ID of the Drive Certificate has not been revoked; then it verifies the second message sent by the drive to check whether the drive pass the nonce-challenging procedure or not. If the above verifications succeed, the host could confirm the validity of the drive, and exchange parameters with it to negotiate a shared Bus Key.

From the above analysis, we think of a special kind of attack aiming at offering a revoked drive the opportunity to bypass the authentication procedure, negotiate a shared Bus Key with a legal host and use this key to exchange necessary information with the host in order to play/record the protected content in the disc. And this attack could be successfully carried out by hiring a third party – a legitimate drive; obviously, this kind of attack, launched by a revoked drive and a hired drive, is what we called "the collusion attack". But the relationship between them is not mutual trust but mutual utilization. To the revoked drive, the hired drive is a lessor who leases out its legitimate identity; and to the hired drive, the revoked drive is just one of the lessees who pay for the use of its identity.

Therefore, there is a restriction lies in this attack mode: Bus Key is the secret merely known to the host and the revoked drive, which implies the hired drive cannot acquire it. Bus Key, in the AACS system, is used for message authentication in the subsequent interaction between the host and the drive, after the authentication protocol is over. Accordingly, in this attack mode, Bus Key is used for messages authentication between the host and the revoked drive after the authentication protocol completed running. Once the hired drive possesses Bus Key, it has the ability to tamper the messages, obstruct the host from acquiring parameters necessary to decrypt the encrypted content in the disc and prevent the revoked drive from playing/recording the disc, which contravenes the goal of the collusion attack. So the purpose of setting the restriction is to make the lessee (the revoked drive) get rid of the influence of the third party (the hired drive) after the authentication protocol completed running, and successfully interact with the host.

Considering the AACS adopts the technique of Elliptic Curve Cryptographic Signature Algorithm (ECDSA) in the key agreement procedure, the crucial factor of implementing the restriction specified above is the parties participating in the Bus Key negotiation. In this attack mode, besides the host and the revoked drive, there should not be a third party participating in the Bus Key negotiation. That is to say, the hired drive should not replace the revoked drive's parameter Dv by its own parameter in order to negotiate the Bus Key with the host itself; and the revoked drive should participate in the negotiation itself, rather than simply obtain a Bus Key generated by the hired drive.

5.2 Formalization of the Collusion Attack

There are three parties in this attack mode: Host, Drive-R and Drive-L.

- Host is just a legal host in the PC-based system;
- Drive-R is a revoked drive whose ID is in the Drive Revocation List located in Host;
- Drive-L is a legitimate drive.

Remarkably, in this attack mode, Drive-R plays the role of Drive and Drive-L plays the role of Intruder. The details about this attack are described as follows:

- If Drive-R wants to interact with Host, it hires Drive-L as its accomplice to employ the attack.
- During the protocol running, Host only can see the certificate of Drive-L and does not know the existence of Drive-R in the whole process of interaction.
- The parameter Dv, calculated by Drive-R based on its 160 bits nonce Dk, the elliptic curve and the Base Point G of ECDSA, could be finally acquired by Host in order to calculate the Bus Key.
- The parameter Hv, calculated by Host based on its 160 bits nonce Hk, the elliptic curve and the Base Point G of ECDSA, could be finally known by Drive-R for the purpose of calculating the Bus Key.
- Because Drive-L is the device hired by Drive-R, Drive-R can pick up necessary information from Drive-L. That is to say, the fact Drive-L knows the parameter Hv is equivalent to the fact that Drive-R knows Hv.
- During the whole process, Drive-L cannot get the Bus Key.

Based on the above analysis, we define eight global Boolean variables:

```
bit HostRunningHD = 0,  HostCommitHD = 0,  HostKnowDv = 0;
bit DriveRunningHD = 0, DriveCommitHD = 0, DriveKnowHv = 0;
bit IntruderKnowHv = 0, HostKnowDcert = 0;
```

HostRunningHD is true iff Host takes apart in a session with Drive. DriveRunningHD is true iff Drive takes apart in a session with Host. HostCommitHD is true iff Host commits to a session with Drive. DriveCommitHD is true iff Drive commits to a session with Host. HostKnowDv is true iff Host knows the parameter Dv. DriveKnowHv is true iff Drive knows the parameter Hv. IntruderKnowHv is true iff Intruder knows the parameter Hv. HostKnowDcert is true iff Host knows Dcert, the certificate of Drive.

The property we want to check could be expressed in the LTL formalism:

$$\Diamond \, (HostKnowDv \&\&(DriveKnowHv \parallel IntruderKnowHv)\&\& \\ !HostKnowDcert\&\&!HostRunningHD\&\&!HostCommitHD) \, . \quad (5)$$

If there is an instance existing in the protocol running that could suffice (5), we could confirm the feasibility of this collusion attack.

5.3   The Experimental Result

Using SPIN, we have found five attack instances shown in Fig. 4 and Fig. 5, and the relevant experimental data is list in Table 2.

Table 2. Attack and Relevant Data

Attack	Attack 1	Attack 2	Attack 3	Attack 4	Attack 5
HostRunningHD	0	0	0	0	0
HostCommitHD	0	0	0	0	0
HostKnowDv	1	1	1	1	1
HostKnowDcert	0	0	0	0	0
DriveRunningHD	0	1	1	0	1
DriveCommitHD	0	1	0	0	0
DriveKnowHv	1	1	1	0	0
IntruderKnowHv	1	1	1	1	1

First, let us focus on Attack 1 and Attack 2. In these two attack instances, the protocol could be successfully completed. In the end of the session, Drive (Drive-R) acquires Hv, and Host gets Dv. (Attack 2 has already been found by J.Sui and D.R. Stinson by simulating the "Unknown Key-Share Attack" in [5].)

In Attack 3, the session does not proceed well. The last message Drive (Drive-R) received has an improper data item: when verifying the signature (Dn‖Hv)SK(Isk) by using Hcert received in the first message, Drive (Drive-R) would detect the invalidity of the signature. According to the rule of this protocol, if the verification fails, Drive (Drive-R) will determine the counterpart is not compliant and abort this session. But in this model, Drive (Drive-R) is not a good boy but a revoked drive. So, after the failure

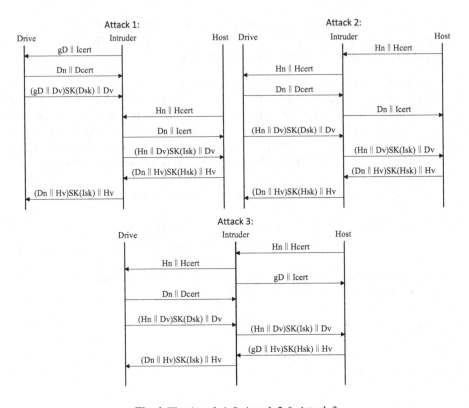

Fig. 4. The Attack 1 & Attack 2 & Attack 3

of the signature verification, it would not only keep the session, but also pick up the parameter Hv from the last message, regardless of the validity of the signature. For the purpose of checking the authenticity of the parameter Hv, Drive (Drive-R) is still required to check the validity of the signature using the certificate of Intruder Icert, which could be got from Intruder before the protocol running, since they are partners.

From the analysis of Attack 3, we can conclude that, in this attack mode, Drive (Drive-R) does not care the rule of the protocol; what it actually cares is whether or not it can get the parameter Hv. And this conclusion could also explain the feasibility of Attack 5, in which Drive (Drive-R) encounters the same problem as in Attack 3.

Moreover, we want to discuss the instances of Attack 4 and Attack 5. It is easy to discover that Drive (Drive-R) could not obtain the parameter Hv at the end of the protocol running; whereas Intruder (Drive-L) has already got Hv at this time. Thus, what Drive (Drive-R) needs to do is just asking Intruder (Drive-L) to send Hv to it. And for the convenience of checking the authenticity of the parameter Hv sent by Intruder (Drive-L), this additional message, written in italics in both attack instances shown in Fig. 5, is requested to follow one of the message modes in the protocol as (Dn||Hv)SK(Isk)||Hv. After receiving this additional message, Drive (Drive-R) would check the validity of the signature using Intruder's certificate Icert which it can get before the protocol running, and pick up the parameter Hv.

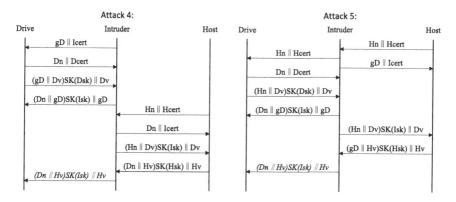

Fig. 5. The Attack 4 & Attack 5

5.4   The Modified Scheme

So far, there are several papers about the AACS drive-host authentication protocol. Particularly, a modified scheme has been advanced, which is declared to be competent of resisting the Unknown Key-Share attack and the Man-In-The-Middle attack in [5].

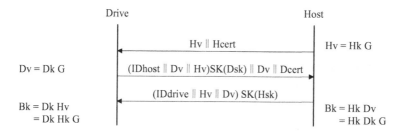

Fig. 6. The Modified Scheme

The modified version is shown in Fig. 6.

Compared with the original one, this modified scheme has two remarkable features: first, Hv and Dv play the role as random challenges, instead of Hn and Dn; second, the ID of the message receiver has been added into the signature.

In this paper, we also carry out an experiment on this modified scheme, and find out that this scheme cannot resist the collusion attack either. In our experiment, in order to check the effectiveness of the modified scheme, we construct a corresponding model on SPIN, and make use of (5) to verify the feasibility of the collusion attack. During the process of verification, we have found four attack instances. These instances are shown in Fig. 7 and Fig. 8, and the relevant experimental data is list in Table 3.

As mentioned earlier, Drive (Drive-R) and Intruder (Drive-L) are allies in the collusion attack, and the purpose of the attack is to let Drive (Drive-R) and Host exchange the parameters Hv and Dv and prevent Host from knowing the existence of Drive in the

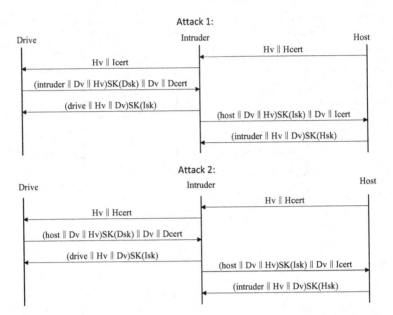

Fig. 7. The Attack 1 & Attack 2

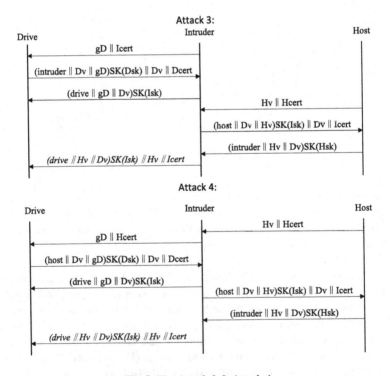

Fig. 8. The Attack 3 & Attack 4

Table 3. Attack and Relevant Data

Attack	Attack 1	Attack 2	Attack 3	Attack 4
HostRunningHD	0	0	0	0
HostCommitHD	0	0	0	0
HostKnowDv	1	1	1	1
HostKnowDcert	0	0	0	0
DriveRunningHD	0	1	0	1
DriveCommitHD	0	0	0	0
DriveKnowHv	1	1	0	0
IntruderKnowHv	1	1	1	1

whole process of the protocol running. In Attack 1 and Attack 2, this purpose could be successfully reached; and in Attack 3 and Attack 4, though failing to get Hv at the end of the protocol, Drive (Drive-R) could get it from Intruder (Drive-L). Similarly, for the convenience of checking the parameter Hv, the additional message, written in italics in both attack instances shown in Fig. 8, is still required to comply with one of the message modes used in the modified scheme – (drive‖Hv‖Dv)SK(Isk)‖Hv‖Icert.

5.5 Relevant Analysis

Apparently, the collusion attack would make a revoked drive bypass the authentication procedure, negotiate a shared Bus Key with a legitimate host and use this key to exchange necessary information with the host in order to play/record the protected content in the disc released by AACS LA after the drive is revoked. All this work could be done with the assistance of a valid drive with a legitimate certificate. This situation is just like once getting the valid serial number and password from a licensed user, one can install and use an unauthorized copy of a legally released software, downloaded from the internet illegally or obtained from illegal DVD/VCD duplicators, unless the software releaser detects this improper action and locks that compromised serial number. Similarly, with the help of a legitimate drive, one could freely use a revoked drive along with a PC host to play/record discs until the AACS LA detects this illegitimate action, which has threatened the security offered by the AACS system seriously.

6 Conclusion

Through the strict model-checking analysis of the AACS drive-host authentication protocol, depending on the variant of the Dolev-Yao attacker model [4], we have discovered a few weaknesses of the target protocol in providing authenticity. Besides, we have advanced a novel collusion attack and found several corresponding attack instances in the original scheme of the target protocol and a modified scheme [5].

In this paper, we have not yet advanced a new scheme to resist that collusion attack. Future work might focus on the modification of the AACS drive-host authentication protocol by introducing the threshold decryption scheme which is mainly used to prevent the collusion attack.

Acknowledgement

This research was funded by grant 90604010 from the National Nature Science Foundation and grant 2007BC311202 of the National Key Foundation Research Plan of China.

References

1. Intel et al. Advanced Access Content System (AACS) – Introduction and Common Cryptographic Elements. Revision 0.91, pp. 32–34 (2006)
2. Khan, A.S., Mukund, M., Suresh, S.P.: Generic Verification of Security Protocols. Technical Report, Chennai Mathematical Institute (2005)
3. Basin, D., Mödersheim, S., Viganò, L.: An On-the-fly Model-Checker for Security Protocol Analysis. In: Snekkenes, E., Gollmann, D. (eds.) ESORICS 2003. LNCS, vol. 2808, pp. 253–270. Springer, Heidelberg (2003)
4. Dolev, D., Yao, A.C.: On the security of public key protocols. IEEE Transactions on Information Theory 29(2), 198–208 (1983)
5. Sui, J., Stinson, D.R.: A Critical Analysis and Improvement of AACS Drive-Host Authentication. Centre for Applied Cryptographic Research (CACR) (2007)
6. Henry, K., Sui, J., Zhong, G.: An Overview of the Advanced Access Content System (AACS). Centre for Applied Cryptographic Research (CACR), 2007 April 12 (2007)
7. Paulson, L.C.: The inductive approach to verifying cryptographic protocols. Journal of computer security 6, 85–128 (1998)
8. Maggi, P., Sisto, R.: Using SPIN to Verify Security Properties of Cryptographic Protocols. In: Bošnački, D., Leue, S. (eds.) SPIN 2002. LNCS, vol. 2318, pp. 187–204. Springer, Heidelberg (2002)
9. Ramanujam, R., Suresh, S.P.: A decidable subclass of unbounded security protocols. In: Proc. IFIP Workshop on Issues in the Theory of Security (WITS–3), Warsaw (Poland), pp. 11–20 (2003)
10. Ramanujam, R., Suresh, S.P.: Decidability of context-explicit security protocols. Journal of Computer Security 13(1), 135–165 (2005)
11. Spin Workshop. Spin-Formal Verification (2008),
    http://spinroot.com/spin/whatispin.html

Appendix: The Sequence Charts of Attack Instances in SPIN

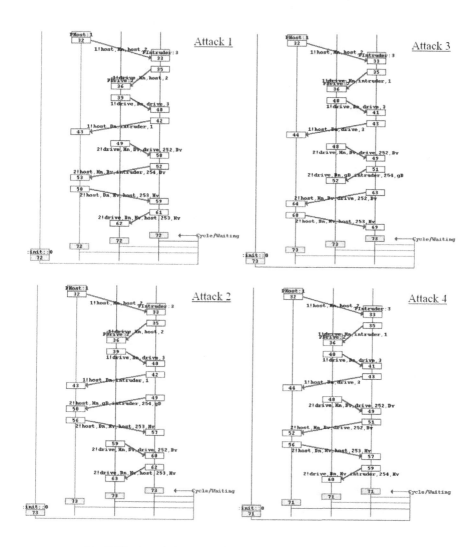

Fig. 9. The Attack Instances Violating the Property of Authenticity

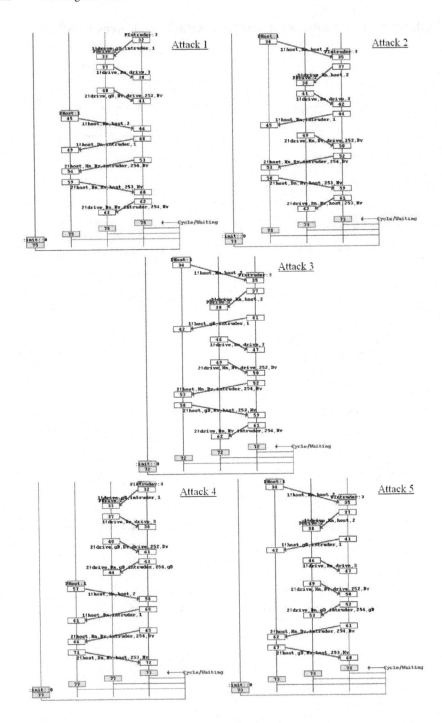

Fig. 10. The Collusion Attack Instances in the AACS Drive-Host Authentication Scheme

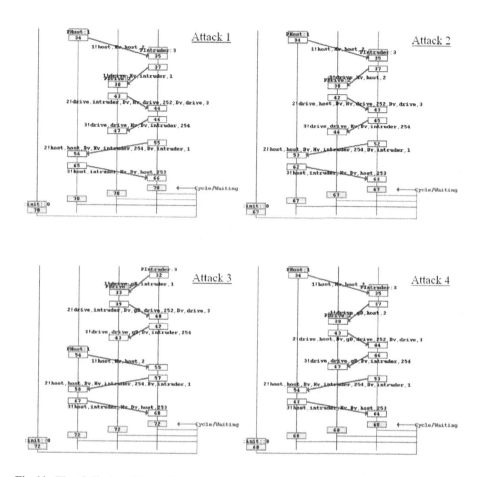

Fig. 11. The Collusion Attack Instances in the Modified AACS Drive-Host Authentication Scheme

Protocol Modeling with Model Program Composition

Margus Veanes and Wolfram Schulte

Microsoft Research, Redmond, WA, USA
{margus,schulte}@microsoft.com

Abstract. Designing and interoperability testing of distributed, application-level network protocols is complex. Windows, for example, supports currently more than 200 protocols, ranging from simple protocols for email exchange to complex ones for distributed file replication or real time communication. To fight this increasing complexity problem, we introduce a methodology and formal framework that uses model program composition to specify behavior of such protocols. A model program can be used to specify an increment of protocol functionality with a coherent purpose, which can be understood and analyzed separately. The overall behavior of a protocol can be defined by a composite model program, which defines how the individual parts interoperate.

1 Introduction

Protocols are abundant; we rely on the reliable sending and receiving of email, multimedia, and business data. But protocols, such as SMB [28], can be very complex and hard to get right. They require careful design to guarantee reliability and failure resilience; they require careful and efficient implementations, to not clog the system; and they require careful documentation and interoperability testing, so that different vendors understand the same protocol.

A protocol typically has many different facets. Each facet provides a partial view of the overall functionality of the protocol with a coherent purpose. An example of a facet is a set of rules that describes how message ids are allowed to be computed and communicated between a client and a server in a client-server protocol.

In this paper we provide a methodology and a formal framework for specifying protocol facets as separate model programs. A model program is a collection of guarded update rules indexed by actions. A model program of a single facet can be subject to liveness and safety analysis, which can be infeasible to perform for the whole protocol model. Instead, one can apply compositional reasoning in the following sence. If a model program satisfies one property and another model program satisfies another property, then the composition of those model programs satisfies both properties. Distilling facet model programs also fosters reuse, since facets, such as an algorithm for request cancellation in a particular client-server protocol, typically reappear in similar protocols.

Model programs of different facets of a protocol can be composed into a single model program. Composition of model programs is syntactic, but the underlying trace semantics is based on the classical theory of labeled transition systems (LTSs) [31,32]. This enables a direct application of the formal LTS based theory of testing using IOCO [9] or

K. Suzuki et al. (Eds.): FORTE 2008, LNCS 5048, pp. 324–339, 2008.

interface automata refinement [15]. The step semantics of model programs is based on the theory of abstract state machines (ASMs) [25] with a rich background universe [6]. This enables explicit state exploration techniques [21] and symbolic analysis techniques that support the needed background theories [36], as well as a range of other ASM technologies [8] to be applied to model programs.

A key property of the composition of model programs is that actions may include parameters as logic variables. When actions are synchronized, values are shared through unification from one model program to another, which is different from communication through actions by composition of input/output automata [33], where input actions in one model are synchronized with output actions in the other model. We provide tool support for analyzing safety and liveness properties for basic and composed model programs within the NModel framework [34]. We have integrated model program composition into a model-based test environment in NModel so that interoperability tests can be driven from those combined models. The NModel framework uses C# for writing model programs and is explained in detail in [30], which also discusses the use of model programs as a practical modeling technique.

To summarize, this paper makes the following contributions.

- We introduce a novel modeling technique for protocols using a decomposition of a protocol into different facets that are modeled separately and composed using model programs.
- We define formally the composition of model programs that simplifies and extends the definition of parallel composition of model programs in [38]. In particular, the composition admits sharing of state variables and can be used for state-dependent scenario control.
- We illustrate the use of this modeling technique and composition on an excerpt of an industrially relevant and non-trivial SMB2 protocol.

The remainder of the paper is organized as follows. Section 2 defines model programs and related notions needed in the sequel. Section 3 defines model program composition. Section 4 illustrates the application of the technique to a sample protocol. Section 5 explains some aspects of the implementation and experiments. Section 6 is about related work. We finish off the paper with a short conclusion.

2 Model Programs

Model programs can be viewed as abstract state machines (ASMs) [25] indexed by actions. The main use of model programs is as high-level specifications in model-based testing tools such as Spec Explorer [1,37] and NModel [34]. In Spec Explorer, one of the supported input languages is the abstract state machine language AsmL [2,26]. AsmL is used in this paper as the concrete specification language for update rules that correspond to basic ASMs with a rich background [6] T including arithmetic, sets, maps, tuples, user defined data types, etc.

We let Σ denote the overall signature of function symbols. Part of the signature, denoted by Σ^{var}, contains function symbols whose interpretation may vary from state to state. The remaining part Σ^{static} contains symbols whose interpretation is fixed by the background theory. A ground term over Σ^{static} is called a *value term*. Formally, the *interpretation* of a value term t is the same in all states and is denoted by $[\![t]\!]$. An example of a value term t, using AsmL syntax, is a *range expression* $\{3..7\}$; whose value $[\![t]\!]$ is the set of all integers from 3 to 7.

A subset of Σ^{static}, denoted by Σ^{action} are free constructors called *action symbols*. An *action* is a value term $f(t_1,\ldots,t_n)$ where f is an action symbol, also called an f-action. We also say *action* for $[\![f(t_1,\ldots,t_n)]\!] = f([\![t_1]\!],\ldots,[\![t_n]\!])$. For all action symbols f with arity $n \geq 0$, and all i, $1 \leq i \leq n$, there is a unique *parameter variable* denoted by $f.i$. We write Σ_f for $\{f.i\}_{1 \leq i \leq n}$. Note that if $n = 0$ then $\Sigma_f = \emptyset$.

Definition 1. A *model program* P is a tuple (V_P, A_P, I_P, R_P), where

- V_P is a finite subset of Σ^{var}, called the *state variables of* P;
- A_P is a finite subset of Σ^{action}, called the *action symbols of* P;
- I_P is a formula over $\Sigma_P = \Sigma^{\text{static}} \cup V_P$, called the *initial state condition of* P;
- R_P is a family $\{R_P^f\}_{f \in A_P}$ of *action rules* $R_P^f = (G_P^f, U_P^f)$, where
  - G_P^f is a formula over $\Sigma_P \cup \Sigma_f$ called the *guard* or *enabling condition of* R_P^f;
  - U_P^f is an update rule over $\Sigma_P \cup \Sigma_f$ called the *update rule of* R_P^f.

We often say *action* to also mean an action rule or an action symbol, if the intent is clear from the context.

Example 1 (Credits). The following model program is written in AsmL. It specifies how a client and a server need to use message ids, based on a sliding window protocol (see Section 4). Here we illustrate the components of the *Credits* model program according to Definition 1.

```
var window as Set of Integer = {0}
var maxId as Integer = 0
var requests as Map of Integer to Integer = {->}

[Action("Req(_,m,c)")]
Req(m as Integer, c as Integer)
  require m in window and c > 0
  requests := Add(requests,m,c)
  window := window difference {m}

[Action("Res(_,m,c,_)")]
Res(m as Integer, c as Integer)
   require m in requests
   require requests(m) >= c
   require c >= 0
   window := window union {maxId + i | i in {1..c}}
   requests := RemoveAt(requests,m)
   maxId := maxId + c
```

Its three state variables are indicated with the keyword `var`. *Credits* has two actions `Req` and `Res`, indicated with the `[Action]` attribute on the corresponding method definition. The initial state condition is given by the initial assignment of values to the state variables. The argument of the `[Action]` attribute provides the arity of the action symbol and the mapping from the formal parameter names used in the method definition to the corresponding parameter variables for the action symbol.[1] Each occurrence of the

---

[1] If the mapping coincides with the method signature, this argument can be omitted.

placeholder '_' indicates that the corresponding parameter variable is not referenced. The Req action rule $R_{Credits}^{Req}$ has the following components. The guard $G_{Credits}^{Req}$ is the conjunction of all of the require-statements. The update rule $U_{Credits}^{Req}$ is defined by the body of the method. Note that the parallel update rule is the default in AsmL, thus both assignments in the Req action are executed in parallel as a single transaction, although in this case a sequential execution would yield the same updates. The Res action rule is analogous. To summarize,

$$V_{Credits} = \{\texttt{window}, \texttt{maxId}, \texttt{requests}\},$$
$$A_{Credits} = \{\texttt{Req}, \texttt{Res}\},$$
$$I_{Credits} = (\texttt{window} = \{0\} \wedge \texttt{maxId} = 0 \wedge \texttt{requests} = \{\mapsto\}),$$
$$G_{Credits}^{Req} = (\texttt{Req}.2 \in \texttt{window} \wedge \texttt{Req}.3 > 0),$$
$$U_{Credits}^{Req} = (\texttt{requests} := \texttt{Add}(\texttt{requests}, \texttt{Req}.2, \texttt{Req}.3) \, \|$$
$$\texttt{window} := \texttt{window} \setminus \{\texttt{Req}.2\}).$$

We introduce a special class of model programs used here for scenario control. A *finite state model program* is a model program all of whose state variables have a finite range. There is a straightforward encoding of regular expressions over the alphabet of actions with placeholders to finite state model programs.[2] Given such a regular expression ρ we write $FSMP(\rho)$ for the corresponding finite state model program.

Example 2 (FSMP(Req(_, 0, 2)*)). The following model program P is a finite state model program, since $V_P = \emptyset$. Intuitively, P describes the closure Req(_,0,2)*.

```
[Action("Req(_,m,c)")]
Req(m as Integer, c as Integer)
  require m = 0 and c = 2
  skip
```

Let P be a fixed model program. A *P-state* is a mapping of V_P to values.[3] Given a P-state S, an extension of S with the parameter assignment $\theta = \{x_i \mapsto v_i\}_{1 \leq i \leq n}$ is denoted by $(S; \theta)$. Given an extended P-state S, the *reduction* of S to V_P is denoted by $S \upharpoonright V_P$. Given an action $a = f(t_1, \ldots, t_n)$, let θ_a denote the parameter assignment $\{f.i \mapsto [\![t_i]\!]\}_{1 \leq i \leq n}$.

Let S be a P-state, and let a be an f-action. We use the notion of *firing* of an update rule U in a state S [25], denoted here by $Fire(S, U)$, that yields the updated state, provided that $Fire(S, U)$ is defined (a consistent update set exists).[4] Then a is *enabled* in S if $(S; \theta_a) \models G_P^f$ and $S' = Fire((S; \theta_a), U_P^f) \upharpoonright V_P$ is defined. Then a *causes a transition from S to S'*.

A *labeled transition system* or *LTS* is a tuple (S, S_0, L, T), where S is a set of *states*, $S_0 \subseteq S$ is a set of *initial states*, L is a set of labels and $T \subseteq S \times L \times S$ is a *transition relation*.

---

[2] Model programs also have an *accepting state condition* that has been omitted from the discussion in this paper.

[3] More precisely, this is the foreground part of the state, the background part is the canonical model of the background theory $\mathcal{T}$.

[4] There is no consistent update set when for example U is a parallel update of two distinct values to the same state variable.

Definition 2. Let P be a model program. The *LTS of P*, denoted by $[\![P]\!]$ is the LTS $(\mathcal{S}, \mathcal{S}_0, L, T)$, where $\mathcal{S}_0$, is the set of all P-states s such that $s \models I_P$; L is the set of all actions over A_P; T and $\mathcal{S}$ are the least sets such that, $\mathcal{S}_0 \subseteq \mathcal{S}$, and if $s \in \mathcal{S}$ and there is an action a that causes a transition from s to s' then $s' \in \mathcal{S}$ and $(s, a, s') \in T$.

A *run* of P is a sequence of transitions $(s_i, a_i, s_{i+1})_{i<\kappa}$ in $[\![P]\!]$, for some $\kappa \leq \omega$, where s_0 is an initial state of $[\![P]\!]$. The sequence $(a_i)_{i<\kappa}$ is called an (*action*) *trace* of P. The run or the trace is *finite* if $\kappa < \omega$. We write *Traces*(P) for the set of all finite traces of P.

To illustrate the notion of a trace, consider $P = FSMP(\text{Req}(\_, 0, 2)^*)$. In this case $[\![P]\!]$ has a single state s_0 that is the empty mapping, because there are no state variables. There is a transition $(s_0, \text{Req}(v, 0, 2), s_0)$ in $[\![P]\!]$ for all values v. Thus a trace of P is any sequence of Req-actions whose second argument is 0 and third argument is 2, which explains the intuition provided in Example 2.

3   Model Program Composition

Under composition, model programs with the same action signature synchronize their steps for the actions. The guards of the actions in the composition are the conjunctions of the guards of the component model programs. The update rules are the parallel compositions of the update rules of the component model programs. We use '$\parallel$' to denote parallel composition of update rules (ASMs) [25].

Definition 3. Let P and Q be model programs such that $A = A_P = A_Q$. The *composition* $P \oplus Q$ is $(V_P \cup V_Q, A, I_P \wedge I_Q, (G_P^f \wedge G_Q^f, U_P^f \parallel U_Q^f)_{f \in A})$.

The following facts follow immediately from the definition of composition. Let P and Q (possibly with indices) denote model programs with the same action signature.

Fact 1 (Commutativity) $[\![P \oplus Q]\!] = [\![Q \oplus P]\!]$.

Fact 2 (Associativity) $[\![(P_1 \oplus P_2) \oplus P_3]\!] = [\![P_1 \oplus (P_2 \oplus P_3)]\!]$.

A straightforward technique to lift two model programs to use the same action signature, that is commonly used to compose FSMs and LTSs, is provided by the following basic action signature extensions.

Definition 4. Let P be a model program and f an action symbol not in A_P. The *enabling extension of P for f*, denoted by P^f, is the extension of P such that $A_{P^f} = A_P \cup \{f\}$ and $R_{P^f}^f = (true, skip)$. The *disabling extension of P for f*, denoted by P^{-f}, is the extension of P such that $A_{P^{-f}} = A_P \cup \{f\}$ and $R_{P^{-f}}^f = (false, skip)$.

Example 3 (OrderedRequests). Consider the following model program, called *OrderedRequests*.

```
var window as Set of Integer

[Action("Req(_,m,_)")]
Req(m as Integer)
  require m = Min(window)
  skip
```

It requires the second argument of a Req action to be the smallest element in window. Note that $I_{OrderedRequests} = true$ because the initial values of the state variables are unspecified, i.e. all states of $[\![OrderedRequests]\!]$ are initial states. The enabling extension $OrderedRequests^{Res}$ adds the action rule $(true, skip)$ for Res to $OrderedRequests$. The model programs $OrderedRequests^{Res}$ and $Credits$ in Example 1 have the same action signature.

The enabling (or disabling) extension of P for a set of action symbols F not in A_P is denoted by P^F (or P^{-F}). Note that $P^{\emptyset} = P^{-\emptyset} = P$. Let P and Q be model programs. Let $P \uplus Q \stackrel{\text{def}}{=} [\![P^{A_Q \setminus A_P} \oplus Q^{A_P \setminus A_Q}]\!]$ and $P \uplus Q \stackrel{\text{def}}{=} [\![P^{-A_Q \setminus A_P} \oplus Q^{-A_P \setminus A_Q}]\!]$. Intuitively, '$\uplus$' is an operator, where all actions whose symbol is not in the shared action signature are interleaved; '$\uplus$' on the other hand disables all such actions.

In the sequel, we overload the composition operator '$\oplus$' so that, for arbitrary model programs P and Q, $P \oplus Q$ stands for $P \uplus Q$.

3.1 Trace Intersection

When composition is used in an unrestricted manner then the end result is a new model program which from the point of view of trace semantics might be unrelated to the original model programs. In general this happens if the composed model programs share state variables. The following proposition follows from [38, Theorem 1].

Proposition 1. *Let P and Q be model programs such that $A_P = A_Q$ and $V_P \cap V_Q = \emptyset$. Then $Traces(P \oplus Q) = Traces(P) \cap Traces(Q)$.*

The main reason why this property is important is that it makes it possible to do compositional reasoning over the traces in the following sence. If all traces of P satisfy a property φ and all traces of Q satisfy a property ψ then all traces of $P \oplus Q$ satisfy both properties φ and ψ.

3.2 Trace Restriction

For scenario control, it is sometimes useful to refer to the state variables of a model program in order to write a scenario for it. In other words, there is a contract model program P and there is a scenario model program Q that may read the state variables of P but it may not change the values of those variables. Let $WriteSet(Q)$ be the set of all state variables of Q that appear as left hand sides of assignment rules in Q.

Proposition 2. *Let P and Q be model programs such that $A_Q \subseteq A_P$, and $WriteSet(Q)$ and V_P are disjoint. Then $Traces(P \oplus Q) \subseteq Traces(P)$.*

In this case composition of P and Q does not introduce traces that were not traces of P. A typical use of such composition is *guard strengthening* that is illustrated in Example 4.

Example 4. Let P be the model program $Credits$ in Example 1 and let Q be the model program $OrderedRequests$ in Example 3. In this case $V_Q = \{window\} \subset V_P$ and $WriteSet(Q) = \emptyset$. In $P \oplus Q$, Q strengthens the guard G_P^{Req} so that all other choices for the parameter m besides the smallest element in windows are eliminated, which is a particular valid scenario for P. It is not possible to achieve this effect easily with "pure" composition as in Proposition 1.

4   Sample Protocol

We consider an excerpt of the new SMB2 protocol, a successor of the Windows file-sharing client-server protocol SMB [28], which is used for filesharing between Vista machines and future Windows hosts. We consider a fixed client and a fixed server. The client sends *requests* to the server and the server sends *responses* back to the client. One can decompose SMB2 into various facets, that, when modeled individually, would comprise between 20 and 30 model programs. We look at two facets that are representative from the point of view of complexity and size. The excerpt is henceforth called SP.

- *Credit negotiation* describes how the client and the server need to use message ids, based on a sliding window algorithm.
- *Cancellation* describes how the client can cancel a previously sent request.

Concrete messages of the protocol are mapped to (abstract) actions where message fields that are not relevant for the given facets have been omitted. We consider three action symbols and the following message fields. Each message has a *command* field that indicates the operation communicated between the client and the server. This command field is either mapped to the first argument of the action, or it is mapped to the action symbol Cancel when the command is a special cancellation command.

- Req is a ternary action symbol that represents a request from the client to execute a command. A *request* is an action $Req(c,m,n)$, where c is a command, m is a message id and n is a number of requested credits.
- Res is an action symbol that takes four arguments and represents responses from the server. A *response* is an action $Res(c,m,n,s)$ where c is a command, m is a message id, n is a number of granted credits, and s is a status value.
- Cancel is a unary action symbol that represents a "meta" request from the client to cancel a previous request. A *cancellation request* is an action $Cancel(m)$ where m is a message id.

4.1   Credit Negotiation

The client can use certain message identifiers to communicate with the server. The set of available message identifiers can be seen as a window of numbers that changes over time. The window is, strictly speaking, not a consecutive interval of numbers because the client does not have to use the available numbers in any particular order. This is an important aspect of the specification that leaves open implementation specific details of the client-side of the protocol. An identifier of a request can only be used once. The client can ask for credits in the requests that it sends to the server in order to expand the window. The server may grant credits in its responses to the client. The number of credits granted in a response determines how the window grows or shrinks as time progresses. Note that the server may grant credits using different implementation specific algorithms the details of which are left open by the specification.

The *Credits* model program is defined uniformly for all of the commands, except for Cancel, see Example 1.

The state variable `window` is the set of all message ids that the client may use to send new requests to the server, `requests` is a map containing all the outstanding credit requests with message ids as keys, and `maxId` is the largest id that has been granted by the server. In the initial state of the model the only possible message id is 0, the maximum id is also 0, and there are no pending requests.

The `Req` action records in the state variable `requests` that message m has an outstanding credit request for c credits, and removes m from the window. The actual command (the first argument) is irrelevant here. The guard of this action rule requires that m appears in the window and that the requested number of credits is positive. The `Res` action updates the window with the new ids and updates the value of the maximum id. This action is enabled if the given id is an outstanding request, and the granted credits do not exceed the requested credits.

Validation. The client *starves* if it runs out of message ids and cannot send further requests. An important safety requirement of the credits algorithm is that the client must not starve. Note that this does not mean that the server always has to grant at least one credit to the client in every response. It may be that the client has pending requests and the server will eventually grant the client more credits. Thus, the state invariant describing this safety condition is that if there are no pending requests then the window must be nonempty.

```
[StateInvariant]
ClientHasEnoughCredits()
    require (requests = {->}) implies (window <> {})
```

A natural question that arises here is if the *Credits* model program has any *unsafe* states, i.e., states that are reachable (through a trace) from the initial state that violate the state invariant. We use the finite state model program $FSMP(\text{Req}(\_,0,2)^*)$ in Example 2 to restrict the number of requested credits to 2 and the message id to 0. $[\![Credits \oplus FSMP(\text{Req}(\_,0,2)^*)]\!]$ is shown in Figure 1 and reveals an unsafe state reached by the trace $\text{Req}(\_,0,2), \text{Res}(\_,0,0,\_)$. The labels on the states show the values of the state variables of the credits model program listed in the same order they appear in Example 1. We need to strengthen the guard of the `Res` action so that if there are no pending requests and the window is empty, then the granted number of credits must be at least one; see Figure 2. Notice that if the window is empty and no credits are

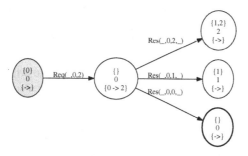

Fig. 1. Exploration of `Credits` $\oplus$ $FSMP(\text{Req}(\_,0,2)^*)$.

```
[Action("Res(_,m,c,_)")]
Res(m as Integer, c as Integer)
    require m in requests
    require requests(m) >= c
    require c >= 0
    require requests.Size > 1 or window <> {} or c > 0
    window := window union {maxId + i | i in {1..c}}
    requests := RemoveAt(requests,m)
    maxId := maxId + c
```

Fig. 2. Correction of the Res action in the *Credits* model program. The guard is stengthened with an additional condition, indicated in boldface.

```
enum Mode
    Sent       //Client has sent the request
    Cancel     //Client has asked to cancel the request

var reqMode as Map of Integer to Mode = {->}

[Action("Req(_,m,_)")]
Req(m as Integer)
    require m in window
    reqMode := Add(reqMode,m,Sent)

[Action]
Cancel(m as Integer)
    if reqMode(m) = Sent
       reqMode := Add(reqMode,m,Cancel)

[Action("Res(_,m,_,status)")]
Res(m as Integer, status as Boolean)
    require m in reqMode.Keys
    require (status or reqMode(m) = Cancel) //status=false means cancelled
    reqMode := RemoveAt(reqMode,m)
```

Fig. 3. *Cancellation* model program

granted then there must be at least two message ids pending when the new condition is checked, because the update rule will remove one of the ids.

4.2 Cancellation

Cancellation enables the client to cancel requests that have been sent to the server. In order to cancel a previously sent request with message id m, the client sends a cancellation message to the server that identifies the request to be cancelled by including its id in the message. The model program is shown in Figure 3. Notice that it is natural to refer to the window of the Credits model program for the valid message ids in a request.

The state variable reqMode records for each message id whether it has been sent or cancelled by the client. Initially, no request has either been sent or cancelled, so the value of reqMode is the empty map.

The Req action records the mode of the message as Sent. The Cancel action is always enabled, it updates a Sent mode to Cancel mode, and ignores the request otherwise (this behavior is needed for robustness). The Res action removes the pending request and requires that the request has indeed been cancelled by the client if the status

Fig. 4. Exploration of *Cancellation* ⊕ *Cancel5*

is *false*. Note that the client may try to cancel a request but is too late to do so, when the server has already completed it but the response has not yet reached the client due to network latencies. Therefore, the status of a response to a request that the client tried to cancel, is either *true* or *false*, so that a potential race condition that would otherwise arise in the specification is avoided.

Validation. *Cancellation* behaves uniformly for all message ids. It is therefore enough to fix a single message id, say 5, to expose all possible isomorphic behaviors. As above, we use a finite state model program to do this.

$$Cancel5 = FSMP(\{\texttt{Cancel(5)},\texttt{Req(\_,5,\_)},\texttt{Res(\_,5,\_,\_)}\}^*)$$

Exploration of ⟦*Cancellation* ⊕ *Cancel5*⟧ is shown in Figure 4. The labels on the states show the value of reqMode. Using more message ids does not provide any additional useful information about *Cancellation*, but blows up the state space exponentially in the number of distinct message ids. With k distinct message ids there are 3^k states.

4.3   Composition

Once the individual facets have been modeled and validated in isolation, we can compose some or all of their model programs to validate their interactions. We use an additional model program called *Commands*: if a request with id m has command c, then the response with id m must also have command c, i.e., the server cannot respond with a command that is different from the one it was requested to execute. Note that it is convenient to refer to window of the *Credits* model program in the *Commands* model program for the domain of message ids. (The definition of the *Commands* model program is straightforward, using a map from message ids to commands.) We assume that the commands are A and B.[5] Note that only the first two arguments of Req and Res actions are relevant in the *Commands* model program. Moreover, we use two scenario model programs: $AB = FSMP(\texttt{Req(A,\_,\_)Req(B,\_,\_)})$ and $M = FSMP(\{\texttt{Cancel(1)},\texttt{Req(\_,\_,2)}\}^*)$. *AB* restricts the client behavior so that a single A request is followed by a single B request. *M* restricts the client behavior so that only message 1 is ever cancelled, and all requests ask for two credits. Exploration of the composition

$$SPscenario = Credits \oplus Cancellation \oplus Commands \oplus AB \oplus M$$

is illustrated in Figure 5. All self-loops of Cancel(1) are hidden. All occurrences of placeholders (for the status argument of responses) indicate that both *true* and *false* are

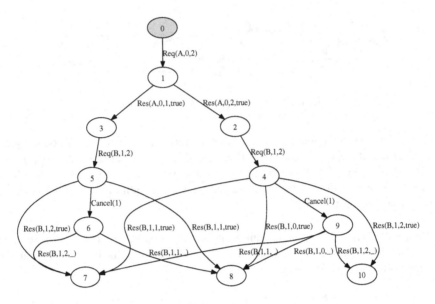

Fig. 5. Exploration of SPscenario

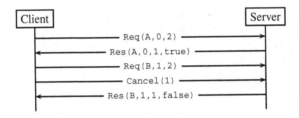

Fig. 6. A trace in Figure 5 from state 0 to state 8

possible. Notice that the server behavior is unconstrained. In the states 7, 8 and 10, the value of window is, respectively, $\{2,3\}$, $\{2\}$, and $\{2,3,4\}$, corresponding to all the possible ways in which the server could grant credits on the way from the initial state. A particular trace from the initial state to state 8 in Figure 5 is illustrated in Figure 6.

5   Implementation and Experiences

All experiments in this paper have been made within the NModel framework using C# as the modeling language. The complete examples, as well as the full source of NModel itself, can be downloaded from [34]. The exploration and the composition examples have been carried out using the *mpv* utility of NModel.

In NModel a model program is scoped by a namespace. Within that namespace, classes can be given a [Feature] attribute that declares that class as a feature or

---

[5] In reality, SMB2 has 19 commands.

submodel program of the full model program. This mechanism can be used to construct separate facet model programs that share state variables, as discussed in this paper. The main composition operator in NModel assumes that the composed model programs do not share state variables.

The *FSMP* construct is supported in NModel by entering a textual representation of a nondeterministic finite automaton or NFA (e.g. in a text file), that is converted to a finite state model program representing a lazy determinization of the NFA based on the Rabin-Scott algorithm, see e.g. [29, Theorem 2.1].

For conformance testing of the server, the client actions are declared *controllable* and the server actions (in this case responses) are declared *observable*. For online (or on-the-fly) test execution, with the *ct* utility of NModel, the composed model program is explored *lazily* by firing the actions one at a time, i.e. building up a trace of the model program incrementally. Due to the lazy exploration, scalability is not an issue. The discussion about *accepting states* has been omitted in this paper. Accepting states are used to define states where a trace may end, thus providing a way to finish a test in a clean way.

Model program analysis in NModel is based on explicit state exploration over abstract states. Much of the algorithmic support builds on earlier work in Spec Explorer [37]. In addition, the exploration includes a pruning technique based on isomorphism checking of states that use objects and unordered data structures [40].

NModel does currently not support symbolic analysis. We are investigating an SMT approach for doing reachability analysis of model programs [36], where we use Z3 [41,5] for our implementation, as it supports background theories [17,16] for arithmetic as well as sets and maps. A prototype is being implemented for a fragment of model programs written in AsmL. Integration of this analysis into NModel is future work.

The entire SMB2 specification contains over 300 pages of natural language specification and corresponds to roughly 20 facets. The specification is written in a way where the different facets are specified in separate sections of the document and therefore the corresponding model programs are closely tied to these sections. Thus, having separate facet model programs matches well with the style of the natural language specs and makes it possible to do requirements tracking in the corresponding model programs.

The internal version of the modeling tool based on model programs is called Spec Explorer 2007 and is being developed and used internally in Windows as a core technology for protocol modeling and model-based testing. In Spec Explorer 2007, model programs and composition are used for modeling and scenario control of industrial application-level network protocols. The entire SMB2 protocol has been modeled. In addition to the contract part of the protocol, over 100 additional model programs were used for scenario control. The use of composition between contract model programs and model programs for scenario control (test purposes) is one of the core techniques for controlling exploration [24]. For complex protocols it may be hard to identify facets due to dependencies. A crude classification of the protocols we have looked at is whether remote procedure call or message passing is being used, where SMB2 belongs to the latter kind. Being able to decompose a large protocol into facets is crucial for the latter kind of protocols.

At least half of the effort in model-based conformance testing of protocols is actually spent in harnessing of the implementation. A big part of this effort goes into implementing a protocol-specific adapter from concrete messages on the wire to abstract actions. When defining a mapping from concrete messages on the wire not all of the fields of messages are relevant. For example, some of the fields in a message are solely related to well-formedness of the message structure, checking of which can be part of a message validation layer that is orthogonal to the behavioral model.

6 Related Work

The notion of facets as behavioral aspects of a protocol is similar to protocol *features*. Feature oriented specifications have a long standing in the telecommunication industry [42], because it makes specifications easy to change and individual features easy to understand, but it also introduces semantic challenges due to unintended feature interactions [10]. More recently, features, as increments of program functionality, are being used in *feature oriented programming* (FOP) for step-wise refinement of systems, and are supported by theory and tools using algebraic specifications [4]. In FOP, features are viewed as program transformations, and the purpose is to support feature oriented development through program synthesis and generative programming [4]. This is quite different from model programs that provide a partial view of the expected behavior of a system as an LTS, where the system itself is a black box, that is typically a combination of different applications from different vendors. However, the relationship between the mathematical underpinnings of model programs and FOP deserves a closer look.

Composition of model programs is a lazy automata-theoretic composition of the underlying LTSs, where actions are composed by unification. The unification between action parameters happens through the conjoined action guards. The motivation comes from the domain of model-based testing and analysis tools such as Spec Explorer [37]. A survey of model-based approaches to software modeling, with an emphasis on testing, is given in the recent book [35]. The notion of model program composition is a simplified and extended version of parallel composition of model programs in [38]. Work related to other forms of composition of automata is discussed in [38]. The use of several feature classes within a single C# model program in NModel [34] allows for sharing of state variables across features. This enables state-dependent parameter generation and guard strengthening, which is, in general, not possible with composition of model programs with disjoint state signatures. Feature classes are also implemented in Spec Explorer 2007 [24]. The semantics of model programs can also be formulated in terms of labeled Kripke structures. This formulation has the advantage that one can adapt techniques that are used for model checking of temporal properties of concurrent software systems, including counterexample-guided abstraction refinement and compositional reasoning [12].

In aspect oriented programming two concerns crosscut when the related method behaviors intersect [19]. In the current paper the crosscutting of concerns corresponds to interacting behaviors between different facets of a protocol. The sharing of information is achieved through unification of actions, that allow data to be shared between traces but make the sharing explicitly visible in action traces. Model program composition might be a viable approach for formalizing certain forms of composition of trace based aspects [18] or model weaving of stateful aspects in aspect oriented modeling [13].

The main application of model programs is for analysis and testing of software systems. In particular, for passive testing or runtime monitoring, a model program can be used as an oracle that observes the traces of a system under test and reports a failure when an action occurs that is not enabled in the model. This is related to aspect oriented approaches to trace monitoring [3]. In the context of testing of reactive systems with model programs [39], the action symbols are separated into controllable and observable ones. In that context the semantics of a model program as an LTS [31,32] is fundamental in order to use IOCO [9], or refinement of interface automata [14], for formalizing the conformance relation.

Model program composition as defined in this paper is independent of the mechanism of exploration or analysis. Various approaches, including explicit state exploration [30] as well as symbolic reachability analysis [36], may be applied. The main difference compared to composition of *action machines* [23] is that composition of model programs is syntactic, whereas composition of action machines is defined in the style of natural semantics using inference rules and symbolic computation that incorporates the notion of computable approximations of subsumption checking between symbolic states. The computable approximations reflect the power of the underlying decision procedures that are being used and are an integral part of the composition, using a three-valued logic. More about model-based testing applications and further motivation for the composition of model programs can be found in [11,23,39,37].

Model programs are also related to symbolic transition systems that have an explicit notion of data and data-dependent control flow [20].

The $FSMP(\rho)$ construction introduced here is a subset of a more general coordination language approach for scenario control called *Cord* [22].

Besides protocol modeling, model program composition is also being investigated as a technique for modeling and analyzing scheduling problems in embedded real-time systems [27].

When considering *interaction* of model programs that require synchronization or communication on objects rather than actions, then composition of model programs may be too limited. A more general foundation can be based on interactive abstract state machines [7].

7   Conclusion

The modeling approach introduced in this paper is being applied in a variety of industrially relevant modeling and testing contexts. In particular, model programs are being adopted as a technique for protocol modeling within Microsoft. The use of composition of model programs is an important part of this effort that enables scenario control as well as a divide-and-conquer approach to model complex protocols. Individual facet model programs can be analyzed separately, they can be composed for interoperability analysis and for constructing the oracle for the full protocol model for test case generation and conformance testing.

References

1. Spec Explorer (released, January 2005), http://research.microsoft.com/specexplorer
2. AsmL, http://research.microsoft.com/fse/AsmL/
3. Avgustinov, P., Bodden, E., Hajiyev, E., Hendren, L., Lhoták, O., de Moor, O., Ongkingco, N., Sereni, D., Sittampalam, G., Tibble, J., Verbaere, M.: Aspects for trace monitoring. In: Havelund, K., Núñez, M., Roşu, G., Wolff, B. (eds.) FATES 2006 and RV 2006. LNCS, vol. 4262, pp. 20–39. Springer, Heidelberg (2006)
4. Batory, D.: A tutorial on feature oriented programming and the AHEAD tool suite. In: Lämmel, R., Saraiva, J., Visser, J. (eds.) GTTSE 2005. LNCS, vol. 4143, pp. 3–35. Springer, Heidelberg (2006)
5. Bjørner, N., de Moura, L.: Z3: An efficient SMT solver. In: Tools and Algorithms for the Construction and Analysis of Systems (TACAS 2008). LNCS, vol. 4963, Springer, Heidelberg (2008)
6. Blass, A., Gurevich, Y.: Background, reserve, and gandy machines. In: Clote, P.G., Schwichtenberg, H. (eds.) CSL 2000. LNCS, vol. 1862, pp. 1–17. Springer, Heidelberg (2000)
7. Blass, A., Gurevich, Y.: Ordinary interactive small-step algorithms, I. ACM Transactions on Computation Logic 7(2), 363–419 (2006)
8. Börger, E., Stärk, R.: Abstract State Machines: A Method for High-Level System Design and Analysis. Springer, Heidelberg (2003)
9. Brinksma, E., Tretmans, J.: Testing Transition Systems: An Annotated Bibliography. In: Cassez, F., Jard, C., Rozoy, B., Dermot, M. (eds.) MOVEP 2000. LNCS, vol. 2067, pp. 187–193. Springer, Heidelberg (2001)
10. Calder, M., Kolberg, M., Magill, E.H., Reiff-Marganiec, S.: Feature interaction: a critical review and considered forecast. Computer Networks 41(1), 115–141 (2003)
11. Campbell, C., Grieskamp, W., Nachmanson, L., Schulte, W., Tillmann, N., Veanes, M.: Testing concurrent object-oriented systems with Spec Explorer (extended abstract). In: Fitzgerald, J.S., Hayes, I.J., Tarlecki, A. (eds.) FM 2005. LNCS, vol. 3582, pp. 542–547. Springer, Heidelberg (2005)
12. Chaki, S., Clarke, E.M., Ouaknine, J., Sharygina, N., Sinha, N.: State/event-based software model checking. In: Boiten, E.A., Derrick, J., Smith, G.P. (eds.) IFM 2004. LNCS, vol. 2999, pp. 128–147. Springer, Heidelberg (2004)
13. Cottenier, T., van den Berg, A., Elrad, T.: Stateful aspects: the case for aspect-oriented modeling. In: AOM 2007, pp. 7–14. ACM, New York (2007)
14. de Alfaro, L.: Game models for open systems. In: Dershowitz, N. (ed.) Verification: Theory and Practice. LNCS, vol. 2772, pp. 269–289. Springer, Heidelberg (2004)
15. de Alfaro, L., Henzinger, T.A.: Interface automata. In: ESEC/FSE 2001, pp. 109–120. ACM, New York (2001)
16. de Moura, L., Bjørner, N.: Efficient E-matching for SMT solvers. In: Pfenning, F. (ed.) CADE 2007. LNCS (LNAI), vol. 4603, pp. 183–198. Springer, Heidelberg (2007)
17. de Moura, L., Bjørner, N.: Model-based theory combination. In: 5th International Workshop on Satisfiability Modulo Theories (SMT 2007), Berlin, Germany, July 2007, pp. 46–57 (2007)
18. Douence, R., Fradet, P., Südholt, M.: Aspect-Oriented Software Development. In: Trace-based Aspects, pp. 201–218. Addison Wesley, Reading (2004)
19. Elrad, T., Aksit, M., Kiczales, G., Lieberherr, K., Ossher, H.: Discussing aspects of AOP. Commun. ACM 44(10), 33–38 (2001)
20. Frantzen, L., Tretmans, J., Willemse, T.: A symbolic framework for model-based testing. In: Havelund, K., Núñez, M., Roşu, G., Wolff, B. (eds.) FATES 2006 and RV 2006. LNCS, vol. 4262, pp. 40–54. Springer, Heidelberg (2006)

21. Grieskamp, W., Gurevich, Y., Schulte, W., Veanes, M.: Generating finite state machines from abstract state machines. In: ISSTA 2002. Software Engineering Notes, vol. 27, pp. 112–122. ACM, New York (2002)
22. Grieskamp, W., Kicillof, N.: A schema language for coordinating construction and composition of partial behavior descriptions. In: 5th International Workshop on Scenarios and State Machines: Models, Algorithms and Tools (SCESM) (2006)
23. Grieskamp, W., Kicillof, N., Tillmann, N.: Action machines: a framework for encoding and composing partial behaviors. IJSEKE 16(5), 705–726 (2006)
24. Grieskamp, W., MacDonald, D., Kicillof, N., Nandan, A., Stobie, K., Wurden, F.: Model-based quality assurance of windows protocol documentation. In: First Intl. Conf. on Software Testing, Verification and Validation, ICST, Lillehammer, Norway (April 2008)
25. Gurevich, Y.: Specification and Validation Methods. In: Evolving Algebras 1993: Lipari Guide, pp. 9–36. Oxford University Press, Oxford (1995), research.microsoft.com/~gurevich/Opera/103.pdf
26. Gurevich, Y., Rossman, B., Schulte, W.: Semantic essence of asml. Theor. Comput. Sci. 343(3), 370–412 (2005)
27. Helander, J., Serg, R., Veanes, M., Roy, P.: Adapting futures: Scalability for real-world computing. In: Proc. 28th IEEE Real-Time Systems Symposium, pp. 105–116. IEEE, Los Alamitos (2007)
28. Hertel, C.: Implementing CIFS: The Common Internet File System. Prentice-Hall, Englewood Cliffs (2003)
29. Hopcroft, J.E., Ullman, J.D.: Introduction to Automata Theory, Languages, and Computation. Addison-Wesley, Reading (1979)
30. Jacky, J., Veanes, M., Campbell, C., Schulte, W.: Model-based Software Testing and Analysis with C#. Cambridge University Press, Cambridge (2007)
31. Keller, R.: Formal verification of parallel programs. Communications of the ACM, 371–384 (July 1976)
32. Lynch, N., Tuttle, M.: Hierarchical correctness proofs for distributed algorithms. In: 6th annual ACM Symposium on Principles of distributed computing, pp. 137–151. ACM, New York (1987)
33. Lynch, N., Tuttle, M.: An introduction to input/output automata. CWI-Quarterly 2(3), 219–246 (1989)
34. NModel (released, May 2007), http://www.codeplex.com/NModel
35. Utting, M., Legeard, B.: Practical Model-Based Testing - A tools approach. Elsevier Science, Amsterdam (2006)
36. Veanes, M., Bjørner, N., Raschke, A.: An SMT approach to bounded reachability analysis of model programs. In: Suzuki, K., Higashino, T., Yasumoto, K., El - Fakih, K. (eds.) FORTE 2008. LNCS, vol. 5048, pp. 53–68. Springer, Heidelberg (2008)
37. Veanes, M., Campbell, C., Grieskamp, W., Schulte, W., Tillmann, N., Nachmanson, L.: Model-Based Testing of Object-Oriented Reactive Systems with Spec Explorer. In: Hierons, R., Bowen, J., Harman, M. (eds.) Formal Methods and Testing. LNCS, vol. 4949, pp. 39–76. Springer, Heidelberg (2008)
38. Veanes, M., Campbell, C., Schulte, W.: Composition of model programs. In: Derrick, J., Vain, J. (eds.) FORTE 2007. LNCS, vol. 4574, pp. 128–142. Springer, Heidelberg (2007)
39. Veanes, M., Campbell, C., Schulte, W., Tillmann, N.: Online testing with model programs. In: Proc. ESEC/FSE-13, pp. 273–282. ACM, New York (2005)
40. Veanes, M., Ernits, J., Campbell, C.: State isomorphism in model programs with abstract data structures. In: Derrick, J., Vain, J. (eds.) FORTE 2007. LNCS, vol. 4574, pp. 112–127. Springer, Heidelberg (2007)
41. Z3 (released, September 2007), http://research.microsoft.com/projects/z3
42. Zave, P.: Feature interactions and formal specifications in telecommunications. Computer 26(8), 20–29 (1993)

Author Index

Lecture Notes in Computer Science

Sublibrary 2: Programming and Software Engineering

For information about Vols. 1– 4350
please contact your bookseller or Springer